AMERICAN GOVERNMENT
AND POLITICS TODAY: THE ESSENTIALS

1994–1995 Edition

1994–1995 EDITION

AMERICAN GOVERNMENT AND POLITICS TODAY: THE ESSENTIALS

Barbara A. Bardes
University of Cincinnati

Mack C. Shelley II
Iowa State University

Steffen W. Schmidt
Iowa State University

West Publishing Company
Minneapolis/Saint Paul ■ New York ■ Los Angeles ■ San Francisco

Copy editor Elaine Levin
Compositor Parkwood Composition Service
Index Maggy Jarpey
Cover photograph Marc Romanelli, The Image Bank
Text photographs Credits appear following index

West's Commitment to the Environment

In 1906, West Publishing Company began recycling materials left over from the production of books. This began a tradition of efficient and responsible use of resources. Today, up to 95 percent of our legal books and 70 percent of our college and school texts are printed on recycled, acid-free stock. West also recycles nearly 27 million pounds of scrap paper annually—the equivalent of 181,717 trees. Since the 1960s, West has devised ways to capture and recycle waste inks, solvents, oils, and vapors created in the printing process. We also recycle plastics of all kinds, wood, glass, corrugated cardboard, and batteries, and have eliminated the use of styrofoam book packing. We at West are proud of the longevity and the scope of our committment to the environment.

Production, Prepress, Printing and Binding by West Publishing Company.

COPYRIGHT ©1986, 1988, 1990, 1992 By WEST PUBLISHING COMPANY
COPYRIGHT ©1994 By WEST PUBLISHING COMPANY
        610 Opperman Drive
        P.O. Box 64526
        St. Paul, MN 55164-0526

Printed in the United States of America

01 00 99 98 97 96 95 94   8 7 6 5 4 3 2 1 0

Library of Congress Cataloging-in-Publication Data

Bardes, Barbara A.
    American government and politics today : the essentials, 1994–1995 edition /
Barbara A. Bardes, Mack C. Shelley, Steffen W. Schmidt.
      p.   cm.
    Includes index.
    ISBN 0-314-02627-4 (alk. paper)
    1. United States—Politics and government. I. Shelley, Mack C.,
1950– . II. Schmidt, Steffen W. III. Title.
JK274.S428 1994
320.973—dc20
                          93-25942
  CIP

CONTENTS IN BRIEF

PART FOUR

Political Institutions 313

PART FIVE

Public Policy 449

CONTENTS

Chapter 3
Federalism 57

PART THREE

People and Politics 173

Chapter 6
Public Opinion 175

Chapter 7
Interest Groups 205

Chapter 11
The Presidency 357

GETTING INVOLVED:
Working for a Clean
Environment 481

Chapter 15
Foreign and Defense Policy 485

PROFILE:
Colin Powell 503

POLITICS AND ETHICS:
Is It Okay to Endanger the Life of a
Foreign Head of State? 508

PREFACE

The United States stands on the threshold of change in 1993. With the election of Bill Clinton as president of the United States, twelve years of Republican control of the White House ended. Clinton's election, which can be explained as the expression of the public's frustration with the politics of "divided government" and the inability of the government to solve the nation's problems, introduces an era of Democratic control of both the White House and the Congress. The voters have spoken for change and for new directions in policy, not only through the election of a Democratic team in Washington but also through their positive response to the "outsider" presidential campaigns of Jerry Brown, Pat Buchanan, and H. Ross Perot.

The new president and the nation face a world of challenges and opportunities. The president can present new policies to deal with health care, education, the environment, and the economy to a new Congress, one that has a Democratic majority in both houses and many new members. Clinton has appointed new officials to head the Cabinet departments and will be able to shape the federal judiciary. It is an exciting time to plan and implement foreign policies: the major adversary of the United States, the Soviet Union, dissolved itself and its successor, Russia, is attempting to establish a market economy; democracy has never been more sought after in the nations of the world; and the United Nations has begun to play a serious and effective role in resolving conflicts.

The American people, however, still face enormous challenges. Any major change in Social Security, in health insurance, and in economic policy has enormous ramifications for each citizen. The federal budget deficit continues to grow while Americans debate how to limit its effects on future life in the United States. While the Cold War has ended, the world is still full of aggressor states, unrelenting ethnic conflicts such as that in the former Yugoslavia, and civil wars that inflict starvation on millions.

Given the challenges that face the citizens of the United States both domestically and abroad, it is even more important that American citizens understand their own political institutions and think critically about the choices the United States must make in the 1990s. Should the United States continue to play the role of global police officer in the coming decades, as it has done in Grenada, Panama, and the Middle East? To what extent can our military forces be reduced and resources diverted to other needs? What are the political priorities of the American people, and can they be met by our system of campaigns and elections? These and many other questions will occupy our student-readers in the future. It is the goal of this edition of *American Government and Politics Today: The Essentials* to enable students to perceive and understand both the dynamics of political change and the institutions and processes that make it possible for the American political system to survive in this changing world. We want students to gain a comprehensive understanding of our political system and its historical origins and at the same time to be stirred by the excitement of current events. We hope to develop the ability of students to think critically about political institutions, political culture, and public policies so that they may be better equipped to act as citizens of the United States and of the world.

1992 Election Results Included and Analyzed

Because we believe that students respond positively to up-to-date information, we have ensured high student interest by including the latest presidential, congressional, and state election results from November 1992. These results are discussed throughout the book, but particularly in Chapter 1 on American democracy and political culture, Chapter 6 on public opinion, Chapter 8 on political parties, Chapter 9 on campaigns, voting and the media, Chapter 10 on Congress, and Chapter 11 on the presidency.

A special feature on the 1992 presidential campaign and the victory of Bill Clinton is included in Chapter 9 as well as the full results of the election-day polling by the CBS/*New York Times* survey division. The voting patterns of women, the younger and older voters, and of party identifiers are discussed in the same chapter. In the chapter on Congress (Chapter 10), a special section discusses the results of the 1992 congressional elections with a particular emphasis on the increased numbers of African-American, Hispanic, and female winners. In addition, the Congress chapter includes the changes in committee chairs that resulted from the 1992 congressional elections.

The 1992 Election: The Winds of Change

For this edition, Barbara Bardes has prepared a student booklet entitled *The 1992 Election: The Winds of Change*. This supplemental monograph gives students extended coverage of the 1992 campaigns and election results, at all levels of government. The race for the presidency is discussed from the pre-primary stages through the conventions and debates up to the election itself. Included in that discussion are sections on the volatility of the polls, the effect of H. Ross Perot's campaign, and the strategies pursued by the Clinton and Bush campaigns. The coverage also includes a comparison of the voting patterns of different groups in 1988 and 1992.

While the presidential election was the focus of media attention, the Congressional elections saw the greatest shift in membership of the House of Representatives in forty years. The booklet highlights the effects of re-districting, the increase in the number of minority and female candidates, and the influence of the scandals that rocked the 102d Congress on the fate of incumbents.

Finally, the booklet discusses some general issues of the 1992 elections: whether this was the "Year of the Woman," the low esteem of governmental institutions, the effect of the media, the problems facing incumbents, the increase in independent and ticket-splitting voters, and the increasing success of minority candidates in 1992. The booklet will provide an opportunity for classes to use the 1992 election as a case study in American electoral politics.

An Analysis of the Break-up of the Soviet Union: *The Rise and Fall of the Soviet Union, 1917–1991.*

To give students the background that they need to understand the challenges that face the United States in carrying out a foreign policy, a student booklet about the dissolution of the Soviet Union is available to adopters. It is called *The Rise and Fall of the Soviet Union, 1917–1991.* The monograph details the attempted conservative coup in the Soviet Union in 1991 with attention to the actions of the Gorbachev regime that led to this crisis. The supplement also provides students with a brief summary of the history and political structure of the former Soviet Union so that they can understand the difficulties that lie ahead of the new Russian government and those of the former republics. Students will also find useful a series of maps, including one of Russia and the former republics and several regional maps that will aid students in seeing how the republics, including Ukraine, Georgia, Moldava, and the Baltics, relate to other nations. After discussing the breakup of the Soviet Union and the difficulties that Russia faces in the future, the supplement leads the student to think about how the decline of America's former adversary affects future foreign policy decisions for the United States.

Handbook of Selected Court Cases

The decisions of the United States Supreme Court play an important role in American political developments, and for that reason, numerous significant Supreme Court decisions are discussed or cited in *American Government and Politics Today.* To further the student's understanding of the Supreme Court's reasoning, a special supplement has been prepared for the 1993–1994 edition. The *Handbook of Selected Court Cases,* which contains thirty-one of the Supreme Court cases mentioned in the text, allows students to read the Court's own words on selected issues. Each case in the *Handbook* opens with a brief statement, in the authors' own words, that describes the essential issue or issues before the Court. Then, a summary of the case as it appears on WESTLAW is presented. Following this summary appear the actual words of the Court, excerpted directly from the Court's written opinion on the case. To assist the student in deciphering the meaning of certain legal terms and case citations, a preface to the *Handbook* provides a guide to legal citations and terminology.

A Total Learning/Teaching Package

This text, along with its numerous supplements, constitutes what we believe to be a total learning/teaching package. Specifically, the text itself contains numerous pedagogical aids and high-interest additions, such as:

1. *A Preview of Contents to Each Chapter.* To give the student an understanding of what is to come, each chapter starts out with a topical outline of its contents.

2. *What If...?* To stimulate student interest in the chapter topics, each chapter begins with a hypothetical situation that we call "What If...?" Some important "What If..." examples are:

- "What If ... We had a National Police Force?" (Chapter 3)
- "What If ... Political Polls Were Banned?" (Chapter 6)
- "What If ... Federal Judges were Elected?" (Chapter 13)

3. *Marginal Definitions.* Because terminology is often a stumbling block to understanding, each important term is printed in boldface, and a definition appears in the margins adjacent to the boldfaced terms. Additionally, all of the marginal definitions are contained alphabetically in a glossary at the end of the text.

4. *Did You Know?* Throughout the text, in the margins, are various facts and figures that we call "Did You Know?" They add relevance, humor, and a certain amount of fun to the student's task of learning about American government and politics. Examples of the "Did You Know" feature are:

- Did You Know ... That the term "Affirmative Action" was first used by a state when New York passed the Fair Employment Practices Law in 1945? (Chapter 5)
- Did You Know ... That there are over 80,000 lobbyists in Washington, D.C., about 20 percent of which represent foreign governments (Chapter 7)
- Did You Know ... That in one month alone the General Accounting Office discovered that twenty federal programs incorrectly paid more than $4.3 million to dead people? (Chapter 12)
- Did You Know ... That all of the personal federal income tax paid by all people west of the Mississippi River would not even pay the interest on the federal deficit of more than $4 trillion? (Chapter 14)

5. *Profiles.* Every chapter is enlivened with a profile of key individuals who have made unique contributions to the American political system.

6. *Politics and ....* Every chapter is further enlivened with special highlighted boxes entitled "Politics and ..." in which we take a closer look at some of the interesting aspects of topics discussed in the chapter. Some of these boxes are:

- Politics and Cultural Diversity.
- Politics and the Environment.
- Politics and Comparative Systems.
- Politics and the Media.

7. *Getting Involved.* Because we believe that the best way for students to get a firmer understanding of the American political system is by direct participation, we offer suggestions on ways for them to get involved in the system. At the end of each chapter, there are suggestions of where to write, whom to call, and what to do. Some examples of this feature are:

- Expressing Your Views: Letters to the Editor (Chapter 3).
- What Does the Government Know about You? (Chapter 12).

8. *Point-by-Point Chapter Summary.* At the end of each chapter, the essential points in the chapter are presented in a point-by-point format for ease of review and understanding.

9. *Questions for Review and Discussion.* To elicit student interest and discussion in and out of class, there are two to five questions for review and discussion at the end of each chapter.

10. *Selected References.* Important and understandable references are given at the end of each chapter. Each reference is annotated to indicate its usefulness and the area that it covers.

11. *Tables, Charts, and Photos.* As you can readily see, the text uses tables and charts, as well as photos, to summarize and illustrate important institutional, historical, or economic facts.

Emphasis on Critical Thinking

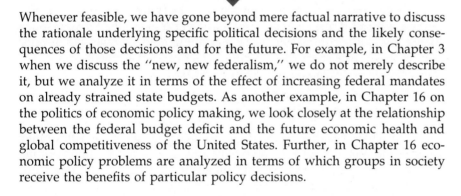

Whenever feasible, we have gone beyond mere factual narrative to discuss the rationale underlying specific political decisions and the likely consequences of those decisions and for the future. For example, in Chapter 3 when we discuss the "new, new federalism," we do not merely describe it, but we analyze it in terms of the effect of increasing federal mandates on already strained state budgets. As another example, in Chapter 16 on the politics of economic policy making, we look closely at the relationship between the federal budget deficit and the future economic health and global competitiveness of the United States. Further, in Chapter 16 economic policy problems are analyzed in terms of which groups in society receive the benefits of particular policy decisions.

The Annotated U.S. Constitution

So that this book can serve as a reference, we have included important documents for the student of American government to have close at hand. Of course, every college American government text includes the U.S. Constitution. We believe that this document—and students' understanding of it—is so important that we have included in this edition a fully annotated U.S. Constitution as Appendix B. Although our brief summaries of constitutional provisions should not be thought of as a substitute for word-for-word analysis, they will help the student understand the finer points within each part of our Constitution.

In addition to a new appendix on how to do research in political science (see the next section) we also have the following appendices:

- *The Declaration of Independence.*
- *A list of presidents of the United States with pertinent biographical information.*
- *Federalist Papers #10 and #51.*

Appendix on How to Do Research in Political Science

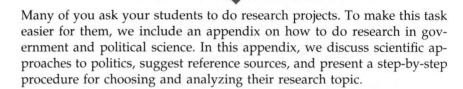

Many of you ask your students to do research projects. To make this task easier for them, we include an appendix on how to do research in government and political science. In this appendix, we discuss scientific approaches to politics, suggest reference sources, and present a step-by-step procedure for choosing and analyzing their research topic.

A Full Supplements Package

In conjunction with a number of our colleagues, we have developed a supplementary teaching materials package that we believe is the best available today.

Study Guide

The student Study Guide was written by James McElyea of Tulsa Junior College, Oklahoma. Each chapter provides learning objectives, a topical outline, a list of terms and concepts, and a variety of self-study questions. The Study Guide contains an essay describing how students can develop and improve their study skills for the American government course. The Study Guide is available for student purchase.

Instructor's Manual with Test Bank

The Instructor's Manual was written by Michael Dinneen of Tulsa Junior College and includes learning objectives and an annotated chapter outline, as well as with numerous teaching suggestions, examples, ideas for presentation, and supplemental lecture ideas. The Test Bank for the 1994–1995 edition has been thoroughly revised with many new items added. The test bank consists of multiple-choice, short-answer, and essay questions.

Computerized Instructor's Manual

The entire Instructor's Manual is now available on disk in ASCII format. It can be coded for practically any word-processing program that you are using. You can modify the Instructor's Manual to meet your own needs and specifications.

Computerized Testing

A computerized testing program, WESTEST, containing the test questions from the Instructor's Manual, is available with this text. WESTEST may be obtained for the IBM PC and compatibles or the Apple Macintosh family of microcomputers. WESTEST allows instructors to create new tests, modify existing tests, change the questions from West's original test bank, and print tests in a variety of formats. Instructors can add questions of their own to the test bank. Instructors should contact their West sales representative to inquire about acquiring WESTEST.

West's Computerized Study Guide—Microguide

A Computerized Study Guide is available with this edition. West's Computerized Study Guide allows students the opportunity to practice taking quizzes and tests on either IBM PC and compatible computers or the Apple Macintosh family of microcomputers. This new software contains a variety of self-testing formats, including multiple-choice and true/false questions. West's Computerized Study Guide is available free to adopters.

A Book of Readings

Accompanying the book is a reader consisting of nineteen chapters keyed to the book topics. Each chapter has from two to four short, interesting, timely, and thought-provoking articles taken from recent sources. The articles focus on subjects discussed in the book and provide the students with additional depth on these topics. Examples include articles on the supposed end of the middle class, on church, state and the supreme court, "green" voters, a new movement on "communitarianism," an article which argues that the old political bosses may not have been such a bad thing. Each section has a short introduction that provides the student with a summary and overview. There are also study and discussion questions at the end of each chapter.

An Introduction to Critical Thinking and Writing in American Politics

In keeping with the emphasis on critical thinking in this edition, we have written a handbook entitled *An Introduction to Critical Thinking and Writing in American Politics*. This handbook introduces students to a series of critical-thinking techniques that will allow them to make better use of the information they receive about the political sphere from campaign speeches, mass media, and privately sponsored publications. Although the examples used in the handbook relate specifically to American politics, the techniques in critical thinking presented can be of value to the students in all their college courses, as well as in their day-to-day activities.

Videotapes

We are pleased to announce that *American Government and Politics Today* was selected as the recommended text for the Dallas County Community College District telecourse, "Government by Consent," which began in 1990. The telecourse is distributed through Dallas Telecourse and the PBS Adult Learning Service to educational institutions.

All qualified adopters of *American Government and Politics Today* are able to select three special half-hour videotapes from this exciting new telecourse. The program is devoted to topics central to the study of American government and includes interviews with major contemporary decision makers. Qualified adopters may also choose from West's Political Science Video Library. A list of tapes if available upon request.

Videodisc

The latest teaching technology involves the use of the videodisc. Similar to the familiar compact disc, a videodisc allows you to instantly find material that you need to illustrate points in a lecture. You can easily go exactly to the spot on the disc that you want. You can still frame for as long as you wish, also. *West's American Government Videodisc* includes, for example, Bill Moyers talking about the Bill of Rights and then interviewing citizens to get their opinions about that important document (in Unit Two) and David Frost interviewing past presidents (in Unit Five).

In addition to the motion sequences, there are hundreds of still frames that can be used in place of overhead transparencies. *West's American Government Videodisc* also has accompanying software, called The Lecture Builder™, described below.

Interactive Videodisc Learning—
Interest Groups and Political Action Committees

A special interest for student learning is the interactive videodisc that we offer. It covers two lessons—interest groups and political action committees (PACs). Your students can interact with the videodisc by answering questions at appropriate spots in the motion-video sequences. This system can be used with any videodisc player that can be controlled by one of the numerous consumer computer systems.

Software

Two software systems are available for the 1993–1994 edition of this text.

The Lecture Builder™.　Those who use the *West's American Government Videodisc* will find that The Lecture Builder™ software allows for complete customization of each separate lecture. This software works with any Macintosh II family computer and any IBM or compatible using the Windows® operating system environment. The Lecture Builder™ permits the instructor to pick and choose the order of the still frames and the motion videos from any part of the videodisc. Also, the motion videos can be edited by the instructor. The Lecture Builder™ also has a fully automated mode with programmable time segments. Ask your West sales representative for a demonstration.

Interactive Software.　This software allows your students to interact with the videodisc that covers interest groups and political action committees.

Transparency Acetates

A set of approximately fifty full-color transparency acetates of key graphs, tables, and diagrams found in the text is available to adopters of this text.

For Users of Previous Editions

First of all, we thank you for your past support. Here we wish to let you know what changes there have been in the 1994–1995 edition.

1. There is more political analysis.

2. The former "Highlights" have been replaced with *Politics and . . .* (with some of the listings already given in this preface). These emphasize more political analysis than the last edition's "Highlights".

3. The following "What If. . ." features are new:

- "What If . . . We Had a World Government?" (Chapter 1).
- "What If . . . We Had an Unwritten Constitution?" (Chapter 2).
- "What If . . . We Had a National Police Force?" (Chapter 3).
- "What If . . . Political Polls Were Banned?" (Chapter 6).
- "What If . . . Interest Group's Contributions Were Limited to $100 per Candidate?" (Chapter 7).
- "What If . . . The Vice President Served as the President's Chief of Staff?" (Chapter 11).
- "What If . . . America Had a Flat Tax?" (Chapter 14).
- "What If . . . the United Nations Enforced Human Rights throughout the World?" (Chapter 15).

4. The key revisions to important chapters are:

- Chapter 2 (The Constitution)—now includes new sections entitled "The Constitution and the Economic Elite," "Republicanism and Federalism in the Constitution," and "The Iroquois Confederacy and American Democratic Principles," as well as an extensively revised section on "Amending the Constitution."
- Chapter 3 (Federalism)—includes a thoroughly revised section on federal grants and a new section on the "new, new federalism."
- Chapter 4 (Civil Liberties)—includes new sections on constitutional freedoms as they relate to obscene speech and abortion rights.
- Chapter 5 (Minority Rights)—includes a new section on the Civil Rights Act of 1991.
- Chapter 7 (Interest groups)—includes new sections entitled "Why are there so many interest groups?" "Interest Groups and Social Movements," "Major Interest Groups," and "Environmental Groups."
- Chapter 8 (Political Parties)—includes a thoroughly revised section on the function of political parties and new sections entitled "The Three Faces of a Party" and the "Party-in-Government."
- Chapter 10 (The Congress)—includes a new section entitled the "Shakeup of 1992" and a totally rewritten section on "How a Bill Becomes a Law," using the Civil Rights Act of 1991 as an example.
- Chapter 12 (The Bureaucracy)—includes a new section comparing the U.S. bureaucracy to that in other countries; a new section entitled "Theories of Bureaucracy"; new exhibits showing the principal duties and most important subagencies of each executive department and the principal duties of selected independent executive agencies, independent regulatory agencies, and government corporations; and

a virtually rewritten section on bureaucrats and politicians as policy makers.

- Chapter 14 (Politics of Economic Policy Making)—extensively revised to include the jobless benefits bill and the savings and loan bailout as examples of the policy-making process; the effects of the federal deficit on American citizens and the American economy; and a new section on global competitiveness and industrial policy.

5. There are three new booklets:
   The 1992 Election: The Winds of Change.
   The Rise and Fall of the Soviet Union 1917–1991.
   Handbook of Selected Court Cases.
6. Videodisc.
7. New Software—The Lecture Builder™ and Interactive Software for Interest Groups and Political Action Committees.
8. A Book of Readings.
9. Expanded annotated notes on the Constitution in Appendix B.
10. Chapter-ending conclusions: A new brief final section ends every chapter. In this section, we reflect on some of the key political developments or events that were covered within the chapter. These sections are designed to place significant topics that were dealt with in detail within the chapter in a broader framework.

Of course all textual materials—text, figures, tables, features, etc.—have been revised as necessary to reflect the political developments that occurred since the last edition. This book has also been extensively updated to reflect the results of all election results from November 1992.

Acknowledgments

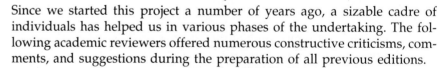

Since we started this project a number of years ago, a sizable cadre of individuals has helped us in various phases of the undertaking. The following academic reviewers offered numerous constructive criticisms, comments, and suggestions during the preparation of all previous editions.

Sharon Z. Alter
William Rainey Harper College

Kevin Bailey
North Harris Community College, Texas

Dr. Charles T. Barber
University of Southern Indiana
Evansville, Indiana

Clyde W. Barrow
Texas A&M University

Lynn R. Brink, Ed.D.
North Lake College
Irving, Texas

Dr. Barbara L. Brown
Southern Illinois University at Carbondale
Carbondale, Illinois

Ralph Bunch
Portland State University

Carol Cassell
University of Alabama

Frank J. Coppa
Union County College
Cranford, New Jersey

Robert E. Craig
University of New Hampshire

Doris Daniels
Nassau Community College, New York

Marshall L. DeRosa, Ph.D.
Louisiana State University
Baton Rouge, Louisiana

Michael Dinneen
Tulsa Junior College

Gavan Duffy
University of Texas at Austin

George C. Edwards, III
Texas A&M University

Mark C. Ellickson
Southwestern Missouri State
University
Springfield, Missouri

Joel L. Franke
Blinn College
Brenham, Texas

Dale Grimnitz
Normandale Community College

Dr. Donald Gregory
Stephen F. Austin State University
Nacogdoches, Texas

Stefan D. Haag
Austin Community College, Texas

Dr. Jean Wahl Harris
University of Scranton
Scranton, Pennsylvania

David N. Hartman
Rancho Santiago College

Robert M. Herman
Moorpark College, California

Paul Holder
McClennan Community College
Waco, Texas

Michael Hoover
Seminole Community College
Sanford, Florida

J. C. Horton
San Antonio College, Texas

Willoughby Jarrell
Kennesaw College, Georgia

Loch K. Johnson
University of Georgia

John D. Kay
Santa Barbara City College, California

Charles W. Kregley
University of South Carolina

Dale Krane
Mississippi State University

Samuel Krislov
University of Minnesota

Ray Leal, Ph.D.
Southwest Texas State University
San Marcos, Texas

Sue Lee
Center for Telecommunications
Dallas County Community College
District

Carl Lieberman
University of Akron, Ohio

Orma Linford
Kansas State University

James D. McElyea
Tulsa Junior College, Oklahoma

William P. McLauchlan
Purdue University

William W. Maddox
University of Florida

S. J. Makielski, Jr.
Loyola University, New Orleans

Jarol B. Manheim
George Washington University

J. David Martin
Midwestern State University, Texas

Bruce B. Mason
Arizona State University

Stanley Melnick
Valencia Community College, Florida

Robert Mittrick
Luzerne County Community College,
Pennsylvania

Stephen Osofsky
Nassau Community College,
New York

John P. Pelissero
Loyola University of Chicago

Charles Prysby
University of North Carolina

Donald R. Ranish
Antelope Valley College,
California

Curt Reichel
University of Wisconsin

Russell D. Renka
Southeast Missouri State University

Eleanor A. Schwab
South Dakota State University

Len Shipman
Mount San Antonio College,
California

Scott Shrewsbury
Mankato State University, Minnesota

Carol Stix
Pace University
Pleasantville, New York

Gerald S. Strom
University of Illinois at Chicago

John R. Todd
North Texas State University

B. Oliver Walter
University of Wyoming

Allan Wiese
Mankato State University, Minnesota

Thomas L. Wells
Old Dominion University, Virginia

Robert D. Wrinkle
Pan American University, Texas

Jean B. White
Weber State College, Utah

The 1994–1995 edition of this text is the result of our working closely with reviewers who each offered us penetrating criticisms, comments, and suggestions for how to improve the text. While we haven't been able to take account of all requests, each of the reviewers listed below will see many of his or her suggestions taken to heart.

Danny M. Adkison
Oklahoma State University

Sharon Z. Alter
William Rainey Harper College, Illinois

Carolyn Grafton Davis
North Harris County College, Texas

Elizabeth N. Flores
Del Mar College, Texas

William A. Giles
Mississippi State University

Forest Grieves
University of Montana

Donald L. Jordan
United States Air Force Academy, Colorado

Bruce L. Kessler
Shippensburg University, Pennsylvania

Steve J. Mazurana
University of Northern Colorado

Thomas J. McGaghie
Kellogg Community College, Michigan

Helen Molanphy
Richland College, Texas

Gregory S. Powell
Kilgore College, Texas

Michael A. Preda
Midwestern State University, Texas

Many individuals helped during the research and editorial stages of this edition. We wish to thank Michael Cik, Eric Hollowell, Lavina Miller, and Suzanne Jasin. Marie-Christine Loiseau also aided in proofreading. Clyde Perlee, Jr., our untiring editor at West Publishing Company, continued to offer strong support and guidance at every phase of this edition. Our project editor, Bill Stryker, helped us in this new design and photo research program. He remains the object of our sincere appreciation as does Jan Lamar for her extensive developmental guidance and her ability to get all the teaching supplements out on time.

Any errors that remain are our own. We welcome any and all comments from instructors and students alike. Comments that we have received on the first three editions have helped us improve this text. Nonetheless, we know that we need to continue to make changes as the needs of instructors and students change.

Barbara Bardes
Mack Shelley
Steffen Schmidt

CHAPTER 1

American Democracy and Political Culture

CHAPTER CONTENTS

WHAT IF ... WE HAD A WORLD GOVERNMENT?

Since the dawn of history, various peoples and nations of the world have engaged in warfare. Indeed, it sometimes seems that armed conflict is an essential and inescapable aspect of human existence. But what if the almost two hundred nations of the world agreed to unite into one political state? What would it be like if there was only one nation—a global nation—on planet Earth?

Let's assume that a global nation exists and that its government is similar to that of the United States under the U.S. Constitution. In other words, we will assume that the world government is based on the consent of the various nations' representatives, governmental powers are shared by the world government and the various nations, and that if a particular nation's law conflicted with a law enacted by the world government, the world government's law would be supreme. Furthermore, we will assume that, as in the United States, the world government has three branches—an executive branch, a legislative branch, and a judicial branch—and a balance of powers exists among the three branches.

What would it mean for the people of the world if a global government of this kind existed? Obviously, there would be many advantages. One of the most significant benefits would be world peace. The armed forces of the global nation would be under the control of the world government. If two or more subordinate nations could not reconcile their differences, they would be compelled to do so by the military might of the world government. Unless they wanted to resort to civil war, the hostile nations would have to comply with the world government.

International trade would also be greatly facilitated. Trade barriers—such as tariffs (taxes) or quotas on imports or exports—would no longer exist, and uniform commercial laws would reduce the risks currently attending international business transactions. Sellers and buyers around the planet could engage in business transactions just as they currently do within the United States, knowing that their respective promises would be enforced by the world court system. There would also be a single world currency unit, instead of the more than one hundred different currencies now existing.

Of course, there would also be disadvantages to having a single global nation. Consider, for example, the fact that our hypothetical world government is a representative democracy (that is, an elected government that has the support of the majority of the nations' peoples). This means that the government would have to be responsive to the economic needs, customs, and social values of many nations and cultures. Compromises would have to be made that might not be acceptable to many. For example, in some countries, religion and government are not separated as in the United States. In some countries of the Moslem world of North Africa and the Middle East, the law of Islam is the law of the state and vice versa. Similarly, in Latin America, the Roman Catholic Church has traditionally played a dominant political, as well as cultural, role. Nations whose politics and religion are thus intertwined might not agree to become members of the world nation unless their customs were recognized, at least in part, by the world constitu-

tion. In a word, the civil rights guaranteed by the world constitution might differ substantially from the civil rights guaranteed by the U.S. Constitution.

Also, what if the world government were taken over by revolutionaries who somehow obtained control of the world government's armed forces? What if the democratic government became a dictatorship? There would be no other national army to defend the world against the dictatorship. And, if the world government took control of the communications network, it would be exceedingly difficult for the various nations to organize a counterattack and regain control of the world government.

Similarly, there would be no sanctuary from the world government's policies and law. There would probably be extradition laws among all nations similar to those among the states in the United States. Those accused of crimes could not escape to another country, such as Brazil, and evade the law. Although this might enhance crime control, it would also mean that if you objected to a law or policy of the world government, you would have no recourse but to obey it or face the consequences of noncompliance.

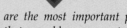

1. *What are the most important policy problems that a world government would have to address?*
2. *How would a world government protect against the possibility that it might be taken over by revolutionaries and turned into a world dictatorship?*

"This country, with all its institutions, belongs to the people who inhabit it. Whenever they shall grow weary of the existing government, they can exercise their constitutional right of amending it, or their revolutionary right to dismember or overthrow it."[1] With these words, Abraham Lincoln underscored the most fundamental concept of American government—that the people control the government, and not vice versa. Furthermore, the people have the right to change the government through established procedures or, if that fails, by more extreme measures.

In the last ten years, we have witnessed the citizens of Eastern Europe and the former Soviet Union claiming the right to control their own destinies and, in many cases, demanding new **institutions** of government that will better meet their needs. For the first time in more than forty years, the citizens of Poland, Hungary, (former) East Germany, Romania, Bulgaria, and (former) Czechoslovakia formed competing political parties, organized election campaigns, and turned out to vote for new political leaders. For them, the fundamental questions of politics—who governs, who makes the decisions that will change people's lives, who enforces the laws and how—are immediate and exhilarating.

In contrast, in the United States, where the right to vote has been ensured for more than two hundred years, only about one-half of the eligible voters usually participate in electing the president. Even fewer vote in state or local contests. For many Americans, the institutions of government are remote and complicated; the problems of daily life outweigh interest in political issues.

If it takes something new, interesting or exciting to get Americans involved in politics, the election of 1992 provided that stimulus. While the campaign of incumbent president George Bush seemed stale and unable to generate momentum, the Clinton-Gore ticket presented fresh faces and a fresh style to the public. More importantly, H. Ross Perot's bid for the

INSTITUTIONS
Long-standing, identifiable structures or associations that perform functions for society.

---

[1]*The Oxford Dictionary of Quotations,* 3d ed. (Oxford, England: Oxford University Press, 1980), p. 314.

Like the people of other Eastern European nations and the former Soviet Union, the voters of Hungary cast their ballots to choose new leaders. As Soviet dominance in Eastern and Central Europe disappeared, political parties and the other mechanisms of elections were created very quickly in many of these nations, to meet national demands. Consultants from United States political parties and citizen groups aided the nations as they established their new political systems.

presidency introduced a new type of campaign to the public and garnered 19 percent of the vote, more than any third party candidate since Theodore Roosevelt in 1912. Perot appealed to independent voters with his "anti-politics as usual" message and his clear articulation of the issues. Although both Clinton and Bush tried to avoid dealing with the Perot campaign, the tone of the presidential debates was certainly changed by the addition of Perot.

Clinton's campaign also reached out to motivate voters with its emphasis on young voters and baby boomers. Bill Clinton's appearances on MTV and late-night television helped boost his credibility with the younger generation. His campaign also worked hard at increasing voter registration, including participation in the "Rock the Vote" campaign with rock music companies. Because independent voters and young voters generally are less likely to go to the polls, the Clinton and Perot campaigns undoubtedly contributed to the unusually high voter turnout seen in 1992.

As Lincoln well understood, politics will only involve Americans if they understand the institutions, the players in the political arena, and the stakes of the game. The goal of this textbook is to reveal the political processes by which people try to influence decisions and the institutions of government in which decisions are made. To begin, we explore the nature of politics and how our political system deals with the universal question of who governs.

What Is Politics?

If there were no government, there would be no **politics** as we understand the concept. Although there are probably as many definitions of politics as there are political scientists, most definitions see politics as a way of resolving **social conflict**.

All modern societies require cohesion and a high level of cooperation among their members to survive and prosper. At the same time, each

POLITICS
According to David Easton, the "authoritative allocation of values" for a society; according to Harold Lasswell, "who gets what, when, and how" in a society.

SOCIAL CONFLICT
Disagreements arising in society because of differing beliefs, values, and attitudes; conflicts over society's priorities and competition for scarce resources.

President Bill Clinton addresses the media following his first meeting with key members of Congress. Pictured here are, from left to right, Vice President Al Gore, Senate Majority Leader George Mitchell, House Majority Leader Richard Gephardt, Senate Minority Leader Bob Dole, House Minority Leader Bob Michel, and House Speaker Tom Foley.

nation must deal with conflict among its citizens. To maintain a vital degree of unity and cooperation, ways must be found to channel and to resolve conflict to keep it from threatening the very existence of the society.

Conflicts arise in societies because their members are distinct individuals with their own unique needs, values, and perspectives. Individuals and groups compete with one another in at least three respects. First, because of their differing beliefs, rooted in religious or personal values, individuals may disagree over basic issues of right and wrong. The intensely bitter debate that has raged in recent years over abortion is an example of this kind of conflict. Second, because of their differing needs and values, individuals may disagree about society's priorities. In the 1990s, Americans are debating whether the government's main concern should be social justice and solving urban problems, saving the environment, or economic growth. Third, individuals compete for scarce resources. Income is a good example. There is never enough of it to go around to satisfy everyone's demands. Thus, many political debates can be analyzed in terms of the distribution of income. Underlying most debates about taxes, for example, is the question of which group will part with more of its income to pay for the nation's priorities.

Harold Lasswell, one of this century's most influential political scientists, fashioned a definition of politics that captures these conflicts: Politics is a process that determines "who gets what, when, and how" for a society. This definition implies that people (the "who") are in conflict over values (the "what"). Another implication is that a society needs to have a set of procedures to resolve the question of who gets what. Thus, politics not only recognizes the reality of social conflict but also the need for ways to resolve these conflicts. It is important to note that conflict is seen as natural and inevitable in any social system. Differences of opinion or values are not inherently bad in a society. The process of resolving conflict can be an opportunity for clarifying values and making change possible.

Another leading political scientist, David Easton, has formulated one of the most widely used definitions of politics, one that is similar to Lasswell's. Easton defines politics as the "authoritative allocation of values" for a society. This means that politics encompasses all of the activities involved in the conflict over who receives benefits from the society. These benefits, or values, may include status, welfare payments, or a law dealing with prayer in the public schools. Easton further specifies that conflict resolution must be authoritative. Authoritative decisions are those that can be backed up by legitimate power. This concept of **authority** is very important for helping us understand politics and the role of government in society.

What Does Government Do?

If politics refers to conflict and conflict resolution, **government** refers to the structured arrangement through which the decisions resolving conflict are made. Some societies, such as families or tribes, may be small enough that they do not need permanent structures to make these decisions. The group may collectively and in very informal ways allocate values for the whole society. This would be a community that has politics but no government. But once a society reaches a certain level of complexity, there is likely to emerge a particular person or group of people who makes de-

AUTHORITY
The features of a leader or an institution that compel obedience, usually because of ascribed legitimacy. For most societies, government is the ultimate authority in the allocation of values.

GOVERNMENT
A permanent structure (institution) composed of decision makers who make society's rules about conflict resolution and the allocation of resources and who possess the power to enforce them.

Did You Know ... That the phrase "In God We Trust" was made the national motto on July 30, 1956, but had appeared on U.S. coins as early as 1864?

BUREAUCRACY
A large organization that is structured hierarchically to carry out particular functions.

PUBLIC POLICIES
What the government decides to do or not to do.

COMPLIANCE
Accepting and carrying out authoritative decisions.

LEGITIMACY
A status conferred by the people on the government's officials, acts, and institutions through their belief that the government's actions are an appropriate use of power by a legally constituted governmental authority following correct decision-making policies. These actions are regarded as rightful and entitled to compliance and obedience on the part of citizens.

POWER
The ability to cause others to modify their behavior and to conform to what the power holder wants.

TOTALITARIAN REGIME
A form of government that controls all aspects of the political and social life of a nation. All power resides with the government. The citizens have no power to choose the leadership or policies of the country.

cisions allocating values for the society. With the formal establishment of these decision makers, we have arrived at the concept of government.

Governments range in size from the chief of a primitive tribe to the massive **bureaucracy** of the People's Republic of China. To carry out its function of making rules to resolve social conflict, governments may consist of multiple decision-making bodies and permanent organizations, such as the bureaucracy. The government's activities range from simply outlining the rules or laws that regulate individual behavior to the implementation of **public policies** that are intended to fulfill specific national goals. As an example of the former, state governments set the age and qualifications necessary to obtain a driver's license. As an example of the latter, the national government has adopted a policy to improve the quality of air by closely regulating the kinds of automobile engines that can be sold and the gasoline that they burn to reduce the level of some pollutants in the air of American cities.

The government's environmental policy requires that individuals use unleaded gasoline, which costs more than leaded fuel, in all cars produced after 1975. Why do most citizens obey this law or, for that matter, any other law? One reason that citizens obey the government is because people believe that it has the authority to make such laws. By authority, we mean the ultimate right to force **compliance** with its decisions. In general, Americans also believe that the laws should be obeyed because they possess the quality of **legitimacy,** that is, they are appropriate and rightful. The laws are an appropriate use of power by the legally constituted government following correct decision-making procedures. To say that authority is legitimate is to suggest strongly an obligation to comply with its decisions—even a moral obligation.

What Is Power?

Another and perhaps more fundamental answer to why we comply with onerous rules is because we understand that the government has the **power** to enforce these laws. Although we may obey the speed limit and acknowledge the legitimacy of pollution control laws, we also support the right of the government to use force to make other citizens obey the same laws.

Power is a particular kind of relationship between two actors. If Smith is able to make Brown do something that Brown would otherwise not do, we say that Smith has power over Brown. That power may be exercised through persuasion, command, or physical coercion, as well as myriad other ways. In the same way, we perceive an interest group such as the National Rifle Association as powerful if it is successful in preventing gun control regulations. Often, we talk of the power of presidents to convince Congress to pass legislation that they have requested. In many respects, power is at the heart of "who gets what."

Who Governs?

One of the most fundamental questions of politics is who or what groups control the government. Who has the power to make laws and enforce obedience in the society? At one extreme are societies that are governed by a **totalitarian regime.** In this form of government, a small group of leaders or a single individual—a dictator—makes all political decisions for the society. Every aspect of political, social, and economic life is controlled by the government. The people have no power to influence the government or select its leadership.

In contrast to totalitarian government is **anarchy,** which is the state of no government. Anarchy exists when every individual governs himself or herself in a society in which there are no laws and no government.

The United States is a **democracy.** Derived from the Greek language, the word means "government by the people." The ultimate power to control the government, including changing its institutions and choosing the political decision makers, rests with the people. Democracy, however, can take many forms. The earliest and purest form was created by the ancient Greeks.

ANARCHY
The state of having no government and no laws. Each member of the society governs himself or herself.

DEMOCRACY
A system of government in which ultimate political authority is vested in the people. Derived from the Greek words *demos* ("the people") and *kratos* ("authority").

The Athenian Model of Direct Democracy

The government of the ancient Greek city-state of Athens is often considered to be the historical model for a **direct democracy.** In fact, the system was not a pure system of direct democracy because the average Athenian was not a participant in every political decision. Nonetheless, all major issues, even if decided by the committees of the ruling Council, were put before the assembly of all citizens for a vote. Moreover, about one in six citizens held some political office in any given year. Because positions were usually held only for one year and rotated from one citizen to another quite often, most citizens did, in fact, participate in governing. The most important feature of Athenian democracy was that the **legislature** was composed of all of the citizens. Women, foreigners, and slaves, not being citizens, were excluded.

Direct democracy in Athens is considered to have been an ideal form of democracy because it demanded a high level of participation from every citizen. All important decisions were put to a vote of the entire

DIRECT DEMOCRACY
A system of government in which political decisions are made by the people directly, rather than by their elected representatives; probably possible only in small political communities.

LEGISLATURE
A government body primarily responsible for the making of laws.

This town meeting in New Hampshire allows every citizen of the town to vote directly and in person for elected officials, for proposed policies, and, in some cases, for the town budget. To be effective, such a form of direct democracy requires that the citizens stay informed about local politics and devote time to discussion and decision making.

INITIATIVE
A procedure by which voters can propose a law or a constitutional amendment.

REFERENDUM
An act of referring legislative (statutory) or constitutional measures to the voters for approval or disapproval.

RECALL
A procedure allowing the people to vote to dismiss an elected official from state office before his or her term has expired.

CONSENT OF THE PEOPLE
The idea that governments and laws derive their legitimacy from the consent of the governed.

citizenry so that public debate over political issues was a constant feature of social life.

Direct democracy also has been practiced in some Swiss cantons, in New England town meetings, and in some midwestern township meetings in the United States. New England town meetings, which include all of the voters who live in the town, continue to make important decisions for the community—such as levying taxes, hiring city officials, and deciding local ordinances—by majority vote. Some states provide a modern adaptation of direct democracy for their citizens: In thirty-nine states, representative democracy is supplemented by the **initiative** or the **referendum**—a process by which the people may vote directly on laws or constitutional amendments. The **recall** process, which is available in thirteen states, allows the people to vote to remove an incumbent from state office.

The Founders' Fear of Direct Democracy

Although they were aware of the Athenian model, the framers of the U.S. Constitution—for the most part—were opposed to such a system. For many centuries preceding this country's establishment, any form of democracy was considered to be dangerous and to lead to instability. But in the eighteenth and nineteenth centuries, the idea of government based on the **consent of the people** gained increasing popularity. Such a government was the main aspiration of the American and French revolutions, as well as of many subsequent ones. Few of the revolutions' advocates, however, were ready to embrace direct democracy on the Athenian model. Generally, the masses were considered to be too uneducated to govern themselves, too prone to the influence of demagogues (political leaders who manipulate popular prejudices), and too likely to abrogate minority rights.

In *The Federalist Papers,* James Madison defended the new scheme of republican government in the Constitution, while warning of the problems inherent in a "pure democracy":

> [A] pure democracy . . . can admit of no cure for the mischiefs of faction [groups pursuing some special interest]. A common passion or interest will, in almost every case, be felt by a majority of the whole . . . and there is nothing to check the inducements to sacrifice the weaker party or an obnoxious individual. Hence it is that such democracies have ever been spectacles of turbulence and contention, and have ever been found incompatible with personal security or the rights of property; and have in general been as short in their lives as they have been violent in their deaths.[2]

Like many other politicians of his time, Madison feared that pure, or direct, democracy would deteriorate into mob rule. What would keep the majority of the people, if given direct decision-making power, from abusing the rights of individuals?

---

[2]James Madison, in Alexander Hamilton, James Madison, and John Jay, *The Federalist Papers,* No. 10 (New York: Mentor Books, 1961), p.81. See Appendix D.

PROFILE

Thomas Jefferson

"I have sworn upon the altar of God eternal hostility against every form of tyranny over the mind of man."

There is perhaps no better representative of the spirit of the early American political climate and no clearer proponent of the modern American political culture than Thomas Jefferson. It was Jefferson's eloquence, for example, that crafted the strong statements in the Declaration of Independence that established the foundation for our views about the relationship between the people and their government:

> We hold these Truths to be self-evident, that all Men are created equal, that they are endowed by their Creator with certain unalienable Rights, that among these are Life, Liberty, and the Pursuit of Happiness—That to secure these Rights, Governments are instituted among Men, deriving their just Powers from the Consent of the Governed, that whenever any Form of Government becomes destructive of these Ends, it is the Right of the People to alter or to abolish it, and to institute new Government, laying its Foundation on such Principles and organizing its Powers in such Form, as to them shall seem most likely to effect their Safety and Happiness.

Not all of Jefferson's views were written into the Declaration of Independence. For example, Jefferson's attacks on King George III of England for failing to abolish the slave trade (even though Jefferson was a slave owner) were stricken from the final version of the document.

Thomas Jefferson was born in Shadwell, Virginia, on April 13, 1743. He attended the College of William and Mary and subsequently studied law, science, and philosophy. After drafting the Declaration of Independence while a member of the Continental Congress, he was elected to the Virginia House of Delegates in 1776. Three years later, he became governor of Virginia. British occupation and political complexities led him to retire to his home at Monticello, Virginia. He became a member of the Continental Congress again in 1783, for which he drafted provisions for the subsequent Northwest Ordinance, which forbade slavery north of the Ohio River.

Jefferson was appointed minister to France in 1785 and secretary of state in 1789. He resigned that cabinet post in 1793 because of continued differences with Secretary of the Treasury Alexander Hamilton over plans for a strong, centralized, executive-centered government bordering on monarchy. He ran as the Democratic-Republican nominee for president in 1796, lost to John Adams, and became Adams's vice president. Jefferson and Aaron Burr received equal numbers of electoral votes in the 1800 presidential contest, but Jefferson became president by a vote of the House of Representatives when Hamilton threw his Federalist support in the House to Jefferson. His first term was highlighted by the Louisiana Purchase (1803), which brought huge western territories into the union. Following reelection against Federalist Charles C. Pinckney in 1804, Jefferson pursued an unpopular embargo policy to try to keep the United States out of the Napoleonic Wars that ravaged Europe.

He retired to Monticello in 1809, later founded the University of Virginia, and developed his interests in education, science, architecture, and music. He died at Monticello on July 4, 1826, the same day that John Adams passed away.

It has been said that the greatest assemblage of intellectual talent that ever gathered in the White House occurred when Thomas Jefferson dined alone.

Did You Know ... That parents are more successful in getting their children to agree with them on what party to support than in getting them to agree with them on policy issues, such as school prayers or free speech?

REPRESENTATIVE DEMOCRACY
A form of government in which representatives elected by the people make and enforce laws and policies.

UNIVERSAL SUFFRAGE
The right of all adults to vote for their representatives.

MAJORITY
More than 50 percent.

MAJORITY RULE
A basic principle of democracy asserting that the greatest number of citizens in any political unit should select officials and determine policies.

Representative Democracy

The framers of the U.S. Constitution settled on a form of republican government known as a **representative democracy.** The people hold the ultimate power over the government through the election process, but policy decisions are all made by national officials. Even this distance between the people and the government was not sufficient; other provisions in the Constitution made sure that the Senate and the president would be selected by political elites rather than by the people. This modified form of democratic government came to be widely accepted throughout the Western world as a compromise between the desire for democratic control and the needs of the modern state.

Principles of Democratic Government.   As practiced in the United States and many European countries, democratic government emphasizes certain values and procedures. All representative democracies rest on the rule of the people as expressed through the election of government officials. In the twentieth century, **universal suffrage** is the rule. In the 1790s, only free white males were able to vote and, in some states, they had to be property owners as well. Women did not receive the right to vote in national elections in the United States until 1920, while the right to vote of African Americans was not really secured until the 1960s.

Granting every person the right to participate in the election of officials recognizes the equal voting power of each citizen. This emphasis on the equality of every individual before the law is central to the American system. Because everyone's vote counts equally, the only way to make fair decisions is by some form of **majority** will. But to ensure that **majority rule** does not become oppressive, modern democracies also provide guarantees of minority rights. If certain democratic principles did not protect

Volunteers register voters in the Spanish Harlem section of New York City. By setting up a table in the neighborhood, the election officials make registration more convenient for voters as well as less threatening. Both political parties often conduct voter registration drives in the months before general elections.

minorities, the majority might violate the fundamental rights of members of certain groups, especially groups that are unpopular or dissimilar to the majority population. In the past, the majority has imposed such limitations on African Americans, Native Americans,[3] and Japanese Americans, to name only a few.

One way to guarantee the continued existence of a representative democracy is to hold free, competitive elections. Thus, the minority always has the opportunity to win elective office. For such elections to be totally open, freedom of the press and speech must be preserved so that opposition candidates may present their criticisms of the government. Americans are not always prepared to tolerate the political opinions of parties or individuals that run counter to the dominant political culture. In times of crisis, our tolerance tends to be even lower.

Constitutional Democracy.   Another key feature of Western representative democracy is that it is based on the principle of **limited government.** Not only is the government dependent on popular sovereignty, but the powers of the government are also clearly limited, either through a written document or through widely shared beliefs. The U.S. Constitution sets down the fundamental structure of the government and the limits to its activities. Such limits are intended to prevent political decisions based on the whims or ambitions of individuals in government rather than on constitutional principles.

Do We Have a Democracy?

The sheer size and complexity of American society make it unsuitable for direct democracy on a national scale. Some scholars suggest that even representative democracy is difficult to achieve in any modern state. They point to the low level of turnout for presidential elections and the even lower turnout for local ones. Polling data have shown that many Americans are neither particularly interested in politics nor well informed. Few are able to name the persons running for Congress in their district, and even fewer can discuss the candidates' positions. Members of Congress claim to represent their constituents, but few constituents follow the issues, much less communicate their views to the representatives. For the average citizen, the national government is too remote, too powerful, and too bureaucratic to be influenced by one vote.

Democracy for the Few

If the ordinary citizens are not really making policy decisions with their votes, who is? One answer suggests that **elites** really govern the United States. Proponents of **elite theory** see society much like Alexander Hamilton, who said,

Did You Know . . . That in 1992 there were 504,501 elected officials in the United States, which was more than all the bank tellers in the country?

LIMITED GOVERNMENT
A form of government based on the principle that the powers of government should be clearly limited either through a written document or through wide public understanding; characterized by institutional checks to ensure that government serves the public rather than private interests.

ELITES
The upper socioeconomic classes that control political and economic affairs.

ELITE THEORY
A perspective holding that society is ruled by a small number of people who exercise power in their self-interest.

---

[3]Certain members of this ethnic group prefer to be called either Native American Indians or American Indians. To be consistent with current usage, we refer to this group as Native Americans throughout this text.

Did You Know ... That the Greek philosopher Aristotle favored enlightened despotism over democracy, which to him meant mob rule?

All communities divide themselves into the few and the many. The first are the rich and the wellborn, the other the mass of the people.... The people are turbulent and changing; they seldom judge or determine right. Give therefore to the first class a distinct, permanent share in the government. They will check the unsteadiness of the second, and as they cannot receive any advantage by a change, they therefore will ever maintain good government.

Elite theory describes an American mass population that is uninterested in politics and willing to let leaders make the decisions. Some versions of elite theory posit a small, cohesive elite class that makes almost all the important decisions regarding the nation,[4] whereas others suggest that voters choose among competing elites. New members of the elite are recruited through the educational system so that the brightest children of the masses allegedly have the opportunity to join the elite stratum.

In such a political system, the primary goal of the government is stability, because elites do not want any change in their status. Major social and economic change only takes place if elites see their resources threatened. This selfish interest of the elites does not mean, however, that they are necessarily undemocratic. Political scientists Thomas Dye and Harmon Ziegler propose that American elites are more devoted to democratic principles and rights than are most members of the mass public.[5]

Elite theory can neither be proved nor disproved because it is not possible to identify with certainty the members of the ruling elite. Some governmental policies, such as tax loopholes for the wealthy, may be perceived as elitist in nature, whereas others benefit many members of the public. Elite theory does increase our awareness of the power of both elected and unelected leaders.

[4]Michael Parenti, *Democracy for the Few,* 4th ed. (New York: St. Martin's Press, 1983).
[5]Thomas Dye and Harmon Ziegler, *The Irony of Democracy*, 8th ed. (Duxbury, Mass.: Wadsworth, 1990).

Elites may have far more power and influence on the political system than do voters from the lower and middle classes. Because they share an educational background from selective schools, a higher income level, and common lifestyles, they are more likely to see government policy makers on a social basis and to form friendships with elected officials.

Democracy for Groups

A different school of thought looks at the characteristics of the American electorate and finds that our form of democracy is based on group interests. Even if the average citizen cannot keep up with political issues or cast a deciding vote in any election, the individual's interests will be protected by groups that represent him or her.

Theorists who subscribe to **pluralism** as a way of understanding American politics believe that people are naturally social and inclined to form associations. These groups of like-minded individuals will present their demands to government. In the pluralists' view, politics is the struggle among groups to gain benefits for their members. Given the structures of the American political system, group conflicts tend to be settled by compromise and accommodation so that each interest is satisfied to some extent.[6]

Pluralists see public policy as resulting from group interactions carried out within Congress and the executive branch. Because there are a multitude of interests, no one group can dominate the political process. Furthermore, because most individuals have more than one interest, conflict among groups does not divide the nation into hostile camps.

There are a number of flaws in some of the basic assumptions of this approach. Among these are the relatively low number of people who formally join interest groups, the real disadvantages of pluralism for the poorer citizens, and pluralism's belief that group decision making always reflects the best interests of the nation.

Both pluralism and elite theory attempt to explain the real workings of American democracy. Neither approach is complete, nor can either be proved. The perspective viewing the United States as run by elites reminds us that the founders were not great defenders of the mass public and suggests that people need constant motivation to stay involved in the political system. In contrast, the pluralist view underscores both the advantages and the disadvantages of Americans' inclination to join, to organize, and to pursue benefits for themselves. It points out all of the places within the American political system in which interest groups find it comfortable to work. With this knowledge, the system can be adjusted to keep interest groups within the limits of the public good.

PLURALISM
A theory that views politics as conflict among interest groups. Political decision making is characterized by bargaining and compromise.

Ideas and Politics: Political Culture

In spite of its flaws and weaknesses, most Americans are proud of their political system and support it with their obedience to the laws, their patriotism, or their votes. Given the diverse nature of American society and the wide range of ethnic groups, economic classes, and other interests, what gives Americans a common political heritage? One of the forces that unites Americans is the **political culture,** which can be defined as a patterned set of ideas, values, and ways of thinking about government and politics. For Americans, the political culture includes such symbolic ele-

POLITICAL CULTURE
The pattern of beliefs and attitudes toward government and the political process held by a community or nation.

---

[6]David Truman, *The Governmental Process* (New York: Knopf, 1951); Robert Dahl, *Who Governs?* (New Haven, Conn.: Yale University Press, 1961).

Certain groups within the United States insist on maintaining their own cultural beliefs and practices. The Amish, pictured here, are descended from German religious sects and live in close communities in Pennsylvania, Ohio, Indiana, and Illinois, as well as in other states. The more conservative Amish groups do not use modern conveniences, such as automobiles or electricity, and have resisted immunizations and mandatory schooling for their children.

POLITICAL SOCIALIZATION
The process through which individuals learn a set of political attitudes and form opinions about social issues. The family and the educational system are two of the most important forces in the political socialization process.

ments as the flag, the Statue of Liberty, and the Lincoln Memorial; ideas such as the belief that one is innocent until proved guilty; and deeply held values, including equality, liberty, and the right to hold property.

The degree to which Americans subscribe to a single set of values is surprising if you consider that virtually all U.S. citizens are descended from immigrants. The process by which such beliefs and values are transmitted to individuals is known as **political socialization.** Historically, the political parties played an important role in teaching new residents how to participate in the system in return for their votes. Frequently, the parties also provided the first economic opportunity in the form of jobs to immigrants and their families.

A fundamental source of political socialization is, of course, the family. The beliefs and attitudes transmitted to children by their parents play a large role in the formation of political views and values. Yet another major force for the socialization of Americans—past and present—has been the school system. The educational process continues to socialize the children of immigrants and native-born Americans by explicitly teaching such basic political values as equality and liberty. Perhaps the school system is even more successful in teaching loyalty to our political system. From introducing a benevolent police officer to first-graders to playing the national anthem at high school graduation, American schools emphasize patriotism and citizenship.

A Political Consensus

Usually, the more homogeneous a population, the easier it is to have a political culture that is based on consensus. One of the reasons that Great Britain maintains a limited government without a written charter is that there exists substantial agreement within the population with respect to the political decision-making process of government. Even when a nation is heterogeneous in geography and ethnic background, such as the United

POLITICS AND CULTURAL DIVERSITY

Increasing the Diversity of Americans

The map shows the number of immigrants expected to settle in each state during the 1990s, according to the U.S. Census Bureau. The shading indicates the new immigrants as a percentage of the 1990 state population. The numbers in the states indicate thousands of immigrants. The politics of the states that receive a large number of immigrants will be changed by the corresponding increase in cultural diversity.

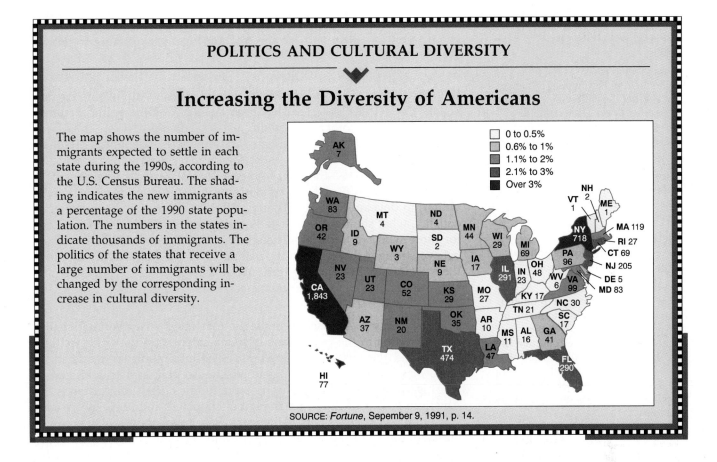

SOURCE: *Fortune*, September 9, 1991, p. 14.

States, it is possible for shared cultural ideas to develop. We have already discussed one of the most fundamental ideas in American political culture—democracy. There are other concepts related to the notion of democracy that are also fundamental to American political culture, although individual Americans may interpret their meaning quite differently. Among these are liberty, equality, and property.

Liberty. **Liberty** can be defined as the greatest freedom of individuals that is consistent with the freedom of other individuals in the society. In the United States, liberty includes religious freedom, both the right to practice whatever religion one chooses and freedom from any state-imposed religion. The basic guarantees of liberty are found not in the body of the U.S. Constitution but in the Bill of Rights, the first ten amendments to the Constitution. The process of ensuring liberty for all Americans did not end with the adoption of the Bill of Rights but has continued through the political struggles of groups such as African Americans, women, and those who hold unpopular opinions.

The concept of liberty has both personal and political dimensions. Most Americans feel that each individual has the right to free expression and to choose whatever path he or she might want to take, economically, socially, and politically. The idea of liberty also has a specific meaning in the political process. Freedom of speech, freedom of the press, and the

LIBERTY
The greatest freedom of individuals that is consistent with the freedom of other individuals in the society.

EQUALITY
A concept that all people are of equal worth.

INALIENABLE RIGHTS
Rights held to be inherent in natural law and not dependent on government; as asserted in the Declaration of Independence, the rights to "life, liberty, and the pursuit of happiness."

PROPERTY
As conceived by the political philosopher John Locke, a natural right superior to human law (laws made by government).

POPULAR SOVEREIGNTY
The concept that ultimate political authority rests with the people.

FRATERNITY
From the Latin *fraternus* ("brother"), the term *fraternity* came to mean, in the political philosophy of the eighteenth century, the condition in which each individual considers the needs of all others; a brotherhood. In the French Revolution of 1789, the popular cry was "liberty, equality, and fraternity."

A "welcome home" parade for the troops that participated in Operation Desert Storm. The crowd typifies the mixture of peoples and cultures that make up American society.

freedom to organize groups for political action are essential to maintaining competition for office and for the free and open discussion of political issues.

Equality.   The Declaration of Independence states, "All men are created equal." Today, that statement has been amended by the political culture to include groups other than white males—women, African Americans, Native Americans, Asian Americans, and others. The definition of **equality,** however, still is unclear to most Americans. Does equality mean simply political equality—the right to register to vote, to cast a ballot, and to run for political office? Does equality mean equal opportunity for individuals to develop their talents and skills? If the latter is the meaning of equality, what should the United States do to ensure equal opportunities for those who are born poor, handicapped, or female? Most Americans believe strongly that all persons should have the opportunity to fulfill their potential, but many disagree about whether it is the government's responsibility to eliminate economic and social differences.

Property.   Many Americans probably remember that the **inalienable rights** asserted in the Declaration of Independence are the rights to "life, liberty, and the pursuit of happiness." The inspiration for that phrase, however, came from the writings of an English philosopher, John Locke, who clearly stated that man's rights were to life, liberty, and **property.** In American political culture, the pursuit of happiness and property are considered to be closely related. Americans place tremendous value on owning land, on acquiring material possessions, and on the monetary value of jobs. Property can be seen as giving its owner political power and the liberty to do whatever he or she wants. At the same time, the ownership of property immediately creates inequality in society. But the desire to own property is so widespread among all classes of Americans that socialist movements, which advocate the redistribution of wealth and property, have had a difficult time securing a wide following here.

Democracy, liberty, equality, and property—these concepts lie at the core of American political culture. Other issues—such as majority rule, **popular sovereignty,** and **fraternity**—are closely related to them. For most Americans, these fundamental principles are so deeply ingrained that they rarely think about what they might mean today.

Subcultures and Political Conflict

Not all Americans share equally in this dominant political culture. Native Americans and Hispanic citizens have tried to preserve their respective cultures and languages in the face of pressure to conform to the national standard. As larger numbers of Asian, Latin American, and East European immigrants join the society, the question of how to integrate these diverse cultures into the dominant American culture becomes more urgent. To what extent can we become a more multicultural society and yet sustain some level of consensus? Some groups in the nation have rejected the majority emphasis on individual economic achievement and material pos-

Hispanic Americans join together to support a political candidate. Like other ethnic groups, these Hispanic voters seek to have their concerns heard by the candidates. In return, political candidates try to show their appreciation for the culture of the ethnic voters by delivering a speech in their language or promising more benefits for the group.

sessions and advocate instead communities based on the sharing of resources and true direct democracy.

In addition to alternative or minority subcultures, which reject part of all of the dominant culture, there exist multiple perspectives on how fundamental values relate to today's policy dilemmas. Indeed, political conflict over the application of these ideas, over choices among policies, and even over which problems are most in need of solving is inevitable and unending. What the political culture does is to provide a common ground for the debate and a common set of rules within which debate, however intense, can be carried on.

Ideas and Politics: Ideology

An **ideology** is a closely linked set of beliefs about the goal of politics and the most desirable political order. True ideologies are well-organized theories that can guide virtually every decision that an individual or society can make. As discussed in the feature on page 20, the major ideologies of our time are usually represented as a continuum from far left to far right according to their view of the power of government. Few Americans, however, derive their views on politics from the more extreme ideologies.

IDEOLOGY
A comprehensive and logically ordered set of beliefs about the nature of people and the institutions of government.

POLITICS AND IDEOLOGY

Competing Visions of Power

Political ideologies offer their adherents well-organized theories. These theories propose goals for the society and the political means by which those goals can be achieved. At the core of every political ideology is a set of values that guides its theory of governmental power. If we compare political ideologies on the basis of how much power the government should have within a society, we can array them on a continuum from left to right, as shown in the first box below.

For each of these ideological positions, the amount of power granted to the government is intended to achieve a certain set of goals within the society, and the perfect society would completely achieve these values. The values are arrayed in the second box below.

In the United States, there are adherents of each of these ideological positions; given widely shared cultural values, however, only two of these belief systems have consistently played a central part in American political debates: liberalism and conservatism.

How Much Power Should the Government Have?

Marxism-Leninism	Socialism	Liberalism	Conservatism	Libertarianism
Central control of economy and political system.	Active government control of major economic sectors.	Positive government action in economy and to achieve social goals.	Positive government action to support capitalism; action to uphold certain values.	Government action only for defense; no regulation of economy or individual behavior.

What Values Should the Government Pursue?

Marxism-Leninism	Socialism	Liberalism	Conservatism	Libertarianism
Total equality and security; unity and solidarity.	Economic equality; community.	Political liberty; economic security; equal opportunity.	Political liberty; economic liberty; order.	Total political and economic liberty for individuals.

LIBERALISM
A set of beliefs that includes the advocacy of positive government action to improve the welfare of individuals, support for civil rights, and a tolerance for political and social change.

CONSERVATISM
A set of beliefs that includes a limited role for the national government in helping individuals, support for traditional values and life-styles, and a preference for the status quo.

In fact, the American political spectrum has been dominated for decades by two relatively moderate ideological positions: **liberalism** and **conservatism.**

American liberals believe that government should take strong, positive action to solve the nation's economic and social problems. They believe it is the obligation of the government to enhance opportunities for economic and social equality for all people. Following this view, liberals tend to support government programs to reduce poverty, to redistribute income from wealthier citizens to poorer ones, and to regulate the activities of business. In general, liberals are also more tolerant of social change and resist efforts to restrict the rights of individuals to choose alternative lifestyles.

Conservatives give a higher priority to the value of property and preservation of the social order than do liberals. Conservatives believe that the individual is primarily responsible for his or her own well-being and achievements. They are less supportive of government policies that attempt to change the social or economic status of individuals. In general, conservatives believe that many activities of the government could be eliminated or could be performed better by the private sector. In recent years, the conservative movement has also espoused a return to traditional social values—strengthening the family, opposing abortion, and supporting prayer in the public schools. Conservatives believe that traditional values will help preserve order in the society, whereas liberals see the imposition of those values as restricting the liberty of individuals.

There are also smaller groups of Americans who consider themselves to be communists, socialists, or libertarians, but these groups play a minor role in the national political arena. The limited role played by these and other alternative political perspectives is reinforced by the fact that they receive little positive exposure in classrooms, the media, or public discourse.

America's presence is felt in Africa with the relief mission to Somalia.

Conclusion: The United States in a Changing World

As the United States looks to the future, it faces many questions about the nation's position in the world and the ability of its political system to deal with massive international change. The dissolution of the Soviet Union has demanded the creation of a new relationship with a former adversary. The increasingly unified European Community poses a challenge to U.S. economic power, and the Pacific Rim nations—Japan, South Korea, Singapore, Taiwan—continue to grow as economic competitors to the United States.

The political system of the nation is stable and well established. Yet the economic health of the nation seems precarious, and race relations may be deteriorating. Also, the very stability of our political system raises questions about whether the political structures, the political parties, and the voters themselves are sufficiently adaptable to respond to the new world that we face. Are the structures of our government—the executive branch, the houses of Congress, the judiciary, the bureaucracy—responsive enough to chart a new role for the United States in world politics? Can the political parties rally themselves to debate that world role? Can the political system really become multicultural and grant political power to all of the old and new minority groups that will make up the nation in the future? Can the Clinton administration propose new policies to keep American industry competitive with a unified Europe, the Pacific Rim, and the newly independent nations of Eastern Europe?

All of these questions and many more will confront the United States in the years to come. The political system is in place. What we look at in the chapters that follow are the institutions and political processes that have been established to govern the nation. What we critically examine is whether that political system has the dynamism to meet the challenges of the future.

GETTING INVOLVED

Seeing Democracy in Action

One way to begin understanding the American political system is to observe a legislative body in action. There are thousands of elected legislatures in the United States at all levels of government. You might choose to visit the city council, a school board, the township board of trustees, the state legislature, or the U.S. Congress. Before attending a business session of the legislature, try to find out how the members are elected. Are they chosen by the "at-large" method of election so that each member represents the whole community, or are they chosen by specific geographical districts or wards? Some other questions you might want to ask are: Is there a chairperson or official leader of the body who controls the meetings and who may have more power than the other leaders? What are the responsibilities of this legislature? Are the members paid political officials or do they volunteer their services? Do the officials serve as full-time or part-time employees?

When you visit the legislature, keep in mind the theory of representative democracy. The legislators or council members are elected to represent their constituents. Observe how often the members refer to the voters or to their constituents or to the special needs of their community or electoral district. Listen carefully for the sources of conflict within a community. If there is a debate, for example, over a zoning decision that involves the issue of land use, try to figure out why some members oppose the decision. Perhaps the greatest sources of conflict in local government

are questions of taxation and expenditure. It is important to remember that the council or board is also supposed to be working toward the good of the whole; listen for discussions of the community's priorities.

If you want to follow up on your visit and learn more about representative government in action, try to get a brief interview with one of the members of the council or board. In general, legislators are very willing to talk to students, particularly students who also are voters. Ask the member how he or she sees the job of representative. How can the wishes of the constituents be identified? How does the representative balance the needs of the ward or district with the good of the whole community? You also might ask the member how he or she keeps in touch with constituents and informs them of the activities of the council.

After your visit to the legislative body, think about the advantages and disadvantages of representative democracy. Do you think the average citizen would take the time to consider all of the issues that representatives must debate? Do you think that, on the whole, the elected representatives act responsibly for their constituents?

To find out when and where the local legislative bodies meet, look up the number of the city hall or county building in the telephone directory and call the clerk of council. For information on the structure of your local government, contact the local chapter of the League of Women Voters.

CHAPTER SUMMARY

1. Politics was defined by Harold Lasswell as the process of "who gets what, when, and how" in a society. David Easton defined it as "the authoritative allocation of values" in a society. The authority of government to make allocative decisions is based on power, legitimacy, and the compliance of the people.

2. Fearing the problems of a direct democracy, the framers of the Constitution set up a representative, or indirect, democracy based on the Madisonian (after James Madison) model of democratic government. The people control the government through the election of representatives. Decisions are made by majority rule, although the rights of minorities are protected.

3. Some scholars believe that most of the power in our society is held by elite leaders who actively influence political deci-

sions, while the masses are apathetic. The pluralist viewpoint suggests that groups that represent the different interests of the people struggle for political power. In pluralist theory, the political process is characterized by bargaining and compromise between groups.

4. The American political system is characterized by a set of cultural beliefs that includes liberty, equality, and property. These beliefs are passed on to each generation of Americans by the process of political socialization. There are, however, subcultures within the United States that may not subscribe to these ideas. Even within the shared culture, there are different perspectives on government responsibility for the solution of problems. These ideological views range from conservative to liberal.

QUESTIONS FOR REVIEW AND DISCUSSION

1. What decisions does the national government make that affect your life and work? What direct power does the national government have over you?

2. Think about how political decisions are made in your city or community. Are there certain individuals or social groups that seem to predominate in decision making? How are such elite groups controlled by the voters?

3. Think about your own family and schooling. How did you learn about the concepts of liberty, equality, and opportunity? How did you find out the difference between Republicans and Democrats? Has your political socialization continued in your adult years? Through what agencies, or sources of information, has that socialization occurred?

SELECTED REFERENCES

Robert A. Dahl, *Modern Political Analysis,* 4th ed. (Englewood Cliffs, N.J.: Prentice Hall, 1991). Definitions and explanations of politics and political analysis, political influence, political systems, and political socialization.

Robert A. Dahl, *A Preface to Economic Democracy* (Berkeley: University of California Press, 1985). Dahl argues that social and political equality in the United States could be achieved within a framework of liberty if "workplace democracy" were to be realized. Liberty, justice, and efficiency, he proposes, could all be achieved with such a radical transformation of the American social vision.

E. J. Dionne, Jr., *Why Americans Hate Politics* (New York: Simon & Schuster, 1991). Dionne argues that the two political ideologies, liberal and conservative, have not provided real solutions to the problems of crime, educational decline, race relations, and other pressing issues; he argues for a new "politics of the center" that will stimulate new participation and leadership.

William Greider, *Who Will Tell the People: The Betrayal of American Democracy* (New York: Simon & Schuster, 1992). According to the author, a governing elite in Washington is running the United States and running it into the ground. The elite is made up of corporate lobbyists and lawyers, think-tank gurus, and aging political parties that have alienated the average American.

Anthony King, ed., *The New American Political System* (Lanham, Md.: AEI Press, 1990). In this collection of essays, well-known and knowledgeable authors discuss their viewpoints on various aspects of the American political system.

Harold Lasswell, *Politics: Who Gets What, When and How* (New York: McGraw-Hill, 1936). A classic work defining the nature of politics.

Steven A. Peterson, *Political Behavior: Patterns in Everyday Life* (Newbury Park, Calif.: Sage, 1990). Professor Peterson, in an unconventional approach to the topic of political behavior, stresses the effect of institutions and everyday experiences on people's perceptions of politics.

Jack C. Plano and Milton Greenberg, *The American Political Dictionary,* 6th ed. (New York: Holt, Rinehart and Winston, 1982). Nearly 1,200 terms, organizations, court cases, and important statutes are defined in this useful reference work.

Donald L. Robinson, *Government for the Third American Century* (Boulder, Colo.: Westview Press, 1989). The author asks whether a system based on an eighteenth-century constitution can meet the challenges of the twenty-first century and then offers interesting ideas for numerous basic constitutional reforms.

Harold W. Stanley and Richard G. Niemi, *Vital Statistics on American Politics,* 3d ed. (Washington, D.C.: Congressional Quarterly Press, 1992). This valuable reference contains over 200 tables and figures on a wide range of topics covering almost all aspects of American politics.

Alexis de Tocqueville, *Democracy in America,* ed. by Phillips Bradley (New York: Vintage Books, 1945). An account of life in the United States by a French writer who traveled through the nation in the 1820s.

Kenneth D. Wald, *Religion and Politics in the United States* (New York: St. Martin's Press, 1987). This book emphasizes the profound influence of religion on American politics and government, and the diversity of conservative and liberal political values that can be traced to the role of religion in American society.

Richard W. Wilson, *Compliance Ideologies: Rethinking Political Culture* (New York: Cambridge University Press, 1992). Wilson describes the interaction between a country's politics and its culture and how that interaction can strengthen the state.

CHAPTER 2
The Constitution

CHAPTER CONTENTS
▼

WHAT IF . . . WE HAD AN UNWRITTEN CONSTITUTION?

The U.S. Constitution is perhaps the most enduring symbol of our nation's political heritage. It is a concise document that outlines in a few thousand words a revolutionary form of government consisting of three separate but co-equal branches (the executive, the legislative, and the judicial branches) and a bill of rights designed to protect the citizenry from abuses of power by the government. It provides the benchmark by which the courts determine whether certain forms of conduct by governmental or private entities are legally permissible.

What if there were no Constitution? Would the absence of a written document preclude the development of a legal system that would protect the rights of citizens? Would we live in an anarchic society characterized by widespread lawlessness and misery? Although these questions are provocative, it seems unlikely that such apocalyptic consequences would result simply because we lacked a written constitution. Indeed, it is possible that our legal system might be similar to the one we have today even if there were no written constitution.

Some argue that the Constitution might not be of crucial importance to the development of such things

as civil rights and religious freedom because the state of the law ultimately reflects the values of society itself. Given the prevailing climate at the time the Constitution was written, the founders felt that written guarantees were necessary. It is true, though, that values tend to change over time. This is illustrated by the fact that the institution of slavery was accepted by many persons in colonial America. Despite its offensiveness, it took four years of bloody civil war to abolish slavery. More than a century later, few people can say anything positive about slavery because our attitudes toward such things as equality and human dignity have changed.

How would the Supreme Court decide cases without a written constitution? It would look to a variety of sources of law, including prior cases, statutes, customs and practices, and academic writings. How it would rule on a case involving religious freedom or racial discrimination, for example, would depend not only on its interpretation of these sources but also on the attitudes of the justices themselves.

A written constitution is not a prerequisite for building a democratic society (although it usually helps greatly). Great Britain has no single

document that serves as a written constitution. Its constitution consists of a body of agreements, some written and some unwritten. Written parts of the British constitution are based on the Magna Carta (1215), the 1689 Bill of Rights, the Reform Act of 1832, laws passed by Parliament, and various charters. It also incorporates judicial decisions through the years that make up British common law. The unwritten part of the British constitution has derived from custom and usage—practices that have gained acceptance over time. Unlike the U.S. Constitution, which describes the selection of the president, for example, there is no written document that describes the process by which the lower house of Parliament chooses or dismisses the prime minister. The practice has instead evolved through tradition.

1. *Can you think of some examples of how the courts' interpretation of the Constitution has been affected by changing societal values and traditions?*
2. *Do you consider the fact that the United States has a written constitution to be an advantage or a disadvantage? Why?*
3. *Do Americans have any rights that are* not *enumerated in the Constitution?*

We the People of the United States, in Order to form a more perfect Union, establish Justice, insure domestic Tranquility, provide for the common defence, promote the general Welfare, and secure the Blessings of Liberty to ourselves and our Posterity, do ordain and establish this Constitution for the United States of America.

Every schoolchild in America has at one time or another been exposed to these famous words from the Preamble to the United States Constitution. The document itself is remarkable: As constitutions go, it is short; and since its ratification on June 21, 1788, relatively few amendments have been added to it. What is even more remarkable is the fact that it has remained largely intact for over two hundred years, making it the oldest written constitution in the world today.

How and why this Constitution was created is a story that has been told and retold. It is worth repeating because the historical and political context in which this country's governmental machinery was formed is essential to understanding American government and politics today. The Constitution was not the result of completely creative thinking. Many of its provisions were grounded in contemporary political philosophy. The delegates to the Constitutional Convention in 1787 brought with them two important sets of influences: their political culture and their political experience. In the years between the first settlements in the New World and the writing of the Constitution, Americans had developed a political philosophy about how people should be governed and had tried out numerous forms of government. These experiences gave the founders the tools with which they constructed the Constitution.

Did You Know . . . That the first English claim to territory in North America was made by John Cabot, on behalf of King Henry VII, on June 24, 1497?

The Starving Time

The first British outpost in North America was set up by Sir Walter Raleigh in the 1580s for the purpose of harassing the Spanish treasure

The first British settlers who landed on the North American continent faced severe tests of endurance. This woodcut depicts a cold existence for the settlers in the late 1500s and early 1600s.

fleets. Located in Roanoke Island Colony, it stands as one of history's great mysteries: After a short absence to resupply the colony, Raleigh's captain, John White, returned in 1590 to find no trace—living or dead—of the small colony's inhabitants. Roanoke has ever after been referred to as the "lost colony."

In 1607, the British government sent over a group of farmers to establish a trading post, Jamestown, in what is now Virginia. The Virginia Company of London was the first to establish successfully a permanent British colony in the Americas. The king of England gave the backers of this colony a charter granting them "full power and authority" to make laws "for the good and welfare" of the settlement. The Jamestown colonists instituted a **representative assembly,** setting a precedent in government that was to be observed in later colonial adventures.

REPRESENTATIVE ASSEMBLY
A legislature composed of individuals who represent the population.

Jamestown was not a commercial success. Of the 105 men who landed, 67 died within the first year. But 800 new arrivals in 1609 added to their numbers. By the spring of the next year, frontier hazards had cut their numbers to 60! Of the 6,000 people who left England for Virginia between 1607 and 1623, 4,000 of them perished. The historian Charles Andrews has called this the "starving time for Virginia."[1]

Pilgrims, the *Mayflower,* and the Compact

The first New England colony was established in 1620. A group of English Puritans, calling themselves pilgrims, came over on the ship *Mayflower* to the New World, landing at Plymouth (Massachusetts). Before going on shore, the adult males—women were not considered to have any political status—drew up the Mayflower Compact, which was signed by forty-one of the forty-four men aboard the ship on November 21, 1620. The reason for the compact was obvious: Being outside the jurisdiction of the Virginia

---

[1]Charles M. Andrews, *The Colonial Period of American History,* Vol. 1 (New Haven, Conn.: Yale University Press, 1934), p. 110.

The signing of the Compact aboard the *Mayflower.* In 1620, the Mayflower Compact was signed by almost all of the men aboard the ship *Mayflower,* just before disembarking at Plymouth, Massachusetts.

Company of London, which had chartered their settlement in Virginia, not Massachusetts, and fearful of the consequences of having no political institutions, the pilgrim leadership wanted to form a government.

The Compact was not a constitution. It was a political agreement in which the signers agreed to submit to majority-rule government, pending the receipt of a royal charter. The Mayflower Compact's historical and political significance is twofold: It depended on the consent of the affected individuals, and it served as a prototype for similar compacts in American history. According to Samuel Eliot Morison, the Compact proved the determination of the English immigrants to live under the rule of law, based on the *consent of the people*.[2]

More Colonies, More Government

A second outpost in New England was set up by the Massachusetts Bay Colony in 1630. Then followed Rhode Island, Connecticut, New Hampshire, and others. By 1732, the last of the thirteen colonies, Georgia, was established. During the colonial period, Americans developed a concept of limited government, which followed from the establishment of the first colonies under Crown charters. Theoretically, London governed the colonies. In practice, partly owing to the colonies' distance from London, the colonists exercised a large measure of self-government. The colonists were able to make their own laws, as in the Fundamental Order of Connecticut in 1639. The Massachusetts Body of Liberties in 1641 supported the protection of individual rights and was made a part of colonial law. In 1682, the Pennsylvania Frame of Government was passed. It, along with the Pennsylvania Charter of Privileges of 1701, established the rationale for our modern Constitution and Bill of Rights. All of this legislation enabled the colonists to acquire crucial political experience. After independence in 1776, the states quickly set up their own constitutions.

British Restrictions and Colonial Grievances

The Navigation Acts of 1651 were the earliest general restrictions on colonial activity. These acts imposed the condition that only English ships (including ships of its colonies) could be used for trade within the British Empire. The Proclamation of 1763 declared that no colonial settlement could be established west of the Appalachians. In 1764, the Sugar Act was passed, in part, to pay for the French and Indian War. Many colonists were unwilling to pay the required tax.

Further regulatory legislation was to come. In 1765, the British Parliament passed the Stamp Act, providing for internal taxation, or, as the colonists' Stamp Act Congress assembled in 1765 called it, "taxation without representation." The colonists boycotted the Stamp Act. The success of the boycott (the Stamp Act was repealed a year later) generated a feeling of unity within the colonies. The British, however, continued to try to raise revenue in the colonies. When duties on glass, lead, paint, and other items were passed in 1767, the colonists boycotted the purchase of English

---

[2]See Morison's "The Mayflower Compact" in *An American Primer*, edited by Daniel J. Boorstin (Chicago: University of Chicago Press, 1966), p. 18.

MILESTONES IN EARLY U.S.
POLITICAL HISTORY

1585	British outpost set up in Roanoke.
1607	Jamestown established, Plymouth Company lands settlers.
1620	Mayflower Compact signed.
1630	Massachusetts Bay Colony set up.
1639	Fundamental Orders of Connecticut adopted.
1641	Massachusetts Body of Liberties adopted.
1682	Pennsylvania Frame of Government passed.
1701	Pennsylvania Charter of Privileges written.
1732	Last of thirteen colonies established.
1756	French and Indian War declared.
1765	Stamp Act; Stamp Act Congress meets.
1770	Boston Massacre.
1774	First Continental Congress.
1775	Second Continental Congress; Revolutionary War begins.
1776	Declaration of Independence signed.
1777	Articles of Confederation drafted.
1781	Last state signs Articles of Confederation.
1783–1789	"Critical period" in U.S. history; weak national government.
1786	Shays' Rebellion.
1787	Constitutional Convention.

King George III (1738–1820) was king of Great Britain and Ireland from 1760 until his death on January 29, 1820. Under George III, the first attempt to tax the American colonies was made. Ultimately, the American colonies, exasperated at renewed attempts at taxation, proclaimed their independence on July 4, 1776.

FIRST CONTINENTAL CONGRESS
The first gathering of delegates from the thirteen colonies, held in 1774.

SECOND CONTINENTAL CONGRESS
The 1775 Congress of the colonies that established the Continental Army.

COMMON SENSE
Thomas Paine's best-selling pamphlet that argued for a new government in the colonies.

commodities in return. The colonists' fury over taxation climaxed in the Boston Tea Party: colonists dressed as Mohawk Indians dumped almost 350 chests of British tea into the Boston Harbor as a gesture of tax protest. In retaliation, the British Parliament passed the Coercive Acts (the "Intolerable Acts") in 1774, which closed Boston Harbor and placed the government of Boston under direct British control. The colonists were outraged—and they responded.

The Colonial Response: The Continental Congresses

New York, Pennsylvania, and Rhode Island proposed the convening of a colonial congress. The Massachusetts House of Representatives requested that all colonies hold conventions to select delegates to be sent to Philadelphia for such a congress. The **First Continental Congress** was held at Carpenter's Hall on September 5, 1774. It was a gathering of delegates from twelve of the thirteen colonies (Georgia did not attend until 1775). At that meeting, there was little talk of independence. The Congress passed a resolution requesting that the colonies send a petition to King George III expressing their grievances. Resolutions were also passed requiring that the colonies raise their own troops and boycott British trade. The British government condemned the Congress's actions, treating them as open acts of rebellion.

The delegates to the First Continental Congress declared that, in every county and city, a committee was to be formed whose mission was to spy on the conduct of friends and neighbors and to report to the press any violators of the trade ban. In spite of the antilibertarian nature of these committees, their formation was an act of cooperation among the colonies, which represented a step toward the creation of a national government.

By the time the **Second Continental Congress** met in May 1775 (this time all the colonies were represented), fighting had already broken out between the British and the colonists. One of the main actions of the Second Congress was to establish an army. It did this by declaring the militia that had gathered around Boston an army and naming George Washington as commander in chief. The participants in that Congress still attempted to reach a peaceful settlement with the British Parliament. One declaration of the Congress stated explicitly that "we have not raised armies with ambitious designs of separating from Great Britain, and establishing independent states." But by the beginning of 1776, military encounters had become increasingly frequent.

Public debate was acrimonious. Then Thomas Paine's *Common Sense* appeared in Philadelphia bookstores. The pamphlet was a colonial bestseller.[3] Many agreed that Paine did make common sense when he argued that

> a government of our own is our natural right: and when a man seriously reflects on the precariousness of human affairs, he will become convinced, that it is infinitely wiser and safer, to form a constitution of our own in a cool and de-

---

[3]To do relatively as well today, a book would have to sell between eight and ten million copies in its first year of publication.

liberate manner, while we have it in our power, than to trust such an interesting event to time and chance.[4]

Students of Paine's pamphlet point out that his arguments were not new—they were common in tavern debates throughout the land. Rather, it was the near poetry of his words—which were at the same time as plain as the alphabet—that struck his readers.

Declaring Independence

The Resolution of Independence

On April 6, 1776, the Second Continental Congress voted for free trade at all American ports for all countries except Great Britain. This act could be intrepreted as an implicit declaration of independence. The next month, the Congress suggested that each of the colonies establish state governments unconnected to Britain. Finally, on July 2, the Resolution of Independence was adopted by the Second Continental Congress:

> RESOLVED, That these United Colonies are, and of right ought to be free and independent States, that they are absolved from allegiance to the British Crown, and that all political connection between them and the state of Great Britain is, and ought to be, totally dissolved.

The actual Resolution of Independence was not legally significant. On the one hand, it was not judicially enforceable, for it established no legal rights or duties. On the other hand, the colonies were already, in their own judgment, self-governing and independent of Britain. Rather, the Resolution of Independence and the subsequent Declaration of Independence were necessary to establish the legitimacy of the new nation in the eyes of foreign governments, as well as in the eyes of the colonists themselves. What the new nation needed most was supplies for its armies and a commitment of foreign military aid. Unless it appeared in the eyes of the world as a political entity separate and independent from Britain, no foreign government would enter into a contract with its leaders.

July 4, 1776—The Declaration of Independence

By June 1776, Thomas Jefferson was already writing drafts of the Declaration of Independence in the second-floor parlor of a bricklayer's house in Philadelphia. On adoption of the Resolution of Independence, Jefferson had argued that a declaration putting forth clearly the causes that compelled the colonies to separate from England was necessary. The Second Congress assigned the task to him, and he set to work, enumerating the major grievances. Some of his work was amended to gain unanimous acceptance (for example, his condemnation of slavery was eliminated to satisfy Georgia and North Carolina), but the bulk of it was passed intact on July 4, 1776. On July 19, the modified draft became "the unanimous

"You know, the idea of taxation with representation doesn't appeal to me very much either."

Drawing by Handelsman; © 1970 The New Yorker Magazine, Inc.

---

[4]*The Political Writings of Thomas Paine*, Vol. 1 (Boston: J. P. Mendum Investigator Office, 1870), p. 46.

Did You Know ... That in the "Boston Massacre" of March 5, 1770, British troops killed five civilians who were allegedly rioting, including Crispus Attucks, an African American who was reportedly a leader of the group?

NATURAL RIGHTS
Rights held to be inherent in natural law, not dependent on governments. John Locke stated that natural law, being superior to human law, specifies certain rights of "life, liberty, and property." These rights, slightly altered to become "life, liberty, and the pursuit of happiness," are asserted in the Declaration of Independence.

UNICAMERAL LEGISLATURES
Legislatures with only one legislative body, as compared with bicameral (two-house) legislatures, such as the United States Congress. Nebraska is the only state in the Union with a unicameral legislature.

Members of the Second Continental Congress signed the Declaration of Independence on July 4, 1776. Minor changes were made in the document in the following two weeks. On July 19, the modified draft became the "unanimous declaration of the 13 United States of America." On August 2, the members of the Second Continental Congress signed it. The first official printed version carried only the signatures of the Congress's president, John Hancock, and its secretary, Charles Thompson.

declaration of the thirteen United States of America." On August 2, it was signed by the members of the Second Continental Congress. The first printed version carried only the signatures of the Congress's president, John Hancock, and secretary, Charles Thompson.

A revolutionary concept in the Declaration was the assumption, inspired by the ideas of John Locke, that people have **natural rights** ("unalienable Rights") including "life, liberty, and the pursuit of happiness." Governments are established to secure these rights, and governments derive their power "from the consent of the governed." The Declaration claimed that whenever any form of government "becomes destructive to these ends, it is the Right of the People to alter or to abolish it, and to institute a new government."

The Rise of Republicanism

Not everyone had agreed with the notion of independence. There were recalcitrant colonists in the middle and lower southern colonies who demanded that independence be preceded by the formation of a strong central government. But the anti-Royalists in New England and Virginia, who called themselves Republicans, were against a strong central government. They opposed monarchy, executive authority, and virtually any form of restraint on the power of local groups. These so-called Republicans were a major political force from 1776 to 1780. Indeed, they almost prevented victory over the British by their unwillingness to cooperate with any central authority.

During this time, all the states adopted written constitutions. Eleven of the constitutions were completely new. Two of them—those of Connecticut and Rhode Island—were old royal charters with minor modifications. Republican sentiment led to increased power for the legislatures. In Pennsylvania and Georgia, **unicameral** (one-body) **legislatures** were un-

checked by executive or judicial authority. Basically, the Republicans attempted to maintain the politics of 1776. In almost all states, the legislature was predominant.

The Articles of Confederation: Promise and Reality

The fear of a powerful central government led to the passage of the Articles of Confederation. The term **confederation** is important; it means a voluntary association of *independent* **states,** in which the member states agree to only limited restraints on their freedom of action. As a result, confederations seldom have an effective executive authority.

Even though Richard Henry Lee first proposed the establishment of the confederation on June 6, 1776, it wasn't until November 15, 1777, that the Second Continental Congress agreed to a draft for the Articles, and it wasn't until March 1, 1781, that the last state, Maryland, agreed to sign.

Under the Articles, the thirteen original colonies, now states, established a government of the states on March 1, 1781—the Congress of the Confederation. The Congress was a unicameral assembly of so-called ambassadors from each state, with each state possessing a single vote. Each year the Congress would choose one of its members as its president, but the Articles did not provide for a president of the United States. The Congress was authorized in Article X to appoint an executive committee of the states "to execute in the recess of Congress, such of the powers of Congress as the United States, in Congress assembled, by the consent of nine [of the thirteen] states, shall from time to time think expedient to vest with them." The Congress was also allowed to appoint other committees and civil officers necessary for managing the general affairs of the United States. The Articles did not establish a separate judicial institution, although Congress had certain judicial functions. In addition, the Congress could regulate foreign affairs and establish coinage and weights and measures. But it lacked an independent source of revenue and any executive machinery to enforce its desires on individual citizens throughout the land. Figure 2-1 illustrates the structure of the confederal government under the Articles of Confederation; Table 2-1 summarizes the powers—and the lack of powers—of Congress under that system.

Article II of the Articles of Confederation guaranteed each state its sovereignty:

> Each state retains its sovereignty, freedom and independence, and every power, jurisdiction, and right, which is not by this Confederation expressly delegated to the United States in Congress assembled.

Accomplishments under the Articles

Although the Articles of Confederation had many defects, there were also some accomplishments during the eight years of their existence. Certain states' claims to western lands were settled. Maryland had objected to the claims of Massachusetts, New York, Connecticut, Virginia, the Carolinas, and Georgia. It was only after these states consented to give up their land claims to the United States as a whole that Maryland signed the Articles of Confederation. Another accomplishment under the Articles was the

Did You Know . . . That on July 4, 1776, on the day the Declaration of Independence was signed, King George III of England wrote in his diary, "Nothing of importance happened today"?

CONFEDERATION
A political system in which states or regional governments retain ultimate authority except for those powers they expressly delegate to a central government. A voluntary association of independent states, in which the member states agree to limited restraints on their freedom of action.

STATE
A group of people occupying a specific area and organized under one government; may be either a nation or a subunit of a nation.

FIGURE 2-1 ■ The Structure of the Confederal Government under the Articles of Confederation

Congress
Congress had one house. Each state had two to seven members, but only one vote. The exercise of most powers required approval of at least nine states. Amendments to the Articles required the consent of all the states.

Committee of the States
A committee of representatives from all the states was empowered to act in the name of Congress between sessions.

Officers
Congress appointed officers to do some of the executive work.

The States

TABLE 2-1 ■ Powers of the Congress of the Confederation

Congress Had Power to	Congress Lacked Power to
■ Declare war and make peace.	■ Provide for effective treaty-making power and control foreign relations; it could not compel states to respect treaties.
■ Enter into treaties and alliances.	
■ Establish and control armed forces.	
■ Requisition men and money from states.	■ Compel states to meet military quotas; it could not draft soldiers.
■ Regulate coinage.	■ Regulate interstate and foreign commerce; it left each state free to set up its own tariff system.
■ Borrow money and issue bills of credit.	
■ Fix uniform standards of weight and measurement.	■ Collect taxes directly from the people; it had to rely on states to collect and forward taxes.
■ Create admiralty courts.	■ Compel states to pay their share of government costs.
■ Create a postal system.	
■ Regulate Indian affairs.	■ Provide and maintain a sound monetary system or issue paper money; this was left up to the states, and monies in circulation differed tremendously in value.
■ Guarantee citizens of each state the rights and privileges of citizens in the several states when in another state.	
■ Adjudicate disputes between states upon state petition.	

passage of the Northwest Ordinance of 1787, which established a basic pattern of government for new territories north of the Ohio River.

Finally, the Articles created a sort of "first draft" for the Constitution of the United States that was to follow. In a sense, it was an unplanned applied experiment to try out some of the principles of government set forth in the Declaration of Independence.

Weaknesses of the Articles

Although Congress had the legal right to declare war and to conduct foreign policy, it did not have the right to demand revenues from the states. It could only *ask* for them. Also, the actions of Congress required the consent of nine states. Any amendments to the Articles required the unanimous consent of the Congress and confirmation by every state legislature. Further, the Articles did not create a national system of courts.

Basically, the functioning of the government under the Articles depended on the good will of the states. Article III of the Articles simply established a "league of friendship" among the states—no national government was intended.

Perhaps the most telling weakness of the Articles was their inability to give the Continental Congress the power to tax. When states refused to send money to support the government (not one state met the financial requests made by Congress under the Articles), Congress resorted to selling off western lands to speculators or issuing bonds that sold for less than their face value. Due to a lack of resources, the Continental Congress was forced to disband the army, even in the face of serious Spanish and British military threats. Although it was permitted to do so, Congress really did not have the power to raise and maintain an army.

Shays' Rebellion and the Need for Revision of the Articles

By 1786, in the city of Concord, Massachusetts, the scene of one of the first battles of the Revolution, there were three times as many people in prison for debt as there were for all other crimes combined. In Worcester County, the ratio was even higher—twenty to one. Most of the prisoners were small farmers who couldn't pay their debts owing to the disorganized state of the economy. In August 1786, mobs of musket-bearing farmers led by former revolutionary captain Daniel Shays seized county courthouses and disrupted the trials of the debtors. Shays' men then launched an attack on the federal arsenal at Springfield, but they were repulsed.

Shays' Rebellion demonstrated that the central government could not protect the citizenry from armed rebellion or provide adequately for the public welfare.

Drafting the Constitution

The Annapolis Convention

The Virginia legislature called for a meeting of all the states at Annapolis, Maryland, on September 11, 1786—ostensibly to discuss commercial problems only. It was evident to those in attendance (including Alexander Hamilton and James Madison) that the national government had serious weaknesses that had to be addressed if it were to survive. Among the

Did You Know . . . That the delegates to the Constitutional Convention signed the document by geographic order, starting with New Hampshire—the northernmost state—and finishing with Georgia—the southernmost state?

George Washington presided over the Constitutional Convention of 1787. Although the Convention was supposed to have started on May 14, 1787, few of the delegates had actually arrived in Philadelphia by that date. It formally opened in the East Room of the Pennsylvania State House (later named Independence Hall) on May 25. Only Rhode Island did not send any delegates.

Did You Know ... That of the fifty-five delegates who attended the Constitutional Convention, sixteen failed to sign the final document and some of the thirty-nine signatories approved only with reservations?

important problems to be solved were the relationship between the states and the central government, the powers of the national legislature, the need for executive leadership, and the establishment of policies for economic stability. At this Annapolis meeting, a call was issued to all the states for a general convention to meet in Philadelphia in May of 1787 "to consider the exigencies of the union." When the Republicans, who favored a weak central government, realized that the Philadelphia meeting would in fact take place, they approved the convention in February 1787, but they made it explicit that the convention was "for the sole and express purpose of revising the Articles of Confederation." Those in favor of a stronger national government—the Federalists, as they were to be called—had different ideas.

The Philadelphia Convention

The designated date for the opening of the convention was May 14, 1787. Because few of the delegates had actually arrived in Philadelphia by that time, however, it was not formally opened in the East Room of the Pennsylvania State House[5] until May 25. By this time, fifty-five of the seventy-four delegates chosen for the convention had arrived. (Of those fifty-five, only about forty played active roles at the convention.) Rhode Island was the only state that refused to send delegates.

Not a Commoner among Them

Who were the fifty-five delegates? They certainly did not represent a cross section of eighteenth-century American society. Indeed, most were members of the upper class. Consider the following facts:

1. Thirty-three were members of the legal profession.
2. Three were physicians.
3. Almost 50 percent were college graduates.
4. Seven were former chief executives of their respective states.
5. Six were large plantation owners.
6. Eight were important businessmen.[6]

They were also relatively young by today's standards: James Madison was thirty-six, Alexander Hamilton was only thirty-two, and Jonathan Dayton of New Jersey was twenty-six. The venerable Benjamin Franklin (see the *Profile* in this chapter), however, was eighty-one and had to be carried in on a portable chair borne by four prisoners from a local jail. Not counting Franklin, the average age was just over forty-two.

The delegates may also be characterized as astute politicians who were attempting to develop a pragmatic plan to save the new nation.[7] With the exception of age, they were quite similar to the members of Congress today. In the 102d Congress (1991–1993), for example, over 180 representatives and

---

[5]The State House was later named Independence Hall. This was the same room in which the Declaration of Independence had been signed eleven years earlier.

[6]Charles Warren, *The Making of the Constitution* (New York: Barnes & Noble, 1967), pp. 55–60.

[7]John Roche, "The Founding Fathers: A Reform Caucus in Action," *American Political Science Review*, Vol. 61 (December 1961), pp. 799–816.

PROFILE

Benjamin Franklin

*"We must indeed all hang to-
gether, or, most assuredly, we
shall all hang separately."*

"Remember that *time* is money. He
that can earn ten shillings a day by
his labour, and goes abroad, or sits
idle, one half of that day, though he
spends but sixpence during his di-
version of idleness, ought not to
reckon *that* his only expense; he has
really spent, or rather thrown away,
five shillings besides." Such were
the words of Benjamin Franklin in
his *Advice to a Young Tradesman,*
published in 1748. A better example
of the cost of time would be hard
to find.

Franklin's aphorisms were undoubtedly colored by his strict Calvinist upbringing. The true Calvinist
was a driven man, described by
British economist R. H. Tawney as
"tempered by self-examination, self-
discipline, self-control . . . the practical ascetic, whose victories are won
not in the cloister, but on the battlefield, in the counting house, and in
the market." Calvin himself referred
to God as the "great task maker"
and looked around for tasks man
should undertake. Ben Franklin
claimed that he was a freethinker,
but his father's continual exhorta-
tions—such as "Seest thou a man
diligent in his business. He shall
stand before kings"—must have
had some effect.

Franklin was born in 1706 and
raised in Boston. Family funds were
insufficient for him to aim for Harvard, so he turned his hand to

printing and went to Philadelphia in
1723. Deciding that London was the
place to perfect his printing knowledge, he spent two years there
working and living the Bohemian
life. Within a few years he began to
prosper as a master printer. His
simple writing style and great clar-
ity of expression also began to be
rewarded. *Poor Richard's Almanac,*
published annually between 1732
and 1757, was one of Franklin's
most profitable enterprises, selling
ten thousand copies a year. When
he was twenty-three years old,
Franklin wrote his first treatise on
economics: *A Modest Inquiry into the
Nature and Necessity of a Paper Currency* (1729). Coincidentally, Franklin
was the first to start printing Pennsylvania paper currency.

Franklin was a crusader for learning and also a good businessman.
He introduced printing and news
publications to many communities
throughout the colonies. He also
helped start the present University

of Pennsylvania in 1751. In 1753, he
was named deputy postmaster general of the colonies.

Ben Franklin was also one of the
first persons in America to use the
techniques of advertising to increase
business. When he started his
General Magazine, he advertised his
own "Pennsylvania Fire Place." The
copy he wrote was persuasive:
Franklin criticized ordinary fire-
places because they caused drafts
that made "women . . . get cold in
the head, rheums, and defluxions,
which fall into their jaws and gums
. . . [destroying] . . . early, many a
fine set of teeth."

During the Revolution, Franklin
helped draft the Declaration of Independence, which he also signed.
Dispatched as an envoy of the new
government to France in 1776, pro-
claiming "our cause is the cause of
all mankind," he began the successful diplomatic mission that enlisted
foreign support for the Revolution.
He signed the first U.S. treaty of alliance with France in 1778 and the
treaty of peace with Great Britain
in 1783. He died in 1790.

To practical men, especially the
officers of savings banks ("a penny
saved is a penny earned"), Ben
Franklin seemed to be the epitome
of good sense and morality. To others, he appeared to be a materialistic
opportunist. But, as John Adams
once said, Franklin's "reputation
was more universal than that of
Leibniz, Newton, or Voltaire, and he
was the first civilized American."

over 60 senators were lawyers, and African Americans, Hispanics, Native Americans, and women were notably underrepresented.

The Working Environment

The conditions under which the delegates worked for 115 days were far from ideal, and were made even worse by the necessity of maintaining total secrecy. The framers of the Constitution felt that if public debate were started on particular positions, delegates would have a more difficult time compromising or backing down to reach agreement. Consequently, the windows were usually shut in the East Room of the State House. Because the summer was quickly upon the delegates, the air became heavy, humid, and hot by noon of each day. Also, when the windows were open, flies swarmed into the room. The delegates did, however, have a nearby tavern and inn to which they retired each evening. The Indian Queen became the informal headquarters of the delegates.

Factions among the Delegates

We know much about the proceedings at the convention because James Madison kept a daily, detailed personal journal. A majority of the delegates were strong nationalists—they wanted a central government with real power, unlike that of the central government under the Articles of Confederation. Washington and Franklin preferred limited national authority based on a separation of powers. But they were apparently willing to accept any type of national government, as long as the other delegates approved it. A few pronationalists, led by Gouverneur Morris of Pennsylvania and John Rutledge of South Carolina, distrusted the ability of the common people to engage in self-government.

Among the nationalists were several monarchists, including Alexander Hamilton, who was chiefly responsible for the Annapolis Convention's call for the Constitutional Convention. In a long speech on June 18, he presented his views: "I have no scruple in declaring . . . that the British government is the best in the world and that I doubt much whether anything short of it will do in America." Hamilton wanted the American president to hold office for life and to have absolute veto power over the legislature.

Another important group of nationalists were of a more democratic stripe. Led by James Madison of Virginia and James Wilson of Pennsylvania, these democratic nationalists wanted a central government founded on popular support.

Still another faction consisted of nationalists who would only support a central government if it were founded on very narrowly defined republican principles and less democratic in nature. This group was a relatively small number of individuals, including Edmund Randolph and George Mason of Virginia, Elbridge Gerry of Massachusetts, and Luther Martin and John Francis Mercer of Maryland.

Most of the other delegates of Maryland, New Hampshire, Connecticut, New Jersey, and Delaware were concerned about only one thing—claims to western lands. As long as those lands became the common property of all states, they were willing to support a central government.

Elbridge Gerry (1744–1814), from Massachusetts, was a patriot during the Revolution. He was a signatory of the Declaration of Independence and later became governor of Massachusetts (1810–1812).

Finally, there was a group of delegates who were totally against a national authority. Two of the three delegates from New York quit the convention when they saw the nationalist direction of its proceedings.

Politicking and Compromises

The debates at the convention started on the first day. James Madison had spent months reviewing European political theory. When his Virginia delegation arrived ahead of most of the others, it got to work immediately. By the time Washington opened the convention, Governor Edmund Randolph of Virginia was immediately able to present fifteen resolutions. In retrospect, this was a masterful stroke on the part of the Virginia delegation: It immediately set the agenda for the remainder of the convention—even though the delegates had, in principle, been sent to Philadelphia for the sole purpose of amending the Articles of Confederation, not to write a new constitution.

The Virginia Plan.   Randolph's fifteen resolutions proposed an entirely new national government under a constitution. It was, however, a plan that not surprisingly favored the large states, including Virginia. Basically, it called for the following:

1. A **bicameral** (two-house) **legislature,** the lower house chosen by the people and the smaller upper house chosen by the lower house from nominees selected by state legislatures. The number of representatives would be proportional to a state's population, thus favoring the large states. The legislature could void any state laws.
2. The creation of an unspecified national executive, elected by the legislature.
3. The creation of a national judiciary appointed by the legislature.

It did not take long for the smaller states to realize they would fare poorly under the Virginia plan, according to which Virginia, Massachusetts, and Pennsylvania would form a majority in the national legislature. The debate on the plan dragged on for a number of weeks. It was time for the small states to come up with their own plan.

The New Jersey Plan.   On June 15, lawyer William Paterson of New Jersey offered an alternative plan. After all, argued Paterson, under the Articles of Confederation all states had equality; therefore, the convention had no power to change this arrangement. He proposed the following:

1. The fundamental principle of the Articles of Confederation—one state, one vote—would be retained.
2. Congress would be able to regulate trade and impose taxes.
3. All acts of Congress would be the supreme law of the land.
4. Several people would be elected by Congress to form an executive office.
5. The executive office would appoint a supreme court.

Basically, the New Jersey plan was simply an amendment of the Articles of Confederation. Its only notable feature was its reference to the **supremacy doctrine,** which was later included in the Constitution.

Did You Know . . . That the First Congress, in 1789, considered 145 proposed amendments to the brand-new Constitution, of which 12 were submitted to the states and 10 were ratified in less than three years?

BICAMERAL LEGISLATURE
A legislature made up of two chambers, or parts. The United States Congress, composed of the House of Representatives and the Senate, is a bicameral legislature.

SUPREMACY DOCTRINE
A doctrine that asserts the superiority of national law over state or regional laws. This principle is rooted in Article VI of the Constitution, which provides that the Constitution, the laws passed by the national government under its constitutional powers, and all treaties constitute the supreme law of the land.

GREAT COMPROMISE
The compromise between the New Jersey and the Virginia plans that created one chamber of the Congress based on population and one chamber that represented each state equally. Also called the Connecticut Compromise.

The "Great Compromise."   The delegates were at an impasse. Most wanted a strong national government and were unwilling even to consider the New Jersey plan. But when the Virginia plan was brought up again, the small states threatened to leave. It wasn't until July 16 that the **Great Compromise** was achieved. Roger Sherman of Connecticut proposed the following:

1. A bicameral legislature in which the House of Representatives would be apportioned according to the number of free inhabitants in each state, plus three-fifths of the slaves.
2. An upper house, the Senate, which would have two members from each state elected by the state legislatures.

This plan, often called the Connecticut Compromise because of the role of the Connecticut delegates in the proposal, broke the deadlock. It did exact a political price, however, because it permitted each state to have equal representation in the Senate. Having two senators represent each state in effect diluted the voting power of citizens living in more heavily populated states and gave smaller states disproportionate political powers. But the Connecticut Compromise resolved the large-state/small-state controversy. It also settled another major issue—how to deal with slaves in the representational scheme. Slavery was legal everywhere except in Massachusetts, but it was concentrated in the South. The South wanted slaves to be counted equally in determining representation in Congress. But equal representation meant equal taxation, and the South wanted to avoid equal taxation. Sherman's three-fifths compromise solved the issue, satisfying those northerners who felt that slaves should not be counted at all and those southerners who wanted them to be counted as free whites. Actually, Sherman's Connecticut plan spoke of three-fifths of "all other persons" (and that is the language in the Constitution itself). It is not hard to figure out, though, who those other persons were.

Slavery and Other Issues.   The slavery issue was not completely eliminated by the three-fifths compromise. Many delegates were opposed to slavery and wanted it banned entirely in the United States. Charles Pinckney of South Carolina led strong southern opposition to this idea. Finally, the delegates agreed that Congress could limit the importation of slaves after 1808. The compromise meant that the issue of slavery itself was never addressed. The South won twenty years of unrestricted slave trade and a requirement that escaped slaves in free states be returned to their owners in slave states.

The agrarian South and the mercantile North were in conflict. The South was worried that the northern majority in Congress would pass legislation unfavorable to its economic interests. Because the South depended on exports of its agricultural products, it feared the imposition of export taxes. In return for acceding to the northern demand that Congress be given the power to regulate commerce among the states and with other nations, the South obtained a promise that export taxes would not be imposed. Even today, such taxes are prohibited. The United States is one of the few countries that does not tax its exports.

There were other disagreements. The delegates could not decide whether to establish only a Supreme Court or to create lower courts as well. They

An American slave market from a painting by Taylor. The writers of the Constitution did not ban slavery in the United States but did agree to limit the importing of new slaves after 1808.

deferred the issue by mandating a Supreme Court and allowing Congress to establish lower courts. They also disagreed over whether the president or the Senate would choose the Supreme Court justices. A compromise was reached, with the agreement that the president would nominate the justices and the Senate would confirm the nomination.

These compromises as well as others resulted from the recognition that if one group of states refused to ratify, the Constitution was doomed.

Working toward Final Agreement

The Connecticut Compromise was reached by mid-July. The makeup of the executive branch and the judiciary, however, was left unsettled. The remaining work of the convention was turned over to a five-man Committee of Detail, which presented a rough draft of the Constitution on August 6. It made the executive and judicial branches subordinate to the legislative branch.

The Madisonian Model.   The major issue of **separation of powers** had not yet been resolved. The delegates were concerned with structuring the government to prevent the imposition of tyranny—either by the majority or by a minority. It was Madison who devised a governmental scheme—sometimes called the **Madisonian model**—to achieve this: The executive, legislative, and judicial powers of government were to be separated so that no one branch had enough power to dominate the others. The separation of powers was by function, as well as by personnel, with Congress passing laws, the president enforcing and administering laws, and the courts interpreting laws in individual circumstances.

Each of the three branches of government would be independent of the others, but they would have to cooperate to govern. Figure 2-2 outlines these **checks and balances.** The president has veto power over congres-

MADISONIAN MODEL
The model of government devised by James Madison in which the powers of the government are separated into three branches: executive, legislative, and judicial.

SEPARATION OF POWERS
The principle of dividing governmental powers among the executive, the legislative, and the judicial branches of government.

CHECKS AND BALANCES
A major principle of the American governmental system whereby each branch of the government exercises a check on the actions of the others. Separation of powers, divided power, and checks and balances limit government's power by pitting power against power. For example, the president checks Congress by holding veto power, Congress has the purse strings, and the Senate approves presidential appointments.

The Supreme Court can declare presidential actions unconstitutional.

The president nominates federal judges; the president can refuse to enforce the Court's decisions.

THE JUDICIARY

The Supreme Court can declare congressional laws unconstitutional.

Congress can rewrite legislation to circumvent the Court's decisions; the Senate confirms federal judges.

The president proposes laws and can veto congressional legislation; the president makes treaties, executive agreements, and executive orders; the president can refuse, and has refused, to enforce congressional legislation.

THE PRESIDENCY

The Congress makes legislation and can override a presidential veto of its legislation; the Congress can impeach and remove a president; the Senate must confirm presidential appointments and consent to the president's treaties based on a two-third's concurrence; the Congress has the power of the purse and provides funds for the president's programs.

THE CONGRESS

FIGURE 2-2 ■ **Checks and Balances**

The major checks and balances among the three branches are illustrated here. Some of these checks are not mentioned in the Constitution, such as judicial review—the power of the courts to declare federal or state acts unconstitutional—or the president's ability to refuse to enforce judicial decisions or congressional legislation. Checks and balances can be thought of as a confrontation of powers or responsibilities. Each branch delays or checks the action of another; two branches in conflict have powers that can result in balances or stalemates, requiring one branch to give in or both to reach a compromise.

ELECTORAL COLLEGE
A group of persons called electors selected by the voters in each state and Washington, D.C.; this group officially elects the president and vice president of the United States. The number of electors in each state is equal to the number of each state's representatives in both houses of Congress. The Twenty-third Amendment to the Constitution permits Washington, D.C., to have as many electors as a state of comparable population.

sional acts. Congress controls the budget and must approve presidential appointments. The Supreme Court consists of judges appointed by the president but with the advice and consent of the Senate.[8] Madison also wanted to prevent the branches from abdicating their power to other branches. Note that our Constitution forces cooperation between at least two branches. But with checks and balances, we see simultaneous protection of the independence of each branch, yet forced dependence: Congress can pass a law; the executive branch must enforce and administer it.

The Executive.   Some delegates favored a plural executive made up of representatives from the various regions. This was abandoned in favor of a single chief executive. Others argued that Congress should choose the executive. To make the presidency completely independent of the proposed Congress, however, an **electoral college** was adopted, probably at

_____
[8]After *Marbury v. Madison* in 1803 (1 Cranch 137; see the Appendix at the end of this chapter, which discusses legal citations), the Supreme Court became part of this checks and balances system through judicial review and the limited right to declare the policies of the other two branches of government unconstitutional. See Chapter 15.

James Wilson's suggestion. To be sure, the electoral college created a cumbersome presidential election process. However, it insulated the president from direct popular control. The seven-year single term that some of the delegates had proposed was replaced by a four-year term and the possibility of reelection.

The Final Document

On September 17, 1787, the Constitution was approved by thirty-nine delegates. Of the fifty-five who had originally attended, only forty-two remained. Only three delegates refused to sign the Constitution. Others disapproved of at least parts of it but signed anyway to begin the ratification debate.

The Constitution that was to be ratified established the following fundamental principles:

1. Popular sovereignty, or control by the people.
2. A republican government in which the people choose representatives to make decisions for them.
3. Limited government with written laws, in contrast to the powerful monarchical English government the colonists had rebelled against.
4. Separation of powers with checks and balances among branches to prevent any one branch from gaining too much power.
5. A federal system that allowed for states' rights because the states feared too much centralized control.

The Difficult Road to Ratification

The founders knew that **ratification** of the Constitution was far from certain. Indeed, because it was almost guaranteed that many state legislatures would not ratify it, the delegates agreed that each state should hold a special convention. Elected delegates to these conventions would discuss and vote on the Constitution. Further departing from the Articles of Confederation, the delegates agreed that as soon as nine states (rather than all thirteen) approved the Constitution, it would take effect and the Congress could begin to organize the new government.

Delaware was the first to ratify, on December 7, 1787, less than three months after the signing of the final document. The vote was unanimous. Pennsylvania and New Jersey ratified soon after, on December 12 and 18, respectively. The Pennsylvania vote was 43 to 23, while the New Jersey convention was unanimous.

The Federalists Push for Ratification

The two opposing forces in the battle over ratification were the Federalists and the Anti-Federalists. The **Federalists**—those in favor of a strong central government and the new Constitution—had an advantage over the **Anti-Federalists,** who wanted to prevent the Constitution (in its then-current form) from being ratified. In the first place, the Federalists had assumed a positive name, leaving their opposition the negative label

RATIFICATION
Formal approval.

FEDERALISTS
The name given to those who were in favor of the adoption of the U.S. Constitution and the creation of a federal union. They favored a strong central government.

ANTI-FEDERALISTS
Those individuals who opposed the ratification of the new Constitution in 1787.

of *Anti*-Federalist. More important, the Federalists had attended the Constitutional Convention and knew of all the deliberations that had taken place. Their opponents had no such knowledge because those deliberations were not open to the public. Thus, the Anti-Federalists were at a disadvantage in terms of information about the document. The Federalists also had time, power, and money on their side. Communications were slow, and those who had access to the best communications were Federalists—mostly wealthy bankers, lawyers, plantation owners, and merchants living in urban areas where communication was better. The Federalist campaign was organized relatively quickly and effectively to elect Federalists as delegates to the state ratifying conventions. The Anti-Federalists, however, had at least one strong point in their favor: They stood for the status quo. In general, the greater burden is placed on those advocating change.

The Federalist Papers.   In New York, opponents of the Constitution were quick to attack it. Alexander Hamilton answered their attacks in newspaper columns over the signature "Caesar." When the Caesar letters had little effect, Hamilton switched to the pseudonym Publius and secured two collaborators—John Jay and James Madison. In a very short period of time, those three political figures wrote a series of eighty-five essays in defense of the Constitution and of a republican form of government. These widely read essays appeared in New York newspapers from October 1787 to August 1788 and were reprinted in the newspapers of other states. Although we do not know for certain who wrote every one, it is apparent that Hamilton was responsible for about two-thirds of the essays. These included the most important ones interpreting the Constitution, explaining the various powers of the three branches, and presenting a theory of judicial review. Madison's *Federalist Paper* No. 10 (see Appendix D), however, is considered a classic in political theory, dealing with the nature of groups—or factions, as he called them. In spite of the rapidity with which *The Federalist Papers* were written, they are considered by many to be perhaps the best example of political theorizing ever produced in the United States.[9]

The Anti-Federalist Response.   The Anti-Federalists used such pseudonyms as Montezuma and Philadelphiensis in their replies. Many of their attacks against the Constitution were also brilliant. They claimed that it was a document written by aristocrats and would lead to aristocratic tyranny. More important, the Anti-Federalists believed the Constitution would create an overbearing and overburdening central government inimical to personal liberty. (The Constitution said nothing about liberty of the press, freedom of religion, or any other individual liberties.) They wanted to include a list of guaranteed liberties, or a bill of rights. Finally, the Anti-Federalists decried the weakened power of the states.

The Anti-Federalists cannot be dismissed as a bunch of unpatriotic extremists. They included such patriots as Patrick Henry and Samuel

---

[9]Some scholars believe that *The Federalist Papers* played only a minor role in securing ratification of the Constitution. Even if this is true, they still have lasting value as an authoritative explanation of the Constitution.

Adams. They were arguing what had been the most prevalent view of the time. This view derived from the French political philosopher Montesquieu, who believed that liberty was only safe in relatively small societies governed by direct democracy or by a large legislature with small districts. The Madisonian view favoring a large republic, particularly expressed in *Federalist Papers* Nos. 10 and 51 (see Appendix D), was actually the more *un*popular view of the time. Madison was probably convincing because citizens were already persuaded that a strong national government was necessary to combat foreign enemies and to prevent domestic insurrections. Still, some researchers believe it was mainly the bitter experiences with the Articles of Confederation, rather than Madison's arguments, that created the setting for the ratification of the Constitution.[10]

The March to the Finish.   The struggle for ratification continued. After Delaware, Pennsylvania, and New Jersey had ratified, Georgia ratified unanimously on January 2, 1788, and, on January 9, Connecticut voted for ratification by a margin of 3 to 1. There was a bitter struggle in Massachusetts, but clever politicking by the Federalists resulted in a close but successful ratification vote on February 6, 1788. (Some historians believe the Anti-Federalists were a majority in the state at that time.) In the spring of 1788, Maryland and South Carolina ratified by sizable majorities. On June 21, 1788, by a 57 to 46 margin, New Hampshire became the ninth state to ratify. The Constitution was now formally in effect, but that meant little without the large states of New York and Virginia. During that summer, New York and Virginia agreed to the new Constitution by slender majorities. It took another sixteen months for North Carolina to ratify. Rhode Island did not ratify until May 29, 1790, and then by a margin of only two votes (see Table 2-2).

Was the Constitution Truly Favored by the Majority?   Political scientists and historians still debate whether the Constitution was actually favored by a popular majority. The delegates at the various state ratifying conventions had been selected by only 150,000 of the approximately four million citizens of that time. That does not seem very democratic—at least not by today's standards. (On election day in 1992, for example, 104 million persons—of 190 million people of voting age—voted in the presidential election.) Even Federalist John Marshall believed that in some of the adopting states a majority of the people opposed the Constitution.[11] We have to realize, however, that the adoption of the Constitution was probably as open a process as was reasonable at that time. Transportation and communication were rudimentary and slow. It would have been difficult to discover the true state of popular opinion, even if the leaders of the new nation had been concerned to do so. In any event, as soon as the Constitution was ratified, the movement to place limits on the power of the national government began.

---

[10]Of particular interest is the view of the Anti-Federalist position contained in Herbert J. Storing, *What the Anti-Federalists Were For* (Chicago: University of Chicago Press, 1981). Storing also edited seven volumes of the Anti-Federalist writings, *The Complete Anti-Federalist* (Chicago: University of Chicago Press, 1981). See also Jackson Turner Main, *The Antifederalist* (Chapel Hill: University of North Carolina Press, 1961).

[11]Charles Beard, *An Economic Interpretation of the Constitution* (New York: Macmillan, 1913), p. 299.

TABLE 2-2 ■ Ratification of the Constitution

State	Date	Vote For–Against
Delaware	Dec. 7, 1787	30–0
Pennsylvania	Dec. 12, 1787	46–23
New Jersey	Dec. 19, 1787	38–0
Georgia	Jan. 2, 1788	26–0
Connecticut	Jan. 9, 1788	128–40
Massachusetts	Feb. 6, 1788	187–168
Maryland	Apr. 28, 1788	63–11
South Carolina	May 23, 1788	149–73
New Hampshire	June 21, 1788	57–46
Virginia	June 25, 1788	89–79
New York	July 26, 1788	30–27
North Carolina	Nov. 21, 1789*	184–77
Rhode Island	May 29, 1790	34–32

*Ratification was originally defeated on August 4, 1788, by a vote of 184–84.

The Bill of Rights

Bills of rights had been included in state constitutions at least as early as 1776, when George Mason of Virginia wrote the Virginia Declaration of Rights. That document was modeled on the traditional rights established in England and present in the British Bill of Rights of 1689.

Ratification in several important states could not have proceeded if the Federalists had not assured the states that amendments to the Constitution would be passed to protect individual liberties against incursions by the national government. Many of the recommendations of the state ratifying conventions included specific rights that were later considered by James Madison as he labored to draft what became the Bill of Rights.

Ironically, Madison had a year earlier told Jefferson, "I have never thought the omission [of the Bill of Rights] a material defect" of the Constitution. But Jefferson's enthusiasm for a bill of rights apparently influenced Madison, as did his desire to gain popular support for his election to Congress. He promised in his campaign letter to voters that, once elected, he would force Congress to "prepare and recommend to the states for ratification, the most satisfactory provisions for all essential rights."

Madison had to cull through more than two hundred state recommendations. It was no small task, and in retrospect he chose remarkably well. (One of the rights appropriate for constitutional protection that he left out was equal protection under the laws—but that was not commonly regarded as a basic right at that time. It wasn't until 1868 that an amendment guaranteeing that no state shall deny equal protection to any person was ratified. The Supreme Court has applied this guarantee to certain actions of the federal government as well.)

LET'S SEE NOW ...WE'LL GIVE THEM FREEDOM, BUT NOT TOO MUCH FREEDOM, LIBERTY BUT NOT TOO MUCH LIBERTY. DEMOCRACY, BUT NOT TOO MUCH DEMOCRACY...

Copyright 1985 Sidney Harris.

The final number of amendments that Madison and a specially appointed committee came up with was seventeen. Congress tightened the language somewhat and eliminated five of the amendments. Of the remaining twelve, two—dealing with the apportionment of representatives and the compensation of the members of Congress—were not immediately ratified by the states. Eventually, Supreme Court decisions led to legislative reforms relating to apportionment. As will be discussed shortly, the amendment relating to compensation of members of Congress was ratified 203 years later—in 1992!

On December 15, 1791, the national Bill of Rights was adopted when Virginia agreed to ratify the ten amendments. The basic structure of American government had already been established. Now the fundamental rights of individuals were protected, at least in theory, at the national level. The proposed amendment that Madison characterized as "the most valuable amendment in the whole lot"—which would have prohibited the *states* from infringing on the freedoms of conscience, press, and jury trial—had been eliminated by the Senate. Thus, the Bill of Rights as adopted did not limit state power, and individual citizens had to rely on the guarantees contained in the particular state constitution or state bill of rights. The country had to wait until the violence of the Civil War before significant limitations on state power in the form of the Fourteenth Amendment became part of the national Constitution.

Altering the Constitution— The Formal Amendment Process

The original U.S. Constitution is short (see Appendix B). It consists of only 7,000 words, whereas the state constitutions of Alabama and New York contain 174,000 words and 80,000 words, respectively. One of the reasons it is short is that the framers intended it to be only a framework for governing, to be interpreted by succeeding generations. One of the reasons it has remained short is because the formal amending procedure does not allow for changes to be made easily. Article V of the Constitution outlines the way in which amendments may be proposed and ratified (see Figure 2-3 on page 48).

Two formal methods of proposing an amendment to the Constitution are available: (1) a two-thirds vote in each house of Congress or (2) a national convention called by Congress at the request of two-thirds of the state legislatures. There has yet to be a successful amendment proposal using the second method, although the balanced-budget amendment—first proposed in 1975—has come close, having been passed by more than thirty state legislatures.

Ratification can occur by one of two methods: (1) by a positive vote in three-fourths of the legislatures of the various states or (2) by special conventions called in the states for the specific purpose of ratifying the proposed amendment and a positive vote in three-fourths of them. The second method has been used only once, to repeal Prohibition. That situation was exceptional because it involved an amendment—the Twenty-first—to repeal an amendment—the Eighteenth, which had created Prohibition. State conventions were necessary for repeal because the "pro-

PROPOSING AMENDMENTS

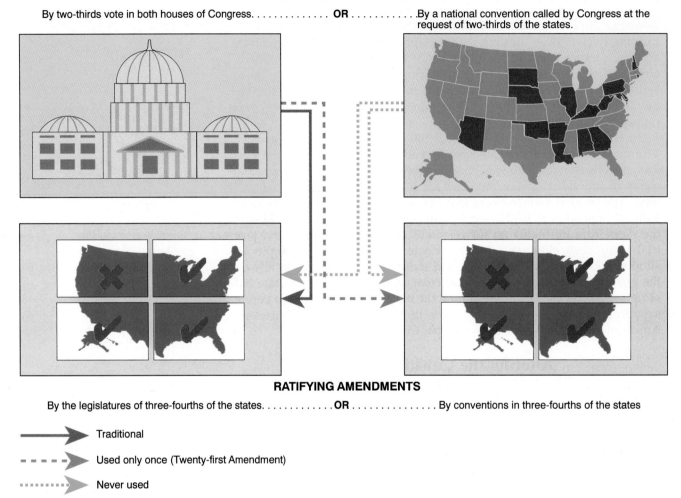

FIGURE 2-3 ■ The Formal Constitutional Amending Procedure

There are two ways of proposing amendments to the U.S. Constitution and two ways of ratifying proposed amendments. Among the four possibilities, the usual route has been proposal by Congress and ratification by state legislatures. Only in the case of the ratification of the Twenty-first Amendment in 1933, which repealed the Eighteenth Amendment (Prohibition), was ratification by state conventions used. The Constitution has never been amended by two-thirds of the states requesting a national convention to be called by Congress and then having the proposed amendment ratified by the legislatures of three-fourths of the states or by state conventions.

dry" legislatures in the more conservative states would never have passed the repeal. (It should be noted that Congress determines the method of ratification to be used by all states for each proposed constitutional amendment.)

Many Amendments Proposed, Few Accepted

Congress has considered more than 7,000 amendments to the Constitution. Only 33 have been submitted to the states after having been passed by Congress, and only 27 have been ratified (see Table 2-3). It should be clear that the process is much more difficult than a chart like Figure 2-3 can indicate. Because of competing social and economic interests, the require-

TABLE 2-3 ■ Amendments to the Constitution

Amendments	Subject	Year Adopted	Time Required for Ratification
1st–10th	The Bill of Rights	1791	2 years, 2 months, 20 days
11th	Immunity of states from certain suits	1795	11 months, 3 days
12th	Changes in electoral college procedure	1804	6 months, 3 days
13th	Prohibition of slavery	1865	10 months, 3 days
14th	Citizenship, due process, and equal protection	1868	2 years, 26 days
15th	No denial of vote because of race, color, or previous condition of servitude	1870	11 months, 8 days
16th	Power of Congress to tax incomes	1913	3 years, 6 months, 22 days
17th	Direct election of U.S. senators	1913	10 months, 26 days
18th	National (liquor) prohibition	1919	1 year, 29 days
19th	Women's suffrage	1920	1 year, 2 months, 14 days
20th	Change of dates for congressional and presidential terms	1933	10 months, 21 days
21st	Repeal of the 18th Amendment	1933	9 months, 15 days
22nd	Limit on presidential tenure	1951	3 years, 11 months, 3 days
23rd	District of Columbia electoral vote	1961	9 months, 13 days
24th	Prohibition of tax payment as a qualification to vote in federal elections	1964	1 year, 4 months, 9 days
25th	Procedures for determining presidential disability, presidential succession, and filling a vice presidential vacancy	1967	1 year, 7 months, 4 days
26th	Minimum voting age cannot be set above 18 in any election	1971	3 months, 7 days
27th	Congress cannot vote itself a raise that takes effect before the next election	1992	203 years

ment that two-thirds of both the House and Senate approve the amendments is difficult to achieve. Thirty-four senators, representing only seventeen sparsely populated states, could block any amendment. After approval by Congress, the process becomes even more arduous. Three-fourths of the state legislatures must approve the amendment. Only those amendments that have wide popular support across parties and in all regions of the country are likely to be approved.

Why was the amendment process made so difficult? The framers feared that a simple amendment process could lead to a tyranny of the majority, which could pass amendments to oppress disfavored individuals and groups.

Limits on Ratification

A reading of Article V of the Constitution reveals that the framers of the Constitution specified no time limit on the ratification process. The Supreme Court has held that Congress can specify a time for ratification as long as it is "reasonable." Since 1919, most proposed amendments have included a requirement that ratification be obtained within seven years. This was the case with the proposed Equal Rights Amendment. When three-fourths of the states had not ratified in time, Congress extended the limit for an additional three years and three months. That extension expired on June 30, 1982, without the amendment having been ratified. Another proposed amendment, which would have guaranteed congressional representation to the District of Columbia, fell far short of the thirty-eight state ratifications needed before its August 22, 1985, deadline.

On May 7, 1992, the Michigan state legislature became the thirty-eighth state to ratify one of the two "lost" amendments of the twelve that originally were sent to the states in 1789. The ten amendments that were passed out of that group became our Bill of Rights, as mentioned previously. Not until 203 years later, though, did the following amendment gain ratification from the required three-fourths of state legislatures:

> No law, varying the compensation for the services of the Senators and Representatives, shall take effect, until an election of Representatives shall have intervened.

The requirement that an election take place before any raise goes into effect gives the voters a measure of control over congressional salaries. Six states ratified the amendment before 1791, after which no other ratifications occurred until Ohio acted in 1873. Then, in 1978, Wyoming's ratification and growing protests over increased congressional salaries stimulated an avalanche of additional ratifications.

Given the fact that most of the amendments proposed in recent years have been given a time limit of only seven years by Congress, it was questionable for a time whether the amendment would become effective even if the necessary number of states ratified it. Is 203 years too long a lapse of time between the proposal and the final ratification of an amendment? It apparently was not because the amendment was certified as legitimate by archivist Don Wilson of the National Archives on May 18, 1992.

The National Convention Provision

The Constitution provides that a national convention requested by the legislatures of two-thirds of the states can propose a constitutional amendment. This procedure has never been used, but there is a possibility that two-thirds of the legislatures will in fact jump on the bandwagon of the proposed amendment to require a balanced federal budget. By 1991, thirty-two of the required thirty-four states had called for a constitutional convention to draft a balanced-budget amendment. What if the required thirty-four states passed resolutions to have such a convention? The Constitution is silent about the procedures to be followed. There is no precedent. Can the convention be limited to one specific issue? Does Congress have the legal authority to set the ground rules? Scholars disagree on these questions, and Congress fears a convention in which unrestrained representatives could propose any amendment, even one calling for a new form of government. There is also another problem: The resolutions passed by the various states and sent to Congress are not identical; they seek at least ten different forms of a constitutional amendment to balance the budget. What would be the format for drafting a single amendment? Congress has proposed (but not passed) a Constitutional Convention Procedures Act to exert control over a constitutional convention if it were to occur.

Informal Methods of Constitutional Change

Formal amendments are one way of changing our Constitution, and, as is obvious by their small number, they have not been resorted to very frequently. If we discount the first ten amendments (the Bill of Rights), which passed soon after the ratification of the Constitution, there have been only seventeen formal alterations of the Constitution in the more than two hundred years of its existence.

But looking at the sparse number of formal constitutional changes gives us an incomplete view. The brevity and ambiguity of the original document has permitted great changes in the Constitution by way of changing interpretations over time. As the United States grew, both in population and territory, new social and political realities emerged. Congress, presidents, and the courts found it necessary to interpret the Constitution's provisions in light of these new realities. The Constitution has proved to be a remarkably flexible document, adapting itself time and again to new events and concerns.

Congressional Legislation

The Constitution gives the Congress broad powers to carry out its duties as the nation's legislative body. For example, Article I, Section 8, of the Constitution gives Congress the power to regulate foreign and interstate commerce. Although there is no clear definition of foreign commerce or interstate commerce in the Constitution, Congress has cited the *commerce clause* as the basis for passing thousands of laws that have defined the meaning of foreign and interstate commerce. Similarly, Article III, Section 1, states that the national judiciary shall consist of one supreme court and "such inferior courts, as Congress may from time to time ordain and establish." Through a series of acts, Congress has used this broad sanction to establish the federal court system of today.

Presidential Actions

Even though the Constitution does not expressly authorize the president to propose bills or even budgets to Congress, presidents since the time of Woodrow Wilson (who served as president from 1913 to 1921) have proposed hundreds of bills to Congress each year. Presidents have also relied on their Article II authority as commander in chief of the nation's armed forces to send American troops abroad into combat, although the Constitution provides that Congress has the power to declare war. Presidents have also conducted foreign affairs by the use of **executive agreements,** which are legally binding documents made between the president and a foreign head of state. The Constitution does not mention such agreements.

Did You Know . . . That a constitutional amendment opposed by the thirteen smallest states with less than 4 percent of the nation's population will not become part of the Constitution even though it has been ratified by the other thirty-seven states, which have 96 percent of the population?

EXECUTIVE AGREEMENTS
Binding international agreements made between chiefs of state that do not require legislative sanction.

JUDICAL REVIEW
The power of the Supreme Court or
any court to declare federal or state
laws and other acts of government
unconstitutional.

Judicial Review

Another way of changing the Constitution—or of making it more flexible—is through the power of **judicial review.** In the landmark case of *Marbury v. Madison*[12] in 1803, the Supreme Court ruled a provision of an act of Congress to be unconstitutional. Chief Justice Marshall declared that it is "the province and duty of the Judiciary department to say what the law is." Although the case was primarily concerned with the power of the Supreme Court in relation to the other two branches of the federal government, the principle of judicial review itself opened the way for Congress and the executive branch to test the elasticity of the Constitution—that is, it allowed them to see how far and in what ways it could be "stretched" without breaking.

Interpretation, Custom, and Usage

The Constitution has also been changed through its interpretation by both Congress and the president. Originally, the president had a staff consisting of personal secretaries and a few others. Today, because Congress delegates specific tasks to the president and the chief executive assumes political leadership, the executive office staff alone has increased to several thousand persons. The executive provides legislative leadership far beyond the intentions of the Constitution.

Changes in the ways of doing political business have also altered the Constitution. The Constitution does not mention political parties, yet these informal, "extraconstitutional" organizations make the nominations for offices, run the campaigns, organize the members of Congress, and in fact change the election system from time to time. The emergence and evolution of the party system, for example, has changed the way of electing the president. The Constitution calls for the electoral college to choose the president. Today the people vote for electors who are pledged to the candidate of their party, effectively choosing the president themselves. Perhaps most strikingly, the Constitution has been adapted from serving the needs of a small, rural republic with no international prestige to providing a framework of government for an industrial giant with vast geographic, natural, and human resources.

Conclusion: An Enduring Achievement

Some say the Constitution has lasted because it furnishes only an outline for government. Much was left unsaid so that political circumstances could be accounted for. Others might give credit for the flexibility of the document to the sharing of power among the three branches and the compromises this sharing encourages. Still others suggest that the doctrine of federalism solved the problems of governing many diverse territories within one nation. Most important, the Constitution articulates certain principles of democratic government—such as representation, majority rule, and protection for minorities—that have become the core of American political culture and that are the accepted "rules of the game" from the smallest town council to the halls of Congress.

---

[12]1 Cranch 137 (1803). See Chapter 15.

GETTING INVOLVED

How Can You Affect the U.S. Constitution?

The Constitution is an enduring document that has survived more than two hundred years of turbulent history. It is also a changing document, however. Twenty-seven amendments have been added to the original Constitution. How can you, as an individual, actively help to rewrite the Constitution?

One of the best ways is to work for (or against) a constitutional amendment. At the time of this writing, national coalitions of interest groups are supporting or opposing proposed amendments concerning the limitations of the size of the government and antiabortion laws. If you want an opportunity to change the Constitution—or to assure that it is not changed—you could work for or with one of the alliances of groups interested in the fate of these amendments.

The following contacts should help you get started on efforts to affect the U.S. Constitution directly.

Government Reform

An organization whose goal is to "reduce the size and cost of federal government to those functions specified in the U.S. Constitution" is the Liberty Amendment Committee of the U.S.A., P.O. Box 20888, El Cajon, CA 92021. The ultimate goal of LACUSA is to see the so-called Liberty Amendment (now pending in Congress) ratified and then to abolish the income tax.

An even more general goal—namely, to encourage Congress to call a constitutional convention (the most open-ended way to change the Constitution)—is pursued by Conservatives for a Constitutional Convention, P.O. Box 582, Desert Hot Springs, CA 92240.

The Movement for Economic Justice, 1638 R St., N.W., Washington, DC, is an activist organization seeking grassroots involvement. Its goals are to encourage greater government responsiveness in such areas as revenue-sharing, inflation, and "fundamental economic reform." It conducts programs and training conferences and issues newsletters.

Abortion

One of the organizations whose primary goal is to secure the passage of the Human Life Amendment is the American Life Lobby, Route 6, Box 162-F, Stafford, VA 22554 (703-659-4193). The Human Life Amendment would recognize in law the "personhood" of the unborn, secure human rights' protections for the fetus from the time of fertilization, and prohibit abortion under any circumstances.

The National Abortion Rights Action League, 1424 K St., N.W., Washington, DC 20005 (202-347-7774), is a political action and information organization working on behalf of "pro-choice" issues—that is, the right of women to have control over reproduction. The organization has roughly 150,000 members.

CHAPTER SUMMARY

1. Early efforts by Great Britain to establish North American colonies were unsuccessful. The first English colonies were established at Jamestown in 1607 and Plymouth in 1620. The Mayflower Compact created the first formal government. By the mid-1700s, other British colonies had been established along the Atlantic seaboard from Georgia to Maine.
2. Following the conclusion of the French and Indian War in 1763, the British tried to reassert control over their increasingly independent-minded colonies through a series of taxes and legislative acts. The colonists responded with boycotts of British products and protests. Representatives of the colonies formed the First Continental Congress in 1774. The delegates sent a petition to the king of England expressing their grievances. The Second Continental Congress established an army in 1775 to defend colonists against attacks by British soldiers.
3. On July 4, 1776, the Second Continental Congress ap-

proved the Declaration of Independence. Perhaps the most revolutionary aspects of the Declaration were its assumptions that people have natural rights to life, liberty, and the pursuit of happiness, that governments derive their power from the consent of the governed, and that people have a right to overthrow oppressive governments. Not all of the colonists supported independence. During the Revolutionary War, however, all of the colonies adopted written constitutions that severely curtailed the power of executives, thus giving their legislatures predominant powers. By the end of the Revolutionary War, the states had signed the Articles of Confederation, creating a weak government with few powers. The Articles proved to be unworkable because the national government had no way to assure compliance by the states with such measures as securing tax revenues.
4. General dissatisfaction with the Articles of Confederation

prompted delegates to call the Philadelphia Convention in 1787. Although the delegates originally convened with the idea of amending the Articles, the discussions soon focused on creating a constitution for a new form of government. The Virginia Plan and the New Jersey Plan were offered but did not garner widespread support. A compromise offered by the state of Connecticut helped to break the large-state/small-state disputes dividing the delegates. The final version of the Constitution provided for the separation of powers and checks and balances.

5. Fears of a strong central government prompted the addition of the Bill of Rights to the Constitution. The Bill of Rights secured a wide variety of freedoms for Americans, including the freedoms of religion, speech, and assembly. It was ini-tially applied to the federal government, but subsequent amendments to the Constitution following the Civil War made it clear that the Bill of Rights also applied to the states.

6. An amendment to the Constitution may be proposed by either a two-thirds vote in each house of Congress or by a national convention called by Congress at the request of two-thirds of the state legislatures. Ratification can occur by either a positive vote in three-fourths of the legislatures of the various states or by special conventions called in the states for the specific purpose of ratifying the proposed amendment and a positive vote in three-fourths of them. Informal methods of constitutional change include congressional legislation, presidential actions, judicial review, and changing interpretations of the Constitution.

QUESTIONS FOR REVIEW AND DISCUSSION

1. The writing of the Constitution can be seen as the first real working of group interest, or pluralism, in the United States. What kinds of bargains or compromises were struck in the writing of this document? How were the various interests in the thirteen colonies protected by the provisions of the Constitution?

2. Although the Constitution calls for separation of powers, a more accurate description of the system might be one of "separate branches sharing powers." What provisions of the Constitution require that the branches cooperate, or "share," power in order for the government to function?

3. List all the ways that the rights of the individual states are protected in the Constitution. Which provisions make it clear that the federal government has the ultimate power?

4. Why have so few amendments been added to the Constitution? How do the amendments that have been adopted reflect broad societal changes that have taken place since 1789?

SELECTED REFERENCES

Charles A. Beard, *An Economic Interpretation of the Constitution* (New York: Macmillan, 1913). This classic interpretation of the motives of the founders of the republic emphasizes the founders' economic interests in the success of the nation.

Richard Beeman, Stephen Botein, and Edward C. Carter II, eds., *Beyond Confederation: Origins of the Constitution and American National Identity* (Chapel Hill, N.C.: University of North Carolina Press, 1987). This collection of essays discusses the debate over the intentions of the framers of the Constitution.

Richard B. Bernstein and Kym S. Rice, *Are We to Be a Nation? The Making of the Constitution* (Cambridge, Mass.: Harvard University Press, 1987). The story of the revolution in political thought that led to the Constitution, presented in words and pictures.

Robert A. Bernstein, *Elections, Representation, and Congressional Behavior: The Myth of Constituency Control* (Englewood Cliffs, N.J.: Prentice Hall, 1989). This book addresses the issue of how citizens and constituents exercise control over the policy positions and decisions of members of Congress and then offers suggestions for changes in the electoral system to improve representation.

Edward S. Corwin, *The Constitution and What It Means Today,* 14th ed., rev. by Harold W. Chase and Craig R. Ducat (Princeton, N.J.: Princeton University Press, 1978). A detailed analysis of the meaning and interpretation of the Constitution through court cases.

Michael Foley, *The Silence of Constitutions: An Essay in Constitutional Interpretation* (New York: Routledge, 1990). In this insightful analysis of the nature of constitutions, both written and unwritten, Foley argues that the presence of gaps in the explicitness of constitutions allows constitutional conflicts to be continually postponed.

Leslie F. Goldstein, *In Defense of the Text: Democracy and Constitutional Theory* (Lanham, Md.: Rowman & Littlefield, 1991). Goldstein offers both an excellent summary of the constitutional theories currently being debated, as well as an exposition of her own theory of constitutional interpretation.

Alexander Hamilton, James Madison, and John Jay, *The Federalist Papers* (Cambridge, Mass.: Harvard University Press, 1961). The complete set of columns from the *New York Packet* defending the new Constitution.

Leonard W. Levy, Kenneth L. Karst, and Dennis J. Mahoney,

eds., *Encyclopedia of the American Constitution* (Riverside, N.J.: Macmillan, 1986). This truly remarkable resource book contains roughly 2,000 articles by 262 leading constitutional scholars, covering every major aspect of the Constitution and including a discussion of all the hotly debated issues.

Clinton Rossiter, *1787: The Grand Convention* (New York: Macmillan, 1966). A readable and interesting account of the Constitutional Convention in Philadelphia.

Sylvia Snowiss, *Judicial Review and the Law of the Constitution* (New Haven, Conn.: Yale University Press, 1990). An examination of the nature and extent of judicial review.

Herbert J. Storing, *The Complete Anti-Federalist,* 7 vols. (Chicago: University of Chicago Press, 1981). An examination of the views of those opposed to the Constitution.

James L. Sundquist, *Constitutional Reform and Effective Government* (Washington, D.C.: Brookings Institution, 1986). The author reviews the heated debate over constitutional reform, first analyzing the basic assumptions of the 1787 debates and then exploring the workable and desirable modifications that could strengthen and modernize American government.

Kenneth W. Thompson, *Governance II: The Presidency, the Congress, and the Constitution: Deadlock or Balance of Powers?* (Lanham, Md.: University Press of America, 1991). A study of the interrelationships of the branches of government and the ways in which the three branches can help or hinder each other.

APPENDIX TO CHAPTER TWO

How to Read Case Citations and Find Court Decisions

Many important court cases are discussed in references in footnotes throughout this book. Court decisions are recorded and published. When a court case is mentioned, the notation used to refer to, or to cite, the case denotes where the published decision can be found.

State courts of appeals decisions are usually published in two places, the state reports of that particular state and the more widely used *National Reporter System* published by West Publishing Company. Some states no longer publish their own reports. The *National Reporter System* divides the states into the following geographic areas: Atlantic (A. or A.2d where 2d refers to second series), South Eastern (S.E. or S.E.2d), South Western (S.W. or S.W.2d), North Western (N.W. or N.W.2d), North Eastern (N.E. or N.E.2d), Southern (So. or So.2d), and Pacific (P. or P.2d).

Federal trial court decisions are published unofficially in West's *Federal Supplement* (F.Supp.), and opinions from the circuit courts of appeals are reported unofficially in West's *Federal Reporter* (F. or F.2d). Opinions from the United States Supreme Court are reported in the *United States Reports* (U.S.), the *Lawyer's Edition of the Supreme Court Reports* (L.Ed.), West's *Supreme Court Reporter* (S.Ct.), and other publications. The *United States Reports* is the official edition of the United States Supreme Court decisions published by the federal government. Many early decisions are missing from these volumes. The citations of the early volumes of the *U.S. Reports* include the names of the actual reporters such as Dallas, Cranch, or Wheaton. *McCulloch v. Maryland,* for example, is cited as 17 U.S. (4 Wheat.) 316. Only after 1874 did the present citation system, in which cases are cited based solely on their volume and page numbers in the *U.S. Reports,* come into being. An unofficial and more complete edition of Supreme Court decisions, the *Lawyer's Edition of the Supreme Court Reports,* is published by the Lawyers Cooperative Publishing Company of Rochester, New York. West's *Supreme Court Reporter* is an unofficial edition of decisions dating from October 1882. These volumes contain headnotes and brief editorial statements of the law involved in the case.

State courts of appeals' decisions are cited by giving the name of the case; the volume, name, and page number of the state's official report (if the state publishes its own reports); the volume, unit, and page number of the *National Reporter;* and the volume, name, and page number of any other selected reporter. Federal court citations are also listed by giving the name of the case and the volume, name, and page number of the reports. In addition to the citation, this textbook lists the year of the decision in parentheses. Consider, for example, the case, *United States v. Curtiss-Wright Export Co.,* 299 U.S. 304 (1936). The Supreme Court's decision of this case may be found in volume 299 of the *United States Reports* on page 304. The case was decided in 1936.

CHAPTER 3
Federalism

CHAPTER CONTENTS

WHAT IF ... WE HAD A NATIONAL POLICE FORCE?

The U.S. Constitution reserves all powers to the states that are not expressly delegated to the federal government. The primary motivation for limiting the national government's powers was to prevent it from encroaching on the rights of the states. But this federalist structure was also adopted because many of the delegates to the 1787 Philadelphia Convention believed that certain governmental functions could be performed more capably by the states.

Nearly every municipality in the United States maintains a police force responsible for protecting its residents. Every state also maintains a police force, such as a state highway patrol, that enforces the laws along highways such as the interstate system. The federal government operates the Federal Bureau of Investigation (FBI). The FBI handles only those types of crimes that are under the jurisdiction of the federal government, such as counterfeiting, interstate auto theft, and smuggling. The FBI often cooperates with state and local officials in such actions as drug seizures.

What if all of the nation's police forces—on the local, state, and national levels—were merged into a single force? Such an arrangement would be similar to that found in many nations having unitary systems of government, such as France. If the United States had a unitary system of government, we would expect to see a centralization of authority and power in Washington. The decisions of local police chiefs could then be overruled by the national office in Washington, D.C. Because a national police force would probably be funded by Congress, state and local offices would have less freedom to decide how to respond to what used to be purely local matters. Any failure to follow the directions of the national government could be punished by cutting off funding and demoting or firing local officials.

A national police force might be more efficient because there would no longer be any problems with disputes over jurisdiction. But this gain might be offset by the need for actions on purely local matters to be approved by the national office. If a murder takes place in Los Angeles, for example, the Los Angeles Police Department is primarily responsible for conducting the investigation and coordinating the efforts to catch the murderer. In a national police system, however, the Los Angeles Police Department's efforts would be overseen by the national office.

Another efficiency of a national police force might be a common computer data base listing all persons having criminal records in the country. This would be a significant improvement over the present situation in which national, state, and local officials often cannot easily track the movements of a criminal because comprehensive data bases do not exist. In addition, having a single police force would make it possible to formulate a single strategy to capture a felon, as opposed to the current situation in which local, state, and federal officials may operate at cross-purposes with one another.

What is the likelihood that we will ever have a national police force? The chances are remote at best. People distrust the federal government in general. They also believe it is too far removed from the local scene to be able to respond effectively to purely local crimes such as bicycle thefts and vandalism. Moreover, many people do not believe that the federal government is better able to solve crimes than are local police agencies, nor do they feel that the operational efficiency of these local agencies would be improved if most major decisions had to be made in Washington, D.C. Most important is the issue of accountability. The residents of a municipality would have little influence over the choice of the police chief if the nation had a single police force. In addition, many people would be concerned that a national police force could pose a political threat to the independence of the government itself.

1. *How might the operational inefficiencies of the present system be improved without merging all local, state, and national agents into a single force?*

2. *Is a national police force more appropriate for a geographically compact country such as France than for a larger country such as the United States? Why?*

How many separate governments do you think exist in the United States? One national government and fifty state governments, plus local governments, create a grand total of more than 80,000 governments in all! The breakdown can be seen in Table 3-1. Those 80,000 governments contain about 500,000 elected officeholders. Visitors from France or Spain are often awestruck by the complexity of our system of government. Consider that a criminal action can be defined by state law, by national law, or by both. Thus, the alleged criminal can be prosecuted in the state court system or in the national court system (or both). Often, economic regulation over exactly the same matter exists at the local level, the state level, and the national level—generating multiple forms to be completed, procedures to be followed, and laws to be obeyed. Numerous programs are funded by the national government but administered by state and local governments.

There are various ways of ordering relations between central governments and local units. Federalism is one of these ways. Understanding federalism and how it differs from other forms of government is important in understanding the current American political system.

Three Systems of Government

There are basically three ways of ordering relations between central governments and local units: (1) a unitary system, (2) a confederal system (confederation), and (3) a federal system. The most popular, both historically and today, is the unitary system.

A Unitary System of Government

A **unitary system** of government is the easiest to define: Unitary systems allow ultimate governmental authority to rest in the hands of the national,

UNITARY SYSTEM
A centralized governmental system in which local or subdivisional governments exercise only those powers given to them by the central government.

TABLE 3-1 ■ **The Number of Governments in the United States Today**

With more than 80,000 separate governmental units in the United States today, it is no wonder that intergovernmental relations in the United States are so complicated. Actually, the number of school districts has decreased over time, but the number of special districts created for single purposes, such as flood control, has increased from only about eight thousand during World War II to almost thirty thousand today.

Federal government		1
State governments		50
Local governments		83,153
Counties	3,042	
Municipalities (mainly cities or towns)	19,205	
Townships (less extensive powers)	16,691	
Special districts (water, sewer, etc.)	29,485	
School districts	14,730	
	83,153	
TOTAL		83,204

SOURCE: U.S. Department of Commerce, *Statistical Abstract of the United States* (Washington, D.C.: U.S. Government Printing Office, 1993).

or central, government. Consider a typical unitary system—France. There are departments in France and municipalities. Within the departments and the municipalities are separate government entities with elected and appointed officials. So far, the French system appears to be very similar to the United States system; but the similarity is only superficial. Under the unitary French system, the decisions of the governments of the departments and the municipalities can be overruled by the national government. Also, the national government can cut off the funding of many departmental and municipal government activities. Moreover, in a unitary system such as that in France, all questions related to education, police, the use of land, and welfare are handled by the national government.[1] Britain, Sweden, Israel, Egypt, Ghana, and the Philippines also have unitary systems of government, as do most countries today.

A Confederal System

CONFEDERAL SYSTEM
A system of government consisting of a league of independent states, each having essentially sovereign powers. The central government created by such a league has only limited powers over the states.

You were introduced to the elements of a **confederal system** of government in Chapter 2, when we examined the Articles of Confederation. A confederation is the opposite of a unitary regime. It is a league of independent states in which a central government or administration handles only those matters of common concern expressly delegated to it by the member states. The central governmental unit has no ability to make laws directly applicable to individuals unless the member states explicitly support such laws. The United States under the Articles of Confederation and the Confederate States during the American Civil War were confederations. There are no pure confederations in the world today (with the exception, perhaps, of the United Nations), although Switzerland officially is a confederation of twenty-three sovereign cantons. At the end of 1991, eleven of the former fifteen republics that made up the former Union of Soviet Socialist Republics formed the Commonwealth of Independent States. It is not yet clear whether this confederation will endure.

A Federal System

FEDERAL SYSTEM
A system of government in which power is divided by a written constitution between a central government and regional, or subdivisional, governments. Each level must have some domain in which its policies are dominant and some genuine political or constitutional guarantee of its authority.

EXTRAORDINARY MAJORITY
A majority that is greater than 50 percent plus one. For example, ratification of amendments to the U.S. Constitution requires the approval of two-thirds of the House and the Senate and three-fourths of the states.

Between the unitary and confederal forms of government lies the **federal system.** In this system, authority is divided, usually by a written constitution, between a central government and regional, or subdivisional, governments (often called constituent governments). The central government and the constituent governments both act directly on the people through laws and through the actions of elected and appointed governmental officials. Within each government's sphere of authority, each is supreme in theory. Contrast a federal system to a unitary one in which the central government is supreme and the constituent governments derive their authority from it. A key feature of all federal systems is that changes in their written constitution must be approved by **extraordinary majorities** of the legislature of both the national government and some of the subnational units (the states, in the United States). Australia, Canada, Mexico, India,

---

[1]In the past decade, legislation has altered somewhat the unitary character of the French political system.

Brazil, and Germany are examples of nations with federal systems. See Figure 3-1 for a comparison of the three systems.

Why a Federal System?

There are currently over 180 countries in the world. None of them has a truly confederal system of government. Almost all have a unitary system. The United States is one of the few nations that has a truly federal system of government power (and one in which both levels of government derive their authority from, and exercise power over, the people).

The Historical Reasons for American Federalism

There are historical, as well as practical, reasons why the United States developed in a federal direction. Some of these reasons are discussed below.

Common Problems.   As you have seen in Chapter 2, the historical basis of the federal system was laid down in Philadelphia at the Constitutional Convention, where strong national government advocates (see the *Profile* of Alexander Hamilton in this chapter) opposed equally strong states' rights advocates. This dichotomy continued through to the ratifying conventions in the several states. The resulting federal system was a compromise. The appeal of federalism was that it retained state traditions and local power, while establishing a strong national government capable of handling common problems.

Size and Regional Isolation.   At the time of the Philadelphia Convention, the thirteen colonies taken together were geographically larger than England or France. Slow travel and communication combined with geographical spread contributed to the isolation of many regions within the colonies. It could, for example, take up to several weeks for all of the colonies to be informed about one particular political decision. Even if the colonial leaders had agreed on the desirability of a unitary system, the

FIGURE 3-1 ■ The Flow of Power in Three Systems

In a unitary system, the flow of power is from the central government to the local and state governments. In a confederal system, the flow of power is in the opposite direction—from the state and local governments to the central government. In a federal system the flow of power is, in principle, both ways.

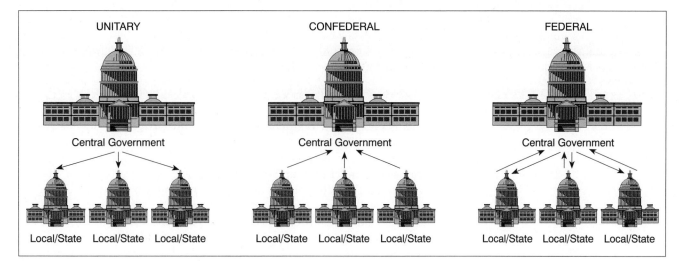

UNITARY	CONFEDERAL	FEDERAL
Central Government	Central Government	Central Government
Local/State Local/State Local/State	Local/State Local/State Local/State	Local/State Local/State Local/State

PROFILE

Alexander Hamilton

"The more close the union of the states, and the more complete the authority of the whole, the less opportunity will be allowed the stronger states to injure the weaker."

The modern form of American federalism, consisting of a strong national government and subsidiary states, was endorsed both in theory and in practice by Alexander Hamilton. A New York lawyer educated at King's College (now Columbia University), Hamilton was a colleague of George Washington and a delegate to the Philadelphia Constitutional Convention. He later led the forces in favor of ratification of the Constitution at the New York state convention. Hamilton's successful politicking for ratification in that state was highlighted by a series of eighty-five public letters, which were printed in New York City newspapers from October 27, 1787, to August 16, 1788. The letters, which represented the joint work of Hamilton, James Madison, and John Jay, have come to be known as *The Federalist Papers*. About two-thirds of them are attributable to Hamilton.

Hamilton's admiration for a strong and energetic national government is evident in *The Federalist*

Papers. He wrote that "the vigor of government is essential to the security of liberty" and that the fledgling nation confronted the alternatives of "adoption of the new Constitution or a dismemberment of the Union." History and common sense showed that "if these States should either be wholly disunited, or only united in partial confederacies, the subdivisions into which they might be thrown would have frequent and violent contests with each other." A divided nation of sovereign states would also be easy prey for the divide-and-conquer tac-

tics of other nations." A firm Union will be of the utmost moment to the peace and liberty of the States as a barrier against domestic faction and insurrection," whereas weak confederations would lead to "incurable disorder and imbecility in the government." The Constitution was not designed to abolish state governments, but to make them "constituent parts of the national sovereignty" by congressional representation.

A vigorous national government working for a common interest would also provide economic benefits from "an active commerce, an extensive navigation, [and] a flourishing marine," and the nation would be able to compete against European commercial power. "An unrestricted intercourse between the States themselves will advance the trade of each by an interchange of their respective productions, not only for the supply of reciprocal wants at home, but for exportation to foreign markets."

Hamilton, who became the nation's first secretary of the treasury in the cabinet of George Washington from 1789 to 1795, worked vigorously to implement these ideas. His views about strong national government have become dominant in U.S. history.

problems of size and regional isolation would have made such a system operationally difficult.

Sectionalism and Political Subcultures.   The American way of life has always been characterized by a number of political subcultures, which divide along the lines of race, wealth, education, religion, and, more recently, age and sexual preferences. Subcultures associated with geography naturally developed because different groups of individuals became concentrated in different regions. For example, the Puritans who founded

New England had, according to Daniel Elazar, a moralist subculture, viewing politics as the road to a good society.[2] The agricultural society of the South generated a traditionalist subculture, stressing not only tradition but also family and community. Finally, the Middle Atlantic states seemed to engender an individualist subculture, in which politics was viewed as simply another business.

The existence of diverse political subcultures would appear to be at odds with a political authority concentrated solely in a central government. Had the United States developed into a unitary system, the various political subcultures certainly would have been less able to influence government behavior (relative to their own regions and interests) than they have done, and continue to do, in our federal system.

Other Arguments for Federalism

The arguments for federalism in the United States and elsewhere involve a complex set of factors, some of which we have already noted. First, for big countries, such as the United States, India, and Nigeria, federalism allows many functions to be "farmed out" by the central government to the states or provinces; the lower levels of government, accepting these responsibilities, can thereby become the focus of political dissatisfaction rather than the national authorities. Second, even with modern transportation and communications systems, the sheer geographic or population size of some nations makes it impractical to locate all political authority in one place. Finally, federalism brings government closer to the people, allowing more direct access to, and influence on, government agencies and policies, rather than leaving the population restive and dissatisfied with a remote, faceless, all-powerful central authority.

In the United States, in particular, federalism historically has had special benefits as well as drawbacks. State government has long been a training ground for future national leaders. Presidents such as Ronald Reagan (1981–1989) and Bill Clinton (1993–   ) first made their political mark as state governors, and many federal judges and members of Congress were initiated into politics and government on state courts or in state legislatures.

Many people argue that the states have also been testing grounds for the introduction of bold new government initiatives. This was true, for example, with unemployment compensation, which began in Wisconsin; the enfranchisement of eighteen-year-old voters, which was pioneered by Georgia; state lotteries, which were established in their modern form in New Hampshire; and air pollution control, which was initiated in California. Of course, not everyone agrees that all of these developments were entirely beneficial, and other actions pioneered at the state level—such as Prohibition or Jim Crow laws—were either disastrous or morally bankrupt.

Arguments against Federalism

Not everyone thinks federalism is such a good idea. Some see it as a way for powerful state and local interests to block progress and impede

---

[2]Daniel J. Elazar, *American Federalism: A View from the States* (New York: Crowell, 1966).

Did You Know ... That under Article I, Section 10, of the Constitution, no state is allowed to enter into any treaty, alliance, or confederation?

national plans. Political scientist William H. Riker condemns American federalism for perpetuating racism.[3] Smaller political units are more likely to be dominated by a single political group, and the dominant groups in some cities and states have resisted implementing equal rights for all minority groups. Others point out, however, that the dominant factions in other places have been more progressive in many areas, such as the environment, than the national government.

The Constitutional Basis for American Federalism

No mention of the designation "federal system" can be found in the United States Constitution. Nor is it possible to find a systematic division of governmental authority between the national and state governments in that document. Rather, the Constitution sets out different types of powers (Figure 3-2). These powers can be classified as (1) the delegated powers of the national government; (2) the reserved powers of the states; (3) concurrent powers; and (4) prohibited powers.

Powers Delegated to the National Government

The delegated powers of the national government include both expressed and implied powers, as well as resulting powers and the special category of inherent powers.

Expressed Powers.   Most of the powers expressly delegated to the national government are found in Article I, Section 8, of the Constitution. Some expressly delegated powers include setting standards for weights and measures, making uniform naturalization laws, admitting new states, establishing post offices, and declaring war.

Implied Powers.   Article I, Section 8, also states that the Congress shall have the power

> to make all laws which shall be necessary and proper for carrying into execution the foregoing powers, and all other powers vested by this Constitution in the Government of the United States, or in any Department or Officer thereof.

ELASTIC CLAUSE, OR NECESSARY AND PROPER CLAUSE
The clause in Article I, Section 8, that grants Congress the power to do whatever is necessary to execute its specifically delegated powers.

This clause is sometimes called the **elastic clause,** or the **necessary and proper clause,** because it provides flexibility to our constitutional system. It gives Congress all those powers that can be reasonably inferred but are not expressly stated in the brief wording of the Constitution. The clause was first used in the Supreme Court decision of *McCulloch v. Maryland* [4] (discussed later in this chapter) to develop the concept of implied powers, through which the national government has succeeded in strengthening the scope of its authority to meet the numerous problems that the framers of the Constitution did not, and could not, anticipate.

[3]William H. Riker, "Federalism," in Fred I. Greenstein and Nelson W. Polsby, eds., *Handbook of Political Science,* Vol. 5 (Reading, Mass.: Addison-Wesley, 1975), p. 154.
[4]4 Wheaton 316 (1819). See the appendix to Chapter 2 for more information about how court decisions are referenced.

Inherent Powers. A special category of national powers that is not implied by the necessary and proper clause consists of what have been labeled the inherent powers of the national government. These powers derive from the fact that the United States is a sovereign power among nations, and, as such, its national government must be the only government that deals with other nations. Under international law, it is assumed that all nation-states, regardless of their size or power, have an *inherent* right to ensure their own survival. To do this, each nation must have the ability to act in its own interest among and with the community of nations—by, for instance, making treaties, waging war, seeking trade, and

FIGURE 3-2 ■ The American Federal System—Division of Powers between the National Government and the State Governments

We can separate the division of powers between national and state governments by looking at the powers granted by the Constitution to both the national governments and the state governments together. Then we look at the powers denied by the Constitution to each level of government.

SELECTED POWERS GRANTED BY THE CONSTITUTION (including amendments)		
National Government	**National and State Governments**	**State Governments**
IMPLIED "To make all laws which shall be necessary and proper for carrying into execution the foregoing powers, and all other powers vested by this Constitution in the Government of the United States, or in any Department or Officer thereof." (Article 1, Section 8, Clause 18)	CONCURRENT ■ To levy and collect taxes ■ To borrow money ■ To make and enforce laws ■ To establish courts ■ To provide for the general welfare ■ To charter banks and corporations	RESERVED TO THE STATES ■ To regulate intrastate commerce ■ To conduct elections ■ To provide for public health, safety, and morals ■ To establish local governments ■ To ratify amendments to the federal constitution ■ To establish a state militia
EXPRESS ■ To coin money ■ To conduct foreign relations ■ To regulate interstate commerce ■ To levy and collect taxes ■ To declare war ■ To raise and support the military ■ To establish post offices ■ To establish courts inferior to the Supreme Court ■ To admit new states		

POWERS DENIED BY THE CONSTITUTION		
National Government	**National and State Governments**	**State Governments**
■ To tax articles exported from any state ■ To violate the Bill of Rights ■ To change state boundaries ■ To suspend the right of *habeas corpus* ■ To make *ex post facto* laws ■ To subject officeholders to a religious test	■ To grant titles of nobility ■ To permit slavery ■ To deny citizens the right to vote because of race, color, or previous servitude ■ To deny citizens the right to vote because of sex	■ To tax imports or exports ■ To coin money ■ To enter into treaties ■ To impair obligations of contracts ■ To abridge the privileges or immunities of citizens or deny due process and equal protection of the laws

Hurricane Andrew's vast destruction left over 250,000 people homeless and caused billions of dollars of damage. Natural disasters, like Andrew, outstrip a state's ability to respond adequately and often require federal relief.

acquiring territory.[5] The national government has these powers whether or not they have been enumerated in the Constitution. Some constitutional scholars categorize inherent powers as a third type of power, completely distinct from the delegated powers (both expressed and implied) of the national government.

Reserved Powers of the State Governments

The Tenth Amendment states that the powers not delegated to the United States by the Constitution, nor prohibited by it to the states, are reserved to the states respectively, or to the people. These are the reserved powers that the national government cannot deny to the states. Such powers include each state's right to regulate commerce within its borders and to provide for a state militia. States also have the reserved power to make laws on all matters not prohibited to the states by the national or state constitutions and not expressly, or by implication, delegated to the national government. The states also have **police power**—the authority to legislate for the protection of the health, morals, safety, and welfare of the people. On occasion, states have used their power to pass discriminatory legislation, such as laws prohibiting interracial marriages. These laws were passed on the assumption that because the Constitution did not grant such regulatory power to the national government, that power was reserved to the states acting through their legislatures. But when such laws were declared to be unconstitutional,[6] they immediately became unenforceable by the states.

POLICE POWER
The authority to legislate for the protection of the health, morals, safety, and welfare of the people. In the United States, most police power is a reserved power of the states. The federal government is able to legislate for the welfare of its citizens through specific congressional powers, such as its power to regulate interstate commerce.

---

[5]See especially *United States v. Curtiss-Wright Export Co.*, 299 U.S. 304 (1936), which upheld the validity of a joint resolution of Congress delegating the power to the president to prohibit arms shipments to foreign belligerents.
[6]*Loving v. Virginia*, 388 U.S. 1 (1967).

POLITICS AND ECONOMICS AMONG THE STATES

▼

The Battle over Water

Las Vegas, Nevada, is in the middle of a desert. You wouldn't know it by visiting that city, however. Water consumption per capita is double that of many other western cities, most of which are located in decidedly less arid environments. Las Vegas does not have a magic well. Indeed, only one-fifth of the water consumed annually by the city comes from the ground. The rest is piped in from the Colorado River. The city's legal ability to do so is based on an agreement dating back to the 1920s.

Clark County (in which Las Vegas is located) is growing faster than most other counties in the United States. Its current population of three quarters of a million is expected to increase to a million by the year 2000. At present water us-age rates, Las Vegas needs a new source of water, even assuming it increases its share from the Colorado River. The solution offered by Las Vegas is to use a state law that allows it to claim unused water. It wants to do this by collecting 3,000 acre-feet of water per year from over a hundred sites within the state and pumping it to the city in enormous pipelines. This cooperative water project would cost anywhere from $2 billion to $7 billion.

Environmentalists and farmers—particularly in the state of California—are worried. They argue that the removal of so much water from the aquifer will turn Nevada into a dust bowl and threaten the existing springs in Death Valley, California. Planners in Nevada state that California can buy up more Colorado River water from Utah and Colorado. Coloradans and planners in Utah respond that so, too, can Nevada. A former governor of Nevada, Mike Ocallhehan, says that everybody is wrong: He claims that it would be cheaper for Nevada to build a desalinization plant on the Pacific for California in exchange for part of California's share of the Colorado River.

Whatever the economics of providing water to thirsty Las Vegas, the ultimate solution will rely more heavily on the political power and negotiating skills of the people in the various states involved. At some point, Congress may step in to require the states to impose higher water usage fees to encourage reductions in the use of this essential natural resource.

Concurrent Powers

In some areas, the Constitution gives national and state governments an equal right to pass legislation and to regulate certain activities. These are called concurrent powers. Most concurrent powers are not specifically stated in the Constitution; they are only implied. An example of a concurrent power is the power to tax. The types of taxation are divided between the levels of government. States may not levy a tariff (a set of taxes on imported goods); the federal government may not tax real estate; and neither may tax the facilities of the other. If the state governments did not have the power to tax, they would not be able to function other than on a ceremonial basis.

Other concurrent powers include the power to borrow money, to establish courts, and to charter banks and corporations. Concurrent powers are normally limited to the geographical area of the state and to those functions not preempted by the Constitution or by the national government—such as the coinage of money and the negotiation of treaties.

The foregoing discussion might give the impression that the power of the states today is derived solely from the Constitution. This would be a mistake, for the independence of the states rests, in large part, on the commitment of American citizens to the idea of local self-government. In addition, and perhaps more important, members of the national legisla-

Did You Know . . . That Abraham Lincoln, the "Great Emancipator," claimed on taking office that he would not attack slavery as an institution and that he even wanted a constitutional amendment to make the right to own slaves irrevocable?

ture—senators and representatives—are elected by their local constituencies. Except for the president, politicians in the national government have obtained their power by satisfying those local constituencies, rather than by satisfying some ill-defined, broad national constituency. Even the president must appeal to local constituencies to some degree, however, because the presidential candidate receiving the largest popular vote in a state wins all of that state's electoral votes (with some exceptions). Furthermore, many of the programs paid for and undertaken by the national government are carried out by the state and local governmental units— for example, the interstate highway system, most of the welfare system, job creation programs, and environmental clean-up programs.

Horizontal Federalism

So far we have examined only the relationship between central and state governmental units. But, of course, the states have numerous commercial, social, and other dealings among themselves. These interstate activities, problems, and policies make up what can be called **horizontal federalism.** The national Constitution imposes certain "rules of the road" on horizontal federalism, which have had the effect of preventing any one state from setting itself apart from the other states. The three most important clauses in the Constitution relating to horizontal federalism, all taken from the Articles of Confederation, require that

1. Each state give full faith and credit to every other state's public acts, records, and judicial proceedings.
2. Each state extend to every other state's citizens the privileges and immunities of its own citizens.
3. Each state agree to render persons who are fleeing from justice in another state back to their home state when requested to do so.

HORIZONTAL FEDERALISM
Activities, problems, and policies that require state governments to interact with one another.

The only indication that a motorist has crossed a state boundary on Interstate 95 is the "Welcome to Maine" sign posted there. There are no border posts, and no visa, passport, or special permission is needed to change states. Different traffic laws may apply however.

The Full Faith and Credit Clause

Article IV, Section 1, of the Constitution provides that "full faith and credit shall be given in each state to the public acts, records, and judicial proceedings of every other state." This clause applies only to civil matters. It ensures that rights established under deeds, wills, contracts, and the like in one state will be honored by other states and that any judicial decision with respect to such property rights will be honored as well as enforced in all states. The **full faith and credit clause** was originally put in the Articles of Confederation to promote mutual friendship among the people of the different states. In fact, it has contributed to the unity of American citizens because it protects their legal rights as they move about from state to state. This is extremely important for the conduct of business in a country with a very mobile citizenry.

Privileges and Immunities

Privileges and immunities are defined as special rights and exemptions provided by law. Article IV, Section 2, indicates that "the citizens of each state shall be entitled to all privileges and immunities of citizens in the several states." This clause indicates that states are obligated to extend to citizens of other states protection of the laws, the right to work, access to courts, and other privileges they grant their own citizens. It means, quite simply, that a resident of Alabama cannot be treated as an alien when that person is in California or New York. He or she must have access to the courts of each state, to travel rights, and to property rights.[7]

Interstate Extradition

Article IV, Section 2, states that "a person charged in any state with treason, felony, or another crime who shall flee from justice and be found in another state, shall on demand of the executive authority of the state from which he fled, be delivered up, to be removed to the state having jurisdiction of the crime." The language here appears clear, yet governors of one state had not been legally required to **extradite** (render to another state) a fugitive from justice until 1987. The federal courts will not order such an action. It is rather the moral duty of a governor to do so, and, in fact, extradition is routinely followed in most cases. Governors who refuse to extradite are inviting retaliation from other states. In many cases, the question is moot because Congress has made it a federal crime to flee across state lines to avoid prosecution for certain felonies. Therefore, apprehension by federal agents puts the fugitive in national government hands, and that person is usually turned over to the state from which he or she fled.

The Peaceful Settlement of Differences between States

States are supposed to settle their differences peacefully. In so doing, they may enter into agreements called **interstate compacts**—if consented to by Congress. In reality, congressional consent is necessary only if such a com-

FULL FAITH AND CREDIT CLAUSE
A section of the Constitution that requires states to recognize one another's laws and court decisions. It ensures that rights established under deeds, wills, contracts, and other civil matters in one state will be honored by other states.

PRIVILEGES AND IMMUNITIES
Special rights and exceptions provided by law. Article IV, Section 2, of the Constitution requires states not to discriminate against one another's citizens. A resident of one state cannot be treated as an alien when in another state; he or she may not be denied such privileges and immunities as legal protection, access to courts, travel rights, or property rights.

EXTRADITE
To surrender an accused or convicted criminal to the authorities of the state from which he or she has fled; to return a fugitive criminal to the jurisdiction of the accusing state.

INTERSTATE COMPACTS
Agreements between two or more states. Agreements on minor matters are made without congressional consent, but any compact that tends to increase the power of the contracting states relative to other states or relative to the national government generally requires the consent of Congress. Such compacts serve as a means by which states can solve regional problems.

---

[7]Out-of-state residents have been denied lower tuition rates at state universities, voting rights, and immediate claim to welfare benefits. Actually, the courts have never established a precise meaning of the term *privileges and immunities.*

POLITICS AND THE ENVIRONMENT

The Not-in-My-Backyard (NIMBY) Syndrome

One of the benefits of having the fifty individual states controlled by one written national Constitution is free trade. It is not easy for one state to impose restrictions on other states' shipment of goods and services across state lines. In fact, it is impossible under most circumstances. But what is true for the shipment of cars from Detroit to Texas or the shipment of watermelons from California to New York is not always true for refuse. As the nation's landfills overflow, many states, particularly those in the Northeast, are now shipping their garbage to less-populated states, typically in the South and Midwest. Everybody seems to be in favor of getting rid of garbage, so long as it is not dumped in their own backyard. This is known as the not-in-my-backyard, or NIMBY, syndrome.

Indiana is a favorite location for the interstate shipment of trash. Republican Senator Dan Coats of Indiana, hoping to halt this practice, sponsored legislation that would allow states to ban out-of-state trash. Environmentalists backed the bill because they saw it as a way to force each state to recycle more trash. The waste management industry is, of course, opposed to such restrictions. Industry spokespersons argue that any such legislation is an unwarranted obstacle to interstate commerce.

When the "garbage" in question happens to be low-radiation waste, the issue gets really heated. Virtually no community likes the idea of having a low-radiation nuclear dump anywhere in its vicinity. The day is still pretty far away when the United States will be shipping its normal garbage to outer space, but it is possible that radioactive waste may eventually end up there. It may not matter if such a solution costs taxpayers 10 or even 1,000 times more than building additional radioactive dump sites within the continental United States. So far, there is no political constituency from outer space that will complain.

pact increases the power of the contracting states relative to other states (or to the national government). Typical examples of interstate compacts are the establishment of the Port of New York Authority by the states of New York and New Jersey and the regulation of the production of crude oil and natural gas by the Interstate Oil and Gas Compact of 1935. The U.S. Supreme Court plays a major role in dealing with legal disputes between the states, as well as between the national government and the state governments. We consider the judicial system in more detail in Chapter 15.

The Supremacy of the National Constitution

The supremacy of the national constitution over subnational laws and actions can be found in the **supremacy clause** of the Constitution. The supremacy clause (Article VI, Paragraph 2) states:

> This Constitution, and the laws of the United States which shall be made in pursuance thereof; and all Treaties made . . . under the Authority of the United States, shall be the supreme law of the Land; and the Judges in every State shall be bound thereby; any Thing in the Constitution or Laws of any State to the Contrary notwithstanding.

In other words, states cannot use their reserved or concurrent powers to thwart national policies. All national and state officers, as well as judges, must be bound by oath to support the Constitution. Hence, any

SUPREMACY CLAUSE
The constitutional provision that makes the Constitution and federal laws superior to all state and local legislation.

legitimate exercise of national governmental power supersedes any conflicting state action.[8] Of course, deciding whether a conflict actually exists
is a judicial matter, as you will soon read about in the case of *McCulloch
v. Maryland.*

Some political scientists believe that national supremacy is critical for
the longevity and smooth functioning of a federal system. Nonetheless,
the application of this principle has been a continuous source of conflict.
Indeed, the most extreme result of this conflict was the Civil War, which
we explore in more detail later.

Milestones in National Government Supremacy

Numerous court decisions and political events and even more numerous
instances of bureaucratic decision making have given our national government a preponderance of significant political power. Such was not the
case during the early days of the American republic. Historically, there
are at least three milestones on the route to today's relatively more powerful national government. They are as follows:

1. The Supreme Court case of *McCulloch v. Maryland* (1819),[9] in which the
doctrine of implied powers of the national government was clarified.
2. The Supreme Court case of *Gibbons v. Ogden* (1824),[10] in which the
national government's power over commerce was defined for the first
time in an expansive way.
3. The Civil War (1861–1865).

McCulloch v. *Maryland* (1819)

The U.S. Constitution says nothing about establishing a national bank.
Article I, Section 8, gives Congress the power "to coin money, regulate
the value thereof, and of foreign coin, and fix the standards of weights
and measures." Nonetheless, at different times Congress chartered two
banks—the First and Second Banks of the United States—and provided
part of their initial capital; they were thus national banks.

Maryland was one of many states that opposed the existence of the
Second Bank of the United States, claiming that it represented unfair competition against state banks and an overextension of centralized political
power. Yielding to pressure from its state banks, the government of Maryland imposed a tax on the Second Bank's Baltimore branch. It was an
attempt to put that branch out of business. The branch's cashier, James
William McCulloch, refused to pay the Maryland tax. Maryland took
McCulloch to its state court. In that court, the state of Maryland won.
Because similar taxes were being levied in other states, the national government appealed the case to the Supreme Court, then headed by Chief
Justice John Marshall.

---

[8]An excellent example of this is President Eisenhower's disciplining of Arkansas Governor
Orval Faubus by calling up the National Guard to enforce the court-ordered desegregation
of Little Rock High School. See R. Neustadt, *Presidential Power: The Politics of Leadership from
FDR to Carter* (New York: Wiley, 1980).
[9]4 Wheaton 316 (1819).
[10]9 Wheaton 1 (1824).

John Marshall (1755–1835)

The Constitutional Question. The question before the Supreme Court was of monumental proportions. The very heart of national power under the Constitution, as well as the relationship between the national government and the states, was at issue. Congress has the authority to make all laws that are "necessary and proper" for the execution of Congress's expressed powers. Strict constitutional constructionists looked at the word *necessary* and contended that the national government had only those powers *indispensable* to the exercise of its designated powers. To them, chartering and contributing capital to a bank was not necessary, for example, to coin money and regulate its value. Nothing was specifically stated in the Constitution about the creation by the national government of a national bank.

Loose constitutional constructionists disagreed. They believed that the word *necessary* could not be looked at in its strictest sense. If one were to interpret the necessary and proper clause literally, it would have no practical effect. As Hamilton once said, "It is essential to the being of the national Government, that so erroneous a conception of the meaning of the word *necessary* should be exploded."

Marshall's Decision. Three days after hearing the arguments in the case, John Marshall announced the decision of the Court. (Some suspect that Marshall probably made his decision in this case even before he heard the opposing arguments.) Marshall's Federalist views are evident in his decision. It is true, Marshall said, that Congress's power to establish a national bank was not expressed in the Constitution. He went on to say, however, that if establishing such a national bank aided the national government in the exercise of its designated powers, then the authority to set up such a bank could be implied. To Marshall, the "necessary and proper" clause embraced "all means which are appropriate" to carry out "the legitimate ends" of the Constitution. Only when such actions are forbidden by the letter and spirit of the Constitution are they thereby unconstitutional. There was nothing in the Constitution, according to Marshall, "which excludes incidental or implied powers; and which requires that everything granted shall be expressly and minutely described." It would be impossible to spell out every action that Congress might legitimately take—the Constitution "would be enormously long and could scarcely be embraced by the human mind."

In perhaps the single most famous sentence ever uttered by a Supreme Court justice, Marshall said, "[W]e must never forget it is a constitution we are expounding." In other words, the Constitution is a living instrument that has to be interpreted to meet the "practical" needs of government. Marshall's decision became the basis for strengthening the national government's power from that day on. The Marshall Court enabled the national government to grow and to meet problems that the Constitution's framers were unable to foresee. Today, practically every expressed power of the national government has been expanded in one way or another by use of the necessary and proper clause.

Gibbons v. Ogden (1824)

One of the more important parts of the Constitution included in Article I, Section 8, is the so-called **commerce clause,** in which Congress is given

COMMERCE CLAUSE
The section of the Constitution in which Congress is given the power to regulate trade among the states and with foreign countries.

the power "to regulate commerce with foreign nations, and among the several states, and with the Indian tribes." What exactly does "to regulate commerce" mean? What does "commerce" entail? The issue here is essentially the same as that raised by *McCulloch v. Maryland*—how strict an interpretation should be given to a constitutional phrase? As can be expected, because Marshall interpreted the necessary and proper clause liberally in *McCulloch v. Maryland,* he also, five years later, used the same approach in interpreting the commerce clause.

The Issue before the Court.   Robert Fulton, inventor of the steamboat, and Robert Livingston, American minister to France, secured a monopoly of steam navigation on the waters in New York State from the New York legislature in 1803. They licensed Aaron Ogden to operate steam-powered ferryboats between New York and New Jersey. Thomas Gibbons decided to compete with Ogden, but he did so without New York's permission. Ogden sued Gibbons. The New York state courts granted Ogden an **injunction,** prohibiting Gibbons from operating in New York waters. Gibbons appealed to the Supreme Court.

Marshall's Decision.   Marshall defined commerce as all commercial intercourse—that is, all business dealings. The Court ruled against Ogden's monopoly, thus reversing the injunction against Gibbons. Marshall used this opportunity not only to expand the definition of commerce but also to validate and increase the power of the national legislature to regulate commerce. Said Marshall, "What is this power? It is the power . . . to prescribe the rule by which commerce is to be governed. This power, like all others vested in Congress, is complete in itself." In other words, the power of the national government to regulate commerce has no limitations, other than those specifically found in the Constitution.

As a result of Marshall's decision, the commerce clause allowed the national government to exercise increasing authority over all areas of economic affairs throughout the land. Some scholars believe that Marshall's decision in *Gibbons v. Ogden* welded the people of the United States into a unit by the force of their commercial interests. Although Congress did not immediately exploit this broader grant of power, today few areas of economic activity remain outside the regulatory power of the national legislature.

INJUNCTION
An order issued by a court to compel or restrain the performance of an act by an individual or government official.

The Civil War

We usually think of the Civil War simply as the fight to free the slaves. The facts are quite different. Freedom for the slaves was an important aspect of the Civil War, but not the only one and certainly not the most important one, say many scholars. At the heart of the controversy that led to the Civil War was the issue of national government supremacy versus the rights of the separate states. The Civil War brought to an ultimate and violent climax the ideological debate that had been outlined by the Federalist and Anti-Federalist parties in the early years of the nation. This debate was sparked anew by the passage of a tariff in 1828. The state of South Carolina attempted to nullify the tariffs, claiming that in cases of conflict between a state and the national government, the state should have the ultimate authority over its citizens.

The Civil War was not fought over just the question of slavery. Rather, the supremacy of the national government was at issue. Had the South won, presumably any state or states would have the right to secede from the Union.

NULLIFICATION
The act of nullifying, or rendering void. John C. Calhoun asserted that a state had the right to declare a national law to be null and void and therefore not binding on its citizens, on the assumption that ultimate sovereign authority rested with the several states.

INTERPOSITION
The act in which a state places itself between its citizens and the national government as a protector, shielding its citizens from any national legislation that may be harmful to them. The doctrine of interposition has been rejected by the federal courts as contrary to the national supremacy clause of Article VI in the Constitution.

CONCURRENT MAJORITY
A principle advanced by John C. Calhoun whereby democratic decisions could be made only with the concurrence of all segments of society affected by the decision. Without their concurrence, a decision should not be binding on those whose interests it violates.

SECESSION
The act of formally withdrawing from membership in an alliance; the withdrawal of a state from the federal union.

Nullification and Secession.   Defending the concept of **nullification** was a well-educated and articulate senator from South Carolina, John C. Calhoun. Not a newcomer to politics, Calhoun had served the national government in several capacities—as vice president, as secretary of state, and as secretary of war. Calhoun viewed the federal system as simply a compact (as in the Articles of Confederation) among sovereign states. The national government was not the final judge of its own power—the ultimate sovereign authority rested with the several states. It followed that the national government could not force a state and its citizens to accept a law against their will. In such cases, Calhoun argued, the state had the right to declare a national law *null and void* and therefore not binding on its citizens. This theory of nullification uses the concept of **interposition,** in which a state places itself between its citizens and the national government as a protector, shielding its citizens from any national legislation that may be harmful to them.[11]

Calhoun also espoused the political doctrine of the **concurrent majority.** He maintained that democratic decisions could be made only with the concurrence of all segments of society affected by the decision. Without that agreement a decision should not be binding on those whose interests it violates.

Calhoun's concurrent majority thesis was used by others later as a justification for the **secession** of the southern states from the Union. The ultimate defeat of the South, however, permanently ended any idea that a state within the Union can successfully claim the right to secede. We live in "the indestructible union of indestructible states," as the Supreme Court has said. It is not without irony that the Civil War, brought about in large part because of the South's desire for increased states' rights, in fact resulted in the opposite—an increase in the political power of the national government.

---

[11]Thomas Jefferson and James Madison also used the theory of interposition in the Kentucky and Virginia Resolutions of 1799, written to protest the Alien and Sedition Acts of 1798.

War and Growth of the National Government.   Thousands of new employees were hired to run the Union war effort and to deal with the social and economic problems that had to be handled in the aftermath of war. A billion-dollar ($1.3 billion, which is over $11 billion in today's dollars) national government budget was passed for the first time in 1865 to cover the increased government expenditures. The first (temporary) income tax was imposed on citizens to help pay for the war. Both the increased national government spending and the nationally imposed income tax were precursors to the expanded role of the national government in the American federal system.[12] Civil liberties were curtailed in the Union and in the Confederacy in the name of the wartime emergency. The distribution of pensions and widows' benefits also boosted the national government's social role. The North's victory set the nation on the path to a modern industrial economy and society.

The Continuing Dispute over the Division of Power

As we have noted, *McCulloch v. Maryland* expanded the implied powers of the federal government. The dispute, and its ultimate outcome, can be viewed as part of a continuing debate about the boundaries between federal and state authority, with the Supreme Court as the boundary setter, or referee. As we might expect, the character of the referee will have an impact on the ultimate outcome of any boundary dispute. While John Marshall was chief justice of the Supreme Court, he did much to permit the increase in the power of the national government and the reduction in that of the states. During the Jacksonian era (1829–1837), a shift back to states' rights began. In particular, the business community preferred state regulation (or, better yet, no regulation) of commerce. The question of the regulation of commerce became one of the major issues in federal–state relations.

The issue was often resolved in favor of the states under U.S. Supreme Court Justice Roger Taney, who headed the Court from 1836 until 1864. Taney's goal was to shift the constitutional emphasis from the national level and return power to the states. He was particularly concerned with shoring up state power in the regulation of business and other activities within state borders, such as public health, safety, and morals. Under Taney, the police power of the states became the basic instrument through which property was controlled in the "public interest."

The continuing dispute over the division of power between the national government and the states can be looked at in terms of the historical phases of federalism in the United States: dual federalism, cooperative federalism, and the new federalism.

Dual Federalism

The doctrine of **dual federalism** emphasized a distinction between federal and state spheres of authority, particularly in the area of **economic**

---

[12]The future of the national government's powerful role was cemented with the passage of the Sixteenth Amendment (ratified in 1913), which authorized the federal income tax. Annual federal government expenditures now exceed one-quarter of annual national economic output.

DUAL FEDERALISM
A system of government in which the states and the national government each remain supreme within their own spheres. The doctrine looks on nation and state as coequal sovereign powers. It holds that acts of states within their reserved powers could be legitimate limitations on the powers of the national government.

ECONOMIC REGULATION
The regulation of business practices by government agencies.

regulation. The distinction between *intra*state commerce (which was not under the control of the national government) and *inter*state commerce (which was under the control of the national government) became of overriding importance. For example, in 1918, the U.S. Supreme Court ruled that a 1916 federal law banning child labor was unconstitutional, because it was a local problem and the power to deal with it was reserved to the states.[13] Even as recently as 1976, the Court held that a federal law regulating wages and overtime pay could not be applied to state government employees, as that would damage the states' ability to function effectively and would violate state sovereignty.[14] A 1985 Supreme Court decision overturned this ruling and stated that Congress, rather than the courts, should decide which state activities the federal government can regulate.[15]

Cooperative Federalism

Franklin D. Roosevelt was inaugurated on March 4, 1933, as the thirty-second president of the United States. In the previous year, nearly 1,500 banks had failed (and 4,000 more would fail in 1933). Thirty-two thousand businesses closed down and one-fourth of the labor force was unemployed. The national government had been expected to do something about the disastrous state of the economy. But for the first three years of the Great Depression, the national government did very little. That changed with the new Democratic administration's energetic intervention in the economy. FDR's "New Deal" included numerous government spending and welfare programs, in addition to voluminous regulations relating to economic activity. The U.S. Supreme Court, still abiding by the

---

[13]*Hammer v. Dagenhart*, 247 U.S. 251 (1918). This decision was overruled in *United States v. Darby*, 312 U.S. 100 (1940).
[14]*National League of Cities v. Usery*, 426 U.S. 833 (1976); altered by *Equal Employment Opportunity Commission v. Wyoming*, 460 U.S. 226 (1982).
[15]*Garcia v. San Antonio Metro*, 469 U.S. 528 (1985).

In the 1800s, very young children worked in coal mines. Today, child labor laws prohibit employers from hiring such young Americans. Some argue that even in the absence of child-labor laws, few if any children would still be working in the mines because the United States is a much richer country than it was a hundred years ago. Presumably parents, no longer at subsistence income levels, would opt to have their children go to school.

legal doctrine of dual federalism, rejected as an unconstitutional interference in state powers virtually all of Roosevelt's national regulation of business. It was not until 1937 that the Court, responding to Roosevelt's Court-packing threat and worsening economic conditions, including the outbreak of violent labor disputes, ruled that manufacturing could be regulated as interstate commerce by the national government.[16]

Some political scientists have labeled the era since 1937 as an era of **cooperative federalism,** in which the states and the national government cooperate in solving complex common problems. Others see the Supreme Court's 1937 decision as the beginning of an era of national supremacy, in which the power of the states has been consistently diminished. In particular, Congress can pass virtually any law that regulates almost any kind of economic activity, no matter where that activity is located. For all intents and purposes, the doctrine of dual federalism has been dead for quite some time, although there were attempts at reviving it during the Reagan administration (1981–1989). Many minorities have expressed a preference for cooperative federalism and national supremacy, believing that their rights are better protected when the federal government has oversight of state government actions.

COOPERATIVE FEDERALISM
The theory that the states and the national government should cooperate in solving problems.

The Growth of National-Level Powers

Even if the Great Depression had not occurred, we probably still would have witnessed a growth of national-level powers as the country became increasingly populated, industrial, interdependent with other countries, and a world power. This meant that problems and situations that were once treated locally would begin to have a profound impact on Americans hundreds or even thousands of miles away.

---

[16]*National Labor Relations Board v. Jones & Laughlin Steel Corp.,* 301 U.S. 1 (1937). For a different view of the historical significance of this decision, see Morton Grodzins, "Centralization and Decentralization in the American Federal System," in Robert A. Goldwin, ed., *A Nation of States: Essays on the American Federal System* (Chicago: Rand McNally, 1963).

This mural in San Francisco was one of the many projects sponsored by the New Deal's Works Progress Administration (WPA) in the 1930s. The federal government's efforts to alleviate unemployment (in this case among artists) during the Great Depression signaled a shift from dual federalism to cooperative federalism.

For example, if one state is unable to maintain an adequate highway system, the economy of the entire region may suffer. If another state maintains a substandard educational system, the quality of the work force, the welfare rolls, and the criminal justice agencies in other states may be affected. So the death of dual federalism and the ascendancy of national supremacy had a very logical and very real set of causes. Our more mobile, industrial, and increasingly interdependent nation demanded more uniform and consistent sets of rules, regulations, and governmental programs. The shift toward a greater role for the central government in the United States can nowhere better be seen than in the shift toward increased central government spending as a percentage of total government spending. Figure 3-3 shows that back in 1929, on the eve of the Great Depression, local governments accounted for 60 percent of all government outlays, whereas the federal government accounted for only 17 percent. After Roosevelt's New Deal had been in place for several years during the Great Depression, local governments gave up half their share of the government spending pie, dropping to 30 percent, and the federal government increased its share to 47 percent. Estimates are that in 1993, the federal government accounts for about 65 percent of all government spending.

The New Federalism

NEW FEDERALISM
A plan to limit the national government's power to regulate and to restore power to state governments. Essentially, the new federalism was designed to give the states greater ability to decide for themselves how government revenues should be spent.

The third phase of federalism, which began in 1969, was labeled by President Richard Nixon as the **new federalism.** Its goal was to reduce the restrictions attached to federal grants—that is, to allow local officials to make the decisions about how the money is to be spent. Under Nixon's program, money was given directly to states and localities without any strings attached. This program, which was known as *revenue sharing,* lasted through 1986.

With Reagan's election in 1980, the administration took steps to privatize various federal programs, including low-cost housing, prisons, and hospitals. Reassigning government programs to the private sector seemed to go well beyond the new federalism. But even with more traditional

FIGURE 3-3 ■ The Shift toward Central Government Spending

Before the Great Depression, local governments accounted for 60 percent of all government spending, with the federal government only accounting for 17 percent. By 1960, federal government spending was up to 64 percent, local governments accounted for only 19 percent, and the remainder was spent by state governments. The estimate for 1993 is that the federal government accounts for 65 percent and local governments for 16 percent.

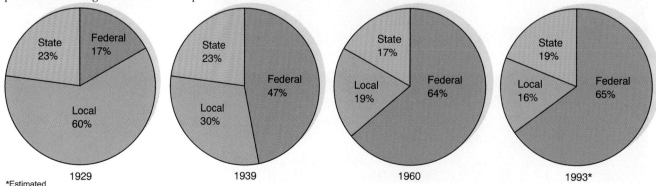

*Estimated

SOURCE: *Government Finances* (U.S. Department of Commerce, Bureau of the Census, 1993.)

The 1992 convention of state governors.

shifting of money to states, analysis shows that the new federalism was probably more talk than action. The politics behind this inaction are relatively straightforward.

Take the case of the revenue-sharing program, in which the federal government simply gave back to the state and local governments a certain portion of federal taxes. This process generated specific constituencies among governments but not among voters. Consequently, there were no well-organized groups of people lobbying Congress to increase revenue sharing. So, when the federal government budget continued to be in the red in the 1980s, it was relatively easy for the members of Congress to let the program die.

Also, particularly under the Reagan and Bush administrations, the number of **federal mandates** to the states in the areas of health, pollution control, and welfare have increased dramatically, a topic to which we return at the end of this chapter.

FEDERAL MANDATES
Requirements in federal legislation that force states and municipalities to comply with certain rules.

Fiscal Federalism: Federal Grants

Today, the national government collects over 60 percent of all tax dollars. As part of our system of cooperative federalism, the national government gives back to the states (and local governments) a significant amount— almost $160 billion estimated in fiscal year 1993. Currently, there are basically two separate methods by which the national government returns nationally collected tax dollars to state and local governments: *categorical grants-in-aid* and *block grants*.

Categorical Grants-in-Aid

Grants from the national government to the states occurred even before the ratification of the Constitution. Some students reading this book may be attending a land-grant college. These are state universities that were

CATEGORICAL GRANTS-IN-AID
Federal grants-in-aid to states or local governments that are for very specific programs or projects.

MATCHING FUNDS
For many categorical grant programs, the state must "match" the federal funds. Some programs only require the state to raise 10 percent of the funds, whereas others approach an even share.

EQUALIZATION
A method for adjusting the amount of money that a state must put up to receive federal funds that takes into account the wealth of the state or its ability to tax its citizens.

PROJECT GRANT
An assistance grant that can be applied for directly by state and local agencies; established under a national program grant. Project grants allow Congress (and the administration) to bypass state governments and thereby to place the money directly where it is supposedly the most needed.

BLOCK GRANTS
Federal programs that provide funding to the state and local governments for general functional areas, such as criminal justice or mental health programs.

built with the proceeds from the sale of land grants given by the national government to the states. Cash grants-in-aid started in 1808 when Congress gave money to the states to pay for the state militia. It wasn't until the twentieth century that the federal grants-in-aid program became significant, however. The major growth began in the 1960s, during which decade they quadrupled.

The major category of grants-in-aid to the states is labeled **categorical grants-in-aid** because they are used for specific programs. Currently, there are over four hundred categories for these types of grants.

The Nuts and Bolts of Giving and Getting Grants-in-Aid.   The restrictions and regulations that accompany categorical grants-in-aid started to mushroom during the administration of Franklin D. Roosevelt (1933–1945). The number and scope of the categorical grants also expanded further as part of the Great Society programs of President Lyndon Johnson (1963–1969). Grants became available in the fields of education, pollution control, conservation, recreation, and highway construction and maintenance. For some of the categorical grant programs, the state and local governments must put up a share of the money, usually called **matching funds.** For other types of programs, the funds are awarded according to a formula that takes into account the relative wealth of the state, a process known as **equalization.**

In general, categorical grants have remained under fairly tight control by Congress. In a move to bypass the states, Congress established the **project grant** approach, which allows state and local agencies to apply directly for assistance to local offices that administer the federal funds. In this way, the funds can be directly placed where—in the eyes of Congress—they are most needed.

Block Grants

As part of the new federalism, governors and mayors succeeded in convincing Washington that fewer restrictions should be placed on the grants-in-aid. No state or local official ever liked all of the strings attached to myriad grants-in-aid.

The solution was to group a number of categorical grants under one broad purpose. Thus, the **block grant** was born in 1966 in the field of health. Out of the numerous block grants that were proposed from 1966 until the election of Ronald Reagan in 1980, only five became law. At the administration's urging, Congress increased the number to nine. By the beginning of the 1990s, such block grants accounted for over 10 percent of all federal aid programs.

Although governors and mayors prefer block grants in principle, they have grown very slowly. The reason is that the coalitions supporting block grants are too diffuse to muster the necessary lobbying muscle to force Congress to increase them. A political rule of thumb is that the less specific the program, the harder it is to pry funds out of Congress to increase the size of that program. After all, members of Congress like to take credit for programs and have some input into who runs them, who receives the money, and so on. Thus, any member of Congress who sees a national problem that needs solving will automatically want to create a (specific) categorical grants-in-aid program, rather than a (general) block grant program, so that Congress, not the states, will decide how the money shall be spent. Also, the broader the range of activities under a block grant, the less likely it is that any one affected group will have enough of a stake in the overall category to spend the resources needed to lobby for an increase in the grant.

Federally Induced
State and Local Governmental Costs

According to some political observers, the remainder of the 1990s will see an increasing conflict between Washington, D.C., and state and local governments. This conflict concerns the burden placed by *federal mandates* on state and municipal governments. President Bush referred to the problem in his 1992 State of the Union message:

> We must put an end to the unfinanced federal government mandates. These are the requirements Congress puts on our cities, counties, and states without supplying the money. And if Congress passes a mandate, it should be forced to pay for it and balance the cost with savings elsewhere.

Examples of recent federal mandates are minimum water purity requirements for specific localities; requirements for access by physically disabled persons to public buildings, sidewalks, and other areas; and mandatory minimum prison sentences for certain crimes.

Preemption of Federal Laws over State Authority

Federal mandates preempt state and local laws and rules in the sense that congressional legislation prevails when it conflicts with state and local laws or regulations. Figure 3-4 on page 82 shows the increase in the number of federal laws that preempt state authority.

Some of the Costs of Federal Mandates

No accurate analysis exists of the overall costs to state and local governments incurred as a result of federal mandates. Certain mandates, however, are clearly very costly. Consider some of the mandates affecting health and safety. Congress passed a law in 1986, for example, that requires the removal of asbestos from school buildings. The projected cost is now $6 billion over thirty years. Other mandates involve eligibility for Medicaid. Medicaid is the federally subsidized, state-run health-care program for low-income Americans. The estimated cost of the program for the states is $44 billion in 1993. Each time Congress increases eligibility for Medicaid, the states pay the bulk of the additional cost. The latest expansion of coverage includes benefits for children, pregnant women, and the elderly. Representative Henry A. Waxman (D., Calif.), chairman of the House Subcommittee on Health and Environment, stated that "we simply can't let pregnant women, infants, and children go without health care."[17] Pennsylvania Governor Robert P. Casey, in response, proposed

Did You Know . . . That local governments, which can be created as well as abolished by their state, have no independent existence according to the Constitution, unlike the state and national governments?

---

[17]Quoted in the *New York Times*, March 24, 1992, p. A14.

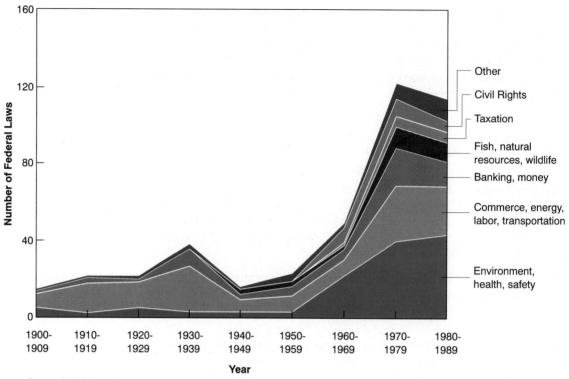

SOURCE: U.S. Advisory Commission on Intergovernmental Relations.

FIGURE 3-4 ■ Federal Laws that Preempt State Laws

This graph shows, by decade, the number of federal laws that preempt state authority. As you can see, the greatest growth in federal preemption is in laws regulating the environment, health, or safety areas: laws affecting commerce, energy, labor, and transportation run a close second.

that some medical benefits for disabled men be eliminated to offset the cost of expanded benefits for children, pregnant women, and the elderly. The message was, the money simply is not there.

Conclusion: The Changing Face of Federalism

The new federalism of the Nixon, Reagan, and Bush administrations had as its goal giving the states more power. This was accomplished, as noted previously, by block grants, revenue sharing, and an attempt to let the states "do their own thing." During the 1980s and early 1990s, overall federal aid to states and local governments declined. But one could hardly call what has occurred in the relationship between federal and state governments the new federalism. At the beginning of this decade, President Bush signed twenty bills into law, all of which included numerous mandates. The National Conference of State Legislatures indicated that those bills alone were costing state and local governments billions of extra dollars a year—yet the national government has provided little help for the states.

Some political scientists have labeled what is occurring the "new, new federalism." Under the new, new federalism, Washington, D.C., continues to reduce funding to the states but at the same time increases federal control. According to Joseph F. Zimmerman, professor of political science at the State University of New York in Buffalo, the current expansion of federal authority over state affairs represents a historic shift in American government since the 1960s. In two studies that he wrote for the Advisory Commission on Intergovernmental Relations, Zimmerman concluded that "Congress, with the acquiescence of the Supreme Court, is slowly usurping the sovereign powers of states and turning them into administrators of national policy."[18] Zimmerman further pointed out that the presumed deregulation under the Reagan administration in the 1980s was "largely ineffective." All that happened was that the federal government passed on more significant regulatory burdens to state and local governments than in almost any other decade. Given that the federal government has recently been running deficits of between $300 and $400 billion a year, the economics of the new, new federalism may make political sense.

The massive riots in Los Angeles and other American cities in the spring of 1992, as well as the $30 billion in damages inflicted on southern Florida by Hurricane Andrew in the late summer of 1992, may affect this issue and other issues related to federal funding. Because state and local resources are often insufficient to meet the needs of many poor local communities or areas devastated by natural disasters, the question as to what role the federal government should play in assisting these communities has once again become a topic of significant debate.

[18]*New York Times,* May 23, 1992, p. B1.

GETTING INVOLVED

Expressing Your Views—Writing Letters to the Editor

Just about every day an issue concerning federalism is discussed in the media. Advocates of decentralization—a shift of power from federal to state or local governments—argue that we must recognize the rights of states to design their own destiny and master their own fate. Advocates of centralization—more power to the national government—see the shift in power under decentralization as undermining the national purpose, common interests, and responsibilities that bind us together in pursuit of national goals. The big question is how much the national government should do for the people. Is it within the power of the national government to decide what the law should be on abortion? Before 1973, each state set its own laws without interference from the national government. Who should be responsible for the homeless? Should the national government subsidize state and local efforts to help them? Who is responsible for the nation's health care? Should the national government expand its role in this area?

You may have valid, important points to make on these or other issues. One of the best ways to make your point is by writing an effective letter to the editor of your local newspaper (or even to a national newspaper such as the *New York Times*). First, you should familiarize yourself with the kinds of letters that are accepted by the newspapers to which you want to write. Then, follow these rules for writing an effective letter:

1. Use a typewriter and double-space the lines. If possible, use a word processor with a spelling checker and grammar checker.
2. Your lead topic sentence should be short, to the point, and powerful.
3. Keep your thoughts on target—choose only one topic to discuss in your letter. Make sure it is newsworthy and timely.
4. If you know that facts were misstated or left out in current news stories about your topic, supply them. The public wants to know.
5. Don't be afraid to express moral judgments. You can go a long way by appealing to the readers' sense of justice.
6. Personalize the letter by bringing in your own experiences.
7. With appropriate changes, send your letter to the editors of more than one newspaper or magazine. Make sure, however, that the letters are not exactly the same.
8. Sign your letter and give your address and your phone number. If your letter is not published, try again. Eventually, one will be.

CHAPTER SUMMARY

1. There are three basic models of ordering relations between central governments and local units: (a) a unitary system, (b) a confederal system, and (c) a federal system. A unitary system, such as in France, is one in which the national government has ultimate authority. This system is most common. A confederal system is a league of independent states, each having esssentially sovereign powers. The central government handles only matters of common concern that have been expressly delegated to it by member states. Somewhere between the unitary and the confederal forms of government lies the federal system. In a federal system, authority is divided between the central government and the regional, or subdivisional, governments.

2. Federalism is probably the best arrangement in large countries because of their size and consequent regional differences and political subcultures. A division of power between local and national governments brings government closer to the people and allows government to meet the local needs of its citizens. State governments in the United States have also served as testing grounds for future national leaders and bold new initiatives.

3. The Constitution expressly delegated certain powers to the national government in Article I, Section 8. In addition to these expressed powers, the national government has implied and inherent powers. Implied powers are those that are reasonably necessary to carry out the powers expressly delegated to the national government. Inherent powers are those held by the national government by virtue of its being a sovereign state with the right to preserve itself.

4. The Tenth Amendment to the Constitution states that powers not delegated to the United States by the Constitution, nor prohibited by it to the states, are reserved to the states respectively, or to the people. In certain areas, the Constitution provides for concurrent powers, which are powers that are jointly held by the national and state governments. The classic example of a concurrent power is the power to tax.

5. The three most important clauses in the Constitution relating to horizontal federalism require that (a) each state give full faith and credit to every other state's public acts, records, and judicial proceedings; (b) each state extend to every other state's citizens the privileges and immunities of its own citizens; and (c) each state agree to return persons who are fleeing from justice to another state back to their home state when requested to do so.

6. The supremacy clause of the Constitution states that the Constitution, congressional laws, and national treaties are the supreme law of the land. States cannot use their reserved or concurrent powers to override national policies.

7. *McCulloch v. Maryland* (1819) enhanced the implied power of the federal government through Chief Justice John Marshall's broad interpretation of the "necessary and proper" clause of Article I of the Constitution. The effects of the decision are part of a continuing debate about the boundaries between federal and state authority.

8. *Gibbons v. Ogden* (1824) enhanced and consolidated national power over commerce. Chief Justice Marshall interpreted the commerce clause of the Constitution broadly and held that the commerce power was complete in itself, with no limitations other than those found specifically in the Constitution. The regulation of commerce became one of the major issues in federal-state relations.

9. At the heart of the controversy that led to the Civil War was the issue of national government supremacy versus the rights of the separate states. The notion of nullification eventually led to the secession of the Confederate states from the Union. But the effect of the South's desire for increased states' rights and the subsequent Civil War was an increase in the political power of the national government.

10. In dual federalism, each of the states and the federal government remain supreme within their own spheres. The era since the Depression has sometimes been labeled as one of cooperative federalism, in which states and the national government cooperate in solving complex common problems. Others view it as the begining of an era of national supremacy. The third phase of federalism was labeled the new federalism by President Nixon and was revived by President Reagan. The goal of the new federalism was to decentralize federal programs, giving more responsibility to the states.

11. There are basically two separate methods by which the national government returns nationally collected tax dollars to state and local governments: (a) categorical grants-in-aid and (b) block grants.

12. Federal government mandates have placed a heavy burden on state and local governments, which do not always have sufficient resources to pay the costs incurred by implementing the mandates.

QUESTIONS FOR REVIEW AND DISCUSSION

1. The Constitution and federal law are supreme over state and local legislation. Can you think of several areas of law over which local governments should have complete authority?

2. Should the national government take full responsibility for protecting the environment?

3. Are the states unlikely to fund social welfare programs on their own if the federal government no longer sends grants for them? Why does the Congress prefer to keep control of such programs at the national level?

4. By choosing a federal form for our government, the framers of the Constitution assured the continued existence of regional differences. Choose four states from different sections of the country and list the ways in which their political interests differ from each other. What kinds of national legislation will cause these differences to surface? How do these differences affect the outcome of presidential elections?

SELECTED REFERENCES

Richard F. Bensel, *Yankee Leviathan: The Origins of Central State Authority* (New York: Cambridge University Press, 1990). In this analysis of state formation, Bensel looks closely at the changes in political structure caused by the Civil War.

Daniel J. Elazar, *American Federalism: A View from the States,* 3rd ed. (New York: Harper and Row, 1985). This classic book focuses on the politics of federalism—bargaining, negotiation, and cooperation. It also emphasizes the political subcultures of America and their impact on the states.

Michael Fix and Daphne A. Kenyon, eds., *Coping with Mandates: What Are the Alternatives?* (Lanham, Md.: University Press of America, 1990). This excellent examination of the mandates issue focuses on the history of mandates and their relationship to policy goals, the burden that mandates place on state and local governments, and the potential of alternative approaches to the mandates issue.

Morton Grodzins, *The American System* (Chicago: Rand McNally, 1974). A classic examination of the modern federal system.

Alexander Hamilton, John Jay, James Madison, *The Federalist:*

A Collection of Essays Written in Favor of the New Constitution, edited by George W. Carey and James McClellan. (Dubuque, Ia.: Kendall/Hunt Publishing Co., 1990). This student-oriented edition makes these classic essays accessible to this generation and includes an introduction, analytical notes, a glossary, and an index.

Robert Higgs, *Crisis and Leviathan: Critical Episodes in the Growth of American Government* (New York: Oxford University Press, 1987). A study of the reasons for the growth in size and power of government in the United States.

David Osborne, *Laboratories of Democracy: A New Breed of Governor Creates Models for National Growth* (Boston: Harvard Business School Press, 1990). The author uses a series of six case studies of governors to describe and analyze the lessons of state-level innovation in areas such as economic development, technology, social policy, and welfare reform.

C. G. Pickvance and E. Preteceille, *State and Locality: A Comparative Perspective on State Restructuring* (Irvington, N.Y.: Columbia University Press, 1991). An insightful comparative study of the relationship between central and local governments in several nations, including the United States.

James C. Smith, *Emerging Conflicts in the Doctrine of Federalism: The Intergovernmental Predicament* (Lanham, Md.: University Press of America, 1984). Intergovernmental problems that interfere with the smooth operation and performance of government institutions, in particular the roles of different levels and jurisdictions, are concisely explored in this study.

Deil S. Wright, *Understanding Intergovernmental Relations,* 2nd ed. (Monterey, Calif.: Brooks/Cole, 1982). Wright explores national political authorities' relations with state and local officials, emphasizing the practice and problems of federalism.

PART TWO

CIVIL RIGHTS AND LIBERTIES

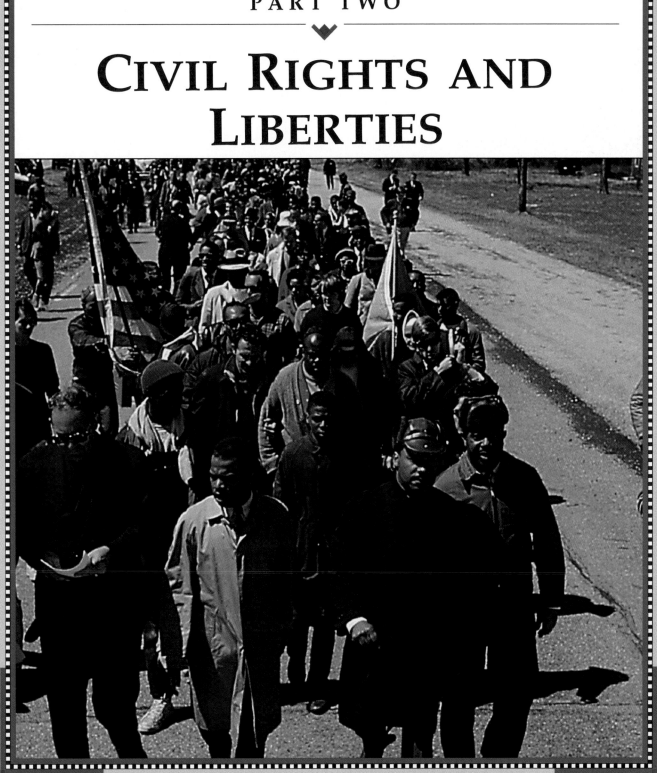

CHAPTER 4
Civil Liberties

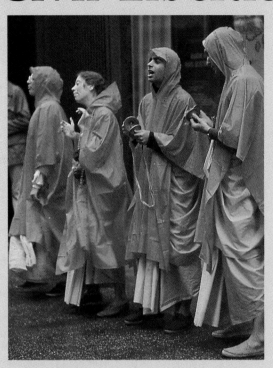

CHAPTER CONTENTS

WHAT IF ... THE *MIRANDA* RULES WERE ELIMINATED?

Since the mid-1960s, the criminal justice process in the United States has been governed largely by what have come to be known as the "*Miranda* rules." These rules, established by a 1966 Supreme Court decision, hold that criminal suspects must be treated in such a manner as to decrease the probability that they will be convicted wrongly of crimes they did not commit. The *Miranda* rules include four warnings and a waiver. Before being interrogated, a person in police custody must be informed of the following: (1) The person has the right to remain silent. (2) Anything the person says can be used against him or her in court. (3) The person has the right to an attorney. (4) If the person cannot afford an attorney but wants one, one will be appointed. The person in custody must waive these rights before any statement he or she makes during the interrogation will be admitted as evidence.

There are some exceptions to the *Miranda* rules. For instance, a confession will be admitted as evidence, even if it is given before a suspect is informed of his or her rights, if the suspect also confesses after being informed. A probationer's confession to his or her probation officer without the warnings is admissible. If the warnings are given, a confession will be admitted, even if the police lie to the suspect's lawyer or fail to tell the suspect that the lawyer wants to see him or her.

What might happen if the *Miranda* rules were eliminated? It is very difficult to know for certain. But some outcomes can be guessed at from the American experience with criminal justice procedures that were

general before the introduction of the *Miranda* rules. It was once common, and might be again, for suspects to be subjected to the "third degree," which ranged from mild psychological pressure to violent physical and mental torture. The past record includes allegations, and proved instances, of beatings, threats of severe punishment, denial of access to legal counsel, incarceration without formal charges being filed, sleep deprivation, suspects being kept in handcuffs (sometimes with their arms wrapped around radiators), and other violations of what we today regard as the rights of criminal suspects. These actions and worse are common in other countries today that do not have *Miranda*-type protections for their citizens.

If you were arrested in a future America that did not have *Miranda* rules, what kind of treatment could you expect? The odds are that many, if not most, police officers and prosecutors would behave decently and with respect for our constitutional rights. But there would without a doubt be a strong incentive for law-enforcement officers to go out of their way to get a conviction. If you were ensnared in such a system, whether you were guilty or not, any of the following might happen. Depending on the seriousness of the offense with which you were charged, you might be arrested in the middle of the night without being told why. Your arms might be handcuffed or tied very uncomfortably, and you would be compelled to accompany the arresting officers to the police station. Once in detention, you probably would not have

the automatic right to make a telephone call to a lawyer who could give you legal advice or to contact your family to let them know what had happened to you.

There are reasons to expect that the excesses of the past might not be repeated if the *Miranda* rules were repealed. Educational levels among police officials are higher than before, and many are college-trained in the social sciences and related disciplines that encourage sensitivity to human rights. Furthermore, experienced law-enforcement officers would have already become used to *Miranda*-governed procedures and trained in proper treatment of criminal suspects, and those habits would take some time to break.

The incidents of police brutality that are reported today indicate that methods of interrogation employed in the pre-*Miranda* past might be used again, however. Also, most public opinion polls indicate a hardening of popular attitudes toward crime and alleged criminals, and many Americans are demanding harsher treatment of drug dealers, rapists, child pornographers, and murderers. In such a climate, police and the public might not make a clear distinction between those who actually are guilty of such offenses and those who may be merely suspected of committing crimes.

---

1. *Which groups would fare worse in the United States without* Miranda *rules, and why?*
2. *What are the costs to society of retaining the* Miranda *rules?*

Most Americans believe that they have more individual freedom than virtually any other people on earth. For the most part, this opinion is accurate. The freedoms that we take for granted—religion, speech, press, and assembly—are relatively unknown in many parts of the world. In many nations today, citizens have little chance of living without government harassment if they choose to criticize openly, through speech or print, the government or its actions. Indeed, if the United States suddenly had the same rules, laws, and procedures about verbal and printed expression that exist in many other countries, American jails would be filled overnight with transgressors.

Civil Rights and the Fear of Government

Without government, people live in a state of anarchy. With unbridled government, men and women may end up living in a state of tyranny. The framers of the Constitution wanted neither extreme. As we pointed out in Chapter 2, the Declaration of Independence was based on the idea of natural rights. These are rights discoverable in nature and history, according to such philosophers as John Locke and John Dickinson, who wrote that natural rights "are born with us; exist with us; and cannot be taken away from us by any human power."[1] Linked directly to the strong prerevolutionary sentiment for natural rights was the notion that a right was first and foremost a *limitation* on any government's ruling power. To obtain ratification of the Constitution by the necessary nine states, the Federalists had to deal with the colonists' fears of a too-powerful national government. The **Bill of Rights** was the result. When we speak of civil liberties in the United States, we are mostly referring to the specific limitations on government outlined in the Bill of Rights.[2] Despite these sentiments, the first ten amendments to the U.S. Constitution were passed by Congress on September 25, 1789, and ratified by three-fourths of the states by December 15, 1791. The two-hundredth anniversary of the ratification of the Bill of Rights was celebrated during the last three months of 1991.

BILL OF RIGHTS
The first ten amendments to the United States Constitution. They contain a listing of the rights a person enjoys and which cannot be infringed upon by the government, such as the freedoms of speech, press, and religion.

The Bill of Rights

The First Amendment to the Constitution is for many the most significant part of the Bill of Rights, as well as the mainstay of the Declaration of Independence statement that all people should be able to enjoy life, liberty, and the pursuit of happiness. It is in this First Amendment that our basic freedoms of religion, speech, the press, assembly, and the right of petition are set forth. The first part of this chapter examines each of these freedoms in detail.

---

[1]Quoted in Bernard Bailyn, *The Ideological Origins of the American Revolution* (Cambridge, Mass.: Harvard University Press, 1967), p. 77.

[2]Note that there is a distinction between the technical definitions of a civil *right* and a civil *liberty*. A civil right represents something that the government must do—guarantee to individuals a power or privilege, such as the right to vote. A civil liberty represents something that the government cannot do—abridge a freedom, such as the freedom of speech.

The Nationalization of the Bill of Rights

Most citizens do not realize that, as originally presented, the Bill of Rights limited only the power of the national government, not that of the states. In other words, a citizen in the state of Virginia in 1795 could not successfully sue in federal court against a law passed in Virginia that violated one of the amendments in the Bill of Rights. Each state had (and still has) its own constitution with its own bill of rights. Whereas the states' bills of rights were similar to the national one, there were some differences, and, perhaps more important, each state's judicial system interpreted the rights differently. A citizen in one state effectively had a different set of civil rights from a citizen in another state. It was not until the Fourteenth Amendment was ratified in 1868 that our Constitution explicitly guaranteed to everyone due process of the law. Section 1 of that amendment provides that

> no State shall make or enforce any law which shall abridge the privileges or immunities of citizens of the United States; nor shall any State deprive any person of life, liberty, or property, without due process of law; nor deny to any person within its jurisdiction the equal protection of the laws.

Section 5 of the amendment explicitly gives Congress the power to enforce by appropriate legislation the provisions of the amendment. Note the use of the terms *citizens* and *person*. *Citizens* have political rights, such as voting and running for office, but no *person*, citizen or alien, can be denied civil liberties (speech, press, and religion) nor have his or her property taken without equal recourse to the legal system.[3]

The Fourteenth Amendment itself was, as Kenneth Karst wrote, an act of "**positive law**," that is, a law made to fit a particular circumstance. At the time of its passage, the sponsors of the Fourteenth Amendment had wished to extend to the South "a system of liberties and equality under the law that already existed elsewhere in the nation."[4]

POSITIVE LAW
Laws made in and by legislatures to fit a particular circumstance.

The Incorporation Issue

The Fourteenth Amendment was passed as a standard that would guarantee both due process and equal protection under the laws for all persons. The courts did not agree. Many jurists still believed, as John Marshall stated in the *Barron v. Mayor of Baltimore* decision, that the states were "distinct governments framed by different persons and for different purposes."[5] Marshall's statement in the *Barron* decision was plain: The Bill of Rights limits only the national government and not the state governments. The *Barron* decision is still the general rule of law. We shall see, though, that it has been greatly modified in practice through later interpretations of the Fourteenth Amendment.

---

[3]Section 2 of the amendment, which concerns voting rights, contains the first use in the Constitution of the word *male*. At the time of the amendment's adoption, women were not allowed to vote.

[4]Kenneth L. Karst, "Not One Law at Rome and Another at Athens: The Fourteenth Amendment in Nationwide Application," *Washington University Law Quarterly*, No. 3 (Summer 1972), p. 383.

[5]*Barron v. Mayor of Baltimore*, 7 Peters 243 (1833).

In 1873, in the *Slaughter-House Cases*,[6] the U.S. Supreme Court upheld the principle of **dual citizenship,** arguing that to deprive states of their authority and their identity would "fetter and degrade state governments." The Court refused to apply the guarantees of the Bill of Rights to the states under the Fourteenth Amendment's privileges and immunities clause. A Louisiana law prohibited livestock yards and slaughterhouses within New Orleans, except for the Crescent City Company's operation. Butchers and others adversely affected sought to have the law declared void, in part under the Fourteenth Amendment. The Supreme Court held that the Fourteenth Amendment creates two types of citizenship—federal and state—and that the privileges and immunities clause extends federal constitutional protection only to the privileges and immunities of national citizenship. The Court reasoned that the Louisiana statute did not infringe on any of the privileges and immunities of national citizenship.

Only gradually, and never completely, did the Supreme Court accept the **incorporation theory**—that no state could act in violation of the U.S. Bill of Rights. By holding that those rights are protected against actions of the states, as well as of the national government, the Court has made their meanings uniform. In doing so, the Court has been deciding which rights are basic or essential to the American concept of ordered liberty. Table 4-1 shows the rights that the Court has incorporated into the Fourteenth Amendment and the case in which it first applied each protection. The practical implementation of the Fourteenth Amendment has taken place relatively slowly, through the doctrine of selective incorporation.

DUAL CITIZENSHIP
The condition of being a citizen of two sovereign political units; being a citizen of both a state and the nation.

INCORPORATION THEORY
The view that most of the protections of the Bill of Rights are incorporated into the Fourteenth Amendment's protection against state governments.

[6]16 Wall 36 (1873).

TABLE 4-1 ■ Incorporating the Bill of Rights into the Fourteenth Amendment

Year	Issue	Amendment Involved	Court Case
1925	Freedom of speech	I	*Gitlow v. New York,* 268 U.S. 652
1931	Freedom of the press	I	*Near v. Minnesota,* 283 U.S. 697
1932	Right to a lawyer in capital punishment cases	VI	*Powell v. Alabama,* 287 U.S. 45
1934	Freedom of religion	I	*Hamilton v. Regents of the University of California,* 293 U.S. 245
1937	Freedom of assembly and right to petition	I	*De Jonge v. Oregon,* 299 U.S. 353
1947	Separation of state and church	I	*Everson v. Board of Education,* 330 U.S. 1
1948	Right to a public trial	VI	*In re Oliver,* 333 U.S. 257
1961	No unreasonable searches and seizures	IV	*Mapp v. Ohio,* 367 U.S. 643
1962	No cruel and unusual punishment	VIII	*Robinson v. California,* 370 U.S. 660
1963	Right to a lawyer in all criminal felony cases	VI	*Gideon v. Wainwright,* 372 U.S. 335
1964	No compulsory self-incrimination	V	*Malloy v. Hogan,* 378 U.S. 1
1965	Right to privacy	I	*Griswold v. Connecticut,* 381 U.S. 479
1966	Right to an impartial jury	VI	*Parker v. Gladden,* 385 U.S. 363
1967	Right to a speedy trial	VI	*Klopfer v. North Carolina,* 386 U.S. 213
1969	No double jeopardy	V	*Benton v. Maryland,* 395 U.S. 784

The last hundred years of Supreme Court decisions have bound the fifty states to accept most of the guarantees for their respective citizens that are contained in the U.S. Bill of Rights. The exceptions have usually involved the right to bear arms and to refuse to quarter soldiers and the right to a grand jury hearing. Thus, for all intents and purposes, the Bill of Rights provisions of the national Constitution must be uniformly applied by individual state governments to their laws and practices.

Just as judicial interpretation of the Fourteenth Amendment required more than a hundred years to "nationalize" the Bill of Rights, judicial interpretation has shaped the true nature of those rights as they apply to individuals in the United States. As we shall see in the following pages, there have been numerous conflicts over the meaning of such simple phrases as freedom of press and freedom of religion. To understand what freedoms we actually have, we have to examine some of those conflicts.

Freedom of Religion

In the United States freedom of religion consists of two principal precepts as they are presented in the First Amendment. The first has to do with separation of church and state, and the second guarantees the free exercise of religion.

The Separation of Church and State

ESTABLISHMENT CLAUSE
The part of the First Amendment prohibiting the establishment of a church officially supported by the national government. It is applied to questions of state and local government aid to religious organizations and schools, of the legality of allowing or requiring school prayers, and of the teaching of evolution versus fundamentalist theories of creation.

The First Amendment to the Constitution states, in part that "Congress shall make no law respecting an establishment of religion." In the words of President Jefferson, the **establishment clause** was designed to create a "wall of separation of Church and State."[7] Perhaps Jefferson was thinking about the religious intolerance that characterized the first colonies. Although many of the American colonies were founded by groups in pursuit

[7]See Frank J. Sorauf, *Wall of Separation* (Princeton, N.J.: Princeton University Press, 1976).

Fundamentalists Vicki Frost and her husband challenged certain textbooks as being too secular and violating their freedom of religion. Other people have argued that public schools cannot teach about religion because that would be a violation of the establishment clause.

of religious freedom, they were nonetheless quite intolerant of religious nonconformity within their communities. He undoubtedly was also aware that state religions were the rule; among the original thirteen American colonies, nine of them had official religions.

As interpreted by the Supreme Court, the establishment clause in the First Amendment means at least the following:

Neither a state nor the federal government can set up a church. Neither can pass laws which aid one religion, aid all religions, or prefer one religion over another. Neither can force nor influence a person to go to or to remain away from church against his will or force him to profess a belief or disbelief in any religion. No person can be punished for entertaining or professing religious beliefs or disbeliefs, for church attendance or nonattendance. No tax in any amount, large or small, can be levied to support any religious activities or institutions, whatever they may be called, or whatever form they may adopt to teach or practice religion. Neither a state nor the federal government can, openly or secretly, participate in the affairs of any religious organizations or groups and vice versa.[8]

The establishment clause covers all conflicts about such matters as state and local government aid to religious organizations and schools, the legality of allowing or requiring school prayers, and the teaching of evolution versus fundamentalist theories of creation.

The Issue of School Prayer. Do the states have the right to promote religion in general, without making any attempt to establish a particular religion? That is the question in the issue of school prayer and was the precise question presented in 1962 in *Engel v. Vitale,*[9] the so-called Regents' Prayer Case in New York. The State Board of Regents of New York had suggested that a prayer be spoken aloud in the public schools at the beginning of each day. The recommended prayer was as follows:

Almighty God, we acknowledge our dependence upon Thee,
And we beg Thy blessings upon us, our parents, our teachers, and our Country.

Such a prayer was implemented in many New York public schools.

A number of students' parents challenged the action of the regents, maintaining that it violated the establishment clause of the First Amendment. At trial, the parents lost. The Supreme Court, however, ruled that the regents' action was unconstitutional because "the constitutional prohibition against laws respecting an establishment of a religion must at least mean that in this country it is no part of the business of government to compose official prayers for any group of the American people to recite as part of a religious program carried on by any government."[10] The Court's conclusion was based in part on the "historical fact that governmentally established religions and religious persecutions go hand in hand."[11] In 1963, the Supreme Court outlawed daily readings of the Bible and recitation of the Lord's Prayer in public schools.[12]

Did You Know . . . That Samuel Argall, governor of Virginia from 1616 to 1618, punished those who failed to attend church with prison terms and forced labor and banned all forms of amusement on Sunday?

Children pray in school. Such in-school prayer is in violation of Supreme Court rulings based on the First Amendment. A Supreme Court ruling does not necessarily carry with it a mechanism for enforcement everywhere in the United States, however.

---

[8]*Everson v. Board of Education,* 330 U.S. 1 (1947).
[9]370 U.S. 421 (1962).
[10]*Ibid.*
[11]*Ibid.*
[12]*Abington School District v. Schempp,* 374 U.S. 203 (1963).

Although the Supreme Court has repeatedly ruled against officially sponsored prayer and Bible-reading sessions in public schools, other means for bringing some form of religious expression into public education have been attempted. In 1983, the Tennessee legislature passed a bill requiring public school classes to begin each day with a minute of silence. This followed several years of efforts by the Tennessee legislature to bring "meditation, prayer, or silent reflection into school." Alabama also had a similar law. In 1985, the Supreme Court struck down as unconstitutional the Alabama law authorizing one minute of silence in all public schools for prayer or meditation. The majority of the Court concluded that because the law specifically endorsed prayer, it appeared to support religion.[13]

Many school districts, particularly in the South, continue to operate in violation of the Court's prayer ban. A coalition of conservatives and southerners has proposed a constitutional amendment that would overturn the 1963 ruling.

Forbidding the Teaching of Evolution.   There have been rather short-lived efforts by certain religious groups to forbid the teaching of evolution in public schools. One such law was passed in Arkansas, only to be struck down by the Supreme Court in the 1968 *Epperson v. Arkansas* case.[14] The Court held that the Arkansas legislation violated the separation of church and state, for it imposed religious beliefs on students. The Arkansas legislature then passed a law requiring the teaching of the biblical story of creation alongside of evolution. In the 1982 Supreme Court case *McLean v. Arkansas,* this law was declared unconstitutional.

Aid to Church-Related Schools.   Throughout the United States, all property owners except religious, educational, fraternal, literary, scientific, and similar nonprofit institutions must pay property taxes. A large part of the proceeds of such taxes goes to support public schools. But not all school-age children attend public schools. Fully 12 percent attend private schools, of which 85 percent have religious affiliations. Numerous cases have reached the Supreme Court in which the Court has tried to draw a fine line between permissible public aid to students in church-related schools and impermissible public aid to religion.

It is at the elementary and secondary levels that these issues have arisen most often. In a series of cases, the Supreme Court has allowed states to use tax funds for lunches, textbooks, speech-and-hearing-problem diagnostic services, standardized tests, and transportation for students attending church-operated elementary and secondary schools.[15] In a number of cases, however, the Supreme Court has held state programs helping church-related schools to be unconstitutional. In *Lemon v. Kurtzman,*[16] the Court judged that direct state aid could not be used to subsidize religious instruction. The Court in the *Lemon* case gave its most general statement on the constitutionality of governmental aid to religious schools, stating

---

[13]*Wallace v. Jafree,* 472 U.S. 38 (1985).
[14]393 U.S. 97 (1968).
[15]See *Everson v. Board of Education,* 330 U.S. 1 (1947); *Meek v. Pittenger,* 421 U.S. 349 (1975); and *Committee for Public Education v. Regan,* 444 U.S. 646 (1980).
[16]403 U.S. 602 (1971).

POLITICS AND RELIGION

The Wall of Separation

At Nathan Bishop Middle School in Providence, Rhode Island, a rabbi was asked by the principal to give a nondenominational benediction at the graduation ceremony. Included as part of the prayer was thanks to God for a "court system where all can seek justice." A father of a student who objected to including the prayer in the graduation ceremony sued school officials. The federal trial and appellate courts that heard the case held that by including the prayer in the graduation, the school violated the Constitution. The case reached the Supreme Court in 1992 as *Lee v. Weisman.**

Traditionally, the United States Supreme Court has applied one of two concepts in cases under the establishment clause. The Court has required neutrality, to promote Jefferson's "wall of separation" between church and state; or the Court has advised accommodation, which tolerates church and state coming together.

Since 1971, in twenty-nine decisions, the Court has used the test set out in *Lemon v. Kurtzman* as a framework for determining neutrality. Under this test, the Court asks whether an activity has a secular aim, whether its primary effect is to advance or inhibit religion, and whether it fosters excessive entanglement between religion and gov-

ernment. Critics complain that the *Lemon* test has led to a narrow secularism.

Over the last fifty years, in all cases in which the Court has dealt with religion in the public schools, the Court has not allowed a prayer at a formal school function. The Court has struck down daily prayers, daily Bible reading, posting the Ten Commandments in classrooms, and daily moments of silence. In one case, the Court permitted voluntary Christian clubs to meet after school on public school grounds. In another case, the Court stated a tolerance for prayers for legislative bodies, so long as the prayers do not proselytize. The Court explained its tolerance for these prayers on the basis that the first Congress, which adopted the Bill of Rights, approved of legislative prayers.

In the last establishment clause case that came before the Court before *Lee v. Weisman*, the justices voted five to four to hold unconstitutional a Christmas display of a Nativity scene in a Pittsburgh courthouse. Since that case was decided, the strongest proponents of separation—Justices Thurgood Marshall and William Brennan—have retired.

With these cases and events in mind, the outcome in *Lee v. Weisman* turned on whether the Court saw the graduation benediction as a public school prayer or as a legislative prayer. Lower federal courts are

split on the issue of whether school-related prayer outside the school breaches Jefferson's wall of separation. Prayers before high-school football games have been rejected. Nonsectarian prayers at graduation ceremonies have been upheld, when the school did not choose the person who gave the prayer nor provide guidelines as to what was said. Indeed, in 1993 the Supreme Court allowed student-organized prayer at graduation ceremonies. In the *Lee* case, because the school chose the rabbi who gave the benediction and offered guidelines as to what he could say, the Supreme Court held that the prayer violated the establishment clause.

Supporters of the school's practice argue that, unlike daily prayers in a classroom, attendance at graduation is voluntary, the ceremony may be held off campus, graduation occurs only once a year, and students generally attend in the company of their parents. Supporters complain that prohibiting the benediction interferes with free speech and promotes secularism by excising all mention of religion, which violates the free exercise clause.

Observers believe that the Court will likely develop a new test for establishment clause cases, shifting away from neutrality and toward accommodation.

*112 S.Ct. 2649 (1992).

FREE EXERCISE CLAUSE
The provision of the First Amendment guaranteeing the free exercise of religion.

that the aid had to be secular in aim, that it could not have the primary effect of advancing or inhibiting religion, and that the government must avoid "an excessive entanglement with religion." All laws under the establishment clause are now subject to the three-part *Lemon* test. In other cases, the Court has denied state reimbursements to religious schools for field trips and for developing achievement tests.

The Free Exercise of Religious Beliefs

The First Amendment constrains Congress from prohibiting the free exercise of religion. Does this **free exercise clause** mean that no type of religious practice can be prohibited or restricted by government? Certainly, a person can hold any religious belief that she or he wants; or a person can have no religious belief. When, however, religious *practices* work against public policy and the public welfare, the government can act. For example, regardless of a child's or parent's religious beliefs, the government can require certain types of vaccinations. Similarly, public school students can be required to study from textbooks chosen by school authorities. The sale and use of marijuana for religious purposes has been held illegal because a religion cannot make legal what would otherwise be illegal. Conducting religious rites that result in beheaded and gutted animals being left in public streets normally is not allowed.

The courts and lawmakers are constantly faced with a dilemma. On the one hand, no law may be made that requires someone to do something contrary to his or her religious beliefs or teachings, because this would interfere with the free exercise of religion. On the other hand, if certain individuals, because of their religious beliefs, are exempted from specific laws, then such exemptions might tend to favor religion and be contrary to the establishment clause. The original view of the Court was that while religious beliefs are protected by the law, acting on those beliefs may not be. For instance, children of Jehovah's Witnesses are not required to say the Pledge of Allegiance at school,[17] but their parents cannot prevent them from accepting medical treatment (such as blood transfusions) if in fact their lives are in danger. The current view of the Court is that in all but a few situations, a state is free to require everyone to comply with a law that is generally valid. In other words, states can punish or deny benefits to people whose religious practices violate a law. A state can make exceptions for religious practices, but the Constitution does not require it to do so.[18]

Freedom of Expression

▼

Perhaps the most frequently invoked freedom that Americans have is the right to free speech and a free press without government interference. These rights guarantee each person a right of free expression by all means of communication and ensure all persons a full discussion of public affairs. Each of us has the right to have our say, and all of us have the right to hear what others say. For the most part, Americans can criticize public

---

[17]*West Virginia State Board of Education v. Barnette*, 319 U.S. 624 (1943).
[18]*Employment Division, Department of Human Resources of Oregon v. Smith*, 494 U.S. 872 (1990).

officials and their actions without fear of reprisal or imprisonment by any branch of the government.

Permitted Restrictions

At various times, restrictions on expression have been permitted. A description of several such restrictions follows.

Clear and Present Danger. When a person's remarks present a clear and present danger to the peace or public order, they can be constitutionally curtailed. Justice Holmes used this reasoning in 1919 when examining the case of a socialist who had been convicted for violating the Espionage Act. Holmes stated:

> The question in every case is whether the words are used in such circumstances and are of such a nature as to create a *clear and present danger* that they will bring about the substantive evils that Congress has a right to prevent. It is a question of proximity and degree. (Emphasis added.)[19]

Thus, according to the **clear and present danger test,** expression may be restricted if evidence exists that such expression would cause a condition, actual or imminent, that Congress has the power to prevent. Commenting on this test, Justice Brandeis in 1920 said, "Correctly applied, it will reserve the right of free speech . . . from suppression by tyrannists, well-meaning majorities, and from abuse by irresponsible, fanatical minorities."[20] A related test includes the **preferred-position test.** Only if the government is able to show that limitations on speech are absolutely necessary to avoid imminent, serious, and important evils are such limitations allowed. Another test is called the **sliding-scale test.** The courts must carefully examine the facts of each individual case before restricting expression.

The Bad-Tendency Rule. According to the **bad-tendency rule,** speech or other First Amendment freedoms may permissibly be curtailed if there is a possibility that such expression might lead to some "evil." In *Gitlow v. New York*,[21] a member of a left-wing group was convicted of violating New York state's criminal anarchy statute when he published and distributed a pamphlet urging the violent overthrow of the United States government. In its majority opinion, the Supreme Court held that although the First Amendment afforded protection against state incursions on freedom of expression, Gitlow could be legally punished in this particular instance because his expression would tend to bring about evils that the state had a right to prevent.

No Prior Restraint. **Prior restraint** is defined as restraining an activity before that activity has actually occurred. It involves censorship as opposed to subsequent punishment. Prior restraint of expression would require, for example, a permit before a speech could be made, a newspaper

CLEAR AND PRESENT DANGER TEST
The test proposed by Justice Holmes for determining when government may restrict free speech. Restrictions are permissible, he argued, only when speech provokes a "clear and present danger" to the public order.

PREFERRED-POSITION TEST
A court test used in determining the limits of free expression guaranteed by the First Amendment, requiring that limitations only be applied on speech to avoid imminent, serious, and important evils.

SLIDING-SCALE TEST
The courts must carefully examine the facts of each individual case before restricting expression.

BAD-TENDENCY RULE
Speech or other First Amendment freedoms may permissibly be curtailed if there is a possibility that such expression might lead to some "evil."

PRIOR RESTRAINT
Restraining an action before the activity has actually occurred. It involves censorship as opposed to subsequent punishment.

---

[19]*Schenck v. United States*, 249 U.S. 47 (1919).
[20]*Schaefer v. United States*, 251 U.S. 466 (1920).
[21]268 U.S. 652 (1925).

published, or a movie or TV show exhibited. Most, if not all, Supreme Court justices have been especially critical of any governmental action that imposes prior restraint on expression:

> A prior restraint on expression comes to this Court with a "heavy presumption" against its constitutionality. . . . The government thus carries a heavy burden of showing justification for the enforcement of such a restraint.[22]

The Protection of Symbolic Speech

Not all expression is in words or in writing. Gestures, movements, articles of clothing, and so on may under certain circumstances be considered **symbolic,** or nonverbal, **speech.** Such speech is given substantial protection today by our courts. During the Vietnam war (1964–1973), when students around the country began wearing black armbands in protest, a Des Moines, Iowa, school administrator issued a regulation prohibiting students in the Des Moines School District from wearing them. The U.S. Supreme Court ruled that such a ban violated the free speech clause of the First Amendment. It reasoned that the school district was unable to show that wearing the black armbands had disrupted normal school activities. Furthermore, the school's ruling was discriminatory as it selected certain forms of symbolic speech for banning; lapel crosses and fraternity rings, for instance, symbolically speak of a person's affiliations, but these were not banned.[23] In 1989, in *Texas v. Johnson,* the Supreme Court ruled that state laws that prohibited the burning of the American flag as part of a peaceful protest also violated the freedom of expression protected by the First Amendment. Congress responded by passing the Flag Protection Act of 1989, which was ruled unconstitutional by the Supreme Court in June 1990. Congress and President Bush immediately pledged to work for a constitutional amendment to "protect our flag."

SYMBOLIC SPEECH
Nonverbal expression of beliefs, which is given substantial protection by the courts.

[22]*Nebraska Press Association v. Stuart,* 427 U.S. 539 (1976). See also *Near v. Minnesota,* 283 U.S. 697 (1931).
[23]*Tinker v. Des Moines School District,* 393 U.S. 503 (1969).

Mary Beth Tinker and her brother John display the armbands they wore to protest the Vietnam war. Their school principal tried to prevent them from wearing such bands while at school. The Supreme Court, however, ruled that the armbands constituted symbolic speech that was protected by the First Amendment.

The Protection of Commercial Speech

Commercial speech is usually defined as advertising statements. Can advertisers use their First Amendment rights to prevent restrictions on the content of commercial advertising? Until the 1970s, the Supreme Court held that such speech was not protected by the First Amendment. By the mid-1970s, however, more and more commercial speech was brought under First Amendment protection. According to Justice Harry A. Blackmun, "Advertising, however tasteless and excessive it sometimes may seem, is nonetheless dissemination of information as to who is producing and selling what product for what reason and at what price."[24] If consumers are to make more intelligent marketplace decisions, there must be a "free flow of commercial information," according to Blackmun and the Court. Thus, for example, the federal government cannot prohibit the mailing of unsolicited advertisements (so-called junk mail), a state cannot prohibit the advertising of drug prices by pharmacies, and a town cannot prohibit the use of "for sale" signs by sellers of homes.

Nonadvertising "speech" by businesses has also achieved First Amendment protection. In *First National Bank v. Belotti*,[25] the Supreme Court examined a Massachusetts statute prohibiting corporations from spending money to influence "the vote on any question submitted to the voters, other than one materially affecting any of the property, business, or assets of the corporation." That statute was struck down as unconstitutional because it unnecessarily restrained "free speech." Some critics of the Court see in such decisions a strong bias toward property rights (the rights of corporations to use their property without regulation) and against the interests of consumers and the general citizenry. Similarly, the Court has held that a law forbidding a corporation from using bill inserts to express its views on controversial issues also violates the First Amendment.[26] In contrast, laws limiting the amount that a corporation or an unincorporated association may contribute to a political candidate have been upheld.[27]

Unprotected Speech: Obscenity

Numerous state and federal statutes make it a crime to disseminate obscene materials. All such state and federal statutes prohibiting obscenity have been deemed constitutional if the definition of obscenity conforms with that of the then-current U.S. Supreme Court. Basically, the courts have not been willing to extend constitutional protections of free speech to what they consider obscene materials. For example, in *Roth v. United States*,[28] the Supreme Court stated, "Obscenity is not within the area of constitutionally protected speech or press."

But what is obscenity? As Justice Potter Stewart once said, even though he could not define it, "I know it when I see it."[29] The problem, of course,

COMMERCIAL SPEECH
Advertising statements that have increasingly been given First Amendment protection.

---

[24]*Virginia State Board of Pharmacy v. Virginia Citizens Consumer Council, Inc.,* 425 U.S. 748 (1976).

[25]435 U.S. 765 (1978).

[26]*Consolidated Edison Co. v. Public Service Commission,* 447 U.S. 550 (1980).

[27]*California Medical Association v. Federal Election Commission,* 453 U.S. 182 (1981).

[28]354 U.S. 476 (1957).

[29]*Jacobellis v. Ohio,* 378 U.S. 184 (1964).

The Constitution does not specifically protect pornography, but rather it guarantees freedom of speech in general. One finds great differences in local laws concerning what is and is not pornographic and therefore in what is and is not legal.

is that even if it were agreed on, the definition of obscenity changes with the times. Victorians deeply disapproved of the "loose" morals of the Elizabethan Age. The works of Mark Twain and Edgar Rice Burroughs have at times been considered obscene (after all, Tarzan and Jane were not legally wed).

The Supreme Court has grappled from time to time with the problem of specifying an operationally effective definition of obscenity. In the *Roth* case in 1957, the Court coined the phrase "utterly without redeeming social importance." Since then, Supreme Court justices have viewed numerous films to determine if they met this criterion. By the 1970s, the justices had recognized the failure of the *Roth* definition. In *Miller v. California*, Chief Justice Burger created a formal list of requirements, known as the Roth-Miller test of obscenity, that currently must be met for material to be legally obscene. Under this test, material is obscene if (1) the average person finds that it violates contemporary community standards, (2) the work taken as a whole appeals to a prurient interest in sex, (3) the work shows patently offensive sexual conduct, and (4) the work lacks serious redeeming literary, artistic, political, or scientific merit.[30]

The problem, of course, is that one person's prurient interest is another person's artistic pleasure. The Court went on to state that the definition of prurient interest would be determined by the community's standards. The Court avoided presenting a definition of obscenity, leaving this determination to local and state authorities. Consequently, the *Miller* case has had widely inconsistent applications. Obscenity is still a constitutionally unsettled area, whether it deals with speech or printed or filmed materials. Some feminists, often in alliance with religious fundamentalists, have begun a drive to enact new antipornography laws on the basis that pornography violates women's rights. In 1982, the Supreme Court upheld state laws making it illegal to sell material showing sexual performances by minors. Most recently, the Court has ruled that states can outlaw the possession of child pornography in the home. The Court reasoned that the ban on private possession is justified because owning the material perpetuates commercial demand for it and for the exploitation of the children involved.[31]

Recently, governments and media groups have been confronted with the issue of regulating the lyrics and covers of record albums, the content of monologues by "shock" comedians, and other issues relating to obscenity in movies and on television. In Cincinnati, in 1990, a jury was asked to determine whether seven photographs displayed as part of a 175-photograph museum exhibit were obscene. The photographs were included in a touring retrospective of Robert Mapplethorpe's work. The jury applied the *Roth–Miller* test of obscenity and found that the photographs met all requirements except the last: They concluded that the photographs did not lack artistic merit. The museum and its director were therefore acquitted.

Unprotected Speech: Slander

Can you say anything you want about someone else? Not really. Individuals are protected from **defamation of character,** which is defined as

DEFAMATION OF CHARACTER
Wrongfully hurting a person's good reputation. The law has imposed a general duty on all persons to refrain from making false, defamatory statements about others.

[30]*Miller v. California,* 413 U.S. 5 (1973).
[31]*Osborne v. Ohio,* 110 S.Ct. 1691 (1990).

wrongfully hurting a person's good reputation. The law has imposed a general duty on all persons to refrain from making false, defamatory statements about others. Breaching this duty orally involves the wrongdoing called **slander.**[32]

Legally, slander is the public uttering of a statement that holds a person up for contempt, ridicule, or hatred. Slanderous public uttering means that the defamatory statements are made to, or within the hearing of, persons other than the defamed party. If one person calls another dishonest, manipulative, and incompetent when no one else is around, that does not constitute slander. The message is not communicated to a third party. If, however, a third party accidentally overhears defamatory statements, the courts have generally held that this constitutes public uttering and therefore slander, which is prohibited. Furthermore, any individual who repeats defamatory statements is legally responsible, even if that person reveals the source of such statements. Hence, some radio stations have instituted seven-second delays for live broadcasts, such as talk shows, allowing them to ''bleep'' out possibly defamatory statements.

Fighting Words and Hecklers' Veto

The Supreme Court has prohibited types of speech "which by their very utterance inflict injury or intend to incite an immediate breach of peace that governments may constitutionally punish."[33] The reference here is to a prohibition on public speakers from using **fighting words.** These may include racial, religious, or ethnic slurs that are so inflammatory that they will provoke the "average" listener to fight. Under the Supreme Court leadership of Chief Justice Burger, fighting words were more and more narrowly construed. For example, a four-letter word used about the draft and emblazoned on a sweater is not considered a fighting word, unless it is directed at a specific person.

Members of a crowd listening to a speech are similarly prohibited from exercising a **hecklers' veto.** When hecklers do so, they are threatening disruption or violence and they are vetoing the essential rights of the speaker.

Freedom of the Press

Freedom of the press can be regarded as a special instance of freedom of speech. Of course, at the time of the framing of the Constitution, the press meant only newspapers, magazines, and perhaps pamphlets. As technology has modified the ways in which we disseminate information, so, too, have the laws touching on freedom of the press been modified. But what can and cannot be printed still occupies an important place in constitutional law.

Ice T, a rap musician, outraged many members of the law-enforcement community with the lyrics to his song, "Cop Killer." The First Amendment to the Constitution protects the performer's right to use the lyrics as long as they do not cause any criminal action.

SLANDER
The public uttering of a statement that holds a person up for contempt, ridicule, or hatred. This means the defamatory statement is made to, or within the hearing of, persons other than the defamed party.

FIGHTING WORDS
Words that when uttered by a public speaker are so inflammatory that they could provoke the average listener to violence; the words are usually of a racial, religious, or ethnic type.

HECKLERS' VETO
Boisterous and generally disruptive behavior by listeners of public speakers that, in effect, vetoes the public speakers' right to speak.

---

[32]Breaching it in writing involves the wrongdoing called *libel,* which is discussed in the next section.
[33]*Cohen v. California,* 403 U.S. 15 (1971).

PROFILE

Lawrence Tribe

"The framers of our Constitution were very wise indeed. They bequeathed us a framework for all seasons, a truly astonishing document whose principles are suitable for all times and all technological landscapes."

Apart from Supreme Court justices and perhaps the attorneys on *L.A. Law,* lawyers rarely become widely known to the American public. Laurence H. Tribe is an exception in this respect. Tribe, a highly successful litigator and professor of law at Harvard Law School, has become well known for his liberal views on civil rights and women's issues. Attacked by his critics as a defender of criminals and perverts, he has gone to battle for such clients as the Reverend Sun Myung Moon and championed such causes as gay sexual rights, affirmative action, busing to integrate schools, and legalized abortion. Tribe has also achieved renown as one of the nation's authorities on constitutional law. His courtroom successes and legal theories and abilities have distinguished him among jurists, politicians, and students alike.

Tribe, a naturalized citizen, was born in 1941 in Shanghai, Republic of China, to Jewish parents who had fled from Eastern Europe. He moved to San Francisco with his family five years later. At the age of sixteen, he entered Harvard University and received his undergraduate degree in mathematics, *summa cum laude,* four years later. In 1966, he graduated from Harvard Law School *magna cum laude* and three years later returned to Harvard Law

School as an assistant professor. Within three years, he was a tenured professor, and by 1977 he was considered one of the ten best law professors in the country. In 1982, he became the Ralph S. Tyler, Jr., Professor of Constitutional Law, a position he still holds.

When asked why he chose a career in law instead of mathematics, Tribe said that he believed law was "a place where ideas could change the world." Tribe's ideas have been influential. In 1978, he served as one of the constitutional delegates who drafted the first constitution for the Marshall Islands. Also in 1978, he authored *American Constitutional Law,* which quickly gained recognition as a major constitutional law casebook. The text, now in its second edition, has been cited by courts worldwide. Other books followed. In all, he has published thirteen—including *Abortion: The Clash of Absolutes* (1990) and *On Reading the Constitution* (1991)—and numerous articles.

Tribe's legal arguments and theories, largely liberal views, strong political connections, and media appearances and journal articles have propelled him into the public spotlight. He achieved his highest public visibility in 1987 when the Senate Judiciary Committee was considering the nomination of Robert H. Bork to the Supreme Court bench. Tribe viewed Bork's conservative interpretation of constitutional rights as a threat to civil liberties. By coaching the Democrats on the Senate Judiciary Committee and testifying himself against Bork, Tribe played a key role in Bork's defeat.

Tribe is not without critics. Some speculate that he wins so many cases because he avoids those that are not likely to succeed. Others claim that he is relentlessly driven by ambition and that the driving force of his career has been an aspiration to gain a seat on the Supreme Court for himself. Because he sides with liberals on some issues and conservatives on others, Tribe has often been accused of being philosophically inconsistent. For Tribe, however, his mixture of liberal and conservative views does not equate to philosophical inconsistency. "There really is no unitary theory that can make sense of the whole Constitution" in Tribe's opinion. Therefore, Tribe contends, "both those liberals who read the Constitution as expressing some single vision of human rights, and those conservatives who read it as expressing some single vision of structural checks and balances are making the same kind of mistake."

Defamation in Writing

As slander is oral defamation, **libel** is defamation in writing. As with slander, libel is an **actionable** wrong only if the defamatory statements are observed by a third party. If one person writes another a private letter wrongfully accusing him or her of embezzling funds, that does not constitute libel. It is interesting that the courts have generally held that dictating a letter to a secretary constitutes communication of the letter's contents to a third party, and therefore, if defamation has occurred, the wrongdoing of libel is actionable.

Newspapers are often involved in libel suits. *New York Times Co. v. Sullivan* explored an important question about public officials and liability.[34] Sullivan, a commissioner of the city of Montgomery, Alabama, sued the *New York Times* for libel because it had printed an advertisement critical of the actions of Montgomery police during the Civil Rights movement. Under Alabama law, the jury found that the statements were in fact libelous on their face, so that damages could be awarded to Mr. Sullivan without proof of the extent of any injury to him. The jury awarded him a half-million dollars, and the Alabama Supreme Court upheld the judgment.

The U.S. Supreme Court, however, unanimously reversed the judgment. It found that Alabama's rule of liability as applied to public officials in performance of their duty deprived critics of their rights of free speech under the First and Fourteenth Amendments.[35] Speaking for the Court, Justice William J. Brennan, Jr., stated that libel laws such as those in Alabama would inhibit the unfettered discussion of public issues. The Court indicated that only when a statement was made with **actual malice** against a public official could damages be obtained. If the Court had upheld the Alabama judgment, virtually any criticism of public officials could be suppressed.

A Free Press versus a Fair Trial: Gag Orders

Another major freedom of the press issue concerns newspaper reports of criminal trials. Amendment VI of the Bill of Rights guarantees a fair trial. In other words, the accused have rights. But the Bill of Rights also guarantees freedom of the press. What if the two appear to be in conflict? Which one prevails?

Jurors certainly may be influenced by reading news stories about the trial in which they are participating. In the 1970s, judges increasingly issued "gag orders," which restricted the publication of news about a trial in progress or even a pretrial hearing. A landmark case was decided by the Supreme Court in 1976,[36] based on the trial of E. C. Simants, who was charged with the murder of a neighboring family. Because the murder occurred in the course of a sexual assault, details of the crime were quite lurid. A local Nebraska judge issued an order prohibiting the press from reporting information gleaned in a pretrial hearing. Because there were

LIBEL
Defamation of character in writing.

ACTIONABLE
Furnishing grounds for a lawsuit.

ACTUAL MALICE
Actual desire and intent to see another suffer by one's actions.

"GAG ORDERS"
Orders issued by judges restricting publication of news about a trial in progress or a pretrial hearing in order to protect the accused's right to a fair trial.

---

[34]376 U.S. 254 (1964).

[35]Remember that the Supreme Court has held that the Fourteenth Amendment "nationalizes" most of the liberties listed in the Bill of Rights.

[36]*Nebraska Press Association v. Stuart*, 427 U.S. 539 (1976).

only 860 people in the town, the judge believed that such publicity would prejudice potential jurors.

The Supreme Court unanimously ruled that the Nebraska judge's gag order had violated the First Amendment's freedom of the press clause. Chief Justice Burger indicated that even pervasive adverse pretrial publicity did not necessarily lead to an unfair trial, and that prior restraints on publication were not justified. Some justices even went so far as to indicate that gag orders are never justified.

In spite of the *Nebraska Press Association* ruling, the Court has upheld certain types of gag orders. In *Gannett Company v. De Pasquale*,[37] the highest court held that if a judge found a reasonable probability that news publicity would harm a defendant's right to a fair trial, the court could impose a gag rule: "Members of the public have no constitutional right under the Sixth and Fourteenth Amendments to *attend* criminal trials." The *Nebraska* and *Gannett* cases, however, involved pretrial hearings. Could a judge impose a gag order on an entire trial, including pretrial hearings? In *Richmond Newspapers, Inc. v. Virginia*,[38] the Court ruled that actual trials must be open to the public except under unusual circumstances.

Confidentiality and Reporters' Work Papers

By the 1980s, the courts had begun to rule in cases concerning the press's responsibility to law-enforcement agencies. In one case, Myron Farber, a *New York Times* reporter who had possession of extensive notes relating to a murder case, was jailed in 1978 in New Jersey for not turning this material over to law-enforcement officials. The Supreme Court refused to review the case.[39]

Moreover, in several cases the police were permitted to search newspaper offices for documents related to cases under investigation. In general, the courts have moved in the direction of requiring the press to cooperate in criminal investigations to a much greater degree than it had before. These cases obviously raise a serious question about the confidentiality of working papers and background information that reporters obtain in the course of doing stories or investigative reporting. The question concerns not only the legitimate ownership of those notes and the reporter's right to privacy, but also whether these decisions compromise the freedom of the press guaranteed by the Constitution.

One important case concerned the *Stanford Daily*.[40] The campus newspaper of Stanford University had its offices searched by police officers with a search warrant. They were looking for photographs that would identify demonstrators who may have been responsible for injuries to the police. In this particular case, the Court ruled that the protection of confidentiality, and therefore the protection of the First Amendment's guarantee of a free press, was less important under the specific circumstances than the needs of law-enforcement agencies to secure information neces-

---

[37]443 U.S. 368 (1979).
[38]448 U.S. 555 (1980).
[39]*New York Times Co. v. Jascalevich*, 439 U.S. 1317 (1978).
[40]*Zurcher v. Stanford Daily*, 436 U.S. 547 (1978).

sary for prosecution. Congress responded to the *Stanford Daily* case by enacting the Privacy Protection Act.[41] This law applies to state as well as federal law-enforcement personnel. It limits their power to obtain evidence from the news media by means of a search warrant and in many instances requires that they use a subpoena. Also, more than half the states have enacted so-called shield laws. These laws protect reporters against having to reveal their sources and other confidential information.

Other Information Channels: Motion Pictures, Radio, and TV

The framers of our Constitution could not have imagined the ways in which information is disseminated today. Nonetheless, they fashioned the Constitution into a flexible instrument that could respond to social and technological changes. First Amendment freedoms have been applied differently to newer forms of information dissemination.

Motion Pictures: Some Prior Restraint. The most onerous of all forms of government interference with expression is prior restraint. As we noted, the Supreme Court has not declared all forms of censorship unconstitutional, but does require an exceptional justification for such restraint. Only in a few cases has the Supreme Court upheld prior restraint of published materials.

The Court's reluctance to accept prior restraint is less evident in the case of motion pictures. In the first half of the twentieth century, films were routinely submitted to local censorship boards. In 1968, the Supreme Court ruled that a film can only be banned under a law that provides for a prompt hearing at which the film is shown to be obscene. Today, few local censorship boards exist. Instead, the film industry regulates itself primarily through the industry's rating system.

Radio and TV: Limited Protection. Of all forms of communication, television is perhaps the most important and radio runs a close second. Radio and television broadcasting has the most limited First Amendment protection. In 1934, the national government established the Federal Communications Commission (FCC) to regulate electromagnetic wave frequencies. No one has a right to use the airwaves without a license granted by the FCC. The FCC grants licenses for limited periods and imposes numerous regulations on broadcasting. Although Congress has denied the FCC the authority to censor what is transmitted, the FCC can impose sanctions on those radio or TV stations broadcasting "filthy words," even if the words are not legally obscene.[42] Also, the FCC has occasionally refused to renew licenses of broadcasters who have presumably not "served the public interest." Perhaps one of the more controversial of the FCC's rulings was its **fairness doctrine,** imposing on owners of broadcast licenses an obligation to present "both" sides of significant public issues. In 1987, the FCC repealed the fairness doctrine. The FCC determined that the doctrine was unconstitutional because it violated broadcasters' freedom of speech under the First Amendment.

FAIRNESS DOCTRINE
An FCC regulation affecting broadcasting media, which required that fair or equal opportunity be given to legitimate opposing political groups or individuals to broadcast their views.

[41]42 U.S.C. Sections 2000aa to 2000aa-12.
[42]*Federal Communications Commission v. Pacifica Foundation*, 438 U.S. 726 (1978).

The Right to Assemble and to Petition the Government

The First Amendment prohibits Congress from making any law that abridges "the right of the people peaceably to assemble and to petition the Government for a redress of grievances." Inherent in such a right is the ability of private citizens to communicate their ideas on public issues to government officials as well as to other individuals. The Supreme Court has often put this freedom on a par with the freedom of speech and the freedom of the press. Nonetheless, it has allowed municipalities to require permits for parades, sound trucks, and demonstrations,[43] so that public officials may control traffic or prevent demonstrations from turning into riots. This became a major issue in 1977 when the American Nazi party wanted to march through the largely Jewish suburb of Skokie, Illinois. The American Civil Liberties Union defended the Nazis' right to march (in spite of its opposition to the Nazi philosophy). The Supreme Court let stand a lower court's ruling that the city of Skokie had violated the Nazis' First Amendment guarantees[44] by denying them a permit to do so.

The right to assemble has been broadly defined. For example, municipal and state governments do not have the right to require any organization to publish its membership list. This was decided in *NAACP v. Alabama*[45] when the state of Alabama required the National Association for the Advancement of Colored People (NAACP) to publish a list of its members. The Supreme Court held that the requirement was unconstitutional because it violated the NAACP's right of assembly, which the Court addressed in terms of freedom of association.

The courts have generally interpreted the right to parade and protest more narrowly than pure forms of speech or assembly. The Supreme

---

[43]*Davis v. Massachusetts,* 167 U.S. 43 (1897).
[44]*Collin v. Smith,* 439 U.S. 916 (1978).
[45]357 U.S. 499 (1958).

With their right to assemble and demonstrate protected by the Constitution, members of the modern Ku Klux Klan march in Wilmington, North Carolina. The police escort is charged with making sure that neither the marchers nor the observers provoke any violence.

Court has generally upheld the right of individuals to parade and protest in public places, but it has ruled against parades and protests when matters of public safety were at issue. In *Cox v. New Hampshire*,[46] for example, the Court ruled that sixty-eight Jehovah's Witnesses had violated a statute prohibiting parading without a permit and upheld the right of a municipality to control its public streets.

More Liberties under Scrutiny: Matters of Privacy

During the past several years, a number of civil liberties that relate to the right to privacy have become important social issues. Among the most important are the right to sexual freedom, the right to have an abortion, and the right to die.

The Right to Privacy

No explicit reference is made anywhere in the Constitution to a person's right to privacy. The courts did not take a very positive approach toward the right to privacy until relatively recently. For example, during Prohibition suspected bootleggers' telephones were routinely tapped and the information obtained was used as a legal basis for prosecution. In *Olmstead v. United States*,[47] the Supreme Court upheld such an invasion of privacy. Justice Louis Brandeis, a champion of personal freedoms, strongly dissented to the majority decision in this case. He argued that the framers of the Constitution gave every citizen the right to be left alone. He called such a right "the most comprehensive of rights and the right most valued by civilized men."

In the 1960s, the highest court began to modify the majority view. In *Griswold v. Connecticut*,[48] in 1965, the Supreme Court overthrew a Connecticut law that effectively prohibited the use of contraceptives, holding that the law violated the right to privacy. Justice William O. Douglas formulated a unique way of reading this right into the Bill of Rights. He claimed that the First, Third, Fourth, Fifth, and Ninth Amendments created "penumbras, formed by emanations from those guarantees that help give them life and substance," and went on to talk about zones for privacy that are guaranteed by these rights. When we read the Ninth Amendment, we can see the foundation for his reasoning: "The enumeration in the Constitution of certain rights, shall not be construed to deny or disparage others retained by the people." In other words, just because the Constitution, including its amendments, does not specifically talk about the right to privacy does not mean this right is denied to the people.

In a reversal of this trend, the Supreme Court ruled in 1986 that the right to privacy does not protect homosexual acts between consenting adults. It ruled that a Georgia law prohibiting sodomy—oral or anal sex—was constitutional.[49] About half the states have so-called sodomy laws, which are generally intended to restrict homosexual activities.

---

[46]312 U.S. 569 (1941).

[47]277 U.S. 438 (1928). This decision was reversed later in *Katz v. United States*, 389 U.S. 347 (1967).

[48]381 U.S. 479 (1965).

[49]*Bowers v. Hardwick,* 478 U.S. 186 (1986).

An important privacy issue, created in part by new technology, is the amassing of information on individuals by government. The average American citizen has personal information filed away in dozens of agencies—such as the Social Security Administration and the Internal Revenue Service. Because of the threat of indiscriminate use of private information by nonauthorized individuals, Congress passed the Privacy Act in 1974. This was the first law regulating the use of federal government information about private individuals. Under the Privacy Act, every citizen has the right to obtain copies of personal records collected by federal agencies and to correct inaccuracies in such records. In addition, the act established a Privacy Protection Study Commission, which has found a wide range of abuses in this area.

The use of lie detectors, or polygraphs, has been under scrutiny for many years. In 1988, Congress prohibited many uses of the polygraph by private employers for random employee examinations and for pre-employment screenings. Such tests may still be used by federal, state, and local governments, by companies doing sensitive work for federal, military, or security agencies, or by companies dealing with controlled substances or those who provide private security services.

The Right to Have an Abortion

Does a woman have the right to have an abortion? The arguments for and against this extremely sensitive issue revolve around the question of who, if anyone, has the right to control reproduction.

Historically, abortion was not a criminal offense before the "quickening" of the fetus (the first movement of the fetus in the uterus, usually between the sixteenth and eighteenth weeks of pregnancy). During the last half of the nineteenth century, however, state laws became more severe. By 1973, performance of an abortion was a criminal offense in most states—the government controlled reproductive rights. In *Roe v. Wade*,[50] the United States Supreme Court accepted the argument that the laws against abortion violated "Jane Roe's" right to privacy under the Constitution.[51] The Court did not answer the question about when life begins. It simply said that the "the right to privacy is broad enough to encompass a woman's decision whether or not to terminate her pregnancy." The Court did not say that such a right was absolute. Instead, it asserted that any state could impose certain regulations that would safeguard the health of the mother and protect potential life after the first three months of pregnancy.

Thus, the Court balanced different interests when it decided that during the first trimester of pregnancy abortion was an issue solely between a woman and her doctor—the state could not limit abortions except to require that they be performed by licensed physicians. During the second trimester, to protect the health of the mother, the state was allowed to specify the conditions under which an abortion could be performed. Dur-

---

[50]410 U.S. 113 (1973).

[51]Jane Roe was not the real name of the woman in this case. It is a common legal pseudonym used to protect a person's privacy.

Both prochoice and antiabortion groups have repeatedly exercised the right to assemble and protest government action. Here, pictures show the prochoice groups protesting outside the Supreme Court building in Washington, D.C., and the prolife groups picketing outside the 1992 Republican National Convention. The main purpose of such protests is to win media attention to their positions.

ing the final trimester, the state could regulate or even outlaw abortions except when necessary to preserve the life or health of the mother.

After *Roe*, the Supreme Court issued decisions in a number of cases defining and redefining the boundaries of state regulation of abortion. Twice the Court has struck down laws that required a woman who wished to have an abortion to undergo counseling designed to discourage abortions.[52] The Court has held, however, that the government can prohibit doctors in medical clinics that receive federal funding from discussing abortion with their patients.[53]

In 1989, the Supreme Court announced its decision in *Webster v. Reproductive Health Services*,[54] a case that challenged very restrictive state laws on abortion. In a narrow five-to-four majority, the Court upheld the restrictions that Missouri placed on the performing of abortions, opening the way for many other states to enact similar or more restrictive laws. Specifically, the ruling allowed states to pass laws that, like the Missouri statute, ban the use of public hospitals or other taxpayer-supported facilities from performing abortions, bar public employees, including doctors and nurses, from assisting in abortions, and require the performance of viability tests on any fetus thought to be at least twenty weeks old. Although the *Webster* decision did not overturn the right to have an abortion, the Court's ruling was a major victory for antiabortion forces. The ultimate effect of the *Webster* decision was to make the right to obtain an abortion much more difficult in some states than in others.

In 1990, the territory of Guam banned all abortions except those necessary to save a woman's life or preserve her health. Similar laws making abortion a crime have been passed in Louisiana and Utah. These laws are seen as direct challenges to *Roe v. Wade*. A federal district court refused to enforce the Guam law, and a federal appeals court affirmed the decision.[55] Sup-

---

[52]*Thornburgh v. American College of Obstetricians and Gynecologists*, 476 U.S. 747 (1986); *City of Akron v. Akron Center for Reproductive Health, Inc.*, 462 U.S. 416 (1983).

[53]*Rust v. Sullivan*, 111 S.Ct. 1759 (1991).

[54]492 U.S. 490 (1989).

[55]*Guam Society of Obstetricians and Gynecologists v. Ada*, 962 F.2d 1366 (9th Cir. 1992). Upon appeal to the U.S. Supreme Court, the Court refused to grant *certioriri*.

porters of the law argued that recent Supreme Court decisions have effectively nullified the principles announced in *Roe*. The appeals court emphasized that the Supreme Court has never expressly overruled *Roe*.

The Pennsylvania Abortion Control Act, parts of which were similar to the Missouri law considered by the Supreme Court in *Webster* in 1989, came before the Court in 1992 in *Planned Parenthood v. Casey*.[56] The act required that a woman who wished to have an abortion receive specific counseling and wait twenty-four hours. A married woman was required to notify her husband. Unmarried girls under the age of eighteen and not self-supporting were required by the act to obtain the consent of one of their parents or the permission of a state judge. A federal appeals court upheld all of the act's provisions except the husband-notification requirement. In a five-to-four decision, the Supreme Court also upheld these provisions of the Pennsylvania law.

Shortly after the inauguration of President Bill Clinton, Justice Byron White announced his retirement from the Supreme Court. Mr. Clinton's nominee to replace him will certainly oppose these anti abortion rulings.

The Right to Die

EUTHANASIA
Killing incurably ill people for reasons of mercy.

The question of whether the right to privacy includes the right to die is now a major point of controversy. Suicide and **euthanasia,** or mercy killing, are both illegal; but many extremely ill people do not want their lives prolonged through expensive artificial measures. These situations often end up in court because hospitals and doctors sympathetic to the patient's wishes do not want to be legally or morally responsible for giving the order to stop treatment, even with the patient's and family's consent.

The 1976 case of Karen Ann Quinlan was one of the first publicized right-to-die cases.[57] The parents of Quinlan, a young woman who had been in a coma since age twenty-one and kept alive by a respirator, wanted her respirator removed. The Supreme Court of New Jersey ruled that the right to privacy includes the right of a patient to refuse treatment and that patients unable to speak can exercise that right through a family or guardian. In its ruling on a 1985 case, the New Jersey Supreme Court set some clear guidelines for when care could be withheld for patients who cannot express their own wishes.[58] Care can be withheld if (1) patient would have definitely refused treatment, (2) evidence suggests that treatment would have been refused, and (3) the burdens of continuing care are greater than the benefits.

In 1992, Washington state became the first place in the world to legalize euthanasia. Essentially, the new law allows physicians to assist terminally ill patients "in dying with dignity." Mentally competent patients certified by two doctors as having less than six months to live can request assisted death. Patients in comas or vegetative states may be removed from life-sustaining machines and artificial food and water tubes. Similar measures have been considered in California, Oregon, and the European Community.

---

[56]112 S.Ct. 2791 (1992).

[57]*In re Quinlan,* 70 N.J. 10, 355 A.2d 647 (1976).

[58]*In re Conroy,* 98 N.J. 321, 486 A.2d 11209 (1985).

The Great Balancing Act: The Rights of the Accused versus the Rights of Society

The United States has one of the highest violent crime rates in the world. The statistics are shocking. So it is not surprising that many citizens have extremely strong opinions about the rights of those accused of criminal offenses. When an accused person, especially one who has confessed to some criminal act, is set free because of an apparent legal "technicality," many people may feel that the rights of the accused are being given more weight than the rights of society and of potential or actual victims. Why, then, give criminal suspects rights? The answer is partly to avoid convicting innocent people, but mostly because all citizens have rights, and suspects are citizens.

The courts and the police must constantly engage in a balancing act of competing rights. At the basis of all discussions about the appropriate balance is, of course, the U.S. Bill of Rights. The Fourth, Fifth, Sixth, and Eighth Amendments specifically deal with the rights of criminal defendants.

Rights of the Accused

The basic rights of criminal defendants can be outlined as follows. When appropriate, the specific amendment on which a right is based is given also.

Limits on the Conduct of Police Officers and Prosecutors

- No unreasonable or unwarranted searches and seizures (Amend. IV)
- No arrest except on probable cause (Amend. IV)
- No coerced confessions or illegal interrogation (Amend. V)
- No entrapment
- Upon questioning, suspect must be informed of rights

Did You Know . . . That a study by sociologist Michael L. Radelet and philosopher Hugo Adam Bedau showed that between 1900 and 1985, 350 innocent persons were convicted of capital offenses, and that 23 of these convicts were executed, with 21 others winning last-minute reprieves?

A still shot from the videotape that documented the beating of Rodney King by members of the Los Angeles police force. The initial acquittal of those police officers of charges of brutality set off the most violent and costly riots in American history. In a subsequent retrial in federal court, two of the four officers were convicted of excessive brutality and of depriving King of his civil rights.

Writ of Habeas Corpus
Literally, "you should have the body."
An order that requires jailers to bring
a party before a court or judge and
explain why the party is being held in
prison.

Defendant's Pretrial Rights

- **Writ of habeas corpus** (Article I, Section 9)
- Prompt arraignment (Amend. VI)
- Legal counsel (Amend. VI)
- Reasonable bail (Amend. VIII)
- Defendant must be informed of charges (Amend. VI)
- Right to remain silent (Amend. V)

Trial Rights

- Speedy and public trial before a jury (Amend. VI)
- Impartial jury selected from cross section of community (Amends. VI and VII)
- Trial atmosphere free of prejudice, fear, and outside interference
- No compulsory self-incrimination (Amend. V)
- Adequate counsel (Amend. VI)
- No cruel and unusual punishment (Amend. VIII)
- Appeal convictions
- No double jeopardy (Amend. V)

Extending the Rights of the Accused: *Miranda* v. *Arizona*

In 1963, near Phoenix, Arizona, a young woman was kidnapped and raped. A twenty-three-year-old mentally disturbed suspect, Ernesto Miranda, was arrested soon after the crime took place. After two hours of questioning, he confessed and was later convicted.

Miranda's counsel appealed his conviction. They argued that the police had never informed Miranda that he had the right to remain silent and the right to be represented by counsel. In 1966, a five-to-four majority of the U.S. Supreme Court ruled in Miranda's favor:

> Prior to any questioning, the person must be warned that he has a right to remain silent, that any statement he does make may be used against him, and that he has a right to the presence of an attorney, either retained or appointed.[59]

The majority voted to reverse the conviction on the basis of the Fifth and Sixth Amendments, but the minority complained that the majority was distorting the Constitution by placing the rights of criminal suspects above the rights of society as a whole—the balancing act was again in question. Police officials sided with the minority view, but many agreed with the majority that criminal law enforcement would be more reliable if it were based on independently secured evidence rather than on confessions obtained under coercive interrogation conditions in the absence of counsel.

Another extension of the rights of the accused was made by the Court in the case of Clarence Earl Gideon, described in this chapter's *Politics and Criminal Justice* feature.

Recent Rulings and Their Impact on *Miranda*

The Supreme Court under Chief Justice Warren Burger did not expand the *Miranda* ruling but rather reduced its scope and effectiveness. Also,

---

[59]*Miranda v. Arizona*, 384 U.S. 436 (1966).

POLITICS AND CRIMINAL JUSTICE

The Case of Clarence Earl Gideon

In 1962, Clarence Earl Gideon sent a petition to the Supreme Court to review his most recent conviction, which was for breaking into a pool hall and stealing some money in Panama City, Florida. That petition would not only change Gideon's life but would become a landmark case in constitutional law as well.

Clarence Gideon had been in trouble with the law during much of his life and in jail at least four times before for various minor crimes. Those who knew him, including his jailers, found him rather likeable and relatively harmless.

Gideon claimed in his petition that his conviction and sentencing to a five-year term in prison violated the due process clause of the Fourteenth Amendment to the Constitution, which says that "no state shall . . . deprive any person of life, liberty, or property, without due process of the law." Gideon reported that at the time of his trial, when he asked for the assistance of a lawyer, the court refused this aid.

The heart of Gideon's petition lay in his notion that "to try a poor man for a felony without giving him a lawyer was to deprive him of due process of law."

The problem with Gideon's argument was that the Supreme Court had established a precedent twenty years earlier in *Betts v. Brady*,* when

*316 U.S. 455 (1942).

it held that criminal defendants were not automatically guaranteed the right to have a lawyer present when they were tried in court except in capital cases.

Gideon was successful, with the help of his court-appointed lawyer, Abe Fortas, who later was named to the Supreme Court by President Johnson. In the case of *Gideon v. Wainwright*,** the Court decided in Gideon's favor, saying that persons who can demonstrate that they are unable to afford to have a lawyer present and are accused of felonies must be given a lawyer at the expense of the government. Gideon was retried, represented by an attorney appointed by the court, and found innocent of the charges.

**372 U.S. 335 (1963).
SOURCE: Anthony Lewis, *Gideon's Trumpet* (New York: Vintage Books, 1964).

Congress in 1968 passed the Omnibus Crime Control and Safe Streets Act, which provided—among other things—that in federal cases a voluntary confession could be used in evidence even if the accused was not informed of his or her rights.

Today, juries can even accept confessions without being convinced they were voluntary.[60] Even in cases that are not tried in federal court, confessions made by criminal suspects who have not been completely informed of their legal rights may be taken into consideration.[61] In 1984, the Court added another exception to the *Miranda* rule by allowing the introduction of evidence into the courtroom that was voluntarily given by the suspect

---

[60]See especially *Lego v. Twomey*, 404 U.S. 477 (1972).
[61]*Michigan v. Tucker*, 417 U.S. 433 (1974).

Did You Know . . . That in 1989, in a five-to-four decision, the U.S. Supreme Court ruled that the police do not need a search warrant to conduct low-altitude helicopter searches of private property?

EXCLUSIONARY RULE
A policy forbidding the admission at trial of illegally seized evidence.

before he had been informed of his rights. The Court held that when "public safety" required action (in this case, to find the loaded gun), police could interrogate the suspect before advising him of his right to remain silent.[62]

The Exclusionary Rule

At least since 1914, judicial policy has prohibited the admission of illegally seized evidence at trials in federal courts. This is the so-called **exclusionary rule.** Improperly obtained evidence, no matter how telling, could not be used by prosecutors. This includes evidence obtained by police in violation of the Fourth Amendment. The Fourth Amendment protects against unreasonable searches and seizures and requires that a search warrant may be issued by a judge to a police officer only on probable cause (a demonstration of facts that permit a reasonable belief that a crime has been committed). The question that must be determined by the courts is what constitutes an "unreasonable" search and seizure.

The reasoning behind the exclusionary rule is that it forces police officers to gather evidence properly, in which case their due diligence will be rewarded by a conviction. There have always been critics of the exclusionary rule who argue that it permits guilty persons to be freed because of innocent errors.

This rule was first applied to state courts in the 1961 Supreme Court decision, *Mapp v. Ohio.*[63] In this case, the Court overturned the conviction of Dollree Mapp for the possession of obscene materials. Police found pornographic books in her apartment after searching it without a search warrant despite her refusal to let them in.

In a more recent case in Massachusetts, the Court seemed to be loosening the severity of the exclusionary rule. A Boston police officer suspected a man of murder and wished to search his residence. He used a technically incorrect search warrant form. The Massachusetts Appeals Court threw out the conviction because of this technical defect. But the U.S. Supreme Court held that the officer acted in good faith and thereby created the "good faith exception."[64]

Capital Punishment: Cruel and Unusual?

Amendment VIII prohibits cruel and unusual punishment. Until a Supreme Court decision in 1972,[65] the death penalty was not considered cruel and unusual punishment. Indeed, a number of states had imposed the death penalty for a variety of crimes and allowed juries to decide when the condemned could be sentenced to death.

But many believed, and in 1972 the Court agreed, that the imposition of the death penalty was random and arbitrary. For example, 53 percent of all persons executed from 1930 to 1965 were African Americans, even though African Americans constituted less than 10 percent of the popu-

[62]*New York v. Quarles,* 467 U.S. 649 (1984).
[63]367 U.S. 643 (1961).
[64]*Massachusetts v. Sheppard,* 468 U.S. 981 (1984).
[65]*Furman v. Georgia,* 408 U.S. 238 (1972).

Capital punishment became a viable alternative after a 1972 Supreme Court ruling. In 1992, Arizona executed its first inmate in twenty-nine years, Delaware its first in forty-six years, and California its first in twenty-five years.

lation during that period. Changing attitudes toward the death penalty could be seen in the fact that the number of individuals who actually were executed had dropped dramatically since the 1930s. From 1930 to 1939, 1,666 persons were executed; from 1960 to 1969, fewer than 200 persons were executed.

The Supreme Court's 1972 decision stated that the death penalty, as then applied, violated the Eighth and Fourteenth Amendments. It ruled that capital punishment is not necessarily cruel and unusual if the criminal has killed or attempted to kill someone. In its opinion, the Court invited the states to make more precise laws so that the death penalty would be applied more consistently. A majority of states have done so. In the 1990s, an increasing number of states are executing death-row inmates.

Issues surrounding the sanity of death-row inmates have come up in the last decade. In 1986, the Supreme Court ruled that the U.S. Constitution bars states from executing convicted killers who have become insane while waiting on death row (*Ford v. Wainwright*).[66] Despite this ruling, in 1989 (in *Penry v. Lynaugh*), the Supreme Court held that mentally retarded persons may be executed for murder.[67] In the same year, the Court found that defendants who were as young as sixteen could be executed if they committed a murder.[68] Finally, in *Murray v. Giarratano*, the court held that indigent death-row inmates have no constitutional right to a lawyer for a second round of state court appeals.[69]

When considering statistical evidence regarding one state's death-sentencing process, which the defendant claimed was racially discriminatory, the Supreme Court held that some disparities are an inevitable part of the criminal justice system and do not necessarily violate the Constitution.[70] In Georgia, in 1978, the defendant, a black man, was convicted

---

[66]477 U.S. 399 (1986).
[67]492 U.S. 302 (1989).
[68]*Stanford v. Kentucky*, 492 U.S. 361 (1989).
[69]492 U.S. 1 (1989).
[70]*McCleskey v. Kemp*, 481 U.S. 279 (1987).

of armed robbery and murder—shooting a white police officer in the face during the robbery of a store. The jury recommended the death penalty, and the trial court followed the recommendation. On appeal, the defendant presented a statistical study based on more than 2,000 murder cases that occurred in Georgia during the 1970s. The study purported to show that the death sentence was imposed more often on black defendants convicted of killing whites than on white defendants convicted of killing blacks. The Supreme Court decided that the statistics did not prove that race enters into capital sentencing decisions or that it was a factor in the defendant's case. The Court stated that the unpredictability of jury decisions does not justify their condemnation, because it is the jury's function to make difficult judgments. The Court explained that any method for determining guilt or punishment has its weaknesses and the potential for misuse. Despite such imperfections, the Court concluded, constitutional guarantees are met when the method has been made as fair as possible.

Capital punishment remains one of the most debated aspects of our criminal justice system. Those in favor of it maintain that it serves as a deterrent to serious crime and satisfies society's need for justice and fair play. Those opposed to the death penalty do not believe it has any deterrent value and hold that it constitutes a barbaric act in an otherwise civilized society. Recent public opinion polls have demonstrated that a large majority of Americans favor using the death penalty more frequently.

Conclusion: The Role of State Governments in Expanding Civil Liberties

During the 1950s, 1960s, and 1970s, the United States Supreme Court made landmark decisions establishing new rights and liberties. Federal judges were seen by many as the champions of civil liberties. By 1980, however, conservatives began to feel that the judges were going too far. During the Reagan presidency (1981–1989), judges appointed to the federal bench, including those nominated to fill vacancies on the Supreme Court, were more conservative. The new conservatives appear less willing to respond positively to legal challenges that expand civil liberties. Persons who seek to expand civil liberties are turning away from federal courts and looking to state courts. Under state constitutions and state bills of rights, state supreme courts are issuing decisions that expand civil liberties beyond what federal courts appear willing to do. United States Supreme Court Chief Justice William Rehnquist has acknowledged the authority of state courts to make rules that are more expansive than those made by federal courts. Former Justice William Brennan believes this is a "significant development" in constitutional law. The trend toward increased state authority in expanding civil liberties, which can be expected to increase through the 1990s, is an example of the continuing flexibility of our American system of government.

GETTING INVOLVED

Your Civil Liberties: Searches and Seizures

What happens if you are stopped by members of the police force? Your civil liberties protect you from having to provide any other information than your name and address. Indeed, you are not really required to produce evidence of identification, although it is a good idea to show this to the officers. Normally, even if you have not been placed under arrest, the officers have the right to frisk you for weapons, and you must let them proceed. The officers cannot, however, check your person or your clothing further if, in their judgment, no weaponlike object is produced. Only if the officers have a search warrant or probable cause that they will likely find incriminating evidence if the search is conducted may they search you. Normally, it is unwise to resist physically the officers' attempt to search you if they do not have probable cause or a warrant; it is usually best simply to refuse orally to give permission for the search, preferably in the presence of a witness. Also, it is usually advisable to tell the officer as little as possible about yourself and the situation that is under investigation. Being polite and courteous, though firm, is better than acting out of anger or frustration and making the officers irritable. If you are arrested it is best to keep quiet until you can speak with a lawyer.

If you are in your car and are stopped by the police, the same fundamental rules apply. Always be ready to show your driver's license and car registration quickly. You may be asked to get out of the car. The officers may use a flashlight to peer inside if it is too dark to see otherwise. None of this constitutes a search. A true search requires either a warrant or probable cause. No officer has the legal right to search your car simply to find out if you may have committed a crime. Passengers in a car that has been stopped by the police are legally required only to give a name and address. Passengers are not even obligated to produce a piece of identification.

If you are in your residence and a police officer with a search warrant appears, you should examine the warrant before granting entry. A correctly made out warrant will state the exact place or persons to be searched, a description of the object sought, the date of the warrant (which should be no more than ten days old), and the signature of a judge or magistrate. If the search warrant is in order, you should not make any statement. If you believe it to be invalid, you should make it clear orally that you have not consented to the search, preferably in the presence of a witness. If the warrant is later proved to be invalid, normally any evidence obtained would be considered illegal. Officers who attempt to enter your home without a search warrant can do so only if they are pursuing a suspected felon into the house. Rarely is it advisable to give permission for a warrantless search. You must be the one to give permission for any evidence obtained to be legal. The landlord, manager, or head of a college dormitory cannot give legal permission. A roommate, however, can give permission for a search of his or her room, which may allow the police to search those areas in which you have personal belongings. If you find yourself a guest in a location that is being legally searched, you may be legally searched also. But unless you have been placed under arrest, you cannot be compelled to go to the police station or into a squad car.

If you would like to find out more about your rights and obligations under the laws of searches and seizures, you might wish to contact the following organizations:

The American Civil Liberties Union
22 East 40th Street
New York, NY 10016
(212) 725-1222

Legal Defense Fund
67 Winthrop Street
Cambridge, MA 02138
(617) 864-8680

CHAPTER SUMMARY

1. To deal with American colonists' fears of a too-powerful national government, after the adoption of the U.S. Constitution, Congress proposed a Bill of Rights. These ten amendments to the Constitution were ratified by the states by the end of 1791. The amendments represent civil liberties—that is, they are limitations on government.

2. Originally, the Bill of Rights limited only the power of the federal government, not that of the states. This is still the general rule. Gradually, however, the Supreme Court accepted the incorporation theory that no state could violate the Bill of Rights. In applying the protections of the Bill of Rights to the states through the Fourteenth Amendment, the Supreme Court has been deciding which rights are necessary to the American concept of ordered liberty. These rights must be applied uniformly by the state governments.

3. The First Amendment protects against government interference with the freedom of religion by requiring a separation of church and state and by guaranteeing the free exercise of religion. The separation of church and state is mandated in the establishment clause. Under this clause, the Supreme Court has ruled against officially sponsored prayer, Bible-reading sessions, and "moments of meditation, prayer, or silent reflection" in public schools. The Court has also struck down laws forbidding the teaching of evolution or requiring the teaching of the biblical story of creation. The government can provide financial aid to religious schools if the aid is secular in aim, the aid does not have the primary effect of advancing or inhibiting religion, and the government avoids "an excessive entanglement with religion." The free exercise of religion is guaranteed by the free exercise clause. Only when religious practices work against public policy or the public welfare can the government interfere. A religion cannot make legal what is otherwise illegal.

4. The First Amendment protects against government interference with the freedom of speech, which includes symbolic speech (wearing black armbands to protest a war, for example). Restrictions are permitted when expression presents a clear and present danger to the peace or public order, or when expression has a bad tendency (that is, when it might lead to some "evil"). Expression may be restrained before it occurs, but such prior restraint has a "heavy presumption" against its constitutionality. Commercial speech (advertising) and noncommmercial speech by businesses have received First Amendment protection. Speech that has not received First Amendment protection includes expression judged to be obscene, utterances considered to be slanderous, and speech constituting fighting words or a heckler's veto.

5. The First Amendment protects against government interference with the freedom of the press, which can be regarded as a special instance of freedom of speech. Publication of news about a criminal trial may be restricted by a gag order under unusual circumstances. The press may be asked to cooperate in criminal investigations by revealing its sources or providing other evidence in response to subpoenas or search warrants. In most states, shield laws protect reporters from having to reveal their sources and confidential information. Speech by the press that does not receive protection includes libelous statements made with actual malice.

6. The First Amendment protects the right to assemble peaceably and to petition the government. Permits may be required for parades, sound trucks, and demonstrations to maintain the public order, and a permit may be denied to protect the public safety. To avoid government interference with freedom of association, an organization cannot be required to publish a list of its members.

7. Under the Ninth Amendment, rights not specifically mentioned in the Constitution are not denied to the people. Among these unspecified rights is a right to privacy, which has been implied through the First, Third, Fourth, Fifth, and Ninth Amendments. This right has been used to strike down a law prohibiting the use of contraceptives and to protect a woman's right to control reproduction. The right to privacy has not been held to protect homosexual acts. Whether the right to privacy includes the right to die is an ongoing controversy.

8. The Constitution includes protections for the rights of persons accused of crimes. Under the Fourth Amendment, no one may be subject to an unreasonable search or seizure or arrested except on probable cause. Under the Fifth Amendment, an accused person has the right to remain silent. Under the Sixth Amendment, an accused person must be informed of the reason for his or her arrest, and has the right to adequate counsel, even if he or she cannot afford an attorney, and the right to a prompt arraignment and a speedy and public trial before an impartial jury selected from a cross section of the community. Under the Eighth Amendment, cruel and unusual punishment is prohibited. Other rights include a right to a fair trial and a right to at least one appeal. When public safety demands it, police may interrogate a suspect before advising him or her of the right to remain silent, and any confession or evidence may be used against the suspect. The exclusionary rule forbids the admission of illegally seized evidence at trials in federal courts. There is a "good faith" exception to the exclusionary rule: Illegally seized evidence need not be thrown out owing to, for example, a technical defect in a search warrant. Whether the death penalty is cruel and unusual punishment continues to be debated.

QUESTIONS FOR REVIEW AND DISCUSSION

1. Although the Communist party was strictly outlawed in the United States for many years, today its candidates compete openly in presidential and other elections. What activities—speeches, printed publications, demonstrations, and other actions—of the Communist party do you think could be considered illegal under the current laws?

2. Most conflicts concerning civil liberties involve the rights of the individual versus the rights of society as a whole. What religious practices might be considered a threat to society? What activities of certain missionary groups may be violating your right to be left alone?

3. The punishment of convicted criminals serves not only as retribution for the crime but also to satisfy the community's sense of justice. How should the courts balance the rights of the criminal against the rights of society—and the rights of the victim—to ensure fair treatment?

4. The electronic era has created many legal situations that are not covered by the Constitution. To what extent should radio and television be covered by freedom of the press? Should videotape rentals be regulated to prevent the spread of pornography, especially to minors? Should computer communications be protected by the right to privacy?

SELECTED REFERENCES

Brookings Task Force on Civil Justice Reform, *Justice for All: Reducing Costs and Delay in Civil Litigation* (Washington, D.C.: Brookings Institute, 1990). This is a short but powerful report from a commission set up to look at ways of streamlining and reducing costs and delays in the American civil justice system.

William A. Carroll and Norman B. Smith, eds., *American Constitutional Rights: Cases, Documents and Commentary* (Lanham, Md.: University Press of America, 1991). This casebook describes the fluctuation, growth, and decline in the constitutional rights of the individual throughout American history.

William C. Culbertson, *Vigilantism: Political History of Private Power in America* (Westport, Conn.: Greenwood Press, 1990). This book examines the American people's history of taking the law into their own hands. The author asserts that private power has been instrumental in creating, distributing, and maintaining socially acceptable values and norms.

William A. Donohue, *The Politics of the American Civil Liberties Union* (New Brunswick, N.J.: Transaction Books, 1985). An interesting study of one of the most visible and active civil liberties groups in the United States, with specific emphasis given to the role of ideology and the political orientation of the American Civil Liberties Union.

Susan P. Fino, *The Role of State Supreme Courts in the New Judicial Federalism* (Westport, Conn.: Greenwood Press, 1987). An assessment of how state law is utilized to fashion rights not mandated by the Supreme Court's interpretation of the United States Constitution.

Nat Hentoff, *The First Freedom: The Tumultuous History of Free Speech in America* (New York: Delacorte, 1980). This is a lively account of the evolution of the freedom of speech.

Anthony Lewis, *Gideon's Trumpet* (New York: Vintage, 1964). Absolutely essential reading for understanding how criminal rights cases reach the Supreme Court.

Steven H. Shriffin, *The First Amendment, Democracy, and Romance* (Cambridge, Mass.: Harvard University Press, 1990). In this highly readable and well-researched work, Shriffin argues that the First Amendment should be interpreted more broadly and that emotion, as well as logic, has its place in the law.

Geoffrey R. Stone, Richard A. Epstein, and Cass R. Sunstein, eds., *The Bill of Rights in the Modern State* (Chicago: University of Chicago Press, 1992). A collection of essays written by prominent constitutional scholars on some of today's most controversial constitutional issues. Such issues as freedom of religion, freedom of speech, and constitutional interpretation are discussed from a variety of perspectives.

D. F. B. Tucker, *Law, Liberalism and Free Speech* (Totowa, N.J.: Rowman and Littlefield, 1986). Using the ideas of major contemporary philosophers, this book explores fundamental principles of freedom of speech and provides specific applications to privacy, the public interest, the media, and authority.

William L. Van Deburg, *New Day in Babylon: The Black Power Movement and American Culture, 1965–1975* (Chicago: University of Chicago Press, 1992). A highly readable account of the Black Power movement in the United States and how it affected African Americans, as well as American culture generally.

CHAPTER 5
The Rights of Minorities and Women

CHAPTER CONTENTS

WHAT IF . . . WE HAD UNRESTRICTED IMMIGRATION?

Until 1875, the United States was open to almost unlimited immigration. Only prostitutes and convicts were excluded. But government policy underwent many permutations since that time, so that by 1993 American immigration laws had become a complicated mix of quotas and special provisions—over thirty different categories. These include quotas by region of the world, country, skill, and economic condition (a special Hong Kong set-aside allowed in a large number of Hong Kong residents provided they would invest at least $1 million in the United States and hire at least ten Americans), relatives of U.S. citizens, refugees, those seeking temporary political asylum, and seasonal laborers (migrant workers). Under the most recent law, so-called "employer sanctions" impose fines and other penalties on persons (companies) knowingly hiring illegal aliens.

What if the United States were to return to an open immigration policy? The world in the 1990s is characterized by easy transportation, mobility, and rapid, sometimes simultaneous, worldwide communications. People in every corner of the world can learn about life in the United States. For many in countries torn by strife and plagued by poverty, the United States still seems a golden land of economic opportunity and political freedom. Moreover, the "American way of life," including its popular culture of emblematic blue jeans, hamburgers, rock music, and other distinctive characteristics, has an enormous allure for people in Eastern Europe

and many other places. Thus, an open immigration policy, no questions asked, would clearly stimulate a huge number of persons to come to the United States or to send their children or other relatives.

With open immigration, the arrival of these millions would have both negative and positive consequences. On the negative side, U.S. institutions would be challenged by the surge of new persons requiring education, housing, health care, and other services. A relatively unmonitored immigration policy would no doubt allow in some new criminals, human rights abusers, and drug dealers. The needs of sick persons seeking medical help and the poor, unskilled, and unemployable among the newcomers would place severe strains on cities, counties, states, and the federal government. Racially, ethnically, and religiously diverse immigrant groups might clash with one another and increase the tension in U.S. neighborhoods. This has happened with Vietnamese and Koreans, on the one hand, and established African Americans, Hispanics, and European Americans, on the other, in New York City and other places.

There would, however, also be great advantages to open immigration. Entrepreneurs and others wishing to move away from places with an uncertain future (Hong Kong, for instance, which reverts to Chinese control in 1997) would bring their capital, skills, and energy, which would stimulate business. The new wave of immigrants also would

bring their culture and, in the manner of traditional immigrant groups, greatly enrich American music, art, dance, and a host of other cultural forms.

Finally, and most important, new immigrants would help ease the looming labor shortage, which (as a result of low U.S. birthrates and an aging population) may threaten U.S. economic prosperity in the twenty-first century. In 1900, there were only 111 older Americans for every 1,000 working people. Now there are almost 300, and this figure is rising. This has resulted in a budget expenditure of over $375 billion in aid to the elderly. In contrast, immigrants are overwhelmingly working age (almost 50 percent are in the "early prime labor force age" of twenty to thirty-nine, compared with only 26 percent of current Americans). These new, young, working Americans would fill the jobs that might go begging and also create new jobs through entrepreneurship. They would pay local and state taxes and Social Security taxes, stimulate new housing and commercial construction, and inject vitality into the educational system, which in some places is shrinking because of a declining school-age population.

1. *When did your family immigrate to the United States? From what country did they come?*
2. *Would they be able to immigrate to the United States today?*
3. *What did they do for a living when they arrived?*

We hold these Truths to be self-evident, that all Men are created equal . . .

These are beautiful words, to be sure. But when they were written in 1776, the term *men* had a somewhat different meaning than it has today. It did not include slaves or women or Native Americans. So individuals in these groups were not considered equal. It has taken this nation over two hundred years to approach even a semblance of equality among all Americans.

The struggle for equality has not been easy. In this chapter, we show that it is continuing. It is a struggle perhaps best described as an effort to strengthen and to expand constitutional guarantees to *all* persons in our society. In this chapter and in the one that follows, we examine the rights of various minorities and groups: African Americans, Mexican Americans and other Hispanics, Native Americans, Asian Americans, women, gays, the elderly, and juveniles.

Minority rights have often been called civil rights, and the quest for the expansion of minority rights has been called the civil rights movement. Because the modern civil rights movement started with the struggle for African-American equality, that story is told first.

African Americans: The Consequences of Slavery

Article I, Section 2, of the Constitution states that congressional representatives and direct taxes are to be apportioned among the states according to their respective numbers, obtained by adding to the total number of free persons "three-fifths of all other Persons." The "other persons" were, of course, slaves. A slave was thus equal to three-fifths of a white person.[1] As Lincoln stated sarcastically, "All men are created equal, except Negroes." Before 1863, the Constitution thus protected slavery and made equality impossible in the sense we use the word today. African-American leader Frederick Douglass pointed out that "Liberty and Slavery—opposite as Heaven and Hell—are both in the Constitution."

The constitutionality of slavery was confirmed just a few years before the outbreak of the Civil War in the famous *Dred Scott v. Sanford*[2] case of 1857. The Supreme Court held that slaves were not citizens of the United States, nor were they entitled to the rights and privileges of citizenship. The Court also ruled that the Missouri Compromise, which banned slavery in the territories north of 36° 30' latitude (the southern border of Missouri), was unconstitutional. The *Dred Scott* decision had grave consequences. Most observers contend that the ruling contributed to making the Civil War inevitable. (In all fairness, it should be noted that the decision was not unanimous—the Court was divided six to three over the issue, and the nine justices filed nine separate opinions in the case.)

With the emancipation of the slaves by President Lincoln's Emancipation Proclamation in 1863 and the passage of the Thirteenth, Fourteenth, and Fifteenth Amendments during the Reconstruction period following the

This portrait is of Dred Scott (1795–1858), an American slave who was born in South Hampton County, Virginia. He was the nominal plaintiff in a test case that sought to obtain his freedom on the ground that he lived in the free state of Illinois. Although the Supreme Court ruled against him, he was soon emancipated and became a hotel porter in St. Louis, Missouri.

---

[1]It may seem ironic that the median wage of blacks today is approximately three-fifths that of whites.

[2]19 Howard 393 (1857).

Did You Know ... That minorities will make up 35 percent of the U.S. population by the year 2010, and by the year 2025, minorities will account for 40 percent of young people ten to twenty-one years of age?

Civil War, constitutional inequality was ended. The Thirteenth Amendment (1865) states that neither slavery nor involuntary servitude shall exist within the United States. The Fourteenth Amendment (ratified on July 9, 1868) tells us that *all* persons born or naturalized in the United States are citizens of the United States. Furthermore, ''No State shall make or enforce any law which shall abridge the privileges or immunities of the citizens of the United States; nor shall any State deprive any person of life, liberty or property without due process of law; nor deny to any person within its jurisdiction the equal protection of the laws.'' The Fifteenth Amendment seems equally impressive: ''The right of citizens of the United States to vote shall not be denied or abridged by the United States or by any State on account of race, color, or previous condition of servitude.'' Pressure was brought to bear on Congress to include in the Fourteenth and Fifteenth Amendments a prohibition against discrimination based on sex, but with no success. As we shall see, the words of these amendments had little immediate effect. Although slavery was legally and constitutionally ended, politically and socially African-American inequality has continued to the present time. In the following sections, we discuss several landmarks in the struggle of African Americans to overcome this inequality.

The Civil Rights Acts of 1865–1877

At the end of the Civil War, President Lincoln's Republican party controlled the national government and most state governments, and the so-called Radical Republicans with their strong antislavery stance controlled that party. The Radical Republicans pushed through the Thirteenth, Fourteenth, and Fifteenth Amendments to the Constitution (the ''Civil War amendments''). From 1865 to 1877, they succeeded in getting Congress to pass a series of civil rights acts that were aimed at enforcing these amendments. Even Republicans who were not necessarily sympathetic to a strong antislavery position wanted to undercut Democratic domination of the South. What better way to do so than to guarantee African-American suffrage? The civil rights acts that were passed from 1865 to 1877 were also supported by pro-industry legislators who believed that agrarian southern Democrats would impede industrialization.

Lincoln reads the Emancipation Proclamation on July 22, 1862. The Emancipation Proclamation did not abolish slavery (that was done by the Thirteenth Amendment, in 1865), but it ensured that slavery would be abolished if and when the North won the Civil War. After the Battle of Antietam on September 17, 1862, Lincoln publicly announced the Emancipation Proclamation and declared that all slaves residing in states that were still in rebellion against the United States on January 1, 1863, would be freed once those states came under the military control of the Union army.

The first Civil Rights Act in the Reconstruction period that followed the Civil War was passed in 1866 over the veto of President Andrew Johnson. That act extended citizenship to anyone born in the United States and gave African Americans full equality before the law. The act further authorized the president to enforce the law with national armed forces. Many considered the law to be unconstitutional, but such problems disappeared in 1868 with the adoption of the Fourteenth Amendment.

Among the six other civil rights acts in the nineteenth century, one of the more important was the Enforcement Act of May 31, 1870, which set out specific criminal sanctions for interfering with the right to vote as protected by the Fifteenth Amendment and by the Civil Rights Act of 1866. Equally important was the Civil Rights Act of April 20, 1872, known as the Anti-Ku Klux Klan Act. This act made it a federal crime for anyone to use law or custom to deprive an individual of his or her rights, privileges, and immunities secured by the Constitution or by any federal law. Section 2 of that act imposed detailed penalties or damages for violation of the act.

The last of these early civil rights acts, known as the Second Civil Rights Act, was passed on March 1, 1875. It declared that everyone is entitled to full and equal enjoyment of public accommodations, theaters, and other places of public amusement and imposed penalties for violators. Unfortunately, the act was virtually nullified by the *Civil Rights Cases* of 1883 discussed below.

The Ineffectiveness of the Civil Rights Acts

The Reconstruction statutes, or civil rights acts, ultimately did little to secure equality for African Americans in their civil rights. Both the *Civil Rights Cases* and the case of *Plessy v. Ferguson* effectively nullified these acts.

The *Civil Rights Cases*. The Supreme Court invalidated the 1875 Civil Rights Act when it held in the *Civil Rights Cases*[3] of 1883 that the enforcement clause of the Fourteenth Amendment was limited to correcting actions by states in their official acts; thus, the discriminatory acts of private citizens were not illegal. ("Individual invasion of individual rights is not the subject matter of the Amendment.") The 1883 Supreme Court decision met with widespread approval throughout most of the United States. Twenty years after the Civil War, the nation was all too willing to forget about the Civil War amendments and the civil rights legislation of the 1860s and 1870s. The other civil rights laws that the Court specifically did not invalidate became dead letters in the statute books, although they were never repealed by Congress.

***Plessy v. Ferguson*: Separate but Equal.** A key decision during this period concerned Homer Plessy, a Louisiana resident who was one-eighth African American. In 1892, he was riding in a train from New Orleans when the conductor made him leave the car, which was restricted to whites, and directed him to a car for nonwhites. At that time, Louisiana had a statute providing for separate railway cars for whites and African Americans.

Did You Know . . . That by the time of the Revolution, African Americans made up nearly 25 percent of the American population of about three million?

---

[3]109 U.S. 3 (1883).

SEPARATE-BUT-EQUAL DOCTRINE
The doctrine holding that segregation in schools and public accommodations does not imply the superiority of one race over another; rather, it implies that each race is entitled to separate but equal facilities.

Jim Crow laws required the segregation of the races, particularly in public facilities such as this theater. The name "Jim Crow" originates from a nineteenth-century vaudeville character who was called Jim (which was a common name) Crow (for a black-colored bird). Thus, the name "Jim Crow" was applied to laws and practices affecting African Americans.

Plessy went to court, claiming that such a statute was contrary to the Fourteenth Amendment's equal protection clause. In 1896, the U.S. Supreme Court rejected Plessy's contention. The Court concluded that the Fourteenth Amendment "could not have been intended to abolish distinctions based upon color, or to enforce social ... equality." The Court indicated that segregation alone did not violate the Constitution: "Laws permitting, and even requiring their separation in places where they are liable to be brought into contact do not necessarily imply the inferiority of either race to the other."[4] So was born the **separate-but-equal doctrine.**

The only justice to vote against this decision was John Harlan, a former slaveowner. He stated in his dissent, "Our Constitution is color-blind, and neither knows nor tolerates classes among citizens." Justice Harlan also predicted that the separate-but-equal doctrine would "in time prove to be ... as pernicious as the decision ... in the Dred Scott Case."

For more than half a century, the separate-but-equal doctrine was accepted as consistent with the equal protection clause in the Fourteenth Amendment. In practical terms, the separate-but-equal doctrine effectively nullified this clause. *Plessy v. Ferguson* became the constitutional cornerstone of racial discrimination throughout the United States. Even though *Plessy* upheld segregated facilities in railway cars only, it was assumed that the Supreme Court was upholding segregation everywhere as long as the separate facilities were equal. The result was a system of racial segregation, particularly in the South, that required separate drinking fountains, separate seats in theaters, restaurants, and hotels, separate public toilets, and separate waiting rooms for the two races—collectively known as Jim Crow laws.

The End of the Separate-but-Equal Doctrine

A successful attack on the separate-but-equal doctrine began with a series of suits in the 1930s to admit African Americans to state professional schools. By 1950, the Supreme Court had ruled that African Americans who were admitted to a state university could not be assigned to separate sections of classrooms, libraries, and cafeterias. In 1951, Oliver Brown decided that his eight-year-old daughter, Linda Carol Brown, should not have to go to an all-nonwhite elementary school, twenty-one blocks from her home, when there was a white school only seven blocks away. The National Association for the Advancement of Colored People (NAACP), formed in 1909, decided to help Oliver Brown. The results were monumental in their impact on American society.

Brown v. Board of Education. The 1954 unanimous decision in *Brown v. Board of Education of Topeka*[5] established that public school segregation of races violates the equal protection clause of the Fourteenth Amendment. Concluding that separate schools are inherently unequal, Chief Justice Warren stated that "to separate [African Americans] from others of similar age and qualifications solely because of their race generates a feeling of inferiority as to their status in the community that may affect their hearts and minds in a way unlikely ever to be undone." Warren said that sep-

---

[4]*Plessy v. Ferguson,* 163 U.S. 537 (1896).
[5]347 U.S. 483 (1954).

aration implied inferiority, whereas the majority opinion in *Plessy v. Ferguson* had said the opposite. Legal purists still argue with the sociological, rather than strictly legal, criteria of the *Brown* decision.

"With All Deliberate Speed." The following year, in *Brown v. Board of Education*[6] (sometimes called the second *Brown* decision), the Court asked for rearguments concerning the way in which compliance with the 1954 decision should be undertaken. The Supreme Court declared that the lower courts must ensure that African Americans would be admitted to schools on a nondiscriminatory basis "with all deliberate speed." The high court told lower federal courts that they had to take an activist role in society. The district courts were to consider devices in their desegregation orders that might include "the school transportation system, personnel, [and] revision of school districts and attendance areas into compact units to achieve a system of determining admission to the public schools on a nonracial basis."

Reactions to School Integration

One unlooked-for effect of the "all deliberate speed" decision was that the term *deliberate* was used as a loophole by some officials who were able to delay desegregation by showing that they were indeed acting with all deliberate speed but still were unable to desegregate. Another reaction to court-ordered desegregation was "white flight." In some school districts, the public school population became 100 percent nonwhite when white parents sent their children to newly established private schools, sometimes known as "segregation academies."

The white South did not let the Supreme Court ruling go unchallenged. Arkansas's Governor Orval Faubus used the state's National Guard to block the integration of Central High School in Little Rock, Arkansas, in September 1957. The federal court demanded that the troops be withdrawn. Finally, President Eisenhower had to nationalize the Arkansas National Guard and send it to quell the violence. Central High became integrated.

The universities in the South, however, remained segregated. When James Meredith, an African-American student, attempted to enroll at the University of Mississippi in Oxford in 1962, violence flared there as it had in Little Rock. Two men were killed and a number injured in campus rioting. President John Kennedy sent federal marshals and ordered federal troops to maintain peace and protect Meredith. One year later, George Wallace, governor of Alabama, promised "to stand in the schoolhouse door" to prevent two African-American students from enrolling at the University of Alabama in Tuscaloosa. Wallace was forced to back down when Kennedy nationalized the Alabama National Guard.

The Controversy Continues: Busing

In most parts of the United States, school integration is made difficult by housing segregation. Although it is true that a number of school boards in northern districts created segregated schools by arbitrarily drawing

Did You Know . . . That the Rhode Island colony enacted the first American law declaring slavery illegal, on May 18, 1652?

---

[6]349 U.S. 294 (1955).

To remedy *de facto* segregation, the courts often imposed busing requirements on school districts. Busing meant transporting children of white neighborhoods to nonwhite schools, and vice versa. Busing has been one of the most controversial domestic policies in the history of this country. Initially, bused students had to be escorted by police because of potential violence. This scene was photographed in Boston in the 1970s.

DE FACTO SEGREGATION
Racial segregation that occurs not as a result of deliberate intentions but because of past social and economic conditions and residential patterns.

DE JURE SEGREGATION
Racial segregation that occurs because of laws or administrative decisions by public agencies.

BUSING
The transportation of public school students from areas where they live to schools in other areas to eliminate school segregation based on residential patterns.

school district lines, the concentration of African Americans and other minorities in well-defined geographical locations—sometimes due to agreements between majority homeowners to exclude minorities—was the reason for the *de facto* **segregation** of northern public schools. The obvious solution to both *de facto* and *de jure* **segregation** seemed to be transporting some African-American schoolchildren to white schools and some white schoolchildren to nonwhite schools. Increasingly, the courts ordered school districts to engage in such **busing** across neighborhoods. Busing led to violence in some northern cities, as in south Boston where African-American students were bused into blue-collar Irish-Catholic neighborhoods.

Busing is unpopular with many groups. In the mid-1970s, almost 50 percent of African Americans interviewed were opposed to busing, and approximately three-fourths of the whites interviewed held the same opinion.[7] Nonetheless, the Supreme Court upheld a number of busing plans. In 1971, the court upheld the right of judges to order school busing in the case of *Swann v. Charlotte-Mecklenburg Board of Education.*[8] In this case, the justices unanimously held that busing was permissible in school districts that had practiced deliberate segregation in the past. Two years later, in *Keyes v. School District No. 1,*[9] the Court ruled that the Denver school board had intentionally segregated a significant number of students. The Court determined that the Denver school board had to desegregate the school system completely. (The *Keyes* decision was reaffirmed in 1979 when the Court upheld crosstown busing plans in Dayton and Columbus, Ohio.[10]) In 1974, the Supreme Court, in a five-to-four vote, rejected a plan to bus

---

[7]Diane Ravitch, "Busing: The Solution That Has Failed to Solve," *New York Times,* December 21, 1975, Section 4, p. 3.
[8]402 U.S. 1 (1971).
[9]413 U.S. 189 (1973).
[10]*Dayton Board of Education v. Brinkman,* 443 U.S. 526 (1979); *Columbus Board of Education v. Penick,* 443 U.S. 449 (1979).

children between Detroit and its suburbs. The Court determined in this case, *Milliken v. Bradley*,[11] that busing could not be ordered between the school districts unless there had been intentional action by the suburban district to segregate the city schools.

In an apparent reversal of previous decisions, the Supreme Court in June 1986 allowed the Norfolk, Virginia, public school system to end fifteen years of court-ordered busing of elementary schoolchildren.[12] Starting in the fall of 1986, the Norfolk schools were allowed to assign children to schools in their neighborhoods, even though ten of the city's thirty-five elementary schools would become 97 to 100 percent nonwhite. The Norfolk school board supported the decision. Its support was prompted by a drop from 32,500 whites attending public schools in 1970 when busing was ordered to fewer than 14,000 in 1985.

Lower federal courts have followed the Supreme Court's lead in allowing school districts to discontinue busing.[13] These and other cases hold that once a school district implements a plan to establish a racially neutral school system, the district is not responsible for any resegregation that results from changing demographics (such as "white flight"). Nevertheless, busing is still approved as a remedy for cases in which school districts are segregating students.[14]

The Civil Rights Movement

The *Brown* decision applied only to public schools. Not much else of the structure of existing segregation was affected. In December 1955, a forty-three-year-old African-American woman, Rosa Parks, boarded a public bus in Montgomery, Alabama (see the *Profile* of Parks in this chapter). When it became crowded and several white people stepped aboard, she was asked to move to the rear of the bus, the "colored" section. She refused, was arrested, and was fined $10; but that was not the end of the matter. For an entire year, African Americans boycotted the Montgomery bus line. The protest was headed by a twenty-seven-year-old Baptist minister, Dr. Martin Luther King, Jr. During the protest period, he went to jail,[15] and his house was bombed; but in the face of overwhelming odds, King won. In 1956, the federal district court issued an injunction prohibiting the segregation of buses in Montgomery. The era of civil rights protests had begun.

King's Philosophy of Nonviolence

The following year, King formed the Southern Christian Leadership Conference (SCLC). King's philosophy of nonviolent civil disobedience was influenced greatly by Mahatma Gandhi's life and teachings. Gandhi had

Did You Know . . . That during the 1964 Mississippi Summer Project, organized by students to register African-American voters, there were 1,000 arrests, 35 shooting incidents, 30 buildings bombed, 25 churches burned, 80 people beaten, and at least 6 murders?

---

[11]418 U.S. 717 (1974).

[12]*Riddick v. School Board of City of Norfolk*, 627 F.Supp. 814 (1984); *certiorari* denied, 479 U.S. 938 (1986).

[13]See, for example, *Flax v. Potts*, 864 F.2d 1157 (5th Cir. 1989); and *Price v. Austin Independent School District*, 729 F.Supp. 533 (W.D. Tex. 1990).

[14]*Keyes v. School District No. 1*, 895 F.2d 659 (10th Cir. 1990).

[15]Read his "Letter from the Birmingham Jail" for a better understanding of this period.

PROFILE

Rosa Parks

"My shoulder ached, I had had a bad day at work, I was tired from sewing all day, and all of a sudden everything was just too much."

She was an unlikely figure to be a rallying point for a major civil rights campaign in the heart of Alabama in the 1950s. On December 1, 1955, Rosa Parks, a forty-two-year-old seamstress, refused to give up her seat on a Montgomery, Alabama, bus to a white passenger. She was arrested for violating Alabama's segregation laws, spent the night in jail, and, by her act, spurred the African-American community to organize a total boycott of the Montgomery bus system. Rosa Parks's simple refusal to move to the back of the bus was the catalyst for the movement of African Americans to end segregation of buses, trains, lunch counters, and other public facilities in the South.

Rosa Parks was born on February 4, 1913, in Tuskegee, Alabama. Her father was a carpenter; her mother taught school. As a child she was soft spoken and mild mannered. Her early years were marked by fear of the Ku Klux Klan and their night raids on African-American families. After studying at Alabama State College, she worked briefly at clerical jobs, finally becoming a tailor's assistant at a Montgomery department store. Her husband, Raymond Parks, was a barber. The only indicator of Rosa Parks's engagement in civil rights was her volunteer work for the NAACP,

where she helped in the campaign to register African-American voters.

After working long days as a seamstress, Mrs. Parks often walked the mile home to her apartment because she found the bus system, with its segregated seating, a trial to endure. She claimed that if you did not passively follow the rules, "whites would accuse you of causing trouble when all you were doing was acting like a normal human being instead of cringing. You didn't have to wait for a lynching. You died a little each time you found yourself face to face with this kind of discrimination." On the day she finally rebelled, Mrs. Parks took the bus because it was too hot to walk. Halfway through the trip, the bus filled up, and the driver ordered

the four African-American riders in Mrs. Parks's row to give up their seats to boarding white passengers. Mrs. Parks refused because, she recalls, "My shoulder ached, I had had a bad day at work, I was tired from sewing all day, and all of a sudden everything was just too much."

After Rosa Parks's arrest and harsh treatment in the Montgomery jail, the African-American community organized a boycott of the bus system that lasted for a year. Although the bus boycott was the beginning of civil rights activism in Alabama, Mrs. Parks suffered for her actions. She was fired from her job within two months, and her husband eventually lost his job as well. They were continually harassed by threatening telephone calls and racist intimidation. Rosa went to work for the group that coordinated the boycott and, within a short time, found herself speaking for civil rights throughout the country. Eventually, Rosa and her husband moved to Detroit, where she became involved in community work and continued to work for civil rights.

Within ten years after Mrs. Parks's action, segregated facilities were outlawed by the Civil Rights Act of 1964, and Congress passed the Voting Rights Act of 1965 to ensure that African Americans could exercise their voting rights. Rosa Parks, the woman who wouldn't move to the back of the bus, was hailed by Martin Luther King, Jr., as "the great fuse that led to the modern stride toward freedom."

led Indian resistance to the British colonial system from 1919 to 1947, using tactics such as demonstrations and marches, as well as purposeful, public disobedience to unjust laws, while remaining nonviolent. King's followers successfully used these methods to widen public acceptance of their case. For the next decade, African Americans and sympathetic whites engaged in sit-ins, freedom rides, and freedom marches. In the beginning, such demonstrations were often met with violence, but the contrasting image of nonviolent African Americans and violent, hostile whites created strong public support for the civil rights movement. When African Americans in Greensboro, North Carolina, were refused service at a Woolworth's lunch counter, they organized a sit-in that was aided day after day by sympathetic whites and other African Americans. Enraged customers threw ketchup on the protestors. Some spat in their faces. But the sit-in movement continued to grow. Within six months of the first sit-in at the Greensboro Woolworth's, hundreds of lunch counters throughout the South were serving African Americans.

The sit-in technique was also successfully used to integrate interstate buses and their terminals, as well as railroads engaged in interstate transportation. Although buses and railroads that were engaged in interstate transportation were prohibited by law from segregating African Americans from whites,[16] they only stopped doing so after the sit-in protests.

The civil rights movement, with King at its head, gathered momentum in the 1960s. One of the most famous of the violence-plagued protests occurred in Birmingham, Alabama, in the spring of 1963, when Police Commissioner Eugene "Bull" Connor unleashed police dogs and used electric cattle prods against the protestors. The object of the protest had been to provoke a reaction by local officials so that the federal government would act. People throughout the country viewed the event on national television with indignation and horror, and such media coverage played a key role in the process of ending Jim Crow conditions in the United States. The ultimate result was the most important civil rights act in the nation's history, passed in 1964.

Police dog attacks, cattle prods, high-pressure water hoses, beatings, bombings, and the March on Washington—all of these events led to an environment in which Congress felt compelled to act on behalf of African Americans. The second era of civil rights acts, the so-called Second Reconstruction period, was underway.

Modern Civil Rights Legislation and Its Implementation

In the wake of the Montgomery bus boycott, public sentiment for stronger civil rights legislation put pressure on Congress and President Dwight David Eisenhower to act. The action taken was relatively symbolic. The Civil Rights Act of 1957 established a Civil Rights Commission and a new Civil Rights Division within the Justice Department. (President Reagan tried to abolish the Commission in 1983; Congress extended its life for

Did You Know ... That by September 1961, more than 3,600 students had been arrested for participating in civil rights demonstrations and that 141 students and 58 faculty members had been expelled by colleges and universities for their part in civil rights protests?

---

[16]See *Morgan v. Commonwealth of Virginia,* 328 U.S. 373 (1946); and *Henderson v. United States,* 339 U.S. 819 (1950).

POLITICS AND RACE

Martin Luther King, Jr.: "I Have a Dream"

On August 28, 1963, in the centennial year of the Emancipation Proclamation, a long-planned mass mobilization of civil rights supporters took place in the "March on Washington for Jobs and Freedom." The march, in which 250,000 African-American and white men and women participated, was a major event in the civil rights movement and in the leadership of Martin Luther King, Jr., head of the Southern Christian Leadership Conference. The March on Washington helped to generate political momentum that resulted in the landmark civil rights legislation of 1964 and 1968. It also propelled Atlanta Baptist minister King to the forefront of the civil rights movement.

Local school bands provided early entertainment for the crowd gathered at the Washington Monument marshaling grounds. Joan Baez sang the anthem of the civil rights movement, "We Shall Overcome," and the mood was further enhanced by the songs of Peter, Paul, and Mary and the resounding voice of Odetta. Several minutes before the scheduled 11:30 A.M. starting time for the march to the Lincoln Memorial, the marchers set out behind the Kenilworth Knights, a local drum and bugle corps. The crowd moved too quickly for its leaders, who rushed to keep up with the marchers while marshals and news reporters tried to slow the human flow along Constitution and Independence Avenues.

At the Lincoln Memorial, more entertainers performed for the crowd massed around the reflecting pool and near the memorial steps. Performances of Bobby Darin, Josh

White, Bob Dylan, Marian Anderson, Lena Horne, Mahalia Jackson, and others were interspersed with speeches by author James Baldwin, actors Paul Newman, Charlton Heston, Burt Lancaster, Sidney Poitier, Marlon Brando, Sammy Davis, Jr., and Harry Belafonte, Nobel Prizewinner Dr. Ralph Bunche, and sports greats Jackie Robinson and Wilt Chamberlain.

The day's program included speeches by civil rights leaders John Lewis, Roy Wilkins, A. Philip Randolph, and Martin Luther King, Jr. The jobs, education, and antidiscrimination programs called for by earlier speakers were summarized in Dr. King's words:

There will be neither rest nor tranquility in America until the Negro is granted his citizenship rights. The whirlwinds of revolt will continue to shake the foundations of our nation until the bright day of justice emerges. . . . I have a dream that my four little children will one day live in a nation where they will not be judged by the color of their skin but

by the content of their character. . . . When we let freedom ring, when we let it ring from every village and every hamlet, from every state and every city, we will be able to speed up that day when all God's children, black men and white men, Jews and Gentiles, Protestants and Catholics, will be able to join hands and sing in the words of that old Negro spiritual, "Free at last! Free at last! Thank God almighty, we are free at last!"

The contribution of Martin Luther King, Jr., to minority rights was officially recognized on October 20, 1983, when, after originally opposing the legislation, President Reagan signed into law an act establishing January 15, Martin Luther King, Jr.'s birthday, as a national holiday beginning in 1986.

SOURCES: David L. Lewis, *King: A Critical Bibliography* (New York: Praeger, 1970), pp. 210–232; Lenwood G. Davis, *I Have a Dream . . .: The Life and Times of Martin Luther King, Jr.* (Westport, Conn.: Negro Universities Press, 1969), pp. 132–140.

another twenty years, after working out a compromise in which the president and congressional leaders would select its members.)

The growing number of demonstrations and sit-ins successfully created further pressure for more legislation through the classic democratic politics of mobilization of public opinion, coordinated with lobbying of political leaders. The Civil Rights Act of 1960 was passed to protect voting rights. Whenever a pattern or practice of discrimination was documented, the Justice Department, on behalf of the voter, could bring suit even against a state. The act also set penalties for obstructing a federal court order by threat of force and for illegally using and transporting explosives. But the 1960 Civil Rights Act, as well as that of 1957, had little substantive impact.

The same cannot be said about the Civil Rights Acts of 1964 and 1968, and the Voting Rights Act of 1965. Those acts marked the assumption by Congress of a leading role in the enforcement of the constitutional notion of equality for *all* Americans, as provided by the Fourteenth and Fifteenth Amendments.

The Civil Rights Act of 1964

As the civil rights movement mounted in intensity, equality before the law came to be "an idea whose time has come," in the words of conservative Senate Minority Leader Everett Dirksen. The 1964 legislation, the most far-reaching bill on civil rights in modern times, forbade discrimination on the basis of race, color, religion, gender, and national origin.

The major provisions of the act were as follows:

1. It outlawed arbitrary discrimination in voter registration.
2. It barred discrimination in public accommodations, such as hotels and restaurants, whose operations affect interstate commerce.
3. It authorized the federal government to sue to desegregate public schools and facilities.
4. It expanded the power of the Civil Rights Commission while extending its life.

Did You Know . . . That in 1963 there were more than 10,000 demonstrations for racial equality?

In 1963, a historic civil rights bill was before Congress. Many opposed the bill as too radical. To galvanize senators and representatives to pass the bill, Martin Luther King, Jr., organized a "March on Washington for Jobs and Freedom." On August 28, 1963, more than 200,000 Americans appeared in Washington to call for its passage. At the time, it was the largest demonstration in the capital's history.

Did You Know . . . That the term *affirmative action* was first used by a state when New York passed the Fair Employment Practices Law in 1945?

FILIBUSTER
In the Senate, unlimited debate to halt action on a particular bill.

CLOTURE
A method invoked to close off debate and to bring the matter under consideration to a vote in the Senate.

5. It provided for the withholding of federal funds from programs administered in a discriminatory manner.
6. It established the right to equality of opportunity in employment.

Discrimination in housing was not covered by the 1964 act.

Several factors led to the passage of the 1964 act. As we noted, there had been a dramatic change in the climate of public opinion owing to violence perpetrated against protesting African Americans and whites in the South. Second, the assassination of President John F. Kennedy in 1963 had, according to some, a significant effect on the national conscience. Many believed the civil rights program to be the legislative tribute that Congress paid to the martyred Kennedy. Finally, the 1964 act could be seen partly as the result of President Lyndon B. Johnson's vigorous espousal of the legislation after his gradual conversion to the civil rights cause.

The act was passed in Congress only after the longest **filibuster** in the history of the Senate (eighty-three days) and only after **cloture** was imposed for the first time to cut off a civil rights filibuster.

The Civil Rights Act of 1968

Martin Luther King, Jr., was assassinated on April 4, 1968. Nine days after King's death, President Johnson signed the Civil Rights Act of 1968, which forbade discrimination in most housing and provided penalties for those attempting to interfere with individual civil rights, giving protection to civil rights workers, among others. Although the open-housing provision seemed important at the time, it was rendered ineffective by that summer when the Supreme Court prohibited discrimination in the sale and rental of all housing, using as a precedent the Civil Rights Act of April 9, 1866.[17] The Court held that Section 1 of the earlier act contains a broad prohibition against any racial discrimination in the sale or rental of property. It therefore forbids private development companies from refusing to rent to an individual simply because she or he is African American. The Court noted that racial discrimination "herds men into ghettos and makes their ability to buy property turn on the color of their skin."

Employment and Affirmative Action

EQUAL EMPLOYMENT OPPORTUNITY COMMISSION (EEOC)
A commission established by the 1964 Civil Rights Act to (1) end discrimination based on race, color, religion, gender, or national origin in conditions of employment and (2) promote voluntary action programs by employers, unions, and community organizations to foster equal job opportunities.

SUBPOENA
A legal writ requiring a person's appearance in court to give testimony.

Title VII of the Civil Rights Act of 1964 is the cornerstone of employment discrimination law, prohibiting discrimination in employment based on race, color, religion, gender, or national origin. Under Title VII, executive orders were issued that banned employment discrimination by firms that received any federal funding. The 1964 Civil Rights Act created a five-member commission, the **Equal Employment Opportunity Commission (EEOC),** to administer Title VII.

The EEOC can issue interpretive guidelines and regulations, but these do not have the force of law. Rather, they give notice of the commission's enforcement policy. The EEOC also has investigatory powers: It has broad authority to require the production of documentary evidence, to hold hearings, and to **subpoena** and examine witnesses under oath.

[17]*Jones v. Mayer*, 329 U.S. 409 (1968).

To put teeth in the 1964 law, President Johnson applied the concept of **affirmative action** in 1965. Affirmative action can be defined as remedial steps taken to improve work opportunities for women, racial and ethnic minorities, and other persons considered to have been deprived of job opportunities in the past on the basis of their race, color, religion, gender, or national origin.

Reverse Discrimination: Backlash

By the early 1970s, Labor Department regulations imposing numerical employment goals and timetables had been applied to every company that did more than $10,000 worth of business of any sort with the national government. Affirmative action plans were also required whenever an employer had been ordered to develop such a plan by a court or by the EEOC because of past discrimination. Finally, labor unions that had been found to discriminate against women or minorities were required to follow affirmative action plans.

Many people became convinced that affirmative action plans had a negative impact on whites, especially white males, and such plans began to be challenged in the courts. In *McDonald v. Santa Fe Trail Transportation Co.*,[18] in 1976, the Supreme Court stated that "Title VII [of the 1964 Civil Rights Act] prohibits racial discrimination against the white petitioners upon the standards as would be applicable were they Negroes." Several employees had misappropriated the property of the Santa Fe Trail Transportation Company. Although the white employees were discharged, the black employees were reinstated. The issue of voluntary affirmative action programs was not, however, addressed in the *Santa Fe* case.

The *Bakke* Case. Alan Bakke, a Vietnam war veteran and engineer who had been turned down for medical school at the Davis campus of the University of California, discovered that his academic record was better than those of some of the minority applicants who had been admitted to the program. He sued the University of California regents, alleging **reverse discrimination.** The Davis medical school had held sixteen places out of one hundred for educationally "disadvantaged students" each year, and the administrators at that campus admitted to using race as a criterion for admission for these particular minority slots. At trial in 1974, Bakke said that his exclusion from medical school violated his rights under the Fourteenth Amendment's provision for equal protection of the laws. The trial court agreed. On appeal, the California Supreme Court agreed also. Finally, the regents of the university appealed to the U.S. Supreme Court.

On June 28, 1978, the Supreme Court handed down its decision in *Regents of the University of California v. Bakke*.[19] The Court did not actually rule against affirmative action programs but did hold that Bakke must be admitted to the UC-Davis Medical School because its admission policy had used race as the *sole* criterion for the sixteen "minority" positions. But Justice Lewis Powell, speaking for the Court, indicated that race can be considered "as a factor" among others in admissions (and presumably

AFFIRMATIVE ACTION
Policies issued in job hiring that give special consideration or compensatory treatment to traditionally disadvantaged groups in an effort to overcome present effects of past discrimination.

REVERSE DISCRIMINATION
The charge that affirmative action programs requiring preferential treatment or quotas discriminate against those who do not have minority status.

---

[18]427 U.S. 273 (1976).
[19]438 U.S. 265 (1978).

hiring) decisions. In other words, it is legal to give special consideration to "afflicted minority groups" in an effort to remedy past discrimination. Race can be one of many criteria for admission, but not the only one. So affirmative action programs, but not specific quota systems, were upheld as constitutional.

The *Weber* Case.   In 1979, the issue of reverse discrimination in employment was addressed in *United Steelworkers of America v. Weber*.[20] The lower courts in that case had relied on the *Santa Fe* decision mentioned earlier and on Section 703(j) of the Civil Rights Act of 1964.

Using the language of *Santa Fe* and Section 703(j) as a basis for their decisions, the district court and the court of appeals held that the use of a racial quota to staff an apprenticeship program violated Title VII. What was at issue was Brian F. Weber's complaint that as a white employee in Kaiser Aluminum and Chemical Corporation's plant in Gramercy, Louisiana, he was denied his rightful place in a training program that would have raised his salary had he successfully completed it. Because of the affirmative action program in his union, he was passed over in favor of African Americans with less seniority.

Even though the lower courts held in his favor, in 1979 the Supreme Court reversed their decisions. The Court stated that the prohibition against racial discrimination in Title VII must be read against the background of the legislative history of Title VII calling for voluntary or local resolution of the discrimination problems and against the historical context from which the 1964 Civil Rights Act arose. In other words, the union apprenticeship program at Kaiser Aluminum violated the words of the Civil Rights Act of 1964, but not the spirit. Essentially, any form of reverse discrimination—even explicit quotas—is permissible provided that it is the result of a legislative, executive, or judicial finding of past discrimination.

The Court's More Recent Record on Reverse Bias

In 1984, in *Firefighters Local Union No. 1784 v. Stotts*,[21] the Court said that the layoffs of Memphis firefighters had to be done by seniority unless there were African-American employees who could prove they were victims of racial bias. But in 1986, in *Wygant v. Jackson Board of Education*,[22] the Court sent the signal that affirmative action could apply to hiring, but not to layoffs. This mixed message came from a case brought by a group of white teachers in Jackson, Michigan, challenging a labor contract that called for laying off three white teachers for every faculty member belonging to a minority group in order to preserve the school system's racial and ethnic ratios. In a five-to-four vote, the Court's majority said that the Jackson plan violated the Fourteenth Amendment's guarantee of equal protection of the laws. In a case involving Alabama state troopers, the use of temporary quotas to expand the access of blacks to the formerly all-white police force was upheld.

[20]443 U.S. 1963 (1979).
[21]467 U.S. 561 (1984).
[22]476 U.S. 267 (1986).

In 1989, the Supreme Court considered whether whites could challenge employment decisions made on the basis of an earlier judgment that included goals for hiring African Americans as firefighters in the city of Birmingham, Alabama. White firefighters who had not been parties in the earlier proceedings alleged that because of their race, they were being denied promotions in favor of less-qualified African Americans. The Supreme Court held that the white firefighters could challenge those employment decisions.[23] In another 1989 decision, the Court overturned a local government minority-preference program, signaling to dozens of cities and states that hundreds of affirmative action programs may also be invalid.[24] On racial discrimination, the Court made it harder for minority workers to sue employers.[25] In another ruling, racial harassment was exempted from a widely used antibias law.[26] The Court also held that employment-discrimination laws do not apply outside the territorial limits of the United States.[27]

The Civil Rights Act of 1991

By 1990, civil rights activists were arguing that the conservative 1989 rulings of the Supreme Court made it difficult for victims of employment discrimination to prove their cases. Believing that the courts could not be counted on to expand civil rights protections, some activists turned to Congress. Congress responded with the Civil Rights Act of 1991, which effectively overturned the conservative rulings. Specifically, the act makes it easier for workers to sue employers. Another section of the act includes racial harassment under the widely used antibias law from which the Supreme Court had exempted it. Also, the act now bars challenges to earlier judgments that include goals for hiring minorities by persons in the same circumstances as the firefighters in the Birmingham case—thus overruling the Supreme Court's 1989 decision on this issue. Another provision extends coverage of employment discrimination laws to U.S. citizens working outside the territorial limits of the United States for American companies. Finally, the act provides for the recovery of more damages, including punitive damages, in intentional discrimination cases and provides for jury trials in cases under Title VII of the Civil Rights Act of 1964.

The Voting Rights Act of 1965

The Fourteenth Amendment provided for equal protection of the laws. The Fifteenth Amendment, ratified on February 3, 1870, stated that "the right of citizens of the United States to vote shall not be denied or abridged by the United States or by any State on account of race, color, or previous condition of servitude." Immediately after the adoption of

---

[23]*Martin v. Wilks*, 490 U.S. 755 (1989).

[24]*Richmond v. J. A. Croson Co.*, 488 U.S. 469 (1989).

[25]*Wards Cove Packing Co. v. Atonio*, 490 U.S. 642 (1989).

[26]*Patterson v. McLean Credit Union*, 491 U.S. 164 (1989).

[27]*Equal Employment Opportunity Commission v. Arabian American Oil Co.*, 111 S.Ct. 1227 (1991).

those amendments, African Americans in the South began to participate in political life—but only because of the presence of federal government troops and northern Radical Republicans who controlled the state legislatures.

Historical Barriers to African-American Political Participation

The brief enfranchisement of African Americans ended after 1877 when southern Democrats regained control of state governments after the federal troops that occupied the South during the Reconstruction era were withdrawn. Social pressure, threats of violence, and the terrorist tactics of the Ku Klux Klan combined to dissuade African Americans from voting. Southern politicians, using everything except race as a formal criterion, passed laws that effectively deprived them of the right to vote.

This was the era of the **white primary** and the "**grandfather clause.**" By using the ruse that political party primaries were private, southern whites were allowed to exclude African Americans. The Supreme Court in *Grovey v. Townsend*[28] upheld such exclusion. Indeed, it was not until 1944 in *Smith v. Allwright*[29] that the highest court finally found the white primary to be a violation of the Fifteenth Amendment. The Court reasoned that the political party was actually performing a state function in holding a primary election, not acting as a private group. By being denied a vote in the primary, African Americans had been prevented from participating in the selection of public officials from the end of Reconstruction until World War II. The grandfather clause restricted the voting franchise to those who could prove that their grandfathers had voted before 1867. Most African Americans were automatically disenfranchised by this provision. In *Guinn v. United States,* the Supreme Court held that grandfather clauses were unconstitutional.[30]

Another device to prevent African Americans from voting was the **poll tax,** requiring the payment of a fee to vote. This practice assured the exclusion of poor African Americans from the political process. It wasn't until the passage of the Twenty-fourth Amendment, ratified in 1964, that the poll tax as a precondition to voting was eliminated. That amendment, however, applied only to federal elections. In *Harper v. Virginia State Board of Elections,*[31] the Supreme Court declared that the payment of any poll tax as a condition for voting in any election is unconstitutional.

By the 1960s, the distribution of seats in state legislatures among state voting districts had become another obstacle to African Americans' political participation. Frequent use of area instead of population as a basis for voting districts led to (white) rural representatives dominating state legislatures. In 1962, the Supreme Court decided that federal courts could hear cases involving state districting, and in 1964, the Court ruled that population is the only acceptable basis for the distribution of seats in a legislative body.[32]

WHITE PRIMARY
A state primary election that restricts voting only to whites; outlawed by the Supreme Court in 1944.

GRANDFATHER CLAUSE
A device used by southern states to exempt whites from state taxes and literacy laws originally intended to disenfrancise African-American voters. It restricted the voting franchise to those who could prove that their grandfathers had voted before 1867.

POLL TAX
A special tax that must be paid as a qualification for voting. The Twenty-fourth Amendment to the Constitution outlawed the poll tax in national elections, and in 1966 the Supreme Court declared it unconstitutional in all elections.

---

[28]295 U.S. 45 (1935).
[29]321 U.S. 649 (1944).
[30]238 U.S. 347 (1915).
[31]383 U.S. 663 (1966).
[32]*Baker v. Carr,* 369 U.S. 186 (1962); *Reynolds v. Sim,* 377 U.S. 533 (1964).

As late as 1960, only 29.1 percent of African Americans of voting age were registered in the southern states, in stark contrast to 61.1 percent of whites. In 1965, Martin Luther King, Jr., took action to change all that. Selma, the seat of Dallas County, Alabama, was chosen as the site to dramatize the voting rights problem. In Dallas County, only 2 percent of eligible African Americans had registered to vote by the beginning of 1965. King organized a fifty-mile march from Selma to the state capital in Montgomery. He didn't get very far. Acting on orders of Governor George Wallace to disband the marchers, state troopers did so with a vengeance— with tear gas, night sticks, and whips.

Once again the national government was required to intervene to force compliance with the law. President Johnson nationalized the National Guard, and the march continued. During the march, the president went on television to address a special joint session of Congress urging passage of new legislation to assure African Americans the right to vote. The events during the Selma march and Johnson's dramatic speech, in which he invoked the slogan of the civil rights movement ("We shall overcome"), were credited for the swift passage of the Voting Rights Act of 1965.

Provisions of the Voting Rights Act of 1965

The act had two major provisions. The first one outlawed discriminatory voter registration tests. The second major section authorized federal registration of persons and federally administered voting procedures in any political subdivision or state that discriminated electorally against a particular group.[33] In part, the act provided that certain political subdivisions could not change their voting procedures without federal approval. The act targeted counties, mostly in the South, in which less than 50 percent of the eligible population was registered to vote. Federal voter registrars were sent to these areas to register African Americans who had been restricted by local registrars. Within one week after the act was passed, forty-five federal examiners were sent to the South. A massive voter-registration drive covered the country.

In 1970, the Voting Rights Act was extended to August 1975. In 1975, Congress extended the act to August 1982, and it was again extended in 1983. The act originally brought federal supervision to areas of the country known for discriminating against African Americans in the voter-registration process. But in 1970 and in 1975, the law was extended to other states and to other groups, including Spanish-speaking Americans, Asian Americans, and Native Americans, including Alaskan natives. As a result of this act and its extensions and of the large-scale voter-registration drives in the South, the number of African Americans registered to vote climbed dramatically, until, by 1980, 55.8 percent of African Americans of voting age in the South were registered.

By 1986, the number of registered African-American voters nationally was more than 11 million. By 1993, there were more than 7,200 black elected officials in the United Sates, including the mayors of Atlanta, Detroit, the District of Columbia, Los Angeles, and Philadelphia. In 1984, the

The Ku Klux Klan, or KKK, is well known for its burning-cross symbol. The KKK was organized during the Reconstruction period after the Civil War for the purpose of preventing ex-slaves from benefiting from the civil rights guaranteed by postwar federal legislation and constitutional amendments. After World War I, the KKK also became anti-Catholic and anti-Semitic.

---

[33]In addition, the act indicated that in Congress's opinion the state poll tax was unconstitutional.

POLITICS AND RACE

Rage and Opportunity

The twentieth century's worst U.S. race riot—and the costliest riot in U.S. history—occurred in Los Angeles in April and May, 1992. Fifty people were killed, and more than 2,000 people were injured. Approximately 17,000 police officers and National Guard and federal troops were sent in or placed on standby. The civil disorder started when it was announced that a jury had acquitted four white police officers of charges relating to a beating in 1991 of Rodney King, an African American and a Los Angeles resident. The beating had been videotaped, and a portion of the videotape was shown on national television.

Many people were incredulous at the news of the acquittal. Some people were also surprised by the reaction of the residents in south central Los Angeles, an area that also saw riots in the "long, hot summers" of the 1960s. Other cities, including Atlanta, New York, San Francisco, and Seattle, also experienced civil disturbances. But not everyone was surprised. More than two decades earlier, Martin Luther King, Jr., said, "A riot is the language of the unheard." For years, African-American leaders warned about the rising level of frustration in America's cities, saying that society must rededicate itself to the goal of equality or endure more strife. They claim that

the root of the problem may be that we have not done enough to attain our goals of equal justice and equal opportunity.

Promoting racial equality and attacking poverty were part of President Lyndon Johnson's Great Society program in the 1960s. Priorities changed over the decades, however. Some observers believe that over the past twenty-five years, elected officials neglected problems caused by racism and poverty. During the 1980s, President Ronald Reagan attempted to reduce what remained of Johnson's Great Society program. Even as the federal budget doubled, aid to cities was cut by more than half, and assistance for low-income housing was reduced by two-thirds.

During the past two decades, other factors that undercut the economy of the cities included the loss of unskilled manufacturing jobs and the increased cost of housing. Los Angeles lost 200,000 jobs in 1991 alone. The illegal drug trade seemed to replace the lost jobs, fostering violence. Changing social attitudes, including a decreased commitment to the family as a social unit, had an especially negative impact in poor urban areas. The chasm between an African-American underclass (one of every three African Americans who reside in large cities lives below the

poverty line) and the rest of American society widened. Some observers say this created two societies—a white suburban society shielded from urban problems and an urban society segregated from the mainstream.

American political leaders responded to the Rodney King verdict and the ensuing violence with varying degrees of awareness. Senator Bill Bradley of New Jersey was direct and eloquent. He said, "The divide among races in our cities deepens, with white Americans more and more unwilling to spend the money necessary to ameliorate the physical conditions or to see why the absence of meaning in the lives of many urban children threatens the future of their own children." What occurred in Los Angeles in the spring of 1992 provided an opportunity to learn from mistakes. As Bradley put it, "If we as a nation continue to ignore the racial reality of our times, tiptoe around it, demagogue it, or flee from it, we're going to pay an enormous price." Bradley proposed a plan to help end violence in the cities, to help families and children, and to renew investment in public works and job training. Bradley noted, "The future of urban America will take one of three paths—abandonment, encirclement, or conversion."

Reverend Jesse Jackson became the first African-American candidate to compete seriously for the Democratic presidential nomination. In 1988, a renewed effort to register thousands more African Americans and other minority voters helped Jackson achieve an impressive total primary and caucus vote. In 1989, Virginia became the first state to elect an African-American governor.

Hispanics in American Society

▼

The second largest minority group in America can be classified loosely as Hispanics—or individuals from Spanish-speaking backgrounds. Even though this minority group represents over 8 percent of the American population, its diversity and geographical dispersion have hindered its ability to achieve political power, particularly at the national level. Mexican Americans constitute the majority of the Hispanic population. Of the over twenty million Hispanics in the United States, Mexican Americans are a majority. The next largest group is Puerto Ricans, then Cubans, and finally Hispanics from Central and South America.

Economically, Hispanics in the United States are less well off than non-Hispanic whites but a little better off than African Americans. About 27 percent of them live in poverty. Unlike the economic situation of African Americans, that of Hispanic Americans is worsening. The percentage of their population below the poverty level rose over three percentage points between 1982 and 1992. The unemployment rate for Hispanics decreased less than the rate for any other group, and Hispanics' real median income actually dropped during that period. Hispanic leaders have attributed these declines to language barriers and lack of training, (which lead to low-paying jobs), and to continuing immigration, (which deflates statistical progress).

Politically, Hispanics are gaining power in some states. By 1993, there were fourteen Hispanics in the United States Congress, about 3.2% of the total membership.

Mexican Americans

Mexicans were not brought to the colonies by force. Some of them were in the southwestern territory of what eventually became the United States before the settlement of the eastern shores by the early English colonists.

Did You Know . . . That the Hispanic population of the United States increased by 39 percent between 1980 and 1990 and is now approximately 21 million? Hispanics make up 8.2 percent of the U.S. population and are expected to surpass African Americans as the largest minority in the next century.

▼

Spanish-language billboards in Miami, Florida, demonstrate the pervasiveness of Spanish-speaking cultures in some sections of the United States. Indeed, southern Florida leads the nation in the number of Americans who speak a language other than English at home. In Dade County, 57 percent of the residents do not speak English at home. In the adjacent city of Hialeah, the figure is 90 percent.

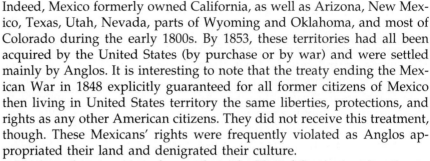

Did You Know . . . That Florida's 1.5 million Hispanics own 32,000 businesses that contribute almost $3 billion annually to the Florida economy?

Indeed, Mexico formerly owned California, as well as Arizona, New Mexico, Texas, Utah, Nevada, parts of Wyoming and Oklahoma, and most of Colorado during the early 1800s. By 1853, these territories had all been acquired by the United States (by purchase or by war) and were settled mainly by Anglos. It is interesting to note that the treaty ending the Mexican War in 1848 explicitly guaranteed for all former citizens of Mexico then living in United States territory the same liberties, protections, and rights as any other American citizens. They did not receive this treatment, though. These Mexicans' rights were frequently violated as Anglos appropriated their land and denigrated their culture.

Mexicans have continued to settle in the United States, immigrating to this country primarily for economic reasons. Some Mexicans look to the United States for employment and a chance to better their lives. Most Mexican Americans still live in the southwestern United States, but many have moved to Indiana, Illinois, Pennsylvania, and Ohio.

Political Participation.   Mexican Americans have a very low level of political participation in national elections. Mexican Americans have faced numerous barriers to voting, as have African Americans. Not the least of these is the language barrier for those unable to read English. The Voting Rights Act extension of 1970 alleviated this problem somewhat by requiring ballots to be printed in both English and Spanish in districts where at least 5 percent of the registered voters are Spanish speaking.

Puerto Ricans

Because Puerto Rico is a U.S. Commonwealth, its inhabitants are American citizens. As such, they may freely move between Puerto Rico and the United States. Most of them who come to the continental United States reside in the New York–New Jersey area.

In Puerto Rico, Puerto Ricans use U.S. currency, U.S. mails, and U.S. courts. In Puerto Rico, they are also eligible for U.S. welfare benefits and food stamps, but they pay no federal taxes unless they move to the continental United States. By 1993, almost three-fourths of Puerto Ricans living in Puerto Rico were eligible for food stamps. Those who come to the mainland do not fare much better, owing to economic and language barriers and racial discrimination.

Puerto Ricans have had few political successes on the mainland. There are more than a million Puerto Ricans living in New York City, constituting at least 10 percent of the city's population, but only about 30 percent are registered to vote. Other statistics show that currently there are only a few Puerto Rican city council members and only one Puerto Rican member of Congress. In New York City's massive bureaucracy, only a small percentage of the administrators are Puerto Rican.

Cuban Americans

Unlike their Hispanic brothers and sisters from Mexico and Puerto Rico, Cuban Americans chose to come to the United States for political, as well as economic, reasons. They left Cuba to escape the communist regime of Fidel Castro. Many of the emigrés came from the educated middle class,

POLITICS AND POWER

Population and Political Involvement

In the largest effort at political empowerment by an American minority group, Hispanics across the United States are demanding increased political power through greater representation at all levels of elective office.

Efforts to attain this goal began with the 1990 census. Political representation is based in part on population. Legislative representatives are elected from political districts, and the boundaries of the districts are redrawn after every census. Under the Voting Rights Act of 1965, districts must be drawn so that minorities have the chance to win an election wherever possible.

From the Puerto Rican community in New York to Mexican-American communities in California and Texas, Hispanics attempted to achieve the fullest count of Hispanic residents in the census. Nationally, in the 1980s, the Hispanic population grew more than five times faster than the average of other ethnic groups. After the census, Hispanics fought for effective representation in the new districts. The census figures include large numbers of immigrants and young people, however. In elections, only voters count.

More than 60 percent of Hispanic adults are citizens, but they register to vote in low numbers. Even those Hispanics who are registered to vote are less likely to actually go to the polls on election day. They are younger, poorer, and less educated than Americans as a whole—factors that are associated with low voter turnout. With the 1990 redistricting, there may be more political involvement. A new district can give them a chance to elect their own representatives.

Hispanic leaders generally have urged members of their communities to become politically involved. Different leaders propose different approaches to Hispanic participation in American society. Some urge Hispanics to move out of their ethnic enclaves and to assimilate socially and economically into the larger society. Others suggest that Hispanics not move from their communities but become fully involved in the political system nonetheless. Despite these differences of opinions, all Hispanic leaders emphasize the importance of voting.

and, although they had to leave most of their financial assets behind, their education and training helped them to become established economically with relative ease. In Miami, for example, one can find numerous examples of former Cuban professionals who started out as taxi drivers and today own banks, retail stores, and law practices.

In 1980, President Carter allowed more than 150,000 Cubans to enter Florida through the so-called Mariel boatlift. This wave of Cuban immigrants was mostly lower class and unskilled. A thousand Mariel Cubans had been released from Cuban prisons and mental institutions. The Mariel Cubans' assimilation into even the heavily Latin-accented culture of Miami was noticeably less successful than that of their earlier compatriots.

A majority of Cuban Americans reside in southern Florida, although some live in New York City and elsewhere. Economically, they constitute a major force in the southern Florida region. Politically, they have been very successful in gaining power within city and county governments. Even Miami's mayor was born in Cuba. As a group, Cuban Americans are known for being staunchly anticommunist and strongly oppose any attempts of the American government to improve relations with communist Cuba. Their political influence will certainly rise as their percentage of the population increases. In Dade County, Hispanics, particularly Cubans, now constitute the majority of the county's population.

Bilingualism

All Hispanic groups are concerned about the preservation of their language and heritage. Bilingual education programs are supported by many Hispanic groups as a civil right. This claim was established by the Supreme Court in 1974, when it required a school district in California to provide special programs for Chinese students with language difficulties if there were a substantial number of these children.[34] There is disagreement over the purpose of bilingual education. Some people feel such programs should be temporary, helping students only until they master English. Others want them to be permanent programs to help immigrant students preserve their cultural heritage.

Bilingualism extends beyond the education system. In many parts of the United States, signs, announcements, advertisements, and government documents are printed in languages other than English. Concern over the number of immigrants who do not speak English led California voters in 1986 to approve a law making English the state's official language. Similar measures were adopted by referendum in 1988 in Arizona, Colorado, and Florida. Members of Congress have even proposed an amendment to the U.S. Constitution making English our national language. Such laws affect government documents and official communication, not private use of language.

Native Americans: An American Tragedy

When America was "discovered," there were about 10 million Native Americans, or "Indians," living in the New World. It is estimated that they had inhabited areas from the north slope of Alaska to the southern tip of South America for at least 30,000 years before Europeans arrived. By 1900, the number of Native Americans in the continental United States had declined to less than half a million owing to the effects of war and diseases brought to the continent by European immigrants. In the latest census, about two million individuals identified themselves as Native Americans. The five states with the largest Native-American populations are Oklahoma, Arizona, California, New Mexico, and Alaska.

Native Americans have not fared well economically, as is evident in Figure 5-1. From the point of view of health, Indians are even worse off than their economic status shows. Death rates per 100,000 of the population are two and sometimes three or more times the national average.

The Appropriation of Indian Lands

When the Confederation Congress passed the Northwest Ordinance in 1787, it stated that "the utmost good faith shall always be observed towards the Indians; their lands and property shall never be taken from them without their consent; and in their property, rights, and liberty, they shall never be invaded or disturbed, unless in just and lawful wars authorized by congress." In 1789, Congress designated the Native-American tribes as foreign

FIGURE 5-1 ■ Native American and White Family Earnings Compared

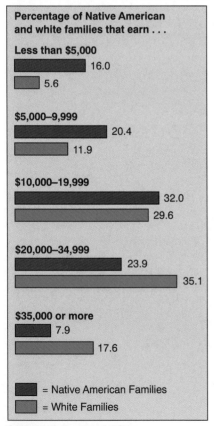

Percentage of Native American and white families that earn . . .

Less than $5,000
16.0
5.6

$5,000–9,999
20.4
11.9

$10,000–19,999
32.0
29.6

$20,000–34,999
23.9
35.1

$35,000 or more
7.9
17.6

■ = Native American Families
▨ = White Families

SOURCE: U.S. Department of Commerce.

[34]*Lau v. Nichols*, 414 U.S. 563 (1974).

nations to enable the government to sign land and boundary treaties with them.

During the next hundred years, many agreements were made with the Native-American tribes; however, many were broken by Congress, as well as by individuals who wanted Native-American lands for settlement or exploration. In 1830, Congress instructed the Bureau of Indian Affairs to remove all Native-American tribes to lands west of the Mississippi River to free land east of the Mississippi for white settlement. From that time on, Native Americans who refused to be "removed" to whatever lands were designated for them were forcibly moved. During the resettlement of the Cherokee tribe in 1838–1839, on a forced march known as the "Trail of Tears," nearly 4,000 of 15,000 Cherokees died. With the passage of the Dawes Act (General Allotment Act) of 1887, the goal of Congress became the "assimilation" of Native Americans into American society. Each family was allotted acreage within the reservation to farm, and the rest was sold to whites. The number of acres in reservation status was reduced from 140 million acres to about 47 million acres. Tribes that refused to cooperate with this plan lost their reservations altogether.

Native-American Political Response

Native Americans have been relatively unsuccessful in garnering political power. This is partly because the tribes themselves have no official representation in government and because the tribes are small and scattered. In the 1960s, the National Indian Youth Council (NIYC) was the first group to become identified with Indian militancy. At the end of the 1960s, a small group of persons identifying themselves as Indians occupied Alcatraz Island, claiming that the island was part of their ancestral lands. In 1972, several hundred Native Americans marched to Washington and occupied the Bureau of Indian Affairs (BIA). (Founded in 1824 as part of the War Department, today the BIA runs the Indian reservation system with the tribes.) They arrived in a caravan labeled "The Trail of Broken Treaties." In 1973, supporters of the American Indian Movement (AIM) took over Wounded Knee, South Dakota, which had been the site of the mas-

Navajo Council in Window Rock, Arizona. The council, which governs tribal affairs, consists of representatives elected from local areas.

sacre of at least 150 Sioux Indians by the U.S. Army in 1890.[35] The goal
of these demonstrations was to protest federal policy and to dramatize
injustices toward Native Americans.

The siege at Wounded Knee focused the anger of Native Americans on
the BIA and the way their affairs were being administered by the agency.
The American Indian Policy Review Commission, established by Congress, agreed in its 1977 report that the BIA mishandled Indian money,
did not protect Indian property rights, and neglected Indian safety. Recently, however, the BIA has let more and more tribes control the police,
job training, educational, and social programs that the BIA used to manage. Nonetheless, there are still numerous conflicts between Indian tribes
and the BIA, as well as between them and state governments.

As more Americans have become aware of the concerns of Native
Americans, Congress has started to compensate for past injustices. Courts,
too, have shown a greater willingness to recognize Indian treaty rights.
For example, cases dealing with the right of present-day Native Americans
to a share of the annual salmon harvest in Washington involved, in part,
enforcement of nineteenth-century treaty provisions.[36] In a decision that
may open the way for other long-standing Native-American claims, the
Supreme Court ruled that three tribes of Oneida Indians could claim damages for the use of tribal land that had been unlawfully conveyed in
1795.[37] Lower court cases decided since this ruling may limit recovery on
other similar claims, however.[38]

Asian Americans

Because Asian Americans have a relatively high median income, they are
typically not thought of as being victims of discrimination. This certainly
was not always the case. The Chinese Exclusion Act of 1882 prevented
persons from China and Japan from coming to the United States to prospect for gold or to work on the railroads or in factories in the West.
Japanese-American students were segregated into special schools after the
1906 San Francisco earthquake so that white children could use their
buildings. The 1941 Japanese bombing of Pearl Harbor intensified the fear
and hatred of the Japanese. Executive Order 9066, signed by President
Franklin D. Roosevelt on February 19, 1942, set up "relocation" camps for
virtually all Japanese Americans living in the United States. The Japanese
were required to dispose of their property, usually at below-market prices.
It wasn't until 1944 and 1945 that the relocation camps were closed and
the prisoners freed after a December 18, 1944, Supreme Court ruling

[35]This famous incident was the subject of Dee Brown's best-selling book, *Bury My Heart at
Wounded Knee* (New York: Holt, Rinehart, and Winston, 1971), published two years before
the siege.
[36]*United States v. Washington*, 384 F.Supp. 312 (W.D. Wash. 1974); affirmed 520 F.2d 676 (9th
Cir. 1975); substantially affirmed, *Washington v. Washington State Commercial Passenger Fishing
Vessel Association*, 443 U.S. 658 (1979).
[37]*County of Oneida v. Oneida Indian Nation*, 470 U.S. 226 (1985).
[38]For example, *Yankton Sioux Tribe of Indians v. South Dakota*, 796 F.2d 241 (9th Cir. 1986).

deemed such activity illegal.[39] Three Japanese Americans who had been jailed for resisting relocation during World War II successfully sued the United States in 1983. They won damages, and their 1942 convictions were overturned because of their claim that the army lied about the possibility of security threats. In 1988, Congress provided funds to compensate former camp inhabitants or their survivors—$1.25 billion for 65,000 people.

Both the Japanese and the Chinese have overcome initial prejudice to lead America's ethnic groups in median income and median education. Recently, however, a new group of Asians have had to fight discrimination—those from Southeast Asia. More than a million Indo-Chinese war refugees, most from Vietnam, have come into the United States in the last twenty years. Like their predecessors, the newer immigrants have quickly increased their median income; only about one-third of all such households receive welfare of any sort. Most have come with families and have been sponsored by American families or organizations, so they have had good support systems to help them get started. As with the Chinese and the Japanese, however, once they become established, they are seen as economic threats by those who believe they are being displaced by the new immigrants.

The Task before Us—Overcoming Our Prejudices

Some observers suggest that "melting pot" is not an accurate metaphor for the racial and ethnic mix in America. Because there appears to be little social interaction among ethnic groups, "salad bowl" might more accurately depict the hodgepodge of groups that make up the population of the United States. Taking this comparison a step further, political circumstances in the United States might be described as "salad dressing." Our ideals profess equality of rights for *all* citizens, but our reality has yet to match our ideals.

Can we practice what we profess? In the United States, the notion that one's own racial or ethnic background is superior to that of others has always infected relations among racial and ethnic groups. In other words, racism probably has always complicated our domestic social and political life.

Of course, prejudice is not limited to relations between African Americans and whites. Relations among all ethnic groups are at least sometimes tainted by the poison of prejudice or racism. Irrespective of ethnicity, relations between men and women are often tainted by the poison of sexism. Can we overcome our prejudices? How this question is answered will determine our future because our nation is now more diverse than at any time in its past. In the 1990s, half of the new entrants into the work force will be African American, Hispanic, or Asian. This trend will increase in the next century. The ability to overcome our prejudices will determine whether the United States becomes, as Ben Wattenberg describes us, the first truly "universal nation" or whether we self-destruct in ethnic and racial conflict.

---

[39]See Dylan S. Meyer, *Uprooted American: The Japanese-American and the War Relocation Authority During World War II* (Tucson: University of Arizona Press, 1971).

Women's Position in Society

In 1776, Abigail Adams reminded her husband, John Adams, to "remember the women." Despite this reminder, women, although considered citizens in the early years of the nation, had no political rights. The first political cause in which women became actively engaged was the slavery abolition movement. Even male abolitionists felt that women should not take an active role on the subject.

In 1848, Lucretia Mott and Elizabeth Cady Stanton organized the first women's rights convention in Seneca Falls, New York. The three hundred persons who attended approved a declaration of sentiments: "We hold these truths to be self-evident: that all men *and women* are created equal." In the following twelve years, groups of feminists held seven conventions in different cities in the Midwest and in the East. With the outbreak of the Civil War, however, advocates of women's rights were urged to put their support behind the war effort, and most agreed.

The Suffrage Issue and the Fifteenth Amendment

"The right of citizens of the United States to vote shall not be denied or abridged by the United States or by any State on account of race, color, or previous condition of servitude." So reads Section 1 of Amendment XV to the Constitution, ratified on March 30, 1870. The campaign for the passage of this amendment split the women's **suffrage** movement. Militant feminists wanted to add "sex" to "race, color, or previous condition of servitude." Other feminists, along with many men, opposed this view; they wanted to separate African-American suffrage and women's suffrage to ensure the passage of the amendment. So, although the African-American press supported the women's suffrage movement, it became separate from the racial equality movement. Still, some women attempted to vote in the years following the Civil War. One, Virginia Louisa Minor, was arrested and convicted in 1872. She appealed to the Supreme Court, but the Court upheld her conviction.[40]

Susan B. Anthony and Elizabeth Cady Stanton formed the National Suffrage Association in 1869. According to their view, women's suffrage was a means to achieve major improvements in the economic and social situation of women in the United States. In other words, the vote was to be used to obtain a larger end. Lucy Stone, however, felt that the vote was the only major issue. Members of the American Women's Suffrage Association, founded by Stone and others, traveled to each state, addressed state legislatures, wrote, published, and argued their convictions. They achieved only limited success. In 1890, the two organizations quit battling and joined forces. The National American Women's Suffrage Association had only one goal—the enfranchisement of women—but it made little progress.

By the early 1900s, small radical splinter groups were formed, such as the Congressional Union headed by Alice Paul. This organization worked

SUFFRAGE
The right to vote; the franchise.

Elizabeth Cady Stanton (1815–1902) was a social reformer and a women's suffrage leader. At her wedding in 1840 to Henry B. Stanton, she insisted on dropping the word "obey" from the marriage vows. She wrote *The History of Women's Suffrage,* which was published in 1886.

---

[40]*Minor v. Happersett,* 21 Wall. 162 (1874). The Supreme Court reasoned that the right to vote was a privilege of state, not federal, citizenship. The Court did not consider privileges of state citizenship to be protected by the Fourteenth Amendment.

solely for the passage of an amendment to the national Constitution. Willing to use "unorthodox" means to achieve its goal, this group and others took to the streets. There were parades, hunger strikes, arrests, and jailings. Finally, in 1920, seventy-two years after the Seneca Falls convention, the Nineteenth Amendment was passed: "The rights of citizens of the United States to vote shall not be denied or abridged by the United States or by any State on account of sex." Women were thus enfranchised.

Although today it may seem that the United States was slow to give women the vote, it was really not too far behind the rest of the world. The first countries to grant women electoral equality with men were New Zealand in 1893, Finland in 1906, Norway in 1913, and Denmark and Iceland in 1915. Toward the end of World War I, or soon after, many more Western nations granted women the right to vote.

Women's Continued Struggle for Equal Status

Obviously, the right to vote does not guarantee political power. It has been more than half a century since women obtained the right to vote in most countries of the Western World, yet the number of women who have held high political positions can be counted on one's fingers. Women have become elected heads of government in India, Sri Lanka, Israel, Bolivia, Argentina, Barbados, the Phillipines, Pakistan, and Great Britain. There have been a few women ministers in a number of countries, but normally these ministries are concerned primarily with so-called "women's interests," such as family affairs or social welfare. In the United States, no woman has yet been nominated for president by a major political party—although public opinion polls suggest ever-increasing support for the idea of a female president. In Congress, the men's club atmosphere prevails. A few women senators have been elected. As of 1993, there were 48 women members of the House of Representatives—only 11 percent of the total. Of the more than 10,000 members of the House of Representatives who have served, only 1 percent have been women. No woman has yet held one of the major leadership positions in the House or in the Senate.

Women have also been meagerly represented in federal political appointments, although this situation is changing. Franklin Roosevelt appointed the first woman to a cabinet post—Frances Perkins, who was secretary of labor from 1933 to 1945. In 1969, President Nixon declared that "a woman can and should be able to do any political job that a man can do." But by the time of his resignation in 1974, he had not appointed a woman to either the cabinet or the Supreme Court. His successor, Gerald Ford, appointed a woman as secretary of housing and urban development. President Carter (1977–1981) had three women in his cabinet and appointed many female judges. Ronald Reagan (1981–1989) appointed women to two major cabinet posts and to head the U.S. delegation to the United Nations. He is also credited with a historical first in his appointment of Sandra Day O'Connor to the Supreme Court in 1981. President Bush appointed two women to cabinet posts, and a woman served as his international trade negotiator. President Clinton named three women to cabinet posts.

Susan B. Anthony (1820–1906) was a leader of the women's suffrage movement who was also active in the anti-alcohol and antislavery movements. In 1869, with Elizabeth Cady Stanton, she founded the National Women's Suffrage Association. In 1888, she organized the International Council of Women and, in 1904, the International Women's Suffrage Alliance, in Berlin.

Women have had more success at attaining elective office in state legislatures and local governments. Several women have been elected to governorships. Over 20 percent of the legislators in each of eighteen states are women, and the same is true of city council members in large and medium-size cities. Chicago, Houston, and San Francisco have had women mayors, as have 17 percent of U.S. cities with populations of more than thirty thousand.

The representation of women in political office does not reflect their participation as voters. The absolute turnout of women voters nationally is higher than that of male voters.

The National Organization for Women (NOW)

Although often identified as middle-class, the modern women's movement seeks to define sexism and to eradicate it from all spheres of life for all women. Perhaps the most prominent of the organizations associated with the women's movement is the National Organization for Women (NOW). NOW was formed in 1966 by writer Betty Friedan and others who were dissatisfied with the lack of aggressive action against sex discrimination by the then-largest women's organizations—the National Federation of Business and Professional Women's Clubs and the League of Women Voters. The specific issue around which NOW coalesced was the failure of the Equal Employment Opportunity Commission (EEOC) to enjoin newspapers from running separate want ads for men and women. NOW grew from its 300 members in 1966 to over 250,000 members in 1993. It has continued to be one of the leading pressure groups in the struggle for women's rights.

The Supreme Court and Sex Discrimination

Laws that include different provisions for men and women are not always struck down by the Supreme Court. The Court has established standards for determining whether gender classifications are acceptable. Laws with racial classifications are always "suspect" and are invalidated unless the government can prove that the classifications are "necessary to a compelling objective" (in fact, laws with racial classifications have been invalidated in almost every case). Laws that classify by sex are permissible if they "substantially relate to important governmental interests." For example, a law punishing males but not females for statutory rape is valid because of the important governmental interest in preventing teenage pregnancy in those circumstances.[41] A law granting a husband, as "head and master" of the house, the right to unilaterally sell or give away property owned jointly with his wife is not valid.[42] This standard for evaluating the acceptability of gender classifications was established by the Court in 1971 in *Reed v. Reed*,[43] a case involving an Idaho law that gave men preference over women in administering estates of dead relatives. In 1973, the Supreme Court struck down a federal law providing that ser-

---

[41]*Michael M. v. Superior Court*, 450 U.S. 464 (1981).
[42]*Kirchberg v. Feenstra*, 450 U.S. 455 (1981).
[43]404 U.S. 71 (1971).

vicemen's wives automatically receive certain benefits but servicewomen's husbands receive these benefits only if they demonstrate a certain degree of need.[44] In this case, some of the justices unsuccessfully tried to apply to gender cases the "suspect" standard applied to race cases.

NOW and the Equal Rights Amendment

Perhaps more than any other women's group, NOW has championed the passage of the Equal Rights Amendment (ERA), which states:

> Equality of rights under the law shall not be denied or abridged by the United States or by any state on account of sex.

ERA was first introduced in Congress in 1923 by leaders of the National Women's Party who felt that getting the vote would not be enough to change women's status. After years during which the amendment was not even given a hearing in Congress, it was finally approved by both chambers in 1972.

As we noted in Chapter 2, any constitutional amendment must be ratified by the legislatures (or conventions) in three-fourths of the states before it can become law. Supporters of ERA initially had until March 22, 1979, to obtain ratification by thirty-eight states.

By March 22, 1973, ERA had been ratified by thirty states—eight less than were needed. At the same time opposing forces were becoming organized and militant.

Opposition to ERA: The Conservative Reaction

Phyllis Schlafly mobilized the sentiments of many women and men against ERA through the Stop-ERA and the Eagle Forum organizations. Schlafly claimed that pro-ERA groups were hostile to all the values women had traditionally held and to the general welfare of women.

The necessary thirty-eight states failed to ratify the amendment within the seven-year period, in spite of the support given to ERA in numerous national party platforms and by six presidents and both houses of Congress. NOW boycotted nonratifying states. Nonetheless, the anti-ERA campaign was successful: As the deadline neared, five approvals were still lacking. Three states rescinded their ratification.[45] Republicans withdrew their support for the amendment in their 1980 party platform. Congress decided to extend the deadline to June 30, 1982, but ERA again failed to receive the required number of ratifications.

Federal Responses to Sex Discrimination in the Workplace

Although ERA did not pass, several efforts were made by the federal government to eliminate sex discrimination in the labor market both before and after the introduction of the amendment.

Did You Know . . . That according to the Population Crisis Committee, Sweden leads the world in the status accorded to women, followed by Finland and then the United States? (Women in Bangladesh suffer the greatest discrimination.)

Phyllis Schlafly, a leading opponent of the Equal Rights Amendment.

---

[44]*Frontiero v. Richardson*, 411 U.S. 677 (1973).

[45]But such rescinding (or taking back one's vote) may not be constitutional. Samuel S. Friedman argued this point in *ERA: May a State Change Its Vote?* (Detroit: Wayne State University Press, 1979).

Did You Know ... That on average, women with four years of college have a lower income than men who have not finished high school?

SEX DISCRIMINATION
Overt behavior in which people are given differential or unfavorable treatment on the basis of sex. Any practice, policy, or procedure that denies equality of treatment to an individual or to a group because of gender.

SEXUAL HARASSMENT
Harassment on the basis of sex, in violation of Title VII. This includes unwanted physical or verbal conduct or abuse of a sexual nature that interferes with a recipient's job performance or carries with it an implicit or explicit threat of adverse employment consequences.

Professor Anita Hill testifies at the hearings for the nomination of Judge Clarence Thomas to the Supreme Court. Ms. Hill's charges of sexual harassment against Thomas opened a national debate both on the nomination and about the ways in which sexual harassment may occur.

Sex Discrimination and Title VII

Sex was included as a prohibited basis for discrimination in the job market under Title VII of the Civil Rights Act of 1964, although Title VII does not cover discrimination based on sexual preferences. Since its enactment, Title VII has been used to strike down so-called protective legislation, which prevents women from undertaking jobs deemed "too dangerous or strenuous by the state." In practice, such protective legislation often "protected" women from higher-paying jobs. Under the Equal Employment Opportunity Commission (EEOC) guidelines, such state statutes may not be used as a defense to a charge of illegal **sex discrimination.**

Sexual Harassment

Sexual harassment has also been outlawed by Title VII. In April 1980, the EEOC issued its first guidelines on the subject. Under the guidelines, all unwelcome sexual advances, requests, or other physical or verbal conduct of a sexual nature constitute illegal sexual harassment if submission to them is a condition of employment or a basis of pay, of promotion, or of other employment decisions. Also, if such unwanted conduct interferes with an employee's job performance or creates an intimidating, hostile, or offensive environment, it is illegal. The courts have gone so far as to hold the employer liable for illegal sexual harassment by supervisors, and EEOC guidelines go one step farther—they hold an employer liable for a supervisor's conduct regardless of the employer's knowledge of such conduct or even when the employer has a policy forbidding such conduct. The right of women to be free from sexual harassment on the job has also been increasingly upheld by the Supreme Court in the last few years. In 1986, the court indicated that creating a hostile environment by sexual harassment, even if job status is not affected, violates Title VII.[46]

The number of sexual-harassment complaints filed through the Equal Employment Opportunity Commission has increased dramatically in recent years, from about five thousand in 1985 to nearly ten thousand in 1992. The issue of sexual harassment received national attention in 1991 when charges of improper behavior were leveled at U.S. Supreme Court nominee Clarence Thomas by law professor Anita Hill. According to Hill, Thomas had sexually harassed her in the early 1980s when they both worked at the EEOC. Although Hill's charges caused a national furor, Thomas's nomination was approved.

The number of cases involving claims of sexual harassment that actually go to trial average no more than forty or fifty each year. Most sexual-harassment cases are settled out of court by employers who do not wish to receive negative publicity.

Pension Fund Contributions

In 1978, in a Title VII-based decision, the Supreme Court ruled that an employer (the City of Los Angeles) could not require female employees to make higher pension-fund contributions than male employees earning

---

[46]*Meritor Savings Bank, FSB v. Vinson*, 477 U.S. 57 (1986).

the same salary.[47] This and similar cases involving differential life insurance premiums for males and females (prohibited by a 1983 ruling) represent another set of issues on which Americans have been slowly redefining gender-based discrimination.[48]

Pregnancy

The 1978 Pregnancy Discrimination Act amended Title VII to include job-related discrimination based on pregnancy, childbirth, or related medical conditions. According to this amendment, health and disability insurance plans must cover pregnancy, childbirth, or related medical conditions in the same way as any other temporary disability. An employer must provide leaves of absence for pregnant women on the same terms and conditions as those given to any other worker for any other temporary disability. Also, simply because a woman is pregnant does not mean that she can be forced to take a maternity leave for any *specified* period of time. As long as she is capable of performing her duties, she must be allowed to work. The 1978 act applies both to married and unmarried women and to any aspect of employment.

Fetal Protection Policies

Fetal protection policies prevent fertile women from working in jobs in which they could be exposed to hazardous substances that could harm them or their unborn children. Men were not usually affected by these restrictions, even though medical studies have revealed that male reproductive systems may also be damaged from prolonged exposure to hazardous materials, such as lead. The policies were regarded as a way to avoid later suits in which mothers or children would accuse a company of having failed to take precautions that might have protected them from harm.

One of the most extreme fetal protection policies was adopted in 1982 by Johnson Controls, Inc., the country's largest producer of automobile batteries. The Johnson policy required all women of childbearing age working in jobs that entailed periodic exposure to lead or other hazardous materials to prove that they were infertile or to transfer to other positions. Women who agreed to transfer often had to accept cuts in pay and reduced job responsibilities. At least one woman who refused to accept a safer job agreed to be sterilized. Employees and their union, United Auto Workers, brought a suit against Johnson, claiming that the fetal protection policy violated Title VII. The Supreme Court agreed that the policy was discriminatory: "Women as capable of doing their jobs as their male counterparts may not be forced to choose between having a child and having a job."[49]

The Equal Pay Act of 1963

The Equal Pay Act was enacted in 1963 as an amendment to the Fair Labor Standards Act of 1938. Since 1979, it has been administered by the Equal

Did You Know ... That the median weekly earnings for women working full time are about 70 percent of men's median weekly full-time earnings?

Women took part in Operation Desert Storm as officers and enlisted personnel. Although a Congressional Act restricted women from holding combat positions, they often performed their jobs in combat zones. In 1993, the Secretary of Defense asked the military to train women for service in combat aircraft.

---

[47]*Los Angeles v. Manhart,* 435 U.S. 702 (1978).
[48]Congressional Quarterly, *Guide to the U.S. Supreme Court* (Washington, D.C., 1979).
[49]*United Auto Workers v. Johnson Controls, Inc.,* 111 S.Ct. 1196 (1991).

Did You Know . . . That in 1922, at age eighty-seven, Rebecca Latimer Felton was the first and oldest woman to serve in the U.S. Senate—although she was appointed as a token gesture and allowed to serve only one day?

COMPARABLE WORTH
The idea that compensation should be based on the worth of the job to an employer and that factors unrelated to the worth of a job, such as the sex of the employee, should not affect compensation. Supporters of the comparable-worth doctrine argue that women should be entitled to comparable wages for doing work that is different from, but of comparable worth and value to, work done by higher-paid men.

Employment Opportunity Commission. Basically, the act prohibits sex-based discrimination in the wages paid for equal work on jobs when their performance requires skill, effort, and responsibility under similar conditions. It is job content rather than job description that controls in all cases. For the equal pay requirements to apply, the act requires that male and female employees must work at the same establishment.

With equal-pay questions, the issue focuses more on the jobs performed by two employees and whether they are substantially equal than on the equivalence of employees' skills and training. But small differences in job content do not justify higher pay for one sex. The courts look to the primary duties of the two jobs. The jobs of a barber and a beautician are considered essentially "equal." So, too, are those of a tailor and a seamstress.

Comparable Worth, or Pay Equity

The concept of **comparable worth,** or pay equity, is that women should receive equal pay not just for equal (that is, the same) work, but also for work of comparable skill, effort, and responsibility. This is an effort to redress the effects of traditional "women's work" being undervalued and underpaid. Indeed, four out of five women hold jobs that have largely become women's work—for example, secretary (99 percent female), telephone operator (88 percent female), and nurse (94 percent female).

In 1981, the Supreme Court ruled that female workers could sue under Title VII even if they were not performing the same jobs as men. In this case, a group of female prison guards, given the title "matrons," in Washington County, Oregon, claimed that they did not receive the same salaries as male prison guards, known as "deputy sheriffs." Their jobs differed from the men's in that they had fewer prisoners to guard and they also performed clerical tasks. The Court ruled that they could sue on the basis of sex discrimination.[50]

In 1983, the American Federation of State, County, and Municipal Employees filed a lawsuit against the state of Washington, charging that state employees in job categories dominated by women were paid less, on average, than workers in other categories requiring comparable skills and background. According to the Washington State Supreme Court, the "evidence is overwhelming that there has been past historical discrimination against women in employment in the state of Washington and that discrimination has been manifested, according to the evidence, by direct, overt, and institutionalized discrimination."[51] The court ruled that the state would have to make amends. Union officials estimated that the state's liability in this case may reach $500 million.

The Status of the Elderly

A major change in our society is the growing number of people age sixty-five or over. People are having fewer children and living longer because

---

[50]*Washington County, Oregon v. Gunther*, 452 U.S. 161 (1981).
[51]*American Federation of State, County and Municipal Employees v. State of Washington*, 33 Fair Empl. Prac. (BNA) 810 (1984).

of advances in medical care. Within a few decades, we will no longer be a nation of young people, with its focus on youth culture. Demographically, we will resemble countries such as France, where the unknowing American immediately remarks on how many ''old'' people there are.

Today, the median age of the population of the United States is slightly over thirty-two, and thirty-two million Americans are sixty-five or over. As can be seen in Figure 5-2, it is estimated that by the year 2020 this figure will have reached forty-two million. Thus the problems of aging and retirement are going to become increasingly important national issues. Because many elderly people rely on income from Social Security to maintain themselves, the funding of Social Security benefits continues to be a major issue on the national political agenda.

Poverty, at least on the surface, appears to be a problem facing older people in America. More than 10 percent of people sixty-five and older have incomes below the poverty level. There are a number of explanations for this phenomenon, which we consider in the following pages.

The Burden of Medical Costs

Many older people find themselves unable to make ends meet because they suffer from chronic illnesses that require constant attention. Medical expenses associated with such illnesses may be a steady drain on already meager resources. Since the introduction of Medicare and Medicaid, however, this problem has been ameliorated for a large number of senior citizens.

Age Discrimination in Employment

The unstated policy of many companies not to hire older people makes it extremely difficult for senior citizens to work even when they want to. In spite of their proven productivity, the elderly have suffered from discrimination in employment for many years. One of their major problems has been **mandatory retirement.**

Court Actions.   Mandatory retirement laws for government employees may result in many otherwise qualified people losing their jobs and thus may not promote efficiency in government. But the laws have been upheld in the courts. In 1976, the Supreme Court, in *Massachusetts Board of Retirement v. Murgia,*[52] upheld a Massachusetts law requiring state troopers to retire at age fifty. The Court said that age could not be considered a ''suspect'' classification. In 1985, however, in *Johnson v. Mayor of Baltimore,*[53] the Court held that a federal statute requiring certain government employees to retire at a specified age (such as requiring federal firefighters to retire at age fifty-five) does not mean that a similar mandatory retirement age can be imposed on employees of other governmental units or on similar private-sector employees.

Congressional Actions.   As age was not included within the protections of the 1964 Civil Rights Act, Congress directed the secretary of labor to

---

[52]427 U.S. 307 (1976).
[53]472 U.S. 353 (1985).

MANDATORY RETIREMENT
Forced retirement when a person reaches a certain age.

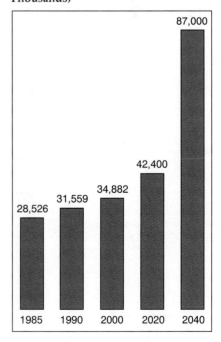

FIGURE 5-2 ■ Population Projections: Persons Age 65 and Older (in Thousands)

				87,000
28,526	31,559	34,882	42,400	
1985	1990	2000	2020	2040

SOURCE: *Statistical Abstract of the United States,* 1992, p. 261.

These senior citizens are marching to save government-provided medical services. Medical-care expenses are a major problem for this nation's elders. A rising percentage of government spending does, however, go for medical care to the aged.

prepare a report on the problem of age discrimination. In 1965, that report, *The Older American Workers—Age Discrimination in Employment,* documented widespread discrimination. The report served as the impetus for passage of the Age Discrimination in Employment Act of 1967. The act, which applies to employers, employment agencies, and labor organizations and covers individuals over the age of forty, prohibits discrimination against individuals on the basis of age unless age is shown to be a bona fide occupational qualification reasonably necessary to the normal operation of the particular business.

Specifically, it is against the law to discriminate by age in wages, benefits, hours worked, or availability of overtime. Employers and unions may not discriminate in providing fringe benefits, such as education or training programs, career development, sick leave, and vacations. It is a violation of the act to publish notices or advertisements indicating a preference limitation or discrimination based on age. Even advertisements that imply a preference for youthful workers over older workers are in violation of the law. Requesting age on an application is not illegal but may be closely scrutinized in light of the employer's hiring practices.

The Age Discrimination in Employment Act of 1967 was amended in 1974 to include state and local governments and to furnish protection to most federal employees. More important, in 1978, Congress made extensive amendments to the 1967 act, prohibiting mandatory retirement of most employees under age seventy. Many states had already passed similar statutes. In 1986, mandatory retirement rules were finally outlawed, except for a few selected occupations. The act's protection was extended to individuals over age seventy to whom it had not previously been available.

The Elderly and Politics

As voters, legislators, and activists, the elderly contribute significantly to American political life.

The Elderly As Voters. If we use voter participation as a measure of political involvement, it is clear that the elderly are very active. Table 5-1

TABLE 5-1 ■ Voter Participation by Age Groups, 1988

Voter participation seems to be positively correlated with age, as we can see in this table. The lowest participation is by 18–20-year-olds and the highest is by those 65 and over.			
Age Group	**Persons of Voting Age (Millions)**	**Percent Reporting They Registered**	**Percent Reporting They Voted**
18–20	10.7	35.4%	18.6%
21–24	15.7	46.6%	24.7%
25–34	41.9	55.8%	35.1%
35–44	33.0	67.9%	49.3%
45–64	44.8	74.8%	58.7%
65 and over	27.7	76.9%	60.9%

SOURCE: *Statistical Abstract of the United States, 1990,* p. 262.

shows that of the six age categories listed, the over-sixty-five age group ranks first in voter registration and in actual turnout on election day. Whereas approximately 46 percent of all persons of voting age claim to have voted, in the over-sixty-five category the voting rate is 60.9 percent.

The Elderly As Legislators. Whereas other minority groups are very poorly represented in the Senate and in the House, such is not the case for the elderly. In 1991, for example, the Senate had 33 members over the age of sixty and the House had 136. Table 5-2 shows the age categories of members of Congress for selected years.

The Elderly As Activists. Today the elderly work for their interests through a number of large and effective political associations. The National Association of Retired Federal Employees, formed in 1921, currently

Did You Know . . . That those eighty-five years of age or older constitute the most rapidly growing segment of the U.S. population and that by the year 2040 this group will constitute 8 percent of the total population?

TABLE 5-2 ■ Ages of Members of Congress for Selected Years

Congressional Chamber and Year	Age					
	Under 40	40–49	50–59	60–69	70–79	80 and Over
Representatives						
1973	45	132	154	80	20	2
1975	69	138	137	75	14	2
1977	81	121	147	71	15	—
1979	86	125	145	63	14	—
1981	94	142	132	54	12	1
1983	86	145	132	57	13	1
1985	71	154	131	59	17	1
1987	63	153	137	56	24	2
1989	38	165	131	79	20	2
1991	27	152	130	108	24	4
Senators						
1973	3	25	37	23	11	1
1975	5	21	35	24	15	—
1977	6	26	35	21	10	2
1979	10	31	33	17	8	1
1981	9	35	36	14	6	—
1983	7	28	39	20	3	3
1985	4	27	38	25	4	2
1987	5	30	36	22	5	2
1989	0	29	41	22	6	2
1991	0	19	48	20	11	2

SOURCE: Harold W. Stanley and Richard G. Niemi, *Vital Statistics on American Politics*, 3d ed. (Washington D.C., Congressional Quarterly, Inc., 1992) p. 183.

has 450,000 members. In 1947, the National Retired Teachers' Association was established, and today it has more than half a million members. The largest of these groups is the American Association of Retired Persons, for those aged fifty and older, founded in 1958, with a current membership of more than thirty million. The latter two groups have united in a powerful joint effort to ensure beneficial treatment for the elderly by lobbying for legislation at the federal and state levels. They use the same staff in Washington and provide almost the same services to their members, including low-priced group insurance and travel programs.

The Rights of the Handicapped

By the 1970s, the handicapped were becoming a political force. Congress passed the Rehabilitation Act in 1973, which prohibited discrimination against the handicapped in programs receiving federal aid. The Department of Health, Education, and Welfare, or HEW (now Health and Human Services, or HHS), however, was slow to issue regulations needed to implement this act. When these regulations had still not been issued by April 1977, members of the American Coalition of Citizens with Disabilities staged a "wheel-in" by occupying several Washington HEW offices. A few weeks after this event, HEW passed the necessary regulations. There was still disagreement about what constituted discrimination. The handicapped wanted the right to physical access so that they could compete more effectively in the marketplace. This meant modifying physical structures so the handicapped could avoid the curbs, stairways, and other obstacles that make mobility difficult for them. A 1978 amendment to the Rehabilitation Act of 1973 established the Architectural and Transportation Barriers Compliance Board. Regulations for ramps, elevators, and the like in all federal buildings were implemented. Cost, however, created somewhat of an impediment. Estimates from as low as $4 billion to more than $7 billion were given as the cost of compliance over the next several decades. Faced with such estimates, the Reagan administration (1981–1989) took some steps to rescind previous advances in this area.

Congress passed the Education for All Handicapped Children Act in 1975. Unofficially, this act has been referred to as the "bill of rights for handicapped youth." It guarantees that all handicapped children will receive an "appropriate" education.

In 1990, Congress passed new legislation to provide expanded access to public facilities, including transportation. The Americans with Disabilities Act of 1990 (the "handicapped's bill of rights") prohibits job discrimination against the 43.6 million Americans with physical and mental disabilities, including those with AIDS, and requires access to public buildings and public services. Physical access means ramps, hand rails, and wheelchair-accessible restrooms, counters, drinking fountains, telephones, and doorways, as well as more accessible mass transit. In addition, other steps must be taken to comply: Car-rental companies must provide cars with hand controls for disabled drivers, and telephone companies are required to have operators to pass on messages from the speech-impaired who use telephones with keyboards.

One group active in the fight for rights for the disabled is Americans Disabled for Accessible Public Transit, or Americans Disabled for Atten-

POLITICS AND THE DISABLED

Special Treatment

Twenty percent of the population of the United States has some form of disability, and there are hundreds of different disabilities. All disabled persons share a common experience, however: discrimination. The United States Supreme Court has recognized "invidious discrimination against the handicapped"—discrimination that is often the product of "thoughtlessness and indifference," causing persons with disabilities "to live among society shunted aside, hidden, and ignored."*

This discrimination motivated the movement to push for the enactment of the Americans with Disabilities Act (ADA) of 1990. It has also prompted many of those with disabilities to change the way they are perceived by society. "We don't want to be dependent any more. We want to be part of society in every way," says Lex Friedan of the Institute for Rehabilitation and Research Foundation. Friedan is a quadriplegic wheelchair user. In other words, disabled persons share not

*Alexander v. Choate, 469 U.S. 287 (1985).

only a common experience but also a common desire: to be treated like everyone else.

Being treated like everyone else does not mean the total absence of special treatment. The disabled want special treatment in the form of regulations mandated by the ADA. They want special treatment in the form of expenditures by government and business. Special treatment is not unique to the disabled—business firms and others receive special treatment in the same forms. Broadly, special treatment for persons with disabilities is designed to give them the opportunity to live without allowing a disability to define them or dominate their lives.

Businesses see disabled persons as a source of customers and employees. On the whole, however, business has been afraid of the increased costs associated with the special treatment required by the ADA. One of the purposes of the ADA is to make disabilities irrelevant in employment decisions. Generally, an employer complies with the ADA if an applicant for employment is con-

sidered on the basis of his or her ability to do the job with reasonable accommodation. As a rule, persons with disabilities are to be judged on the basis of the average level of performance by their peers. An employer violates the ADA if an applicant is rejected on the basis of stereotypes or generalizations about his or her disability or disabilities in general. There is a dispute over what constitutes "reasonable accommodation" and what it will cost. The dispute may be settled only in the courts.

Perhaps a better way to view the provisions of the ADA is to consider what they will *not* cost. The ADA reduces the dependency of disabled persons on federal and state funds and opens a way for the disabled to earn a living and pay taxes like everyone else. This is the special treatment that disabled persons seek, and this is the way they wish to be perceived. This goal may not be exclusive to those who are disabled. To be treated like everyone else is the same special treatment that most, if not all, of us desire.

dant Programs Today (ADAPT). Formed in 1983 to fight for wheelchair lifts on public buses, ADAPT achieved its goal with the inclusion in the Americans with Disabilities Act of 1990 of a provision that all new buses be equipped with hydraulic lifts for people in wheelchairs. ADAPT's other objectives include Medicaid funding for attendants for disabled persons, allowing them to live relatively independently. Currently, Medicaid pays for nursing home care only. ADAPT asks that 20 percent of Medicaid funds paid to nursing homes be diverted to attendant programs. Such legislation highlights the question of the economic trade-offs that have to be made when resources are allocated to benefit specially selected groups in society. It is not enough to state simply that the handicapped (or the elderly or any other disadvantaged group) should be given better treatment in America. We must also ask the question of who will bear the costs of this improved treatment. This is both an economic and a political question.

PROFILE

Bree Walker Lampley

"It's the rest of the world that creates handicaps. If the world celebrated our differences, things wouldn't be like this."

In the summer of 1991, Jane Norris, during her Los Angeles radio talk show, passionately criticized a California woman with a genetic disorder who was going to have a baby. The mother-to-be was Bree Walker Lampley, news anchor for KCBS-TV in Los Angeles. Lampley has ectrodactyly, an inherited disease that causes the toes and fingers to fuse together. Norris questioned the "social responsibility" of Lampley's decision—"which affects us all"—to bear a child, when Lampley knew that there was a fifty-fifty chance that the child would inherit the disease. Norris asked her listeners, "Is it fair to pass along a genetically disfiguring disease to your child? I have to say, I don't think I could do it."

Lampley and her husband, Jim Lampley, currently a sportscaster for HBO, had already faced this question. When she was pregnant with her first child, Andrea, Lampley discovered through an ultrasound procedure that the baby had ectrodactyly. Their second child, Aaron—whom she was carrying at the time of Norris's broadcast—also has the disease. He was born with one "finger" on each hand, and his toes are also fused together.

Norris's remarks are revealing of society's preoccupation with physically "normal" babies. For a large number of Americans, disability is sometimes regarded as a fate worse than death. One of the arguments used by those in favor of legalized abortion is that a woman should have the right to abort her pregnancy if she learns, through prenatal testing, that the child she is carrying is physically deformed in some way or has Down's syndrome. It has also been argued that parents should have the right to withhold life-saving medical care from disabled infants. Our culture's fear of disabled babies has come under increasing scrutiny by disabled and pregnant women such as Bree Walker Lampley, as well as by those in the disability rights movement and others in society who are strongly committed to reproductive freedom.

Born and raised in Austin, Minnesota, to a loving and encouraging family, Lampley has struggled throughout her life against a society that places a high value on physical perfection. She and her brother, Eryk, both inherited ectrodactyly from her mother. Even the most loving family could not shield her from the hurt and pain inflicted on her by her peers, some of whom called her "butterfingers," "monster hands," or some equally derogatory epithet.

After earning a degree in journalism from the University of Minnesota, Lampley applied for a job as a reporter for the *Minneapolis Tribune* but did not land the job because typing was too difficult for her. She eventually went into radio. After several years as a successful disc jockey, she finally landed a television job, anchoring the nightly news program for a San Diego station. At first, she wore prosthetic gloves to make her hands look more normal. In 1980, she abandoned the gloves, which were not only clumsy but deceived her audience. Her action was supported by hundreds of viewers. In the years since, Lampley has received numerous awards and honors for excellence in newscasting and investigative reporting.

Lampley is actively involved in the disability rights movements, her major focus being disability awareness by the media. She was appointed to the California Media Task Force on Disability in 1981 and to the President's Committee on Employment for the Handicapped in 1983. In 1985 and 1989, she received the Media Access Award for "creating more media awareness of disability issues." She has been featured in various magazines, including *Redbook*, *Newsweek*, and *Glamour*. In 1992, in her home state of Minnesota, she was presented with the National Courage Award. On receiving the award, Lampley stated, "I don't think of myself as courageous. I've seen real courage. Everyday people who are real heroes. That's why this is so humbling. What sets me apart from 43 million disabled Americans is that I have a voice on television. I have a job with a microphone."

The Rights and Status of Juveniles

There are sixty-three million children who are American citizens. The definition of *children* ranges from under age sixteen to under age twenty-one. But, however defined, children form a large group of individuals in the United States and have the fewest rights and protections. The reason for this lack is the common presumption of society and its lawmakers that children are basically protected by their parents. This is not to say that children are the exclusive property of the parents, but rather that an overwhelming case in favor of *not* allowing parents to control the actions of their children must be presented before the state will intervene.

The Rights of Children in Civil and Criminal Proceedings

Children today have limited rights in civil and criminal proceedings in our judicial system. Different procedural rules and judicial safeguards apply in civil and criminal laws. **Civil law** relates in part to contracts among private individuals or companies. **Criminal law** relates to crimes against society that are defined by society acting through its legislatures.

Private Contract Rights. Children are defined exclusively by state law with respect to private contract negotiations, rights, and remedies. The legal definition of **majority** varies from eighteen to twenty-one years of age, depending on the state. If an individual is legally a minor, as a rule, she or he usually cannot be held responsible for contracts entered into. In most states, only contracts entered into for so-called **necessaries** (things necessary for subsistence, as determined by the courts) can be enforced against minors. Also, when minors engage in negligent behavior, typically their parents are liable. If, for example, a minor destroys a neighbor's fence, the neighbor may bring suit against the child's parents but not against the child.

Criminal Rights. One of the main requirements for an act to be criminal is intent. The law has given children certain defenses against criminal prosecution because of their presumed inability to have criminal intent.

Under the **common law,** children up to seven years of age were considered incapable of committing a crime because they did not have the moral sense to understand that they were doing wrong. Children between the ages of seven and fourteen were also presumed to be incapable of committing a crime, but this presumption could be challenged by showing that the child understood the wrongful nature of the act. Today, states vary in their approaches, but most states retain the common law approach, although age limits vary from state to state. Other states have simply set a minimum age for criminal responsibility.

All states have juvenile court systems that handle children below the age of criminal responsibility who commit delinquent acts. The aim of juvenile courts is allegedly to reform rather than to punish. In states that retain the common law approach, children who are above the minimum age but are still juveniles can be turned over to the criminal courts if the juvenile court determines that they should be treated as adults.

CIVIL LAW
The law regulating conduct between private persons over noncriminal matters. Under civil law, the government provides the forum for the settlement of disputes between private parties in such matters as contracts, domestic relations, and business relations.

CRIMINAL LAW
The law that defines crimes and provides punishment for violations. In criminal cases, the government is the prosecutor because crimes are against the public order.

MAJORITY
Full age; the age at which a person is entitled by law to the management of his or her own affairs and to the full enjoyment of civil rights.

NECESSARIES
In contract law, necessaries include whatever is reasonably necessary for suitable subsistence as measured by age, state, condition in life, and so on.

COMMON LAW
Judge-made law that originated in England from decisions shaped according to prevailing customs. Decisions were applied to similar situations and thus gradually became common to the nation. Common law forms the basis of legal procedures in the United States.

This juvenile is being arrested in the same way as an adult would be, but he does not have the rights under criminal law of an adult. Juveniles receive less severe punishment than adults do for similar crimes, however.

Procedural Rights in Criminal Trials.   Previously, if a child was picked up for illegal activities, that child could have been sentenced in juvenile court without a lawyer, without the child's parents being allowed to see the complaint against him or her, and without being able to cross-examine whoever made the complaint. In addition, in most states the child would have been unable to appeal his or her punishment to a higher court. Basically, the Bill of Rights did not apply to the young.

In 1967, all that changed. In a watershed case, the father of a child who had been sentenced in juvenile court to six years in an industrial school for one obscene phone call took his case all the way to the Supreme Court. The father argued that the Bill of Rights protects children and noted that his child did not have a lawyer, the parents did not see the complaint against the child, and no one could cross-examine the person who complained that the child had made the obscene phone call. Amazingly, if the child had been an adult (over eighteen), the maximum sentence in the state in which the presumed phone call was made would have been three months in jail or a fine of from five to fifty dollars.

The Supreme Court, in *In re Gault*,[54] held that

> the Due Process Clause of the Fourteenth Amendment requires that in respect to proceedings to determine [juvenile] delinquency which may result in commitment to an institution in which the juvenile's freedom is curtailed, the child and his parent must be notified of the child's right to be represented by counsel retained by them, or if they are unable to afford counsel, that counsel will be appointed to represent the child.

In its majority opinion, the Court, after reviewing reports on juvenile court proceedings, concluded that "juvenile court history has again demonstrated that unbridled discretion, however benevolently motivated, is frequently a poor substitute for principle and procedure." Finally, the Court stated that "under our Constitution, the condition of being a boy does not justify a **kangaroo court.**"

KANGAROO COURT
A mock hearing in which norms of justice and judicial procedure are ignored.

---

[54]387 U.S. 1 (1967).

In spite of *In re Gault*, children still do not have the right to trial by jury or to bail. Also, parents can still commit their minor children to state mental institutions without allowing the child a hearing.

The Rights and Status of Gays

Studies by Alfred Kinsey and his associates in the late 1940s and early 1950s, coupled with more recent research, indicate that there are perhaps twenty-five million Americans with varying degrees of homosexual orientation.[55] Gays, as they are most commonly called, therefore represent one of the most important minorities in the United States. Nonetheless, the rights of gays did not surface as a major issue on the American political and legal scene until the 1970s.

The Law and Public Attitudes

The status of gays came to national attention in 1977, when Anita Bryant, of Florida orange juice and television commercial fame, organized a "Save Our Children" campaign. Its purpose was to rescind the law protecting gays' legal rights in Dade County, Florida. The Dade County law protected homosexuals from discrimination in public accommodations, housing, and employment. Bryant's campaign against the gay community's effort to keep the law on the books was successful. In June 1977, Miami citizens voted two to one to repeal the law protecting gays. Similar laws were repealed in Eugene, Oregon; Wichita, Kansas; and St. Paul, Minnesota. In the 1990 primary, Broward County, Florida, voters defeated a proposal designed to give gay people greater protection against discrimination (the so-called "human rights referendum") by a margin of three to two. Today, twenty-nine states still have antihomosexual laws on the books. And in the summer of 1986, the Supreme Court upheld an antigay law in the state of Georgia that made homosexual conduct between two adults a crime.[56] In 1992, the citizens of Colorado passed a state-wide referendum prohibiting laws that specifically protect homosexuals.

Attitudes toward gays are changing, however. Recent Gallup polls show that 47 percent of Americans believe that private homosexual relations between consenting adults should not be considered illegal. Almost one hundred cities throughout the United States currently have laws prohibiting discrimination against homosexuals in the areas of housing, education, banking, labor union employment, and public accommodations. Since 1982, Wisconsin has had on its books a general law prohibiting all discrimination against homosexuals. In 1989, Massachusetts passed a law specifically stating that the state does not endorse homosexuality nor recognize homosexual partnerships, but that no discrimination against homosexuals shall exist. In 1990, St. Paul, Minnesota, passed a new

---

[55]Rhonda Rivera, "Homosexuality and the Law," in William Paul, James D. Weinrich, John C. Gonsirock, and Mary E. Hoxtedt, eds., *Homosexuality: Social, Psychological, and Biological Issues* (Beverly Hills, Calif.: Sage, 1982), pp. 25–26.

[56]*Bowers v. Hardwick*, 478 U.S. 186 (1986).

Did You Know ... That a recent Gallup poll found that 45 percent of adults would ''vote against a public official regardless of other factors'' if the candidate were a homosexual?

ordinance prohibiting discrimination on the basis of sexual orientation in housing, education, employment, and public accommodations. In a number of states and localities, laws against ''hate crimes'' include actions taken against gays, even though the genesis of those laws was crimes against African Americans and Hispanics.

Gays and Politics

The number of gay organizations grew from fifty in 1969 to more than a thousand by the end of the 1970s. These groups have been active in exerting pressure on legislatures, the media, schools, and churches. In 1973, gay organizations succeeded in having the American Psychiatric Association remove homosexuality from its list of disorders. During the 1970s and 1980s, more than half the states repealed sodomy laws. The Civil Service Commission eliminated its ban on the employment of gays. In 1980, the Democratic party platform included a gay rights plank.

Politicians have not overlooked the potential significance of homosexual issues in American politics. Conservative politicians have been generally critical of gays. Liberals, however, have by and large begun to speak out for gay rights. Walter Mondale, former vice president of the United States and the winning contender for the Democratic party nomination for president in 1984, addressed a gay convention and openly bid for gays' political support.

In cities such as San Francisco, which is considered to be the gay capital of the United States, and Washington, D.C., the homosexual vote is considered to be a critical factor in politics. In 1979, gay political activist David Scott forced San Francisco Mayor Dianne Feinstein into a runoff primary election. In that same year, active gay voters in Washington, D.C., helped to elect Mayor Marion Barry. The gay community also supported Jesse Jackson's 1988 bid for the presidency and his ''Rainbow Coalition.'' Gays have been elected to public offices, and gays in increasing numbers and from all walks of life declare themselves publicly. Americans still do not

Gays have become an important political force in American politics today. These demonstrators believe that constitutional civil rights and liberties, including equal protection of the laws, should extend to gays and that laws permitting discrimination against gays should be repealed.

appear to have accepted homosexuality as a normal and legitimate way of life, however. On taking office, President Clinton ordered the military to end its ban on gays and to integrate them into the armed forces. The immediate result was resistance from military leaders and a storm of protest from conservative opponents of gay rights. The controversy over the role of gays in American society will continue to occupy a great deal of public debate.

Conclusion: The Continuing Debate over Equality

Over the last thirty years, the gains of gay people, the handicapped, the elderly, women, and children have been impressive. But fear of people who are different and a general fear of change continue to exist. Consequently, controversy over the roles that these groups play, or should play, in American society will continue to foster public debate. One part of the debate concerns what gains these groups should make—what kind of benefits the elderly and the handicapped should receive, for example—and the other part concerns how to pay for resources allocated to their benefit. These are important political and economic questions.

Only by intense political efforts have these groups made progress. Their efforts will certainly continue. In the 1990s, women will try for more seats in Congress, possibly through the efforts of a new feminist political party. Gays will continue to fight for antidiscrimination laws at state and local levels. Once such laws are enacted, gays will continue to fight against their repeal. The elderly and the handicapped will continue to seek better, less expensive medical care and safer, easier access to public facilities.

Acknowledging new rights of specially selected groups is usually not enough, however. Resources must be allocated to pay for the benefits— better medical care, for instance, costs more. Positive attitudes toward equality do not always translate into economically feasible programs. What resources are allocated to pay for what benefit will continue to occupy public debate.

GETTING INVOLVED

What to Do about Discrimination

When you apply for a job, you may be subjected to a variety of possibly discriminatory practices—based on your race, color, gender, religion, age, national origin, sexual preference, or disability. You may also be subjected to a battery of tests, some of which you may feel are discriminatory. At both state and federal levels, the government has continued to examine the fairness and validity of criteria used in job-applicant screening. If you believe that you have been discriminated against by a potential employer, you may wish to consider the following steps:

1. Evaluate your own capabilities and determine if you are truly qualified for the position.
2. Analyze the reasons that you were turned down (or dismissed); do you feel that others would agree with you, or would they uphold your employer's claim?
3. If you still believe that you have been unfairly treated, you have recourse to several agencies and services.

You should first speak to the personnel director of the company and politely explain that you feel you have not been adequately evaluated. If asked, give the specifics of your concerns. If necessary, go into explicit detail and indicate that you feel that you may have been discriminated against. If a second evaluation is not forthcoming, contact the local branch of your state employment agency. If you still do not obtain adequate help, contact one or more of the following agencies, usually found by looking in your telephone directory under "state government" listings:

1. If a government entity is involved, a state ombudsman or citizen aide who will mediate may be available.
2. You may wish to contact the state civil rights commission, which will at least give you advice if it does not wish to take up your case.
3. The state attorney general's office will normally have a division dealing with discrimination and civil rights.
4. There may be a special commission or department specifically set up to help you, such as a women's status commission or a commission on Hispanic or Asian Americans. If you are a member of such a minority or a woman, contact these commissions.
5. Finally, at the national level, you can contact the American Civil Liberties Union, and you can also contact the most appropriate federal agency: Equal Employment Opportunity Commission, 2401 E St., N.W., Washington, DC 20506.

CHAPTER SUMMARY

1. The United States is more heterogeneous in terms of race and religion than Western European nations. In our country, as part of the ongoing struggle for equality, there is an effort to strengthen and to expand constitutional guarantees to *all* persons in our society. These guarantees are often called civil rights, and this struggle is often called the civil rights movement.

2. The civil rights movement started with the struggle by African Americans for equality. Before the Civil War, African Americans were slaves, and slavery was protected by the Constitution and the Supreme Court—African Americans were not considered citizens or entitled to the rights and privileges of citizenship. In 1863 and the years after the Civil War, the Emancipation Proclamation and the Thirteenth, Fourteenth, and Fifteenth Amendments (the Civil War amendments) legally and constitutionally ended slavery.

3. Politically and socially, African-American inequality continued. The *Civil Rights Cases* (1883) and *Plessy v. Ferguson* (1896) effectively nullified the civil rights acts of

1865–1877. In the *Civil Rights Cases,* the Supreme Court held that the Fourteenth Amendment did not apply to private invasions of individual rights. In *Plessy,* the Court upheld the separate-but-equal doctrine, declaring that segregation did not violate the Constitution. African Americans were excluded from the voting process through poll taxes, grandfather clauses, white primaries, and literacy tests.

4. African Americans fought unceasingly for equality. Legal segregation was declared unconstitutional by the Supreme Court in *Brown v. Board of Education of Topeka* (1954), in which the Court stated that separation implied inferiority. In *Brown v. Board of Education* (1955), the Supreme Court ordered federal courts to ensure that public schools were desegregated "with all deliberate speed." Also in 1955, the modern civil rights movement began with a boycott of segregated public transportation in Montgomery, Alabama. Headed by Martin Luther King, Jr., the movement obtained an injunction against the segregation of Montgomery buses and, employing nonviolent tactics, gained other victories in other cities and states.

The Twenty-fourth Amendment and a Supreme Court decision outlawed poll taxes. Other court decisions supported other aims of the movement. Congress passed a new series of laws to enforce civil rights, assuming a significant role in enforcing the constitutional notion of equality for all Americans. Of particular impact have been the Civil Rights Acts of 1964 and the Voting Rights Act of 1965.

5. Affirmative action was perceived by many whites as negative. In *McDonald v. Santa Fe Trail Transportation Co.* (1976), the Supreme Court stated that the Civil Rights Act of 1964 prohibits reverse discrimination—discrimination against whites. In *Regents of the University of California v. Bakke* (1978), the Supreme Court held that race as a sole criterion for admission to a university is improper. In *United Steelworkers of America v. Weber* (1979), the Supreme Court held that an employer's use of a racial quota to staff an apprenticeship program is improper. In the *Weber* case, however, the Court stated that reverse discrimination is permissible if it results from a legislative, executive, or judicial finding of past discrimination. In the 1980s, the Supreme Court and other federal courts allowed school districts to discontinue busing.

6. Today, Hispanics make up the second largest minority group in the United States. Their diversity and geographical dispersion, however, hinder their ability to exercise unified political power, particularly at the national level. Hispanics have faced discriminatory barriers to political participation.

7. In 1787, Congress declared Native-American tribes to be foreign nations to enable the government to sign land and boundary treaties with them. Over the next century, many treaties were made and most were broken, with Native Americans being forced westward as white settlement expanded. Congress passed the Dawes Act (General Allotment Act) in 1887, to assimilate Native Americans. Generally, assimilation was forced on Native Americans so the government could acquire their land and resources. Partly because their numbers were so diminished and the tribes so scattered, Native Americans have been unsuccessful in attaining political power.

8. The Chinese Exclusion Act of 1882 prevented Chinese from coming to work in the western United States in certain occupations. After the San Francisco earthquake of 1906, Japanese-American children were segregated so that white children could use their schools. In 1942, at a time of intensified fear and hatred of the Japanese because of the bombing of Pearl Harbor, the president ordered the relocation of West Coast residents of Japanese descent to internment camps. In 1988, Congress provided funds to compensate those Americans and their survivors.

9. In the early years of the United States, women were considered citizens, but they were citizens without political rights. After the first women's rights convention in 1848, the women's movement gained momentum. It was not until 1920, when the Nineteenth Amendment was passed, that women gained the right to vote.

10. The right to vote has not guaranteed political power. Women have been, and continue to be, greatly underrepre-

sented in Congress, as well as in the other branches of the federal government. Women have had more success at state and local levels. Nowhere does the representation of women in political office reflect their participation as voters—their national turnout is higher than that of men.

11. The modern women's movement seeks to define sexism and to eradicate it from all spheres of life for all women. Laws that include different provisions for men and women are not always struck down by the Supreme Court. It holds that laws involving classifications on the basis of sex are permissible if they "substantially relate to important governmental interests." The National Organization for Women (NOW) worked for the passage of the Equal Rights Amendment (ERA) to the Constitution. ERA is seen as a way to invalidate state laws that maintain the inferior status of women by discriminating against them.

12. Federal government efforts to eliminate sex discrimination in the labor market include prohibiting sex as a basis for discrimination under Title VII of the Civil Rights Act of 1964. Title VII has been used to invalidate "protective" laws that kept women out of jobs deemed dangerous or onerous by a state. Under Equal Employment Opportunity Commission (EEOC) guidelines, these laws may not be used as a defense to a charge of sex discrimination. The Supreme Court has upheld the right of women to be free from sexual harassment on the job. The Court has also held that an employer cannot require female employees to make higher pension-fund contributions than males earning the same salaries. Under the Pregnancy Discrimination Act (an amendment to Title VII), job-related discrimination cannot be based on pregnancy, childbirth, or related medical conditions. Title VII has also been used by the Supreme Court to invalidate fetal protection policies. The Equal Pay Act of 1963 (an amendment to the Fair Labor Standards Act), which is administered by the EEOC, prohibits sex discrimination in wages paid for equal work at the same establishment.

13. Problems associated with aging and retirement are becoming increasingly important as the number of elderly in the United States increases. The Age Discrimination in Employment Act of 1967 prohibits job-related discrimination against individuals over the age of forty on the basis of age, unless age is shown to be a bona fide occupational qualification reasonably necessary to the normal operation of the business. The act applies to virtually all aspects of employment and most employers, including the federal government and state and local governments. As a group, the elderly contribute significantly to American political life, ranking first in voter registration and turnout and being well represented in Congress.

14. The handicapped, too, have become an effective political force. In 1973, Congress passed the Rehabilitation Act, which prohibits discrimination against the handicapped in programs receiving federal aid. The handicapped pushed for, and obtained, regulations implementing the act and regulations for ramps, elevators, and the like in all federal buildings. The Education for All Handicapped Children Act (1975) provides that all handicapped children receive an "appropriate" education. The Americans with Disabilities Act of 1990 prohibits job discrimination against persons with physical and mental disabilities, requiring that positive steps be taken to comply. The act also requires expanded access to public facilities, including transportation, and to services offered by such private concerns as car-rental and telephone companies.

15. Though children form a large group of Americans, they have the fewest rights and protections, in part because it is commonly presumed that parents protect their children. Only contracts entered into for necessaries can be enforced against minors. When minors engage in negligent acts, their parents may be held liable. Minors have some defense against criminal prosecution because of their presumed inability at certain ages to have criminal intent. For those below the age of criminal responsibility, there are state juvenile courts. In *In re*

Gault (1967), the Supreme Court held that in juvenile court proceedings, a child is entitled to a lawyer, to see the complaint against him or her, to cross-examine the complainant, and to appeal, but a child has no right to trial by jury or to bail. When minors are tried as adults, they receive all of the rights accorded to adults.

16. Gay rights surfaced as a major issue on the American political and legal scene only in the 1970s, despite the large number of people with some degree of homosexual orientation in the United States. More than half of the states have antihomosexual laws, and a state law that made homosexual conduct between consenting adults a crime has been upheld by the Supreme Court. Since 1969, gay organizations have lobbied actively for the repeal of antihomosexual rules and laws.

QUESTIONS FOR REVIEW AND DISCUSSION

1. According to the Supreme Court in *Brown v. Board of Education of Topeka*, "separate but equal" is "inherently unequal." Why did the Court reject the separate-but-equal doctrine in 1954? Why didn't segregation really provide equal opportunities for African Americans in the United States?

2. Even though the North fought the Civil War in part to liberate the slaves, the southern states were able to reestablish white domination within a generation after the war. Why did the North allow the disenfranchisement of African Americans in the South, even though it violated the Constitution? How did the Supreme Court's views of the proper powers of government work to support segregation in the South and industrialization in the North?

3. To what extent can the "American" culture absorb other, non-Anglo-Saxon cultures, such as those of Native Americans, Hispanics, or Asians? How would "American culture" be changed if we came to have a multilingual, multiethnic society?

4. Think about the concept of equal pay for comparable work. What kinds of jobs traditionally performed by men would be comparable in effort, skill, and worth, say, to an executive secretary or switchboard operator? How would the economy be affected if the wages for many "women's jobs" were greatly increased?

5. What changes in our patterns of family life and in societal values have led to the political activism of senior citizens?

SELECTED REFERENCES

Martha F. Albertson and Nancy S. Thomadsen, *At the Boundaries of Law: Feminism and Legal Theory* (New York: Routledge, 1990). A series of essays exploring the effect that legal intervention and political injustice have had, and continues to have, on women's lives.

Herman Belz, *Equality Transformed: A Quarter-Century of Affirmative Action* (New Brunswick, N.J.: Transaction, 1990). Belz explores the changing nature of affirmative action policies over time.

Dee Brown, *Bury My Heart at Wounded Knee* (New York: Holt, Rinehart & Winston, 1971). An important examination of the treatment of Native Americans as the frontier pushed westward.

Kristin Bumiller, *The Civil Rights Society* (Baltimore, Md.: The Johns Hopkins University Press, 1992). In this provocative and insightful analysis of the effect of civil rights legislation on American minorities, Bumiller argues that laws prohibiting discrimination achieve an unintended result—they serve to reinforce the social identity of minorities as victims and thus enhance their sense of powerlessness in American society.

Gary Burtless, ed., *Work, Health, and Income among the Elderly* (Washington, D.C.: The Brookings Institute, 1987). A collection of papers examining the economic implications of changing patterns among the elderly.

Stokely Carmichael and Charles V. Hamilton, *Black Power: The Politics of Liberation in America* (New York: Vintage Books, 1967). A classic expression of the politics of racism in the United States and of the struggle to overcome white domination.

Peter Collier and David Horowitz, eds., *Second Thoughts about Race in America* (Lanham, Md.: University Press of America, 1991). This book deals with the metamorphosis of the civil rights movement over the last quarter-century and its relationship to the recent phenomenon of political correctness.

Elizabeth O. Colton, *The Jackson Phenomenon: The Man, The Power, The Message* (New York: Doubleday, 1989). This book offers a very interesting and personal perspective on Jesse Jackson's 1988 presidential campaign from the vantage point of an insider who was his campaign press secretary.

Stephen Cornell, *The Return of the Native: American Indian Political Resurgence* (New York: Oxford University Press, 1988). Considered to be the best study of Native Americans as an important and increasingly politicized ethnic minority.

Susan Faludi, *Backlash: The Undeclared War against American Women* (New York: Crown Publishers, 1991). The author suggests that the women's movement is losing ground because the media and the New Right of American politics have created a backlash against women's equality.

Marilyn French, *The War against Women* (New York: Simon & Schuster, 1992). This book catalogs what the author views as the losing battle of the sexes being waged by women. French discusses the subjugation of women by tradition, religion, and the state; institutional discrimination that prevents women from attaining economic independence, political power, and control over their own bodies; cultural hatred of women; and physical assaults against women.

Sylvia Ann Hewlett, *A Lesser Life: The Myth of Women's Liberation in America* (New York: Morrow, 1986). In one of the most controversial books on the women's struggle, Hewlett unfavorably compares the record of the United States with other countries, especially in Europe, in the area of women's social support and social legislation (maternity leave and day care, for example).

Richard Kluger, *Simple Justice* (New York: Alfred A. Knopf, 1975). The history of the 1954 Supreme Court ruling on *Brown v. Board of Education of Topeka* and African Americans' struggle for equality.

William W. Lammers, *Public Policy and the Aging* (Washington, D.C.: Congressional Quarterly Press, 1983). The author describes how the rapidly growing older population will affect the development of programs for the elderly. Specific public policies are explored in detail.

Robert A. Licht, *The Framers and Fundamental Rights* (Lanham, Md.: University Press of America, 1991). In this collection of essays, several authors examine the question of fundamental constitutional rights and provide a framework within which the rights being asserted by various groups today can be understood more clearly.

Aldon D. Morris, *The Origins of the Civil Rights Movement* (New York: The Free Press, 1985). This interesting book traces the alliances among African-American groups and the tactics they used in accelerating the civil rights movement in the United States.

Camille Paglia, *Sexual Personae: Art and Decadence from Nefertiti to Emily Dickenson* (New Haven: Yale University Press, 1991). This is one of the most controversial books on gender to be published in recent years. Paglia, a feminist, stands on end most of the principles of politically correct feminism.

Arthur Schlesinger, *The Disuniting of America* (New York: Norton, 1991). The author warns of the dangers of ethnic particularism, of the rejection by some minorities of "Eurocentrism" in culture and curriculum, and of the emergence of "political correctness" in the United States.

Lee Sigelman, *Black Americans' Views of Racial Equality: The Dream Deferred* (New York: Cambridge University Press, 1991). A statistical analysis, based on surveys, of African-American attitudes about racial inequality and injustice with respect to age, gender, and economic status.

Gilbert Y. Steiner, *Constitutional Inequality: The Political Fortunes of the Equal Rights Amendment* (Washington, D.C.: Brookings Institute, 1985). This case study of the Equal Rights Amendment dissects the difficulties in accomplishing fundamental policy changes through constitutional amendments.

Patricia A. Vardin and Ilene N. Brody, eds., *Children's Rights: Contemporary Perspectives* (New York: Teachers College Press, 1979). A valuable collection of essays on the rights of children in American society.

Sidney Verba and Gary R. Orren, *Equality in America: The View from the Top* (Cambridge, Mass.: Harvard University Press, 1985). This fascinating book used an elite survey of 2,762 American leaders from a wide range of groups (business, labor, feminists, and so on) to determine the meanings and implications of equality and attitudes about equality in America.

C. Vann Woodward, *The Strange Career of Jim Crow* (New York: Oxford University Press, 1957). The classic study of segregation in the southern United States.

PART THREE

PEOPLE AND POLITICS

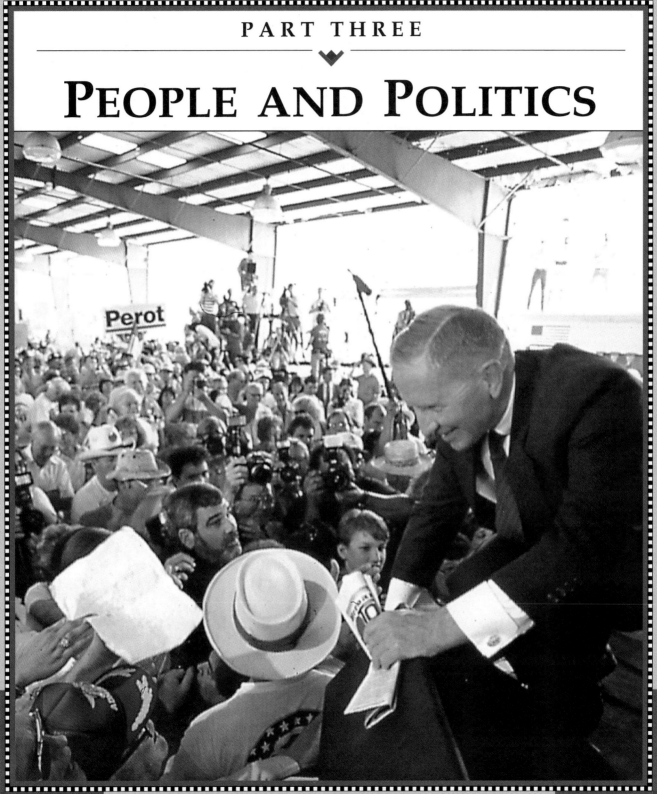

CHAPTER 6
Public Opinion

CHAPTER CONTENTS

WHAT IF ... POLITICAL POLLS WERE BANNED?

In election year 1992, one of the reasons that many Americans responded enthusiastically to presidential candidate H. Ross Perot was his promise to make up his own mind and not decide the issues according to the latest polls. These voters were angry at candidates and elected officials who seemed to take positions only after public opinion was revealed by the media and the pollsters.

Public opinion polls abound. They are commissioned by public agencies to help identify public needs or to measure public satisfaction with services. They are sponsored by private corporations to tap public attitudes toward their products. Newspapers, television stations, and entire networks either contract with commercial pollsters to gather data or, as the *New York Times* does, set up their own polling operations. Finally, political parties and candidates also commission polls to identify the public's preferences on policies and candidates.

Even to the relatively inattentive voter, it seems that political candidates design their campaigns in reaction to polling data. If the polls show that the public thinks the candidate is too interested in international politics, then the candidate's stump speech suddenly focuses on domestic issues. Public discomfort with a candidate's personality traits may lead to deliberate attempts by the candidate to change his or her public image.

What would campaigns and elections be like if all such political polls were banned? Federal regulations might allow, for example, polls taken by public or other agencies that focus on policies or issues but ban polls that ask for opinions about individuals or parties. In particular, no polls that ask how a person might vote would be allowed.

Much of the information generated by polls would probably not be missed. As columnist Brian Dickinson put it, "What does it mean that 48 percent of the voters think that the Supreme Court is too conservative?" After all, the Court is not elected; the Constitution makes it perfectly clear that the president nominates candidates and the Senate confirms them. Besides, do voters mean that the Court is politically conservative, or too pro-business, or socially conservative? The likelihood that such polling data are based on a common set of definitions is extremely low.

Information generated by polls is often published to create a news story. If there were no daily or weekly readings on the president's popularity, would it change the way that Americans evaluate how the government is really performing? Probably not. Instead of leaning on the latest presidential popularity figures to decide whether to support a presidential proposal, members of Congress would have to make their own judgments of the chief executive's initiative.

Most important, the character of American elections would be changed by a ban on political polling. Candidates would have to plan their campaigns and choose the issues they think are most crucial without regard to immediate public reaction. They would be unable to change their campaign strategy whenever the polls indicated that they were lagging behind in the "horse race." Journalists would not be able to issue daily reports on that same horse race. Instead, more attention might be paid to the candidates' speeches. Some journalists might try to find out what other public officials say about a candidate or analyze the feasibility of a candidate's proposals.

Finally, the voters would have to cast their votes without knowing which candidate is ahead in the polls. In some elections, the polls have found the race to be so close that no winner could be projected. Such elections tend to increase voter turnout owing to the excitement of the contest. Banning polls might have a similar effect on voter participation, as well as limit some of the more manipulative campaign strategies.

1. *Is polling the public just reporting the facts, like any kind of news reporting? Should poll reporting be protected by the First Amendment?*
2. *How does knowing which candidate is ahead shape campaign strategy? How does knowing the latest poll results affect voters' decisions?*

In an era of widespread public opinion polling, what role does public opinion play in the American political system? If the United States is a representative democracy, how powerful is the voice of the public, as it is expressed through polls, and how powerful should it be? Because our representatives in Washington and in our state legislatures must make decisions on policies and issues that affect the country throughout the year, it would seem that the views of the public, as measured by polls, would help politicians in voting on the laws.

Public opinion as expressed by polls, however, may be limited in its usefulness by its very character. After all, the pollster wrote the question, called the voters, and perhaps forwarded the results to the politicians. Public opinion, as gathered by commercial or academic polls, is not equivalent to constituents' writing to their representatives, nor does answering a poll require the effort of going out to vote. In fact, public opinion polls normally include the views of many individuals who do not vote.

How Powerful Is Public Opinion?

At various times in the recent history of the United States, public opinion has played a powerful role in presidential politics. Beginning in 1965, as public opinion became more divided over the war in Vietnam, numerous public expressions of opposition to the war took place, as measured by the polls and demonstrations in many cities. By 1968, when Lyndon Johnson was preparing to run for another term, public opinion against the war was expressed through a surge of support for antiwar candidate Senator Eugene McCarthy in the New Hampshire primary. Faced with public disapproval, Johnson dropped out of the race.

As the Watergate scandal of 1972 unfolded, revealing the role of President Nixon through congressional hearings and through tape recordings from his office, a similar groundswell of opinion against the president occurred. In this case, the disastrous fall in the president's approval ratings to less than 25 percent coincided with the decision by the House Judiciary Committee to initiate impeachment proceedings against the president. Nixon, facing an impeachment trial, resigned from office.

Both of these cases illustrate the power of public opinion when there is great public dissatisfaction with the government or with an official. On the positive side, high approval ratings for a president, such as George Bush maintained until late 1990, can be used to persuade Congress to support the president's program. Rarely, however, is public opinion so strongly expressed over a long period of time.

In most situations, public opinion is used by legislators, politicians, and presidents to shore up their own arguments. It provides a kind of evidence for their own point of view. If the results of polls do not support their position, they can either commission their own poll or ignore the polls. Public opinion favored passage of the Equal Rights Amendment, but the necessary total of thirty-eight state legislatures could not be persuaded to ratify it. In the weeks before President Bush ordered the beginning of the air war against Iraq, only about 50 percent of the public believed that the use of force was the right thing to do to drive Iraq out of Kuwait. Within a few days after the beginning of the air war, more than 85 percent of all

Americans believed that Bush had acted correctly by attacking Iraq. In neither of these cases, however, was public opinion overwhelmingly on one side or the other, initially. Thus, elected officials, although aware of the polls, could carry on their politics with little fear of reprisal from the voters and, in the case of Bush, with the hope that the public would rally to support him. Public opinion, then, is neither all-powerful nor powerless.

Defining and Measuring Public Opinion

There is no one public opinion because there are many different "publics." In a nation of more than 250 million people, there may be innumerable gradations of opinion on an issue. What we do is describe the distribution of opinions among the public about a particular question. Thus we define **public opinion** as follows:

> Public opinion is the aggregate of individual attitudes or beliefs shared by some portion of adults.

Although it might be said, for example, that public opinion favored the passage of the Equal Rights Amendment, a more accurate description of public opinion on that issue would be that 60 percent of the public supported the amendment, whereas 40 percent opposed it or had no opinion.

How is public opinion made known in a democracy? In the case of the Vietnam war, it was made known by numerous antiwar protests, countless articles in magazines and newspapers, and continuing electronic media coverage of antiwar demonstrations. Normally, however, public opinion becomes known in a democracy through elections and, in some states, initiatives or referenda. Other ways are through lobbying and interest group activities, which are also used to influence public opinion.

Public opinion can be defined most clearly by its effect. As political scientist V. O. Key, Jr., said, public opinion is what governments "find it prudent to heed."[1] This means that for public opinion to be effective, enough people have to hold a particular view with such strong conviction that a government feels its actions should be influenced by it.

An interesting question arises as to when *private* opinion becomes *public* opinion. Everyone probably has a private opinion about the competence of the president, as well as private opinions about more personal concerns, such as the state of a neighbor's lawn. We say that private opinion becomes public opinion when the opinion is publicly expressed and if the opinion concerns public issues. When someone's private opinion becomes so strong that the individual is willing to go to the polls to vote for or against a candidate or an issue—or to participate in a demonstration, to discuss the issue at work, to be willing to speak out on local television, or to participate in the political process in any one of a dozen other ways—then that opinion becomes public opinion.

PUBLIC OPINION
The aggregate of individual attitudes or beliefs shared by some portion of adults. There is no one public opinion because there are many different "publics."

---

[1]*Public Opinion and American Democracy* (New York: Alfred A. Knopf, 1961), p. 10.

Union members protest a cut in benefits. A strike can be seen as an expression of public opinion, but if the union does not get support from others, politicians will feel no effect.

The Qualities of Public Opinion

At the beginning of the Vietnam war in the 1960s, public opinion about its conduct was not very clear, like a camera that is not focused. As the war progressed and U.S. involvement deepened, public opinion became increasingly clarified. Public opinion has identifiable qualities that change over time. Political scientists have identified at least five specific qualities relating to public opinion: (1) intensity, (2) fluidity, (3) stability, (4) quiescence, and (5) relevance. In addition, political knowledge affects opinion, and the distribution of opinion on an issue indicates the possibilities for conflict or compromise.

Intensity

How strongly people are willing to express their private opinions determines the **intensity** of public opinion. Consider an example that seems to be regularly in the news—gun control. Most Americans who have opinions about gun control do not have very strong opinions. A small percentage has extremely intense convictions pro or con. But the average intensity is still quite mild. In contrast, public opinion about the Iranian hostages in 1979 and 1980 was quite intense, on average. Most Americans were in favor of taking drastic measures to free the hostages. Of those who did have an opinion, only a few were just mildly interested in saving the hostages.

Intensity of public opinion is often critical in generating public *action*. Intense minorities can win on an issue of public policy over less intense majorities. Public policy makers often equate the intensity of opinion on an issue with the issue's relevance.

INTENSITY
The strength of a pro or con position concerning public policy or an issue. Intensity is often critical in generating public action; an intense minority can often win on an issue of public policy over a less intense majority.

Fluidity

Public opinion can change drastically in a very short period of time. When this occurs, we say that public opinion is fluid.

Did You Know ... That James Madison and others argued in *The Federalist Papers* that public opinion was potentially dangerous and should be diffused through a large republic with separation of government powers?

FLUIDITY
The extent to which public opinion changes over time.

SOLID SOUTH
A term describing the disposition of the post–Civil War southern states to vote for the Democratic party. (Voting patterns in the South have changed.)

STABILITY
The extent to which public opinion remains constant over a period of time.

LATENT PUBLIC OPINION
Unexpressed political opinions that have the potential to become manifest attitudes or beliefs.

At the end of World War II, the American people were about evenly divided in their opinions of the United States's wartime ally, the ex-Soviet Union. A 1945 Roper poll showed that about 39 percent of Americans saw the Soviets as peace loving, while 38 percent felt they were aggressive. During the years of the cold war (1947 to, roughly, 1985), American opinion about the aims of the Soviet Union was very consistent. Between 13 and 17 percent of the American people believed that the Soviet Union was peace loving, and more than 60 percent saw it as aggressive. Mikhail Gorbachev's leadership of the Soviet Union and his policy of openness toward the West created an extremely fluid state of opinion among Americans. As Americans watched his attempts at internal reform and his willingness to allow the Eastern European nations to pull away from the Communist orbit, American opinion about the Soviet Union changed quickly. Over a four-year period, between 1985 and the beginning of 1990, the number of Americans who saw the Soviet Union as peace loving increased from 17 to 36 percent. In an even quicker turnaround, during the same period, the proportion of the American public that held an unfavorable opinion about the Soviet Union dropped from 41 to 13 percent. The **fluidity** of American opinion was a response to the rapidly changing conditions in the Soviet Union and world politics.[2] Such fluidity in public opinion reflects public awareness of government policy and in turn influences government decision making.

Stability

Many individual opinions remain constant over a lifetime. Taken together, individual opinions that constitute public opinion may also be extremely stable, persisting for many years. Consider the effect of the Civil War on political attitudes in the South. It was the Republicans under Abraham Lincoln who, in the eyes of southerners, were responsible for the Civil War and the ensuing humiliations experienced by a defeated South. Consequently, the South became strongly Democratic. Until the post–World War II period, it was called the **Solid South** because Democratic candidates always won. We can say that public opinion in the South in favor of Democrats and against Republicans had great **stability**.

Quiescence

Not all political opinions are expressed by the holders of opinions. There may be potential political opinions—those not yet realized. Political scientists call these **latent,** or quiescent, **public opinions.** Some say, for example, that Hitler exploited the latent public opinion of post–World War I Germany by forming the National Socialist party. The public was ripe for a leader who would militarize Germany and put Germany back on its feet. Latent public opinion offers golden opportunities for political leaders astute enough to perceive it and act on it politically.

When average citizens are asked to respond to highly complex issues about which they have imperfect knowledge, their opinions may remain latent. This was true, for example, of the antiballistic missile (ABM) program debated by the Senate in 1969. A Gallup poll in July of that year indicated that 59 percent of Americans were undecided about the value

[2]*New York Times,* December 3, 1989.

of the ABM program even though they knew about it. What the views of those citizens would have been if they had been better informed is unknown. Poll questions dealing with views on foreign nations also produce a high proportion of responses indicating that many people rarely think about these kinds of issues.

Relevance

Relevant public opinion for most people is simply public opinion that deals with issues concerning them. If a person has a sick parent who is having trouble meeting medical bills, then the relevant public opinion for that person will be an opinion that is focused on the issues of Medicare and Medicaid. If another person likes to go hunting with his or her children, gun control becomes a relevant political issue. Of course, **relevance** changes according to events. Public concern about inflation, for example, was at an all-time low during the late 1980s and early 1990s. Why? Because the United States had relatively little inflation during that period. Public opinion about the issue of unemployment was certainly relevant during the Great Depression, but not during the 1960s when the nation experienced 102 months of almost uninterrupted economic growth from 1961 to 1969.

Certain popular books can make a particular issue relevant. The publication of *The Population Bomb*[3] by Paul Ehrlich in 1968 sparked nationwide concern with uncontrolled population growth. The population issue, although still far from resolved, is less in the public mind today. Indeed, public opinion polls rarely sample attitudes about it.

Political Knowledge

People are more likely to base their opinions on knowledge about an issue if they have strong feelings about the topic. Just as relevance and intensity are closely related to having an opinion, individuals who are strongly interested in a question will probably take the time to read about it.

Looking at the population as a whole, the level of political information is quite low. Survey research tells us that slightly less than 46 percent of adult Americans can give the name of their congressperson, and just 39 percent can name both U.S. senators from their state. Only 30 percent know that the term of their congressional representative is two years, although almost 70 percent know the majority party in Congress. What these data tell us is that Americans do not expend much effort remembering political facts that may not be important to their daily lives.

Americans are also likely to forget political information quite quickly. Facts that are of vital interest to citizens in a time of crisis lose their significance after the crisis has passed. In the 1985 *New York Times*/CBS News Survey on Vietnam, marking the tenth anniversary of the end of that conflict, 63 percent of those questioned knew that the United States sided with the South Vietnamese in that conflict. Only 27 percent remembered, however, which side in that conflict launched the Tet offensive, which was a major political defeat for American and South Vietnamese forces.[4]

If political information is perceived to be of no use for an individual or is painful to recall, it is not surprising that facts are forgotten. What is

RELEVANCE
The extent to which an issue is of concern at a particular time. Issues become relevant when the public views them as pressing or of direct concern to them.

"Are you uninformed or apathetic?"
"I don't know and I don't care."

"Why Are Your Papers in Order?" © 1984 by Peter C. Vey.

---

[3]New York: Ballantine Books, 1968.
[4]*New York Times*/CBS News Survey, February 23–27, 1985.

Did You Know ... That for the 1984 presidential election between Ronald Reagan and Walter Mondale, the last preelection Gallup poll missed the actual percentage of Reagan's popular vote support by only 0.2 percentage points?

CONSENSUS
General agreement among the citizenry on an issue.

DIVISIVE OPINION
Public opinion that is polarized between two quite different positions.

OPINION POLL
A method of systematically questioning a small, selected sample of respondents who are deemed representative of the total population. Widely used by government, business, university scholars, political candidates, and voluntary groups to provide reasonably accurate data on public attitudes, beliefs, expectations, and behavior.

more disturbing than forgetting the past is the inability of many citizens to give basic information about current issues. Recent polls on U.S. military involvement in Europe found that only 60 percent of the public knew that United States was a member of the North Atlantic Treaty Organization (NATO), which it has been since 1949, and 21 percent thought that the Soviet Union was also a member (NATO was founded to provide a unified defense against the Soviet Union).[5] Clearly, many people have not cared to learn much about U.S. military commitments.

Consensus and Division

There are very few issues on which most Americans agree. The more normal situation is for opinion to be distributed among several different positions. Looking at the distribution of opinion can tell us how divided the public is on a question and give us some indication of whether compromise is possible. The distribution of opinion can also tell us how many individuals have not thought about an issue enough to hold an opinion.

When a large proportion of the American public appears to express the same view on an issue, we say that a **consensus** exists, at least at the moment the poll was taken. Figure 6-1 shows the pattern of opinion that might be called consensual. Issues on which the public holds widely differing attitudes result in **divisive opinion** (Figure 6-2). If there is no possible middle position on such issues, we expect that the division will continue to generate political conflict.

Figure 6-3 shows a distribution of opinion indicating that most Americans either have no information about the issue or are not interested enough in the issue to formulate a position. This figure illustrates latent, or quiescent, opinion. Politicians may feel that the lack of knowledge gives them more room to maneuver, or they may be wary of taking any action for fear that the opinion will crystallize after a crisis. It is possible that we would see the latent pattern most often if survey respondents were totally honest. Research has shown that some individuals will express fabricated opinions to an interviewer on certain topics rather than admit their ignorance.

Measuring Public Opinion: Polling Techniques

The History of Opinion Polls

Although some idea of public opinion can be discovered by asking persons we know for their opinions or by reading the "Letters to the Editor" sections in newspapers, most descriptions of the distribution of opinions are based on **opinion polls.** During the 1800s, certain American newspapers and magazines spiced up their political coverage by doing face-to-face straw polls or mail surveys of their readers' opinions. In this century, the magazine *Literary Digest* further developed the technique of opinion polls by mailing large numbers of questionnaires to individuals, many of whom were its own subscribers. From 1916 to 1936, more than 70 percent of the magazine's election predictions were accurate.

---

[5]*New York Times*/CBS News Survey, May 5–11, 1989.

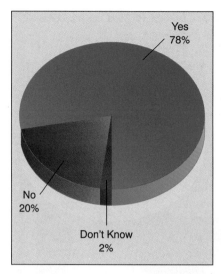

FIGURE 6-1 ■ Consensus Opinion

When asked if U.S. school children should be required to pledge allegiance to the flag in all U.S. schools, a majority of Americans agree.
SOURCE: Survey by the Gallup Organization, May 23–26, 1991.

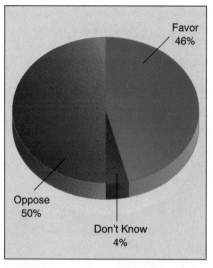

FIGURE 6-2 ■ Divisive Opinion

Americans are almost evenly divided on using U.S. troops in a foreign nation to fight drug traffickers. Since the Vietnam war, Americans have strong differences over the use of troops abroad.
SOURCE: *Gallup Report,* October 1989.

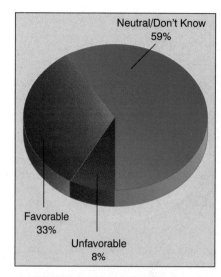

FIGURE 6-3 ■ Latent Opinion

Few Americans have strong feelings about the Philippines in either direction, probably because they have little knowledge about the nation. What types of events might cause Americans to change their views?
SOURCE: *New York Times*/CBS News Survey, September 21–22, 1987.

The *Literary Digest,* however, suffered a major setback in its polling activities when it predicted that Alfred Landon would win over Franklin Delano Roosevelt in 1936, based on more than two million returned questionnaires. Landon won in only two states. A major problem with the *Digest's* polling technique was its continuing use of nonrepresentative respondents. In 1936, at the bottom of the Great Depression, those people who were the magazine's subscribers were, for one thing, considerably more affluent than the average American.

Several newcomers to the public opinion poll industry accurately predicted Roosevelt's landslide victory. The organizations of these newcomers are still active in the poll-taking industry today: the Gallup poll of George Gallup, and Roper and Associates founded by Elmo Roper. Gallup and Roper, along with Archibald Crossley, developed the modern polling techniques of market research. Using personal interviews with small samples of selected voters (a few thousand), they showed that they could predict with accuracy the behavior of the total voting population. We shall see how this is possible.

Government officials during World War II were keenly interested in public opinion about the war effort and about the increasing number of restrictions placed on civilian activities. Improved methods of sampling were used, and by the 1950s a whole new science of survey research was developed, which soon spread to Western Europe, Israel, and other countries. Survey research centers sprang up throughout the United States, particularly at universities. Some of these survey groups are the American Institute of Public Opinion at Princeton, New Jersey; the National Opinion Research Center at the University of Chicago; and the Survey Research Center at the University of Michigan.

POLITICS AND POLLS

When Polls Are Wrong

Between 1920 and 1932, the *Literary Digest* accurately projected the winners of each presidential election. The poll consisted of approximately ten million voters who received a mailing and returned their responses on presidential preference. In 1936, the results were tallied and reported on October 31: for Landon 57 percent, with 1,293,699 votes; for Franklin D. Roosevelt 43 percent and 972,897 ballots. When American voters actually went to their polling places in November, the results were quite different: Roosevelt got 62.5 percent of the vote and carried every state except Maine and Vermont.

What went wrong? First, the sample was selected from telephone directories and lists of automobile owners, creating a biased sample. Second, of the ten million questionnaires mailed, only about 20 percent were returned; thus, there was a strong self-selection among those who chose to answer. Third, the time lag between the early September mailing of the questionnaire and the election could not anticipate any changes in voter perception, campaign events, or even world or national events that by November would cause a shift in voter preferences. Finally, the poll neglected to take into account the fact that in 1936 the United States was still in the throes of a major national crisis. People were shifting allegiances. The New Deal coalition that Roosevelt was constructing recombined different and new groups of people; the working class and the less affluent were rallying behind FDR. The poll underrepresented this constituency.

Polling techniques greatly improved in subsequent years. The

quota sampling technique of George Gallup, Jr., used census data to identify the necessary percentages of relevant groups in the population (by religion, gender, race, and so on) to make a poll more accurate. Nonetheless, a second erroneous poll occurred in 1948 when Gallup projected that Thomas Dewey would defeat Harry Truman: The poll indicated that Truman would get 44.5 percent of the vote; actually, he obtained 49.9 percent and won. The *Chicago Daily Tribune* predicted the winner before the election results were tallied with a banner headline that read "DEWEY DEFEATS TRUMAN."

Studies have demonstrated that quota sampling tends to underrepresent certain groups, in particular the poor, minorities, and the less educated, because in filling the assigned quotas, pollsters tend to avoid dangerous neighborhoods and other difficult polling obstacles. An entire quota may be filled from a single, relatively easy location (such as a "nice" apartment building where all of, say, the African-American quota can be completed).

Moreover, in 1948, Gallup did his last poll two weeks before the election, thereby missing a last-minute shift toward Truman. Subsequent polls have tried to correct these flaws by polling up to election day.

In spite of great refinements, a third major national polling failure occurred in 1980. Most polls showed the race between Reagan and Carter to be "too close to call." When Reagan beat Carter 51 percent to 41 percent, pollsters and the public were amazed at the magnitude of Reagan's victory. What went wrong? In essence, it was the major enemy of pollsters: last-minute changes in opinion. Almost up to election day, relatively large numbers of voters were undecided (some polls showed as many as 13 percent). In hindsight, it appears that almost all of the "undecided" went to Reagan. Polls that were taken closest to election day revealed this trend. In fact, Carter's pollster, Patrick Caddell, looked at his figures the day before the election and told Carter aboard Air Force One that he would not win the election.

Sampling Techniques

How can interviewing several thousand voters tell us what tens of millions of voters will do? Clearly, it is necessary that the sample of several thousand individuals be representative of all voters in the population. Consider an analogy. Let us say we have a large jar containing pennies of various dates, and we want to know how many pennies were minted within certain decades—1940–1949, 1950–1959, and so on. There are 10,000 pennies in the jar. One way to estimate the distribution of the dates on the pennies—without examining all 10,000—is to take a representative sample. This sample would be obtained by mixing the pennies up well and then removing a handful of them—perhaps 100 pennies. The distribution of dates might be as follows:

- *1940–1949: 5 percent*
- *1950–1959: 5 percent*
- *1960–1969: 20 percent*
- *1970–1979: 30 percent*
- *1980–present 40 percent*

If the pennies are very well mixed within the jar and if you take a large enough sample, the resulting distribution would probably approach the actual distribution of the dates of all 10,000 coins.

The most important principle in sampling, or poll taking, is randomness. Every penny or every person should have a known chance, and especially an *equal chance*, of being sampled. If this happens, then a small sample should be representative of the whole group both in demographic characteristics (age, religion, race, living area, and the like) and in opinions. The ideal way to sample the voting population of the United States would be to put all voter names into a jar—or a computer—and randomly sample, say, 2,000 of them. Because this is too costly and inefficient, pollsters have developed other ways to obtain good samples. One of the most interesting techniques is simply to choose a random selection of telephone numbers and interview the respective households. This technique produces a relatively accurate sample at a low cost.

To ensure that the random samples include respondents from relevant segments of the population—rural, urban, Northeast, South, and so on—most survey organizations randomly choose, say, urban areas that they will consider as representative of all urban areas. Then they randomly select their respondents within that area. A generally less accurate technique is known as *quota sampling*. For this type of poll, survey researchers decide how many persons of certain types they need in the survey—such as minorities, women, or farmers—and then send out interviewers to find the necessary number of these types. This method is often not only less accurate, but it also may be biased if, say, the interviewer refuses to go into certain neighborhoods or will not interview after dark. Generally, the national survey organizations take great care to select their samples randomly because their reputations rest on the accuracy of their results. Usually, the Gallup or Roper polls interview about 1,500 individuals, and their results have a very high probability of being correct—within a margin of 3 percent. The accuracy with which the Gallup poll has predicted national election results is reflected in Table 6-1.

Did You Know . . . That public opinion pollsters typically measure national sentiment among the more than 185 million adult Americans by interviewing only about 1,500 people?

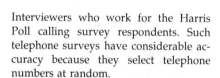

Interviewers who work for the Harris Poll calling survey respondents. Such telephone surveys have considerable accuracy because they select telephone numbers at random.

TABLE 6-1 ■ Record of Gallup Poll Accuracy

YEAR	Gallup Final Survey*		Election Result*		Deviation†
1992	44.0%	Clinton	43%	Clinton	+1.0
1988	53.0	Bush	54.0	Bush	−1.0
1986	n.a.	Democratic	n.a.	Democratic	n.a.
1984	59.0	Reagan	59.2	Reagan	−0.2
1982	55.0	Democratic	56.1	Democratic	−1.1
1980	47.0	Reagan	50.8	Reagan	−3.8
1978	55.0	Democratic	54.6	Democratic	+0.4
1976	48.0	Carter	50.0	Carter	−2.0
1974	60.0	Democratic	58.9	Democratic	+1.1
1972	62.0	Nixon	61.8	Nixon	+0.2
1970	53.0	Democratic	54.3	Democratic	−1.3
1968	43.0	Nixon	43.5	Nixon	−0.5
1966	52.5	Democratic	51.9	Democratic	+0.6
1964	64.0	Johnson	61.3	Johnson	+2.7
1962	55.5	Democratic	52.7	Democratic	+2.8
1960	51.0	Kennedy	50.1	Kennedy	+0.9
1958	57.0	Democratic	56.5	Democratic	+0.5
1956	59.5	Eisenhower	57.8	Eisenhower	+1.7
1954	51.5	Democratic	52.7	Democratic	−1.2
1952	51.0	Eisenhower	55.4	Eisenhower	−4.4
1950	51.0	Democratic	50.3	Democratic	+0.7
1948	44.5	Truman	49.9	Truman	−5.4
1946	58.0	Republican	54.3	Republican	+3.7
1944	51.5	Roosevelt	53.3[1]	Roosevelt	−1.8
1942	52.0	Democratic	48.0[2]	Democratic	+4.0
1940	52.0	Roosevelt	55.0	Roosevelt	−3.0
1938	54.0	Democratic	50.8	Democratic	+3.2
1936	55.7	Roosevelt	62.5	Roosevelt	−6.8

*The figure shown is the winner's percentage of the Democratic–Republican vote except in the elections of 1948, 1968, 1976, and 1980. Because the Thurmond and Henry Wallace voters in 1948 were largely split-offs from the normally Democratic vote, final preelection estimates of the division of the vote were made for the four candidates Truman, Dewey, Wallace, and Thurmond. Therefore, the percentages for Truman shown for 1948 are based on the total vote for the four candidates. In 1968, George Wallace's candidacy was supported by such a large minority that he was clearly a major candidate, and the 1968 percentages are based on the total Nixon–Humphrey–Wallace vote. In 1976, because of interest in McCarthy's candidacy and its potential effect on the Carter vote, the final Gallup poll report included estimates of the share of the vote for Carter, Ford, and McCarthy, as well as an estimate for all other candidates combined. Therefore, the percentages for Carter shown for 1976 are based on the total vote for all candidates. The same is true of 1980, when Anderson's candidacy drew a sizable minority vote.

†Average deviation for twenty-five national elections: 2.1 percentage points.

Average deviation for eighteen national elections since 1950 inclusive: 1.4 percentage points.

Trend in deviation:

Elections	Average Error
1936–1950	3.6
1952–1960	1.7
1962–1970	1.6
1972–1992	1.2

[1]Civilian vote 53.3 + Roosevelt soldier vote 0.5 = 53.8 Roosevelt. Gallup final survey based on civilian vote.

[2]Final report said Democrats would win control of the House, which they did even though the Republicans won a majority of the popular vote.

SOURCES: *The Gallup Report*, August/September 1984, p. 61; *The Gallup Report*, September 1985, p. 33; *Congressional Quarterly Weekly Report*, November 7, 1992, p. 3550.

Similar sampling techniques are used in many other, nonpolitical situations. For the Nielsen ratings of TV programs, for example, representative households are selected by the A. C. Nielsen Company and a machine is attached to each household's TV set. The machine monitors viewing choices twenty-four hours a day and transmits this information to the company's central offices. A one-point drop in a Nielsen rating can mean a loss of revenue of millions of dollars to a TV network. A one-point drop indicates about 800,000 fewer viewers are watching a particular show. This means that advertisers are unwilling to pay as much for viewing time. Indeed, advertising rates are based in many cases solely on Nielsen ratings. When you consider that only about 3,000 families have that little machine attached to their TV sets, it is apparent that the science of selecting representative samples has come a long way—at least far enough to convince major advertisers to accept advertising fees based on the results of those samples.

Did You Know . . . That a radio station in Iowa conducts "The Cess Poll" to assess voters' primary election preferences for president by measuring the drop in water pressure when people express their support for a candidate by flushing their toilets when the candidate's name is read over the air?

The Polls and the 1992 Presidential Election

As the 1992 election drew near and the polls still showed President Bush trailing Bill Clinton (see Figure 6-4), the president took to referring to the myriad surveyors of the public as "those nutty pollsters" and insisted that their results did not reflect the true sentiment of the voters. Of course, Mr. Bush's campaign was well supplied with its own polling data, which showed about the same margins as the media polls. Bush's disparagement of the polls underlined how important they had become to the campaign plans of the candidates. At the same time, Mr. Clinton had become more cautious on the campaign trail, carefully protecting his lead in the states in which the polls showed him to be a clear winner. H. Ross Perot, on the other hand, simply refused to discuss the polls and continued to lavishly fund his campaign for the presidency.

FIGURE 6-4 ■ Tracking the New York Times/CBS News Poll

SOURCE: *New York Times*, October 25, 1992, p. 12; and *New York Times*, November 3, 1992, p. 9.

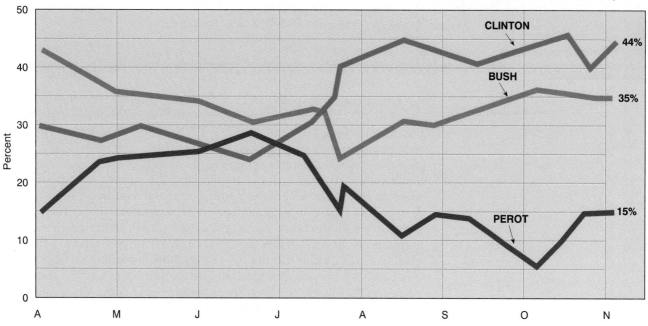

PROFILE

Chester James Carville, Jr.

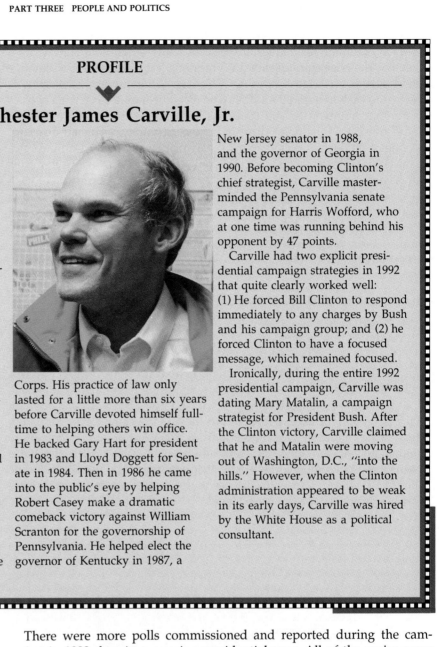

"I think that when it's written about, this is going to be a kind of campaign that signaled not just a change in the way we govern, but in the way we run for office."

James Carville was not just President Clinton's chief campaign strategist, but, according to the *New York Times,* also the campaign's "diviner and spiritual center." These were strong words for someone who was once considered a struggling political consultant.

Carville, born in Benning, Georgia, went to high school, college, and law school in Louisiana. Louisiana is considered by some to be a state in which the national pastime isn't baseball, but rather politics. That is where he started his political career, working for an unsuccessful state legislative candidate whose campaign motto was "I want you, I need you, and I'll fight for you."

Carville's stay at Louisiana State University lasted seven years because of a stint with the U.S. Marine

Corps. His practice of law only lasted for a little more than six years before Carville devoted himself full-time to helping others win office. He backed Gary Hart for president in 1983 and Lloyd Doggett for Senate in 1984. Then in 1986 he came into the public's eye by helping Robert Casey make a dramatic comeback victory against William Scranton for the governorship of Pennsylvania. He helped elect the governor of Kentucky in 1987, a

New Jersey senator in 1988, and the governor of Georgia in 1990. Before becoming Clinton's chief strategist, Carville masterminded the Pennsylvania senate campaign for Harris Wofford, who at one time was running behind his opponent by 47 points.

Carville had two explicit presidential campaign strategies in 1992 that quite clearly worked well: (1) He forced Bill Clinton to respond immediately to any charges by Bush and his campaign group; and (2) he forced Clinton to have a focused message, which remained focused.

Ironically, during the entire 1992 presidential campaign, Carville was dating Mary Matalin, a campaign strategist for President Bush. After the Clinton victory, Carville claimed that he and Matalin were moving out of Washington, D.C., "into the hills." However, when the Clinton administration appeared to be weak in its early days, Carville was hired by the White House as a political consultant.

There were more polls commissioned and reported during the campaign in 1992 than in any prior presidential year. All of the major news organizations—NBC, ABC, CBS, CNN—and the major national newspapers commissioned polls throughout the campaign. Many newspapers ran weekly features comparing the results of the most recent polls. Some journalists tried to avoid emphasizing the polling data and focused more on the issues behind the numbers, but the data won out in the last few weeks of the campaign. Polls were commissioned after every debate to report which candidate "won" the debate. The Bush campaign received a strong positive jolt when the CNN/*USA Today* poll reported that the president was quickly closing the gap on Bill Clinton ten days before the election. No other polling organization, however, could find the same phenomenon that weekend. Even the news anchors started discussing how the polls chose their respondents and how the results were tallied.

How Public Opinion Is Formed

Most Americans are willing to express opinions on political issues when asked. How do individuals acquire these opinions and attitudes? Most views that are expressed as political opinions are acquired through a process known as **political socialization.** By this we mean that individuals acquire their political attitudes, often including their party identification, through relationships with their families, friends, and coworkers. The most important influences in this process are the following: (1) the family, (2) the educational environment and achievement of the individual, (3) the influence of peers, (4) the influence of religion, (5) economic status, (6) political events, (7) opinion leaders, (8) the media, and (9) race and other demographic traits. We discuss each of these influences below, as well as the fairly recent phenomenon of the gender gap.

POLITICAL SOCIALIZATION
The process by which individuals acquire political beliefs and attitudes.

The Importance of the Family

The family is the most important force in political socialization. Not only do our parents' political attitudes and actions affect our adult opinions, but also the family links us to other socialization forces. We acquire our ethnic identity, our notion of social class, our educational opportunities, and our early religious beliefs from our families. Each of these factors can also influence our political attitudes.

The clearest legacy of the family is partisan identification. If both parents identify with one party, there is a strong likelihood that the children will begin political life with the same party preference. Children do not "learn" such attitudes in the same way as they learn how to ride a bike. Rather, they learn by absorbing their parents' casual comments about political parties, their actions and conversation during election campaigns, and other intended clues.

In their study of political attitudes among adolescents, M. Kent Jennings and Richard G. Niemi[6] probed the partisan attachments of high school seniors and their parents during the mid-1960s. That parents successfully transmit their party identification to their children is evident from Table 6-2. Democratic parents tend to produce Democratic children about two-

Patriotism is instilled in children through the process of political socialization. The children in this picture know that their parents approve of this display of support for the flag, thus enhancing their patriotic feelings.

[6]*The Political Character of Adolescence: The Influence of Families and Schools* (Princeton, N.J.: Princeton University Press, 1974).

TABLE 6-2 ■ Student Party Identification by Parent Party Identification (in Percentages)

High School Students	Parents		
	Democratic	Independent	Republican
Democratic	66	29	13
Independent	27	55	36
Republican	7	17	51

SOURCE: M. Kent Jennings and Richard G. Niemi, *The Political Character of Adolescence: The Influence of Family and Schools* (Princeton, N.J.: Princeton University Press, 1974), p. 41.

thirds of the time, and Independent and Republican parents both transmit their beliefs about parties only slightly less well. There is still a sizable amount of cross-generational slippage, however. In all, Jennings and Niemi found that 59 percent of the children agreed with their parents' party ties.

In a 1973 reinterview of the same children and their parents,[7] Jennings and Niemi found that the younger people had become notably more independent of partisan ties, whereas their parents went through very little change. By 1973, a majority of the children deviated from their parents' partisanship.

These researchers also noted wide variance between the attitudes of the parents and children about specific political issues. They investigated parent–student attitudes on four issues: school integration, school prayers, allowing communists to hold elective office, and allowing speeches against churches and religion. There was only a moderate relationship between the generations' views on the first two issues and virtually no relationship at all on the last two issues. The younger group's political attitudes were obviously strongly affected by their experiences during the time period between the two interviews. By 1973, many of the high school seniors had completed college or spent time in the work force. Even more significantly, by the time of the second interview, many of the younger group had served in—or participated in protests against—the Vietnam war.

Educational Influence on Political Opinion

From the early days of the republic, schools were perceived to be important transmitters of political information and attitudes. Children in the primary grades learn about their country mostly in patriotic ways. They learn to salute the flag, to say the pledge of allegiance, and to celebrate national holidays. Later, in the middle grades, children learn more historical facts and come to understand the structure of government and the functions of the president, judges, and Congress. By high school, students have a more complex understanding of the political system, may identify with a political party, and may take positions on issues.

Education is a powerful influence on an individual's political attitudes and on political behavior. Generally, the more education a person receives, the more liberal his or her opinions become. Students who go on to graduate training continue to become more liberal in their opinions. By *liberal*, we mean that the student is more likely to be tolerant of social change, to support social welfare programs, and to think that the United States should be active in international affairs. Individuals who have limited educational backgrounds are more likely to be isolationist in their foreign policy positions, more conservative in their social opinions, and less likely to support civil rights and civil liberties.

Peers and Peer Group Influence

Once a child enters school, the child's friends become an important influence on behavior and attitudes. As young children, and later as adults,

---

[7]*Generations and Politics* (Princeton, N.J.: Princeton University Press, 1981).

"Glad you brought that up, Jim. The latest research on polls has turned up some interesting variables. It turns out, for example, that people will tell you any old thing that pops into their heads."

Drawing by Saxon © 1984 The New Yorker Magazine, Inc

friendships and associations in **peer groups** are influential on political attitudes. We must, however, separate the effects of peer group pressure on opinions and attitudes in general from peer group pressure on political opinions. For the most part, associations among peers are nonpolitical. Political attitudes are more likely to be shaped by peer groups when the peer groups are involved directly in political activities.

Individuals who join interest groups based on ethnic identity may find, for example, a common political bond through working for the group's civil liberties and rights. Members of a labor union may feel strong political pressure to support certain prolabor candidates. African-American activist groups may consist of individuals who join together to support government programs that will aid the African-American population.

Religious Influence

Religious associations tend to create definite political attitudes, although why this occurs is not clearly understood. Surveys show that Roman Catholic respondents tend to be more liberal on economic issues than Protestants. Apparently, Jewish respondents are more liberal on all fronts than either Catholics or Protestants.[8] In terms of voting behavior, it has been observed that northern white Protestants are more likely to vote Republican, whereas northern white Roman Catholics more often vote Democratic; and everywhere in the United States, Jews mostly vote Democratic. These associations between religious background and political attitudes

PEER GROUPS
Groups consisting of members sharing common relevant social characteristics. They play an important part in the socialization process, helping to shape attitudes and beliefs.

---

[8]See Robert S. Erikson, Norman R. Luttbeg, and Kent L. Tedin, *American Public Opinion: Its Origins, Content, and Impact*, 2d ed. (New York: John Wiley, 1980).

are partly derived from the ethnic background of certain religious groups and the conditions at the time their forebears immigrated to the United States. Germans who immigrated before the Civil War tend to be Republican regardless of their religious background, whereas Eastern European Catholics, who arrived in the late nineteenth century, adopted the Democratic identity of the cities in which they made their homes. The relationship between religion and party affiliation is shown in Figure 6-5.

Sometimes a candidate's religion enters the political picture, as it did in the 1960 presidential election contest between Democrat John Kennedy and Republican Richard Nixon. The fact that Kennedy was a Catholic—the second Catholic to be nominated by a major party—polarized many voters. Among northern whites, Kennedy was supported by 83 percent of voting Catholics and by 93 percent of Jewish voters but only by 28 percent of the Protestants who voted.

The Influence of Economic Status and Occupation

How wealthy you are and the kind of job you hold are also associated with your political views. Social-class differences emerge on a wide range of issues. Poorer people are more inclined to favor government social welfare programs but are likely to be conservative on social issues such as abortion. The upper middle class is more likely to hold conservative economic views but to be tolerant of social change. People in lower economic strata also tend to be more isolationist on foreign policy issues and are more likely to identify with the Democratic party and vote for Democratic candidates. Support for civil liberties and tolerance of different points of view tend to be greater among those with higher social status and lower among those with lower social status. Probably, it is educational differences more than the patterns of life at home or work that account for this.

The Influence of Political Events

People's political attitudes may be shaped by political events and the nation's reactions to them. In the 1960s and 1970s, the war in Vietnam—

FIGURE 6-5 ■ Religion and Party Affiliation

SOURCE: *New York Times*, April 10, 1991.

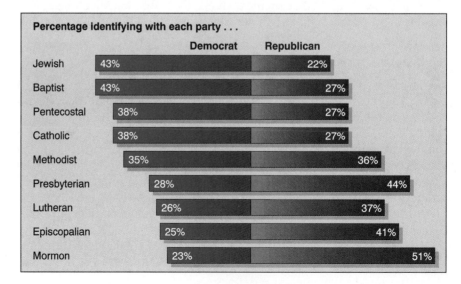

including revelations about the secret bombing in Cambodia—and the Watergate break-in and subsequent cover-up fostered widespread cynicism toward government. In one study of the impact of Watergate, Christopher Arterton[9] found that school children changed their image of the president from a "benevolent" to a "malevolent" leader as the scandal unfolded. Negative views also increased about other aspects of politics and politicians.

When the events of an era produce a long-lasting political impact, **generational effects** result. Voters who grew up in the 1930s during the Great Depression were likely to form life-long attachments to the Democratic party, the party of Franklin D. Roosevelt. There was some evidence that the years of economic prosperity under Ronald Reagan during the 1980s may have influenced young adults to identify with the Republican party. A 1990 poll showed that 52 percent of thirteen-to-seventeen-year-olds thought of themselves as Republicans, while 32 percent of this age group thought of themselves as Democrats.[10] This trend was dramatically reversed, however, in the 1992 presidential race.

GENERATIONAL EFFECTS
The long-lasting effects of events of a particular time period on the political opinions or preferences of those who came of political age at that time.

Opinion Leaders' Influence

We are all influenced by those with whom we are closely associated or whom we hold in great respect—friends at school, family members and other relatives, teachers, and so on. In a sense, these people are **opinion leaders,** but on an informal level; that is, their influence over us is not necessarily intentional or deliberate. We are also influenced by formal opinion leaders, such as a president, a lobbyist, a congressperson, or a news commentator, who have as part of their job the task of swaying people's views. Their interest lies in defining the political agenda in such a way that discussions about policy options will take place on their terms.

OPINION LEADERS
Those who are able to influence the opinions of others because of position, expertise, or personality. Such leaders help to shape public opinion either formally or informally.

Media Influence

Newspapers, television, and other **media** act as sources of information, commentary, and images. Newspapers and news magazines (such as *Time* or *Newsweek)* are especially rich sources of knowledge about political issues. Some argue that newspaper editorials normally have a heavily pro-Republican and conservative slant, especially for presidential endorsements, and that columnists are often selected to reflect such biases. Journalists are perceived as having a counteracting Democratic and liberal bias. Television, the media source relied on by most Americans, conveys only limited political information about issues or candidates' qualifications. There seems to be no strongly partisan or ideological bias in television coverage, although the visual and mental images conveyed by TV clearly have a powerful impact.

MEDIA
The technical means of communication with mass audiences. The media have become extremely important in American political life as a means of informing and influencing millions of citizens.

The Influence of Demographic Traits

African Americans show a much stronger commitment than whites to steady or more rapid racial desegregation. African Americans tend to be

---

[9]"The Impact of Watergate on Children's Attitudes toward Authority," *Political Science Quarterly*, Vol. 89 (June 1984), pp. 269–288.
[10]*The Public Perspective*, May/June 1990, p. 105.

POLITICS AND ECONOMICS

Competing Influences: Race and Wealth

Two major influences that seem to shape the opinions of Americans are race and income. As noted in the text, African Americans are more likely to be liberal on welfare and government-spending issues than are whites, on the average, whereas individuals who earn higher incomes tend to be conservative on welfare and government spending issues. Presumably, high-income individuals perceive that it is in their best interest to have the government spend less on these programs because the wealthier classes pay more taxes and receive few of the benefits. Poorer Americans, whether African Americans or white, tend to approve of government spending on welfare programs because they are the principal beneficiaries of such expenditures.

One question that has interested social scientists and politicians has to do with the political opinions of people who achieve a high income. Does becoming wealthy change the individual's political opinions? Specifically, do African Americans who rise to the upper middle class become more Republican and conser-

vative, or do they remain loyal to the interests of other African Americans who have not done as well?

Recent research shows that over the last fifteen years, African Americans as a group have maintained their liberal views. African-American respondents are almost twice as likely as whites to support government efforts to improve the standard of living for the poor. When the African-American respondents are divided into income groups, it becomes clear that wealthy African Americans do not become more conservative than those who have lower incomes. As the accompanying figure indicates, support for spending more on welfare does decline slightly among African Americans as their income increases, but the overall level of support for such government spending is twice as high as it is for whites of the same economic class. Not only do African Americans of the upper-income groups keep their liberal views, but they also stay within the Democratic party. In 1984, surveys showed that 11 percent of the upper-income African

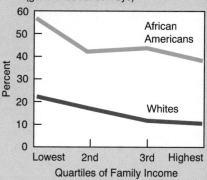

Support for Spending More on Welfare (general social surveys)

Americans were Republicans, as compared with 8 percent of lower-income African Americans. According to Scott Keeter and Elliott Banks, "African Americans evidently continue to view political issues more in terms of their collective group situation than in terms of their personal economic circumstances."

SOURCE: Scott Keeter and Elliott Banks, "An Examination of the Growth of Conservatism among Black Americans." Paper presented at the annual meeting of the American Association for Public Opinion Research, Toronto, Canada, May 1988.

more liberal than whites on social welfare issues, civil liberties, and even foreign policy. Party preferences and voting among African Americans since the 1930s have very heavily supported the Democrats, and, as the *Politics and Economics* feature in this chapter indicates, wealth has little impact on African-American attitudes.

It is somewhat surprising that a person's chronological age has comparatively little impact on political preferences. Still, young adults are somewhat more liberal than older people on most issues, and they are considerably more progressive on such issues as marijuana legalization, pornography, civil disobedience, and racial and sexual equality.

The generally greater conservatism of older Americans may be explained in one or more ways: (1) Simply becoming older makes people more conservative; (2) people carry with them the values they learned when they first became politically aware, which are now considered relatively conservative; and (3) people's attitudes are shaped by the events that unfold as they grow up. The most important of these explanations seems to be the third; that is, a person's views are mainly determined by when he or she happened to be born. If someone grew up in an era of Democratic party dominance, then that person will be more likely to remain a Democrat throughout his or her life.[11]

Finally, attitudes vary from region to region, although such patterns probably are accounted for mostly by social class and other differences. Regional differences are relatively unimportant today. There is still a tendency for the East and West to be more liberal than most of the Midwest and the South, and for the South and East to be more Democratic than the West and the Midwest. More important than region is a person's residence—urban, suburban, or rural. Big cities tend to be more liberal and Democratic because of their greater concentration of minorities and newer ethnic groups, and smaller communities are more conservative and, outside the South, more Republican.

The Gender Gap

Until the 1980s, there was little evidence that men's and women's political attitudes were very different. The election of Ronald Reagan in 1980, however, soon came to be associated with a **gender gap.** In a May 1983 Gallup poll, 43 percent of the women polled approved of Reagan's performance in office and 44 percent disapproved, versus 49 percent of men who approved and 41 percent who disapproved.[12]

In the 1988 election, the gender gap reappeared but in a modified form. Although the Democrats hoped that women's votes would add significantly to their totals, a deep split between men and women did not occur. The final polls showed that men voted 54 percent for George Bush, as did 50 percent of the women. The 1992 presidential election again found women more likely than men to vote for the Democrats: 46 percent of women voted for Clinton compared to 41 percent of the men. Additionally, women were less likely to vote for Ross Perot than were men.

Women also appear to hold different attitudes from their male counterparts on a range of issues other than presidential preferences. They are much more likely to oppose capital punishment, as well as the use of force abroad. A 1982 poll sponsored by the Chicago Council on Foreign Relations showed that only 34 percent of American women favored the government selling military equipment to other nations, whereas 50 percent of men supported this strategy. Women's reluctance to support the use of force reinforced the gender gap in 1991. As the troop buildup in Saudi Arabia increased, women's approval of Bush lagged 10 to 14 percentage points behind that of men. Other studies have shown that women are more concerned about risks to the environment, particularly from nuclear power, and are more supportive of social welfare than are men.[13] These differences of opinion appear to be growing and may become an important factor in future elections at national and local levels.

Did You Know . . . That young children first think of politics in terms of a benevolent president and a helpful police officer?

GENDER GAP
Most often used to describe the difference between the percentage of votes a candidate receives from women voters and the percentage the candidate receives from men. The term was widely used after the 1980 presidential election.

---

[11]Erikson, Luttbeg, and Tedin, *op. cit.,* pp. 170–175.
[12]*The Gallup Report,* May 1983.
[13]Katherine Frankovic, "Sex and Politics—New Alignments, Old Issues," *PS,* 1982, pp. 439–448.

The Political Culture of Americans

Americans are divided into a multitude of ethnic, religious, regional, and political subgroups. In many cases, members of these groups hold a particular set of opinions about government politics, about the goals of the society, and about the rights of their group and the rights of others. Given the diversity of American society and the wide range of opinions contained within it, how is it that the political process continues to function without being stalemated by conflict and dissension?

One explanation is rooted in the concept of the **political culture,** which can be described as a set of attitudes and ideas about the nation and the government. Our political culture is widely shared by Americans of many different backgrounds. To some extent, it consists of symbols, such as the American flag, the Liberty Bell, and the Statue of Liberty. One of the reasons that the renovation of the statue so strongly engaged the imagination of the citizens is because it symbolizes two major aspects of American political culture: the pursuit of liberty and the fact that most Americans are descended from immigrants who sought liberty and equality.

The elements of our political culture also include certain shared beliefs about the most important values in the American political system. Research by Donald Devine[14] suggests there is a set of key values that is central to the political culture. Among the most important are three of the values from the revolutionary period: (1) liberty, equality, and property; (2) support for religion; and (3) a high value on community service and personal achievement. The structure of the government—particularly federalism, the political parties, the powers of Congress, and popular rule—were also found to be important values.

The political culture provides a general environment of support for the political system. If the people share certain beliefs about the system and a reservoir of good feeling exists toward the institutions of government, the nation will be better able to weather periods of crisis, such as Watergate. This foundation of goodwill may combat cynicism and increase the level of participation in elections as well. During the 1960s and 1970s, survey research showed that the overall level of **political trust** declined steeply. A considerable proportion of Americans seemed to feel that they could not trust government officials and that they could not count on officials to care about the ordinary person. This index of political trust reached an all-time low in 1992, reflecting Americans' cynicism about the government and the presidential election campaign (see Table 6-3).

One way to test whether Americans really believe in the values that are central to the political culture is to examine the degree of **political tolerance** they are willing to show toward those who hold views differing strongly from their own. Researchers asked Americans if they would be willing to permit demonstrations by a number of groups who espouse particular opinions.[15] More than 80 percent of those asked were willing to permit demonstrations opposing crime in the community and pollution. About 60 percent felt that it would be acceptable to permit African-

POLITICAL CULTURE
That set of beliefs and values regarding the political system that are widely shared by the citizens of a nation.

POLITICAL TRUST
The degree to which individuals express trust in the government and political institutions. This concept is usually measured through a specific series of survey questions.

POLITICAL TOLERANCE
The degree to which individuals are willing to grant civil liberties to groups that have opinions differing strongly from their own.

[14]Donald Devine, *Political Culture of the United States* (Boston: Little, Brown, 1972).
[15]David G. Lawrence, "Procedural Norms and Tolerance: A Reassessment," *American Political Science Review,* Vol. 70 (1976), p. 88.

TABLE 6-3 ■ **Trends in Political Trust**

	1964	1968	1972	1974	1976	1978	1980	1982	1984*	1986*	1988*	1990*	1992*
QUESTION: How much of the time do you think you can trust the government in Washington to do what is right—just about always, most of the time, or only some of the time?													
Percent saying:													
Always/Most of the time	76	61	53	36	33	29	25	32	46	42	44	27	23
Some of the time/Never	22	36	45	61	63	67	73	64	51	55	54	73	75

SOURCE: The University of Michigan Survey Research Center, National Election Studies.
*The *New York Times*/CBS News Surveys.

American militants or radical students to demonstrate, whereas only 40 percent would support efforts to march for the legalization of marijuana. Although we do not find that all Americans are willing to extend political tolerance to groups indiscriminately, it appears that the political culture is strong enough to provide freedom for many points of view.

Public Opinion about Government

A vital component of public opinion in the United States is the considerable ambivalence with which the public regards many major national institutions. Table 6-4 shows trends from 1973 to 1991 in Gallup public opinion polls asking respondents at regularly spaced intervals "how much

TABLE 6-4 ■ **Confidence in Institutions Trend**

QUESTION: I am going to read a list of institutions in American society. Would you please tell me how much confidence you, yourself, have in each one—a great deal, quite a lot, some, or very little?										
	Percent Saying "Great Deal" or "Quite a Lot"									
	1973	1975	1977	1979	1981	1983	1985	1987	1989	1991
Church or organized religion	66%	68%	65%	65%	64%	62%	66%	61%	52%	56%
Military	NA	58	57	54	50	53	61	61	63	69
U.S. Supreme Court	44	49	46	45	46	42	56	52	46	39
Banks & banking	NA	NA	NA	60	46	51	51	51	42	30
Public schools	58	NA	54	53	42	39	48	50	43	35
Congress	42	40	40	34	29	28	39	NA	32	18
Newspapers	39	NA	NA	51	35	38	35	31	NA	32
Big business	26	34	33	32	20	28	31	NA	NA	22
Television	37	NA	NA	38	25	25	29	28	NA	24
Organized labor	30	38	39	36	28	26	28	26	NA	22

NA = Not asked.
SOURCE: *The Gallup Report*, October 1991.

TABLE 6-5 ■ Most Important Problem Trend 1970–1993

Year	Problem
1993	Health care, deficit
1992	Unemployment, budget deficit
1991	Economy
1990	War in Middle East
1989	War on drugs
1988	Economy, budget deficit
1987	Unemployment, economy
1986	Unemployment, budget deficit
1985	Fear of war, unemployment
1984	Unemployment, fear of war
1983	Unemployment, high cost of living
1982	Unemployment, high cost of living
1981	High cost of living, unemployment
1980	High cost of living, unemployment
1979	High cost of living, energy problems
1978	High cost of living, energy problems
1977	High cost of living, unemployment
1976	High cost of living, unemployment
1975	High cost of living, unemployment
1974	High cost of living, Watergate, energy crisis
1973	High cost of living, Watergate
1972	Vietnam
1971	Vietnam, high cost of living

SOURCE: The Gallup Report, 1993.

confidence you, yourself, have" in the institutions listed. Over the years, military and religious organizations have ranked highest, but note the decline in confidence in churches following the numerous scandals concerning television evangelists in the late 1980s. Note also the heightened regard for the military after the Persian Gulf War in 1991. The U.S. Supreme Court, which many people do not see as a particularly political institution although it is clearly involved in decisions with vitally important consequences for the nation, also scored well, as did banks and banking until recently. A series of unpopular Supreme Court decisions from 1989 to 1991 and the savings and loan scandals of recent years caused the public's confidence in both of those institutions to drop significantly by 1991. Even less confidence is expressed in newspapers, big business, television, and organized labor, all of which are certainly involved directly or indirectly in the political process. In 1991, following the check-kiting scandal and other embarassments, confidence in Congress fell to a record low of 18 percent.

Although people may not have much confidence in government institutions, they nonetheless turn to government to solve what they perceive to be the major problems facing the country. Table 6-5, which is based on Gallup polls conducted over the years 1973 to 1993, shows that the leading problems have clearly changed over time. The public tends to emphasize problems that are immediate. It is not at all unusual to see fairly sudden and even apparently contradictory shifts in public perceptions of what government should do. Note the years 1975–1977 and 1980–1983, when both "high cost of living" and "unemployment" were at the top of the public's action agenda. These two problems are quite possibly contradictory. Reducing unemployment, everything else constant, is likely to produce inflationary pressures, and attempts to reduce inflation may have to be accompanied by more people unemployed so as to reduce inflationary pressures. In some instances, government cannot respond well to these contradictory demands from the public. Jimmy Carter (1977–1981), for example, was largely unable to resolve this dilemma. In contrast, Ronald Reagan (1981–1989) was much more successful in confronting much the same set of demands from public opinion, although Reagan benefited from very fortunate declines in energy prices and a climate of opinion that would tolerate very high rates of unemployment for a couple of years (1981–1982).

This gives rise to a critically important question: Is government really responsive to public opinion? A study by political scientists Benjamin I. Page and Robert Y. Shapiro[16] suggests that in fact the national government is very responsive to the public's demands for action. In looking at changes in public opinion poll results over time, Page and Shapiro show that when the public supports a policy change, 43 percent of the time policy changes in a direction congruent with the change in public opinion, 22 percent of the time policy changes in a direction opposite to the change in opinion, and 33 percent of the time policy does not change at all. So, overall, the national government could be said to respond to changes in public opinion about two-thirds of the time. Page and Shapiro also show,

[16]"Effects of Public Opinion on Policy," *American Political Science Review*, Vol. 77 (1985), pp. 175–190.

as should be no surprise, that when public opinion changes more dramatically, say, by 20 percentage points rather than by just 6 or 7 percentage points, government policy is much more likely to follow changing public attitudes.

Political Ideology

Political candidates and officeholders in the United States are frequently identified as liberals or conservatives. In recent years, variations on these labels include post–Cold War liberals and neoconservatives. These terms refer loosely to a spectrum of political beliefs that are commonly arrayed on a continuum from left to right. Each of the terms has changed its meaning from its origins and continues to change as the issues of political debate change. In the United States, however, the terms most frequently refer to sets of political positions that date from the Great Depression.

Liberals are most commonly understood to embrace national government solutions to public problems, to believe that the national government should intervene in the economy to ensure its health, to support social welfare programs to assist the disadvantaged, and to be tolerant of social change. Today, liberals are often identified with pro-women's rights positions, pro-civil rights policies, and opposition to increased defense spending. New York Governor Mario Cuomo and Massachusetts Senator Edward Kennedy are usually tagged as liberals.

In contrast, conservatives usually feel that the national government has grown too large, that the private sector needs less interference from the government, that social welfare programs should be limited, that state and local governments should be able to make their own decisions, and that the nation's defense should be strengthened. Some conservatives express grave concerns about the decline of family life and traditional values in this country; they would not be tolerant of gay rights laws, for example. Arizona Senator Barry Goldwater represented conservatism in the 1960s, whereas Senator Jesse Helms and presidential candidate Pat Buchanan are examples of today's variety.

When asked, Americans are usually willing to identify themselves on the liberal–conservative spectrum. More individuals are likely to consider themselves moderates than either liberal or conservative. As Table 6-6 shows, the number of conservatives increased and the number of liberals declined in the early years of the Reagan administration, but, by 1986, the proportions were about the same as ten years earlier.

Most Americans, however, do not fit into the categories as nicely as do Edward Kennedy or Pat Buchanan. Such political leaders, who are quite conscious of their philosophical views and who hold a carefully thought out and a more or less consistent set of political beliefs, can be described as **ideologues.** Partly because most citizens are not highly interested in all political issues and partly because Americans have different stakes in politics, most people have mixed sets of opinions that do not fit into one ideological framework. Election research suggests that only a small percentage of all Americans, perhaps less than 10 percent, could be identified

Senator Ted Kennedy (top) of Massachusetts has been a liberal voice throughout his tenure in Congress. Patrick Buchanan (bottom), who opposed President George Bush during the Republican primaries in 1992, is an outspoken conservative. Buchanan has built a career in television as a political commentator.

IDEOLOGUE
A term applied to an individual whose political opinions are carefully thought out and relatively consistent with one another. Ideologues are often described as having a comprehensive world view.

TABLE 6–6 ■ Ideological Self-Identification, 1976–1990

There has been relatively little change in the distribution of liberals and conservatives even after the elections of self-described liberal or conservative presidents.

Year	Liberal	Moderate	Conservative	No Opinion
1976	21%	41%	26%	12%
1977	21	38	29	12
1978	21	35	27	17
1979	21	42	26	12
1980	19	40	31	11
1981	18	43	30	9
1982	17	40	33	11
1984	17	41	31	11
1986	20	45	28	7
1988	18	45	33	4
1990	20	48	28	6

SOURCES: Gallup Reports, *New York Times*/CBS News Surveys.

as ideologues. The rest of the public conceived of politics more in terms of the parties or of economic well-being.

Some critics of the American political system have felt that elections would be more meaningful and that the nation could face important policy problems more effectively if Americans were more ideological in their thinking. Public opinion research suggests that for most Americans, political issues are not usually as important as events in their daily lives are. There is no evidence to suggest that forces are in place to turn Americans into highly motivated ideological voters.

Conclusion: Public Opinion and the Political Process

Surveys of public opinion, no matter what fascinating questions they ask or how quickly they get the answers, are not equivalent to elections in the United States. Because not all Americans are equally interested in politics or equally informed, public opinion polls can suggest only the general distribution of opinion on issues. Many times, only a few citizens have formulated a preference, and these preferences will be changed by events.

Politicians, whether in office or in the midst of a campaign, see public opinion as important to their careers. The president, members of Congress, governors, and other elected officials realize that strong support by the public as expressed in opinion polls is a source of power in dealing with other politicians. It is far more difficult for a senator to say no to the president if he is immensely popular and if polls show approval of his policies. Public opinion also helps political candidates identify the most important concerns among the public and may help them shape their campaigns successfully.

Although opinion polls cannot give exact guidance on what the government should do in a specific instance, the opinions measured in polls do set an informal limit on government action. For example, consider the highly controversial issue of abortion. Most Americans are moderates on this issue; they do not approve of abortion as a means of birth control, but they do feel that it should be available under certain circumstances. Yet sizable groups of people express very intense feelings both for and against abortion. Given this distribution of opinion, most elected officials would rather not try to change policy to favor either of the extreme positions. To do so would clearly violate the opinion of the majority of Americans. In this case, as in many others, public opinion does not make public policy; rather, it restrains officials from taking truly unpopular actions. If officials do act in the face of public opposition, the consequences of such actions will be determined at the ballot box.

GETTING INVOLVED

How to Read a Public Opinion Poll

Americans are inundated with information from public opinion polls. The polls, often reported to us through television news, the newspaper, *Time* or *Newsweek* magazines, or radio, purport to tell us a variety of things: whether the president's popularity is up or down, whether gun control is more popular now than previously, or who is leading the pack for the next presidential nomination.

What must be kept in mind with this blizzard of information is that not all the poll results are equally good or equally believable. As a citizen, you need to be aware of what makes one set of public opinion poll results valid and other results useless or even dangerously misleading. You should be able to evaluate the results that are being presented to you by the media or by political groups or candidates.

The first question has to do with how the people who were interviewed were selected. Pay attention only to opinion polls that are based on scientific, or random, samples, in which a known probability was used to select every person who was interviewed. These *probability samples*, as they are also called, can take a number of different forms. The simplest to understand is known as a *simple random sample*, in which everybody had a known, and possibly an equal, chance of being chosen to be interviewed. Other satisfactory ways of selecting samples are *systematic samples*, in which every tenth person, for example, might be selected from an alphabetized list of names; *stratified sampling*, in which the pollster has purposely selected a particular proportion or number of poll respondents who are, say, black, Jewish, or farmers and who otherwise might not get sufficient representation in the sample; or *cluster sampling*, in which people have been interviewed in randomly chosen geographical areas. As a rule, do not give credence to the results of opinion polls that consist of person-in-the-shopping-mall interviews broadcast on local television news segments. The main problem with this kind of opinion taking, which is a special version of a so-called *accidental sample*, is that not everyone had an equal chance of being in the mall when the interview took place. Also, it is almost certain that the people in the mall are not a reasonable cross section of a community's entire population (shopping malls would tend to attract people who are disproportionately younger, female, mobile, and middle class). In general, if a pollster cannot be specific about the odds of the results of the poll being correct, it means that some nonrandom, or nonprobability, sample has been taken and that the results are probably not very useful.

Probability samples are useful (and nonprobability samples are not) for the following reason: When you know the odds that the particular sample would have been chosen randomly from a larger population, you can calculate the "sampling error," or the range within which the real results for the whole population would fall if everybody had been interviewed. Well-designed probability samples will allow the pollster to say, for example, that he or she is 95 percent sure that 61 percent of the public, plus or minus 4 percentage points, supports national health insurance. The range around the sample result becomes smaller, meaning that the guess about the actual proportion of national health insurance supporters is more precise, as the size of the sample gets bigger. It turns out that if you want to become twice as precise about a poll result, you would need to collect a sample four times as large. This tends to make accurate polls quite expensive and difficult to collect. Typically, national public opinion polls by, for example, the Gallup organization seldom interview more than about 1,500 respondents. With a sample of that size, Gallup is able to be correct to within about 3 percentage points of the probably true figures in 95 samples out of every 100.

There are other important points to keep in mind when you see opinion poll results. How were people contacted for the poll—by mail, by telephone, in person in their homes, or in some other way? By and large, because of its lower cost compared with interviewing people in person, polling firms have recently turned more and more to telephone interviewing. This method usually can produce highly accurate results. Its disadvantage is that telephone interviews typically need to be short and deal with questions that are fairly easy to answer. Interviews in person are better for getting useful information about why a particular response was given to a question. They take much longer to complete, however, and are not as useful if results must be generated quickly. Results from mail questionnaires should be taken with a grain of salt. Usually, only a small percentage of people complete them and send them back. Also, the kinds of people who fill them out are typically better educated, with higher incomes and more prestigious jobs, and are therefore not representative of the general population or its likely attitudes.

When you see the results from public opinion polls in this book, they are usually from probability samples, with the results having been gathered in personal interviews or over the telephone. The next time you see an opinion poll anywhere else, try to find out how the results were collected before you form an opinion based on the poll's results.

CHAPTER SUMMARY

1. Public opinion is the aggregate of individual attitudes or beliefs shared by some portion of adults. It has at least five special qualities: (a) intensity—the strength of an opinion; (b) fluidity—the extent to which opinion changes; (c) stability—the extent to which opinion remains constant; (d) quiescence—latent opinions; and (e) relevance—the extent to which an issue is of concern at a particular time. Opinions are distributed among the public in different ways. Consensus issues are those on which most people agree, whereas divisive issues are those about which people strongly disagree.

2. Most descriptions of public opinion are based on the results of opinion polls. The accuracy of polls is based on sampling techniques that ensure randomness in the selection of respondents. Polls only measure opinions held on the day they are taken and will not reflect rapidly changing opinions. Certain methodological problems may reduce the accuracy of polls.

3. Opinions and attitudes are produced by a combination of socialization, information, and experience. Young people, for example, are likely to be influenced by their parents' political party identification. Education has an effect on opinions and attitudes, as do peer groups, religious affiliation, economic status, ethnicity, and gender. Political events may have generational effects, shaping the opinions of a particular age group.

4. A political culture exists in the United States because so many Americans hold similar attitudes and beliefs about how the government and the political system should work. In addition, most Americans are able to identify themselves as liberals, moderates, or conservatives, even though they may not articulate a consistent philosophy of politics, or ideology.

5. Public opinion can play an important part in the political system by providing information to candidates, by indicating support or opposition to the president and Congress, and by setting limits on government action through public pressure.

QUESTIONS FOR REVIEW AND DISCUSSION

1. How does public opinion influence the formation of national policies? Is public opinion more powerful as a positive force for change or as a negative force opposing change?

2. Think about a current political problem—for example, U.S. policy towards Eastern Europe or oil politics in the Middle East. How have the opinions of your parents, your friends, or your teachers affected your own attitudes? To what extent are your views colored by your own political party identification?

3. Do you consider yourself to be a liberal, a conservative, or a moderate on political issues? Try to list all of the beliefs that you hold that create such an identity. To what extent do you feel close to politicians or elected officials who identify themselves in the same way as you do?

SELECTED REFERENCES

Irving Crespi, *Public Opinion, Polls and Democracy* (Boulder, Colo.: Westview Press, 1989). Crespi explores the reciprocal influences of polling, politics, and the media. He offers solutions to the often inappropriate uses of polls and suggests reforms in media reporting methods.

Benjamin De Mott, *The Imperial Middle Class: Why Americans Can't Think Straight about Class* (New York: William Morrow, 1990). This interesting book explains why Americans do not accept social class as a relevant factor in identity; rather, the school experience and pop culture, especially television, are the crucial factors.

Robert Donovan and Ray Scherer, *Unsilent Revolution: Television News and American Public Life, 1948–1991* (New York: Cambridge University Press, 1992). An exploration of the effect that television has had on such institutions as politics, current events, and public opinion over the last half-century.

Michael Margolis and Gary A. Mauser, eds., *Manipulating Public Opinion: Essays on Public Opinion As a Dependent Variable* (Pacific Grove, Calif.: Brooks/Cole, 1989). This collection of empirical studies examines the ability of political elites to manage public opinion in election campaigns, in the development of public policy, and in the process of political socialization.

Arthur Sanders, *Making Sense of Politics* (Ames: Iowa State University Press, 1990). The author explores the complexities of public opinion by using in-depth interviews of a small group of people in Utica, New York, as a means of defining ideology and other factors influencing public opinion.

Jerry L. Yeric and John R. Todd, *Public Opinion: The Visible Politics*, 2d ed. (Itasca, Ill.: F. E. Peacock, 1989). The relationship of public opinion to polling, public policy, and demographic factors is explained in this text.

John R. Zaller, *The Nature and Origins of Mass Opinion* (New York: Cambridge University Press, 1992). Zaller focuses on the role of the mass media in generating public opinion on public policy, civil rights issues, trust in government, presidential actions, and other matters.

CHAPTER 7
Interest Groups

CHAPTER CONTENTS

WHAT IF ... INTEREST GROUPS' CONTRIBUTIONS WERE LIMITED TO $100 PER CANDIDATE?

In 1990, the Realtors' Political Action Committee gave more than $3 million to congressional candidates to use in their election campaigns. Under the current campaign financing law, political action committees (PACs) representing interest groups can give up to $5,000 to each candidate for each election. Thus, the realtors could give contributions of $5,000 for both the primary and general elections to about 300 incumbent legislators or their challengers. What do the realtors expect to get for these contributions? With many interest groups in the PAC contribution game, it is unlikely that $5,000 will exert much influence on a congressperson for a particular vote. Most legislators agree, however, that such support from an interest group will guarantee access for the lobbyists of the organization. Particularly if the candidate is in a tougher race than usual, PAC contributions may earn a polite hearing for the realtors' political needs.

How would the system for gaining access to legislators change if interest groups were limited in their campaign contributions to only $100 per candidate? In the case of the National Association of Realtors, the total expenditure for supporting every member of the House and his or her opponent would be about $87,000, down $2.9 million from the current situation. Obviously, with interest groups able to contribute far less than ordinary citizens, who are now able to give up to $1,000 per candidate per election (with an overall limit of $25,000 per election), PAC contributions would simply be symbolic, signifying the group's basic support for a legislator or challenger. No group could claim a position of special financial importance in a legislator's campaign, and it would be less likely that a group could gain a hearing for its views.

If the limits for the contributions of individuals to campaigns were not also changed, it is likely that interest groups would try to organize their members to make maximum contributions to legislators or candidates who were favorable to their cause. This would be a much harder task, and, in the end, interest groups could not claim that the group itself was responsible for the contributions. It is also likely that interest groups would try to gain access to the legislators by providing other kinds of contributions to the campaign—such as individuals to work for the candidate at the grass-roots level or loaning the candidate an office.

Limiting interest-group contributions to $100 could have a considerable impact on the extremely high reelection rate of incumbent legislators. No longer could incumbent committee chairpersons such as Dan Rostenkowski (chair of the House Ways and Means Committee) build campaign war chests through the traditional maximum PAC contributions. Currently, the greatest proportion of interest-group contributions goes to incumbent legislators who hold positions of power in the majority party either as congressional leaders or as committee chairpersons. These PAC contributions are made to ensure access to the corridors of power regardless of whether the legislator faces a serious electoral challenge.

Limiting interest-group contributions could so restrict their activities that groups might be willing to support public financing for congressional campaigns. Although public financing is already a reality for the general presidential election, Congress has been unable to agree on a public financing law for itself. Republicans charge that any plan proposed by the Democrat-controlled Congress will ultimately favor incumbents, who are mostly Democrats. In contrast, Republican proposals are likely to have special incentives for challengers that Democrats see as a threat. Besides, Republicans often have access to greater personal wealth to finance their campaigns.

In any event, a limit on PAC contributions would likely change the landscape of campaigning. Without the assurance of thousands of PAC dollars for each campaign, legislative candidates would have to forgo much of the media advertising that they use today. In making their choices, candidates and voters might have to rely on reading about candidates' positions and studying the issues rather than depending on television advertising. Many Americans might regard this as a healthy development.

1. *What kinds of influence do interest groups gain from making campaign contributions to candidates?*
2. *Would reducing the size of contributions make interest groups more likely to support challengers rather than incumbent legislators?*

The Role of Interest Groups

After the 1986 tax reform bill was passed, the details of the political machinations that were involved in the bill's passage were published in a book entitled *Showdown at Gucci Gulch*.[1] The title refers to the lineup of lobbyists clad in designer shoes who waited outside the committee rooms to discuss every detail of the proposed bill with the emerging legislators. Each lobbyist represented an interest group or corporation that felt the need to defend its economic or political stake in the tax negotiations. It is worth noting that lobbyists are generally so well paid for their services that they can afford expensive footwear, even if the groups they represent may not be composed of elites.

In contrast to the fashionable lobbyists who frequent the halls of Congress are the more down-to-earth representatives of children and parents who ask for less-crowded schools, homeless citizens who look for housing assistance, or handicapped people in wheelchairs who call for more accessible accomodations in public buildings. In each case, citizens are exercising their right to seek assistance from the government and to gain attention from government decision makers either through quiet negotiations or through public demonstrations. When dissatisfied with their government, Americans look to group action as an effective and acceptable method to make public officials more responsive. In addition to using their voting power to influence elected officials, citizens also look to interest groups to expand that influence.

What Is an Interest Group?

We have already used the term **interest group,** also called pressure group and sometimes lobby, but have not yet explicitly defined it. We may define this kind of group as follows:

> An interest group is any organized group whose members share common objectives. An interest group actively attempts to influence government policy makers through direct and indirect methods, including the marshalling of public opinion, lobbying members of Congress, and electioneering. Interest groups work to persuade decision makers in all three branches of government and at all levels of government.

How Widespread Are Interest Groups?

Alexis de Tocqueville observed in 1834 that "in no country of the world has the principle of association been more successfully used or applied to a greater multitude of objectives than in America."[2] But de Tocqueville probably could not have conceived of the more than 100,000 associations existing in the United States in the 1990s. It is estimated that about two-thirds of the U.S. population is formally associated with some type of

INTEREST GROUP
An organized group of individuals sharing common objectives who actively attempt to influence government policy makers through direct and indirect methods, including the marshalling of public opinion, lobbying, and electioneering.

Alexis de Tocqueville (1805–1859), the French social historian and traveler who first commented on Americans' predilection for group action.

---

[1]Jeffrey Birnbaum and Alan Murray, *Showdown at Gucci Gulch* (New York: Random House, 1987).
[2]*Democracy in America*, Vol. 1, ed. Phillips Bradley (New York: Alfred A. Knopf, 1980), p. 191.

Did You Know . . . That the National Rifle Association has a full-time Washington, D.C., staff of over 300 persons?

group. Of course, the majority of these 100,000 groups do not strictly fit our definition of an interest group because they are not actively seeking to change or influence government policy. But we can be sure that the purpose of the roughly 1,200 organizations whose names begin with the word *National* listed in the Washington, D.C., telephone directory is to do just this. To this list, we can add many of the 600 organizations listed in the D.C. telephone directory that begin with the word *American* or *Americans*. According to Norman J. Ornstein and Shirley Elder,[3] well·over 10,000 separate groups exist for the purpose of influencing government policies.

Why Are There So Many Interest Groups?

The structure of our political system makes it possible for individuals and groups to exert influence at many different points in the system. Most American governments have legislative, executive, and judicial branches. If, for example, the state legislature passes a law that may hurt a local industry, then the representatives of that industry, the employees whose jobs may be affected, and the citizens of the town in which it is located may well feel that they should express their dissatisfaction and try to have the law changed. They may attempt to influence the governor, who could veto the legislation, or they may concentrate on the bureaucracy to forestall the law's implementation. The newly formed interest group may try to block the legislation in the courts. At the next election, the group may try to defeat those representatives who voted for the bill. If they receive no satisfaction at the state level, they may try to move the debate to the federal level. All of the institutions of government offer them similar access under the First Amendment to the Constitution, which guarantees citizens the right to assemble and petition the government for the redress of grievances.

Individuals join interest groups for a variety of reasons. For some individuals, interest groups offer **solidary incentives** for their members. Solidary incentives include companionship, a sense of belonging, and the pleasure of associating with others. Although the National Audubon Society was founded originally to save the snowy egret from extinction, most members join today to learn more about birds and to meet and share their pleasure with other individuals who enjoy birdwatching as a hobby. Even though the incentive might be solidary for many members, the society nonetheless also pursues an active political agenda, working to preserve the environment and to protect endangered species. Most members may not play any part in working toward larger, more national goals unless the organization can convince them to take political action or unless some local environmental issue arises.

For other individuals, interest groups offer direct **material incentives**. A case in point is the American Association of Retired Persons (AARP), which provides discounts, insurance plans, and organized travel opportunities for its members. Because of its exceptionally low dues ($5 annually) and the benefits gained through membership in AARP, it has become the largest—and a very powerful—interest group in the United

SOLIDARY INCENTIVES
Reasons or motives having to do with the desire to associate with others and to share with others a particular interest or hobby.

MATERIAL INCENTIVES
Reasons or motives having to do with economic benefits or opportunities.

---

[3]*Interest Groups, Lobbying and Policymaking* (Washington, D.C.: Congressional Quarterly Press, 1978), p. 23.

States. AARP can claim to represent the interests of millions of senior citizens and can show that they actually have joined the group. For most seniors, the material incentives outweigh the membership costs.

Many other interest groups offer indirect material incentives for their members. Such groups as the American Dairy Association or the National Association of Automobile Dealers do not give discounts or freebies to their members, but they do offer indirect benefits and rewards by, for example, protecting the material interests of their members from government policy making that is injurious to their industry or business.

Finally, interest groups offer the opportunity for individuals to pursue political, economic, or social goals through joint action. Such **purposive incentives** offer individuals the satisfaction of taking action for the sake of their beliefs or principles. The individuals who belong to right-to-life groups or to the National Abortion Rights Action League have joined because they are concerned about the issue of whether abortions should be made available to the public. People join such groups because they feel strongly enough about the issues to support the groups' work with money and time.

Obviously, the proliferation of interest groups and the growth in their membership requires a reciprocity of interests. An interest group must give individuals an incentive to become members of the group, and members of the group must have their needs satisfied through the group's activities, or they will no longer participate.

PURPOSIVE INCENTIVES
Reasons or motives having to do with ethical beliefs or ideological principles.

Interest Groups and Social Movements

Interest groups are often spawned by mass **social movements**. Such movements represent demands by a large segment of the population for change in the political, economic, or social system. Social movements are often the first expression of latent discontent with the contemporary system. They may be the authentic voice of weaker or oppressed groups in society that do not have the means or standing to organize as interest groups. For example, the women's movement of the mid-nineteenth century suffered social disapproval from most mainstream political and social leaders. Because women were unable to vote or take an active part in the political system, it was difficult for women who desired greater freedoms to organize formal groups. After the Civil War, when more women became active in professional life, the first real women's rights group, the National Women's Suffrage Association, came into being.

African Americans found themselves in an even more disadvantaged situation after the end of the Reconstruction period. Not only were they unable to exercise political rights in many southern and border states, but also participation in any form of organization could lead to economic ruin, physical harassment, or even death. The civil rights movement of the 1950s and 1960s was clearly a social movement. Although there were several formal organizations that worked to support the movement—including the Southern Christian Leadership Conference, the National Association for the Advancement of Colored People, and the Urban League—only a social movement could generate the kinds of civil disobedience that took place in hundreds of towns and cities across the country.

SOCIAL MOVEMENT
A movement that represents the demands of a large segment of the public for political, economic, or social change.

Social movements are often precursors of interest groups. They may generate interest groups with specific goals that successfully recruit members through the incentives the group offers. In the case of the women's movement of the 1960s, the National Organization for Women formed out of a demand to end sex-segregated job advertising in newspapers.

Major Interest Groups

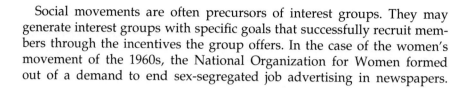

Thousands of groups exist to influence government. Among the major types of interest groups are those that represent the main sectors of the economy—business, labor, and agricultural groups. In addition, there are many groups whose purpose is to protect the interests of professionals and public employees. In more recent years, a number of "public interest" organizations have been formed to represent the needs of the general citizenry, including environmental groups and some "single-issue" groups. The interests of foreign governments and foreign businesses are also represented in the American political arena. Table 7-1 lists some of the interest groups currently lobbying Congress and the interests that they represent.

Business Interest Groups

There are thousands of trade organizations, but most of them are quite ineffective in influencing legislation and administrative regulations. Three big business pressure groups are consistently effective: (1) the National Association of Manufacturers (NAM), (2) the United States Chamber of Commerce, and (3) the Business Roundtable. The annual budget of the NAM is more than $8 million, which it collects in dues from about 14,000 relatively large corporations. Organized in Cincinnati in 1895 as a predominantly small business association, the NAM became during the Great Depression of the 1930s primarily a proponent of the interests of large corporations. Of particular interest to the NAM is legislation that affects labor laws, minimum wage rates, corporate taxes, and trade regulations. The NAM's Washington national headquarters staff numbers about one hundred, of whom a dozen are full-time lobbyists.

Sometimes called the National Chamber, the U.S. Chamber of Commerce represents more than 100,000 businesses. Dues from its members, which include upward of 3,500 local chambers of commerce, approach $30 million a year.

Two hundred of the largest corporations in the United States send their chief executive officers to the Business Roundtable. This organization is based in New York, but it does its lobbying in Washington, D.C. Established in 1972, the Roundtable was designed to promote a more aggressive view of business interests in general, cutting across specific industries. Dues paid by the member corporations are determined by the companies' wealth. Roundtable members include American Telephone and Telegraph, General Motors, USX Corporation, and International Business Machines. The Roundtable opposed common-site picketing legislation, the proposed Consumer Protection Agency, automobile emissions standards, and industrial pollution control.

TABLE 7-1 ■ Selected Lobby Registrations

The following groups, corporations, and individuals were among those registering with the Office of Records and Registration of the House of Representatives during one month in 1992.

Lobby	Type	Interest
American Association of Acupuncture and Oriental Medicine	Professional association	Approval of acupuncture by federal health-related agencies.
Banca Nazionale del Lavaro	Foreign corporation	Congressional investigations.
Distilled Spirits Council of the United States	Trade association	Taxes, health warning labels, alcohol abuse.
Hallmark Cards, Inc.	U.S. corporation	Transfer of ownership of FCC-licensed TV facilities.
Marriott Corp.	U.S. corporation	Taxes, human resources, and labor.
National Electro-Magnetic Fields Research Program	Interest group	Energy.
National Newspaper Association	Trade association	Family leave, labor, taxes, telecommunications, advertising, etc.
Naviera del Pacifico, C.A.	Foreign corporation	Maritime shipping.
New Mexico State University, College of Business Administration and Economics	State university	Environment and trade.
Nintendo of America, Inc.	U.S. corporation	Software protection.
People's Republic of the Sudan	Foreign government	U.S.-Sudan relations
Society of American Florists	Trade association	Floriculture, horticulture, agriculture, education, research, commerce, etc.
Society of Geriatric Ophthalmology	Professional association	Guidelines for cataract surgery.

SOURCE: *Congressional Quarterly*, October 31, 1992.

Agricultural Interest Groups

American farmers and their workers represent about 2 percent of the United States' population. In spite of this, farmers' influence on legislation beneficial to their interests has been enormous. In 1992, American farmers received more than $40 billion in direct and indirect subsidies from the federal government. Farm programs designed to keep farm incomes high include price supports, target prices, soil conservation, and myriad other policies. Farmers have succeeded in their aims through very strong interest groups. The American Farm Bureau Federation, established in 1919, has three million members. It was instrumental in getting government guarantees of "fair" prices during the Great Depression in the 1930s.[4] In principle, the federation, controlled by wealthier farmers, is no longer in favor of government price supports. These farmers, who are engaged in

[4]The Agricultural Adjustment Act of 1933 (declared unconstitutional) was replaced by the 1937 Agricultural Adjustment Act and later changed and amended several times.

Dairy farmers are one of the best organized agricultural interest groups. The distribution of milk with school lunches is but one of the ways that the government tries to support milk prices and protect the industry.

large-scale farming, do not need government price supports to compete effectively.

Another important agricultural special interest organization is the National Farmers' Union (NFU). The NFU was founded in 1902 and claims a membership of more than a quarter of a million today. The oldest farm lobby organization is the National Grange, founded in 1867. With a membership of more than half a million, it finds its support among New England, Middle Atlantic, and, to a lesser extent, Pacific dairy farmers. It champions basically the same causes as the NFU, including higher agricultural support prices.

Labor Interest Groups

LABOR MOVEMENT
In general, the term refers to the full range of economic and political expression of working-class interests; politically, it describes the organization of working-class interests.

Interest groups representing the **labor movement** date back to at least 1886 with the formation of the American Federation of Labor (AFL). In 1955, the AFL joined forces with the Congress of Industrial Organizations (CIO). Today, the combined AFL–CIO is an enormous union with a membership exceeding thirteen million workers. In a sense, the AFL-CIO is a union of unions.

The political arm of the AFL-CIO is the Committee on Political Education (COPE). COPE's activities are funded by voluntary contributions from union members. COPE has been active in state and national campaigns since 1956. In principle, it is used to educate workers and the general public on issues and candidates of interest to labor. Some critics of COPE allege that union members are pressured into making contributions to the organization. Other critics claim that its "education" is simply partisan political propaganda favorable to the Democratic party. The AFL–CIO, through COPE, has established policies on such issues as Social Security, housing, health insurance, and foreign trade.

Other unions are also active politically. One of the most widely known of these is the International Brotherhood of Teamsters, which was led by

Union strikers line the streets outside the Caterpillar factory protesting the use of nonunion workers, or "scabs," to replace them on the assembly line.

Jimmy Hoffa until his expulsion in 1967 because of alleged ties with organized crime. The Teamsters Union was established initially in 1903 and today has a membership of three million and an annual budget of $73 million.

Another independent union is the United Auto Workers, founded in 1935. It now has a membership of 1.5 million with an annual budget of $230 million. Also very active in labor lobbying is the United Mine Workers union, representing about 200,000 members.

Labor group pressure on Congress has been only partly successful. Although unions successfully allied themselves with civil rights groups in the 1960s, they lost on such issues as the Taft–Hartley Act of 1948, which put some limits on the right to strike and the right to organize workers. They were also frustrated in their efforts in 1975 and in 1977 to enact a bill designed to facilitate the picketing of construction sites.

The role of unions in American society has weakened in recent years, as is witnessed by a decline in union membership from 1945 to the present (Figure 7-1). The strength of union membership traditionally lay with blue-collar workers. But in the age of automation and with the rise of the **service sector,** blue-collar workers in basic industries (autos, steel, and the like) represent a smaller and smaller percentage of the total working population. Because of this decline in the industrial sector of the economy, national unions are looking to nontraditional areas for their membership, including migrant farm workers, service workers, and, most recently, public employees—such as police officers, fire-fighting personnel, and teachers, including college professors.

SERVICE SECTOR
The sector of the economy that provides services—such as food services, insurance, and education—in contrast to the sector of the economy that produces goods.

Public Employee Interest Groups

The degree of unionization in the private sector has declined since 1965, but this has been offset by growth in the unionization of public employees.

Membership in the three largest unions of government employees rose

FIGURE 7-1 ■ Decline in Union Membership as a Percentage of Nonagricultural Employment from 1945 to 1993

SOURCE: Leo Troy and Neil Sheflin, *U.S. Union Sourcebook* (West Orange, N.J.: Industrial Relations Data and Information Services, 1985), and Bureau of Labor Statistics.

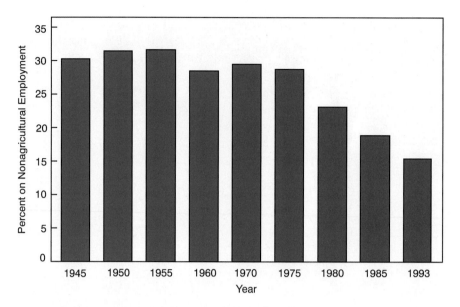

dramatically from 1960 to 1992. Table 7-2 shows the number of members in the three largest public employee unions, which grew more than 500 percent from 1960 to 1992.

Both the American Federation of State, County, and Municipal Employees and the American Federation of Teachers are members of the AFL-CIO's Public Employee Department. Originally, the public employee unions started out as social and professional organizations. Over the years, they have become quite militant and are often involved in strikes. Many of these strikes are illegal because certain public employees do not have the right to strike and essentially sign a contract so stating. In August 1981, the Professional Air Traffic Controllers Organization (PATCO), in defiance of a court order, went on strike. The issues included wage levels, long hours, excess stress, insensitive Federal Aviation Administration management, and other problems. President Reagan, convinced that public opinion was on his side, fired the strikers. Supervisors, nonstrikers, military personnel, and new trainees were rounded up to handle the jobs vacated by the terminated 16,000 air traffic controllers. On July 27, 1982, the union folded as a trustee padlocked the PATCO headquarters office. (A major irony is that PATCO was one of only a few unions to endorse Ronald Reagan's candidacy in 1980.)

TABLE 7-2 ■ The Growth in Public Employee Unionism

Union Name	1960	1979	1992
American Federation of State, County, and Municipal Employees	185,000	889,000	1,103,000
American Federation of Government Employees	70,000	236,000	164,000
American Federation of Teachers	56,000	423,000	483,000
Total	311,000	1,548,000	1,750,000

A powerful interest group lobbying on behalf of public employees is the National Education Association (NEA), a nationwide organization of about 1.8 million administrators, teachers, and others connected with education. The NEA lobbies intensively for increased public funding of education. The NEA sponsors regional and national conventions each year and has an extensive program of electronic media broadcasts, surveys, and the like.

Interest Groups of Professionals

Numerous professional organizations exist, including the American Bar Association, the Association of General Contractors of America, the Institute of Electrical and Electronic Engineers, the Screen Actors Guild, and others. In terms of money spent on lobbying, however, one professional organization stands out head and shoulders above the rest—the American Medical Association (AMA). Founded in 1947, it is now affiliated with more than 2,000 local and state medical societies and has a total membership of 237,000 and an administrative staff of 1,000. Together with the American Dental Association, the AMA spent an estimated $3.2 million in 1990 congressional campaign contributions in its efforts to influence legislation.

The AMA's most notable, but largely unsuccessful, lobbying effort was against the enactment of Medicare, which provides health insurance coverage for the elderly. In the early 1960s, the AMA launched a national advertising campaign to convince the public that Medicare was tantamount to "socialized medicine" and that private plans would offer better protection. This indirect lobbying, combined with direct pressure on members of Congress, delayed passage of the legislation until 1965 and ensured that the bill's language would protect and enhance doctors' incomes. More recently, the AMA has lobbied against the fees for more input into the Clinton administration's health insurance plan.

Environmental Groups

Environmental interest groups are not new. The Audubon Society was founded in 1905 to protect the snowy egret from the commercial demand for hat decorations, and the patron of the Sierra Club, John Muir, worked for the creation of national parks more than ninety years ago. But the blossoming of national environmental groups with mass memberships is a recent phenomenon. Since the first Earth Day, organized in 1972, many interest groups have sprung up to protect the environment in general or unique ecological niches. The groups range from the National Wildlife Federation, with a membership of more than 4.5 million and an emphasis on education, to the fairly elite Environmental Defense Fund, with a membership of 60,000 and a focus on influencing federal policy. Other groups include the Nature Conservancy, which seeks members' contributions so the organization can buy up threatened natural areas and either give them to state or local governments or manage them itself, and the more radical Greenpeace Society and Earth First groups. Greenpeace has become famous for its well-documented and widely disseminated efforts to stop Russian and Japanese whalers at sea, putting their own lives in jeopardy.

Did You Know . . . That the first labor organization in the United States was created by shoemakers' and coopers' guilds in Boston, Massachusetts, in 1648?

The *Rainbow Warrior*, flagship of the Greenpeace organization, is both a symbol for the environmental interest group and a resource that can be used for actions at sea to protect the environment. The *Rainbow Warrior* has acted to save the dolphins, to protest oil spills, and to stop whaling by the Japanese and the Russians.

At the most radical end of the spectrum is Earth First, an organization that has spiked redwood trees with large nails to stop lumbering. Although this practice makes the trees much less valuable to harvest, it has also caused serious injuries to loggers. The Sierra Club and World Wildlife Fund have appealed to young upper-middle-class professionals who not only want to contribute to saving the environment but also to enjoy the groups' travel programs and merchandise offerings.

Public Interest Groups

PUBLIC INTEREST
The best interests of the collective, overall community; the national good, rather than the narrow interests of a self-serving group.

Public interest is a difficult term to define because, as we noted earlier, there are many publics in our nation of more than 250 million. It is nearly impossible for one particular public policy to benefit everybody, which makes it practically impossible to define the public interest. Nonetheless, over the past few decades, a variety of law and lobbying organizations have been formed "in the public interest." The most well known and perhaps the most effective are those public interest groups organized under the leadership of consumer activist Ralph Nader.

The story of Ralph Nader's rise to the top began in the mid-1960s after the publication of his book *Unsafe at Any Speed*, a lambasting critique of the purported attempt by General Motors (GM) to keep from the public detrimental information about GM's rear-engine Corvair. Partly as a result of Nader's book, Congress began to consider testimony in favor of an automobile safety bill. GM made a clumsy attempt to discredit Nader's background. Nader sued, the media exploited the story, and, when GM settled out of court for several hundred thousand dollars, Nader became the recognized champion of consumer interests. Since then, Nader has turned over much of his income to the various public interest groups he has formed or sponsored. Now, there are numerous national "Naderite" organizations promoting consumer interests.

Partly in response to the Nader organizations, numerous conservative public interest law firms have sprung up that are often pitted against the consumer groups in court. Some of these are the Mountain States Legal Defense Foundation, the Pacific Legal Foundation, the National Right-to-Work Legal Defense Foundation, the Washington Legal Foundation, and the Mid-Atlantic Legal Foundation.

One of the largest public interest pressure groups is Common Cause, founded in 1968, whose goal is to reorder national priorities toward "the public" and to make governmental institutions more responsive to the needs of the public. Anyone willing to pay dues of $15 a year can become a member. Members are polled regularly to obtain information about local and national issues requiring reassessment. Some of the activities of Common Cause have been (1) helping to assure passage of the Twenty-sixth Amendment (giving eighteen-year-olds the right to vote), (2) achieving greater voter registration in all states, (3) supporting the complete withdrawal of all U.S. forces from South Vietnam in the 1970s, and (4) promoting legislation that would limit campaign spending.

Other public interest pressure groups are active on a wide range of issues. The goal of the League of Women Voters, founded in 1920, is to educate the public on political matters; although generally nonpartisan, it has lobbied for the Equal Rights Amendment and for government reform. The Consumer Federation of America is an alliance of about two hundred local and national organizations interested in consumer protection. The American Civil Liberties Union dates back to World War I, when, under a different name, it defended draft resisters. It generally enters into legal disputes related to Bill of Rights issues.

Ralph Nader began the movement to create public interest groups through the publication of his book *Unsafe at Any Speed*, which criticized General Motors for underplaying the dangers of its Corvair automobile. Since that time, he has founded a number of not-for-profit public interest groups that track business and governmental actions in specific policy arenas.

Single-Interest Groups

In recent years, a number of interest groups have formed that are focused on one issue. The abortion debate has created various antiabortion groups such as Right to Life and prochoice groups such as the National Abortion Rights Action League. Narrowly focused groups such as these may be able to call more attention to their respective causes because they have simple and straightforward goals and because their members tend to care intensely about the issues. Thus, they can easily motivate their members to contact legislators or to organize demonstrations in support of their policy goals.

Foreign Governments

Home-grown interests are not the only players in the game. Washington, D.C., is also the center for lobbying by foreign governments as well as private foreign interests. Large research and lobbying staffs are maintained by governments of the largest U.S. trading partners, such as Japan, Korea, the Philippines, and the European Community (EC) countries. Even smaller nations, such as those in the Caribbean, engage lobbyists when vital legislation affecting their trade interests is considered. Frequently, these foreign interests hire ex-representatives or ex-senators to promote their positions on Capitol Hill.

PROFILE

Marian Wright Edelman

"We must place our kids first in both our private actions and our public actions."

Children cannot vote, nor can they form political organizations and march on Capitol Hill. If they tried to take independent political action, they might be arrested as juvenile delinquents. They have, however, a champion in Marian Wright Edelman. Edelman is the founder and leader of the Children's Defense Fund, a Washington-based research and lobbying organization that works for the interests of American children, particularly those from poor families. Known as the children's crusader, Edelman has spent twenty years directing research on the status of children in the United States, formulating policy proposals for government, and lobbying for the passage of legislation.

Edelman was born in 1939 in Bennettsville, South Carolina, the youngest of five children. Her father, Arthur Wright, was a Baptist minister who worked to improve the lives of African Americans in his small southern town. He stressed the need to persevere in achieving one's goals and especially, to get an education. Young Marian, who was named after the opera diva Marian Anderson, attended Spelman Col-

lege in Atlanta and Yale Law School. She became the first female African American to be admitted to the bar in the state of Mississippi. During the civil rights movement, Marian Wright applied her legal talents to defend civil rights workers and to investigate poverty in the South for Senator Robert Kennedy. Later, she married Peter Edelman, a Kennedy assistant, whom she first met in Mississippi.

Edelman began her research and lobbying career with the Washington Research Project in 1968 and founded the Children's Defense Fund in 1973. Since that time, she has been tireless in her efforts to call attention to the extent of hunger, poverty, and illness among the nation's children. She has lobbied for better child care, for increased Head

Start funds, and for education to prevent teenage pregnancy.

Voicing her philosophy, Edelman says that "parenting . . . nurturing the next generation is the most important function of this society. . . . We must place our kids first in both our private actions and our public actions. . . . We talk about family values but when we look at our policies, we don't do it."* One way that the government can support the family is through access to good child care for all American families. A major proponent of the Act for Better Child Care, Edelman worked hard to push Democrats and Republicans, the National Education Association, and church groups to agree on a compromise measure that would both increase the number of child-care facilities and help low- and moderate-income families to pay for child care. The coalition did not hold, and a less comprehensive bill passed in 1990.

In spite of this setback, Edelman sees a bright future for child-care legislation because of the growing number of working women of all economic classes. She plans to continue her efforts to put the welfare of children first on the public agenda.

*Glen Elsasser, "Lessons For Life," *Chicago Tribune*, May 10, 1992, Section 6, p. 3.

Interest Group Strategies

Interest groups employ a wide range of techniques and strategies to promote their policy goals. Although few groups are successful at persuading Congress and the president to endorse their programs completely, many are able to prevent legislation injurious to their members from being considered or to weaken such legislation. The key to success for interest groups is the ability to have access to government officials. To achieve this, interest groups and their representatives try to cultivate long-term relationships with legislators and government officials. The best of such relationships are based on mutual respect and cooperation. The interest group provides the official with excellent sources of information and assistance, and the official in turn gives the group opportunities to express its views.

The techniques used by interest groups may be divided into those that are direct and indirect. **Direct techniques** include all those ways in which the interest group and its lobbyists approach the officials personally to press their case. **Indirect techniques,** in contrast, include strategies that use the general public or individuals to influence the government for the interest group.

Direct Techniques

Lobbying, publicizing ratings of legislative behavior, and providing campaign assistance, are the three main direct techniques used by interest groups.

Lobbying Techniques. As might be guessed, the term **lobbying** comes from the activities of private citizens regularly congregating in the lobbies of legislative chambers before a session to petition legislators. In the latter part of the nineteenth century, railroad and industrial interests openly bribed state legislators to pass legislation beneficial to their interests, giving lobbying a well-deserved bad name. Today, standard lobbying techniques still include buttonholing senators and representatives in state capitols and in Washington, D.C., while they are moving from their offices to the voting chambers. Lobbyists, however, do more than that.

Lobbyists engage in an array of activities to influence legislation. These are, at a minimum, the following:

1. Engaging in private meetings with public officials to make known the lobbyist's clients' interests. Although acting on behalf of a client, often lobbyists furnish needed information to senators and representatives (and government agency appointees) that they could not hope to obtain on their own. It is to the lobbyist's advantage to provide accurate information so that the policy maker will rely on this source in the future.
2. Testifying before congressional committees for or against proposed legislation.
3. Testifying before executive rule-making agencies, such as the Federal Trade Commission or the Consumer Product Safety Commission, for or against proposed rules.
4. Assisting the legislators or bureaucrats in drafting legislation or prospective regulations. Often, lobbyists can furnish legal advice on the specific details of legislation.
5. Inviting legislators to social occasions such as cocktail parties, boating expeditions, and other events. Most lobbyists feel that contacting legislators in a more relaxed social setting is effective. The extent to which legislators feel obligated to lobbyists for entertaining them is hard to gauge.
6. Providing political information to legislators and other government officials. Often the lobbyists will have better information than the party leadership about how other legislators are going to vote. In this case, the political information they furnish may be a key to legislative success.

DIRECT TECHNIQUES
Interest group activities that involve interaction with government officials to further the group's goals.

INDIRECT TECHNIQUES
Strategies employed by interest groups that use third parties to influence government officials.

LOBBYING
The attempt by organizations or by individuals to influence the passage, defeat, or contents of legislation and the administrative decisions of government. The derivation of the term may be traced back to over a century ago, when certain private citizens regularly congregated in the lobby outside the legislative chambers before a session to petition legislators.

Lobbyists gather outside a committee room to talk to committee members about the details of a bill. Through this action, the lobbyists are exercising the constitutional right of citizens to assemble and petition the government for the redress of grievances.

TABLE 7-3 ■ ADA Ratings for 1991

Americans for Democratic Action, a liberal political organization, tracks the votes of all senators and representatives on the set of issues that ADA thinks is most important. The "score" for each legislator is the percentage of correct votes from the ADA's point of view. Many other interest groups also engage in the ratings game.

Senator	Highest Rating
Cranston, D., California	100%
Akaka, D., Hawaii	100
Kennedy, D., Massachusetts	100
Lautenberg, D., New Jersey	100
Harkin, D., Iowa	94
Mikulski, D., Maryland	94
Kerry, D., Massachusetts	94
Bradley, D., New Jersey	94
Moynihan, D., New York	94
Pell, D., Rhode Island	94
Leahy, D., Vermont	94
Adams, D., Washington	94
Kohl, D., Wisconsin	94

Senator	Lowest Rating
Mack, R., Florida	0%
Coats, R., Indiana	0
McConnell, R., Kentucky	0
Cochran, R., Mississippi	0
Lott, R., Mississippi	0
Nickles, R., Oklahoma	0
Gramm, R., Texas	0
Armstrong, R., Colorado	6
McClure, R., Idaho	6
Symms, R., Idaho	6
Lugar, R., Indiana	6
Burns, R., Montana	6
Helms, R., North Carolina	6
Thurmond, R., South Carolina	6
Kasten, R., Wisconsin	6
Wallop, R., Wyoming	6

SOURCE: *Congressional Quarterly Weekly Report*, March 3, 1992, p. 705.

POLITICAL ACTION
COMMITTEES (PACs)
Committees set up by and representing corporations, labor unions, or special interest groups; PACs raise and give campaign donations on behalf of the organizations or groups they represent.

The Ratings Game.   Many interest groups attempt to influence the overall behavior of legislators through their rating systems. Each year, the interest group selects those votes on legislation that it feels are most important to the organization's goals. Legislators are given a score based on the percentage of times that he or she voted with the interest group. The usual scheme ranges from 0 to 100 percent. If a legislator has a score of, for example, 90 percent on the Americans for Democratic Action (ADA) rating, it means that she supported their positions to a high degree (Table 7-3). Such a high ADA score is usually interpreted as very liberal. The groups that use rating systems range from the Americans for Constitutional Action (considered to be conservative) to the League of Conservation Voters (environmental). The league identifies the twelve legislators having what the league sees as the worst records on environmental issues and advertises them as the "Dirty Dozen."[5] Needless to say, a senator or representative normally does not want to earn membership on this list.

Campaign Assistance.   Interest groups have additional strategies to use in their attempts to influence government policies. Groups recognize that the greatest concern of legislators is to be reelected, so they focus on their campaign needs. Associations with large memberships, such as labor unions or the National Education Association, are able to provide workers for political campaigns, including precinct workers to get out the vote, volunteers to put up posters and pass out literature, and people to staff telephone banks for campaign headquarters.

In many states, where membership in certain interest groups is large, candidates vie for the groups' endorsements in the campaign. Gaining those endorsements may be automatic, or it may require that the candidates participate in a debate or interview with the interest groups. Endorsements are important because an interest group usually publicizes its choices in its membership publication and because the candidate can use the endorsement in his or her campaign literature. Traditionally, labor unions such as the AFL–CIO and the UAW have endorsed Democratic party candidates. Republican candidates, however, often try to persuade union locals to, at the minimum, refrain from any endorsement. Making no endorsement can then be perceived as disapproval of the Democratic party candidate.

PACs and Political Campaigns.   In the last two decades, the most important form of campaign help from interest groups has become the political contribution from a group's **political action committee (PAC).** The 1974 Federal Election Campaign Act and its 1976 amendments allow corporations, labor unions, and special interest groups to set up PACs to raise money for candidates. For a PAC to be legitimate, the money must be raised from at least fifty volunteer donors and must be given to at least five candidates in the federal election. PACs can contribute up to $5,000 to each candidate in each election. Each corporation or each union is limited to one PAC. As you might imagine, corporate PACs obtain funds from executives in their firms, and unions obtain PAC funds from their members.

---

[5]Bill Keller, "The Trail of the Dirty Dozen," *Congressional Quarterly Weekly Report*, March 21, 1981, p. 510.

The number of PACs has grown astronomically, as has the amount they spend on elections. There were about 600 political action committees in 1976; by 1992, there were more than 3,700. Corporate PACs are increasing at a rate greater than other varieties. The total amount of spending by PACs grew from $19 million in 1973 to an estimated $400 million in 1991–1992. Of the $678 million in campaign money spent by congressional candidates in 1982, about $180 million came from PACs.[6]

Interest groups funnel PAC money to candidates who they think can do the most good for them. Frequently, they make the maximum contribution of $5,000 per election to candidates who face little or no opposition. The summary of PAC contributions given in Figure 7-2 shows that the great bulk of campaign contributions goes to incumbent candidates rather than to challengers. Corporations are particularly likely to give money to Democrats in Congress as well as to Republicans, because many Democratic incumbents chair important committees or subcommittees. In the Senate, the Republicans held committee chairs from 1980 until 1986, so they reaped corresponding benefits in PAC money. Why, might you ask, would business leaders give to Democrats who may be more liberal than themselves? Interest groups see PAC contributions as a way to ensure access to powerful legislators, even if they may disagree with them some of the time. PAC contributions are, in a way, an investment in a relationship.

The campaign finance regulations clearly limit the amount that a PAC can give to any one candidate, but there is no limit on the amount that a PAC can spend on an independent campaign, either on behalf of a candidate or party or in opposition to one. During the 1970s and early 1980s,

Did You Know . . . That the overlapping membership in environmental interest groups that lobby Washington is over two million people and growing fast?

---

[6]"With So Many Seats Open in '92, Campaign Spending Rose 52%," *Congressional Quarterly Weekly Review*, March 20, 1993, p. 691.

FIGURE 7-2 ■ **PAC Contributions to Congressional Candidates, 1972–1990**

SOURCE: *Congressional Quarterly Weekly Report*, March 22, 1986, p. 657; *Federal Election Commission Report, 1987, 1989, 1991.*

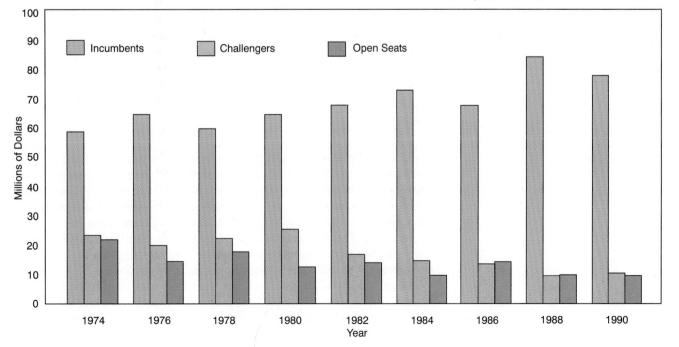

Did You Know . . . That the leading Senate recipient of political action committee (PAC) money in the 1983–1988 period (earning him the title of biggest "PAC-MAN") was Lloyd Bentsen, Democrat of Texas and the 1988 vice presidential candidate, who got over $2.6 million?

CLIMATE CONTROL
The use of public relations techniques to create favorable public opinion toward an interest group, industry, or corporation.

one of the most prominent PACs in the United States was the National Conservative Political Action Committee, or NCPAC. This interest group espoused a conservative philosophy, opposing abortion, supporting prayer in school, and supporting a strong defense policy. NCPAC targeted specific senators and representatives for defeat, spending large sums of money against them in primary and general elections. In general, NCPAC has not been successful in these efforts since 1980.

Indirect Techniques

By working through third parties—which may be constituents, the general public, or other groups—interest groups can try to influence government policy. Indirect techniques mask the interest group's own activities and make the effort appear to be spontaneous. Furthermore, legislators and government officials are often more impressed by contacts from constituents than from an interest group's lobbyist.

Generating Public Pressure.   In some instances, interest groups try to produce a "groundswell" of public pressure to influence the government. Such efforts may include advertisements in national magazines and newspapers, mass mailings, television publicity, and demonstrations. Computers and satellite links make communication efforts even more effective. (See the feature entitled *Politics and Technology* in this chapter.) Interest groups may commission polls to find out what the public sentiments are and then publicize the results. The intent of this activity is to convince policy makers that pubic opinion overwhelmingly supports the group's position.

Some corporations and interest groups also engage in a practice that might be called **climate control.** This strategy calls for public relations efforts that are aimed at improving the public image of the industry or group and not necessarily related to any specific political issue. Contributions by corporations and groups in support of public television programs, sponsorship of such events as "Hands Across America," and commercials extolling the virtues of corporate research are examples of climate control. By building a reservoir of favorable public opinion, groups believe it less likely that their legislative goals will be met with opposition by the public.

Using Constituents as Lobbyists.   One of the most effective interest group activities is the use of constituents to lobby for the group's goals. In the "shotgun" approach, the interest group tries to mobilize large numbers of constituents to write or phone their legislators or the president. Often, the group provides postcards or form letters for constituents to fill out and mail. These efforts are only effective on Capitol Hill when there is an extraordinary number of responses, because legislators know that the voters did not initiate the communication on their own.

A more influential variation of this technique uses only important constituents. Known as the "rifle" technique, or the "Utah plant manager's theory," the interest group contacts an influential constituent, such as the

POLITICS AND TECHNOLOGY

High-Tech Lobbying

Interest group activity has exploded in recent years. One particularly important aspect of lobbying in this new era is the use of modern technology to enhance the role of pressure groups. Such use is particularly striking in the case of the New Right groups on the conservative side of the political spectrum.

Lobbying organizations have for many years employed "grass-roots" tactics for influencing the outcomes of government decisions. These tactics have included soliciting citizens to send letters to members of Congress, mobilizing protest movements, and endorsing or attacking candidates during election campaigns.

What is new, exciting, and potentially crucial in the struggle over who will have access to the levers of power in government is the availability of computer-based technology and expanded telecommunications facilities for communicating more effectively and more quickly to targeted segments of the population. Elected representatives may in fact not know which interest group was involved in the "write-your-congressperson" campaign. They may even be unaware that any group was behind sophisticated letter-writing efforts in which every letter reads slightly differently and at least appears to have come from a different person with an equally intense interest in the issue at hand. Groups also generate massive telephone call-in efforts with instructions to members to emphasize a slightly different aspect of an issue that most concerns them. The goal of such campaigns, made possible by computer-controlled mass mail-

ings to targeted citizens, is to produce at least the appearance that the interest group has a massive, unified, intense, and growing block of supporters.

The use of direct-mail methods to solicit small monetary contributions is among the most important reasons for the growth of conservative pressure groups in recent years. These methods have produced not only a considerable amount of money with which to finance conservative political action committees but also very large lists of contributors and activists for future mobilization. They have also allowed the New Right to bombard average Americans with their views. Mailing lists are readily tapped by the organizers of right-wing groups to generate pressure on Washington officials or on state and local political leaders. The critical thing to understand about these lists, which are maintained by Richard Viguerie in Falls Church, Virginia, is that they allow the pressure groups to bypass the traditional media sources for communicating their views to the general public.

Not only computers but also advanced television technology has allowed New Right pressure groups to increase their role in American politics. The Reverend Jerry Falwell, leader of the Moral Majority, uses more than six hundred television and radio stations to carry his political messages during his weekly broadcasts of the "Old Time Gospel Hour." Conservative activist Paul Weyrich has created National Empowerment Television (NET). NET is a satellite network that allows local groups to see public officials

debate the issues and to ask questions through an interactive connection. Broadcasting three shows per month, Weyrich believes that the impact of his viewing groups and their live complaints, comments, and concerns on elected officials is much stronger than the usual letters and telegrams. In fact, Weyrich claims that his program on the Clarence Thomas nomination forced two Democratic senators to vote for Thomas's confirmation.

Business pressure groups have adopted the tactics that have been so successful for the New Right. Apart from the more traditional efforts of soliciting letters, telegrams, and phone calls to elected officials, the National Chamber of Commerce has a major high-technology communications system available to send its interpretations of pending legislation and other matters to members; a monthly magazine (*Nation's Business*) with a circulation of 1.25 million; a weekly newsletter (*Washington Report*) that is sent to nearly a million members and friends of the chamber; a weekly television program ("It's Your Business") that is carried on more than one hundred stations; a radio show ("What's the Issue?") that discusses major national topics on more than four hundred stations; and Biznet, a highly ambitious closed-circuit, tax-exempt television network, which in theory would allow the chamber to mobilize its members and supporters in only a matter of hours. Future developments in high-tech lobbying will be limited only by the speed with which new technological innovations can be put in place.

ACT UP, a group dedicated to increasing awareness of the AIDS epidemic, stages a protest in Albany, New York. ACT UP members try to focus the public's attention on the need to increase funding for research into the causes of, and cures for, the disease.

manager of a local plant in Utah, to contact the senator from Utah.[7] Because the constituent is seen as responsible for many jobs or other resources, the legislator is more likely to listen carefully to his or her concerns about legislation than to a paid lobbyist.

Building Alliances.　　Another indirect technique used by interest groups is to form an alliance with other groups concerned about the same legislation. Often, these groups will set up a paper organization with an innocuous name, such as the Coalition for American Rivers, to represent their joint concerns. In this case, the sponsoring groups, which included railroads, environmentalists, and others who opposed the construction of the Alton Lock and Dam, contributed money to the "front" alliance, loaned lobbyists to it in Illinois, and paid the rent for its office.[8] The advantages of an alliance are that it looks as if larger public interests are at stake, and it hides the specific interests of the individual groups involved. It is also an efficient device for keeping like-minded groups from duplicating one another's lobbying efforts.

---

[7]Kay Lehman Schlozman and John T. Tierney, *Organized Interests and American Democracy* (New York: Harper and Row, 1986), p. 293.
[8]See T. R. Reid, *Congressional Odyssey* (San Francisco: W. H. Freeman, 1980) for a complete account of such lobbying activities.

Regulating Lobbyists

🔻

Congress made its first attempt to control lobbyists and lobbying activities through Title III of the Legislative Reorganization Act of 1946, otherwise known as the Federal Regulation of Lobbying Act. The act actually provided for public disclosure more than for regulation and neglected to specify which agency would enforce its provisions. Its specific provisions are as follows:

1. Any person or organization that receives money to be used principally to influence legislation before Congress must register.

2. Any individual lobbyist or a representative of a group who is registering must, under oath, give his or her name, address, place of employment, salary, amount and purpose of expenses, and duration of employment.

3. Every registered lobbyist must give quarterly reports on his or her activities; these reports are published in the *Congressional Record*.

4. Anyone failing to satisfy the specific provisions of the act can be fined up to $10,000 and receive a five-year prison term.

In a famous case relating to the constitutionality of the 1946 lobbying act,[9] the Supreme Court emphasized that the intention of the act was simply to enable Congress to discover "who is being hired, who is putting up the money, and how much." The Court stated that the lobbying law does not violate due process, freedom of speech or press, or freedom to petition. But the Court narrowly construed the application of the act to only those lobbyists who *directly* seek to influence federal legislation. Any lobbyist indirectly seeking to influence legislation simply through public opinion does not fall within the scope of the activities regulated by the act.

Currently, about 7,000 lobbyists are registered under the act (Table 7-4). The act has probably had no effect on the amount of money spent on lobbying and the types of activities engaged in by lobbyists. No enforcement agency has been created by Congress, and the public is almost totally ignorant of the information disclosed in the quarterly reports. The problem facing Congress, of course, is that any stricter regulation of lob-

Did You Know . . . That in the 1992 congressional elections, political action committees gave over 80 percent of their campaign funds to incumbents?

🔻

---

[9]*United States v. Harriss,* 347 U.S. 612 (1954).

TABLE 7-4 ■ **What Proportion of Lobbyists Are Registered?**

Total number of registered lobbyists	6,880
Registered as congressional lobbyists	5,935
Registered as foreign agents	785
Registered as executive branch agents	160
Estimated total number of persons lobbying in Washington	80,000
ANSWER: Fewer than 10% are registered.	

SOURCE: *Wall Street Journal,* May 30, 1991, p. A16.

bying will run into constitutional problems because of the potential abridgement of First Amendment rights. Also, so long as the Supreme Court does not view indirect lobbying as falling under the purview of the act, lobbying will be difficult to control.

After the Watergate scandal in 1972, Congress attempted to pass a new bill that would make strict registration and reporting provisions a requirement. This 1976 bill, supported by Common Cause, failed under the combined attack of business, labor, and, interestingly enough, Ralph Nader. By 1978, however, Congress succeeded in passing legislation that addressed the problem of ethics in government. (See the *Politics and Ethics* feature in this chapter for an account of a prosecution under the 1978 Ethics in Government Act.)

Conclusion: Why Interest Groups Have So Much Power

It has been claimed that we are a nation of special interests. Organized interest groups have obtained special benefits for their members and blocked legislation that clearly seems to be supported by most citizens. The power of interest groups in the American political system probably results from a number of factors, some of which are inherent in the groups themselves and some of which are derived from the structure of our government.

Not all interest groups have an equal influence on government. Each has a different combination of resources to use in the policy-making process. Some groups are composed of members who have high social status and enormous economic resources, such as the National Association of Manufacturers. Other groups, such as labor unions, derive influence from their large membership. Still other groups, such as environmentalists, have causes that can claim strong public support even from those people who have no direct stake in the issue. Groups such as the National Rifle Association are well organized and have highly motivated members. This enables them to channel a stream of mail toward Congress with a few days' effort.

Even the most powerful interest groups do not always succeed in their demands. Whereas the National Chamber of Commerce may be accepted as having a justified interest in the question of business taxes, many legislators might feel that the chamber should not engage in the debate over the size of the federal budget deficit. In other words, groups are seen as having a legitimate concern in the issues closest to their interests but not necessarily in broader issues. This may explain why some of the most successful groups are those that focus on very specific issues—such as tobacco farming, funding of abortions, handgun control—and do not get involved in larger conflicts.

The structure of American government also invites the participation of interest groups. The governmental system has many points of access or places in the decision-making process where interest groups may focus an attack. If a bill opposed by a group passes the Senate, the lobbying efforts shift to the House of Representatives or to the president to seek a veto. If

POLITICS AND ETHICS

Lobbying by Former Government Officials

In 1978, Congress passed the Ethics in Government Act as a reaction to the Watergate scandal during the Nixon administration. The main purpose of the act was to provide for independent investigations of present or former high-ranking government officials, unless the charges filed against an official are judged by the attorney general to be without merit. The act forbids former senior government employees to lobby their former agency on any matter for a year after leaving, to lobby any department for two years on an issue in which they had a direct responsibility, or to lobby for the rest of their lives on issues in which they participated "personally and substantially."

On May 29, 1986, Whitney North Seymour was appointed by a three-judge federal court to serve as a special prosecutor to investigate conflict-of-interest charges against former deputy White House Chief of Staff Michael K. Deaver. Deaver left the White House staff in May 1985 to become a highly paid lobbyist for foreign governments and business corporations. Deaver discussed with Robert McFarlane, the president's national security adviser at the time, some objections his client, the Commonwealth of Puerto

Rico, had to a proposed revision in tax laws. The proposed revision would eliminate tax advantages for American businesses that invested in Puerto Rico and could cause perhaps $600 million in economic losses. McFarlane was at the time directly involved in looking into the possible revocation of this tax break. This occurred about two or three months after Deaver left office, in violation of the one-year prohibition

on direct lobbying of his former White House colleagues.

In addition to these incidents, Deaver's work on behalf of the Daewoo Corporation, a large steel company in South Korea, and the U.S. defense contractor Rockwell International Corporation was also examined, following a series of allegations by Democrats on the Senate Judiciary Committee, by the General Accounting Office, and by the Office of Government Ethics. Finally, Deaver's work for the government of Canada in its dispute with the United States over acid rain also allegedly violated the 1978 law.

For his efforts, Deaver was paid well by his clients: $105,000 by Canada, $250,000 by Rockwell International, $250,000 by Daewoo, and an undisclosed amount by Puerto Rico.

After a seven-week trial in late 1987, Deaver was found guilty and became the first person convicted under the Ethics in Government Act.

During the transition period before his inaugural, President Bill Clinton announced ethics rules for appointed members of his administration. These rules also barred lobbying efforts by former executives.

in spite of all efforts the legislation passes, the group may even lobby the executive agency or bureau that is supposed to implement the law and hope to influence the way in which the legislation is applied. In some cases, interest groups carry their efforts into the court system either by filing lawsuits or filing briefs as "friends of the court." The constitutional features of separation of powers and checks and balances encourage interest groups in their efforts.

GETTING INVOLVED

The Gun Control Issue

Is the easy availability of handguns a major cause of crime? Do people have a right to firearms to defend home and hearth? These questions are part of a long-term and heated battle between organized profirearm and antifirearm camps. The disagreements run deeply and reflect strong sentiments on both sides. The fight is fueled by the one million gun incidents occurring in the United States each year—the murders, suicides, assaults, accidents, robberies, and injuries in which guns are involved. Proponents of gun control seek new restrictions on gun purchases—if not a ban on them entirely—while decreasing existing arsenals of privately owned weapons. Proponents of firearms are fighting back. They claim that firearms are a cherished tradition, a constitutional right, a vital defense need for individuals. They contend that the problem lies not in the sale and ownership of the weapons themselves but in the criminal use of firearms.

Michael Beard, director of the National Coalition to Ban Handguns, favors a total ban because "the only way to prevent the tragic loss of life—the thirty-two thousand lives a year we're losing to handguns—is to say: We no longer need handguns. They serve no valid purpose, except to kill people." Neal Know, director of the Institute for Legislative Action of the National Rifle Association of America, op-

poses a ban "because, among other reasons, it wouldn't work. It would not reduce the number of crimes committed. Are we going to assume that a person who will violate a law against rape, robbery, or murder will suddenly obey a gun law? I doubt it. There is no city, no state, no nation that has reduced its crime rate by the enactment of a gun law."*

The debate is intense and bitter. Gun control proponents accuse their adversaries of being "frightened little men living in a pseudomacho myth." Gun control opponents brand the other side as "new totalitarians" intent on curbing individual freedom.

The National Rifle Association (NRA), founded in 1871, is currently one of the most powerful single-issue groups on the American political scene. With some two million members and an annual budget of $30 million, the NRA claims to represent the seventy million gun owners in the United States. Although a majority of Americans support some regulation of semiautomatic weapons and handguns, the NRA has continued to defeat gun control legislation, elect officials sympathetic to its cause, and defeat candidates supporting gun control. If you agree with the NRA's position and want to get involved in its efforts in opposition to gun control legislation, contact:

The National Rifle Association
1600 Rhode Island Ave., N.W.
Washington, DC 20036
202-828-6000

If, however, you are concerned with the increase in gun-related crimes and feel that stricter gun laws are necessary, you can get involved through these organizations:

Committee for the Study of Handgun Misuse
109 N. Dearborn St., Suite 704
Chicago, IL 60602
312-641-5593

The National Coalition to Ban Handguns
100 Maryland Ave., N.E.
Washington, DC 20002
202-544-7190

Handgun Control, Inc.
810 18th St., N.W., Suite 705
Washington, DC 20006
202-638-4723

James and Sarah Brady, leading the movement for handgun control after he was seriously wounded in the assassination attempt on President Reagan in 1981.

*"Should Handguns Be Outlawed?" *U.S. News & World Report*, December 22, 1980, p. 23.

CHAPTER SUMMARY

▼

1. An interest group is an organized group of individuals who share common objectives and who actively attempt to influence government policy. Interest groups proliferate in the United States because they can influence government at many points in the political structure and because they offer solidary, material, and purposive incentives to their members. Interest groups are often created out of social movements.

2. Major types of interest groups include business, labor, agricultural, environmental, professional, and public employee groups. Other important groups may be considered public interest groups. In addition, single-issue groups and foreign governments lobby the government.

3. Interest groups use direct and indirect techniques to influence government. Direct techniques include testifying before committees and rule-making agencies, providing information to legislatures, making campaign contributions, and rating legislators' voting records. Contributions are made through political action committees, or PACs. Most PAC money is given to incumbents to ensure access for the group. Indirect techniques include campaigns to rally public sentiment, letter-writing campaigns, influencing the climate of opinion, and using constituents to lobby for the group's interest.

4. The 1946 Legislative Reorganization Act was the first attempt to control lobbyists and their activities through registration requirements. The Supreme Court narrowly construed the act as applying only to lobbyists who directly seek to influence federal legislation. Fewer than 10 percent of individuals who lobby in Washington are registered.

QUESTIONS FOR REVIEW AND DISCUSSION

▼

1. The American political system is sometimes described as one having "multiple cracks," or points of access for interest groups. If Congress is about to pass a law that adversely affects an interest group to which you belong, how can you lobby against it? How would you plan to lobby Congress, the executive branch, and the Supreme Court? How could you influence public opinion to support your point of view?

2. Think about your own interests—ethnic identity, religious affiliation, occupation, union, profession, hobby interests, and so on. How many interest groups might you belong to? Are you formally a member of any of these? If you are not a member, how are your interests represented? Which group represents the interests of the general public, say, for clean air or for lower taxes?

3. At the present time, PACs give disproportionate amounts of campaign contributions to incumbent legislators. How would the political process be changed if PACs were required to give equal amounts to challengers and incumbents, or if there were a limit on the percentage of campaign funds that could come from PACs? Where do PACs get their money?

SELECTED REFERENCES

▼

Jeffrey M. Berry, *The Interest Group Society* (Glenview, Ill.: Scott, Foresman/Little, Brown, 1989). A comprehensive study of how interest groups are created, how they raise money, how they are staffed, and how they lobby. The role of interest groups in a democracy receives special attention.

Alan J. Cigler and Burdette A. Loomis, eds., *Interest Group Politics,* 2nd ed. (Washington, D.C.: Congressional Quarterly Press, 1986). An in-depth discussion of what interest groups are, how they emerge and grow, and how they influence the legislative process.

A. Lee Fritschler and Bernard H. Ross, *How Washington Works: An Executive Guide to Government* (Cambridge, Mass.: Ballinger Publishing Co., 1987). This book provides a useful, practical perspective on how business executives can influence the federal government, how regulations are developed, how government supports business, and who the key government actors are.

William Greider, *Who Will Tell the People?: The Betrayal of American Democracy* (New York: Simon & Schuster, 1992). Greider argues that the American political process has degenerated into a "grand bazaar" in which interest groups' money is exchanged for political power and influence.

David Rapp, *How the U.S. Got into Agriculture and Why It Can't Get Out* (Washington, D.C.: Congressional Quarterly Press, 1988). Explores how one pressure group became effective.

Lawrence S. Rothenberg, *Linking Citizens to Government: Interest Group Politics at Common Cause* (New York: Cambridge University Press, 1992). This in-depth exploration and analysis of one of the largest common interest groups in America, Common Cause, focuses on the demographics, organization, and policies of the group.

Kay Lehman Schlozman and John T. Tierney, *Organized Interests and American Democracy* (New York: Harper & Row, 1986). A systematic investigation of the activities and strategies of interest groups based on interviews with lobbyists and representatives of 175 groups.

Bruce C. Wolpe, *Lobbying Congress: How the System Works* (Ridgely, Md.: Congressional Quarterly, 1990). This is a combination of a how-to manual and a case-study collection dealing with basic lobbying theory, lobbying dos and don'ts, and specific cases in which lobbying has been effective.

CHAPTER 8
Political Parties

CHAPTER CONTENTS

WHAT IF ... WE HAD A MULTIPARTY POLITICAL SYSTEM IN THE UNITED STATES?

The two-party system is an enduring feature of American government. In most elections, the contest is between two candidates, one from each of the major parties. In modern times, most members of Congress and state legislatures and all of the presidents have been either Democrats or Republicans.

Minor third parties have entered the arena, but historically it has been mostly a two-party affair. With few exceptions, the two major parties have accounted for about 90 percent of the total popular vote since the 1800s.

What if we had a multiparty system instead? Actually, such a system with competing political parties is much more common in Western democracies than the two-party system. As a modern, complex society with a wide variety of interests and opinions, it would seem the United States might be a likely candidate for a multiparty system.

Along with such a system, we would probably have proportional representation. Legislative seats would be allocated to parties in proportion to the percentage of votes they won in the nation or a region. If a party or its candidates received 20 percent of the total vote, the party would have 20 percent of the seats in the legislature. It would be

unlikely for one party to have exclusive government control. In a proportional representation scheme, for example, if Democrats received 53 percent of the total vote for the House of Representatives, they would have 231 seats, a small majority compared with the 258 they won in 1992.

Each party would be similar to a large interest group. Although still acting like a party, it would perform functions that in a two-party system only an interest group can perform. Parties representing interests would bargain with each other instead of interest groups bargaining with each other within a party. Each party would not have to win support from the large and heterogeneous groups they now need, but would achieve success by appealing to special groups.

It is difficult to say how many parties the United States would be needed to represent the diversity of American society. Would we need five or five hundred? We would likely have parties representing many different groups: a farmer's party, a Hispanic party, a western party, a labor party, and so on. A multiparty system would mean that *no* party would hold a majority of legislative seats. To gain support for his or her other programs, the president would have to build a coalition of several parties by persuading each party that its members would benefit from the coalition. The major difficulty in a multiparty political system is, of course, the fact that parties will withdraw from the coalition when they fail to benefit from it. Holding a coalition together for more than one issue is sometimes impossible.

1. *Why do we have only two parties, and how have they survived for more than one hundred years?*
2. *Why do American parties take such moderate positions, and how do they keep their electoral coalitions united?*
3. *What groups are better served by a multiparty system?*

What Is a Political Party?

What are you? If that question were asked during a presidential election campaign, the answer would probably be "I'm a Republican" or "I'm a Democrat" or "I'm an Independent."[1] The answer would refer to a person's actual or perceived affiliation with a particular political party. In the United States, being a member of a political party does not require paying dues, passing an examination, or swearing an oath of allegiance. Well, if nothing is really required to be a member of a political party, what then is a **political party?**

A formal definition might be as follows:

A political party is a group of political activists who organize to win elections, to operate the government, and to determine public policy.

With this definition, we can see the difference between an interest group and a political party. Interest groups do not want to operate government and they do not put forth political candidates—even though they support candidates who will promote their interests if elected or reelected. Another important distinction is that, whereas interest groups tend to sharpen issues, American political parties tend to blur their issue positions in order to attract voters.

A political party is not a **faction** (see Chapter 2). Factions, which historically preceded political parties, were simply groups of individuals who joined together to win a benefit for themselves, like the interest groups of today. They were limited to the period in our political history when there were relatively few elective offices and only a small percentage of the population could meet the requirements for voting. Today, we still use the term *faction*, but only for a particular group within a political party. For example, we speak of the conservative factions within the Republican and Democratic parties. A faction is founded on a particular philosophy, personality, or even geographical region. Sometimes a faction can be based on a political issue. The main feature differentiating a faction from a political party is that the faction generally does not have a permanently organized structure.

POLITICAL PARTY
A group of political activists who organize to win elections, to operate the government, and to determine public policy.

FACTION
A group or bloc in a legislature or political party acting together in pursuit of some special interest or position.

Clinton supporters lead the cheers for the candidate during the convention. Studies have found that the delegates to the Democratic convention are usually more liberal than party followers while delegates to the Republican convention are usually more conservative than rank-and-file members.

Functions of Political Parties in the United States

Political parties in the United States engage in a wide variety of activities, many of which are discussed in this chapter. Through these activities, parties perform a number of functions for the political system. These functions include the following:

1. *Recruiting Candidates for Public Office.* Because it is the goal of parties to gain control of government, they must work to recruit candidates for all elective offices. Often this means recruiting candidates to run against powerful incumbents or for unpopular jobs. Yet if parties did not search out and encourage political hopefuls, far more offices would be uncontested and voters would have limited choices.

---

[1]In rare instances the answer might be "I'm a Libertarian" or "I'm a Socialist" or might refer to some other less common political group.

POLITICS AND COMPARATIVE POLITICAL PARTIES

Political Parties in Other Countries

Countries vary widely in the number of political parties they have and in the way political power is apportioned. Mexico has one dominant political party, but within it are relatively conservative and relatively liberal factions. This party is known as the *Partido Revolucionario Institucional* (Institutional Revolutionary Party), and its somewhat contradictory name conveys the nature of Mexican politics. The party grew out of popular revolutionary struggles in the late nineteenth and early twentieth centuries; however, today it must address the desires of modern Mexicans for stability.

In Italy, in contrast, a variety of parties have vied for control and influence. Voters have been splintered among the Christian Democrats, the former Communists, the Socialists, and a large number of minor parties. In 1993, however, massive corruption and continued political instability associated with organized crime's influence over Italian society resulted in the overwhelming approval of a national referendum that limited the role of small parties.

In many countries, political parties have much closer linkages to members of the electorate than do American parties. In some cases, the linkage is through interest groups or institutions. For example, British labor unions elect representatives to the executive councils of the Labor party. In some European nations, the Catholic Church is informally linked to the Christian Democratic parties. Members are also kept informed of party positions by major newspapers published by the party organization. Some parties organize social and athletic events throughout the year to reinforce members' loyalty and support.

Different party structures grew out of historical events unique to each nation, as well as electoral laws that may favor either small parties (as in Italy) or only the biggest parties (as in the United States). What we are used to—that is, two relatively moderate political parties alternating in power peacefully—is not likely to exist in countries that have evolved differently from the United States.

2. *Organizing and Running Elections.* Although elections are a government activity, political parties actually organize the voter registration drives, recruit the volunteers to work at the polls, provide most of the campaign activity to stimulate interest in the election, and work to increase participation.

3. *Presenting Alternative Policies to the Electorate.* The difference between political parties and factions is that factions are often centered on individual politicians, while parties are focused on a set of political positions. The Democrats or Republicans in Congress who vote together do so because they represent constituencies that have similar expectations and demands.

4. *Accepting Responsibility for Operating the Government.* When the party elects the president or governor and members of the legislature, it accepts the responsibility for running the government. This includes staffing the executive branch with managers from the party and developing linkages among the elected officials to gain support for policies and their implementation.

5. *Acting as the Organized Opposition to the Party in Power.* The "out" party, or the one that does not control the executive branch, is expected to articulate its own policies and oppose the winning party when appropriate. By organizing the opposition to the "in" party, the opposition party forces debate on the policy alternatives.

Students of political parties such as Leon D. Epstein[2] point out that the major functions of American political parties are carried out by a small, relatively loose-knit **cadre,** or nucleus, of party activists. This is quite a different arrangement from the more highly structured, mass-membership party organization typical of European working-class parties. American parties concentrate on winning elections rather than signing up large numbers of deeply committed, dues-paying members who believe passionately in the party's program.

A Short History of Political Parties in the United States

Political parties in the United States have a long tradition, dating back to the earliest years of this nation's history. The function and character of these political parties, as well as the emergence of the two-party system itself, have much to do with the unique historical forces operating from this country's beginning as an independent nation. It was not until the 1790s that political parties emerged in the United States (see Figure 8-1).

[2]*Political Parties in Western Democracies* (New Brunswick, N.J.: Transaction, 1980).

CADRE

The nucleus of political party activists carrying out the major functions of American political parties.

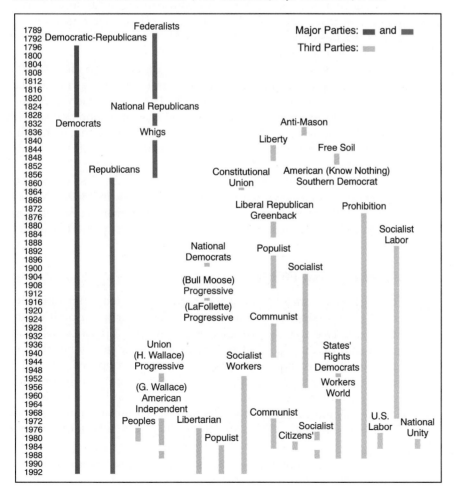

FIGURE 8-1 ■ American Political Parties Since 1789

The chart indicates the years parties either ran presidential candidates or held national conventions. The lifespan for many political parties can only be approximated because parties existed at the state or local level before they ran candidates in presidential elections, and parties continued to exist at local levels long after they ceased running presidential candidates. Not every party fielding a presidential candidate is represented in the chart. For instance, in 1988 at least nine other parties fielded a presidential candidate in at least one state.

SOURCES: Congressional Quarterly, *Congressional Quarterly's Guide to U.S. Elections,* 2d ed. (Washington, D.C.: Congressional Quarterly, 1985), p. 224; *Congressional Quarterly Weekly Report* (1988), p. 3184.

Generally, we can divide the evolution of our nation's political parties into six periods:

1. The creation of parties in the 1790s.
2. The era of one-party rule, or personal politics, in the 1820s.
3. The period from Andrew Jackson's presidency to the Civil War, during which the Democrats and the Whigs were solidly established national parties.
4. The post–Civil War period, ending in 1896.
5. The progressive period, from 1896 to 1921.
6. The modern period, from Franklin Roosevelt's New Deal until today.

The Formative Years: Federalists and Anti-Federalists

The first partisan political division in the United States occurred prior to the adoption of the Constitution. The **Federalists** proposed adoption of the Constitution, while the **Anti-Federalists** were against ratification.

In September 1796, George Washington, who had served as president for almost two full terms, decided not to run again. In his farewell address, he made a somber assessment of the nation's future. Washington felt that the country might be destroyed by the "baneful effects of the spirit of party." He viewed parties as a threat to both national unity and the concept of popular government. Early in his career, Thomas Jefferson did not like political parties either. In 1789, he stated, "If I could not go to heaven but with a party, I would not go there at all."[3]

What Americans found out during the first decade or so after ratification of the Constitution was that even a patriot-king (as Washington has been called) could not keep everyone happy. There is no such thing as a neutral political figure who is so fair-minded that everyone agrees with him or her. During this period, it became obvious to many that something more permanent than a faction would be necessary to identify candidates for the growing number of citizens who would be participating in elections. Thus, according to many historians, the world's first democratic political parties were established in this country. Also, in 1800, when the Federalists lost the presidential election to the Jeffersonian Republicans (also known as Democratic Republicans), one of the first peaceful transfers of power from one party to another was achieved.

The Era of Personal Politics

From 1816 to 1828, a majority of voters regularly elected Jeffersonian Republicans to the presidency and to Congress. **Two-party competition** did not really exist. This was the so-called **era of personal politics,** when attention centered on the character of individual candidates rather than on party identification. Although during elections they opposed the Federalist call for a stronger, more active central government, the Jeffersonian Republicans acquired the Louisiana Territory and Florida, established a national bank, enforced a higher tariff, and resisted European intrusion in the Western Hemisphere. Domestic tranquility was sufficiently in evi-

FEDERALISTS
The first American political party, led by Alexander Hamilton and John Adams. Many of its members had strongly supported the adoption of the new Constitution and the creation of the federal union.

ANTI-FEDERALISTS
The Anti-Federalists opposed the adoption of the Constitution because of its centralist tendencies and attacked the failure of the Constitution's framers to include a bill of rights.

TWO-PARTY COMPETITION
Two strong and solidly established political parties in competition for political control; both parties have a strong chance of winning an election.

ERA OF PERSONAL POLITICS
An era when attention centers on the character of individual candidates rather than on party identification.

Thomas Jefferson, founder of the Democratic Republicans. His election to the presidency in 1800 was decided in the House of Representatives because the Democratic Republican party did not carry enough electoral votes.

---

[3]Letter to Francis Hopkinson written from Paris while Jefferson was minister to France. In John P. Foley, ed., *The Jeffersonian Cyclopedia* (New York: Russell & Russell, 1967), p. 677.

dence that the administration of James Monroe came to be known as the **era of good feeling.**

National Two-Party Rule: Democrats and Whigs

During the era of personal politics, one-party rule did not prevent Jeffersonian Republican factions from competing against each other. Indeed, there was quite a bit of intraparty rivalry. Finally, in 1824 and 1828, Jeffersonian Republicans who belonged to the factions of Henry Clay and John Quincy Adams split with the rest of the party to oppose Andrew Jackson in those elections. Jackson's supporters and the Clay–Adams bloc formed separate parties as **Democrats** and **Whigs,** respectively. That same Democratic party is now the oldest continuing political party in the Western World.

The Whigs were those Jeffersonian Republicans who were often called the "National Republicans." At the national level, the Whigs were able to elect two presidents—William Henry Harrison in 1840 and Zachary Taylor in 1848. The Whigs, however, were unable to maintain a common ideological base when the party became increasingly divided over the issue of slavery in the late 1840s. During the 1850s, the Whigs fell apart as a national party.

The Post–Civil War Period

The existing two-party system was disrupted by the election of 1860, in which there were four major candidates. Abraham Lincoln, the candidate of the newly formed **Republican party,** was the victor with a majority of the electoral vote, although with only 39.9 percent of the popular vote. This newly formed Republican party—not to be confused with the Jeffersonian Republicans—was created in the mid-1850s from the various groups that sought to fill the vacuum left by the disintegration of the Whigs. It took the label of Grand Old Party, or GOP. Its first national convention was held in 1856, but its presidential candidate, John C. Frémont, lost.

After the end of the Civil War, the South became heavily Democratic (the Solid South), and the North became heavily Republican. This era of Republican dominance was highlighted by the election of 1896 when the Republicans, emphasizing economic development and modernization under William McKinley, resoundingly defeated the Democratic and Populist candidate, William Jennings Bryan. The Republicans' control was solidified by winning over the urban working-class vote in northern cities. From the election of Abraham Lincoln until the election of Roosevelt in 1932, the Republicans won all but four presidential elections.

The Progressive Movement

In 1912, a major schism occurred in the Republican party when former Republican President Theodore Roosevelt ran for the presidency as a Progressive. Consequently, there were three significant contenders in that presidential contest. Woodrow Wilson was the Democratic candidate, William Howard Taft was the regular Republican candidate, and Roosevelt was the Progressive candidate. The Republican split allowed Wilson to be

Andrew Jackson earned the name of "Old Hickory" for his exploits during the War of 1812. In 1828, Jackson was elected president as the candidate of the new Democratic party.

ERA OF GOOD FEELING
The years from 1817 to 1825 when James Monroe was president and there was, in effect, no political opposition.

DEMOCRATS
One of the two major American political parties evolving out of the Democratic Republican (Jeffersonian) group supporting Thomas Jefferson.

WHIGS
One of the foremost political organizations in the United States during the first half of the nineteenth century, formally established in 1836. The Whig party was dominated by the same anti-Jackson elements that organized the National Republican faction within the Jeffersonian Republicans and represented a variety of regional interests. It fell apart as a national party in the early 1850s.

REPUBLICAN PARTY
One of the two major American political parties, which emerged in the 1850s as an antislavery party. It was created to fill the vacuum caused by the disintegration of the Whig party. The Republican party traces its name—but not its ideology—to Jefferson's Democratic Republican party.

This is an example of a handbill that was used in the election campaign of 1860. Handbills served the same purpose as today's direct-mail advertisements, appealing directly to the voters with the candidate's message.

William McKinley, campaigning in 1896 on a platform draped with the flag. The decorations are not different from those that candidates used almost a century later.

elected. The Wilson administration, although Democratic, ended up enacting much of the Progressive party's platform. Left without any reason for opposition, the Progressive party collapsed in 1921.

Republican Warren Harding's victory in 1920 reasserted Republican domination of national politics until the Republicans' defeat by Franklin Roosevelt in 1932 in the depths of the Great Depression.

The Modern Era: From the New Deal to the Present

Franklin Delano Roosevelt was elected in 1932 and reelected in 1936 and 1940 and again in 1944. The impact of his successive Democratic administrations and the New Deal that he crafted is still with us today. Roosevelt used his enormous personal appeal to unify Democrats under his leadership, and he established direct communication between the president and the public through his radio "fireside chats." It wasn't until 1940 that the Republicans made even a small dent in the Democratic hegemony, when Wendell Wilkie reduced Roosevelt's popular vote to 54.8 percent from the 60.5 percent and the 57.4 percent of the two previous elections.

In April 1945, Roosevelt died; Vice President Harry Truman became president through succession and in 1948 through election. The New Deal coalition, under Truman's revised theme of the Fair Deal, continued. It was not until Republican Dwight Eisenhower won the 1952 election that the Democrats lost their control of the presidency. Eisenhower was reelected in 1956.

From 1960 through 1968, the Democrats, led first by John F. Kennedy and then by Lyndon B. Johnson, held national power. Republicans again

came to power with Richard Nixon's victory in 1968 and retained it in 1972, but they lost prestige after the Watergate scandal forced Nixon's resignation on August 8, 1974. Although Republican Vice President Gerald Ford (the first person ever *appointed* to the vice presidency to become president) took over for the remainder of Nixon's second term, the Republicans were severely damaged by Nixon's resignation. For this and other reasons, the Democrats were back in power in 1976. But Democratic President Jimmy Carter was unable to win reelection against Ronald Reagan in 1980. The Republicans also gained control of the Senate in 1980 and retained it in the elections of 1982 and 1984. The 1984 reelection of Ronald Reagan appeared to some pollsters to signal the resurgence of the Republican party as a competitive force in American politics as more people declared themselves to be Republicans than in the last several decades.

In 1988, George Bush won the White House for the Republicans without converting many votes to the party. He had very short coattails: Democrats gained seats in the House of Representatives and one seat in the Senate. The same phenomenon occurred in 1992. Bill Clinton won the presidency, but the Democrats lost ten seats in the House.

The Three Faces of a Party

Although American parties are known by a single name and, in the public mind, have a common historical identity, each party is really composed of three major subunits. The first subunit is the **party-in-electorate.** This phrase refers to all those individuals who claim a linkage to the political party. They need not be members in the sense that they pay dues or even participate in election campaigns. Rather, the party-in-electorate is the large number of Americans who feel some loyalty to the party or who use partisanship as a cue to decide who will earn their vote. This is a rather fluid and unstable group, one that can become disenchanted with the candidates and policies offered by the Democrats or Republicans and that can freely switch parties or be drawn to independent or third-party candidates. Needless to say, the party leaders pay rather close attention to the affiliation of their members in the electorate.

The second subunit, the **party organization,** provides the structural framework for the political party by recruiting volunteers to become party leaders, identifying potential candidates, and organizing caucuses, conventions, and election campaigns for its candidates. It is the party organization and its active workers that keep the party functioning between elections, as well as making sure that the party puts forth electable candidates and clear positions in the elections. When individuals accept paid employment for a political party, they are considered party professionals. Among that group are found campaign consultants; fund raisers; local, state, and national executives; and national staff members. If the party-in-electorate declines in numbers and loyalty, the party organization must try to find a strategy to rebuild the grass-roots following.

The **party-in-government** is the third subunit of American political parties. The party-in-government consists of those elected and appointed officials who are identified with a political party. Generally, elected officials

Did You Know . . . That in 1824 the voters were offered the choice between "John Quincy Adams who can write and Andy Jackson who can fight"?

PARTY-IN-ELECTORATE
Those members of the general public who identify with a political party or who express a preference for one party over the other.

PARTY ORGANIZATION
The formal structure and leadership of a political party, including elective committees, local, state, and national executives, and paid professional staff.

PARTY-IN-GOVERNMENT
All of the elected and appointed officials who identify with a political party.

cannot also hold official party positions within the formal organization. Executives such as the president, governors, and mayors often have the informal power to appoint party executives, but their duties in office preclude them from active involvement in the party organization most of the time. Ties to a political party are essential to the functioning of government and the operation of the political process in the United States. Republican representatives, senators, and governors expect to receive a hearing at a Republican-controlled White House if they request it. In return, Republican presidents call on party loyalty when they ask the legislators to support their programs. Finally, the electorate is asked to judge the party-in-government by its policies and candidates at the polls. American political parties, while not nearly as ideological as many European parties, do claim to present alternative positions to the voters. If the party organization and party-in-government are in conflict, the party-in-electorate is likely to look for other party leadership to articulate its preferences.

Party Organization

There are two ways to describe the Democratic and Republican parties: in theory and in reality. In theory, each of the American political parties has a standard, pyramid-shaped organization (see Figure 8-2). The politicians operating within this structure do not find it so simple, however. The pyramid does not accurately reflect the relative power and strengths of the individual parts of the party organization. If it did, the national chairperson of the Democratic or Republican party, along with the national committee, could simply dictate how the organization was to be run, just as if it were Exxon Corporation or Ford Motor Company.

FIGURE 8-2 ■ A Theoretical Structure of the American Political Party

The relationship between state and local parties varies from state to state. Further, some state parties resist national party policies.

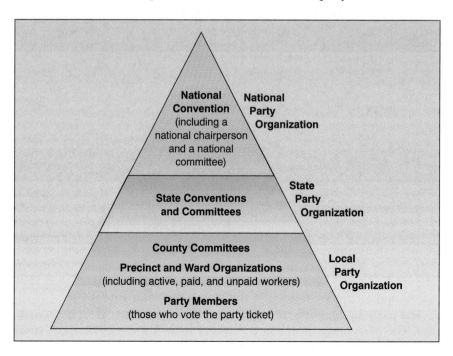

At the conclusion of her speech to the 1992 Republican convention, First Lady Barbara Bush is joined by her husband, her children, and her grandchildren. The large Bush family provided an example of the kinds of family values that the convention endorsed.

In reality, the formal structure of political parties resembles a layer cake with autonomous strata more than it does a pyramid. Malcolm E. Jewell and David M. Olson point out that

> there is no command structure within political parties. Rather, each geographic unit of the party tends to be autonomous from the other units at its same geographic level.[4]

The National Party Organization

Each party has a national organization whose clearly institutional part is the **national convention,** held every four years. The convention is used to nominate the presidential and vice presidential candidates. In addition, the **party platform** is written, ratified, and revised at the national convention. The platform sets forth the party's position on the issues and makes promises to initiate certain policies if the party wins the presidency. Often, platforms represent compromises among the various factions of a party, in an attempt to make peace before the campaign begins.

After the convention, the platform is frequently neglected or ignored by party candidates who disagree with it. Because candidates are trying to win votes from a wide spectrum of voters, it is counterproductive to emphasize the fairly narrow and sometimes controversial goals set forth in the platform. The work of Gerald Pomper[5] has shown, however, that once elected, the parties do try to carry out platform promises and that roughly three-fourths of the promises eventually become law. Of course, some general goals, such as economic prosperity, are included in both parties' platforms.

NATIONAL CONVENTION
The meeting held every four years by each major party to select presidential and vice presidential candidates, to write a platform, to choose a national committee, and to conduct party business. In theory, the national convention is at the top of a hierarchy of party conventions (the local and state conventions are below it) that considers candidates and issues.

PARTY PLATFORM
A document drawn up by the platform committee at each national convention, outlining the policies, positions, and principles of the party; it is then submitted to the entire convention for approval.

---

[4]*American State Political Parties and Elections,* rev. ed. (Homewood, Ill.: Dorsey Press, 1982), p. 73.
[5]Gerald M. Pomper with Susan S. Lederman, *Elections in America: Control and Influence in Democratic Politics,* 2d ed. (New York: Longman, 1980).

NATIONAL COMMITTEE
A standing committee of a national political party established to direct and coordinate party activities during the four-year period between national party conventions.

Choosing the National Committee.   At the national convention, each of the parties formally chooses a national standing committee, elected by the individual state parties. This **national committee** is established to direct and coordinate party activities during the following four years. The Democrats include at least two members, a man and a woman, from each state, from the District of Columbia, and from the several territories. Governors, members of Congress, mayors, and other officials may be included as at-large members of the national committee. The Republicans, in addition, add state chairpersons from every state carried by the Republican party in the preceding presidential, gubernatorial, or congressional elections. The selections of national committee members are ratified by the delegations to the national convention.

One of the jobs of the national committee is to ratify the presidential nominee's choice of a national chairperson, who in principle acts as the spokesperson for the party. Even though we have placed the national committee at the top of the hierarchy of party organization (see Figure 8-2), it has very little direct influence. Basically, the national chairperson and the national committee simply plan the next campaign and the next convention, obtain financial contributions, and publicize the national party.

Picking a National Chairperson.   In general, the party's presidential candidate chooses the national chairperson (see this chapter's *Profile*).[6] The major responsibility of that person is the management of the national elec-

Governor Bill Clinton gives his acceptance speech at the 1992 Democratic Convention. In this speech, the presidential candidate appealed to the voters to support a "new covenant" between the government and the people.

[6]If that candidate loses, however, the chairperson is often changed.

PROFILE

Ronald Brown

"We've got to reach out to the American people and give them a reason to vote for Democratic presidential candidates."

It seemed to be a contradiction—a chairman of the Democratic National Committee (DNC) who belonged to a prestigious Washington law firm and spared no effort to portray himself as a member of society's elite. Yet this was not the only surprise sprung by the national organization of "the party of the common people" in 1989: The aristocratic DNC chairman is, among other things, an African American.

Ronald Brown, whose father managed a hotel, grew up in the Harlem section of New York City. His family placed a high value on education, sending him to elite private schools in which he was often the only African American.

Brown, after serving as an army officer in Europe, received a law degree from St. John's University in New York. He was quickly drawn into politics, becoming the National Urban League's chief lobbyist in 1967. In 1980, he became the director of Senator Ted Kennedy's Senate staff. After a short time in this position, he returned to the private practice of law. Politics seemed to pursue him, however, and in the spring of 1988, Jesse Jackson asked Ron Brown to be his manager at the Democratic national convention in Atlanta. His election by party professionals to the national leadership was both a recognition of his political skill and a bold political gambit by the Democrats.

Ron Brown's assumption of the national leadership of the Democrats came at a time of crisis in the party's history. It had lost the last three presidential elections, and five of the last six; areas once solidly Democratic, such as the South, were experiencing steady inroads by the Republicans; middle-class, traditionally Democratic voters were leaving the party because they saw it as favoring higher taxes and unfair advantages for racial minorities. Indeed, some analysts foresaw the end of the Democratic party as a viable national force. The election of Ron Brown as chief national strategist, organizer, and fund raiser was a bold response to these problems. Because he is an African American, Democratic liberals and moderates hoped he would maintain the his-

toric loyalty of the poor and racial minorities to the party. His organizational skills, talent for compromise, and establishment demeanor would, it was hoped, heal the rift between liberals and conservatives within the party and bring middle-class voters back into the Democratic fold. The thinking that generated support for Brown as chairman was risky, however: Many southern Democrats opposed Brown because of his race, and some Democratic officials in that region actually changed their party affiliation to Republican after he assumed the chairmanship.

The strategy that elevated Brown to the leadership of the party was successful: By persuading various Democratic candidates for state and local offices to work together, the party won important elections in Indiana, Virginia, and New York City in the spring of 1989. The national committee's willingness to invest time and money in these elections—a move that resulted from Brown's efforts—also helped bring victory for the party. During the 1992 campaign, Brown worked with Bill Clinton to bring traditionally Democratic voters back to their party.

On December 12, 1992 Bill Clinton named Ron Brown as Secretary of Commerce. The Democratic National Committee named David Wilhelm as the new national chairperson.

STATE CENTRAL COMMITTEE
The principal organized structure of each political party within each state. Responsible for carrying out policy decisions of the party's state convention.

UNIT RULE
All of a state's electoral votes are cast for the presidential candidate receiving a plurality of the popular vote.

PATRONAGE
Rewarding faithful party workers and followers with government employment and contracts.

tion campaign. In some cases, a strong national chairperson has considerable power over state and local party organizations. There is no formal mechanism with which to exercise direct control over subnational party structures, however. The national chairperson does such jobs as establish a national party headquarters, raise and distribute campaign funds, and appear in the media as a party spokesperson.

The national chairperson, along with the national committee, attempts basically to maintain some sort of liaison among the different levels of the party organization. The fact is that the real strength and power of a national party is at the state level.

The State Organization

There are fifty states in the Union, plus the territories and the District of Columbia, and an equal number of party organizations for each major party. Therefore, there are more than a hundred state parties (and even more if we include local parties and minor parties). Because every state party is unique, it is impossible to describe what an "average" state political party is like. Nonetheless, state parties have several organizational features in common.

This commonality can be described in one sentence: Each state party has a chairperson, a committee, and a number of local organizations. In principle, the **state central committees**—the principal organized structure of each political party within each state—have similar roles in the various states. The committee, usually composed of those members who represent congressional districts, state legislative districts, or counties, has responsibility for carrying out the policy decisions of the party's state convention, and in some states the state central committee will direct the state chairperson with respect to policy making.

Also, like the national committee, the state central committee has control over the use of party campaign funds during political campaigns. Usually, the state central committee has little if any influence on party candidates once they are elected. In fact, state parties are fundamentally loose alliances of local interests and coalitions of often bitterly opposed factions.

State parties are also important in national politics because of the **unit rule,** which awards electoral votes in presidential elections as an indivisible bloc (except in Maine and Nebraska). Presidential candidates concentrate their efforts in states in which voter preferences seem to be evenly divided or in which large numbers of electoral votes are at stake.

Local Party Machinery: The Grass Roots

The lowest layer of party machinery is the local organization, supported by district leaders, precinct or ward captains, and party workers. Much of the work is coordinated by county committees and their chairpersons. In the past, the institution of **patronage**—rewarding the party faithful with government jobs or contracts—held the local organization together. For immigrants and the poor, the political machine often furnished important services and protections. The big-city party machine was the archetypical example, and Tammany Hall, or the Tammany Society, which dominated New York government for nearly two centuries, was perhaps the highest refinement of this political form. (See the *Politics and Ethics* in this chapter.)

POLITICS AND ETHICS

Tammany Hall: The Quintessential Local Political Machine

The Tammany Society dominated New York City politics for more than a century. Founded in 1786 with the express purpose of engaging in cultural, social, and patriotic activities, the society evolved into a major political force and became known as Tammany Hall. In the beginning, it organized and provided social services for the foreign born who made up the bulk of the Democratic party in New York City. One of its more notorious leaders was William Tweed, head of the so-called Tweed ring, whose scandals were unearthed by the *New York Times* in 1871. Readers were entertained and horrified by stories of millions of dollars in kickbacks received from giving out government contracts, of how civil and criminal violations were being overlooked, and of phony leases and padded bills that were paid to members of the Tweed ring. As a result of the exposé, Tweed was imprisoned; but the other members of the ring managed to flee the country (as very wealthy men and women). Richard Crocker took over the leadership of Tammany Hall in 1886 and kept it until 1901.

Tammany Hall's influence declined when its slate of candidates was defeated in a reform movement in 1901. It was not until Franklin

TWEEDLEDEE AND SWEEDLEDUM.
(A New Christmas Pantomime at the Tammany Hall.)
Clown (to Pantaloon). "Let's Blind them with *this*, and then take *some more.*"

TWEED'S GIFT OF FIFTY THOUSAND DOLLARS TO THE POOR OF HIS NATIVE WARD.—"HARPER'S WEEKLY," JANUARY 14, 1871.

Roosevelt's victory in 1932 that Tammany lost its political clout almost completely—but only for a couple of decades. In the 1950s there was a short-lived resurgence in the influence of the Tammany Society. It has enjoyed no political influence in New York City politics since then.

The last big-city local political machine to exercise a great deal of power was run by Chicago's Mayor Richard J. Daley, who was also an important figure in national Democratic politics. Daley, as mayor, ran the Chicago Democratic machine from 1955 until his death in 1976. The Daley organization, largely Irish in candidate origin and voter support, was split by the successful candidacy of African-American Democrat Harold Washington in the racially divisive 1983 mayoral election. He was reelected in 1987 but died within a year. A Washington supporter, Eugene Sawyer, became

Richard M. Daley, mayor of Chicago. Son of the former mayor, Daley won office in a racially divisive election.

mayor after another bitter intraparty fight. In 1989, the son of Mayor Daley, Richard M. Daley, defeated Sawyer in the primary and became mayor. Although most African-American voters supported the African-American candidate, Daley garnered support from white, Hispanic, and Asian-American voters.

City machines are now dead, mostly because their function of providing social services (and reaping the reward of votes) has been taken over by state and national agencies. This trend began in the 1930s when the social legislation of the New Deal established Social Security and unemployment insurance. The local party machine has little, if anything, to do with deciding who is eligible to receive these benefits.

Local political organizations, whether located in cities, townships, or at the county level, still can contribute a great deal to local election campaigns. These organizations are able to provide the foot soldiers of politics, individuals who pass out literature and get out the vote on election day, which can be crucial in local elections. In many regions, local Democratic and Republican organizations still exercise some patronage, such as awarding courthouse jobs, contracts for street repair, and other lucrative construction contracts. Local party organizations are also the most important vehicles for recruiting young adults into political work, because politics at the local level offers activists many opportunities to gain experience.

The Party and Its Members

The two major American political parties are often characterized as being too much like Tweedledee and Tweedledum, the twins in Lewis Carroll's *Through the Looking Glass.* When both parties nominate moderates for the presidency, the similarities between the parties seem to outweigh their differences. Yet the political parties do generate strong conflict for political offices throughout the United States, and there are significant differences between the parties, both in the characteristics of their members and in their platforms.

Although Democrats and Republicans are not divided along religious or class lines to the extent of some European parties, certain social groups are more likely to identify with each. Since the New Deal of Franklin Roosevelt, The Democratic party has appealed to the more disadvantaged groups in society. African-American voters are far more likely to identify with the Democrats, as are members of union households, Jewish voters, and individuals who have less than a high school education. Republicans draw more of their support from college graduates, upper-income families, and professionals or businesspersons. In recent years, more women than men have tended to identify themselves as Democrats than as Republicans.

The coalition of minorities, the working class, and various ethnic groups has been the core of Democratic party support since the presidency of Franklin Roosevelt. The social programs and increased government intervention in the economy that were the heart of Roosevelt's New Deal were intended to ease the strain of economic hard times on these groups. This goal remains important for many Democrats today. In general, Democratic

TABLE 8-1 ■ Which Party Is Better?

Better for	Republican	Democrat	Same/Don't Know
QUESTION: In the view of the public, which party serves the interests of groups in society better?			
Business and professional people	65%	19%	16%
White-collar workers	56	25	19
Skilled workers	58	40	22
Small business people	36	45	19
Farmers	27	49	24
Retired people	28	51	21
Unemployed people	20	59	21
Women	26	45	29
Labor union members	22	55	23
African Americans	17	59	24

SOURCE: *The Gallup Report,* 1991.

identifiers are more likely to approve of social welfare spending, to support government regulation of business, to approve of measures to improve the situation of minorities, and to assist the elderly with their medical expenses. Republicans are more supportive of the private marketplace, and many feel that the federal government should be involved in fewer social programs. Table 8-1 shows that the general public shares these views on which groups are served by each party. It would seem that a larger proportion of the population falls into those groups that most people think are better served by the Democratic party than by the Republican party, yet the Republican party has captured the presidency in five of the last seven elections. Turning from the interests of specific groups to the interest of the nation as a whole, Table 8-2 shows the percentages of the people who think that the Republican or Democratic party

TABLE 8-2 ■ Public Perceptions of the Parties on Peace and Prosperity

Which Party Is Better for Keeping Peace?			Which Party Is Better for Prosperity?		
Year	Republican	Democratic	Year	Republican	Democratic
1980	25%	42%	1980	35%	36%
1982	29	38	1982	34	43
1984	38	38	1984	49	33
1986	34	29	1986	41	30
1988	43	33	1988	52	34
1991	42	33	1991	49	32

SOURCE: *The Gallup Report,* 1991.

Did You Know ... That the political party with the most seats in the House of Representatives chooses the speaker of the House, makes any new rules it wants, gets a majority of the seats on each important committee and chooses their chairs, and hires most of the congressional staff?

is better for preserving peace and promoting prosperity. Since 1984, a greater proportion of the public has felt that the Republican party was better able than the Democratic party to keep peace and to keep the country prosperous. If it is true, as some researchers suggest, that voters are more likely to consider the good of the whole nation rather than their individual interests in choosing a presidential candidate, the success of the Republican party at the presidential level is due to public perceptions of its effectiveness on the issues of peace and the economy.

The differences separating party identifiers are greatly magnified among the leadership of the Democrats and Republicans. Generally, a much greater percentage of Democratic leaders consider themselves to be liberals than do their followers, and Republican elites are far more likely to identify their philosophy as conservative than are their followers. Polls of the national convention delegates, such as that reported in Table 8-3, demonstrate the wide gap in policy preferences between elites and general party identifiers. Such differences are reflected in the party platforms that are adopted at each party's convention. Democratic platforms recently have stressed equality of opportunity, the government's responsibility to

TABLE 8-3 ■ Comparing Convention Delegates to Party Identifiers

During the 1988 national party conventions, the *New York Times* surveyed the delegates to both conventions. The table shows the contrast between the political philosophy and policy preferences of Democratic delegates and Democratic identifiers in the general public and the same comparison for Republicans. The percentage of those surveyed agreeing with the policy is given below.

Position	Dem. Delegate	Dem. Voter	Rep. Voter	Rep. Delegate
Consider self conservative	5%	22%	43%	60%
Consider self liberal	39	25	12	1
Favor federal spending on day care	87	56	44	36
Keep abortion legal	72	43	39	29
Increase federal spending on education	90	76	67	41
Continue today's military spending	32	59	73	84
Worry more about communists in Central America than U.S. role	12	25	55	80

SOURCE: *New York Times*, August 14, 1988, p. 32.

help citizens, and ending tax loopholes for business. Recent Republican platforms seek to ban abortions, oppose quotas to remedy discrimination, and support prayer in schools. It is worth noting, however, that the strong differences between the attitudes of party elites and platforms tend to disappear during the election campaign as candidates try to win votes from partisans of all ideological persuasions and from independent voters as well.

Did You Know . . . That the Democrats and Republicans each had exactly one woman delegate at their conventions in 1900?

The Party-in-Government

After the election is over and the winners are announced, the focus of party activity shifts from getting out the vote to organizing and controlling the government. As you will see later in the text, party membership plays an important role in the day-to-day operations of Congress, with partisanship determining everything from office space to committee assignments and power on Capitol Hill. For the president, the political party furnishes the pool of qualified applicants for political appointments to run the government. Although it is uncommon to do so, presidents can and do occasionally appoint executive personnel, such as cabinet secretaries, from the opposition party. There are not as many of these positions as presidents might like, and presidential power is limited by the permanent bureaucracy. Judicial appointments, however, offer a great opportunity to the winning party. For the most part, presidents are likely to appoint federal judges from their own party.

All of these party appointments suggest that the winning political party, whether at the national, state, or local level, has a great deal of control in the American system. Because of the checks and balances and the relative lack of cohesion in American parties, such control is an illusion. In fact, many Americans, at least implicitly, prefer a "divided government," with the executive and legislative branches controlled by different parties. Figure 8-3 demonstrates that the trend of splitting votes between president

Speaker of the House Tom Foley discusses the 1992 Democratic party convention for a television show. Conventions can boost party loyalty through television coverage.

FIGURE 8-3 ■ Congressional Districts with Split Voting Results between the President and House Members (in Percentages)

SOURCE: Martin Wattenberg, *The Decline of American Political Parties, 1952–1988* (Cambridge, Mass.: Harvard University Press, 1989), p. 19.

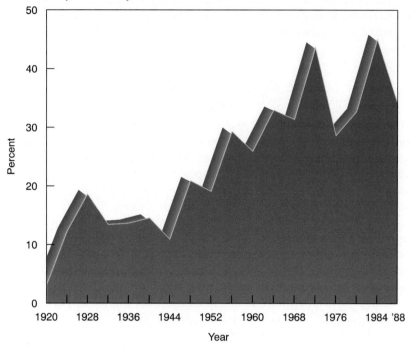

and House members has increased sharply since 1944. Voters seem comfortable with a president affiliated with one party and a Congress controlled by the other. This practice may indicate a lack of trust in government or the relative weakness of party identification among many voters.

Why Do We Have a Two-party System?

It would be difficult to imagine a political system in the United States in which there were four, five, six, or seven major political parties. The United States has a **two-party system,** and that system has been around from about 1800 to the present. But considering the range of political ideology among voters and the variety of local and state party machines, the fact that we still have just two major political parties is somewhat unusual.

Strong competition between the parties at the national level has in general not filtered down to the state level. From 1900 to 1980, the Republicans won eleven presidential elections and the Democrats ten. In state and local elections, however, one-party dominance is the rule in many regions of the United States. The Solid South was almost totally Democratic at all levels of government from 1880 to 1944. The northeastern states and much of the Midwest were solidly Republican from approximately 1860 to 1930. Almost 60 percent of the states are dominated by either the Republican or Democratic party.

TWO-PARTY SYSTEM
A political system in which only two parties have a reasonable chance of winning.

There are several reasons why two major parties have dominated the political landscape in the United States for almost two centuries. These have to do with (1) the historical foundations of the system, (2) the self-perpetuation of the parties, (3) the commonality of views among Americans, (4) the winner-take-all electoral system, and (5) state and federal laws favoring the two-party system.

Did You Know ... That it took 103 ballots for John W. Davis to be nominated at the Democratic national convention in 1924?

The Historical Foundations of the Two-party System

As we have seen, the first two opposing groups in United States politics were the Federalists and the Anti-Federalists. The Federalists, who remained in power and solidified their identity as a political party, represented those with commercial interests, including merchants, shipowners, and manufacturers. The Federalists supported the principle of a strong national government. The Anti-Federalists, who gradually became known as the Democratic Republicans, represented artisans and farmers. They strongly supported states' rights. These interests were also fairly well split along geographic lines, with the Federalists dominant in the North and the Democratic Republicans dominant in the South.

Two relatively distinct sets of interests continued to characterize the two different parties. During Andrew Jackson's time in power, eastern commercial interests were pitted against western and southern agricultural and frontier interests. Before the Civil War, the major split again became North versus South. The split was ideological—over the issue of slavery—as well as economic—the Northeast's industrial interests versus the agricultural interests of the South. After the Civil War and until the 1920s, the Republicans found most of their strength in the Northeast, the Democrats in the Solid South. The West and the Midwest held the balance of power at that time. The period from the Civil War to the 1920s has been called one of **sectional politics.**

Sectional politics gave way to **national politics** as the cities became more dominant and as industry flowed to the South and to the West. Some political scientists classify the period from 1920 to today as one of **class politics,** the Republicans generally finding support among groups of higher economic status and the Democrats appealing more to working-class constituencies. The modern parties also have reversed their traditional views on the issue of states' rights versus a strong central government. Now, it is the Democrats who advocate a stronger role for the national government, whereas the Republicans want the central government to play a lesser role in the political and economic life of the nation.

SECTIONAL POLITICS
The pursuit of interests that are of special concern to a region or section of the country.

NATIONAL POLITICS
The pursuit of interests that are of concern to the nation as a whole.

CLASS POLITICS
Political preferences based on income level and/or social status.

Self-Perpetuation of the Two-party System

As we saw in Chapter 6, most children identify with the political party of their parents. Children learn at quite a young age to think of themselves as either Democrats or Republicans. Relatively few are taught to think of themselves as Libertarians or Socialists or even independents. This generates a built-in mechanism to perpetuate a two-party system. According to most studies of the process of political socialization, psychological attachment to party identity intensifies during adulthood.[7]

---

[7]See, for example, Lester W. Milbrath, *Political Participation: How and Why Do People Get Involved in Politics?* (Chicago, Ill.: Rand McNally, 1965), pp. 134–135.

Republicans look to the future, using campaign buttons to identify their favorites for 1996.

Also, many politically oriented people who aspire to work for social change consider that the only realistic way to capture political power in this country is to be either a Republican or Democrat. Of course, the same argument holds for those who involve themselves in politics largely for personal gain. Thus, political parties offer avenues for the expression of the personal ambitions of politicians and supply government with men and women anxious to serve the public by satisfying their own goals.[8]

The Political Culture of the United States

Another determining factor in the perpetuation of our two-party system is the commonality of goals among Americans. Most Americans want continuing material prosperity. They also believe this goal should be achieved through individual rather than collective initiative. There has never been much support for establishing the government as the owner of the major means of production. Left-wing political movements wish to limit the ownership of private property. Most Americans take a dim view of such an attitude—private property is considered a basic American value, and the ability to acquire and use it the way one wishes is commonly regarded as a basic American right.

Another reason we have had a basic consensus about our political system and the two major parties is that we have largely managed to separate religion from politics. Religion was an issue in 1928, when Governor Alfred Smith of New York became the first Roman Catholic to be nominated for the presidency (he was defeated by Republican Herbert Hoover) and again in 1960 when John F. Kennedy was running for president. But religion has never been a dividing force triggering splinter parties. There has never been a major Catholic party or a Protestant party or a Jewish party or a Moslem party.

The major division in American politics has been economic. As we mentioned earlier, the Democrats have been known—at least since the 1930s—as the party of the working class, in favor of government intervention in the economy and more government redistribution of income from the wealthy to those with lower incomes. The Republican party has been known in modern times as the party of the middle and upper classes and commercial interests, in favor of fewer constraints on the market system and less redistribution of income.

Not only does the political culture support the two-party system, but also the parties themselves are adept at making the necessary shifts in their platforms or electoral appeal to gain new members. Because the general ideological structure of the parties is so broad, it has been relatively easy for them to change their respective platforms or to borrow popular policies from minor parties to attract voter support. Both parties perceive themselves as broad enough to accommodate every group in society; the Republicans try to woo support from the African-American community, and the Democrats strive to make inroads among professional and business groups.

---

[8]This is the view of, among others, Joseph Schlesinger. See his *Ambition and Politics: Political Careers in the United States* (Chicago, Ill.: Rand McNally, 1966).

The Winner-Take-All Electoral System

At virtually every level of government in the United States, the outcome of elections is based on the plurality, winner-take-all principle. A plurality system is one in which the winner is the person who obtains the most votes, even if a majority is not obtained. Whoever gets the most votes gets everything. Because most legislators in the United States are elected from single-member districts in which only one person represents the constituency, the candidate who finishes second in such an election receives nothing for the effort.

The winner-take-all system also operates in the **electoral college** (see Chapter 9). Each state's electors are pledged to presidential candidates chosen by their respective national party conventions. During the popular vote in November, in each of the fifty states and in the District of Columbia, the voters choose one slate of electors from those on the state ballot. If the slate of electors wins a plurality in a state, then usually *all* the electors so chosen cast their ballots for the presidential and vice presidential candidates of the winning party. That means that if a particular candidate's slate of electors receives a plurality of 40 percent of the votes in a state, that candidate will receive all the state's electoral votes. Minor parties have a difficult time competing under such a system, even though they may influence the final outcome of the election. Because voters know that minor parties cannot succeed, they often will not vote for minor party candidates, even if they are ideologically in tune with them.

Not all countries, or all states in the United States, use the plurality, winner-take-all electoral system. Some hold run-off elections until a candidate obtains at least one vote over 50 percent of the votes. Such a system also may be used in countries with multiple parties. Small parties hope to be able to obtain a sufficient number of votes to at least get into a run-off election. Then the small-party candidate can form an alliance with one or more of those parties that did not make the run-off. Such alliances also occur in the United States, but with the winner-take-all system these coalitions must normally be made before the first election because usually there is no run-off.

ELECTORAL COLLEGE
A group of persons called electors who are selected by the voters in each state; this group officially elects the president and the vice president of the United States. The number of electors in each state is equal to the number of each state's representatives in both houses of Congress.

State and Federal Laws Favoring the Two Parties

Many state and federal election laws offer a clear advantage to the two major parties. In some states, the established major parties need gather only a few signatures to place their candidates on the ballot, whereas a minor party or an independent candidate must get many more signatures. The criterion for making such a distinction is often based on the total party vote in the last general election, penalizing the new political party that did not compete in the election.

At the national level, minor parties face different obstacles. All of the rules and procedures of both houses of Congress divide committee seats, staff members, and other privileges on the basis of party membership. A legislator who is elected on a minor party ticket, such as the Liberal party of New York, must choose to be counted with one of the major parties to get a committee assignment. The Federal Election Commission (FEC) rules for campaign financing also place restrictions on minor party candidates.

Such candidates are not eligible for federal matching funds in either the primary or general election. In the 1980 election, John Anderson, running as an independent, sued the FEC for campaign funds, and the commission finally agreed to repay part of his campaign costs after the election in proportion to the votes he received.

The Role of Minor Parties in U.S. Political History

Minor parties have a difficult, if not impossible, time competing within the two-party-dominated American system. Nonetheless, minor parties have had an important place in our political life. Frequently, dissatisfied groups have split from major parties and formed so-called **third parties**,[9] which have acted as barometers of changes in political mood. Such barometric indicators have forced the major parties to recognize new issues or trends in the thinking of Americans. Political scientists also believe that third parties have acted as a safety valve for dissident political groups, perhaps preventing major confrontations and political unrest.

Historically Important Minor Parties

Most minor parties that have endured have had a strong ideological foundation that is typically at odds with the majority mind-set. Ideology has at least two functions. First, the members of the minor party regard themselves as outsiders and look to one another for support; ideology provides tremendous psychological cohesiveness. Second, because the rewards of ideological commitment are partly psychological, these minor parties do not think in terms of immediate electoral success, and a poor showing at the polls does not dissuade either the leadership or the grass-roots participants from continuing their quest for change in American society. Some of the notable third parties that are still active include the following:

1. The Socialist Labor party, started in 1877.
2. The Socialist party, founded in 1901.
3. The Communist party, started in 1919 as the radical left wing that split from the Socialist party.
4. The Socialist Workers' party, formerly a Trotskyite group, started in 1938.
5. The Libertarian party, formed in 1972 and still an important minor party.

As we can see from their labels, several of these minor parties have been Marxist oriented. The most successful was Eugene Debs's Socialist party, which captured 6 percent of the popular vote for president in 1912 and elected more than a thousand candidates at the local level. About eighty mayors were affiliated with the Socialist party at one time or another. It owed much of its success to the corruption of big-city machines and to antiwar sentiment. Debs's Socialist party was vociferously opposed to American entry into World War I, an opposition shared by many Americans. The other more militant parties of the left (the Socialist Labor,

THIRD PARTY
A political party other than the two major political parties (Republican and Democratic). Usually, third parties are composed of dissatisfied groups that have split from the major parties. They act as indicators of political trends and as safety valves for dissident groups.

Eugene V. Debs, founder of the Socialist party and candidate for president on that ticket five times. Despite its longevity, the party has had little impact on the American political system.

---

[9]This term is erroneous because sometimes there have been third, fourth, fifth, and even sixth parties, but because it has endured, we will use it here.

Socialist Workers', and Communist parties) have never enjoyed wide electoral success.

At the other end of the ideological spectrum, the Libertarian party supports a laissez-faire capitalist economic program combined with a hands-off policy on regulating matters of moral conduct.

In 1986, another minor party created a sensation by capturing the Democratic nominations for lieutenant governor and secretary of state in Illinois. Supporters of Lyndon LaRouche, an ultraconservative, self-sponsored candidate for president, had submitted petitions for the offices as Democrats and were elected over the candidates of the regular Democratic party in the primary. The LaRouche candidates had spent only a few hundred dollars on their campaigns, running on the platform that AIDS victims should be quarantined and drug dealers subjected to capital punishment. With almost no publicity and unidentified by the news media or the Democratic party, the LaRouche candidates capitalized on their ballot positions and the lack of voter information. Other LaRouche followers undertook a similar strategy. After a few LaRouche victories, the Democratic and Republican parties worked aggressively to identify the LaRouche supporters for the voters, and all were defeated.

Spin-off Minor Parties

The most successful minor parties have been those that split from major parties. The impetus for these **spin-off parties,** or factions, has usually been a situation in which a particular personality was at odds with the major party. The most famous spin-off was the Bull Moose Progressive party, which split from the Republican party in 1912 over the candidate chosen to run for president. Theodore Roosevelt rallied his forces and announced the formation of the Progressive party, leaving the regular Republicans to support William Howard Taft. Although the party was not successful in winning the election for Roosevelt, it did succeed in splitting the Republican vote so that Democrat Woodrow Wilson won.

Among the Democrats, there have been three splinter third parties since the late 1940s: (1) the Dixiecrat (States Rights) party of 1948, (2) Henry Wallace's Progressive party of 1948, and (3) the American Independent party supporting George Wallace in 1968.

The strategy employed by Wallace in the 1968 election was to deny Nixon or Humphrey the necessary majority in the electoral college. Many political scientists (but not all) believe that Humphrey still would have lost to Nixon in 1968, even if Wallace had not run, because most Wallace voters would probably have given their votes to Nixon. The American Independent party mostly emphasized racial issues and to a lesser extent foreign policy. Wallace received 9.9 million popular votes and 46 electoral votes.

Other Minor Parties

There have been numerous minor parties that have coalesced around specific issues or aims. The goal of the Prohibition party, started in 1869, was to ban the sale of liquor. The Free Soil party, active from 1848 to 1852, was dedicated to preventing the spread of slavery.

Did You Know . . . That Millard Fillmore, former Whig president, ran for president in 1856 as the candidate of the Know-Nothing (or American) party?

SPIN-OFF PARTY

A new party formed by a dissident faction within a major political party. Usually, spin-off parties have emerged when a particular personality was at odds with the major party.

Theodore Roosevelt, president of the United States from 1901–1909. He became president after McKinley was assassinated and was reelected in 1904. In 1912, unable to gain the nomination of the Republican party, Roosevelt formed a splinter group named the Bull Moose party but was unsuccessful in his efforts to win the presidency.

Some minor parties have had specific economic interests as their reason for being. When those interests are either met or made irrelevant by changing economic conditions, these minor parties disappear. Such was the case with the Greenback party, which lasted from 1876 to 1884. It was one of the most prominent farmer-labor parties that favored government intervention in the economy. Similar to the Greenbacks, but with broader support, was the Populist party, which lasted from about 1892 to 1908. Farmers were the backbone of this party, and agrarian reform was its goal. In 1892, it ran a presidential candidate, James Weaver, who received one million popular votes and twenty-two electoral votes. The Populists for the most part joined with the Democrats in 1896 when both parties endorsed the Democratic presidential candidate, William Jennings Bryan.

The Impact of Minor Parties

Minor parties clearly have had an impact on American politics. What is more difficult to ascertain is how great that impact has been. Simply by showing that third-party issues were taken over some years later by a major party really does not prove that the third party instigated the major party's change. The case for the importance of minor parties may be strongest for the splinter parties. Splinter parties do indeed force a major party to reassess its ideology and organization. There is general agreement that Teddy Roosevelt's Progressive party in 1912 and Robert LaFollette's party (also called the Progressive party) in 1924 caused the major parties to take up business regulation as one of their major issues.

Calling the United States a two-party system is an oversimplification. The nature and names of the major parties have changed over time, and smaller parties have almost always enjoyed a moderate degree of success. Whether they are splinters from the major parties or expressions of social and economic issues not addressed adequately by factions within the major parties, the minor parties attest to the vitality and fluid nature of American politics.

Did You Know ... That New York sent two delegations to the 1848 Democratic convention—the Barnburners and the Hunkers?

Conclusion: Is the Party Over?

Figure 8-4 shows trends in **party identification**, as measured by standard polling techniques from 1937 to 1992. What is quite evident is the rise of the independent voter combined with a more recent surge of support for the Republican party, so that the traditional Democratic advantage in party identification is relatively small today.

In the 1940s, only about 20 percent of voters classified themselves as independents. By 1975, this percentage had increased to about 33 percent, and more recent polls show it holding steady at about that level. The Democrats have at times captured the loyalty of about half the electorate, and the Republicans until 1960 had more than 30 percent support. By 1992, the Democrats could count on less than 40 percent and the Republicans about 30 percent of the electorate.

PARTY IDENTIFICATION
Linking oneself to a particular political party.

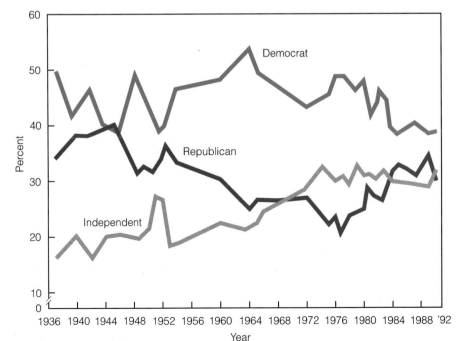

FIGURE   8-4 ■ Party   Identification from 1937 to 1992

SOURCES: *The Gallup Report*, May 1987; *The Gallup Opinion Index*, July 1979; *The Gallup Report*, May 1990; *The Public Perspective*, July/August 1992, p. 17.

TICKET SPLITTING
Voting for candidates of two or more parties for different offices. For example, a voter splits her ticket if she votes for a Republican presidential candidate and for a Democratic congressional candidate.

Not only have ties to the two major parties weakened in the last three decades, but also voters are less willing to vote a straight ticket—that is, to vote for all the candidates of one party. The percentage of voters who are *ticket splitters* has increased from 12 percent in 1952 to more than 28 percent in the presidential election of 1988. This trend, along with the increase in the number of voters who call themselves independents, suggests that parties have lost much of their hold on the loyalty of the voters. **Ticket splitting** and the rise of the independent voter have important policy effects. Because voters are quite likely to vote for a president of one party and a senator from another, it becomes less likely that one party will control both the executive branch and the legislature, thereby making conflict between the branches more frequent. Only in a situation like that of 1981, following the Reagan landslide, are members of Congress likely to follow the president's bidding eagerly.

The increasing trend to ticket-splitting and the relative weakness of party identification among the electorate undoubtedly aided Ross Perot's 1992 campaign for the presidency. Running as an independent candidate, Perot attacked both major parties as ineffective and appealed directly to the voters. His strategy was very successful, garnering 19 percent of the popular vote.

There is considerable debate over the reasons for the upsurge in independent voters and split tickets. The increased importance of the media in American politics, the higher educational levels of Americans, and the mobility of American voters may all work to weaken party ties. This trend makes it more difficult for one party to win congressional seats and the White House and may increase the likelihood of stalemate in policy making.

GETTING INVOLVED

Electing Convention Delegates

The most exciting political party event, staged every four years, is the national convention. Surprising as it might seem, there are opportunities for the individual voter to become involved in nominating delegates to the national convention or in becoming such a delegate. For both the Republican and Democratic parties, most delegates must be elected at the local level—either the congressional district or the state legislative district. These elections take place at the party primary election or at a neighborhood or precinct caucus. If the delegates are elected in a primary, persons who want to run for these positions must file petitions with the board of elections in advance of the election. If you are interested in committing yourself to a particular presidential candidate and running for the delegate position, check with the local county committee or with the party's national committee about the rules you must follow.

It is even easier to get involved in the grass-roots politics of presidential caucuses. In some states, Iowa being the earliest and most famous one, delegates are first nominated at the local precinct caucus. According to the rules announced for the Iowa caucuses, anyone can participate in the caucus if he or she is eighteen years old, a resident of the precinct, and registered as a party member. These caucuses, as well as being the focus of national media attention in January or February, select delegates to the county convention who are pledged to specific presidential candidates. This is the first step toward going to the national convention.

At both the county caucus and convention level, both parties try to find younger members to fill some of the seats. Get in contact with the state or county political party to find out when the caucuses or primaries will be held. Then gather local supporters and friends and prepare to join in an occasion where political persuasion and debate are practiced at their best.

For further information about these opportunities (some states have caucuses and state conventions in every election year), contact the state party office or your local state legislator for specific dates and regulations, or write to the national committees for their informational brochures on how to become a delegate.

Republican National Committee
Republican National Headquarters
310 1st St., S.E.
Washington, DC 20003
202-484-6500

Democratic National Committee
Democratic National Headquarters
1625 Massachusetts Ave., N.W.
Washington, DC 20036
202-797-5900

CHAPTER SUMMARY

1. A political party is a group of political activists who organize to win elections, operate the government, and determine public policy. Political parties perform a number of functions for the political system. These functions include recruiting candidates for political office, organizing and running elections, presenting alternative policies to the voters, assuming responsibility for operating the government, and acting as the opposition to the party in power.
2. The evolution of our nation's political parties can be divided into six periods: (1) the creation and formation of political parties beginning in the 1790s; (2) the era of one-party rule, or personal politics, in the 1820s; (3) the period from Andrew Jackson's presidency to the Civil War, during which the Democrats and Whigs were the two solidly established national parties; (4) the post–Civil War period, ending in 1896

with solid control by the modern Republican party; (5) the progressive period, from 1896 to 1921; and (6) the modern period, from Franklin Roosevelt's New Deal until today.
3. The party is composed of the party-in-electorate, the party organization, and the party-in-government. Each party element maintains linkages to the others to keep the party strong. In theory, each of the political parties has a pyramid-shaped organization with a hierarchical command structure. In reality, each level of the party—local, state, and national—has considerable autonomy. The national party organization is responsible for holding the national convention in presidential election years, writing the party platform, choosing the national committee, and conducting party business.
4. While it may seem that the two parties do not differ substantially on the issues, each has a different core group of

supporters. The general shape of the parties' coalitions reflects the party divisions of Franklin Roosevelt's New Deal. It is clear, however, that party leaders are much further apart in their views than are the party followers.

5. The party-in-government comprises all of the elected and appointed officeholders of a party. The linkage of party is crucial to building support for programs between the branches and levels of government.

6. Two major parties have dominated the political landscape in the United States for almost two centuries. The reasons for this include: (1) the historical foundations of the system, (2) the self-perpetuation of the parties, (3) the commonality of views among Americans, (4) the winner-take-all electoral system, and (5) state and federal laws favoring the two-party system. Minor parties have emerged from time to time, often

as dissatisfied splinter groups from within major parties, and have acted as barometers of changes in political moods. Spin-off parties, or factions, usually have emerged when a particular personality was at odds with the major party, as when Teddy Roosevelt's differences with the Republican party resulted in formation of the Bull Moose Progressive party. Numerous other minor parties, such as the Prohibition party, have formed around single issues.

7. From 1937 until recently, independent voters have formed an increasing proportion of the electorate, with a consequent decline of strongly Democratic or strongly Republican voters. The upsurge in independent voters has been seen most dramatically among new voters—the young and previously disenfranchised. In the 1980s, support increased for the Republican party.

QUESTIONS FOR REVIEW AND DISCUSSION

1. Some commentators have suggested that political parties are becoming obsolete in the United States. What functions of the parties are now being performed by the media? By the individual candidate or campaign organization? By the national government?

2. Although the political parties seem to have a formal organization and structure, the national offices are usually con-

sidered to be unimportant. Why is the power in American parties primarily at the county and state level? Why can't the national party control local parties?

3. What are the major differences on issues and in membership between the Democratic and Republican parties? What elements in the American political system tend to make them both move toward the political center?

SELECTED REFERENCES

Cornelius P. Cotter *et al., Party Organizations in American Politics* (Pittsburgh: University of Pittsburgh Press, 1989). This excellent examination of the organization, finances, and electoral strength of state party organizations looks at how state parties have been transformed in recent years.

Ralph M. Goldman, *The National Party Chairmen and Committees: Factionalism at the Top* (Armonk, N.Y.: M. E. Sharpe, 1990). This book traces party leadership from the founding of the United States to the present time and focuses on the management and socialization of conflict.

Robert Kuttner, *The Life of the Party: Democratic Prospects in 1988 and Beyond* (New York: Penguin, 1987). The author argues that the Democratic party has pursued a self-defeating strategy of moving away from progressive economic populism and towards becoming a technocratic, managerial party imitating the Republican party.

David R. Mayhew, *Placing Parties in American Politics* (Princeton, N.J.: Princeton University Press, 1986). Using sketches of each of the fifty states, this fascinating book analyzes the form, distribution, and effect of local political parties in the United States.

Dean McSweeney and John Zvesper, *American Political Parties: The Formation, Decline, and Reform of the American Party System* (New York: Routledge, 1991). This work discusses in detail the evolution of, and influences on, today's American political party system.

Steven J. Rosenstone, Roy L. Behr, and Edward H. Lazarus, *Third Parties in America: Citizen Response to Major Party Failure* (Princeton, N.J.: Princeton University Press, 1984). The authors' general theory of third-party voting is based on the factors of major party decline, attractive third-party candidates, and new voters with no loyalty to the two major parties.

James L. Sundquist, *Dynamics of the Party System: Alignment and Realignment of Political Parties in the United States* (Washington, D.C.: Brookings Institute, 1973). An analysis of three major realignments in party strength, why they happened, and what they meant.

Martin P. Wattenberg, *The Decline of American Political Parties, 1952–1988* (Cambridge, Mass.: Harvard University Press, 1989). Wattenberg examines the decline in party identification and the increase in split-ticket voting at the same time that campaigns are becoming more image-oriented and media-driven. All of these factors contribute to a decline in the strength of parties but not to their complete disappearance.

CHAPTER 9

Campaigns, Elections and the Media

CHAPTER CONTENTS

WHAT IF . . . VOTING WERE COMPULSORY?

Casting a ballot is often seen as the prime symbol of a democracy. It is the way we choose our leaders, a source of legitimacy for our government, and a means by which citizens can influence public policy. For most Americans, voting is the only form of political participation they experience. Yet a large number of Americans do not vote. In 1990, only about one-third of those old enough to vote actually showed up at the polls to select their representatives and senators. In the 1992 presidential elections, only about half of those eligible actually voted. Voter participation in the United States appears to be much lower than in other democracies, where 80 to 90 percent of the population go to the polls on voting day.

In the United States, our laws give Americans the right to vote, but they do not require us to vote. In some countries, voting is compulsory. What if we had such a law making it compulsory for all eligible citizens to vote, perhaps by levying a fine on those who did not? What would the outcome be if *all* eligible U.S. citizens *had* to vote?

The immediate effects might not be that significant. Studies indicate that nonvoters' attitudes are similar to those of voters, so the results of elections would likely be very much the same. There would be about the

same proportion of Democrats, about 4 percent fewer Republicans, and a similar proportion of independent voters.* Because nonvoters are usually less interested in politics and lack firm positions on issues, the new voters would probably not change issue preferences in the electorate. Nonvoters are not distinctly liberal or conservative.

The longer-term consequences are harder to calculate, but they may be more significant. Those who stay away from the polls tend to be the least educated—the poor, the young, the elderly, minorities, southerners, and the unemployed. Parties and candidates do not have to make specific appeals to these groups because of their low voter turnout. But if these constituencies were compelled by law to vote, their interests might be given more attention. Perhaps the population would be better represented on the whole. The political influence of younger people—who are most often nonvoters—would likely be enhanced significantly.

*Raymond Wolfinger and Steven Rosenstone, *Who Votes?* (New Haven, Conn.: Yale University Press, 1980), Ch. 6.

Younger candidates who are less partisan in appeal could win the younger voters. Policies favoring job opportunities, home ownership, and possibly child care would appeal to this group.

Some argue that the country would be worse off if its least-interested and least-informed citizens voted, and that people who consider voting more trouble than it is worth are likely to make poor choices. Further, it would be unhealthy for a democracy to compel people to vote.

Others say that voting is not only a right but an obligation in a country that claims to have a representative government. Through elections, the people express approval or disapproval of the government's actions, and there would be a stronger sense of the government's legitimacy and of the worthiness of its elected officials if everyone voted. They would argue that when almost half the population avoids the polls, democracy functions badly.

1. *How would compulsory voting change the outcomes of national elections?*
2. *Which groups might be better represented by compulsory voting? Which interests might be poorly served?*

The People Who Run for Political Office

In the winter of 1992, a fairly unlikely cast of characters competed for the Democratic nomination for the presidency. Senator Tom Harkin of Iowa, Senator Bob Kerrey of Nebraska, Governor Douglas Wilder of Virginia, Governor Bill Clinton of Arkansas, Paul Tsongas (former senator of Massachusetts), and Jerry Brown (former governor of California) tramped the fields of New Hampshire to earn primary votes. Two of these contenders—Jerry Brown and Paul Tsongas—were semiretired politicians. Brown was governor more than a decade ago, and Tsongas had retired from the Senate to fight cancer six years earlier. None of the others had the national recognition or big-state backing to be likely candidates.

What they had, instead, were campaign strategies. Clinton had spent several years fund raising, making friends throughout the Democratic party, and convincing the press that he was a bright, effective moderate governor from the New South. Tsongas, the first to announce, pursued a strategy of "speaking the truth" about economic issues that attracted many educated voters. Brown attacked the system as an outsider and promised not to accept large campaign contributions. His constant reminder to voters to call an "800 number" to give money to his campaign netted him great publicity as well as cash. Harkin ran as a left-of-center populist, while Kerrey traded on his youth and Vietnam veteran status. Wilder, a southerner, was the first African-American governor. He also made a moderate pitch.

Of all these campaigns, the most traditional strategy worked best: Clinton's years of making grass-roots contacts, of gaining support in big states, and of building a campaign-financing base in Arkansas, New York, and Washington, D.C., eventually eliminated all of the competitors but Brown, who lasted until the convention.

In the face of Clinton's winning primary strategy and Bush's advantage as an incumbent, the real surprise of 1992 was the rise of H. Ross Perot, a Texas businessperson and billionaire, as an undeclared independent candidate. Until he bowed out of the race in July, Perot threatened to turn the presidential race into a three-way contest and amazed political pundits with his broad support. After a hiatus of two months, Perot re-entered the presidential race in October 1992 and captured 19 percent of the votes cast for president in November.

Why They Run

People who choose to run for office can be divided into two groups—those who are "self-starters" and those who are recruited. The volunteers, or self-starters, get involved in political activities to further their careers, to carry out specific political programs, or in response to certain issues or events. The campaign of Senator Eugene McCarthy in 1968 to deny Lyndon Johnson's renomination was rooted in McCarthy's opposition to the Vietnam war. H. Ross Perot's run for the presidency in 1992 was a response to public alienation and discontent with the parties' candidates.

Issues are important, but self-interest and personal goals—status, career objectives, prestige, and income—are central in motivating some candi-

POLITICS AND PEOPLE

The Clinton Victory: Campaign Strategy or Inevitable Win?

The race for the presidency in 1992 was highly unusual, full of surprises and exciting enough to increase electoral turnout. Yet, the result could have been predicted by political analysts based on economic statistics, regardless of the candidates and their elaborate campaign strategies. Whether Bill Clinton would have won the election even without such a well-organized and successful campaign is a question that will be debated for years to come.

After the Democratic convention, where he named Senator Albert Gore of Tennessee to be his running mate, Clinton wasted no time in reaching out to the voters.

The Republican convention, rather than being a showcase for George Bush and his accomplishments, became a detriment to the Republican ticket. Several of the speakers, among them Patrick Buchanan, articulated very "right-wing" themes and launched attacks on gays and on the policy stands of Hillary Clinton. In general, these attacks alienated voters from the Republican party, even though they may have supported Mr. Bush.

Clinton's campaign was masterful in its themes and its organization. The candidate attacked President Bush, not on his foreign policy record or on his social policies but on the economy. As the economic indicators continued to show high unemployment and a sluggish economy, Clinton spoke of revitalizing the economy. He neutralized Bush's foreign policy successes by asserting that a strong economy was the true base for national security.

The "wild card" in the election was H. Ross Perot, the Texas billionaire who ran as an independent candidate. Perot entered the campaign in the spring, dropped out in July, and then reentered in October. Both campaigns feared the effect of the Perot campaign on their respective voter bases. Perot sparked the debates with his plain speech and his willingness to tackle the issues. He spent more than $60 million of his own fortune for campaign advertising, including thirty-minute-long discussions of the economy. In the end, it is hard to assess Perot's influence on the outcome of the election. He drew voters from Clinton,

from Bush, and from the ranks of the independent voters. There can be little doubt that his campaign energized many citizens who were alienated from the political system. In the final count, Perot garnered 19 percent of the vote, a surprisingly powerful showing for this nonpolitician.

Clinton's victory in November reflected the country's desire for a change, the success of his campaign in rousing the younger voters and attracting suburban voters, and the importance of the economic issue. Although the economy began to show marked improvement in October 1992, Bush was unable to capitalize on the new statistics to improve his support. Whether he would have been reelected if the Clinton campaign had been less effective is a question that will never be answered.

dates to enter political life. Political scientist Joseph Schlesinger suggests that personal ambition is a major force in politics, as political office is often seen as the stepping stone to achieving certain career goals. A lawyer or an insurance agent may run for office only once or twice and then return to private life with enhanced status. Other politicians may aspire to long-term political office—for example, county offices such as commissioner or sheriff that sometimes offer attractive opportunities for power, status, and income and that are in themselves career goals. Finally, we think of ambition as the desire for ever-more-important offices and higher status. Politicians who run for lower office and then set their sights on Congress or a governorship may be said to have "progressive" ambitions.[1]

---

[1]Joseph Schlesinger, *Ambition in Politics: Political Careers in the United States* (Chicago: Rand-McNally, 1966), p. 6.

Although we tend to pay far more attention to the flamboyant politician or to the personal characteristics of those with presidential ambitions than to their "lesser" colleagues, it is important to note that there are far more opportunities to run for office than there are citizens eager to take advantage of them. To fill the slate of candidates for election to such jobs as mosquito-abatement district commissioner, the political party must recruit individuals to run. The problem of finding candidates is compounded in states or cities where the majority party is so dominant that the minority candidates have virtually no chance of winning. In these situations, candidates are recruited by party leaders on the basis of loyalty to the organization and civic duty.

Who Runs?

There are few constitutional restrictions on who can become a candidate in the United States. As detailed in the Constitution, the formal requirements for a national office are as follows:

1. President: Must be a natural-born citizen, have attained the age of thirty-five years, and be a resident of the country for fourteen years by the time of inauguration.
2. Vice President: Must be a natural-born citizen, have attained the age of thirty-five years, and not be a resident of the same state as the candidate for president.
3. Senator: Must be a citizen for at least nine years, have attained the age of thirty by the time he or she takes office, and be a resident of the state from which elected.
4. Representative: Must be a citizen for at least seven years, have attained the age of twenty-five by the time of taking office, and be a resident of the state from which elected.

The qualifications for state legislators are set by the state constitutions and likewise relate to age, place of residence, and citizenship. (Usually, the requirements for the upper house are somewhat higher than for the lower house.) The legal qualifications for running for governor or other state office are similar.

In spite of these minimal legal qualifications for office at both the national and state levels, a quick look at the slate of candidates in any election—or at the U.S. House of Representatives—will reveal that not all segments of the population take advantage of these opportunities. Holders of political office in the United States are overwhelmingly white and male. Until this century, politicians were also of northern European origin and predominantly Protestant. Laws enforcing segregation in the South and many border states, as well as laws that effectively denied voting rights, made it impossible to elect African-American public officials in many areas in which African Americans constituted a significant portion of the population. As a result of the passage of major civil rights legislation in the last several decades, the number of African-American public officials has increased throughout the United States.

Until recently, women were generally considered to be suited only for lower-level offices, such as state legislator or school board member. The last ten years have seen a tremendous increase in the number of women who run for office, not only at the state level, but for the U.S. Congress

Did You Know . . . That you can be listed on the New Hampshire primary ballot merely by paying a $1,000 filing fee?

MAMIE
START PACKING
the
KENNEDYS
are
COMING

as well. Figure 9-1 shows the increase in women candidates. (In 1992, 170 women ran for Congress and 52 were elected). Whereas African Americans were restricted from running for office by both law and custom, women were generally excluded by the agencies of recruitment—parties and interest groups—because they were thought to have no chance of winning or because they had not worked their way up through the party organization. They also had a more difficult time raising campaign funds. Today, it is clear that women are just as likely as men to participate in many political activities, and a majority of Americans say they would vote for a qualified woman or for an African American for president of the United States.

Not only are candidates for office more likely to be male and white than female or African American, but they are also likely to be professionals, particularly lawyers, businesspersons, and teachers. Political campaigning and officeholding are simply easier for some occupational and economic groups than for others, and political involvement can make a valuable contribution to certain careers. Lawyers, for example, have more flexible schedules than other professionals, can take time off for campaigning, and can leave their jobs to hold public office full time. Furthermore, holding political office is good publicity for their professional practice, and they usually have partners or associates to keep the firm going while they are in office. Perhaps most important, many jobs that lawyers aspire to—federal or state judgeships, state attorney offices, or work in a federal

FIGURE 9-1 ■ Women Running for Congress

SOURCE: *New York Times,* May 24, 1992, p. E5.

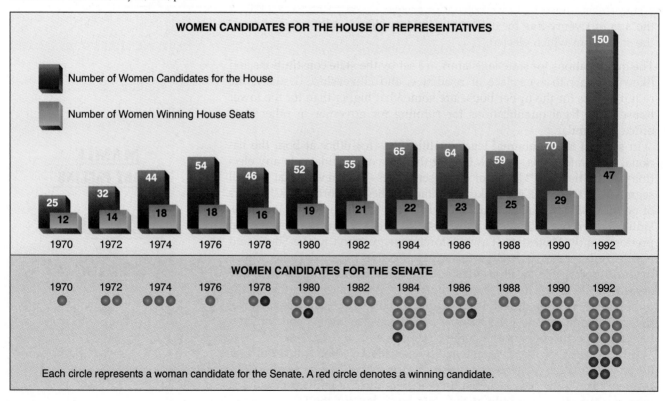

agency—can be attained by political appointment. Such appointments most likely come to loyal partisans who have served their party by running for, and holding, office. Personal ambitions, then, are well served for certain groups by entering the political arena, whereas it could be a sacrifice for others whose careers demand full-time attention for many years.

The Modern Campaign Machine

American political campaigns are extravagant, year-long events that produce campaign buttons and posters for collectors, hours of film and sound to be relayed by the media, and eventually winning candidates who become the public officials of the nation. Campaigns are also enormously expensive; the total expenditures for 1992 were estimated at well over $1 billion for all congressional and local races in that year. Political campaigns exhaust candidates, their staff members, and the journalists covering the campaign—to say nothing of the public's patience.

The Changing Campaign

Campaigns seem to be getting longer and more excessive each year. The goal of all the frantic activity of campaigns is the same for all of them— to convince voters to choose a candidate or a slate of candidates for office. Part of the reason for the increased intensity of campaigns in the last decade is that they have changed from being party-centered to being candidate-centered. The candidate-centered campaign emerged in response to changes in the electoral system and to technological innovations, such as computers (see the *Politics and Technology* feature which discusses how computers are used in campaigns).

To run a successful and persuasive campaign, the candidate's organization must be able to raise funds for the effort, to get coverage from the media, to produce and use paid political commercials and advertising, to schedule the candidate's time effectively with constituent groups and prospective supporters, to convey the candidate's position on the issues, to conduct research on the opposing candidate, and to get the voters to go to the polls. When party identification was stronger among voters and before the advent of television campaigning, a strong party organization on the local, state, or national level could furnish most of the services and expertise that the candidate needed. Political parties provided the funds for campaigning until the 1970s; parties used their precinct organizations to distribute literature, to register voters, and to get out the vote on election day. Less effort was spent on advertising for a single candidate's positions and character because the party label communicated that information to many of the voters.

One of the most important reasons that campaigns no longer depend on parties is that fewer people identify with them (see Chapter 8). For example, in 1952, about 47 percent of the voters declared themselves Democrats and 27 percent said they were Republicans; but in 1992, only 40 percent claimed to be Democrats, while 31 percent were Republicans. In 1952, only 22 percent of the voters were **independent voters;** in 1992, almost 29 percent classified themselves this way. Independent voters in-

Geraldine Ferraro, the first woman to be nominated for vice president by a major party.

INDEPENDENT VOTERS
Voters who disavow any party affiliation and cast their ballots based on their views of who is the best candidate.

POLITICS AND TECHNOLOGY

Politicians Discover the Computer Age

In a game in which handshaking and the personal touch are considered to be the most important way to gain votes, computers have come into their own as an important adjunct for the players. In the 1992 presidential campaign, desktop computers completely replaced typewriters. Campaign managers are increasingly aware of the wide range of tasks that computers can do for them. Experts estimate that some three hundred companies currently specialize in computer services and software for political campaigns.

Computers have taken on an amazing variety of jobs. Taking a cue from the business sector, Richard Gephardt, in 1988, used computers to dial voters in Michigan and give them a tape-recorded message. The Gephardt campaign also used computers to establish a network among all of the campaign offices with electronic mailboxes for the workers.

One of the things that computers do best is to sort voters into categories—male, female, upper income,

African American, and so on. The biggest use for this sorting ability is to create specialized mailing lists for fund raising. The 1988 Dukakis presidential campaign also used this sorting ability to create a bank of information about convention delegates. In both 1988 and 1992, the Bush campaign's computer went a step further; it sent each newly elected Bush delegate a letter signed by the vice president, a questionnaire, and a certificate honoring his or her selection. The computer also kept information about each delegate's birthday, anniversaries, and other special information. Of course, the computer automatically prepared the correct letter or card and sent it to the delegate over the vice president's signature.

Other, more complicated uses for the computer include the Reagan–Bush computerized buying plan for political advertising. Special software was developed to keep track of rates, pricing, and scheduling data for the nation's television markets.

By 1992, political experts realized the power of "on-line" information services such as CompuServe and Prodigy. One Democratic campaign worker discovered a copy of the Bush campaign's memo to workers outlining Clinton's weaknesses. He quickly posted the availability of the information on a Prodigy (electronic network) bulletin board. Within three days, sixty people had sent him messages asking for a copy of the memo. Taking a clue from this kind of bulletin-board usage, Prodigy has established several services for its subscribers. Members can dial up the service from their home computers and look at biographies of political candidates, scan the League of Women Voters' guide to registration laws, and even see paid advertising for candidates on their computer screens at home. This new form of computer use to engage citizens is called by some "teledemocracy."

clude not only those voters who are well educated and issue oriented but also many voters who are not very interested in politics or well informed about candidates or issues. One campaign goal is to give such voters the most information about the political stance of each candidate.

The Professional Campaign

Whether the candidate is running for state legislator, for governor, for the U.S. Congress, or for the presidency, every campaign has some fundamental tasks to accomplish. What is most striking about today's campaigns is that many of these tasks are now put into the hands of paid professionals rather than volunteers or amateur politicians.

The most sought-after and possibly the most criticized expert is the **political consultant,** who, for a large fee, devises a campaign strategy,

POLITICAL CONSULTANT
A paid professional hired to devise a campaign strategy and manage a campaign. Image building is the crucial task of the political consultant.

thinks up a campaign theme, and possibly chooses the campaign colors and candidate's portrait for all literature to be distributed. The paid consultant suggests new campaign ideas to the candidate day by day and decides what new advertising spots are needed. The consultants and the firms they represent are not politically neutral; most will work only for candidates from one party or only for candidates of a particular ideological persuasion.

As more and more political campaigns are run exclusively by professional campaign managers, critics of the campaign system are becoming increasingly vociferous. Their worry is this: Professional campaign managers are concerned almost solely with personalities rather than with philosophies and issues. A professional campaign manager is a public relations person. He or she looks at an upcoming election as a contest of personalities rather than as a contest between two opposing parties or opposing principles. According to critics, professional campaign managers are willing to do anything to get their candidate to win, even if this means reshaping the public image of the candidate so that it bears little relation to reality.

Image building is seen to be the crucial task of campaign consultants and is increasingly necessary to a successful campaign. Using public and private opinion polls as guidelines, consultants mold the candidate's image to meet the campaign's special needs. Image building is a far cry from the "ear to the ground" technique used by party leaders in the past to select candidates and platforms. Yet the alternative to such image building is almost certain failure—regardless of the candidate's stand on significant issues. As Patrick Caddell, Jimmy Carter's pollster and consultant, once lamented, "Too many good people have been defeated because they tried to substitute substance for style."[2]

IMAGE BUILDING
Using public and private opinion polls, the candidate's image is molded to meet the particular needs of the campaign. Image building is done primarily through the media.

The Strategy of Winning

The goal of every political campaign is the same: to win the election. In the United States, unlike some European countries, there are no rewards for a candidate who comes in second; the winner takes all. The campaign organization must plan a strategy to maximize the candidate's chances of winning. In making these strategic choices, a number of factors should be considered. One of the most important concerns is how well known the candidate is. If he or she is a highly visible incumbent, there may be little need for campaigning except to remind the voters of the officeholder's good deeds. If, however, the candidate is an unknown challenger or a largely unfamiliar character attacking a well-known public figure, the campaign must devise a strategy to get the candidate before the public.

In the case of the **independent candidate** or the candidate representing a minor party, the problem of name recognition is serious. There are usually a number of **third-party candidates** in each presidential election (see Table 9-1 for a list of the most successful third-party candidates in American history), and such candidates must present an overwhelming case for

INDEPENDENT CANDIDATE
A political candidate who is not affiliated with a political party.

THIRD-PARTY CANDIDATE
A political candidate running under the banner of a party other than the two major political parties.

[2]Quoted in Peter Woll, *Behind the Scenes in American Government: Personalities and Politics* (Boston: Little, Brown, 1983), p. 128.

TABLE 9-1 ■ The Most Successful Third-Party Candidates

As the Table shows, H. Ross Perot's 19 percent of the vote made him the third most successful third-party candidate in American history. But he did not carry a state and won no electoral votes.

Candidate	Year	Percent of Vote
Theodore Roosevelt (Progressive)	1912	27.4
Millard Fillmore (Whig-American)	1856	21.5
H. Ross Perot (Independent)	**1992**	**19.0**
John C. Breckinridge (Southern Democrat)	1860	18.1
Robert M. La Follette (Progressive)	1924	16.6
George C. Wallace (American Independent)	1968	13.5
John Bell (Constitutional Union)	1860	12.6
Martin Van Buren (Free Soil)	1848	10.1

SOURCE: *Congressional Quarterly Weekly Report,* November 7, 1992, p. 3551.

the voter to reject the major party candidate. Both the Democratic and the Republican candidates use the strategic ploy of labeling third-party candidates as "not serious" and therefore not worth the voter's time.

Because neither of the major parties can claim a majority of voters in its camp, the task that faces them is threefold. Each party and its presidential candidate must reinforce the party loyalty of its followers, motivate the undecided or independents to vote for their candidate, and—the most difficult task—try to convince some followers of the other major party to cross party lines. The Republicans, having fewer adherents than the Democrats, spend more time and money trying to attract independents and Democrats, whereas the Democrats know that they can win if they can secure all of the votes of their party plus a significant share of the independents. To accomplish these tasks, the campaign organization, whether at the presidential level or otherwise, plans a mix of strategies—including televised campaign appearances, debates, and position papers—to sway the voters.

A precinct worker talking to a voter outside the polling place.

Where Does the Money Come From?

In a book published in 1932 entitled *Money in Elections,* Louise Overacker had the following to say about campaign financing:

> The financing of elections in a democracy is a problem which is arousing increasing concern. Many are beginning to wonder if present-day methods of raising and spending campaign funds do not clog the wheels of our elaborately constructed mechanism of popular control, and if democracies do not inevitably become plutocracies.[3]

---
[3]Louise Overacker, *Money in Elections,* (New York: Macmillan, 1932), p. vii.

PROFILE

Ann Richards

"I'm doing what I said I'd do for Texas and I'm finding the bitter reality: change is hard to bring about."

Ann Richards first took the national spotlight as the keynote speaker at the 1988 Democratic National Convention. To many Americans, she was a new kind of politician: a southern woman who held the Texas treasurer's office and who obviously had a quick wit and strong stage presence.

Richards's political career followed a path similar to that pioneered by many other women candidates. Born to an extremely poor family in Waco, Texas, she married a young lawyer, David Richards, who began a practice in Dallas. Ann and David Richards both became involved in local politics, working for liberal candidates and causes. For most of her adult life, Ann Richards stayed at home, raising the couple's four children and working as a political volunteer. In 1975, the Democratic party approached her husband to run for county commissioner. He was reluctant to do so and stepped aside for Ann, who became the party's candidate. She won the race and ended up supervising the road crews, "a truck-driving, front-end-loader operation," as she described it.

When the Texas Democratic party healed the old division between its liberal and conservative wings in 1982, Ann Richards became a candi-

date for state treasurer and easily won the office. She moved to update the state financial system and won praise for her reforms. In 1988, as a new star in the Democratic party, she was tapped for the national address at the convention.

Ann Richards entered the governor's race in 1990 as a decided underdog. She first had to defeat a number of rivals in an extremely tough primary race. The primary was particularly bitter: One of her opponents called attention to her history of alcoholism and accused her of using drugs. After the primary, some of her supporters deserted her because they felt she had backed off from her liberal positions to win conservative Democratic voters—even going dove hunting to

prove that she was not a proponent of gun control.

Richards's general election opponent was Clayton (Claytie) Williams, a millionaire businessperson with a corporate jet, a 10,000-square-foot home, and a swimming pool shaped like a boot. Williams had real advantages going into the campaign—he was a successful corporate leader, self-reliant, and conservative—an archetype of "Bubba," the macho-type southern male. Williams attacked Richards for her feminism, for her liberalism, and for changing her positions. He made a few verbal gaffes, however, that lost the votes of Republican women, including suggesting that rape victims should "just relax and enjoy it." He also refused to shake hands with Richards following a joint appearance of the candidates and was accused of bad manners and a lack of chivalry.

Ann Richards won the election by a narrow margin and was sworn in as the forty-fifth governor of Texas in 1991. True to her campaign promises, she named minorities and women to many statewide offices, started an audit of government expenditures to stop waste and inefficiency, and proposed new ethics legislation to regulate Texas lobbyists. At the same time that she took these reform-minded actions, she wooed the state legislators with lunches, dinners, and visits to the Capitol.

Did You Know ... That a candidate can buy lists of all the voters in a precinct, county, or state for only about two cents per name from a commercial firm?

Although writing more than sixty years ago, Overacker touched on a sensitive issue in American political campaigns: the connection between money and elections. It is estimated that over $1.75 billion was spent at all levels of campaigning in 1992. At the federal level, a total of more than $248 million is estimated to have been spent in races for the House of Representatives, $180 million in senatorial races, and $220 million in the presidential campaign. Except for the presidential campaign in the general election, all of the other money had to be provided by the candidates and their families, borrowed, or raised by other means. For the general presidential campaign, most of the money comes from the federal government.

The road to election is long and takes, among other things, a lot of money (see the feature entitled *Politics and Economics* in this chapter). That money, as we have seen, is used for TV commercials, media consultants, campaign managers, and a host of other professional services. According to Mat Reese, president of Mat Reese and Associates, a campaign management firm, the single most important barrier in running for the House (and presumably the Senate) is the ability to pay for a modern campaign.

Regulating Campaign Financing

Although the total number of dollars being spent on financing campaigns is certainly not decreasing, the way in which campaigns are financed has changed rather dramatically in the last two decades. In the wake of the scandals uncovered after the 1972 Watergate break-in, Congress and the Supreme Court reshaped the nature of campaign financing. It was discovered during the Watergate investigations that large amounts of money had been illegally funneled to Nixon's Committee to Reelect the President (CREEP). Congress acted quickly to prevent the recurrence of such a situation. Presumably, those who make large campaign contributions require something in return.

Candidates Clinton and Gore re-use an old campaign tactic. Instead of using a train to reach small towns, the Democratic team campaigned through small towns and rural areas on a bus. Part of the strategy was to create strong visual images for the rest of the nation to watch on television.

POLITICS AND ECONOMICS

The Inflation of Campaign Expenses

	1988	1992	Change
A guaranteed thirty-second commercial slot during prime time on WAGA-TV, a CBS affiliate in Atlanta	$1,500–7,500	$ 1,800–$10,000	+20.0–33.3%
Double room, one night, Atlanta Ritz-Carlton	$170	$200	+17.6%
A.T.&T. phone system with two incoming lines and six phones	$3,500	$2,000	−42.8%
One bumper sticker (bought in lots of 1,000)	12¢	20¢	+81.8%
One ream of Xerox paper	$3.67	$5	+36.2%
One campaign flier (one page, three-fold, bought in lots of 1,000)	11¹/₂¢	15¢	+30.4%
First-class postage stamp	22¢	29¢	+31.8%
One campaign button (bought in lots of 1,000)	25¢	30¢	+20.0%
Overall limit on pre-nomination spending if federal funds are accepted	$23.0 million	$33.1 million	+43.9%
Overall limit on individual contributions to campaign	$1,000	$1,000	No change

SOURCE: *New York Times*, March 3, 1992.

There have been a variety of federal **corrupt practices acts** designed to regulate campaign financing. The first, passed in 1925, limited primary and general election expenses for congressional candidates. In addition, it required disclosure of election expenses and in, principle, put controls on contributions by corporations. Numerous loopholes were found in the restrictions on contributions, and the acts proved to be ineffective.

The **Hatch Act** (Political Activities Act) of 1939 was passed in another attempt to control political influence buying. That act forbade a political committee to spend more than $3 million in any campaign and limited individual contributions to a committee to $5,000. Of course, such restrictions were easily circumvented by creating additional committees.

CORRUPT PRACTICES ACTS
A series of acts passed by Congress in an attempt to limit and regulate the size and sources of contributions and expenditures in political campaigns.

HATCH ACT
Passed in 1939, this act prohibited a political committee from spending more than $3 million in any campaign and limited individual contributions to a committee to $5,000. The act was designed to control political influence buying.

The Federal Election Campaign Acts of 1972 and 1974

It was not until the 1970s that more effective regulation of campaign financing was undertaken. The Federal Election Campaign Act of 1972 essentially replaced all past laws and instituted a major reform. The act placed no limit on overall spending, but restricted the amount that could be spent on mass media advertising, including television. It limited the amount that candidates and their families could contribute to their own campaigns and required disclosure of all contributions and expenditures in excess of $100. In principle, the 1972 act limited the role of labor unions and corporations in political campaigns. It also provided for a voluntary

$1 check-off on federal income tax returns for general campaign funds to be used by major party presidential candidates (first applied in the 1976 campaign).

But the act still did not go far enough. In 1974, Congress passed another Federal Election Campaign Act. It did the following:

1. Created the **Federal Election Commission,** consisting of six nonpartisan administrators whose duties are to enforce compliance with the requirements of the act.
2. Provided public financing for presidential primaries and general elections. Any candidate running for president who is able to obtain sufficient contributions in at least twenty states can obtain a subsidy from the U.S. Treasury to help pay for primary campaigns. Each major party was given $11 million for the national convention in 1992. The major party candidates have federal support for almost all of their expenses, provided they are willing to accept campaign-spending limits.
3. Limited presidential campaign spending. Any candidate accepting federal support has to agree to limit campaign expenditures to the amount prescribed by federal law.
4. Limited contributions. Citizens can contribute up to $1,000 to each candidate in each federal election or primary; the total limit of all contributions from an individual is $25,000 per year. Groups can contribute up to a maximum of $5,000 to a candidate in any election.
5. Required disclosure. Periodic reports must be filed by each candidate with the Federal Election Commission, listing who contributed, how much was spent, and what the money was spent for.

The 1972 act limited the amount that each individual could spend on his or her own behalf. Senator Jim Buckley of New York challenged that aspect of the law, and the Supreme Court declared the provision unconstitutional in 1976.[4]

---

[4]*Buckley v. Valeo,* 424 U.S. 1 (1976).

FEDERAL ELECTION COMMISSION Created by the 1974 Federal Election Campaign Act to enforce compliance with the requirements of the act; the commission consists of six nonpartisan administrators.

The purpose of signs like these is to increase name recognition, yet it is doubtful that any one name will be recognized when signs proliferate in number and crowd together as they do here.

The Impact of the 1974 Act.   Who would benefit by severe limitations on the amount an individual could spend on her or his own campaign and the total amount that could be spent on a campaign altogether? Obviously, incumbents would benefit by such restrictions. Unfortunately for congressional incumbents, the 1976 Supreme Court decision eliminated restrictions on campaign spending for congressional seats. The Court ruled that the overall campaign-spending ceilings infringed First Amendment rights. In a second opinion, it held that it was unconstitutional to restrict in any way the amount congressional candidates or their immediate families could spend on their own behalf: "The candidate, no less than any other person, has a First Amendment right to engage in the discussion of public issues and vigorously and tirelessly to advocate his own election." The Court let stand the 1974 limits on individual contributions and on contributions by groups such as political action committees (PACs). Candidates who do not want to have to depend on the kindness of strangers can do something else—take out loans.

The Growth in Political Action Committees (PACs).   The 1974 act, as modified by certain amendments in 1976, allows corporations, labor unions, and special interest groups to set up political action committees (PACs) to raise money for candidates. For a PAC to be legitimate, the money must be raised from at least fifty volunteer donors and must be given to at least five candidates in the federal election. Each corporation or each union is limited to one PAC. As you might imagine, corporate PACs obtain funds from executives, employees, and stockholders in their firms, and unions obtain PAC funds from their members.

On March 27, 1990, in the case of *Austin* v. *Michigan State Chamber of Commerce,*[5] the U.S. Supreme Court ruled six to three that the federal and state governments have the power to restrict the involvement of business corporations in political campaigns, by barring the expenditure of campaign funds on independent efforts on a candidate's behalf, such as newspaper advertisements. Corporations were left free to make political contributions through their political action committees. At the time of the Court's action, both federal law and the laws of twenty-one states contained the limitation on corporate political spending.

Running for President: The Longest Campaign

The American presidential election is the culmination of two different campaigns linked by the parties' national conventions. The **presidential primary** campaign lasts officially from January until June of the election year, and the final presidential campaign heats up around Labor Day.

Primary elections were first mandated in 1903 in Wisconsin. The purpose of the primary was to open the nomination process to ordinary party members and to weaken the influence of party bosses in the nomination process. Until 1968, however, there were fewer than twenty primary elections for the presidency. They were generally "**beauty contests**" in which the contending candidates for the nomination competed for popular votes,

[5]494 U.S. 652 (1990).

Did You Know . . . That voter turnout in presidential elections as a proportion of eligible voters declined every year from 1960 to 1980?

PRESIDENTIAL PRIMARY
A statewide primary election of delegates to a political party's national convention to help a party determine its presidential nominee. Such delegates are either pledged to a particular candidate or unpledged.

BEAUTY CONTEST
A presidential primary in which contending candidates compete for popular votes but the results have little or no impact on the selection of delegates to the national convention, which is made by the party elite.

but the results had little or no impact on the selection of delegates to the national convention. National conventions were meetings of the party elite—legislators, mayors, county chairpersons, and loyal party workers—who were mostly appointed to their delegations. These party faithful frequently voted as a bloc under the direction of their leaders. Chicago's Mayor Richard Daley was famous for the control he exercised over the Illinois delegation to the Democratic convention. National conventions saw numerous trades and bargains among competing candidates and the leaders of large blocs of delegate votes.

Reforming the Primaries

In recent years, the character of the primary process and the makeup of the national convention have changed dramatically. The mass public, rather than party elites, now controls the nomination process, owing to extraordinary changes in the party rules. After the massive riots outside the doors of the 1968 Democratic convention in Chicago, many party leaders pushed for serious reforms of the convention process. They saw the general dissatisfaction with the convention, and the riots in particular, as stemming from the inability of the average party member to influence the nomination system.

The Democratic National Committee appointed a special commission to study the problems of the primary system. Known as the McGovern–Fraser Commission, the group over the next several years formulated new rules for delegate selection that had to be followed by state Democratic parties. Although some of the state parties did not agree with the rules, the commission held the ultimate threat: If a state party organization did not comply with the rules, its delegation would not be seated at the national convention. This penalty was carried out against Mayor Daley of Chicago in 1972.

The reforms instituted by the Democratic party, which were imitated in most states by the Republicans, revolutionized the nomination process for the presidency. The most important changes require that convention delegates cannot be nominated by the elites in either party; they must be elected by the voters in primary elections, in caucuses held by local parties, or at state conventions. Delegates are mostly pledged to a particular candidate, although the pledge is not formally binding at the convention. The delegation from each state must also include a proportion of women, younger party members, and representatives of the minority groups within the party. At first, virtually no special privileges were given to elected party officials, such as senators or governors, but in 1984, many of these officials returned to the Democratic convention as superdelegates.

Some political scientists believe these presidential primaries perform several useful functions. First, it is through primaries that a relatively unknown candidate can get his or her "bandwagon" going. Primaries also provide an opportunity for candidates to organize their campaigns and to try out different issue positions before the public. The long primary season stretching from February until mid-June can even be regarded as an endurance test, in which the voters can see how candidates stand up under stress. Finally, the primaries may put pressure on an incumbent to change his or her policy. Lyndon B. Johnson decided not to run for the presidency again after the 1968 New Hampshire primary showed that he was losing party support.

Critics of the system argue that the primaries drag out the presidential election to such a length that by the time they are over, the public is tired of the whole business. The result is that people may take less interest in the general election.

The states that do not have presidential primaries use the **caucus** to choose convention delegates. The original definition of a caucus is a secret meeting of party leaders for the purpose of nominating the party's candidates. In the early years of this century, the caucus was frequently referred to as "the smoke-filled room." Caucuses are still in use by local parties in many states and counties to determine which candidates will be endorsed by the party in primary elections. For the presidential nominating process, caucuses can be used to nominate the delegates to the national convention or to county and state conventions at which the official delegates will be chosen. In the latter case, the caucus must be open to all members of the political party who live within the specified geographic area—which may be a precinct, a legislative district, or a county. These neighbors gather, discuss presidential candidates, decide who the delegates will be, and determine whether the delegates will be pledged to one or more presidential candidates. Some critics of the primary system feel that the caucus is a better way of finding out how loyal party workers feel about the candidates and that its more widespread use would lead to stronger political parties.

Types of Primaries

The two most common types of primaries are the *closed primary* and the *open primary*. In addition, there are the *blanket primary* and the *run-off primary*.

Closed Primary. In a **closed primary,** the selection of a party's candidates in an election is limited to avowed or declared party members. In other words, voters must declare their party affiliation, either when they

Did You Know ... That only slightly more than one-third of eligible voters were estimated to have voted in the 1990 congressional elections?

CAUCUS
A closed meeting of party leaders to select party candidates or to decide on policy. Also, a meeting of party members designed to select candidates and propose policies.

CLOSED PRIMARY
The most widely used primary, in which voters may participate only in the primary of the party with which they are registered.

Party members hold a caucus in the firehouse to choose delegates. It takes considerable confidence to speak up for less popular candidates in the caucus situation.

OPEN PRIMARY
A direct primary in which voters may cast ballots in the primary of either party without having to declare their party registration. Once voters choose which party primary they will vote in, they must select among only the candidates of that party.

BLANKET PRIMARY
A primary in which all candidates' names are printed on the same ballot, regardless of party affiliation. The voter may vote for candidates of more than one party.

RUN-OFF PRIMARY
An election that is held to nominate candidates within the party if no candidate receives a majority of the votes in the first primary election.

CREDENTIALS COMMITTEE
A committee used by political parties at their national convention to determine which delegates may participate. The committee inspects the claim of each prospective delegate to be seated as a legitimate representative of his or her state.

Citizens voting in the New Hampshire primary. This presidential primary has a strong influence on the presidential campaign because it is the first primary.

register or at the primary election. A closed-primary system makes sure that registered voters cannot cross over into the other party's primary in order to nominate the weakest candidate of the opposing party or to affect the ideological direction of that party. Regular party workers favor a closed primary because it promotes party loyalty and responsibility. Independent voters do not like closed primaries because they exclude such voters from participating in the nominating process.

Open Primary.   An **open primary** is a direct primary in which voters can vote in either party primary without disclosing their party affiliation. Basically, the voter makes the choice in the privacy of the voting booth. The voter must, however, choose one party's list from which to select candidates. Open primaries place no restrictions on independent voters. Few states use such a system.

Blanket Primary.   A **blanket primary** is one in which the voter may vote for candidates of more than one party. Alaska, Louisiana, and Washington all have blanket primaries.

Run-off Primary.   Some states have a two-primary system. If no candidate receives a majority of the votes in the first primary, the top two candidates must compete in another primary, called a **run-off primary.**

On to the National Convention

Presidential candidates have been nominated by the convention method in every election since 1832. The delegates are sent from each state and are apportioned on the basis of state representation. There are delegate bonuses for states that had voting majorities for the party in the preceding elections. Parties also accredit delegates from the District of Columbia, the territories, and certain overseas groups.

At the convention, each political party uses a **credentials committee** to determine which delegates may participate. The credentials committee usually prepares a roll of all delegates entitled to be seated. Controversy arises when rival groups claim to be the official party organization for a county, district, or state. At that point, the credentials committee will make a recommendation, which is usually approved by the convention without debate or even a roll call. On occasion, conventions have rejected recommendations of the credentials committee, and in some cases that decision has been a decisive factor in the selection of the presidential nominee.

The Mississippi Democratic party split along racial lines in 1964 at the height of the civil rights movement in the Deep South. Separate all-white and mixed white and African-American sets of delegates were selected, and both factions showed up at the national convention. After much debate on party rules, the committee decided to seat the pro–civil rights forces and exclude those who opposed racial equality.

The goal of any presidential hopeful at the national convention is to obtain a majority of votes on the earliest ballot. Because post-reform delegates generally arrive at the convention committed to presidential candidates, no convention since 1952 has required more than one ballot to choose a nominee. This surprising result is accomplished by a lengthy single ballot during which delegations shift and realign so that the appearance, if not the actuality, of unity may be conveyed to the TV audience. Since the reforms of 1972, candidates have usually come into the convention with enough committed delegates to win.

It is interesting to note that there is no federal regulation of conventions. Each party makes its own rules and policies as it sees fit. The typical convention lasts only a few days. The first day consists of speech making, usually against the opposing party. During the second day, there are committee reports, and during the third day, there is presidential balloting. On the fourth day, a vice presidential candidate is usually nominated, and the presidential nominee gives the acceptance speech.

Did You Know . . . That noncitizens were allowed to vote in some states until the early 1920s?

The Electoral College

Most voters who vote for the president and vice president think that they are voting directly for a candidate. In actuality, they are voting for a slate of **electors** who will cast their ballots in the **electoral college.** Article II, Section 1, of the Constitution outlines in detail the number and choice of electors for president and vice president. The framers of the Constitution wanted to avoid the selection of president and vice president by the excitable masses. Rather, they wished the choice to be made by a few supposedly dispassionate, reasonable men (but not women).

The Choice of Electors

Each state's electors are selected during each presidential election year. The selection is governed by state laws and by the applicable party apparatus (see Table 9-2). After the national party convention, the electors are pledged to the candidates chosen. The total number of electors today is 538, equal to 100 senators, 435 members of the House, plus 3 electors for the District of Columbia, subsequent to the Twenty-third Amendment, ratified in 1961. Each state's number of electors equals that state's number of senators (two) plus its number of representatives.

The Electors' Commitment

If a **plurality** of voters in a state chooses one slate of electors, then those electors are pledged to cast their ballots later in December at the state capital for the presidential and vice presidential candidates for the winning party.[6] The Constitution does not, however, require the electors to cast their ballots for the candidate of their party.

The ballots are counted and certified before a joint session of Congress early in January. The candidates who receive a majority of the electoral votes (270) are certified as president-elect and vice president-elect. According to the Constitution, in cases in which no candidate receives a majority of the electoral vote, the election of the president is decided in the House from among the three highest candidates (decided by a plu-

ELECTOR
The partisan slate of electors is selected early in the presidential election year by state laws and applicable political party apparatus, and the electors cast ballots for president and vice president. The number of electors in each state is equal to that state's number of representatives in both houses of Congress.

ELECTORAL COLLEGE
The constitutionally required method for the selection of the president and the vice president. To be elected president or vice president, the candidate must have a majority of the electoral votes (currently, 270 out of 538).

PLURALITY
The winning of an election by a candidate who receives more votes than any other candidate but not necessarily a majority. Most national, state, and local electoral laws provide for winning elections by a plurality vote.

---

[6]One of the exceptions to this winner-take-all rule is Maine, where since 1969 two electors are chosen on the basis of the statewide vote and the other two according to which party carries each congressional district.

TABLE 9-2 ■ Elector Selection Methods and Ballot Listing

State	Party Convention	Party Committee	Primary	Other	Electors' Names Not on Ballot	Electors' Names Appear on Ballot
Ala.	X[2]	X[1]			X	
Alaska						X
Ariz.			X			X
Ark.	X				X	
Calif.	X[4]			X[3]	X	
Colo.	X[2]			X[4]	X	
Conn.	X[2]				X	
Del.		X			X	
D.C.		X			X	
Fla.				X[5]	X	
Ga.	X[6]	X[6]			X	
Hawaii	X				X	
Idaho	X					X
Ill.	X				X	
Ind.	X				X	
Iowa	X				X	
Kan.	X[2]	X[1]				X
Ky.	X	X[6]			X	
La.		X[1]				X
Me.	X				X	
Md.	X[6]	X[6]			X	
Mass.	X[7]		X		X	
Mich.	X	X[6]			X	
Minn.	X[7]				X	
Miss.			X			X
Mo.	X[6]	X[6]			X	
Mont.	X[2]				X	
Neb.	X				X	
Nev.	X				X	
N.H.	X[7]				X	
N.J.		X			X	
N.M.	X				X	
N.Y.		X			X	
N.C.	X[2]				X	
N.D.	X					X
Ohio	X				X	
Okla.	X					X
Ore.	X[6]	X[6]			X	
Pa.				X[8]	X	
R.I.	X[7]				X	
S.C.		X				X
S.D.	X					X
Tenn.		X[1]				X
Tex.	X[2]				X	
Utah	X				X	
Vt.	X[7]				X	
Va.	X				X	
Wash.	X[2]				X	
W. Va.	X					X
Wis.	X[7]				X	
Wyo.	X				X	

[1] State law allows parties to choose means of selecting electors. Both parties chose to use party committees.

[2] State law allows parties to choose means of selecting electors. Both parties chose to use party conventions.

[3] California law contains separate provisions for the methods to be used by the Democratic and Republican parties in selecting electors. Each Democratic nominee for U.S. representative and the last two Democratic nominees for U.S. senator designate an elector. Certain Republican officials are designated as electors, and the Republican State Central Committee appoints the remaining electors.

[4] State law allows parties to choose means of selecting electors. The state Democratic party chose to use the party convention method. The state Republican party chose to have the party chairman select the electors based on recommendations of party officials.

[5] In Florida, the governor officially chooses the electors; however, the governor must choose only those electors selected by the parties' state executive committees.

[6] State law allows the parties to choose the method of selecting electors. The state Republican party chose to use the party convention method, and the state Democratic party chose to use the party committee method.

[7] Although termed a "convention," state law designates the party officials who meet to select electors.

[8] Pennsylvania law provides that the national Democratic and Republican parties' presidential nominees name their electors for Pennsylvania.

SOURCES: Thomas M. Durbin and Michael V. Seitzinger, *Nomination and Election of the President and Vice President of the United States* (Washington, D.C.: U.S. Government Printing Office, 1980); *Congressional Quarterly Weekly Report*, October 25, 1980, p. 3184.

rality of each state delegation), each state having one vote. The selection of the vice president is determined by the Senate in a choice between the two highest candidates, each senator having one vote. Congress was required to choose the president and vice president in 1801 (Jefferson and Burr), and the House chose the president in 1825 (John Quincy Adams).

It is possible for a candidate to become president without obtaining a majority of the popular vote. There have been numerous minority presidents in our history, including Abraham Lincoln, Woodrow Wilson, Harry S Truman, John F. Kennedy, and Richard Nixon (in 1968). Such an event can always occur when there are third-party candidates.

Perhaps more distressing is the possibility of a candidate being elected when the candidate's major opposition receives a larger popular vote. This occurred on three occasions—in the elections of John Quincy Adams in 1824, Rutherford B. Hayes in 1876, and Benjamin Harrison in 1888, all of whom won elections without obtaining a plurality of the popular vote.

Criticisms of the Electoral College

Besides the possibility of a candidate becoming president even though his or her major opponent obtains more popular votes, there are other complaints about the electoral college. The idea of the Constitution's framers was to have electors use their own discretion to decide who would make the best president. But electors no longer perform the selecting function envisioned by the founders because they are committed to the candidate who has a plurality of popular votes in their state in the general election.[7]

One can also argue that the current system, which gives all of the electoral votes to whoever has a statewide plurality, is unfair to other candidates and their supporters. The unit system of voting also means that presidential campaigning will be concentrated in those states that have the largest number of electoral votes and in those states in which the outcome is likely to be close. All of the other states generally get second-class treatment during the presidential campaign.

It can also be argued that there is something of a less-populous-state bias in the electoral college, because including Senate seats in the electoral vote total partly offsets the more-populous-states' edge in the House. A state such as Alaska (with two senators and one representative) gets an electoral vote for roughly each 183,000 people (based on the 1990 census), whereas Iowa gets one vote for each 308,000 people, and New York has a vote for every half-million inhabitants.

Proposed Reforms

Many proposals for reform of the electoral college system have been advanced. The most obvious is to get rid of it completely and simply allow candidates to be elected on a popular-vote basis; in other words, have a direct election, by the people, for president and vice president. This was proposed as a constitutional amendment by President Carter in 1977, but it failed to achieve the required two-thirds majority in the Senate in a 1979 vote. An earlier effort in 1969 passed the House, but a Senate vote defeated

Did You Know . . . That on July 1, 1990, forty-eight days after the Nebraska Democratic primary for governor, Ben Nelson was finally declared the winner by the State Board of Conveners (he won by 42 votes out of 89,400 votes cast, which was a margin of only .05 of 1 percent, making it the closest primary or general election for governor in modern American politics)?

"FAITHLESS" ELECTORS
Electors voting for candidates other than those within their parties. They are pledged, but not required by law, to vote for the candidate who has a plurality in the state.

---

[7]Note, however, that there have been revolts by so-called **"faithless electors"**— in 1796, 1820, 1948, 1956, 1960, 1968, 1972, 1976, and 1988.

the proposed amendment due to the efforts of senators from less populous states and the South.

A less radical reform is a federal law that would require each elector to vote for the candidate who has a plurality in the state. Another system would eliminate the electors but retain the electoral vote, which would be given on a proportional basis rather than on a unit basis (winner take all). This method was endorsed by President Nixon in 1969.

The major parties are not in favor of eliminating the electoral college, fearing that it would give minor parties a more influential role. Also, less populous states are not in favor of direct election of the president because they feel they would be overwhelmed by the large urban vote.

How Are Elections Conducted?

The United States uses the **Australian ballot**—a secret ballot that is prepared, distributed, and counted by government officials at public expense. Since 1888, all states have used the Australian ballot. Before that, many states used the alternatives of oral voting and differently colored ballots prepared by the parties. Obviously, knowing which way a person was voting made it easy to apply pressure to change his or her vote, and vote buying was common.

Office-Block and Party-Column Ballots

There are two types of ballots in use in the United States in general elections. The first, called an **office-block ballot,** or sometimes a **Massachusetts ballot,** groups all the candidates for each elective office under the title of each office. Politicians dislike the office-block ballot because it places more emphasis on the office than on the party; it discourages straight-ticket voting and encourages split-ticket voting.

A **party-column ballot** is a form of general election ballot in which the candidates are arranged in one column under their respective party labels and symbols. It is also called the **Indiana ballot.** In some states, it allows voters to vote for all of a party's candidates for local, state, and national offices by simply marking a single "X" or by pulling a single lever. Most states use this type of ballot. As it encourages straight-ticket voting, majority parties favor this form. When a party has an exceptionally strong presidential or gubernatorial candidate to head the ticket, the **coattail effect** is increased by the party-column ballot.

Counting the Votes and Avoiding Fraud

State and local election officials tabulate the results of each election after the polls are closed. Although most votes are tallied electronically, there is still the possibility of voting fraud. To minimize this possibility, the use of canvassing boards is common. A **canvassing board** is an official body that tabulates and consolidates the returns and forwards them to the state canvassing authority. The authority will usually certify the election of the winners within a few days.

To avoid fraud at the polling places themselves, each party may appoint **poll watchers** to monitor elections. In virtually all polling places through-

Election judges check the registration of each voter before giving out the ballot. Most local election boards require judges from both political parties at each precinct.

out the country during partisan elections, major parties have their own poll watchers. Poll watching is particularly important when there is a challenge to an entrenched, local political machine. At any time, a poll watcher may make a **challenge,** which is an allegation that a potential voter is either unqualified or that his or her vote is invalid. Once a challenge is made, a bipartisan group of election judges in each precinct will decide on the merits of the challenge.

Vote fraud is something regularly suspected but seldom proved. Voting in the nineteenth century, when secret ballots were rare and people had a cavalier attitude toward the open buying of votes, was probably much more conducive to fraud than modern elections are. Nonetheless, stories persist in places such as Cook County, Illinois, about dead people miraculously voting, people voting more than once, or opponents' votes sinking into the Chicago River.

CHALLENGE
An allegation by a poll watcher that a potential voter is unqualified to vote or that a vote is invalid; designed to prevent fraud in elections.

Voting in National, State, and Local Elections

In 1992, there were 189 million eligible voters. Of that number, 132 million, or 70 percent, actually registered to vote in the general presidential election. Of those who registered, 101 million actually went to the polls. The participation rate during the 1992 presidential election was only 76 percent of registered voters and 55 percent of eligible voters (see Table 9-3).

Figure 9-2 shows that the **voter turnout** in the United States compared with that of other countries places Americans in the bottom 20 percent. Figure 9-3 shows voter turnout for presidential and congressional elections from 1896 to 1992. The last year of high turnout for the presidential elections was 1960, when almost 65 percent of the eligible voters actually voted. We can also see that voting for U.S. representatives is greatly influenced by whether there is a presidential election in the same year.

VOTER TURNOUT
The percentage of citizens taking part in the election process; the number of eligible voters that actually "turn out" on election day to cast their ballots.

TABLE 9-3 ■ **Elected by a Majority?**

Most presidents have won a majority of the votes cast in the election. We generally judge the extent of their victory by whether they have won more than 51 percent of the votes. Some presidential elections have been proclaimed *landslides,* meaning that the candidates won by an extraordinary majority of votes cast. As indicated below, however, no modern president has been elected by more than 38 percent of the total voting-age electorate.

Year—Winner (Party)	Percentage of Total Popular Vote	Percentage of Voting-Age Population
1932 — Roosevelt (D)	57.4	30.1
1936 — Roosevelt (D)	60.8	34.6
1940 — Roosevelt (D)	54.7	32.2
1944 — Roosevelt (D)	53.4	29.9
1948 — Truman (D)	49.6	25.3
1952 — Eisenhower (R)	55.1	34.0
1956 — Eisenhower (R)	57.4	34.1
1960 — Kennedy (D)	49.7	31.2
1964 — Johnson (D)	61.1	37.8
1968 — Nixon (R)	43.4	26.4
1972 — Nixon (R)	60.7	33.5
1976 — Carter (D)	50.1	26.8
1980 — Reagan (R)	50.7	26.7
1984 — Reagan (R)	58.8	31.2
1988 — Bush (R)	53.4	26.8
1992 — Clinton (D)	43.3	23.1

SOURCES: *Congressional Quarterly Weekly Report,* January 31, 1989, p. 137; *New York Times,* November 5, 1992.

The same is true at the state level. When there is a race for governor, more voters participate both in the general election for governor and in the election for state representatives. Voter participation rates in gubernatorial elections are also greater in presidential election years. The average turnout in state elections is about 14 percentage points higher when a presidential election is held.

Now consider local elections. In races for mayor, city council, county auditor, and the like, it is fairly common for only 25 percent or less of the electorate to vote. Is something amiss here? It seems obvious that people would be more likely to vote in elections that directly affect them. At the local level, each person's vote counts more (because there are fewer voters) and the issues—crime control, school bonds, sewer bonds, and so on— touch the immediate interests of the voters. The facts, however, do not fit the theory. Potential voters are most interested in national elections when a presidential choice is involved. Otherwise, voter participation in our representative government is very low (and, as we have seen, it is not overwhelmingly great even at the presidential level).

FIGURE 9-2 ■ Voter Turnout in the United States Compared with Other Countries in Elections during the 1980s.

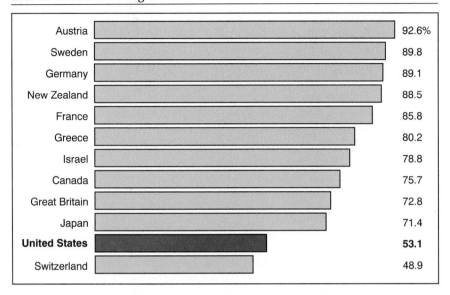

Austria	92.6%
Sweden	89.8
Germany	89.1
New Zealand	88.5
France	85.8
Greece	80.2
Israel	78.8
Canada	75.7
Great Britain	72.8
Japan	71.4
United States	**53.1**
Switzerland	48.9

The Effect of Low Voter Turnout

There are two schools of thought concerning low voter turnout. Some view the decline in voter participation as a clear threat to our **representative democratic government.** Fewer and fewer individuals are deciding who wields political power in our society. Also, low voter participation presumably signals apathy about our political system in general. It also may signal that potential voters simply do not want to take the time to

REPRESENTATIVE
DEMOCRATIC GOVERNMENT
A democracy in which representatives are empowered by the people to act on behalf of those represented.

FIGURE 9-3 ■ Voter Turnout for Presidential and Congressional Elections, 1896–1992

SOURCE: Historical Data Archive, Inter-university Consortium for Political and Social Research: U.S. Bureau of the Census, *Statistical Abstract of the United States: 1980*, 101st ed. (Washington, D.C.: U.S. Government Printing Office, 1980), p. 515; William H. Flanigan and Nancy H. Zingale, *Political Behavior of the American Electorate*, 5th ed. (Boston: Allyn and Bacon, 1983), p. 20; *Congressional Quarterly*, various issues.

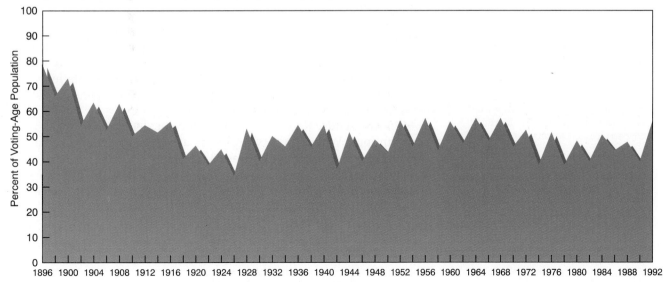

TABLE 9-4 ■ Voting in the 1988 Presidential Election by Age Group (in Percent)

Age	Reported Turnout
18–24	36
25–44	54
45–64	68
65 and over	69

SOURCE: U.S. Bureau of the Census, reported in *National Journal*.

learn about the issues. When only a handful of people do take the time, it will be easier, say the alarmists, for an authoritarian figure to take over our government.

Others are less concerned about low voter participation. They believe that a decline in voter participation simply indicates more satisfaction with the status quo. Also, they believe that representative democracy is a reality even if a very small percentage of eligible voters vote. If everyone who does not vote believes that the outcome of the election will accord with his or her own desires, then representative democracy is working. The nonvoters are obtaining the type of government—with the type of people running it—that they want to have anyway. It has further been suggested that rather than sounding an alarm for the future of American democracy, declining voter participation may really reflect a better-informed voting public. According to political scientists William H. Flanigan and Nancy H. Zingale,

> The high rate of turnout in the nineteenth century may not have resulted from political involvement by an interested, well-informed electorate, but on the contrary it may have been possible at all only because of low levels of information and interest. During the last half of the nineteenth century, a largely uninformed electorate was aroused to vote by means of extreme and emotional political appeals.... [B]y and large, the parties manipulated the electorate—a manipulation possible because the electorate was not well informed.[8]

Factors Influencing Who Votes

A clear association exists between voter participation and the following characteristics: age, educational attainment, minority status, income level, and the existence of two-party competition.

1. Age. Look at Table 9-4, which shows the breakdown of voter participation by age group for the 1988 presidential election. It would appear from these figures that age is a strong factor in determining voter turnout on election day. The reported turnout increases with older age groups. Greater participation with age is very likely due to the fact that older voters are more settled in their lives, are already registered, and have had more time to experience voting as an expected activity.

2. Educational attainment. Education also influences voter turnout. In general, the more education you have, the more likely you are to vote. This pattern is clearly evident in the 1988 election results, as we can see in Table 9-5. Reported turnout was over 30 percentage points higher for those who had some college education than it was for people who had never been to high school.

3. Minority status. Race is important, too, in determining the level of voter turnout. Whites in 1988 voted at a 59 percent rate, whereas the African-American turnout rate was 51.5 percent.

4. Income levels. Differences in income can also lead to differences in voter turnout. Wealthier people tend to be overrepresented in the electorate. In 1988, turnout among whites varied from less than 40 percent of

TABLE 9-5 ■ Voting in the 1988 Presidential Election by Education Level (in Percent)

Years of School Completed	Reported Turnout
8 years or less	36.7
9–11 years	41.3
12 years	54.7
More than 12 years	71

SOURCE: *Statistical Abstract of the United States: 1990* (Washington, D.C.: Government Printing Office, 1990), p. 262.

[8]William H. Flanigan and Nancy H. Zingale, *Political Behavior of the American Electorate*, 5th ed. (Boston: Allyn and Bacon, 1983), p. 9.

those with annual family incomes under $15,000 to about 70 percent for people whose annual family incomes were $50,000 and over.

5. Two-party competition. Another factor in voter turnout is the extent to which elections are competitive within a state. More competitive states generally have higher turnout rates, although the highest average percentage turnout for the past two decades has been in states in which Republicans were elected to most state offices.

The foregoing statistics reinforce one another. For example, rich, white, educated, elderly Minnesotans vote more often than poor, nonwhite, uneducated, young people in Texas.

Legal Restrictions on Voting

Legal restrictions on voter registration have existed since the founding of the nation. Most groups in the United States have been concerned with the suffrage issue at one time or another.

Historical Restrictions

In colonial times, only white males who owned property with a certain minimum value were eligible to vote, leaving a far greater number of Americans ineligible to take part in the democratic process. Because many government functions are in the economic sphere and concern property rights and the distribution of income and wealth, some of the founders of our nation felt it was appropriate that only people who had an interest in property should vote on these issues. Of paramount concern to the backers of the Constitution was that the government should be as insulated as possible from the shifting electoral will of the population. A restricted vote meant a more stable government.

The logic behind this restriction of the **franchise** to property owners was seriously questioned by Thomas Paine in his pamphlet *Common Sense:*

> Here is a man who today owns a jackass, and the jackass is worth $60. Today the man is a voter and goes to the polls and deposits his vote. Tomorrow the jackass dies. The next day the man comes to vote without his jackass and cannot vote at all. Now tell me, which was the voter, the man or the jackass?[9]

The writers of the Constitution resolved the issue by allowing the states to decide who should vote. Thus women were allowed to vote in Wyoming in 1870 but not in the entire nation until the Nineteenth Amendment was ratified in 1920.

It was not until the Jacksonian era of the 1830s that the common man (but not woman) began to be heralded as the backbone of democracy. Men without property were first given the right to vote in the western states. By about 1850, most white adult males in virtually all the states could vote without any property qualification. North Carolina was the last state to eliminate its property test for voting—in 1856.

Extension of the franchise to African-American males occurred with the passage of the Fifteenth Amendment in 1870. This enfranchisement was

Douglas Wilder, the first African American to be elected governor of Virginia.

FRANCHISE
The legal right to vote, extended to African Americans by the Fifteenth Amendment, to women by the Nineteenth Amendment, and to all citizens age eighteen and over by the Twenty-sixth Amendment.

---

[9]Thomas Paine, *Common Sense* (London: H. D. Symonds, 1792), p. 28.

short-lived, however, as the "redemption" of the South by white racists rolled back these gains by the end of the century. As discussed in Chapter 5, only in the 1960s were African Americans, both male and female, able to participate in large numbers in the electoral process. Women received full national voting rights with the Nineteenth Amendment in 1920. The most recent extension of the franchise occurred when the voting age was reduced to eighteen by the Twenty-sixth Amendment in 1971.

Current Eligibility and Registration Requirements

REGISTRATION
The entry of a person's name onto the list of eligible voters for elections. Registration requires meeting certain legal requirements, such as age, citizenship, and residency.

Voting requires **registration,** and registration requires satisfying voter qualifications, or legal requirements. These requirements are the following: (1) citizenship, (2) age (eighteen or older), and (3) residence—the duration varying widely from state to state and with types of elections. In addition, most states disqualify mental incompetents, prison inmates, convicted felons, and election-law violators.

Each state has different qualifications for voting and registration. In every state except North Dakota, registration must take place before voting. Also, many states still require a personal appearance at an official building during normal working hours to register.[10] In general, a person must register well in advance of an election, although voters in Maine, Minnesota, Oregon, and Wisconsin are allowed to register up to, and on, election day.

Some argue that these registration requirements are responsible for much of the nonparticipation in our political process. One study[11] showed that they reduce national voter turnout by about 9 percent. Certainly, since their introduction in the late nineteenth century, registration laws have had the effect of reducing the voting participation of African Americans and immigrants.

There also is a partisan dimension to the debate over registration and nonvoting. When Congress considered the National Voter Registration Act of 1989, support among Republican legislators was stronger than it had been in the past, when Republicans generally feared that an expanded electorate would help to elect more Democrats. The bill required that states provide voter registration forms as part of their applications for drivers' licenses, that all states allow voters to register by mail, and that voter registration forms be made available at a wider variety of public places and agencies. President Bush vetoed the bill.

Early in the Clinton administration, the "motor voter" bill was revived. Republicans forced Democrats in the Senate to delete sections of the bill that required states to provide voter registration forms at unemployment offices and welfare agencies. Republicans claimed that such a provision would make the poor believe that registering to vote was required in order to obtain benefits.

The question arises as to whether registration is really necessary. If it decreases participation in the political process, perhaps it should be dropped altogether. Still, as those in favor of registration requirements

Signs in English and Spanish encourage voters to register for the next election. The Supreme Court has ruled that registration and ballots must be available in other languages if a specified proportion of the citizens speak a language other than English.

---

[10]Twenty states now allow registration by postcard, however.
[11]Raymond E. Wolfinger and Steven J. Rosenstone, "The Effect of Registration Laws on Voter Turnout," *American Political Science Review* (March 1978), pp. 22–48.

argue, such requirements may prevent fraudulent voting practices, such as multiple voting or voting by noncitizens.

How Do Voters Decide?

Political scientists and survey researchers have collected much information about voting behavior. This information sheds some light on which people vote and why people decide to vote for particular candidates. We have already discussed factors influencing voter turnout. Generally, the factors that influence voting decisions can be divided into two groups: socioeconomic and demographic factors, and psychological factors.

Socioeconomic and Demographic Factors

As Table 9-6 indicates, a number of factors appear to influence voting behavior, including (1) education, (2) income and **socioeconomic status,** (3) religion, (4) ethnic background, (5) sex, (6) age, and (7) geographic region. These influences all reflect the voter's personal background and place in society. Some factors have to do with the family into which a person is born: race, religion (for most people), and ethnic background. Others may be the result of choices made throughout an individual's life: place of residence, educational achievement, or profession. It is also clear that many of these factors are related. People who have more education are likely to have higher incomes and to hold professional jobs. Similarly, children born into wealthier families are far more likely to complete college than children from poorer families. Furthermore, some of these demographic factors relate to psychological factors—as we shall see.

Education.   More education seems to be correlated with voting Republican, although this was not the case in 1992. As can be seen in Table 9-6, 39 percent of college graduates voted for Bush in the 1992 election, while 44 percent voted for Clinton. Another exception to the rule that more educated voters vote Republican occurred in 1964, when college graduates voted 52 percent for Democrat Johnson and 48 percent for Republican Goldwater. Typically, those with less education are more inclined to vote for the Democratic nominee. In 1984, Mondale received 43 percent and Reagan 57 percent of the vote from high school graduates, whereas those with only a grade-school education voted 51 percent for Mondale and 49 percent for Reagan. The same pattern held in 1992 when 39 percent of the college graduates voted for Bush compared with 28 percent of those who had not completed high school.

Income and Socioeconomic Class.   If we measure socioeconomic class by profession, then professionals and businesspersons, as well as white-collar workers, tend to vote Republican. Manual laborers, factory workers, and especially union members are more likely to vote Democratic. The effects of income are much the same: The higher the income, the more likely it is that a person will vote Republican. Conversely, a much larger percentage of low-income individuals vote Democratic. But there are no hard and fast rules. There are some very poor individuals who are de-

SOCIOECONOMIC STATUS
A category of people within a society who have similar levels of income and similar types of occupations.

voted Republicans, just as there are some extremely wealthy supporters of the Democratic party. In some recent elections, the traditional pattern did not hold. In 1980, for example, many blue-collar Democrats voted for Ronald Reagan, although the 1992 election showed those votes going to Bill Clinton.

Religion.   In the United States, Protestants have traditionally voted Republican, and Catholics and Jews have voted Democratic. As with the other patterns discussed, however, these are somewhat fluid. Nixon obtained 52 percent of the Catholic vote in 1972, and Johnson won 55 percent

TABLE 9-6 ■ **Vote by Groups in Presidential Elections since 1960 (in Percent)**

	1960		1964		1968			1972		1976		
	JFK	Nixon	LBJ	Goldwater	Humphrey	Nixon	Wallace	McGovern	Nixon	Carter	Ford	McCarthy
NATIONAL	50.1	49.9	61.3	38.7	43.0	43.4	13.6	38	62	50	48	1
SEX												
Male	52	48	60	40	41	43	16	37	63	53	45	1
Female	49	51	62	38	45	43	12	38	62	48	51	*
RACE												
White	49	51	59	41	38	47	15	32	68	46	52	1
Nonwhite	68	32	94	6	85	12	3	87	13	85	15	*
EDUCATION												
College	39	61	52	48	37	54	9	37	63	42	55	2
High school	52	48	62	38	42	43	15	34	66	54	46	*
Grade school	55	45	66	34	52	33	15	49	51	58	41	1
OCCUPATION												
Professional	42	58	54	46	34	56	10	31	69	42	56	1
White collar	48	52	57	43	41	47	12	36	64	50	48	2
Manual	60	40	71	29	50	35	15	43	57	58	41	1
AGE (Years)												
Under 30	54	46	64	36	47	38	15	48	52	53	45	1
30–49	54	46	63	37	44	41	15	33	67	48	49	2
50 and older	46	54	59	41	41	47	12	36	64	52	48	*
RELIGION												
Protestants	38	62	55	45	35	49	16	30	70	46	53	*
Catholics	78	22	76	24	59	33	8	48	52	57	42	1
POLITICS												
Republicans	5	95	20	80	9	86	5	5	95	9	91	*
Democrats	84	16	87	13	74	12	14	67	33	82	18	*
Independents	43	57	56	44	31	44	25	31	69	38	57	4
REGION												
East	53	47	68	32	50	43	7	42	58	51	47	1
Midwest	48	52	61	39	44	47	9	40	60	48	50	1
South	51	49	52	48	31	36	33	29	71	54	45	*
West	49	51	60	40	44	49	7	41	59	46	51	1
MEMBERS OF LABOR UNION FAMILIES	65	35	73	27	56	29	15	46	54	63	36	1

*Less than 1 percent.

Note: 1976 and 1980 results do not include vote for minor party candidates.

of the Protestant vote in 1964. The Catholic vote was evenly split between
Carter and Reagan in 1980 but went heavily for Reagan in 1984. In 1992,
Republican candidate Bush obtained fewer votes from Catholics than did
Democratic candidate Clinton.

Ethnic Background.   Traditionally, the Irish have voted for Democrats.
So too have Slavs, Poles, and Italians. But Anglo-Saxon and northern European ethnic groups have voted for Republican presidential candidates.

TABLE 9-6 (Continued) ■ **Vote by Groups in Presidential Elections since 1960 (in Percent)**

	1980			1984		1988		1992		
	Carter	Reagan	Anderson	Mondale	Reagan	Dukakis	Bush	Clinton	Bush	Perot
NATIONAL	41	51	7	41	59	45	53	43	38	19
SEX										
Male	38	53	7	36	64	41	57	41	38	21
Female	44	49	6	45	55	49	50	46	37	17
RACE										
White	36	56	7	34	66	40	59	39	41	20
Nonwhite	86	10	2	87	13	86	12	NA	NA	NA
EDUCATION										
College	35	53	10	39	61	43	56	44	39	18
High school	43	51	5	43	57	49	50	43	36	20
Grade school	54	42	3	51	49	56	43	56	28	NA
OCCUPATION										
Professional	33	55	10	34	66	40	59	NA	NA	NA
White collar	40	51	9	47	53	42	57	NA	NA	NA
Manual	48	46	5	46	54	50	49	NA	NA	NA
AGE (Years)										
Under 30	47	41	11	40	60	47	52	44	34	22
30–49	38	52	8	40	60	45	54	42	38	20
50 and older	41	54	4	41	59	49	50	50	38	12
RELIGION										
Protestants	39	54	6	39	61	33	66	33	46	21
Catholics	46	47	6	39	61	47	52	44	36	20
POLITICS										
Republicans	8	86	5	4	96	8	91	10	73	17
Democrats	69	26	4	79	21	82	17	77	10	13
Independents	29	55	14	33	67	43	55	38	32	30
REGION										
East	43	47	9	46	54	49	50	47	35	NA
Midwest	41	51	7	42	58	47	52	42	37	NA
South	44	52	3	37	63	41	58	42	43	NA
West	35	54	9	40	60	46	52	44	34	NA
MEMBERS OF LABOR UNION FAMILIES	50	43	5	52	48	57	42	55	24	NA

*Less than 1 percent.
Note: 1976 and 1980 results do not include vote for minor party candidates.
SOURCES: *The Gallup Report,* November 1984, p. 32; *New York Times,* November 10, 1988, p. 18; *New York Times,* November 5, 1992, p. B9.

These patterns were disrupted in 1980, when Reagan obtained much of his support from several of the traditionally Democratic ethnic groups, with the help of fundamentalist religious groups.

African Americans voted principally for Republicans until Roosevelt's New Deal. Since then, they have largely identified with the Democratic party. Indeed, Democratic presidential candidates have received, on average, more than 80 percent of the African-American vote since 1956.

Gender.   Until recently, there seemed to have been no fixed pattern of voter preference by gender in presidential elections. One year, more women than men would vote for the Democratic candidate; another year, more men than women would do so. Some political analysts believe that a "gender gap" became a major determinant of voter decision making in the 1980 presidential election. Ronald Reagan obtained 15 percentage points more than Carter among male voters, whereas women gave about an equal number of votes to each candidate. In 1984, the gender gap amounted to 9 percent nationally, with 64 percent of male voters casting their ballots for Ronald Reagan and 55 percent of the female voters doing the same. The gender gap decreased in 1988 to about 7 percentage points and in 1992 to only 5 percentage points.

Age.   Age clearly seems to relate to an individual's voting behavior. Younger voters have tended to vote Democratic; older voters have tended to vote Republican. It was only the voters under thirty who clearly favored Carter during the Carter–Reagan election in 1980. This trend was reversed in 1984, when voters under thirty voted heavily for Ronald Reagan and again voted Republican in 1988. In 1992, Clinton won back the young voters by ten percentage points.

Geographic Region.   As we noted earlier, the formerly Solid (Democratic) South has crumbled. In 1972, Republican Nixon obtained 71 percent of the southern vote, whereas McGovern only obtained 29 percent. Reagan drew 52 percent of the southern vote in 1980 and 58 percent in 1984.

As part of his campaign's outreach to younger voters and to the "baby boomer" generation, Bill Clinton appeared as a guest on the Arsenio Hall show and on MTV.

Democrats still draw much of their strength from large northern and eastern cities. Rural areas tend to be Republican (and conservative) throughout the country except in the South, where the rural vote still tends to be heavily Democratic. On average, the West has voted Republican in presidential elections. Except for the 1964 election between Goldwater and Johnson, and again in the 1992 election, the Republicans have held the edge in western states in every presidential election since 1956.

Psychological Factors

In addition to socioeconomic and demographic explanations for the way people vote, there are at least three important psychological factors that play a role in voter decision making. These factors, which are rooted in attitudes and beliefs held by voters, are (1) party identification, (2) perception of the candidates, and (3) issue preferences.

Party Identification. With the possible exception of race, party identification has been the most important determinant of voting behavior in national elections. As we pointed out in Chapter 6, party affiliation is influenced by family and peer groups, by age, and by psychological attachment. During the 1950s, independent voters were a little more than 20 percent of the eligible electorate. In the middle to late 1960s, however, party identification began to weaken, and by the 1970s independent voters had become roughly 30 percent of all voters. In 1988, the estimated proportion of independent voters was 33 percent. Independent voting seems to be most concentrated among new voters, particularly among new young voters. Thus we can still say that party identification for established voters is a major determinant in voter choice.

Perception of the Candidates. The image of the candidate also seems to be important in a voter's choice for president. We do not know as much about the effect of candidate image as we do about party identification, however, because it is difficult to make systematic comparisons of candidate appeal over time. The evidence is mixed. Data complied by Warren Miller and others[12] show some important differences in the strength of this factor on voter choice from one election to the next. These researchers found that perceptions of *both* candidates were positive in 1952, 1960, and 1976, whereas in 1956 Eisenhower's image was highly favorable, and Stevenson's was neutral. In 1964, very positive ratings for Johnson contrasted with very negative perceptions of Goldwater. Nixon's positive 1968 and 1972 ratings allowed him to defeat his negatively evaluated opponents. In 1980, both Reagan and Carter had negative images. The researchers also determined that, except in 1964 and 1976, Republican candidates were evaluated more favorably by the voters than were the Democratic candidates. To some extent, voter attitudes toward candidates are based on emotions (such as trust) rather than on any judgment about experience or policy. In 1992, voter decisions were largely guided by their perceptions of who they could trust to run the economy. Bush tried to reduce the voters' trust in Clinton but failed to make an impact.

Did You Know ... That California has 54 electoral college votes, which is one-fifth of the 270 votes needed to elect a president?

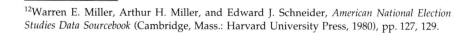

---

[12]Warren E. Miller, Arthur H. Miller, and Edward J. Schneider, *American National Election Studies Data Sourcebook* (Cambridge, Mass.: Harvard University Press, 1980), pp. 127, 129.

Did You Know ... That the greatest declines in voter turnout between 1984 and 1988 occurred among young voters, the less educated, and minorities?

ISSUE VOTING
Voting for a candidate based on how he or she stands on a particular issue.

Issue Preferences. Issues make a difference in presidential and congressional elections. Although personality or image factors may be very persuasive, most voters have some notion of how the candidates differ on basic issues or at least know that they want a change in the direction of government policy.

Historically, economic issues have the strongest influence on voters' choices. When the economy is doing well, it is very difficult for a challenger, particularly at the presidential level, to defeat the incumbent. In contrast, increasing inflation, a rising rate of unemployment, or a high interest rate is likely to work to the disadvantage of the incumbent. Studies of how economic conditions affect the vote differ in their conclusions: Some indicate that people vote on the basis of their personal economic well-being, whereas other studies seem to show that people vote on the basis of the nation's overall economic health.

Foreign policy issues become more prominent in a time of crisis. Although the parties and candidates have differed greatly over policy toward South Africa, for example, foreign policy issues are only truly influential when armed conflict is a possibility. Clearly, public dissension over the war in Vietnam had an effect on elections in 1968 and 1972. In 1980, the Reagan campaign capitalized on Soviet initiatives and the Iranian hostage crisis to persuade the voters that the United States was declining in power and respect.

Some of the most heated debates in American political campaigns take place over the social issues of abortion, the role of women, the rights of lesbians and homosexuals, and prayer in the public schools. In general, presidential candidates would prefer to avoid such issues because voters who care about these questions are likely to be offended if the candidate does not share their view.

All candidates try to set themselves apart from their opposition on crucial issues in order to attract voters. What is difficult to ascertain is the extent to which issues overshadow partisan loyalty or personality factors in the voters' minds. It appears that some campaigns are much more issue oriented than others. Some research has shown that **issue voting** was most important in the presidential elections of 1964, 1968, and 1972, moderately important in 1980, and less important in 1992.

The Media and Its Functions

Historian Daniel J. Boorstin said, "Nothing is 'really' real unless it happens on television."[13] It is not surprising that in a Roper poll, when asked which news source they thought was most credible, most Americans chose the national TV news commentators.[14]

Any study of people and politics, including public opinion, political parties, campaigns, elections, and voter behavior, must take as a given the enormous importance that the media have in American politics today. Not only are the newscasters and their programs the most trusted information

---

[13]*The Quotable Quotations Book,* ed. Alec Lewis (New York: Cornerstone Library, 1981), p. 283.
[14]*U.S. News & World Report,* February 21, 1983, p. 49.

sources in our society, but the media also depend on the political system for much of the news they report. The relationship between the media and politics can best be described as reciprocal: The media need politics and politicians to report on, and political leaders need the media to campaign, to persuade, and to influence. This mutual dependence has sometimes led each party to feel mistreated. Republican leaders frequently complain that the press is too liberal (that is, too critical of Republicans), whereas Democrats argue that the media are controlled by big business (read "Republicans").

The mass media perform a number of different functions in any country. In the United States, we can list at least six. Almost all of them can have political implications, and some are essential to the democratic process. These functions are as follows: (1) entertainment, (2) reporting the news, (3) identifying public problems, (4) socializing new generations, (5) providing a political forum, and (6) making profits.

Did You Know ... That the first "wire" story transmitted by telegraph was sent in 1846?

Entertainment

By far the greatest number of radio and television hours are dedicated to entertaining the public. The battle for prime-time ratings indicates how important successful entertainment is to the survival of networks and individual stations. There is no direct linkage between entertainment and politics; however, network dramas often introduce material that may be politically controversial and that may stimulate public discussion. For example, one controversial segment of *L.A. Law* discussed the "right-to-die" of a paralyzed woman. Made-for-TV movies have focused on many controversial topics, including AIDS, incest, and wife-battering.

Reporting the News

The mass media in all their forms—newspapers, radio, television, cable, magazines—have as their primary goal the reporting of news. The media convey words and pictures about events, facts, personalities, and ideas. The protections of the First Amendment are intended to keep the flow of news as free as possible because it is an essential part of the democratic process. If citizens cannot get unbiased information about the state of their community and their leaders' actions, how can they make voting decisions? Perhaps the most incisive comment about the importance of the media was made by James Madison, who said:

> A people who mean to be their own governors must arm themselves with the power knowledge gives. A popular government without popular information or the means of acquiring it, is but a prologue to a farce or a tragedy or perhaps both.[15]

Identifying Public Problems

The power of information is important, not only in revealing what the government is doing but also in determining what the government ought

---

[15]Quoted in "Castro vs. (Some) Censorship," editorial in the *New York Times*, November 22, 1983, p. 24.

to do—in other words, in setting the public agenda. The mass media identify public problems, such as the scandal of "missing children," and sometimes help to set up mechanisms to deal with them (in this example, the missing children hotline, "Childfind"). American journalists also work in a long tradition of uncovering public wrongdoing, corruption, and bribery and of bringing such wrongdoing to the public's attention. Closely related to this investigative function is that of presenting policy alternatives. Because public policy is often complex and difficult to make entertaining, programs devoted to public policy are not often scheduled for prime-time television. Several networks, however, have produced "white papers" on foreign policy and on other issues.

Socializing New Generations

The media are a major influence on the ideas and beliefs of all adults, but they particularly influence the younger generation and recent immigrants. Through the transmission of historical information (sometimes fictionalized), the presentation of American culture, and the portrayal of all the diverse regions and groups in the United States, the media teach young people and immigrants about what it is to be an American. The extensive coverage of elections is a socializing process for these groups.

Providing a Political Forum

As part of their news function, the media also provide a political forum for leaders and the public. Candidates for office use news reporting to sustain interest in their campaigns, whereas officeholders use the media to gain support for their policies or to present an image of leadership. Presidential trips abroad are an outstanding way for the chief executive to get colorful, positive, and exciting news coverage that makes the president look "presidential." The media also offer a way for citizens to participate in public debate, either through letters to the editor or televised editorials.

Satellite vans for the news services covering the convention. This development in technology allows for more television stations to broadcast live to their own cities and towns.

Making Profits

Most of the news media in the United States are private, for-profit corporate enterprises. One of their goals is to make profits—for employee salaries, for expansion, and for dividends to the stockholders who own the company. Profits are made, in general, by charging for advertising. Advertising revenues are usually directly related to circulation or listener/viewer ratings.

Several well-known outlets are publicly owned—public television stations in many communities and National Public Radio. These operate without commercials and are locally supported and often subsidized by the government and corporations.

Added up, these factors form the basis for a complex relationship among the media, the government, and the public. Throughout the rest of this chapter, we examine some of the many facets of this relationship. Our purpose is to set a foundation for understanding how the media influence the political process.

The Primacy of Television

Television is the most influential of the media. It also is big business. National news TV personalities like Dan Rather may earn in excess of $2 million per year from their TV news-reporting contracts alone. They are paid so much because they command large audiences, and large audiences command high prices for advertising on national news shows. Indeed, news *per se* has become a major factor in the profitability of TV stations. In 1963, the major networks—ABC, CBS, and NBC—devoted only eleven minutes daily to national news. By 1993, the amount of time on the networks devoted to news-type programming had increased to three hours. In addition, a twenty-four-hour-a-day news cable channel—CNN—started operating in 1980. News is obviously good business.

Television's influence on the political process today is recognized by all who engage in it. Its special characteristics are worthy of attention. Television news is often criticized for being superficial, particularly compared with the detailed coverage available in the *New York Times*, for example. In fact, television news is constrained by its peculiar technical characteristics, the most important being the limitations of time; stories must be reported in only a few minutes. The most interesting aspect of television is, of course, the fact that it relies on pictures rather than words. Therefore, the videotapes or slides that are chosen for a particular political story have exaggerated importance. The viewer does not know what other photos may have been taken or events recorded except those appearing on his or her screen. Television news can also be exploited for its drama by well-constructed stories. Some critics suggest that there is pressure to produce television news that has a "story line," like a novel or movie: The story should be short, with exciting pictures, and a clear plot. In the extreme case, the news media is satisfied with a **sound bite,** a several-second comment selected or crafted for its immediate impact on the viewer. (See the *Politics and People* feature in this chapter).

As you are aware, real life is usually not dramatic, nor do all events have a neat or an easily understood plot. Political campaigns are contin-

Did You Know . . . That there are approximately 1,250 full-time radio, TV, and newspaper correspondents in Washington, D.C.?

SOUND BITE
A brief, memorable comment that can easily be fit into news broadcasts.

POLITICS AND PEOPLE

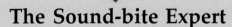

The Sound-bite Expert

Perhaps the most sought-after person by the media is not the candidate or the officeholder but the individual who can produce the most effective or most memorable comment using the fewest words. Because television news stories must be so brief and the message of the story condensed to less than a minute or two, the person who makes the most amusing, witty, outrageous, or wise comment about a situation or issue is likely to get television exposure. These very brief comments are called *sound bites*, meaning a very small snippet of tape that can be played within the news. Some of the commentators or consultants who become well known for their brief comments are regulars on television talk shows. One of these sound-bite experts is Steve Hess, formerly a speechwriter for Eisenhower and an aide to Nixon. Hess has also worked on Capitol Hill and served as a U.S. representative to the United Nations. On a typical day, he will speak on seven to ten radio or television news shows throughout the country, taking the calls from his office or home. He gives public lectures to both interest-group associations and academic groups, while maintaining his position as a scholar at the Brookings Institution.

Hess once wrote an article charging that "TV news is increasingly dishonest . . . reporters tend to interview only those who fit a preconceived notion of what the story will be." Although people stopped asking him for sound bites for a few days, his talk-show comments were quickly in demand again.*

*Howard Kurtz, "Washington's Sound-bite Superstars," *Washington Post National Weekly Edition,* July 22–28, 1991, pp. 6–8.

uing events, lasting perhaps two years or more. The significance of their daily turns and twists are only apparent later. The "drama" of Congress, with its 535 players and dozens of important committees and meetings, is also difficult for the media to present. But TV needs dozens of daily three-minute stories. It has been suggested that these formatting characteristics—or necessities—of TV increase its influence on political events. For example, news coverage of a single event, such as the results of the Iowa caucuses or the New Hampshire primary, may be the most important factor in having the candidate seen as the "front-runner" in presidential campaigns. To a somewhat lesser extent, newspapers and news magazines are also limited by their formats.

The Media and Political Campaigns

All forms of the media—television, newspapers, radio, and magazines—have an enormous political impact on American society. Media influence is most obvious during political campaigns. Because television is the primary news source for the majority of Americans, candidates and their consultants spend much of their time devising strategies to use television to their benefit. Three types of TV coverage are generally used in campaigns for the presidency and other offices: paid-for political announcements, management of news coverage, and campaign debates.

Paid-for Political Announcements

Perhaps one of the most effective **paid-for political announcements** of all time was a short, thirty-second spot created by President Lyndon Johnson's media adviser. In this ad, a little girl stood in a field of daisies. As she held a daisy she pulled the petals off and quietly counted to herself. Suddenly, when she reached number ten, a deep bass voice cut in and began a countdown: 10, 9, 8, 7, 6. . . . When the voice intoned "zero," the unmistakable mushroom cloud of an atom bomb began to fill the screen. Then President Johnson's voice was heard: "These are the stakes. To make a world in which all of God's children can live, or to go into the dark. We must either love each other or we must die." At the end of the commercial, the message read, "Vote for President Johnson on November 3."

To understand how effective this daisy-girl commercial was, you must know that Johnson's opponent was Barry Goldwater, a Republican conservative candidate known for his expansive views on the role of the American military. The implication was that Goldwater would lead the United States into nuclear war. Although the ad was withdrawn within a few days, it has a place in political campaign history as the classic negative campaign announcement. Since the Daisy girl advertisement, negative advertising has come into its own. Candidates vie with each other to produce "attack" ads and then to counterattack when the opponent responds. The public claims not to like negative advertising, but, as one consultant put it, "negative advertising works." Advertising "works" when viewers or

PAID-FOR POLITICAL ANNOUNCEMENT
A message about a political candidate conveyed through the media and designed to elicit positive public opinion.

President Johnson's "Daisy" ad contrasted the innocence of childhood with the horror of an atomic attack.

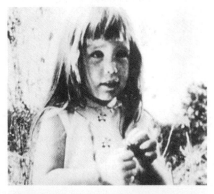

SPIN
An interpretation of campaign events or election results that is most favorable to the candidate's campaign strategy.

SPIN DOCTORS
Political campaign advisers who try to convince journalists of the truth of a particular interpretation of events.

listeners remember an ad. It is clear that negative ads are more memorable than ones that praise the candidate's virtues. The purpose of campaigns is to confirm the votes of the supporters and attract the votes of independents. Negative advertising, which supporters and independents remember longer than positive advertising, works well. For those members of the other party or supporters of the candidate under attack, no vote gain is expected anyway.

Management of News Coverage

Using paid-for political announcements to get a message across to the public is a very expensive tactic. Coverage by the news media is, however, free; it simply demands that the campaign assure that coverage takes place. In recent years, campaign managers have shown increasing sophistication in creating newsworthy events for journalists to cover. They are aware that, as Christopher Arterton points out,

> the media and campaigns need each other; journalists define presidential politics as an important story to be reported fully; campaigners want to reach voters through the news reporting process.[16]

To take advantage of the media's interest in campaign politics, whether at the presidential level or perhaps in a Senate race, the campaign staff tries to influence the quantity and type of coverage the campaign receives. First, it is important for the campaign staff to understand the technical aspects of media coverage—camera angles, necessary equipment, timing, and deadlines—and to plan their political events to accommodate the press. Second, the campaign organization learns that political reporters and their sponsors—networks or newspapers—are in competition for the best stories and can be manipulated through the granting of favors, such as a personal interview with the candidate. Third, an important task for the scheduler in the campaign is the planning of events that will be photogenic and interesting enough for the evening news. A related goal, although one that is more difficult to attain, is to convince reporters that a particular interpretation of an event is correct. By 1992, the art of putting the appropriate **"spin"** on a story or event had become highly developed. Each presidential candidate's press advisers, known as **"spin doctors,"** tried to convince the journalists in 1992 that their interpretation of the primary results was correct. For example, Clinton's people tried to convince the press that he didn't really expect to win the New Hampshire primary anyway, while the Tsongas camp insisted that winning the New England state was a great and unexpected victory. Journalists began to report on the different spins and how the candidates tried to manipulate campaign news coverage.

The Media and the Voters

The question of how much influence the media have on public opinion is difficult to answer. Although one of the media's greatest powers is the ability to shape the public agenda by focusing attention on public prob-

[16]"The Media Politics of Presidential Campaigns," in James David Barber, ed., *Race for the Presidency* (Englewood Cliffs, N.J.: Prentice Hall, 1978), p. 51.

lems and on particular political leaders, studies have shown that the media may not have as much power to change the minds of the people as has been thought. Generally, individuals watch television or read newspapers with certain preconceived ideas about political issues and candidates. These attitudes and opinions act as a kind of perceptual screen that filters out information that makes people feel uncomfortable or that does not fit with their own ideas.

Voters watch campaign commercials and news about political campaigns with "selective attentiveness." That is, they tend to watch those commercials that support the candidate they favor and tend to pay attention to news stories about their own candidates. This process of selectivity also affects perceptions of the content of the news story or commercial and whether it is remembered. Apparently, the media are most influential with those persons who have not formed an opinion about political candidates or issues. Studies have shown that the flurry of television commercials and debates immediately before election day has the most impact on those voters who are truly undecided. Few voters who have already formed their opinions change their minds under the influence of the media.

Going for the Knock-out Punch—Presidential Debates

Perhaps of equal importance to paid-for political advertisements is the performance of the candidate in a televised presidential debate. After the first such debate, which took place in 1960, candidates became aware of the great potential of television for changing the momentum of a campaign. In that first meeting, John Kennedy, the young senator from Massachusetts, took on the vice president of the United States, Richard Nixon. Kennedy's fresh, energetic appearance on television gave him an advantage over the vice president, who looked tired, unshaven, and haggard. Polls taken by Gallup indicated that 43 percent of the respondents felt that

A family watching the 1960 Kennedy and Nixon debates on TV. After the debate, TV viewers thought Kennedy won, whereas radio listeners thought Nixon won.

The format of the second presidential debate of the 1992 campaign proved to be especially well suited to Clinton. His responses to ordinary citizens' questions were often deemed to be more effective than Perot's or Bush's.

Kennedy was the leader in the race after the first debate. By the end of the third debate, Nixon, who had a slight lead in September, was three percentage points behind.[17] What the Kennedy–Nixon debate emphasized was the importance of the candidate's televised image to the campaign.

In general, challengers have much more to gain from debating than do incumbents. Challengers hope that the incumbent may make a mistake in the debate and undermine his "presidential" image. Incumbent presidents are loath to debate the challenger because it puts their opponent on an equal footing with the president. In the Ford–Carter debate of 1976, Gerald Ford, the incumbent, agreed to debate Jimmy Carter because Ford was already running behind in the polls and he hoped to improve his chances through the debate. There is little doubt in most analysts' minds that the 1976 debates helped Carter, the challenger, win the election by a narrow margin.

The presidential debates of 1992 were distinguished by the addition of the independent candidate, H. Ross Perot, and by the use of two different formats. The first and third debates were more formal, with a panel of journalists asking questions of the three candidates. Perot constantly surprised the panel and the audience with his down-to-earth humor and common-sense responses. Bush's performances in the first two debates were lackluster, with some of his fighting spirit appearing in the third one. The innovative format of the second debate certainly increased the interest of the viewing public. All three candidates fielded questions from members of the studio's nonpartisan audience. Clinton seemed to be at home with this format, while Bush was more uncomfortable and Perot had fewer opportunities to capitalize on the forum. Most observers of the three debates noted that the questions posed by the audience were as complex and probing as any raised by the media during the campaign.

The crucial fact about the practice of televising debates is that, although debates are publicly justified as an opportunity for the voters to find out how candidates differ on the issues, what the candidates want is to capitalize on the power of television to project an image. They view the debate as a strategic opportunity to improve their own images or to point out the failures of their opponent. Candidates are very aware that not only is the actual performance important, but also the morning-after interpretation of the debate by the news media may play a crucial role in what the public thinks. Regardless of the risks of debating, the potential for gaining votes is so great that candidates will undoubtedly continue to seek televised debates.

The Media and the Government

Investigating the Government

The mass media not only wield considerable power when it comes to political campaigns but they also can, in one way or another, wield power over the affairs of government and over government officials. Perhaps the most notable example in recent times concerns the activities of *Washington*

[17]Theodore H. White, *The Making of the President, 1960* (New York: Atheneum Publishers, 1961), pp. 294–295.

Post reporters Bob Woodward and Carl Bernstein. Assigned to cover the **Watergate break-in,** these two reporters undertook an investigation that eventually led to the resignation of President Nixon (and later to a best-selling book and a film, *All the President's Men*). More recent investigations have included the Iran–contra scandal, the savings and loan debacle, and the congressional check-kiting scandals. Investigative reporting—with its antecedents in the muckraking journalism of the first decades of this century—became increasingly popular, and journalism as a career attracted a new crop of inquisitive, probing reporters intent on going beyond the news by digging for hidden facts.

The Media and the Presidency

A love–hate relationship clearly exists between the president and the media. During the administration of John F. Kennedy, the president was seen in numerous photos scanning the *New York Times*, the *Washington Post*, and other newspapers each morning to see how the press tallied his successes and failures. This led to frequent jocular comments about his speed-reading ability.

In the United States, the prominence of the president is cultivated by a **White House press corps** that is assigned full time to cover the presiency. Most of the time, they simply wait for the daily or twice-daily briefing by the president's **press secretary.** Because of the press corps's physical proximity to the president, the chief executive cannot even take a brief stroll around the presidential swimming pool without it becoming news. Perhaps no other nation allows the press such access to its highest government official. Consequently, no other nation has its airwaves and print media so filled with absolute trivia regarding the personal life of the chief executive and his family.

President Franklin D. Roosevelt brought new spirit to a demoralized country and led it through the Great Depression through his effective use of the media, particularly radio broadcasts. His radio **"fireside chats"** brought hope to millions. Roosevelt's speeches were masterly in their ability to forge a common emotional bond among his listeners. His decisive announcement in 1933 on the reorganization of the banks calmed a jittery nation and prevented the collapse of the banking industry, which was threatened by a run on banks in which nervous depositors were withdrawing their assets. His famous Pearl Harbor speech, following the Japanese attack on the U.S. Pacific fleet on December 7, 1941 ("a day that will live in infamy"), mobilized the nation for the sacrifices and effort necessary to win World War II.

Perhaps no president exploited the electronic media more effectively than Ronald Reagan. The "great communicator," as he was called, was never more dramatic than in his speech to the nation following the October 1983 U.S. invasion of Grenada.

The early days of the Clinton presidency were marked by stormy press relations. Eventually, Clinton hired David Gergen, a former Reagan aide, to smooth the relationship.

The relationship between the media and the president has thus been reciprocal. Both institutions have used each other, sometimes positively, sometimes negatively. The presidency and the news media are mutually dependent.

WATERGATE BREAK-IN
The 1972 illegal entry into the Democratic campaign offices engineered by participants in Nixon's reelection campaign.

WHITE HOUSE PRESS CORPS
A group of reporters assigned full time to cover the presidency.

PRESS SECRETARY
The individual responsible for representing the White House before the media. The press secretary writes news releases, provides background information, sets up press conferences, and so on.

FIRESIDE CHATS
Warm, informal talks by Franklin D. Roosevelt to a few million of his intimate friends—via the radio. Roosevelt's fireside chats were so effective that succeeding presidents have been urged by their advisers to emulate him by giving more radio and television reports to the nation.

President Franklin D. Roosevelt, the first president to fully exploit the airwaves for his benefit, reported to the nation through radio "fireside chats."

PUBLIC AGENDA
Issues that are commonly perceived by members of the political community as meriting public attention and governmental action. The media play an important role in setting the public agenda by focusing attention on certain topics.

Setting the Public Agenda

Given that government officials have in front of them an array of problems with which they must deal, the process of setting the **public agenda** is constant. To be sure, what goes on the public agenda for discussion, debate, and ultimately policy action depends on many factors—not the least being each official's personal philosophy.

According to a number of studies, the media play an important part in setting the agenda, as well as in helping government officials to better understand society's needs and desires (see the *Politics and Technology* feature in this chapter for another way to set the agenda). W. P. Davison went so far as to claim that diplomats obtain the bulk of their information about what is happening in the world not from other diplomats, but from the press.[18]

In recent years, television coverage has brought a number of issues to public attention and, consequently, to the attention of policy makers. Videotaped footage of the refugee camps in Ethiopia was captured by journalists. The painful images of thousands of children starving while relief shipments were stopped by the combatants in the conflict aroused public concern around the globe. Private efforts were mounted by groups and individuals, including the staging of a massive rock concert benefit, called "Live Aid," to raise money for famine relief. Although many foreign policy decision makers were aware of the situation in Ethiopia, media attention caused them to increase pressure on Ethiopian officials to allow the shipments of food and medical supplies through to the camps.

Interest groups understand well the power of the media. After campaigning unsuccessfully for years against the tuna industry's practice of using fishing nets that also captured dolphins, one group infiltrated a

---

[18]W. P. Davison, "News and Media and International Negotiation," *Public Opinion Quarterly,* No. 38 (Summer 1974), 174–191.

POLITICS AND TECHNOLOGY

The Electronic Town Meeting

One of the more severe charges that presidential candidate H. Ross Perot made against politicians is that they cannot take a position without summoning the pollsters to see what the public thinks. Perot also wanted government to respond to the public and proposed that we use our electronic technology to construct national town meetings.

Perot demonstrated the power of this proposal during the hectic weeks of his first run for the presidency as an independent candidate. He set up satellite feeds from six different states to a central studio and invited thousands of people to attend the event. With two-way tele-vision transmissions and big-screen television monitors, Perot could speak to all of the groups simultaneously. Members of these six audiences could then take turns asking him questions on live television. This use of modern technology led many voters to ask why elected officials do not seek their opinions in a similar fashion, rather than seeming to avoid public contact, particularly in front of an audience.

Although he used the satellite hookup for campaigning, Perot proposed using a similar electronic town meeting to ascertain what the people think about policy issues. As he put it, "With interactive televi-sion, we could take one major issue, go to the American people, cover it in great detail, have them respond, and show by congressional district what people want."

After his inaugural, President Bill Clinton used the electronic town hall format to discuss his proposed economic program with the public. Not only did he respond to questions from the live audience in Detroit but he also took telephone queries from callers around the nation.

---

fishing crew and shot video film of the slaughter of hundreds of dolphins. The broadcast of this tape led to public outrage, congressional investigations of the industry, and a self-imposed ban on the practice by the major tuna-marketing firms in the United States.

The relationship of the media to agenda setting is complex. Evidence is strong that whatever public problems receive the most media treatment will be cited by the public in contemporary surveys as the most important problems. Yet politicians, whether at home or abroad, are able to manipulate media coverage to control some of its effects as well as exploit the media to press their agendas with the public. And media coverage of political campaigns focuses less on campaign issues and the public agenda than on who's ahead in the "horse race" according to the latest poll results.

Government Regulation of the Media

The United States has perhaps the freest press in the world. Nonetheless, regulation of the media does exist, particularly of the electronic media. Many aspects of this regulation were discussed in Chapter 4, when we examined First Amendment rights and the press.

The Electronic Media and Government Control

The First Amendment does not mention the electronic media, which did not exist when the Bill of Rights was written. For many reasons, the government has much greater control over the electronic media than it does over printed media. Through the Federal Communications Commission (FCC), the number of radio stations has been controlled for many years, in spite of the fact that technologically we could have many more radio stations than now exist. Also, the FCC created a situation in which the three major TV networks have dominated the airwaves. Only recently did the FCC bow to public and political pressure to open up the TV airwaves to all the new technological devices now available. Most FCC rules have dealt with ownership of news media, such as how many stations a network can own.

In general, the broadcasting industry has successfully avoided government regulation of content by establishing its own code. This code consists of a set of rules developed by the National Association of Broadcasters, the lobby for the TV and radio industry, which regulate the amount of sex, violence, nudity, profanity, and so forth that is allowed on the air. It should be noted that abiding by the code is voluntary on the part of networks and stations.

Since 1980, there has been continued public debate over whether the government should attempt to control polling and the "early calling" of presidential elections. On election night in 1980, the networks predicted that Ronald Reagan had been elected before numerous states had closed their polls. In 1984, this controversy over network predictions based on exit polls surfaced again. The concern expressed by many was that voters on their way to vote might not bother because the victor had already been declared. It was feared that the resulting drop in turnout would particularly affect state and local races. Because some types of voters, such as factory workers, are more likely to vote late in the day, the outcomes of elections and referenda might be seriously affected.

In 1984, the networks were careful to say that they would not project winners in any state until the polling places *in that state* were closed. With the different time zones and with a concentration of population (and electoral college votes) in the Northeast and Midwest, however, the networks were able to project a winner by 8 P.M. Eastern time, which was 5 P.M. on the West Coast.

Some legislators and citizens have called for a ban on exit polls or on releasing them before *all* polling places in the continental United States are closed. Others have called for a federal law establishing a uniform closing time for voting so that voting would end at the same time all over the country, and thus exit polls could not be a factor. In any event, although turnout has been lower than expected in many western states, studies suggest that the early announcement of election results based on exit polls has little effect on election outcomes.

Does National Security Justify Suppression of the News?

On October 25, 1983, the United States, supported by the island nations of Antigua, Barbados, Dominica, Jamaica, St. Lucia, and St. Vincent, invaded the island of Grenada. The purpose of the invasion, as stated by the president, was to rescue Americans on the island following a violent *coup d'etat* and to replace a hard-line Marxist government. No advance notice was given to the media on the planned operation. Once the assault on Grenada began, no American reporters were allowed on the island for several days. Reporters who tried to get there on a chartered boat were ordered away by the U.S. forces. The U.S. government claimed that this news blackout was necessary to ensure a surprise attack.

The reaction of the American news media was strong and swift. By denying independent access, the government threatened American freedom and the role that the media play in keeping Americans informed. The media and other observers saw the blackout as censorship, and some denounced the military's control of information about the invasion as a blatant propaganda effort.

At the time of the U.S. invasion of Panama in 1989, the Pentagon agreed to send a small pool of reporters to cover the military operation. In fact, the press were allowed into the streets of Panama several hours after the invasion began. The first television pictures sent via satellite showed victorious American troops waving at friendly Panamanians. There were virtually no pictures of deaths and, even several days later, no stories about the civilian casualties in Panama.

The news media were criticized for their coverage of the Panamanian operation on two counts: First, journalists followed the lead of the administration and focused only on the "hunt for Noriega"; and second, neither the print nor the electronic media tried to investigate the question of civilian casualties.

Operation Desert Storm in 1991 saw a repetition of the Panamanian situation with some new twists. Reporters were briefed daily by military spokespersons in Saudi Arabia. Although journalists were skeptical about the optimistic reports, they had no other sources of information. Several journalists, frustrated by military controls on news gathering, went out to the Iraqi border with their escorts and were captured by Iraqi forces. When the coalition's ground offensive began, selected "pools" of reporters accompanied military units. For the most part, the media reported the administration's view.

Did You Know ... That Americans generally have a favorable view of the news media—82 percent report favorably on network TV news, 80 percent on local TV news, and 77 percent on daily newspapers?

Bernard Shaw covered the outbreak of the 1991 American air attack on Baghdad from his hotel room in that city. The continued coverage of the war by CNN correspondents in Iraq raised issues of censorship and control for the media.

Did You Know ... That it has been estimated that the U.S. government retains about 50 percent of the radio broadcast spectrum for government and military uses?

The most unusual coverage was provided by CNN, which continued to broadcast from Baghdad during the air attack and later, as the war progressed. While Americans were fascinated by the coverage from the Iraqi capital, Peter Arnett, the CNN anchor who stayed there, was criticized for continuing his broadcasts under Iraqi censorship. Arnett, however, made it clear to the viewers that he was under the watchful eye of Iraqi officials as he broadcast to the United States.

After Operation Desert Storm ended, journalists were permitted to see more of the military reports generated during the conflict. It became clear that American weaponry had not been as effective as originally reported and that there were many occasions in which the weapons had missed their targets. Criticism of the entire war effort also increased when the extent of Iraqi civilian deaths and the extent of environmental damage to the Persian Gulf—due to the attempted destruction of Kuwait's oil fields—became known. Once again, journalists vowed to be more critical the next time that the United States went to war.

Conclusion: Campaigns and the Media

Modern political campaigns have moved far from the party-centered, mass-based politics of the early twentieth century. The structures and rules for elections have changed. The introduction of the direct primary election, the reform of delegate-selection practices, and campaign-finance reform have all weakened the control that the party organizations formerly exercised over candidates.

At the same time, technology and shifting currents in American society have changed the way in which candidates transmit their appeals to the voter. Television is the medium of choice, both because of its visual power and because most voters choose to get their information from that medium. Two-career families, a population shift to the suburbs and the primacy of television, coupled with the structural changes in election procedures, have given rise to the personality-centered campaign. No longer do state or national candidates worry about how many precinct workers they will have. Rather, they are concerned about hiring the right consultant, designing the best advertising campaigns, and, often most important, raising enough money to pay for the expenses of running.

Voters watch the campaigns unfold, trying to identify the issue positions that are most important to them. Their character assessments of the candidates are based on media coverage and the candidates' own advertising presentations. If the voter is a strong Democrat or Republican, then the party cue is likely to outweigh other characteristics. In addition, voters are exposed to commentary by journalists and other candidates about how the campaign is being conducted. Some commentators have suggested that a decline in voter turnout is a sign that voters are disenchanted with the long campaign season and the emphasis on imagery and media manipulation. As the 1992 presidential election demonstrated, an interesting race, accompanied by a real emphasis on voter registration and turnout, can dramatically increase voter participation. In contrast to the 1988 presidential election, in which voter turnout was 50.2 percent, in 1992, voter turnout was about 54 percent.

GETTING INVOLVED

Voting

In nearly every state, before you are allowed to cast a vote in an election, you must first register. Registration laws vary considerably from state to state, and, depending on how difficult a state's laws make it to register, some states have much higher rates of registration and voting participation than do others.

What do you have to do to register and cast a vote? Most states require that you meet minimum residence requirements. In other words, you must have lived in the state in which you plan to be registered for a specified period of time. You may retain your previous registration, if any, in another state, and you can cast an absentee vote if your previous state permits that. The minimum residency requirement is very short in some states, such as one day in Alabama or ten days in New Hampshire and Wisconsin, but in other states, as much as fifty days (in Arizona or Tennessee) must elapse before you can vote. Other states with voter residency requirements have minimum-day requirements in between these extremes. Twenty states do not have any minimum residency requirement at all.

Nearly every state also specifies a closing date by which you must be registered before an election. In other words, even if you have met a residency requirement, you still may not be able to vote if you register too close to the day of the election. The closing date is different in certain states (Connecticut, Delaware, and Louisiana) for primary elections than for other elections. The closing date for registration varies from election day itself (Maine, Minnesota, Oregon, and Wisconsin) up to fifty days (Arizona). Delaware specifies the third Saturday in October as the closing date.

In most states your registration can be revoked if you do not vote within a certain number of years. This process of automatically "purging" the voter registration lists of nonactive voters happens every two years in about a dozen states, every three years in Georgia, every four years in more than twenty other states, every five years in Maryland and Rhode Island, every eight years in North Carolina, and every ten years in Michigan. Ten states do not require this purging at all.

What you must do to register and remain registered to vote varies from state to state and even from county to county within a state. In general, you must be a citizen of the United States, at least eighteen years old on or before election day, and a resident of the state in which you intend to register.

Using Iowa as an example, you would normally register through the local county auditor. If you move to a new address within the state, you must also change your registration to vote by contacting the auditor. Postcard registrations must be postmarked or delivered to the county auditor no later than the twenty-fifth day before an election. Party affiliation may be changed or declared when you register or reregister, or you may change or declare a party at the polls on election day. Postcard registration forms in Iowa are available at many public buildings, from labor unions, at political party headquarters, at the county auditors' offices, or from campus groups. Mobile registrars may be made available by calling your party headquarters or your county auditor.

For more information on voting registration, you should contact your county or state officials, party headquarters, labor union, or local chapter of the League of Women Voters.

CHAPTER SUMMARY

1. People may choose to run for political office to further their careers, to carry out specific political programs, or in response to certain issues or events. Others are recruited by political parties, interest groups, close friends, or family. The legal qualifications for holding political office are minimal at both the state and local levels, but holders of political office are predominantly white and male and are likely to be from the professional class.

2. American political campaigns are lengthy and extremely expensive. In the last decade, they have become more candidate centered rather than party centered in response to technological innovations and decreasing party identification. Candidates have begun to rely less on the party and more on paid professional consultants to perform the various tasks necessary to wage a political campaign. The campaign organization devises a campaign strategy to maximize the candidate's chances of winning.

3. The amount of money spent in financing campaigns is

steadily increasing. There have been a variety of corrupt practices acts designed to regulate campaign finance. The Federal Election Campaign Acts of 1972 and 1974 instituted major reforms by limiting spending and contributions; the acts allowed corporations, labor unions, and interest groups to set up political action committees (PACs) to raise money for candidates.

4. After the 1968 Democratic convention, the McGovern–Fraser Commission was appointed to study the problems of the primary system. It formulated new rules, which were also adopted by Republicans in many states. These reforms opened up the nomination process for the presidency to all voters.

5. A presidential primary is a statewide election to help a political party determine its presidential nominee at the national convention. Other states use the caucus method of choosing convention delegates. Different types of presidential primaries include the closed primary, the open primary, the blanket primary, and the run-off primary. Some argue for a single, nationwide presidential primary election to replace the state-by-state system.

6. The United States uses the Australian ballot, a secret ballot that is prepared, distributed, and counted by government officials. The office-block ballot groups candidates according to office. The party-column ballot groups candidates according to party labels and symbols.

7. In making a presidential choice on election day, the voter technically does not vote directly for a candidate but chooses between slates of presidential electors. The slate that wins the most popular votes throughout the state gets to cast all the electoral votes for the state. The candidate receiving a majority (270) of the electoral votes wins. Both the mechanics and the politics of the electoral college have been sharply criticized. There have been many proposed reforms, including a direct election in which candidates would be elected on a popular-vote basis.

8. Voter participation in the United States is low (and declining) compared with that of other countries. There is an association between nonvoting and a person's age, education, minority status, and income level. Another factor affecting voter turnout is the extent to which elections are competitive within a state.

9. In colonial times, only white males with a certain minimum amount of property were eligible to vote. The suffrage issue has concerned, at one time or another, most groups in the United States. Current voter eligibility requires registration, citizenship, and specified age and residence requirements. Each state has different qualifications. It is argued that these requirements are responsible for much of the nonparticipation in the political process in the United States.

10. Socioeconomic or demographic factors that influence voting decisions include (a) education, (b) income and socioeconomic class, (c) religion, (d) ethnic background, (e) sex, (f) age, and (g) geographic region. Psychological factors that influence voting decisions include (a) party identification, (b) perception of candidates, and (c) issue preferences.

11. The media are enormously important in American politics today. They perform a number of functions, including (a) entertainment, (b) news reporting, (c) identifying public problems, (d) socializing new generations, (e) providing a political forum, and (f) making profits.

12. The media wield enormous political power during political campaigns and over the affairs of government and government officials by focusing attention on their actions. Today's political campaigns use paid-for political announcements and expert management of news coverage. Of equal importance for presidential candidates is how they appear in presidential debates.

13. The media play an important role in investigating the government, in getting government officials to better understand the needs and desires of American society, and in setting the public agenda. The relationship between the media and the president is close; both have used each other—sometimes positively, sometimes negatively.

14. The media in the United States, particularly the electronic media, are subject to government regulation, although the United States has possibly the freest press in the world. Most Federal Communications Commission rules have dealt with ownership of TV and radio stations.

15. When the United States invaded the island of Grenada on October 25, 1983, the media were not allowed on the island for national security reasons. This blackout raised the question of how the public's "right to know" should be balanced against the need to protect the national interests. The invasion of Panama and Operation Desert Storm raised similar issues.

QUESTIONS FOR REVIEW AND DISCUSSION

1. Think about the U.S. senators from your own state. How did each begin in politics? To what extent are they "self starters?" Did either of your senators hold political office before running for the national legislature? What are the major sources of support and campaign funding for each of the senators?

2. Suppose you were going to run for election on the Democratic ticket in your community. What demographic groups in the population would you try to recruit as supporters and voters?

3. What is the relationship between the primary elections in the states and the national convention of the political party?

Who are the delegates to the national convention and whom do they represent?

4. Suppose that you are the campaign manager for a U.S. Senate candidate in your state. What kinds of "media events" would you try to set up so that your candidate would get coverage? What meetings, parades, celebrations, and rallies would you have your candidate attend to provide good pictures for TV news? What kinds of assistance could you give to the newspeople to make them generally favorable to your campaign?

5. Compare the coverage of a political event, such as an election, or a speech, such as the State of the Union message, by the newspapers, the news magazines, television, and radio. How are pictures used to convey the story compared with words? How does "editing" change the content and the effect of such a story?

SELECTED REFERENCES

Karen M. Arlington and William L. Taylor, eds., *Voting Rights in America: Continuing the Quest for Full Participation* (Lanham, Md.: University Press of America, 1992). These twelve papers on voting rights in America delineate the history of elections and the expansion of voting rights over the years and discuss suggested improvements to the voting system.

Larry Bartels, *Presidential Primaries and the Dynamics of Public Choice* (Princeton, N.J.: Princeton University Press, 1987). A study of the primary process and the dynamics that propel one candidate to the nomination.

Walter Berns, ed., *After the People Vote: A Guide to the Electoral College*, rev. ed. (Lanham, Md.: University Press of America, 1991). This collection of essays looks at the role played by the electoral college in American elections and at what happens in a variety of unusual situations, including the death of a presidential candidate before the November election and the failure of any presidential candidate to get an electoral college majority.

Peter J. Coughlin, *Probabilistic Voting Theory* (New York: Cambridge University Press, 1991). A statistical work on the anticipation of candidate behavior and the corresponding voter response.

Robert Donovan and Ray Scherer, *Unsilent Revolution: Television News and American Public Life, 1948–1991* (New York: Cambridge University Press, 1991). An exploration of the effect that television has had on such institutions as politics, current events, and public opinion over the last half-century.

Doris A. Graber, *Media Power in Politics*, 3d ed. (Washington, D.C.: Congressional Quarterly Press, 1990). This book explores the profound impact of the mass media on the political system. It has both an historical and a topical focus.

Mark Hertsgaard, *On Bended Knee: The Press and the Reagan Presidency* (New York: Random House, 1989). Using over 175 interviews, this interesting book discusses and analyzes the methods used by the Reagan White House public relations staff to manipulate and influence the media and create a favorable image of Reagan, as well as to generate acceptance of his policies.

Kathleen Hall Jamieson, *Packaging the Presidency: A History and Criticism of Presidential Campaign Advertising* (New York: Oxford University Press, 1992). An insightful discussion of presidential campaign advertising as it has evolved over time from printed handbills to television coverage of carefully orchestrated events.

Phyllis Kaniss, *Making Local News* (Chicago, Ill.: University of Chicago Press, 1991). This candid and revealing study of the motives of people involved in the media discusses the economic interests of station owners, the professional goals and constraints of news reporters, and the media strategies of politicians.

Douglas Kellner, *Television and the Crisis of Democracy* (Boulder, Colo.: Westview, 1990). In this quasi-Marxist critique of television, the author argues that the medium is a compliant tool of the conservative interests that own the networks. He concludes that television is a threat to healthy, open debate and thus undermines American democracy.

John R. MacArthur, *Second Front: Censorship and Propaganda in the Gulf War* (New York: Hill and Wang, 1992). This book evaluates media coverage of the war against Iraq as having been overly susceptible to manipulation by the military and the Bush administration. The author advocates a more adversarial form of reporting.

Russell W. Neuman, *The Future of the Mass Audience* (New York: Cambridge University Press, 1992). A study of how modern technological and economic innovations in the mass-media industry affect public communication.

Michael Parenti, *Inventing Reality: The Politics of the Mass Media* (New York: St. Martin's Press, 1986). The author looks at how and why the print and television news media distort important aspects of social and political life. Emphasis is placed on suppression of news, underlying ideological values, mechanisms of information control, media ownership, and the role of newspeople, publishers, advertisers, and the government.

Frances Fox Piven and Richard A. Cloward, *Why Americans Don't Vote* (New York: Pantheon, 1988). The authors trace the decline in voter turnout to the nineteenth century and examine the social-class basis for different levels of voter turnout among Americans.

Neil Postman, *Amusing Ourselves to Death: Public Discourse in the Age of Show Business* (New York: Viking, 1985). Postman offers a serious critique of the way television conveys information and how it undermines the public's ability to analyze the news.

Stephen A. Salmore and Barbara G. Salmore, *Candidates, Parties, and Campaigns: Electoral Politics in America* (Washington, D.C.: Congressional Quarterly Press, 1989). Identifies the central characteristics of successful and unsuccessful campaigns and discusses challenges to the role of the political parties and how the parties have responded.

Martin P. Wattenberg, *The Rise of Candidate-Centered Politics: Presidential Elections in the 1980s* (Cambridge, Mass.: Harvard University Press, 1991). In this important book, the author argues that the decline of political parties in presidential elections produces less issue content, lower levels of candidate popularity, and higher levels of polarization among voters.

PART FOUR

POLITICAL INSTITUTIONS

CHAPTER 10
The Congress

CHAPTER CONTENTS

WHAT IF . . . MEMBERS OF CONGRESS WERE LIMITED TO TWO TERMS?

We all know that members of the U.S. House of Representatives serve terms that last for two years, that members of the U.S. Senate serve terms that last for six years, and that both House and Senate members can be reelected indefinitely. In fact, some members of Congress have been able to achieve reelection so easily and so often that occasionally they have served for as long as half a century in the national legislature! Most members, of course, serve far less time in office than that, but, once elected, representatives and senators are usually hard to dethrone. What might happen, though, if members of the U.S. Congress were limited to serving say, only two terms (four years in the House or twelve years in the Senate)?

The most obvious impact of the two-term limit would come in the area of seniority. Seniority, or the length of continuous service on the record of a member of Congress in either chamber, is the single most important factor in determining who gets to be the chair of a committee, who becomes a party leader, who becomes speaker of the House or president pro tempore of the Senate, who is influential in floor debate, and who has an easier time getting his or her legislative measures adopted on the floor of Congress. With everyone limited to just two terms in office, distinctions of rank based on seniority would all but vanish. Other criteria would have to be adopted to make it possible to tell the difference between more and less influential members. As was true in the early history of Con-

gress, greater influence would probably go to those who are the best natural leaders because of telegenic magnetism, spellbinding oratorical powers, or intricate knowledge of the rules of procedure. Power on committees would likely become even more diffuse than it is now. And very young legislators would be in a much better position to make a name for themselves and to pass laws to their liking.

Relationships between Congress and the White House would quite likely be affected, too, by a change to a two-term limit on membership in Congress. Presidents, assuming that their own terms were not changed, would know that they could easily last in office longer than most members of Congress. Hence, they would not have to confront in their policy battles with Congress such powerful members as, for example, Representative Jamie Whitten from Mississippi. Whitten has been called "the permanent Secretary of Agriculture" owing to his forty-one years as chairman of the House Appropriations Committee's subcommittee on agriculture. From the presidential viewpoint, then, the two-term limit would seem to even the odds of success when dealing with members of Congress. At the same time, however, the two-term limit might increase all the more the executive power that senators and representatives fear and that has grown so greatly since World War II.

From the voters' perspective, we would all have to get used to an entirely new set of people running for

the House and Senate every few years. That would make it imperative that voters have "cues" about the personalities and issue positions taken by these new sets of candidates so they can determine how to vote. Voters would have to depend, as they do today, on political parties and interest groups to furnish information about the candidates' positions and qualifications. Unless campaigns receive equal public funding, rich or well-funded candidates would have a great advantage in buying media exposure—as is also the case today.

Interest groups might not be very interested in backing candidates, however, because a two-term legislator probably could do little for them. In fact, these short-term representatives might ignore not only interest groups but also the voters, figuring they might as well cast their congressional votes on the basis of their personal preferences.

Colorado already has term limits for legislators, and in 1992, term limits were included on the ballots in fourteen states and passed in each case. These new laws limiting the terms of legislators are facing constitutional challenges, however, and their future is therefore uncertain.

1. *Would two-term members of Congress be more in touch with the voters?*
2. *In a Congress in which members could serve for only two terms, what would seniority mean?*

Most Americans spend little time thinking about the Congress of the United States, and when they do, their opinions are frequently unflattering. After the Clarence Thomas–Anita Hill hearings and the check-overdraft scandals of 1991, the *New York Times* reported that only 23 percent of the American people approved of the job that Congress was doing. But 56 percent still approved of the performance of their own representatives. This is one of the paradoxes of the relationship between the people and the Congress. The public holds the institution in low regard while expressing satisfaction with their individual representatives.

Part of the explanation for these seemingly contradictory appraisals is that members of Congress spend considerable time and effort serving their constituents. If the federal bureaucracy makes a mistake, the senator's office tries to resolve the issue. So, what most Americans see of Congress is the work of their own representatives in their home states. The Congress, however, was created to work not just for the constituents, but for the nation as a whole. Understanding the nature of the institution and the process of lawmaking is an important part of understanding how the policies that shape our lives are made.

Why Was Congress Created?

The founders of the American republic believed that the bulk of the power that would be exercised by a national government should be in the hands of the legislature. As you will recall from Chapter 2, the authors of the Constitution were strongly influenced by their fear of tyrannical kings and powerful, unchecked rulers. They were also aware of how ineffective the confederal Congress had been during its brief existence under the Articles of Confederation.

The leading role envisioned for Congress in the new government is apparent from its primacy in the Constitution. Article I deals with the structure, the powers, and the operation of Congress, beginning in Section

John Lewis, former civil rights worker, was elected to Congress in 1986, representing a state in which he had been denied political participation twenty-five years earlier.

1 with an application of the basic principle of separation of powers: "All legislative Powers herein granted shall be vested in a Congress of the United States, which shall consist of a Senate and House of Representatives." These legislative powers are spelled out in detail in Article I and elsewhere.

The **bicameralism** of Congress—its division into two legislative houses—was in part an outgrowth of the Connecticut Compromise, which tried to balance the big-state population advantage, reflected in the House, and the small-state demand for equality, which was satisfied in the Senate. Beyond that, the two chambers of Congress also reflected the social class biases of the founders. They wished to balance the interests and the numerical superiority of the common citizen with the property interests of the less numerous landowners, bankers, and merchants. This goal was achieved by providing in Sections 2 and 3 of Article I that the House of Representatives should be elected directly by "the People," whereas the Senate was to be chosen by the elected representatives sitting in state legislatures.

The elected House, then, was to be the common person's chamber, and the nonelected Senate was to be the chamber of the wealthy, similar to the division between the House of Commons and the House of Lords in England. Also, the House was meant to represent people, whereas the Senate was meant to represent the states, in accordance with the intent of the Connecticut Compromise. The issue of who counted as part of "the People" for electing members of the House was left up to the states. As a practical matter, the electorate as defined in state laws originally included only property-owning adult white males. Women, African Americans, the impoverished, many common workers, and Native Americans could not vote for congressional representatives. The logic of separate constituencies and separate interests underlying the bicameral Congress was reinforced by differences in length of tenure. Members of the House were required to face the electorate every two years, whereas senators could serve for a much more secure term of six years—even longer than the four-year term provided for the president. Furthermore, the senators' terms were staggered so that only one-third of the senators would face election with all of the House members.

The Powers of Congress

The Constitution is both highly specific and extremely vague about the powers that Congress may exercise. The first seventeen clauses of Article I, Section 8, specify most of the **enumerated powers** of Congress—that is, powers expressly given to that body.

Expressed Powers

The enumerated, or expressed, powers of Congress include the right to impose taxes and import tariffs, borrow money, regulate interstate commerce and international trade, establish procedures for naturalizing citizens, make laws regulating bankruptcies, coin (and print) money and

BICAMERALISM
The division of a legislature into two separate assemblies.

ENUMERATED POWERS
The powers specifically granted to the national government by the Constitution. The first seventeen clauses of Article I, Section 8, specify most of the enumerated powers of Congress.

regulate its value, establish standards of weights and measures, punish counterfeiters, establish post offices and postal roads, regulate copyrights and patents, establish lower federal courts, punish pirates and others committing illegal acts on the high seas, declare war, raise and regulate an army and navy, call up and regulate the state militias to enforce laws, to suppress insurrections and to repel invasions, and to govern the District of Columbia.

The most important of the domestic powers of Congress, listed in Article I, Section 8, are the rights to collect taxes, to spend money, and to regulate commerce, whereas the most important foreign policy power is the power to declare war. Other sections of the Constitution give Congress a wide range of further powers. Generally, Congress is also able to establish rules for its own members, to regulate the electoral college, and to override a presidential veto.

Some functions are restricted to only one house. Under Article II, Section 2, the Senate must advise on, and consent to, the ratification of treaties and must accept or reject presidential nominations of ambassadors, Supreme Court justices, and "all other Officers of the United States." But the Senate may delegate to the president, the courts, or department heads the power to make lesser appointments. Congress may regulate the appellate jurisdiction of the Supreme Court, regulate relations between states, and propose amendments to the Constitution.

The amendments to the Constitution provide yet another source of congressional power. Congress must certify the election of a president and a vice president or itself choose these officers if no candidate has a majority of the electoral vote (Twelfth Amendment), may levy an income tax (Sixteenth Amendment), and determines who will be acting president in case of the death or incapacity of the president or vice president (Twentieth Amendment, Sections 3 and 4, and Twenty-fifth Amendment, Sections 2, 3, and 4). In addition, Congress is explicitly given the power to enforce, by appropriate legislation, the provisions of several other amendments.

The Necessary and Proper Clause

Beyond these numerous specific powers, Congress enjoys the right under Article I, Section 8 (the "elastic," or "necessary and proper," clause), "to make all Laws which shall be necessary and proper for carrying into Execution the foregoing Powers [of Article I], and all other Powers vested by this Constitution in the Government of the United States, or in any Department or Officer thereof." This vague statement of congressional responsibilities has set the stage for a greatly expanded role for the national government relative to the states. It has also constituted, at least in theory, a check on the expansion of presidential powers. By continuing to delegate powers to the executive branch, however, Congress has over time reduced the role it might otherwise play in national and international affairs.

The Constitution provides the foundation of congressional powers. Yet a complete understanding of the role that Congress plays requires a broader study of the functions that the national legislature performs for the American political system.

Did You Know . . . That under Senate rules, based on the number of voting-age constituents in the state, a senator from New York was entitled to mail over twenty-seven million sheets of government-supplied paper in the form of newsletters in 1992?

The Functions of Congress

Congress, as an institution of government, is expected by its members, by the public, and by other centers of political power to perform a number of functions. Our perceptions of how good a job Congress is doing overall are tied closely to evaluations of whether and how it fulfills certain specific tasks. These tasks include the following:

1. Lawmaking activities.
2. Service to constituents.
3. Representation of diverse interests.
4. Oversight of the manner in which laws are implemented.
5. Educating the public about national issues and setting the terms for national debate.
6. Resolving conflicts in American society.

The Lawmaking Function

LAWMAKING
The process of deciding the legal rules that govern our society. Such laws may regulate minor affairs or establish broad national policies.

The principal and most obvious function of any legislature is **lawmaking**. Congress is the highest elected body in the country charged with making binding rules for all Americans. Lawmaking requires decisions about the size of the federal budget, about issues such as abortion or school busing, and about the long-term prospects for war or peace. This does not mean, however, that Congress initiates most of the ideas for legislation that it eventually considers. Most of the bills that Congress acts on originate in the executive branch, and many other bills are traceable to interest groups and political party organizations. Through processes of compromise and **logrolling** (offering to support a fellow member's bill in exchange for that member's promise to support your bill in the future), backers of legislation attempt to fashion a winning majority coalition.

LOGROLLING
An arrangement by which two or more members of Congress agree in advance to support each other's bills.

Service to Constituents

CASEWORK
Personal work for constituents by members of Congress.

Individual members of Congress are expected by their constituents to act as brokers between private citizens and the imposing, often faceless, federal government. **Casework** is the usual form taken by this function of providing service to constituents. The legislator and his or her staff spend a considerable portion of their time on casework activity, such as tracking down a missing Social Security check, explaining the meaning of particular bills to people who may be affected by them, promoting a local business interest, or interceding with a regulatory agency on behalf of constituents who disagree with proposed bureaucratic rules and regulations. Legislators and analysts of congressional behavior regard this **ombudsman** role as an activity that strongly benefits the members of Congress. A government characterized by a large, confusing bureaucracy and complex public programs offers innumerable opportunities for legislators to come to the assistance of (usually) grateful constituents. Morris Fiorina suggests somewhat mischievously that senators and representatives prefer to maintain bureaucratic confusion in order to maximize their opportunities for performing good deeds on behalf of their constituents:

OMBUDSMAN
An individual in the role of hearing and investigating complaints by private individuals against public officials or agencies.

Some poor, aggrieved constituent becomes enmeshed in the tentacles of an evil bureaucracy and calls upon Congressman St. George to do battle with the dragon. . . . In dealing with the bureaucracy, the congressman is not merely one vote of 435. Rather, he is a nonpartisan power, someone whose phone call snaps an office to attention. He is not kept on hold. The constituent who receives aid believes that his congressman and his congressman alone got results.[1]

The Representation Function

If constituency service carries with it nothing but benefits for most members of Congress, the function of **representation** is less certain and even carries with it some danger that the legislator will lose his or her bid for reelection. Generally, representation means that the many competing interests in society should be represented in Congress. It follows that Congress should be a body acting slowly and deliberately and that its foremost concern should be to maintain a carefully crafted balance of power among competing interests.

The Trustee View of Representation.   How is representation to be achieved? There are basically two points of view on this issue. The first approach is that legislators should act as **trustees** of the broad interests of the entire society and that they should vote against the narrow interests of their constituents as their conscience and their perception of national needs dictate.

The Instructed-Delegate View of Representation.   Directly opposed to the trustee view of representation is the notion that the members of Congress should behave as **instructed delegates;** that is, they should mirror the views of the majority of the constituents who elected them to power in the first place. On the surface, this approach is plausible and rewarding. For it to work, however, we must assume that constituents actually have well-formed views on the issues that are decided in Congress and, further, that they have clear-cut preferences about these issues. Neither condition is likely to be satisfied very often. Most people generally do not have well-articulated views on major issues, and, among those who do, there frequently is no clear majority position but rather a range of often conflicting minority perspectives.

In a major study of the attitudes held by members of Congress about their proper role as representatives, Roger Davidson found that neither a pure trustee view nor a pure instructed-delegate view was held by most legislators. Davidson's sampling of members of Congress showed that about the same proportion endorsed the trustee approach (28 percent) and delegate approach (23 percent) to representation, but the clear preference was for the **politico** position—which combines both perspectives in a pragmatic mix.[2]

Did You Know . . . That you can get information on the status of legislation in either the House or the Senate, whether committee hearings have been held, and the dates of upcoming hearings by calling the Legislative Status Office of Congress, at (202) 225-1772?

REPRESENTATION
The function of Congress as elected officials to represent the views of their constituents.

TRUSTEES
The idea that a legislator should act according to his or her conscience and the broad interests of the entire society, often associated with the British statesman Edmund Burke.

INSTRUCTED DELEGATES
The concept that legislators are agents of the voters who elected them and that they should vote according to the views of their constituents regardless of their own personal assessments.

POLITICO
The legislative role that combines the delegate and trustee concepts. The legislator varies the role according to the issue under consideration.

---

[1]Morris Fiorina, *Congress: Keystone of the Washington Establishment* (New Haven, Conn.: Yale University Press, 1977), pp. 44–47.
[2]Roger Davidson, *The Role of the Congressman* (New York: Pegasus, 1969), p. 117.

OVERSIGHT
The responsibility Congress has for following up on laws it has enacted to ensure that they are being enforced and administered in the way in which they were intended.

LEGISLATIVE VETO
A provision in a bill reserving to Congress or to a congressional committee the power to reject an act or regulation of a national agency by majority vote; declared unconstitutional by the Supreme Court in 1983.

AGENDA SETTING
The power to determine which public policy questions will be debated or considered by Congress.

The Oversight Function

Oversight of the bureaucracy is essential if the decisions made by Congress are to have any force. **Oversight** is the process by which Congress follows up on the laws it has enacted to ensure that they are being enforced and administered in the way Congress intended. This is done by holding committee hearings and investigations, changing the size of an agency's budget, and cross-examining high-level presidential nominees to head major agencies. Also, until 1983, Congress could refuse to accede to proposed rules and regulations by resorting to the **legislative veto,** which allowed one, or sometimes both, chambers of Congress to disapprove of an executive rule within a specified period of time by a simple majority vote and thereby prevent its enforcement. In 1983, however, the Supreme Court ruled that such a veto violated the separation of powers mandated by the Constitution, because the president had no power to veto the legislative action. Thus, the legislative veto was declared unconstitutional.[3]

Senators and representatives increasingly see their oversight function as a critically important part of their legislative activities. In part, oversight is related to the concept of constituency service, particularly when Congress investigates alleged arbitrariness or wrongdoing by bureaucratic agencies.

The Public-Education Function

Educating the public is a function that is exercised whenever Congress holds public hearings, exercises oversight over the bureaucracy, or engages in committee and floor debate on such major issues and topics as political assassinations, aging, drugs, or the concerns of small businesses. In so doing, Congress presents a range of viewpoints on pressing national questions. Congress also decides what issues will come up for discussion and decision; **agenda setting** is a major facet of its public education function.

The Conflict-Resolution Function

Congress is commonly seen as an institution for resolving conflicts within American society. Organized interest groups and representatives of different racial, religious, economic, and ideological interests look on Congress as an access point for airing their grievances and possibly for stimulating government action on their behalf. A logical extension of the representation function, this focus on conflict resolution puts Congress in the role of trying to resolve the differences among competing points of view by passing laws to accommodate as many interested parties as possible. Clearly, this is not always achieved. Every legislative decision results in some winners and some losers. Congress is commonly regarded as the place to go in Washington to get a friendly hearing or a desired policy result. To the extent that Congress does accommodate competing interests, it tends to build support for the entire political process by all branches of government.

---

[3]*Immigration and Naturalization Service v. Chadha,* 454 U.S. 812 (1983).

House–Senate Differences

▼

The preceding functions of Congress describe how that body is expected to perform and what it does as a whole. To understand better what goes on in the national legislature, however, we need to examine the effects of bicameralism, for Congress is composed of two markedly different—although coequal—chambers. Although the Senate and the House of Representatives exist within the same legislative institution, each has developed certain distinctive features that clearly distinguish life on one end of Capitol Hill from conditions on the other (the Senate wing is on the north side of the Capitol building, and the House wing is on the south side). A summary of these differences is given in Table 10-1.

Size and Rules

The central difference is simply that the House is much larger than the Senate. There are 435 representatives, plus delegates from the District of Columbia, Puerto Rico, Guam, and the Virgin Islands (who have very limited voting opportunities), in the House, compared with just 100 senators.[4] This size difference means that a greater number of formal rules are needed to govern activity in the House, whereas correspondingly looser procedures can be followed in the less crowded Senate. This dif-

---

[4]In 1993, the Democratic majority in the House voted in a rule giving delegates from the District of Columbia and the territories votes in the Committee of the Whole. However, if those votes decide the issue, the vote must be cast again immediately without the delegates. *Congressional Quarterly Weekly Review*, March 13, 1993, p. 573.

TABLE 10-1 ■ **Differences between the House and the Senate**

House*	Senate*
Members chosen from local districts	Members chosen from an entire state
Two-year term	Six-year term
Originally elected by voters	Originally (until 1913) elected by state legislatures
May impeach (indict) federal officials	May convict federal officials of impeachable offenses
Larger (435 voting members)	Smaller (100 members)
More formal rules	Fewer rules and restrictions
Debate limited	Debate extended
Floor action controlled	Unanimous consent rules
Less prestige and less individual notice	More prestige and media attention
Originates bills for raising revenues	Power to advise the president on, and consent to, presidential appointments and treaties
Local or narrow leadership	National leadership

*Some of these differences, such as the term of office, are provided for in the Constitution, while others, such as debate rules, are not.

Did You Know ... That fewer than three in ten people can name the House member from their district and fewer than half can name even one of the two senators from their state?

RULES COMMITTEE
A standing committee of the House of Representatives that provides special rules under which specific bills can be debated, amended, and considered by the House.

FILIBUSTERING
In the Senate, unlimited debate to halt action on a particular bill.

CLOTURE
A method to close off debate and to bring the matter under consideration to a vote in the Senate.

ference is most obvious in the rules governing debate on the floors of the two chambers.

The Senate normally permits extended debate on all issues that arise before it, whereas the House operates with an elaborate system in which its **Rules Committee** normally proposes time limitations on debate for any bill, and a majority of the entire body accepts or modifies those suggested time limits. As a consequence of its stricter time limits on debate, and despite its greater size, the House is often able to act on legislation more quickly than the Senate.

Debate and Filibustering

According to historians, the Senate tradition of unlimited debate, which is known as **filibustering,** dates back to 1790, when a proposal to move the United States capitol from New York to Philadelphia was stalled by such time-wasting tactics. This unlimited-debate tradition—which also existed in the House until 1811[5]—is not absolute, however.

Under Senate Rule 22, debate may be ended by invoking **cloture,** or shutting off discussion on a bill. Recently amended in 1975 and 1979, Rule 22 states that debate may be closed off on a bill if sixteen senators sign a petition requesting it and if, after two days have elapsed, three-fifths of the entire membership (sixty votes, assuming no vacancies) vote for cloture. After cloture is invoked, each senator may speak for a maximum of one hour on a bill before a vote is taken.

The Senate made further changes in its filibuster rule in 1979. It extended Rule 22 to provide that a final vote must take place within one hundred hours of debate after cloture has been imposed, and it further limited the use of multiple amendments to stall postcloture final action on a bill.

Prestige

As a consequence of the greater size of the House, representatives generally cannot achieve as much individual recognition and public prestige as can members of the Senate. Senators, especially those who openly express presidential ambitions, are better able to gain media exposure and to establish careers as spokespersons for large national constituencies. To obtain recognition for his or her activities, a member of the House must either survive in office long enough to join the ranks of the leadership on committees or within the party or become an expert on some specialized aspect of legislative policy—such as tax laws, the environment, or education.

Other Differences

Other major differences between the House and the Senate are unrelated to the size of each chamber. The Constitution, in Article I, provides that members of the House serve shorter terms (two years) than senators (six

[5]William J. Keefe and Morris S. Ogul, *The American Legislative Process,* 7th ed. (Englewood Cliffs, N.J.: Prentice Hall, 1989).

Senator Strom Thurmond leaves the chamber after completing a filibuster that lasted for twenty-four hours and eighteen minutes.

years). All 435 voting members of the House must run for reelection in November of even-numbered years, but only about one-third of the Senate seats are contested in the same biennial election. Before passage of the Seventeenth Amendment in 1913, all senators were not even elected by direct popular vote; they were instead appointed by state legislatures. The longer term in office generally gives senators more time to act as national leaders before facing the electorate again.

Government institutions are given life by the people who work in them and shape them as political structures. Who, then, are the members of Congress, and how are they elected?

Congresspersons and the Citizenry: A Comparison

Members of the U.S. Senate and the U.S. House of Representatives are not typical American citizens (Table 10-2). Members of Congress are, of course, older than most Americans, partly because of constitutional age requirements and partly because a good deal of political experience is normally an advantage in running for national office. Members of Congress are also disproportionately white, male, Protestant, and trained in higher-status occupations.

Some recent trends in the social characteristics of Congress should be noted, however. The average age of members of the 103d Congress is 52.9 years—a slight decrease from an average age of 53 three decades ago. The Protestant domination of Congress has been loosened, with substantial increases being made in the representation of Jews and Roman Catholics. "Higher-status" Protestant denominations, notably Episcopalians and Presbyterians, are overrepresented in Congress, whereas Baptists and Lutherans are underrepresented, relative to their numbers among American Protestants.

Lawyers are by far the largest occupational group among congresspersons: 58 senators and 181 representatives in the One Hundred and Third Congress reported that they were trained in the legal profession.

TABLE 10-2 ■ Characteristics of the 103d Congress (1993–1995)

	U.S. Population (1990)	House	Senate
Age (Median)	33.0	51.7	58
Percent Minority	28.0	15	4
Religion			
Percent church members	61.0	94	94
Percent Roman Catholic	39.0	27	23
Percent Protestant	56.0	60	61
Percent Jewish	4.0	7.3	10
Percent Female	51.9	11	6
Percent with College Degrees	21.4	98	99
Occupation			
Percent lawyers	2.8	42	58
Percent blue-collar workers	20.1	0	0
Family Income			
Percent of families earning over $50,000 annually	22.0	100	100
Personal Wealth			
Percent of population with assets over $1 million	0.7	16	33

The proportion of lawyers in the House is lower now than at nearly any time in the last thirty years, however. Members of this Congress reported other previous occupations as follows: 27 in agriculture, 155 business-persons or bankers, 77 educators, 5 engineers, 33 journalists, 61 labor leaders, 10 law enforcement officers, 6 medical doctors, 9 in politics and public service, 3 clergymen, 2 in aeronautics, 2 in the military, 4 in professional sports, and 2 actors—Fred Grandy (R., Iowa), who starred in the series "Love Boat," and Ben Jones (D., Ga.), who acted in the "Dukes of Hazzard."

Congressional Elections

The process of electing members of Congress is decentralized. Congressional elections are operated by the individual state governments, which must conform to the rules established by the Constitution and by national statutes. The Constitution states that representatives are to be elected every second year by popular ballot, and the number of seats awarded to each state is to be determined by the results of the decennial census. Each state has at least one representative, with most congressional districts having about a half million residents. Senators are elected by popular vote (since the passage of the Seventeenth Amendment) every six years; approximately one-third of the seats are chosen every two years. Each state has two senators. Under Article I, Section 4, of the Constitution, state legislatures are given control over "The Times, Places and Manner of holding Elections for Senators and Representatives"; however, "the Congress may at any time by Law make or alter such Regulations."

PROFILE

Ileana Ros-Lehtinen

"Now it's time for healing. I know there are a lot of people out there who feel alienated."

In a special congressional election in Florida in 1989, the Republican candidate won a seat that had been Democratic for the past forty years and was held much of that time by one person, Claude Pepper. Even more unusual than the change of parties were the characteristics of the victor. Ileana Ros-Lehtinen, a naturalized American citizen who was born in Cuba, defeated a native-born American citizen for the seat.

Ros-Lehtinen left Cuba as a child when her parents fled the Castro regime. During her time in the state legislature, she was known for her service to constituents. Her views are generally conservative; she favors the prolife position on abortion, for example. As a member of Congress, one of the major challenges confronting her is not ideology but rather the job of smoothing relations between the Hispanic community and other ethnic groups.

During the campaign, Ros-Lehtinen's Latin American heritage overshadowed most other issues. Her opponent urged voters to keep the congressional position "an American seat." The voting was described as "an ethnic war," with turnout sharply divided along racial and ethnic lines. Such conflict is not new in Miami, which is part of the congressional district Ros-Lehtinen serves. Her victory, however, was

regarded by some as a turning point in the political balance of power between Hispanic and non-Hispanic residents of the area. The election demonstrated the political effect of the growth in the number of new Americans coming from Latin America and Asia.

The attempt to portray Ros-Lehtinen as un-American was not only ethically questionable but also misleading. She is a conservative Republican who spent seven years in the Florida legislature before running for Congress. Perhaps more important, she beat her opponent by mastering the rules of American democracy—by using a successful campaign strategy and building the necessary organization to implement it. The issue of Ros-Lehtinen's ethnic heritage was, in fact, used by both sides in the campaign; it turned out to be an advantage for her. By 1992, she had increased her winning margin to 67 percent, demonstrating her popularity with voters of many ethnic backgrounds.

Candidates for Congressional Elections

Candidates for seats in Congress are generally recruited by local political party activists. Potential candidates who are selected or self-selected usually share many of the social characteristics of their prospective constituents. Religion, race, and ethnic background are especially important considerations. Prior political experience may be an important asset, especially in states with strong political parties or restrictive nominating systems.

The Nomination Process. Since the early part of the century, control over the process of nominating congressional candidates has been shifting from party conventions—which reformers charged with being corrupt and

DIRECT PRIMARIES
An intraparty election in which the voters select the candidates who will run on a party's ticket in the subsequent general election.

PARTY IDENTIFIERS
Those who identify themselves with a political party.

boss-controlled—to **direct primaries** in which **party identifiers** in the electorate select the candidate who will carry that party's endorsement into the actual election. All fifty states currently use the direct primary to select party nominees for senator or representative. In general, there are more candidates running and the competition is more intense when a party is strong and a November victory is likely.

Who Wins, and Why?   Most candidates win through the effectiveness of their personal organizations, although sometimes with assistance from the state party organization. It is important to realize that congressional candidates have only a loose affiliation to the party at the national and state level. Even the effect of presidential "coattails," in which a victorious president helps bring into office legislators who would not have won otherwise, is minimal. For example, Richard Nixon's smashing victory over George McGovern in 1972, with 61 percent of the popular vote and 520 out of 538 electoral votes, resulted in a gain of only twelve Republican seats in the House.

In midterm congressional elections—those held between presidential contests—voter turnout falls sharply. In these elections party affiliation of the voters who turn out is a stronger force in deciding election outcomes, and the party controlling the White House normally loses seats in Congress. Table 10-3 shows the pattern for midterm elections since 1942. The result is a fragmentation of party authority and a loosening of ties between Congress and the president.

The Power of Incumbency

The power of incumbency in the outcome of congressional elections cannot be overemphasized. Table 10-4 shows that the overwhelming majority of representatives and a smaller proportion of senators who decide to run for reelection are successful. This conclusion holds for both presidential-election and midterm-election years.

David R. Mayhew argues that the pursuit of reelection is the strongest motivation behind the activities of members of Congress.[6] The reelection goal is pursued in three major ways: by *advertising*, by *credit claiming*, and by *position taking*. Advertising includes using the mass media, making personal appearances with constituents, and sending newsletters—all to produce a favorable image and to make the incumbent's name a household word. Members of Congress try to present themselves as informed, experienced, and responsive to people's needs. Credit claiming focuses on the things a legislator claims to have done to benefit his or her constituents—by fulfilling the congressional casework function or by supplying material goods in the form of, say, a new post office or a construction project, such as a dam or a highway. Position taking occurs when an incumbent explains his or her voting record on key issues, makes public statements of general support for presidential decisions, or indicates that he or she specifically supports positions on key issues, such as gun control or anti-inflation policies. Position taking carries with it certain risks, as the

TABLE 10-3 ■ Midterm Losses by the Party of the President: 1942–1990

Seats Lost by the Party of the President in the House of Representatives	
1942	−45 (D)
1946	−55 (D)
1950	−29 (D)
1954	−18 (R)
1958	−47 (R)
1962	− 4 (D)
1966	−47 (D)
1970	−12 (R)
1974	−48 (R)
1978	−15 (D)
1982	−26 (R)
1986	− 5 (R)
1990	− 8 (R)

[6]David R. Mayhew, *Congress: The Electoral Connection* (New Haven, Conn.: Yale University Press, 1974).

incumbent may lose support by disagreeing with the attitudes of large numbers of constituents. Another view, put forward by Richard Fenno, Jr., is that members develop a "homestyle" to build support among their constituents.

The Shakeup of 1992

Following the Iran–contra and savings and loan imbroglios and a period of legislative deadlock, the 1990 midterm elections were expected to result in a large number of defeats for Republican incumbents. Instead, the Democrats gained only nine seats. This loss of Republican incumbents for a sitting president was quite tolerable when compared with Reagan's loss of twenty-six seats in 1982 and Carter's loss of fifteen seats in the 1978 midterm contests.

Then came the check-kiting scandal of 1991 and other embarrassments, plus continued gridlock in Congress. Public disgust was reflected in term-limitation legislation in several states. A record number of the legislators who were up for reelection in 1992 decided to retire rather than face bitter campaigns. In some cases, the redistricting of congressional seats left two sitting members competing against each other, or district boundaries were

Did You Know . . . That in 1992, senators and their staff sent more than two million pages of fax messages—20,000 per senator—and printed 431,172,000 pages of material?

TABLE 10-4 ■ **The Power of Incumbency**

	Presidential-year Elections							Midterm Elections					
	1968	1972	1976	1980	1984	1988	1992	1970	1974	1978	1982	1986	1990
House													
Number of incumbent candidates	409	390	384	398	409	409	368	401	391	382	393	393	407
Reelected	396	365	368	361	390	402	325	379	343	358	352	385	391
Percentage of total	96.8	93.6	95.8	90.7	95.4	98.3	88.9	94.5	87.7	93.7	90.1	98.0	96.1
Defeated	13	25	16	37	19	7	43	22	48	24	39	8	16
In primary	4	12	3	6	3	1	19	10	8	5	10	2	1
In general election	9	13	13	31	16	6	24	12	40	19	29	6	15
Senate													
Number of incumbent candidates	28	27	25	29	29	27	28	31	27	25	30	28	32
Reelected	20	20	16	16	26	23	23	24	23	15	28	21	31
Percentage of total	71.4	74.1	64.0	55.2	89.6	85	82.1	77.4	85.2	60.0	93.3	75.0	96.9
Defeated	8	7	9	13	3	4	5	7	4	10	2	7	1
In primary	4	2	0	4	0	0	1	1	2	3	0	0	0
In general election	4	5	9	9	3	4	4	6	2	7	2	7	1

SOURCES: Norman Orstein, Thomas Mann, and Michael Malbin, *Vital Statistics on Congress, 1991–1992* (Washington, D.C.: Congressional Quarterly Press, 1992), pp. 56–57; *Congressional Quarterly Weekly Report*, November 7, 1992, pp. 3551, 3576.

Did You Know ... That Congress has been exempt from the Occupational Safety and Health Act, the Freedom of Information Act, the Civil Rights Act of 1964, the Equal Pay Act, the Privacy Act, the Age Discrimination in Employment Act, and the District of Columbia health, fire, safety, and building construction codes, among other laws?

redrawn in such a way as to make reelection of the incumbent impossible. For a few representatives there was a financial incentive as well: They belonged to the group that would be allowed to convert campaign funds to personal use if they retired before the 1992 elections.

When the polls closed on November 2, 1992, it was clear that this had been an unusual congressional election. With only forty-three incumbent Representatives defeated in the election, it appeared that the voters were not so angry at Congress as the public outrage at the various scandals had suggested earlier in the year. However, forty-three incumbent losses was the greatest number since the Watergate disaster of 1974, when forty-eight representatives lost.

The 1992 congressional election changed the makeup of the legislature much more by electing historic numbers of minority legislators and female legislators. In the 103d Congress, 15 percent of the members represented ethnic minorities. At the same time, the number of women elected to the House of Representatives doubled, with forty-eight women taking seats in that chamber in the 103d Congress.

The so-called "Year of the Woman" also affected the United States Senate. Four new female senators—Barbara Boxer and Diane Feinstein of California, Carol Moseley Braun of Illinois, and Patty Murray of Washington—joined the two already in the chamber—Barbara Mikulski of Maryland and Nancy Landon Kassebaum of Kansas. All four of the new female senators are Democrats with liberal positions on many issues, and one, Carol Moseley Braun, is the first female African American ever to join the upper chamber. The 103d Congress also saw the second Native American senator, Ben Nighthorse Campbell (see the *Profile* in this chapter) take his seat.

Voters clearly split their tickets in the congressional election of 1992. Although Bill Clinton received 43 percent of the vote for president and won a solid victory in the electoral college, he had no coattails in Congress. Republicans actually gained ten seats in the House of Representatives, although some analysts had expected them to gain more from redistricting. In the Senate, the Democrats maintained their majority over the Republicans, although several incumbents on both sides were defeated. President Bill Clinton began his term of office with a Democratic majority

The 1992 elections brought four new women to the U.S. Senate. *From left to right:* Barbara Boxer, California; Carol Moseley Braun, Illinois; Dianne Feinstein, California; Patty Murray, Washington.

PROFILE

Ben Nighthorse Campbell

"Sometimes I think there ought to be more Indians in Congress, or else no Indians, because its damn tough being the only Indian."

The seventh Native American ever to serve in the House of Representatives, Ben Nighthorse Campbell has established a reputation in Congress as an independent Democrat who is not afraid to speak up for his constituents in rural Colorado, as well as for his own heritage.

Raised in Auburn, California, Campbell spent part of his childhood in an orphanage—his father, a Cheyenne jeweler, was an alcoholic, and his mother had tuberculosis. Campbell worked his way through college as a truck driver and later became a police officer. He earned a gold medal for judo in the 1964 Olympics. Later, Campbell turned to ranching in western Colorado where he breeds and trains quarter horses. He has also followed his father's vocation as a jeweler.

By the 1980s, Campbell claims, he was frustrated by "plastic politicians—professional politicians who have nothing to do with their lives"—and decided to run for election to Congress.* He defeated an incumbent Republican in his first

race. Since then, Campbell has been reelected twice with landslide margins. His easy victories and ability to represent the interests of rural westerners put pressure on him to run for higher office. In 1992, after the decision by Senator Tim Wirth to step down, Campbell decided to run for the Senate and won, becoming the second Native American ever to hold a Senate seat.

Campbell's political positions are rooted in his experiences and his ethnicity. He is conservative on many economic matters, voting with Republicans against some liberal measures, particularly if the measures would place a significant burden on small businesses. He is very

conscious of the difficulties of running a business and sometimes expresses impatience with colleagues who have never worked in an enterprise. He is also fairly conservative on environmental issues, voting against environmental laws that he believes will take away the land of ranchers. As he puts it, "I've never met an environmentalist yet who is in favor of an oil well, a coal mine, or a dam. You'd like to think that people out here, who make a living from the land, would have something more to say about it."**

Campbell is supportive of the Indian people, although only 1.4 percent of his constituents are of Native-American descent. He sponsored a bill to change the name of the Custer Battlefield National Monument in Montana, a name that memorializes the white man, to the Little Bighorn Battlefield National Monument. He also has not shied away from issues concerning the relations between Native Americans and whites, even though his constituents are predominantly white.

*Alison A. Knocke and Albert G. Holzinger, "Business People in Congress," *Nation's Business*, March 1989, p. 58R.
**Dirk Johnson, "Uneasy Role of Congress's Sole Indian," *New York Times*, August 28, 1991.

in both houses and pledges of cooperation from the Democratic leadership who looked forward to working with a Democratic White House for the first time since 1976.

Congressional Reapportionment

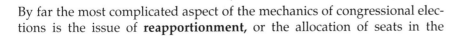

By far the most complicated aspect of the mechanics of congressional elections is the issue of **reapportionment,** or the allocation of seats in the

REAPPORTIONMENT
The redrawing of legislative district lines to accord with the existing population distribution.

REDISTRICTING
The redrawing of district lines within the states.

JUSTICIABLE QUESTION
A question that may be raised and reviewed in court.

House to each state after each census, and **redistricting,** the redrawing of the boundaries of the districts within each state.

In a landmark six-to-two vote in 1962, the Supreme Court made reapportionment a **justiciable** (that is, a reviewable) **question** in the Tennessee case of *Baker v. Carr*[7] by invoking the Fourteenth Amendment principle that no state can deny to any person "the equal protection of the laws." This principle was applied directly in the 1964 ruling, *Reynolds v. Sims,*[8] when the Court held that *both* chambers of a state legislature must be apportioned with equal populations in each district. This "one man, one vote" principle was applied to congressional districts in the 1964 case of *Wesberry v. Sanders,*[9] based on Article I, Section 2, of the Constitution, which requires that congresspersons be chosen "by the People of the several States."

Severe malapportionment of congressional districts prior to *Wesberry* had resulted in some districts containing two or three times the populations of other districts in the same state, thereby diluting the effect of a vote cast in the larger districts. This system had generally benefited the

[7]369 U.S. 186 (1962).
[8]377 U.S. 533 (1964).
[9]376 U.S. 1 (1964).

FIGURE 10-1 ■ The Original Gerrymander

The practice of "gerrymandering"—the excessive manipulation of the shape of a legislative district to benefit a certain incumbent or party—is probably as old as the republic, but the name originated in 1812. In that year, the Massachusetts legislature carved out of Essex County a district that historian John Fiske said had a "dragonlike contour." When the painter Gilbert Stuart saw the misshapen district, he penciled in a head, wings, and claws and exclaimed: "That will do for a salamander!"—to which editor Benjamin Russell replied: "Better say a Gerrymander"—after Elbridge Gerry, then governor of Massachusetts.
SOURCE: *Congressional Quarterly's Guide to Congress,* 3d ed. (Washington, D.C.: Congressional Quarterly Press, 1982), p. 695.

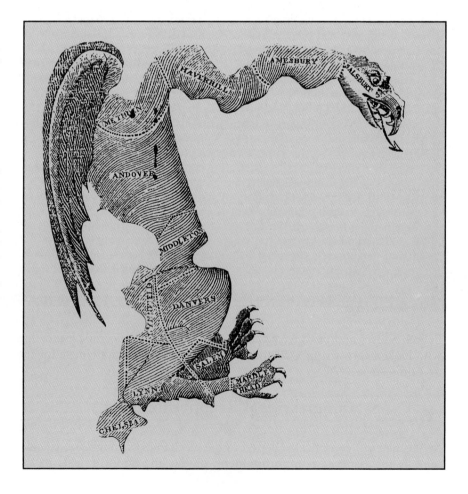

conservative populations of rural areas and small towns and harmed the interests of the more heavily populated and liberal urban areas. In fact, suburban areas have benefited the most from the *Wesberry* ruling, as suburbs account for an increasingly larger proportion of the nation's population, and cities include a correspondingly smaller segment of the population.

Although the general issue of reapportionment has been dealt with fairly successfully by the one man, one vote principle, the specific case of **gerrymandering** has not yet been resolved. This term refers to the legislative boundary-drawing tactics that were used by Elbridge Gerry, the governor of Massachusetts, in the 1812 elections (see Figure 10-1). A district is said to have been gerrymandered when its shape is substantially altered by the dominant party in a state legislature to maximize its electoral strength at the expense of the minority party. This can be achieved by either concentrating the opposition's voter support in as few districts as possible or diffusing the minority party's strength by spreading it thinly across many districts.

In 1986, the Supreme Court heard a case that challenged gerrymandered congressional districts in Indiana. The Court ruled for the first time that redistricting for the political benefit of one group could be challenged on constitutional grounds. In this specific case, *Davis v. Bandemer*,[10] the Court, however, did not agree that the districts were unfairly drawn because it could not be proved that a group of voters would be consistently deprived of its influence at the polls as a result of the new districts. Figure 10-2 shows a contemporary gerrymander.

---

[10]478 U.S. 109 (1986).

GERRYMANDERING
The drawing of legislative district boundary lines for the purpose of obtaining partisan or factional advantage. A district is said to be gerrymandered when its shape is manipulated by the dominant party in the state legislature to maximize electoral strength at the expense of the minority party.

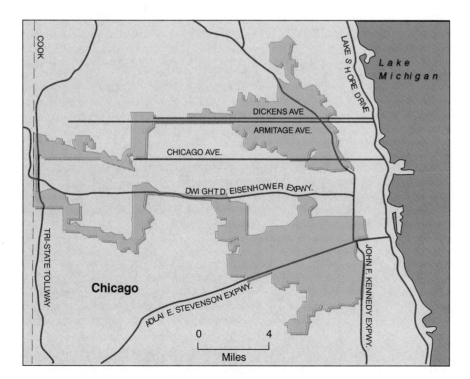

FIGURE 10-2 ■ A Modern Gerrymander

After the 1990 census, Illinois Republicans won control of the redistricting process for the first time in two decades. They worked creatively to change the balance of power to favor Republican candidates for the House of Representatives and for the Illinois General Assembly, while at the same time creating opportunities for minority representation. One example of their work is the Fourth Congressional District in Chicago. Known as the ''earmuff'' district because it looks like a pair of earmuffs, the district stretches fifteen miles from the northwest side of the city west to the county line and then returns east another fifteen miles. These corridors create a majority Hispanic district by joining the Puerto Rican and Mexican communities.

Pay, Perks, and Privileges

Compared with the average American citizen, members of Congress are well paid. In 1993, annual congressional salaries were $129,500. Honoraria from outside speeches are limited to $26,850 for House members and $35,800 for senators. In addition, legislators elected before 1980 can convert unused campaign funds to their personal use after retirement. As described in the *Politics and People* feature in this chapter, legislators have many benefits not available to most workers.

Members of Congress also benefit in other ways from belonging to a select group. They have access to private Capitol Hill gymnasium facilities, get low-cost haircuts, receive free, close-in parking at National and Dulles airports near Washington, and get six free parking spaces in Capitol Hill garages—plus one free outdoor Capitol parking slot. They also avoid parking tickets because of their congressional license plates and are not required to comply with labor laws in dealing with their staffs. They eat in a subsidized dining room and take advantage of free plants from the Botanical Gardens for their offices, free medical care, an inexpensive but generous pension plan, liberal travel allowances, and special tax considerations.

FRANKING
A policy that enables members of Congress to send material through the mail by substituting their facsimile signature (frank) for postage.

Members of Congress are also granted generous **franking** privileges that permit them to mail newsletters, surveys, and other letters to their constituents. The annual cost of congressional mail has risen from $11 million in 1971 to almost $200 million today. Typically, the costs for these mailings rise enormously during election years.

Permanent Professional Staffs

More than 38,660 people are employed in the Capitol Hill bureaucracy. About half of this total consists of personal and committee staff members. The personal staff includes office clerks and secretaries; professionals who deal with media relations, draft legislation, and satisfy constituency requests for service; and staffers who maintain local offices in the member's home district or state. The average Senate office on Capitol Hill employs about thirty staff members, and twice that number work on the personal staff of senators from the most populous states. House office staffs are typically about half as large as those of the Senate.

Congress also benefits from the expertise of the professional staff of agencies that were created to produce information for members of the House and Senate—resources comparable to those available to the president and the rest of the executive branch. The Congressional Research Service (CRS), a section of the Library of Congress, is an information and fact-finding center for legislators and their assistants. It furnishes a computer-based record of the contents and current legislative status of major bills that are under consideration. This record can be reviewed by staff members using computer terminals available in most offices. The General Accounting Office (GAO) audits the spending of money by federal agencies, investigates agency practices, and makes policy recommendations to Congress, especially concerning financial activities of the government. The Office of Technology Assessment (OTA), as yet little used, is designed to evaluate national technology policy in such areas as

---

POLITICS AND PEOPLE

It's a Tough Job, but It Has Great Benefits

Approval of Congress dropped to a new low in 1992. Only 23 percent of Americans approved of the legislature's performance. The discontent was fueled by the check-kiting scandal in the House bank, which cast a new light on the many perquisites of being a legislator. Ordinary Americans were angered by the seeming congressional indifference to the problem of bouncing checks and by the legislators' surprise that the public disapproved of congressional perks.

Not only did members of the House of Representatives have a private bank from which they could borrow against future paychecks, but they also received numerous other privileges not available to most Americans. Members of Congress now receive a salary of $129,500, far above that of most managers in the private sector. Among their perks are the following:

■ The House sergeant-at-arms sees to it that D.C. parking tickets are dismissed if the legislator says that he or she was on official business.

■ Stationery stores in the House and Senate sell gift items as well as stationery at cost.

■ Airport parking is free for 147 members at a time. The spaces are available on a first come, first served basis.

■ Haircuts are cheap—$5.00 on the House side and $4.50 on the Senate side. (These prices are for men. There are no comparable services for women members.)

■ Free health care, including physical examinations and tests, is available.

■ Members are able to reserve accommodations in five lodges run by the National Park Services in the Grand Tetons, Cape Hatteras, Shenandoah National Park, and the Virgin Islands, and on Catoctin Mountain. The lodges are not available to the public.

■ Congressional members and staff receive free assistance from the Internal Revenue Service from February to April 15 each year.

■ There are secret offices within the basement and corners of the Senate for 77 of the 100 senators. Many of these have been decorated with antique furniture from the collection of the sergeant-at-arms. No one has a key to these private hideaways except the senators and those to whom they choose to give keys.

Many legislators defend these perks as small benefits that make them more efficient as legislators. In fact, it does a constituent little good to have his or her representative spend hours looking for a parking space at the airport. But when legislators regard these benefits as routine and fail to show appreciation for them— or abuse them—they risk public hostility. Indeed, many of the freshman legislators in 1993 initiated efforts to curtail some of these privileges.

---

energy and the environment. The Congressional Budget Office (CBO) advises Congress on the anticipated effect on the economy of government expenditures and estimates the cost of proposed policies.

Privileges and Immunities under the Law

Members of Congress also benefit from a number of legal privileges and immunities. Under Article I, Section 6, of the Constitution, they "shall in all Cases, except Treason, Felony, and Breach of the Peace, be privileged from Arrest during their Attendance at the Session of their respective Houses, and in going to and returning from the same; and for any Speech or Debate in either House, they shall not be questioned in any other Place." While the arrest immunity clause is not really an important provision today, the "speech or debate" clause means that a member may

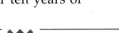

make any allegations or other statements he or she wishes in connection with official duties and not normally be sued for libel or slander or be otherwise subject to legal action.

The Committee Structure

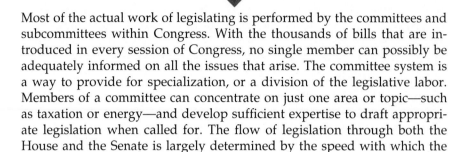

Most of the actual work of legislating is performed by the committees and subcommittees within Congress. With the thousands of bills that are introduced in every session of Congress, no single member can possibly be adequately informed on all the issues that arise. The committee system is a way to provide for specialization, or a division of the legislative labor. Members of a committee can concentrate on just one area or topic—such as taxation or energy—and develop sufficient expertise to draft appropriate legislation when called for. The flow of legislation through both the House and the Senate is largely determined by the speed with which the members of these committees act on bills and resolutions.

Commonly known as "little legislatures,"[11] committees usually have the final say on pieces of legislation. Committee actions may be overturned on the floor by the full House or Senate, but this rarely happens. Legislators normally defer to the expertise of the chairperson and other members of the committee who speak on the floor in defense of a committee decision. Chairpersons of full committees exercise control over the scheduling of both hearings and formal action on a bill and decide which subcommittee will act on legislation falling within their committee's jurisdiction. Committees are very rarely deprived of control over a bill—although this kind of action is provided for in the rules of each chamber. In the House, if a bill has been considered by a standing committee for thirty days, the signatures of a majority (218) of the House membership on a **discharge petition** can pry a bill out of an uncooperative committee's

---

[11]This term is from Woodrow Wilson, *Congressional Government* (New York: Meridian Books, 1956 [first published in 1885]).

DISCHARGE PETITION
A procedure by which a bill in the House of Representatives may be forced out of a committee (discharged) that has refused to report it for consideration by the House. The discharge motion must be signed by an absolute majority (218) of representatives and is used only on rare occasions.

A committee hearing on a constitutional amendment to balance the budget. Starting from the chair of the committee in the center, Democratic senators sit on the left in order of seniority on the committee, while Republicans take the seats on the right in order of seniority.

hands. From 1909 to 1990, however, although 909 such petitions were made, only 26 resulted in successful discharge efforts, and of those, 20 passed the House.[12]

Types of Congressional Committees

Over the past two centuries, Congress has created several different types of committees, each of which serves particular needs of the institution.

Standing Committees. By far the most important committees are the **standing committees**—permanent bodies established by the rules of each chamber of Congress that continue from session to session. A list of the standing committees of the 103d Congress is presented in Table 10-5. In

STANDING COMMITTEE
A permanent committee within the House or Senate that considers bills within a certain subject area.

[12]*Congressional Quarterly's Guide to Congress*, 3d ed., p. 426, and authors' research.

TABLE 10-5 ■ Standing Committees of the 103d Congress (1993–1995)

House Committees	Chair	Senate Committees	Chair
Agriculture	Kika de la Garza, D., Tex.	Agriculture, Nutrition, and Forestry	Patrick Leahy, D., Ver.
Appropriations	William Natcher, D., Ky.	Appropriations	Robert C. Byrd, D., W. Va.
Armed Services	Ronald V. Dellums, D., Calif.	Armed Services	Sam Nunn, D., Ga.
Banking, Finance, and Urban Affairs	Henry B. Gonzalez, D., Tex.	Banking, Housing, and Urban Affairs	Donald W. Riegle, Jr., D., Mich.
Budget	Martin Sabo, D., Minn.	Budget	Jim Sasser, D., Tenn.
District of Columbia	Pete Stark, D., Calif.	Commerce, Science, and Transportation	Ernest Hollings, D., S.C.
Education and Labor	William Ford, D., Mich.	Energy and Natural Resources	J. Bennett Johnston, D., La.
Energy and Commerce	John Dingell, D., Mich.	Environment and Public Works	Max Baucus, D., Mont.
Foreign Affairs	Lee H. Hamilton, D., Ind.		
Government Operations	John Conyers, Jr., D., Mich.	Finance	Daniel P. Moynihan, D., N.Y.
House Administration	Charles Rose, D., N.C.	Foreign Relations	Claiborne Pell, D., R.I.
Judiciary	Jack Brooks, D., Tex.	Governmental Affairs	John Glenn, D., Ohio
Merchant Marine and Fisheries	Gerry E. Studds, D., Mass.	Judiciary	Joseph Biden, Jr., D., Del.
Natural Resources	George Miller, D., Calif.	Labor and Human Resources	Edward Kennedy, D., Mass.
Post Office and Civil Service	William Clay, D., Mo.	Rules and Administration	Wendell Ford, D., Ky.
Public Works and Transportation	Norman Y. Mineta, D., Calif.	Small Business	Dale Bumpers, D., Ark.
Rules	Joe Moakley, D., Mass.	Veterans Affairs	Dennis DeConcini, D., Ariz.
Science and Technology	George E. Brown, Jr., D., Calif.		
Small Business	John J. LaFalce, D., N.Y.		
Standards of Official Conduct	Julian Dixon, D., Calif.		
Veterans Affairs	G. V. "Sonny" Montgomery, D., Miss.		
Ways and Means	Dan Rostenkowski, D., Ill.		

addition, most of the standing committees have created several subcommittees to carry out their work. In the 103d Congress, there were 103 subcommittees in the Senate and 139 in the House.[13]

Each standing committee is given a specific area of legislative policy jurisdiction, and almost all legislative measures are considered by the appropriate standing committees. Because of the importance of their work and the traditional influence of their members in Congress, certain committees are considered to be more prestigious than others. If a congressperson seeks to be influential, he or she will usually aspire to a seat on the Appropriations Committee in either chamber or on the Ways and Means Committee in the House. Significant public policy committees are the House Education and Labor Committee and the Senate Foreign Relations Committee.

Each member of the House serves generally on two standing committees, except when that member sits on the Appropriations, Rules, or Ways and Means Committee—in which case he or she serves on only that one standing committee. Each senator may serve on two major committees and one minor committee (only the Rules and Administration Committee and the Veterans Affairs Committee are considered minor).

Select Committees.   A **select committee** is normally created for a limited period of time and for a specific legislative purpose. For example, a select committee may be formed to investigate a public problem, such as nutrition or aging. Select committees are disbanded when they have reported to the chamber that created them. They rarely create original legislation.

Joint Committees.   A **joint committee** is formed by the concurrent action of both chambers of Congress and consists of members from each chamber. Joint committees, which may be permanent or temporary, have dealt with the economy, taxation, and the Library of Congress.

Conference Committees.   **Conference committees** are special types of joint committees. They are formed for the purpose of achieving agreement between the House and the Senate on the exact wording of legislative acts when the two chambers pass legislative proposals in different forms. No bill can be sent to the White House to be signed into law unless it first passes both chambers in identical form. Sometimes called the "third house" of Congress, conference committees are in a position to make significant alterations in legislation and frequently become the focal point of policy debates. This was the case, for example, with the passage of the tax reform legislation of 1986 and the Clean Air Act of 1991, both of which required long and difficult negotiations in the House–Senate conference committee to reconcile conflicting versions.

The House Rules Committee.   Because of its special "gatekeeping" power over the terms on which legislation will reach the floor of the House of Representatives, the House Rules Committee holds a uniquely powerful position. A special committee rule sets the time limit on debate and determines whether and how the bill may be amended. This practice

---

SELECT COMMITTEE
A temporary legislative committee established for a limited time period for a special purpose.

JOINT COMMITTEE
A legislative committee composed of members from both houses of Congress.

CONFERENCE COMMITTEES
Special joint committees appointed to reconcile differences when bills pass the two houses of Congress in different forms.

Senator Sam Nunn, Chairman of the Senate Armed Services Committee.

---

[13]*Congressional Directory* (Washington, D.C.: Government Printing Office, 1992–1993).

dates back to 1883. The members of the Rules Committee have the unusual power to meet while the House is in session, to have its resolutions considered immediately on the floor, and to initiate legislation on its own.

The Selection of Committee Members

In the House, representatives are appointed to standing committees by the Steering and Policy Committee (for Democrats) and by the Committee on Committees (for Republicans). Committee chairpersons are normally appointed according to seniority.

The rule regarding seniority specifies that majority party members with longer terms of continuous service on the committee will be given preference when committee chairpersons—as well as holders of other significant posts in Congress—are selected. This is not a law but an informal, traditional process. The **seniority system,** although deliberately unequal, provides a predictable means of assigning positions of power within Congress.

The general pattern until the 1970s was that members of the House or Senate who represented **safe seats** would be continually reelected and would eventually accumulate enough years of continuous committee service to enable them to become the chairpersons of their committees—if their party gained control of the appropriate chamber of Congress. Traditionally, this avenue of access to power benefited southern Democrats and midwesterners within the Republican party, who seldom faced serious, organized opposition either in their own party's primaries or during the general election. This resulted in a predominance of committee chairpersons from the more conservative ranks of both political parties.

In the 1970s, a number of reforms in the chairperson selection process somewhat modified the seniority system. The reforms introduced the use of a secret ballot in electing House committee chairpersons and established rules for the selection of subcommittee chairpersons that resulted in a greater dispersal of authority within the committees themselves.

Did You Know . . . That the Constitution does not require that the speaker of the House of Representatives be an elected member of the House?

SENIORITY SYSTEM
A custom followed in both houses of Congress specifying that members with longer terms of continuous service will be given preference when committee chairpersons and holders of other significant posts are selected.

SAFE SEAT
A district that returns the legislator with 55 percent of the vote or more.

The Formal Leadership

The limited amount of centralized power that exists in Congress is exercised through party-based mechanisms. Congress is organized by party. When the Democratic party, for example, wins a majority of seats in either the House or the Senate, Democrats control the official positions of power in that chamber, and every committee has a Democratic chairperson and a majority of Democratic members. The same process holds when Republicans are in the majority. Every member of Congress, except for occasionally successful independent candidates, was elected through a partisan electoral process. Senators and representatives therefore usually have some sense of loyalty to their party in Congress.

We consider the formal leadership positions in the House and in the Senate separately, but, as you will note, there are some broad similarities in the way that leaders are selected and in the ways they exercise power in the two chambers.

Leadership in the House

The House leadership is made up of the speaker, the majority and minority leaders, and the party whips.

SPEAKER OF THE HOUSE
The presiding officer in the House of Representatives. The speaker is always a member of the majority party and is the most powerful and influential member of the House.

The Speaker. The foremost power holder in the House of Representatives is the **speaker of the House.** The speaker's position is technically a nonpartisan one, but in fact, for the better part of two centuries, the speaker has been the official leader of the majority party in the House. When a new Congress convenes in January of odd-numbered years, each party nominates a candidate for speaker. In one of the very rare instances of perfect party cohesion, all Democratic members of the House ordinarily vote for their party's nominee, and all Republicans support their alternative candidate.

House leadership is exercised primarily by the speaker, the majority leader, the minority leader, and the majority and minority whips. The election of the speaker thus automatically puts the majority party in control of the powers that are available to that office.

The influence of modern-day speakers is primarily based on their personal prestige, persuasive ability, and knowledge of the legislative process—plus the acquiescence or active support of other representatives. The major formal powers of the speaker include the following:

1. Presiding over meetings of the House.
2. Appointing members of joint committees and conference committees.
3. Scheduling legislation for floor action.
4. Deciding points of order and interpreting the rules with the advice of the House parliamentarian.
5. Referring bills and resolutions to the appropriate standing committees of the House.

A speaker may take part in floor debate and vote, as can any other member of Congress, but recent speakers usually have voted only to break a tie.

In general, the powers of the speaker are related to his or her control over information and communications channels in the House. This is a

Speaker of the House Tom Foley (D., Wash.) and Senate Majority Leader George Mitchell (D., Maine) speak to the press.

significant power in a large, decentralized institution in which information is a very important resource. With this control, the speaker attempts to ensure the smooth operation of the chamber and to integrate presidential and congressional policies.

In 1975, the powers of the speaker were expanded when the House Democratic caucus gave its party's speaker the power to appoint the Democratic Steering Committee, which determines new committee assignments for House party members.

The Majority Leader. The **majority leader of the House** has been a separate position since 1899, when a power that had usually been exercised by the chairperson of the Ways and Means Committee was transferred to a new office. The majority leader is elected by a caucus of party members to foster cohesion among party members and to act as a spokesperson for the party. The majority leader influences the scheduling of debate and generally acts as the chief supporter of the speaker. Majority leaders conduct most procedural debate and also much of the substantive debate on the House floor. They are most deeply involved in debates on the important partisan issues that separate Democrats from Republicans. The majority leader cooperates with the speaker and other party leaders, both inside and outside Congress, to formulate the party's legislative program and to guide that program through the legislative process in the House. The majority leader's post is a very prestigious one because of the power and responsibility inherent in the office and also because, at least among Democrats, future speakers are recruited from that position.

The Minority Leader. The **House minority leader** is the candidate nominated for speaker by a caucus of the minority party. Like the majority leader, the leader of the minority party's primary responsibility is to maintain cohesion within the party's ranks. As the official spokesperson for the minority party, he or she consults with the ranking minority members of the House committees and encourages them to adhere to the party platform. The minority leader also acts as a morale booster for the generally less well-informed and usually less successful minority, and speaks on behalf of the president if the minority party controls the White House. In relations with the majority party, the minority leader consults with both the speaker and the majority leader on recognizing members who wish to speak on the floor, on House rules and procedures, and on the scheduling of legislation. Minority leaders have no actual power in these areas, however.

Whips. The formal leadership of each party includes assistants to the majority and minority leaders, who are known as **whips.** These positions have existed throughout this century. Over the past fifty years, they have developed into a complex network of deputy and regional whips supervised by the chief party whip. The whips assist the party leader by passing information down from the leadership to party members and by ensuring that members show up for floor debate and record votes on important issues. Whips conduct polls among party members about the members' views on major pieces of legislation, inform the leaders about whose vote is doubtful and whose is certain, and may exert pressure on members to

MAJORITY LEADER OF THE HOUSE
A legislative position held by an important party member in the House of Representatives. The majority leader is selected by the majority party in caucus or conference to foster cohesion among party members and to act as spokesperson for the majority party in the House.

HOUSE MINORITY LEADER
The party leader elected by the minority party in the House.

WHIPS
Assistant floor leaders who aid the majority and minority floor leaders.

Representative Robert H. Michel of Illinois, House minority leader.

support the leader's position. The Democratic whip was historically appointed by the party leader in consultation with the Democratic speaker, whereas the Republican whip has been elected in a party caucus since 1965. Beginning with the 100th Congress, though, the position of House Democratic whip has been filled by a vote of the Democratic caucus. In all, several dozen members take part in this formal effort to maintain party discipline.

Leadership in the Senate

The Senate is less than one-fourth the size of the House. This fact alone probably explains why a formal, complex, and centralized leadership structure is less necessary in the Senate than it is in the House.

The two highest-ranking formal leadership positions in the Senate are essentially ceremonial in nature. Under the Constitution, the vice president of the United States is the president (that is, the presiding officer) of the Senate and may vote to break a tie. The vice president, however, only rarely is present for a meeting of the Senate. The Senate elects instead a **president pro tempore** ("pro tem") to preside over the Senate in the vice president's absence. Ordinarily, the president pro tem is the member of the majority party with the longest continuous term of service in the Senate. The president pro tem does not have powers analogous to those of the speaker of the House, although he or she does appoint, jointly with the speaker, the director of the Congressional Budget Office. The most junior senators are usually chosen by the president pro tem and the majority leader to chair portions of each day's session.

The real leadership power in the Senate rests in the hands of the **majority floor leader,** the **minority floor leader,** and their respective whips. The Senate majority and minority leaders have the right to be recognized first in debate on the floor and generally exercise the same powers available to the House majority and minority leaders. They control the scheduling of debate on the floor in conjunction with the majority party's Policy Committee, influence the allocation of committee assignments for new members or for senators attempting to transfer to a new committee, influence the selection of other party officials, and participate in selecting members of conference committees. The leaders are expected to mobilize support for partisan legislative initiatives or for the proposals of a president who belongs to the same party. The leaders act as liaisons with the White House when the president is of their party, try to get the cooperation of committee chairpersons, and seek to facilitate the smooth functioning of the Senate through the senators' unanimous consent. Floor leaders are elected by their respective party caucuses.

Democratic leaders of the Senate potentially have more power than Republican leaders. The Democratic floor leader is also simultaneously the chairperson of the Democratic Conference (caucus); the Steering Committee, which makes committee assignments; and the Policy Committee, which schedules legislation for floor action. In contrast, four different Republican senators hold these comparable positions, in a much more decentralized pattern of leadership.

Senate party whips, like their House counterparts, maintain communication within the party on platform positions and try to assure that party

PRESIDENT PRO TEMPORE
The temporary presiding officer of the Senate in the absence of the vice president.

MAJORITY FLOOR LEADER
The chief spokesperson of the major party in the Senate who directs the legislative program and party strategy.

MINORITY FLOOR LEADER
The party officer in the Senate who commands the minority party's opposition to the policies of the majority party and directs the legislative program and strategy of his or her party.

Robert Dole, (R., Kan.), Senate minority floor leader.

CHAPTER 10 THE CONGRESS

colleagues are present for floor debate and important votes. The Senate whip system is far less elaborate than its counterpart in the House, simply because there are fewer members to keep track of.

A list of the formal party leaders of the 103d Congress is presented in Table 10-6.

Party leaders are a major source of influence over the decisions about public issues that senators and representatives must make every day. We consider the nature of partisan and other pressures on congressional decision making in the next section.

How Members of Congress Decide

Why congresspersons vote as they do is difficult to know with any certainty. One popular perception of the legislative decision-making process is that legislators take cues from other trusted or more senior colleagues. This model holds that because most members of Congress have neither the time nor the incentive to study the details of most pieces of legislation, they frequently arrive on the floor with no clear idea about what they are voting on or how they should vote. Their decision is simplified, according to the cue-taking model, by quickly checking how key colleagues have voted or intend to vote. More broadly, verbal and nonverbal cues can be

TABLE 10-6 ■ Party Leaders in the 103d Congress (1993–1995)

Position	Incumbent	Party/State	Leader Since
House			
Speaker	Tom Foley	D.-Wash.	June 1989
Majority leader	Richard Gephardt	D.-Mo.	June 1989
Majority whip	David Bonior	D.-Mich.	June 1991
Chairperson of the Democratic Caucus	Steny H. Hoyer	D.-Md.	June 1989
Minority leader	Robert Michel	R.-Ill.	Dec. 1980
Minority whip	Newt Gingrich	R.-Ga.	Mar. 1989
Chairperson of the Republican Conference	Dick Armey	R.-Texas	Jan. 1993
Senate			
President pro tempore	Robert C. Byrd	D.-W.Va.	Jan. 1989
Majority floor leader	George J. Mitchell	D.-Maine	Jan. 1989
Assistant majority leader	Wendell H. Ford	D.-Ky.	Dec. 1990
Secretary of the Democratic Caucus	David Pryor	D.-Ark.	Jan. 1989
Minority floor leader	Robert Dole	R.-Kan.	Jan. 1987
Assistant minority leader	Alan K. Simpson	R.-Wyo.	Jan. 1987
Chairperson of the Republican Conference	Thad Cochran	R.-Miss.	Dec. 1990

CONSERVATIVE COALITION
An alliance of Republicans and southern Democrats that can form in the House or the Senate to oppose liberal legislation and support conservative legislation.

TABLE 10-7 ■ Party Voting in Congress

Percentage of all roll calls when a majority of Democratic legislators voted against a majority of Republican legislators.

Year	House	Senate
1992	64.0	53.0
1991	55.0	49.0
1990	49.0	54.0
1989	55.0	35.0
1988	47.0	42.0
1987	64.0	41.0
1986	57.0	52.0
1985	61.0	50.0
1984	47.1	40.0
1983	55.6	43.6
1982	36.4	43.4
1981	37.4	47.8
1980	37.6	45.8
1979	47.3	46.7
1978	33.2	45.2
1977	42.2	42.4
1976	35.9	37.2
1975	48.4	47.8
1974	29.4	44.3
1973	41.8	39.9

SOURCE: *Congressional Quarterly Weekly Report,* December 19, 1991, p. 3849.

taken from fellow committee members and chairpersons, party leaders, state delegation members, or the president.

A different theory of congressional decision making places the emphasis on the policy content of the issues being decided and on the desires of a congressperson's constituents and the pressures brought to bear by his or her supporters. The degree of constituency influence on congressional voting patterns depends on the extent to which a state or district is urbanized, the region and state that a member represents, and the blue-collar proportion of the labor force.

Most people who study the decision-making process in Congress agree that the single best predictor for how a member will vote is the member's party membership. Republicans tend to vote similarly on issues, as do Democrats. Of course, even though liberals predominate among the Democrats in Congress and conservatives predominate among the Republicans, the parties still may have internal disagreements about the proper direction that national policy should take. This was generally true for the civil rights legislation of the 1950s and 1960s, for example, when the greatest disagreement was between the conservative southern wing and liberal northern wing of the Democratic party.

One way to measure the degree of party unity in Congress is to look at how often a majority of one party votes against the majority of members from the other party. Table 10-7 displays the percentage of all roll-call votes in the House and the Senate when this type of party voting has occurred. Note that party voting occurs at a much higher rate in the House in the odd-numbered years, which happen to be the years when congressional elections are not held.

Regional differences, especially between northern and southern Democrats, may overlap and reinforce basic ideological differences among members of the same party. One consequence of the North–South split among Democrats has been the **conservative coalition** policy alliance between southern Democrats and Republicans. This conservative, cross-party grouping can be counted on to form regularly on votes concerning controversial issues in Congress. It is usually highly successful.

How a Bill Becomes Law

Each year, Congress and the president propose and approve many laws. Some are budget and appropriation laws that require extensive bargaining but must be passed for the government to continue to function. Other laws are relatively free of controversy and are passed with little dissension between the branches of government. Still other proposed legislation is extremely controversial and reaches to the roots of differences between Democrats and Republicans and between the executive and legislative branches. Such a piece of legislation was the Civil Rights Act of 1991, which was signed after two years of conflict between the president and Congress. By examining that law and its road to passage, we can better understand the complexities of the legislative process. (Figure 10-3 diagrams the process with two hypothetical bills.)

During the late 1980s, the Supreme Court articulated a number of decisions that restricted the power of federal civil rights laws. The decisions

FIGURE 10-3 ■ How a Bill Becomes Law

This illustration shows the most typical way in which proposed legislation is enacted into law. The process is illustrated with two hypothetical bills, House bill No. 100 (HR 100) and Senate bill No. 200 (S 200). Bills must be passed by both houses in identical form before they can be sent to the president. The path of HR 100 is traced by a blue line, that of S 200 by a red line. In practice, most bills begin as similar proposals in both houses.

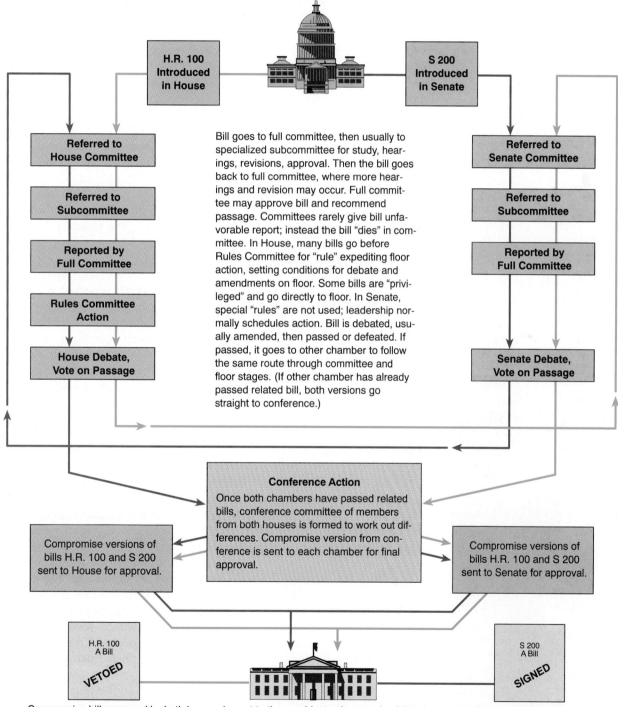

H.R. 100 Introduced in House

S 200 Introduced in Senate

Referred to House Committee

Referred to Subcommittee

Reported by Full Committee

Rules Committee Action

House Debate, Vote on Passage

Bill goes to full committee, then usually to specialized subcommittee for study, hearings, revisions, approval. Then the bill goes back to full committee, where more hearings and revision may occur. Full committee may approve bill and recommend passage. Committees rarely give bill unfavorable report; instead the bill "dies" in committee. In House, many bills go before Rules Committee for "rule" expediting floor action, setting conditions for debate and amendments on floor. Some bills are "privileged" and go directly to floor. In Senate, special "rules" are not used; leadership normally schedules action. Bill is debated, usually amended, then passed or defeated. If passed, it goes to other chamber to follow the same route through committee and floor stages. (If other chamber has already passed related bill, both versions go straight to conference.)

Referred to Senate Committee

Referred to Subcommittee

Reported by Full Committee

Senate Debate, Vote on Passage

Conference Action

Once both chambers have passed related bills, conference committee of members from both houses is formed to work out differences. Compromise version from conference is sent to each chamber for final approval.

Compromise versions of bills H.R. 100 and S 200 sent to House for approval.

Compromise versions of bills H.R. 100 and S 200 sent to Senate for approval.

H.R. 100 A Bill VETOED

S 200 A Bill SIGNED

Compromise bill approved by both houses is sent to the president, who can sign it into law or veto it and return it to Congress. Congress may override veto by a two-thirds majority vote in both houses; bill then becomes law without president's signature.

surprised civil rights and women's groups that believed they could, if necessary, litigate to ensure that employment opportunities would not be withheld from women and minorities through discrimination. The Court curbed these opportunities through a series of decisions that restricted lawsuits to hiring decisions, forced the employee to prove the existence of practices that discriminated against minorities, and generally put the burden of proof of discrimination on the employee, rather than on the employer.

On February 9, 1990, a coalition of senators, representatives, and interest groups announced that it would sponsor new legislation that would essentially overturn these Supreme Court decisions. The resolution was sponsored in the Senate by Senator Ted Kennedy and in the House by Representative Augustus Hawkins. Employers and large businesses opposed the legislation, claiming that it made businesses so liable to lawsuits from unhappy employees who claimed discrimination that companies would simply adopt quotas for minorities and women to prevent the lawsuits. This soon was called the "quota" bill by Republicans, especially President Bush.

After deliberation in the Senate Labor and Human Resources Committee, the Senate passed its version on July 18, 1990. The House Education and Labor Committee approved the bill in early May, even though Republican committee members had walked out of the meetings twice. Because the bill included a number of provisions concerning lawsuits, it went next to the House Judiciary Committee, which reported it out on July 25. The full House approved the bill in July. After the Conference Committee constructed a single bill, both chambers approved the conference report in October but not with enough votes to override a veto. The president vetoed the bill on the grounds that it would force businesses to adopt quotas in hiring and promotion. He also opposed punitive damages in employee lawsuits. Neither chamber of Congress was able to override his veto.

The "quota bill" became an issue in the 1990 elections. Republicans charged that Democrats were willing to hurt business, and Democrats charged that Republicans were creating a false issue.

Undeterred by defeat and determined to overturn the Supreme Court decisions, civil rights groups pondered their next move. By early 1991, Representative William Ford, chairman of the House Education and Labor Committee, reintroduced the civil rights bill. The bill again sought punitive damages against employers and put the burden of proof regarding employment practices on employers. Democrats tried to cast the bill as a women's employment rights bill as much as a minorities' bill. It quickly passed both the House Education and Labor Committee and the House Judiciary Committee. Before going to the floor of the House, the sponsor opened talks with a major interest group representing big business, the Business Round Table. The intent of the talks was to seek agreement on some of the main issues so as to gain the support of President Bush. In other words, if the Round Table could agree, then Bush would sign the bill.

Talks between the Business Round Table and civil rights supporters ended in late April 1991. Then other business groups lobbied the big business group to oppose the bill. At the same time, the liberal sponsors of

President Bill Clinton along with Senator Barbara Mikulski, Senate Majority Leader George Mitchell, and House Speaker Tom Foley, meet with the press.

President Clinton signs the Family Medical Leave Act of 1993.

the bill decided that they did not want further compromises. Senator George Mitchell noted that there was little grass-roots support for the bill, saying, "People aren't out there clamoring for any bill as far as I can see"[14]

The decision to compromise came in mid-May. Democrats decided to accept limits on punitive damages for claims of intentional discrimination brought by women and minorities. Certain other changes in the legal language that had been sought by business groups were also accepted. The compromise angered some women in Congress, but southern Democrats now felt that they might be able to vote for the bill without hurting local businesses. This version passed the House on June 5 but not by enough votes to override a veto. To achieve a passable bill, Senator John Danforth (R., Mo.) proposed a Republican substitute that was more business oriented than Kennedy's version and possibly acceptable to the president. After a summer of discontent and recriminations, a Danforth–Kennedy bill passed the Senate by a margin of ninety-three to five. The House approved the Danforth–Kennedy proposal on November 7 by an overwhelming margin, and President Bush signed the measure on November 21.

The Civil Rights Act of 1991 illustrates many aspects of the legislative process. It took two sessions to pass the law. Both sides—liberals and conservatives—had to compromise. Interest groups—civil rights groups, women's groups, small and large business groups, and conservative groups—all played a part in the process. In the end, the work of several individuals, Kennedy and Danforth among them, carried the bill to passage.

How Much Will the Government Spend?

The Constitution is extremely clear about where the power of the purse lies in the national government: All money bills, whether for taxing or

---

[14]*Congressional Quarterly Weekly Report,* April 27, 1991, p. 1064.

spending, must originate in the House of Representatives. Today, much of the business of the Congress is concerned with approving government expenditures through the budget process and with raising the revenues to pay for government programs.

From 1922, when Congress required the president to prepare and present to the legislature an **executive budget**, until 1974, the congressional budget process was so disjointed that it was difficult to visualize the total picture of government finances. The president presented the executive budget to Congress in January. It was broken down into thirteen or more appropriations bills. Some time later, after all of the bills were debated, amended, and passed, it was possible to estimate total government spending for the next year.

Frustrated by the president's ability to impound funds and dissatisfied with the entire budget process, Congress passed the Budget and Impoundment Control Act of 1974 to regain some control over the nation's spending. The act required the president to spend the funds that Congress had appropriated, frustrating his ability to kill programs he disapproved of by withholding funds. The other major accomplishment of the act was to force Congress to examine total national taxing and spending at least twice in each budget cycle.

The budget cycle of the federal government is described in the following sections. (See Figure 10-4 for a graphic illustration of the budget cycle.)

Preparing the Budget

The federal government operates on a **fiscal year** (FY). The fiscal year runs from October through September, so that fiscal 1994, or FY94, runs from October 1, 1993, through September 30, 1994. Eighteen months before a

EXECUTIVE BUDGET
The budget prepared and submitted by the president to Congress.

FISCAL YEAR
The twelve-month period that is used for bookkeeping, or accounting, purposes. Usually, the fiscal year does not coincide with the calendar year. For example, the federal government's fiscal year runs from October 1 through September 30.

FIGURE 10-4 ■ The Budget Cycle

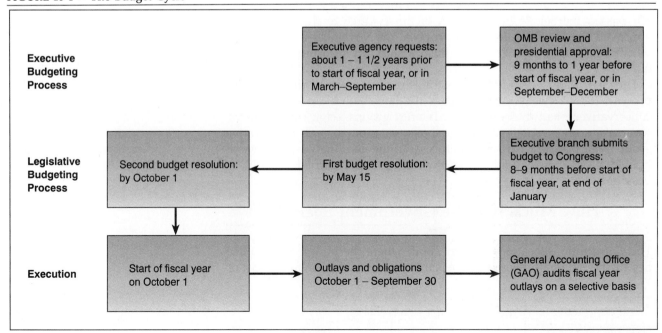

fiscal year starts, the executive branch begins preparing the budget. The Office of Management and Budget (OMB) receives advice from the Council of Economic Advisers (CEA) and the Treasury Department. The OMB outlines the budget and then sends it to the various departments and agencies. Bargaining follows, in which—to use only two of many examples—the Department of Health and Human Services argues for more welfare spending, and the armed forces argue for fewer defense spending cuts.

Even though the OMB has only six hundred employees, it is known as one of the most powerful agencies in Washington. It assembles the budget documents and monitors the agencies throughout each year. Every year, it begins the budget process with a **spring review,** in which it requires all of the agencies to review their programs, activities, and goals. At the beginning of each summer, the director of the OMB sends out a letter instructing agencies to submit their requests for funding for the next fiscal year. By the end of the summer, each agency must submit a formal request to the OMB.

In actuality, the "budget season" begins with the **fall review.** At this time, the OMB looks at budget requests and in almost all cases routinely cuts them back. Although the OMB works within guidelines established by the president, specific decisions are often left to the director and the director's associates. By the beginning of November, the director's review begins. The director meets with cabinet secretaries and budget officers. Time becomes crucial. The budget must be completed by January so it can go to the printer to be included in the *Economic Report of the President.*

Congress Faces the Budget

In January, nine months before the fiscal year starts, the president takes the OMB's proposed budget and submits it to Congress. Then the congressional budgeting process takes over. Congressional committees and subcommittees look at the proposals from the executive branch. The Congressional Budget Office (CBO) advises the different committees on economic matters, just as the OMB and the CEA advise the president. The **first budget resolution** by Congress is supposed to be passed in May. It sets overall revenue goals and spending targets and, by definition, the size of the deficit (or surplus, if that were ever to occur again).

During the summer, bargaining among all the concerned parties takes place. Spending and tax laws that are drawn up during this period are supposed to be guided by the May congressional budget resolution. By September, Congress is supposed to pass its **second budget resolution,** one that will set "binding" limits on taxes and spending for the fiscal year beginning October 1. Bills passed before that date that do not fit within the limits of the budget resolution are supposed to be changed.

In actuality, between 1978 and 1992, Congress did not pass a complete budget by October 1. In other words, generally, Congress does not follow its own rules. Budget resolutions are passed late, and when they are passed, they are not treated as binding. In each fiscal year that starts without a budget, every agency operates on the basis of **continuing resolutions,** which enable the agencies to keep on doing whatever they were doing the previous year with the same amount of funding. Even continuing resolutions have not always been passed on time.

Did You Know . . . That less than half of all Americans polled believe that members of Congress have a high personal moral code of conduct or care deeply about the problems of ordinary citizens?

SPRING REVIEW
Every year, the Office of Management and Budget requires federal agencies to review their programs, activities, and goals and submit their requests for funding for the next year.

FALL REVIEW
Every year, after receiving formal federal agency requests for funding for the next fiscal year, the Office of Management and Budget reviews the requests, makes changes, and submits its recommendations to the president.

FIRST BUDGET RESOLUTION
A resolution passed by Congress in May that sets overall revenue and spending goals and hence, by definition, the size of the deficit for the following fiscal year.

SECOND BUDGET RESOLUTION
A resolution passed by Congress in September that sets "binding" limits on taxes and spending for the next fiscal year beginning October 1.

CONTINUING RESOLUTIONS
Temporary laws that Congress passes when various appropriations bills have not been decided by the beginning of the new fiscal year on October 1.

Did You Know ... That under the 1990 budget agreement, a supermajority of sixty senators is required to pass a tax cut, but only fifty-one votes are needed to raise taxes?

In the fall of 1990, the voters witnessed the worst budget stalemate since the initiation of the new budget process. After President Bush reneged on his pledge of "No new taxes," Republicans battled Democrats in Congress over which taxes to raise. The new fiscal year 1991 budget had to provide enough revenue to begin reducing the federal deficit. A compromise bill crafted by congressional leaders and representatives of President Bush was soundly defeated by majorities of both the Republican and Democratic contingents in the House. Several weeks later, after the president threatened to shut the government down, another budget bill passed, raising taxes on some wealthy Americans and adding to the federal "sin taxes" on cigarettes and alcohol. The budget struggle did little to raise the voters' esteem for Congress or the executive branch.

Although many critics feel that the new budget process is neither efficient nor effective, there is little doubt that focusing on the bottom line has made legislators much more conscious of the federal budget deficit. Furthermore, there is some evidence that members of Congress now see the budget as the most important way to set the nation's agenda. Recent voting patterns in Congress reveal that members of each party are most united on the budget votes, because each party, Democratic and Republican, is fighting for its own preferences in spending.

The Question of Congressional Ethics

Ethics is the most serious public relations problem confronting Congress today. Perhaps nothing has so tarnished the public's perception of Congress as the revelations concerning the abuse of staff members, the misuse of public funds, and the personal indiscretions of several members of that institution. The extent of public disenchantment with the state of congressional ethics was suggested by a Gallup poll conducted in early 1980.[15] Seventy-eight percent of a national sample answered yes when asked if they believed "there are senators and representatives now serving in Congress who won election by using unethical and illegal methods in their campaigns." Forty percent of the same sample felt that one-fifth or more of the present members of Congress "got there by using unethical or illegal campaign methods."

Congress's response to revelations of member misconduct has been mixed. The House Democratic caucus in June 1980 voted 160 to 0 to require that chairpersons of committees or subcommittees be stripped of their posts automatically if they have been censured or indicted on a felony charge carrying a prison sentence of at least two years. This rule can be waived, however, by the same caucus.

Public financing of congressional campaigns may offer a partial solution to recurring problems of financial misconduct. Nonetheless, Congress has refused to use tax money for, or to impose spending limits on, its members' campaigns, even though it adopted such provisions for presidential campaigns in 1974. Part of the campaign-funding problem is illustrated by the former congressman who used leftover campaign funds to make a down payment on a fifty-five-foot houseboat in Florida and to finance a

---

[15]*The Gallup Poll 1980* (Wilmington, Del.: Scholarly Resources, 1981), p. 65.

POLITICS AND ETHICS

Ethics: Congress Examines Its Own for Improprieties

In 1989, both House speaker Jim Wright (D., Tex.) and the House majority whip Tony Coelho (D., Calif.) resigned from Congress. Wright came under investigation on dozens of charges, including influence peddling, accepting a job and car for his wife from a supporter, and violating campaign finance laws by selling a book of his speeches to contributors and keeping the royalties. Coelho resigned while under investigation for his dealings with the convicted financier Michael Milkin.

Beyond the financial improprieties, several House members were investigated in 1989 by the House Ethics Committee for sexual improprieties. Gus Savage (D., Ill.) was accused of making sexual advances to a Peace Corps volunteer while he was on an official trip to Africa. He lost the following primary election. Donald "Buz" Lukens (R., Ohio) was charged with, and convicted for, having sex with a sixteen-year-old girl. He was defeated in the next election. Representative Jim Bates (D., Calif.) was accused of sexually harassing women on his staff. The Ethics Committee had the most dif-

ficult time with the Barney Frank case. The Democratic congressperson from Massachusetts, who had disclosed in 1987 that he was a homosexual, was accused of hiring a former sex partner as a personal assistant. The House Ethics Committee could not decide how to handle this situation and finally reprimanded Frank for using his office improperly to help the man.

The Senate has had its share of ethics problems as well. In 1990, the Senate Ethics Committee investigated Senator David Durenberger (R., Minn.). He was charged with receiving illegal reimbursements for housing expenses and for backdating his purchase of a share in a condominium. The Senate formally denounced Durenberger in July 1990 and ordered him to make restitution for his financial misconduct.

As the trial of Arizona financier Charles Keating for bilking savings and loan depositors proceeded, it became known that several United States senators had used their influence to limit the regulation of Keating's savings bank. The "Keating Five," as they came to be known,

were Alan Cranston (D., Calif.), Dennis DeConcini (D., Ariz.), Donald Riegle, Jr., (D., Mich.), John Glenn (D., Ohio), and John McCain (R., Ariz.). After a long investigation, the Senate Ethics Committee decided that Senator Cranston's behavior was the most flagrant. They avoided taking the harsh step of censuring, owing partly to Cranston's failing health and announced retirement. The committee issued a report "strongly and severely" reprimanding Senator Cranston for accepting more than $850,000 in contributions to voter-registration groups that he sponsored in return for intervening on Keating's behalf with bank regulators. The other four senators were mildly reprimanded for their conduct.

Such investigations of improprieties show that the House and the Senate are able to identify the unethical conduct of their members and publicly discuss it. The continued revelations of such conduct, however, as well as the overall view that Congress has little control over these actions, continue to fuel public suspicion of the institution.

limousine carrying the congressional seal. The practice of diverting unused campaign funds to personal use was outlawed in January 1980, but current members of Congress were exempted from coverage by the law. By the early 1990s, the public's regard for Congress had reached an all-time low. (See the *Politics and Ethics* in this chapter.)

Conclusion: Congress in Disarray

Winds of uncertain change have blown through Congress in the last few years. The old seniority system, once a virtually sure path to power through the committee structure, has been eroded. Power has been decentralized and diffused in many respects, mainly by the growth of subcommittees. The greater number and increased importance of subcommittees has reduced control over information and material resources formerly in the hands of full committee chairpersons and party leaders.

A response to this fragmentation of power in Congress has been the increased importance of the party caucuses, especially on the Democratic side, though this too has meant that party and committee leaders are more answerable to the will of each party member. Numerous mini-caucuses have formed around the specific personal or constituency interests of different members of Congress. These sources of inside lobbying include such groups as the Congressional Black Caucus, the New England Congressional Caucus, the Northeast–Midwest Economic Advancement Coalition, the Congresswomen's Caucus, and the Textile Caucus. These groups have appeared in the House but not yet in the Senate.

Many of the recent changes in Congress resulted from reforms that were intended to "liberalize" the legislative body. The decentralization of power and increasing importance of individual members, however, have tended to make compromise more difficult and to slow down the legislative process. The recent disclosures of ethical misconduct and other scandals have reduced public approval of Congress to a historic low. It seems that the public will change its view only if there is a major turnover in congressional membership or a shift in the political climate.

GETTING INVOLVED

How to Be an Intern in Washington, D.C.

John Stuart Mill, the British political philosopher and economist, wrote in the last century, "There are many truths of which the full meaning cannot be realized until personal experience has brought it home." Hundreds of students each year flock to Washington, D.C., for a summer, a semester, or a full year to gain personal experience in one of the myriad institutions of the nation's capital. For those with "Potomac fever," an internship in Washington earning college credit while working is an extraordinary opportunity. If you are interested in a Washington experience, here are some things to keep in mind.

First, make sure that you discuss your internship plan with your faculty adviser. He or she will have useful tips. Some colleges have strict rules on who may obtain credit for internships, what preparation is necessary, in what year students are allowed to participate in internships, and other such matters. Internships are most useful if you are in your junior or senior year.

There are several ways to plan an internship: First, contact an existing program, such as the Washington Center (514 10th St. N.W., Suite 600, Washington, DC 20004, Tel. 202-289-8680). Such an organization will assist you in finding a suitable internship in government, the private sector, business, foundations, and nonprofit or volunteer organizations, and in considering other opportunities. "Organized" internship programs will also find you housing and usually provide field trips, special seminars, internship advisers, and other support. Ask if your college or university is affiliated with a Washington program or has an internship program of its own.

Second, find your own internship. There are several avenues for identifying and pursuing opportunities. Contact the local office of your representative or senator, which is usually listed in the telephone directory under "United States Government." Many members of Congress have internship coordinators and large, well-supervised programs. Some may even be able to pay part of your expenses.

Yet another route to finding your own internship is to study carefully one of the many directories on internships, such as the *Directory of Washington Internships*, which can be obtained from the Society for Internships and Experimental Education, 122 St. Mary's St., Raleigh, NC 27605.

Always make sure that you explore in detail what a specific job offers. Think carefully about internships that are glorified secretarial jobs in which all you do is typing and filing. Good internships should give you an insider's view on how a profession works. It should furnish some real "hands on" opportunities to do research, deal with the public, learn about legislation, and watch government officials in action.

Remember that most internships are nonpaying. Make sure that you understand all the costs involved and arrange for financing through your college, a guaranteed student loan, personal savings, or family support.

Finally, keep in mind that there are also internships in most members' district offices close to home. Such jobs may not have the glamour of Washington, but they may offer excellent opportunities for political experience.

A very useful booklet with which you should start is *Storming Washington: An Intern's Guide to National Government* by Stephen E. Frantzich, available from the American Political Science Association, 1527 N. Hampshire Ave., N.W., Washington, DC 20036, Tel. 202-483-2512.

CHAPTER SUMMARY

1. The authors of the Constitution, believing that the bulk of national power should be in the legislature, set forth the structure, power, and operations of Congress in Article I of the Constitution. Article I, Section 2, of the Constitution states that Congress will consist of two chambers. Partly an outgrowth of the Connecticut Compromise, this bicameral structure established a balanced legislature with the membership in the House of Representatives based on population and the membership in the Senate based on the equality of states.

2. The first seventeen clauses of Article I, Section 8, of the Constitution specify most of the enumerated, or expressed, powers of Congress, including the right to collect taxes, to spend money, to regulate commerce, and to declare war. Besides its enumerated powers, Congress enjoys the right to "make all Laws which shall be necessary and proper for carrying into Execution the foregoing Powers, and all other Powers vested by this Constitution in the Government of the United States, or in any Department or Officer thereof." This is called the elastic, or necessary and proper, clause.

3. Functions of Congress include (a) lawmaking activities,

(b) service to constituents, (c) representation of diverse interests, (d) oversight of the manner in which laws are implemented, (e) educating the public about national issues and setting the terms for national debate, and (f) resolving conflicts.

4. There are 435 members in the House of Representatives and 100 members in the Senate. Owing to its larger size, the House has a greater number of formal rules. The Senate tradition of unlimited debate, or filibustering, dates back to 1790 and has been used over the years to frustrate the passage of bills. Under Senate Rule 22, cloture can be used to shut off debate on a bill.

5. Congressional elections are operated by the individual state governments, which must abide by rules established by the Constitution and national statutes. The process of nominating congressional candidates has shifted from party conventions to the direct primaries currently used in all states. The overwhelming majority of incumbent representatives and a smaller proportion of senators who run for reelection are successful. The most complicated aspect of the mechanics of congressional elections is reapportionment—the allocation of legislative seats to constituencies. The Supreme Court's one man, one vote rule has been applied to equalize the populations of state legislative and congressional districts.

6. Most of the actual work of legislating is performed by committees and subcommittees within Congress. This is the method for dividing legislative, appropriations, and investigatory functions among small, specialized groups. Legislation introduced into the House or Senate is assigned to the appropriate standing committees for review. Select committees are created for a limited period of time for a specific legislative purpose. Joint committees are formed by the concurrent action of both chambers and consist of members from each chamber. Conference committees are special joint committees set up to achieve agreement between the House and the Senate on the exact wording of legislative acts passed by both chambers in different forms. The seniority rule specifies that longer-serving members will be given preference when committee chairpersons and holders of other important posts are selected.

7. The foremost power holder in the House of Representatives is the speaker of the House. Other leaders are the House majority leader, the House minority leader, and the majority and minority whips. Formally, the vice president is the presiding officer of the Senate, with the majority party choosing a senior member as the president pro tem to preside when the vice president is absent. Actual leadership in the Senate rests with the majority floor leader, the minority floor leader, and their respective whips.

8. A bill becomes law by progressing through both houses of Congress and their appropriate standing and joint committees to the president.

9. The budget process for a fiscal year begins with the preparation of an executive budget by the president. This is reviewed by the Office of Management and Budget and then sent to Congress, which is supposed to pass a final budget by September. Since 1978, Congress has not followed its own time rules.

10. Ethics is the most serious public relations problem facing Congress. Financial misconduct, sexual improprieties, and other unethical behavior on the part of several House and Senate members have resulted in a significant lowering of the public's regard for the institution of Congress. Despite congressional investigations of ethical misconduct and, in some cases, reprimands of members of Congress, the overall view of the public is that Congress has little control over the actions of its members in respect to ethics.

QUESTIONS FOR REVIEW AND DISCUSSION

1. Two of the most important functions of Congress are representation and lawmaking. Think of several instances where these two functions present a conflict for an individual legislator. What should a congressperson do if a vote for a cut in defense spending means reducing jobs in a defense plant in his or her district?

2. Why are so many incumbent congresspersons reelected to office? How do they build so much support in their constituencies? Do voters know enough about congressional activity to make an intelligent choice for their representatives?

3. If legislators on Capitol Hill are mostly wealthy, well-educated lawyers, how can they know the needs and desires of their constituents? Would Congress be different if there were more women, minorities, and working-class people elected?

4. What functions does the leadership of the parties perform in Congress? Why is the leadership organization important to individual members?

5. Is the process of lawmaking too complicated? Does it give too many opportunities to block needed legislation?

SELECTED REFERENCES

Douglas R. Arnold, *The Logic of Congressional Action* (New Haven, Conn.: Yale University Press, 1990). Arnold examines the logic and motivation behind congressional economic, tax-related, and energy policies and gives a clear, decisive analysis of congressional decision-making processes.

Michael Barone and Grant Ujifusa, *The Almanac of American Politics 1993* (Washington, D.C.: National Journal, 1992). A comprehensive summary of current political information on each member of Congress, his or her state or congressional district, recent congressional election results, key votes and ratings of roll call votes by various organizations, sources of campaign contributions, and records of campaign expenditures.

Robert A. Berstein, *Elections, Representation, and Congressional Voting Behavior* (Englewood Cliffs, N.J.: Prentice Hall, 1989). Berstein looks closely at the myth that constituents control their congressional representatives and concludes that voters rarely know what their representatives are doing and do not reward or punish their representatives for their performance.

Paul F. Boller, *Congressional Anecdotes* (New York: Oxford University Press, 1991). Boller's lively and informative history of Congress is filled with revealing stories about members of Congress and entertaining anecdotes made by, or about, congresspersons over the years.

David W. Brady, *Critical Elections and Congressional Policy Making* (Stanford, Calif.: Stanford University Press, 1988). This book analyzes the House of Representatives during critical periods—the Civil War, the 1890s, and the New Deal—when it legislated major policy changes.

Morris P. Fiorina, *Congress: Keystone of the Washington Establishment,* 2d ed. (New Haven, Conn.: Yale University Press, 1989). An extensive update to the 1977 original, this book examines the sources of the criticism that the unconstrained pursuit of personal goals by members of Congress has resulted in their failure to meet the responsibilities imposed by the nation.

John Hibbing, ed., *The Changing World of the U.S. Senate* (Berkeley, Calif.: Institute of Governmental Studies Press, 1990). This book on the Senate, which is one of the best available, provides an excellent history of the institution and its internal operations, as well as a thoughtful debate on the need for more theoretical exploration and analysis of this institution.

John W. Kingdon, *Congressmen's Voting Decisions,* 3d ed. (Ann Arbor: University of Michigan Press, 1990). This is considered to be one of the best studies of the ways in which members of Congress vote and includes the roles played in this process by constituents, colleagues, interest groups, the executive branch, and staff.

John Marini, *The Politics of Budget Control: Congress, the Presidency, and the Growth of the Administrative State* (Bristol, Pa.: Crane Russak, 1992). This text examines the management of the federal budget from the early 1900s to the early 1990s and stresses the centrality of the budget in defining the respective powers of the legislative and executive branches.

Norman J. Ornstein, Thomas E. Mann, and Michael J. Malbin, *Vital Statistics on Congress, 1991–1992* (Washington, D.C.: Congressional Quarterly Press, 1992). The authors bring together from various sources information on eight areas related to Congress including data on the members themselves, on elections, campaign finances, budgeting, committees, and so on.

Robert L. Peabody and Nelson W. Polsby, *New Perspectives on the House of Representatives,* 4th ed. (Baltimore, Md.: The Johns Hopkins University Press, 1992). A comprehensive, behind-the-scenes look at practices and procedures in the House of Representatives.

David W. Rohde, *Parties and Leaders in the Postreform House* (Chicago, Ill.: University of Chicago Press, 1991). Rohde argues that the sectional divisions within the Democratic and Republican parties, particularly between the northern and southern Democrats, have been reduced due to a realignment of electoral forces and that there is an increased divergence between the parties on many significant issues brought before Congress.

James A. Thurber, ed., *Divided Democracy: Cooperation and Conflict between the President and Congress* (Washington, D.C.: Congressional Quarterly Press, 1990). This collection of insightful essays by noted congressional scholars examines the roles of, and the relationship between, the legislative and executive branches of the federal government.

CHAPTER 11
The Presidency

CHAPTER CONTENTS

WHAT IF . . . THE VICE PRESIDENT SERVED AS THE PRESIDENT'S CHIEF OF STAFF?

Traditionally, vice presidents are chosen to "balance the ticket" by appealing to a regional, ethnic, religious, or philosophical perspective different from that of the presidential candidate. After the election, they perform the duties assigned by the Constitution—namely, presiding over the Senate occasionally and doing whatever the president asks them to do. In recent times, presidential candidates have frequently announced their intention to pick a skillful and talented vice president and then to give him or her very important duties.

The problem with this good intention is that it is more difficult than it seems. Vice presidents cannot act as effective liaisons with Congress because the legislators resent it. Vice presidents cannot run cabinet departments because that would create a conflict of interest. Vice presidents can attend funerals of heads of states and perform other honorary duties, but they are *not* the president and are often regarded as unimportant substitutes by foreign nations.

It seems that the vice president's abilities are underused, while presidents continue to be overburdened by their official, ceremonial, and political duties. To cope with their responsibilities, modern presidents have tried numerous organizational schemes for the White House and have exhausted aides in the process. Why not solve both problems by having the president pick an effective, closely allied politician for vice president who could then act as the president's chief of staff?

Giving the chief of staff job to the vice president means that he or she would be responsible for running the White House, screening visitors to the president, keeping tabs on the president's popularity, and making sure that the president gets the kind of advice and assistance that he or she needs from advisers and federal executives. The job would demand excellent organizational and political skills. The vice president would have to be able to speak for the president on some matters and command the respect of other federal and state officials. In effect, the vice president would become the president's closest assistant and adviser.

To choose a vice president for this new responsibility would totally upset the traditional way of building a ticket. Instead of looking for a vice president whose political strengths make up for the presidential candidate's weaknesses, the ideal candidate would complement the president in ideology, partisanship, and policy positions. This might be

seen as a disadvantage to the national ticket because people who did not like the presidential nominee's views would not like the vice presidential nominee's either. If both parties adopted this strategy, there might be a large number of Americans who could find no one on either ticket to support. Furthermore, some groups within each party would claim to have lost their representation and threaten to leave the political family.

More important, presidents would have to change their view of their next-in-command—their vice presidents. Although a presidential nominee always wants a running mate who will be an asset to the ticket, the chief executive does not want a vice president who is more popular with the people than the president. By making the vice president the White House chief of staff, the president either would have to limit the vice president's authority, thus making him or her less able to do the job, or be prepared to see a vice president grow in power and public reputation. Vice presidents have often moved on to compete for the top post. Being chief of staff might sharpen the number two executive's ambition and speed up his or her timetable to the White House.

1. *What kind of running mate would a president need for that person to be an effective chief of staff?*
2. *Would the vice president as chief of staff gain or lose popularity with the public and Congress in taking on this difficult task?*

It is ironic that the Founding Fathers, rejecting so emphatically the model of a king, created an office presently invested with authority far beyond that of any surviving king and only to be rivaled by the powers of absolute monarchs.[1]

The writers of the Constitution created the presidency of the United States without any models to draw on. Nowhere else in the world was there a democratically selected chief executive. What the founders did not want was a king. In fact, given their previous experience with royal governors in the colonies, many of the delegates to the Constitutional Convention wanted to create a very weak executive who could not veto legislation. In part because the delegates knew that George Washington—whose character and integrity were clear—would be the first occupant of the office, they created a chief executive who had enough powers granted in the Constitution to balance those of the Congress.

The power exercised by each president who has held the office has been scrutinized and judged by historians, political scientists, the media, and the public. Indeed, it would seem that Americans are fascinated by presidential power. In this chapter, after first looking at who can become president and at the process involved, we examine closely the nature and extent of the constitutional powers held by the president.

Who Can Become President?

The requirements for becoming president, as outlined in Article II, Section 1, of the Constitution, are not overwhelmingly stringent:

> No person except a natural-born Citizen, or a Citizen of the United States, at the time of the Adoption of this Constitution shall be eligible to the Office of President; neither shall any Person be eligible to that Office who shall not have attained to the Age of 35 Years, and been fourteen Years a Resident within the United States.

The only question that arises about these qualifications relates to the term *natural-born citizen*. Does that mean only citizens born in the United States and its territories? What about a child born to a U.S. citizen (or to a couple who are U.S. citizens) while visiting or living in another country? Although the question has not been dealt with directly by the Supreme Court, it is reasonable to expect that someone would be eligible if his or her parents were Americans. The first presidents, after all, were not even American citizens at birth, and others were born in areas that did not become part of the United States until later. This issue became important when George Romney,[2] who was born in Chihuahua, Mexico, made a serious bid for the Republican presidential nomination in the 1960s.

The great American dream is symbolized by the statement that "anybody can become president of this country." It is true that in modern times presidents have included a haberdasher (Truman—for a short period of time), a peanut farmer (Carter), and an actor (Reagan). But if you examine Appendix C, you will see that the most common previous occupation of

Abraham Lincoln is usually classified as one of the greatest presidents because of his dedication to preserving the Union.

---

[1] Page Smith, *The Constitution: A Documentary and Narrative History* (New York: William Morrow, 1978), p. 528.
[2] Governor of Michigan from 1963 to 1969.

At John F. Kennedy's inauguration, Robert Frost read a special poem.

TWELFTH AMENDMENT
An amendment to the Constitution, adopted in 1804, that specifies the separate election of the president and vice president by the electoral college.

presidents in this country has been the legal profession. Out of forty-two presidents, twenty-five have been lawyers, and many have been wealthy.

Although the Constitution states that the minimum-age requirement for the presidency is thirty-five years, most presidents have been much older than that when they assumed office. John F. Kennedy, at the age of forty-three, was the youngest elected president, and the oldest was Ronald Reagan, at age sixty-nine. The average age at inauguration has been fifty-four. There has clearly been a demographic bias in the selection of presidents. All have been male, white, and Protestant, except for John F. Kennedy, a Roman Catholic. Presidents have been men of great stature—such as Washington—and men in whom leadership qualities were not so pronounced—such as Warren Harding.

The Process of Becoming President

Major and minor political parties nominate candidates for president and vice president at the national conventions every four years. The nation's voters do not elect a president and vice president directly but rather cast ballots for presidential electors who then vote for president and vice president in the electoral college. The electors are chosen from all the states and the District of Columbia.

On occasion, the electoral college has failed to give any candidate a majority. At this point, the election is thrown into the House of Representatives, in which the president is chosen from among the three candidates having the most electoral college votes. Each state's House delegation has one vote. To win the election, a candidate must receive a majority of the votes that are cast in the House of Representatives. By House rule, each state's vote is given to the candidate preferred by a majority of the state's delegation in the House. In the event that there is a tie within any state's House delegation, that state's vote is not counted.

Only two times in our past has the House had to decide on a president. Thomas Jefferson and Aaron Burr tied in the electoral college in 1800. This happened because the Constitution had not been explicit in indicating which of the two electoral votes was for president and which was for vice president. In 1804, the **Twelfth Amendment** clarified the matter. In 1824, the House had to make a choice among William H. Crawford, Andrew Jackson, and John Quincy Adams. It chose Adams, even though Jackson had more electoral and popular votes.

What if the House fails to choose a president? Then the vice president, who has been chosen by the electoral college—or, failing that, chosen by the Senate—acts as president. There is no explicit provision in the Twelfth Amendment or elsewhere in the Constitution about what will happen if neither a president nor a vice president can be selected by Congress. Failure to select a vice president, however, is very unlikely because the Senate makes its choice with all members voting for one of the top two candidates. A Senate deadlock is still possible, however. Either a new election could be called, or the speaker of the House could succeed to the presidency until the matter could be resolved.

PROFILE

George Washington

"I do not conceive we can exist long as a nation without having lodged somewhere a power which will pervade the whole union in as energetic a manner as the authority of the state governments extends over the several states."

George Washington was born more than two and a half centuries ago. In spite of voluminous research and the millions of words written about him, he still retains his aura of greatness. Not surprisingly, his contemporaries offered him as much respect as schoolchildren do today.

If Washington were alive today and scrutinized with the same standards we use with our contemporary presidents, however, this aura might be diminished. Consider his reading habits. They certainly were not as sophisticated as those of John Fitzgerald Kennedy, who, when asked what his ten favorite books were, listed works of biography, history, and politics. Washington, a how-to-do-it expert, enjoyed books about manure and animal husbandry.

Washington was not a world traveler. Indeed, he never went to Europe. He spoke no foreign languages—and he was a poor public speaker. The single outstanding characteristic of his military career was perseverance. It was perseverance that won the Battle of Trenton, which brought the Revolution back to life and convinced France to commit itself to the American cause. Military analysts of today, however, do not have high praise for the technical expertise of Washington's military campaign. Crossing the Delaware River, his troops could not fire their guns because the powder was soaked by freezing rain. His officers wanted to call off the attack, but his men fought with bayonets. The Battle of Trenton was won because Washington was determined, not because he was a military genius.

In his day, Washington was one of the wealthiest individuals in the nation. He was proud and aristocratic in manner and never attempted to give the impression that he was a great democrat. The story goes that Gouverneur Morris, an old friend and supporter, once put his hand on Washington's shoulder to show his close relationship with the chief executive. Washington removed Morris's hand almost immediately.

Contemporaries of the first president and historians of today agree that Washington had the necessary qualities to be the "father of our country"; he was a natural leader. As the chief executive, he organized the administration, maintained dignity in office, and kept the early decisions of the nation free from partisanship.

The Many Roles of the President

The Constitution speaks briefly about the duties and obligations of the president. Based on a brief list of powers and the precedents of history, the presidency has grown into a very complicated job that requires balancing at least five constitutional roles. These are (1) *chief of state*, (2) *chief executive*, (3) *commander in chief* of the armed forces, (4) *chief diplomat*, and (5) *chief legislator* of the United States. Here we examine each of these significant presidential functions, or roles. It is worth noting that one person plays all these roles simultaneously and that the needs of these roles may at times be contradictory.

Did You Know ... That Thomas Jefferson was the first president to be inaugurated in Washington, D.C., where he walked to the Capitol from a boarding house, took the oath, made a brief speech in the Senate chamber, and then walked back home?

CHIEF OF STATE
The role of the president as ceremonial head of the government.

Chief of State

Every nation has at least one person who is the ceremonial head of state. In most democratic governments, the role of **chief of state** is given to someone other than the chief executive. In Britain, for example, the chief of state is the queen. In France, where the prime minister is the chief executive, the chief of state is the president. But in the United States, the president is both chief executive and chief of state. According to William Howard Taft, as chief of state, the president symbolizes the "dignity and majesty" of the American people. In his capacity as chief of state, the president engages in a number of activities that are largely symbolic or ceremonial in nature, such as the following:

- Decorating war heroes.
- Throwing out the first ball to open the baseball season.
- Dedicating parks and post offices.
- Launching charity drives.
- Receiving visiting chiefs of state at the White House.
- Going on official state visits to other countries.
- Making personal telephone calls to congratulate the country's heroes.

Many students of the American political system believe that having the president serve as both the chief executive and the head of state drastically limits the time available to do "real" work. Not all presidents have agreed with this conclusion, however—particularly those presidents who have been able to blend skillfully these two roles with their role as politician. Being chief of state gives the president tremendous public exposure. When that exposure is positive, it helps the president deal with Congress over proposed legislation and increases his chances of being reelected—or getting his party's candidates elected.

One effect of the president's role as chief of state is that his life is put on public display day in and day out. Everything the president and the "first family" does has become intensely interesting to the American public—and indeed to the world. One reason why many Americans are so absorbed by the trivia of presidential activities is that the president is also the personal symbol of the nation, in the same way that kings and queens are. This symbolic role leads to an emotional investment by citizens and explains why, even if the president is not liked by many individuals, they still feel great anxiety when his life is threatened. It seems like a threat to the nation, not just to the person in the office.

Chief Executive

CHIEF EXECUTIVE
The role of the president as head of the executive branch of the government.

According to the Constitution, "The executive Power shall be vested in a President of the United States of America. . . . He may require the Opinion, in writing, of the principal Officer in each of the Executive Departments, upon any Subject relating to the Duties of their respective Offices . . . and he shall nominate, and by and with the Advice and Consent of the Senate, shall appoint . . . Officers of the United States. . . . He shall take Care that the Laws be faithfully executed."

As **chief executive** the president is constitutionally bound to enforce the acts of Congress, the judgments of federal courts, and treaties signed by the United States. To assist in the various tasks of the chief executive, the president has a federal bureaucracy (see Chapter 12), which currently consists of some three million civilian employees and which spends over a trillion dollars per year.

The Powers of Appointment and Removal. Because the president is head of the largest bureaucracy in the United States, you might think that he wields enormous power. The president, however, only nominally runs the executive bureaucracy, for most of its jobs are protected by **civil service.**[3] Therefore, even though the president has **appointment power,** it is not very extensive, being limited to cabinet and subcabinet jobs, federal judgeships, agency heads, and about two thousand lesser jobs. In Table 11-1, we show what percentage of the total employment in each executive department is available for political appointment by the president.

The president's power to remove from office officials who are doing a poor job or who do not agree with the president is not explicitly granted by the Constitution and has been limited. In 1926, however, a Supreme Court decision prevented Congress from interfering with the president's ability to fire those executive-branch officials that the president had appointed with Senate approval.[4]

---

[3]See Chapter 12 for a discussion of the Civil Service Reform Act.
[4]*Meyers v. United States*, 272 U.S. 52 (1926).

CIVIL SERVICE
A collective term for the body of employees working for the government. Generally, civil service is understood to apply to all those who gain government employment through a merit system.

APPOINTMENT POWER
The authority vested in the president to fill a government office or position. Positions filled by presidential appointment include those in the executive branch, the federal judiciary, commissioned officers in the armed forces, and members of the independent regulatory commissions.

TABLE 11-1 ■ Total Employment in Cabinet Departments Available for Political Appointment by the President

Executive Department	Total Number of Employees	Political Appointments Available	Percent
Agriculture	118,403	473	0.40
Commerce	40,092	304	0.76
Defense	1,009,371	505	0.05
Education	4,862	134	2.75
Energy	18,712	170	0.91
Health and Human Services	126,768	203	0.16
Housing and Urban Development	13,745	154	1.12
Interior	77,808	148	0.19
Justice	87,265	585	0.67
Labor	18,123	145	0.80
State	25,534	498	1.95
Transportation	68,049	129	0.19
Treasury	175,150	631	0.36
Veterans Affairs	255,217	14	0.01
Total	2,039,099	3,923	0.19

SOURCES: Committee on Post Office and Civil Service, House of Representatives, 96th Congress, 2nd Session, *Policy and Supporting Positions*, November 18, 1980; *Statistical Abstract of the United States*, 1992.

Did You Know . . . That President William Henry Harrison gave the longest inaugural address of any American president, lasting two hours? The weather was cold and stormy, Harrison caught a cold, got pneumonia and pleurisy, and died a month later.

The ten agencies whose directors the president can remove at any time are as follows:

1. ACTION (coordinates volunteer programs).
2. Arms Control and Disarmament Agency.
3. Commission on Civil Rights.
4. Energy Research and Development Agency.
5. Environmental Protection Agency.
6. Federal Mediation and Conciliation Service.
7. General Services Administration.
8. National Aeronautics and Space Administration.
9. Postal Service.
10. Small Business Administration.

In addition, the president can remove all heads of cabinet departments and all individuals in the Executive Office of the President.

Harry Truman spoke candidly of the difficulties a president faces in trying to control the executive bureaucracy. Upon leaving office, he referred to the problems that Eisenhower, as a former general of the army, was going to have: "He'll sit here and he'll say do this! do that! and nothing will happen. Poor Ike—it won't be a bit like the Army. He'll find it very frustrating."[5]

REPRIEVE
The president has the power to grant a reprieve to postpone the execution of a sentence imposed by a court of law; usually done for humanitarian reasons or to await new evidence.

PARDON
The granting of a release from the punishment or legal consequences of a crime; a pardon can be granted by the president before or after a conviction.

The Power to Grant Reprieves and Pardons.   Section 2 of Article II of the Constitution gives the president the power to grant **reprieves** and **pardons** for offenses against the United States except in cases of impeachment. All pardons are administered by the Office of the Pardon Attorney in the Department of Justice. In principle, pardons are granted to remedy a mistake made in a conviction.

The Supreme Court upheld the president's right to reprieve in a 1925 case concerning the pardon granted by the president to an individual convicted of contempt of court.[6] The judiciary had contended that only judges had the authority to convict individuals for contempt of court when court orders were violated and that the courts should be free from interference by the executive branch. The Supreme Court simply stated that the president could reprieve or pardon all offenses "either before trial, during trial, or after trial, by individuals, or by classes, conditionally or absolutely, and this without modification or regulation by Congress."[7] In a controversial decision, President Gerald Ford pardoned former President Richard Nixon for his role in the Watergate affair before any charges were brought in court.

Commander in Chief

The president, according to the Constitution, "shall be Commander in Chief of the Army and Navy of the United States, and of the militia of the several States, when called into the actual service of the United States." In other words, the armed forces are under civilian, rather than military, control.

[5]Quoted in Richard E. Neustadt, *Presidential Power* (New York: John Wiley, 1960), p. 9.
[6]*Ex parte Grossman*, 267 U.S. 87 (1925).
[7]*Ibid.*

During Operation Desert Storm, President Bush acted as commander-in-chief, receiving frequent updates on the conflict from General Colin Powell and Secretary of Defense Dick Cheney in the situation room of the White House.

Certainly those who wrote the Constitution had George Washington in mind when they made the president the **commander in chief.** Although we no longer expect our president to lead the troops to battle, presidents as commanders in chief have wielded dramatic power. Harry Truman made the awesome decision to drop the atomic bomb on Hiroshima and Nagasaki in 1945 to force Japan to surrender and thus bring to an end World War II. Lyndon Johnson ordered bombing missions against North Vietnam in the 1960s, and he personally selected the targets. Nixon decided to invade Cambodia in 1970, and Ronald Reagan sent troops to Lebanon and Grenada in 1983 and ordered American fighter planes to attack Libya in 1986 in retaliation for terrorist attacks on American citizens. Bush sent troops to Panama in 1989 and to the Middle East in 1990.

The president is the ultimate decision maker in military matters. Everywhere he goes, so too goes the "football"—a briefcase filled with all the codes necessary to order a nuclear attack. Only the president has the power to order the use of nuclear force.

In his role as commander in chief, the president has probably exercised more authority than in any other role. Constitutionally, Congress has the sole power to declare war, but the president can send the armed forces into a country in situations that are certainly the equivalent of war. When William McKinley ordered troops into Peking to help suppress the Boxer Rebellion in 1900, he was sending them into a combat situation. Harry Truman dispatched troops to Korea as part of a "police action" in 1950. Kennedy, Johnson, and Nixon waged an undeclared war in Vietnam, where 57,000 Americans were killed and 300,000 were wounded. In none of these situations did Congress declare war.

In an attempt to gain more control over such military activities, in 1973 Congress passed a **War Powers Act**—over President Nixon's veto—requiring that the president consult with Congress before sending American forces into action. Once they are sent, the president must report to Congress within forty-eight hours. Unless Congress has passed a declaration

COMMANDER IN CHIEF
The role of the president as supreme commander of the military forces of the United States and of the state national guard units when they are called into federal service.

WAR POWERS ACT
A law passed in 1973 spelling out the conditions under which the president can commit troops without congressional approval.

Did You Know . . . That Theodore Roosevelt was the first president to leave the country on an official trip during his term, the first president to ride in a submarine and an airplane, and the first president to have a telephone on his desk?

of war within sixty days or has extended the sixty-day time limit, the forces must be withdrawn. The War Powers Act was tested in the fall of 1983 when Reagan requested that troops be left in Lebanon. The resulting compromise was a congressional resolution allowing troops to remain there for eighteen months. Shortly after the resolution was passed, however, more than 240 sailors and marines were killed in the suicide bombing of a U.S. military housing compound in Beirut. That event provoked a furious congressional debate over the role American troops were playing in the Middle East, and all troops were withdrawn shortly afterward.

In spite of the War Powers Act, the powers of the president as commander in chief are more extensive today than they were in the past. These powers are closely linked to the president's powers as chief diplomat, or chief crafter of foreign policy.

Chief Diplomat

The Constitution gives the president the power to recognize foreign governments; with the **advice and consent** of the Senate, to make treaties; and to make special agreements with other heads of state that do not require congressional approval. In addition, the president nominates ambassadors. As **chief diplomat,** the president dominates American foreign policy.

Recognition Power.   An important power of the president as chief diplomat is **recognition power,** or the power to recognize—or refuse to recognize—foreign governments. In his role as ceremonial head of state, the president has always received foreign diplomats. In modern times, the simple act of receiving a foreign diplomat has been equivalent to accrediting the diplomat and officially recognizing his or her government. Such recognition of the legitimacy of another country's government is a prerequisite to diplomatic relations or negotiations between that country and the United States.

ADVICE AND CONSENT
The power vested in the U.S. Senate by the Constitution (Article II, Section 2) to give its advice and consent to the president concerning treaties and presidential appointments.

CHIEF DIPLOMAT
The role of the president in recognizing foreign governments, making treaties, and making executive agreements.

RECOGNITION POWER
The president's power, as chief diplomat, to extend diplomatic recognition to foreign governments.

President Clinton and President Yeltsin at their 1993 summit meeting in Vancouver.

Deciding when to recognize a foreign power is not always a simple task. The United States, for example, did not recognize the Soviet Union until 1933—sixteen years after the Russian Revolution of 1917. It was only after all attempts to reverse the effects of that revolution—including military invasion of Russia and diplomatic isolation—had proved futile that Franklin Roosevelt extended recognition to the Soviet government. U.S. presidents faced a similar problem with the Chinese communist revolution and the emergence of a new communist government in mainland China. The former government had fled to the island of Taiwan, establishing its headquarters there, and so two rival Chinese governments existed—both claiming legitimacy. In December 1978, long after the communist victory in China, Jimmy Carter granted official recognition to the People's Republic of China and downgraded diplomatic relations with the rival government of the Republic of China in Taiwan. Nixon's earlier "ping-pong diplomacy"[8] and subsequent trip to China did much to prepare the way for diplomatic recognition of that country by the United States, but Carter's policy nonetheless elicited much criticism from anticommunist hardliners. On April 7, 1979, Carter again used his recognition powers as chief diplomat when he broke diplomatic ties with the revolutionary Khomeini government in Iran.

When Lithuania declared its independence from the Soviet Union in 1990, President Bush was placed in a difficult position. The United States had never recognized the Soviet occupation of the Lithuanian republic after World War II. Should Bush have sent an ambassador as soon as Lithuania declared its freedom? Bush moved cautiously, giving Lithuania moral support but avoiding direct recognition so as to avoid disrupting newly cordial relations with the Soviet Union. Similarly, when Croatia and Slovenia declared independence from Yugoslavia, Bush again moved slowly, only recognizing these new nations after many other European nations had done so.

Proposal and Ratification of Treaties. The president has the sole power to negotiate treaties with other nations. These treaties must be presented to the Senate, where they may be modified and must be approved by a two-thirds vote. After ratification, the president can approve the senatorial version of the treaty. Approval poses a problem when the Senate has tacked on substantive amendments or reservations to a treaty, particularly when such changes may require reopening negotiations with the other signatory governments. Sometimes a president may decide to withdraw a treaty if the senatorial changes are too extensive—as Wilson did with the Versailles Treaty in 1919. Wilson felt that the senatorial reservations would weaken the treaty so much that it would be ineffective. His refusal to accept the senatorial version of the treaty led to the eventual refusal of the United States to join the League of Nations.

President Carter was more successful in lobbying for the treaties that provided for the return of the Panama Canal to Panama by the year 2000 and neutralizing the canal. He was unsuccessful, however, in his attempts to gain ratification of the Strategic Arms Limitation Talks treaty, known

Did You Know . . . That more than $150 million has been spent since 1980 to pay living and security expenses for former presidents Nixon, Ford, Carter, Reagan, and Bush?

---

[8]The Nixon administration first encouraged new relations with the People's Republic of China by allowing a cultural exchange of ping-pong teams.

U.S. President Jimmy Carter, Egyptian president Anwar el-Sadat, and Israeli Prime Minister Menachem Begin signing the Camp David accords, bringing peace between Egypt and Israel.

as SALT II. That treaty, which provided for limits on nuclear-armed, long-range bombers and intercontinental ballistic missiles, encountered fierce opposition from Senate conservatives and from the subsequent Reagan administration. The treaty was withdrawn by President Reagan. In 1988, Ronald Reagan succeeded in getting Senate approval of the intermediate-range nuclear forces (INF) treaty with the Soviet Union, which reduced the intermediate-range missiles of both nations.

Executive Agreements.　Presidential power in foreign affairs is greatly enhanced by the use of **executive agreements** made between the president and other heads of state. Such agreements do not require Senate approval, although the House and Senate may refuse to appropriate the funds necessary to implement them. Whereas treaties are binding on all succeeding administrations, executive agreements are not binding without each new president's consent.

Among the advantages of executive agreements are speed and secrecy. The former is essential during a crisis; the latter is important when the administration fears that open senatorial debate may be detrimental to the best interests of the United States or to the interests of the president. There have been far more executive agreements (about 9,000) than treaties (about 1,300). Franklin Roosevelt used executive agreements to bypass congressional isolationists in trading American destroyers for British Caribbean naval bases and in arranging diplomatic and military affairs with Canada and Latin American nations. Many executive agreements contain secret provisions calling for American military assistance or other support.

EXECUTIVE AGREEMENTS
International agreements made by the president, without senatorial ratification, with heads of foreign states.

Chief Legislator

Constitutionally, the president must recommend to the Congress legislation that he judges necessary and expedient. Not all presidents have wielded their powers as **chief legislator** in the same manner. President John Tyler was almost completely unsuccessful in getting his legislative

CHIEF LEGISLATOR
The role of the president in influencing the making of laws.

programs implemented by Congress. Presidents Theodore Roosevelt, Franklin Roosevelt, and Lyndon B. Johnson, however, saw much of their proposed legislation put into effect.

In modern times, the president has played a dominant role in creating the congressional agenda. In the president's annual **State of the Union message,** which is required by the Constitution (Article II, Section 3) and usually given in late January shortly after Congress reconvenes, the president as chief legislator presents his program. The message gives a broad, comprehensive view of what the president wishes the legislature to accomplish during its session. It is as much a message to the American people and to the world as it is to Congress, and its impact on public opinion can determine the way in which Congress responds to the president's agenda.

Getting Legislation Passed. The president can propose legislation, but Congress is not required to pass any of the administration's bills. How, then, does the president get those proposals made into law? One way, of course, is to draft the bills that he wants to see passed. But perhaps equally important is the power of persuasion. The president writes to, telephones, and meets with various congressional leaders; makes public announcements to force the weight of public opinion onto Congress in favor of a legislative program; and, as head of the party, exercises legislative leadership through the congresspersons of the president's party.

To be sure, presidents whose party represents a majority in both houses of Congress have an easier time getting their legislation passed than do presidents facing hostile Congresses. But one of the ways in which a president who faces a hostile Congress can still wield power is through the ability to veto legislation.

Saying No to Legislation. The president has the power to say no through use of the veto,[9] by which the White House returns a bill unsigned to the legislative body with a **veto message** attached. Because the Constitution requires that every bill passed by the House and the Senate must be sent to the president before it becomes law, the president must act on each bill.

1. If the bill is signed, it becomes law.
2. If the bill is not sent back to Congress after ten congressional working days, it becomes law.
3. The bill can be vetoed and sent back to Congress with a message setting forth objections. Congress then can change the bill, hoping to secure presidential approval and repass it. Or it can simply reject the president's objections by overriding the veto with a two-thirds roll-call vote of the members present in each house.
4. If the president refuses to sign the bill and Congress adjourns within ten working days after the bill has been submitted to the president, the bill is killed permanently for that session of Congress. If Congress wishes the bill to be reconsidered, it must be reintroduced during the following session. This is called a **pocket veto.**

---

[9]*Veto* in Latin means "I forbid."

Did You Know . . . That the expression "O.K.," which is used worldwide, was coined in the presidential campaign of 1840 in reference to Martin Van Buren who was called "Old Kinderhook" after his birthplace? His New York supporters formed the "O.K." club and shouted the expression at political rallies and parades.

STATE OF THE UNION MESSAGE
An annual message to Congress in which the president proposes a legislative program. The message is addressed not only to Congress but also to the American people and to the world. It offers the opportunity to dramatize policies and objectives and to gain public support.

VETO MESSAGE
The president's formal explanation of a veto when legislation is returned to the Congress.

POCKET VETO
A special veto power exercised by the chief executive after a legislative body has adjourned. Bills not signed by the chief executive die after a specified period of time. If Congress wishes to reconsider such a bill, it must be reintroduced in the following session of Congress.

TABLE 11-2 ■ Presidential Vetoes, 1789–1992

Note that few bills were vetoed until after the Civil War.

Years	President	Regular Vetoes	Vetoes Overridden	Pocket Vetoes	Total Vetoes
1789–1797	Washington	2	0	0	2
1797–1801	J. Adams	0	0	0	0
1801–1809	Jefferson	0	0	0	0
1809–1817	Madison	5	0	2	7
1817–1825	Monroe	1	0	0	1
1825–1829	J. Q. Adams	0	0	0	0
1829–1837	Jackson	5	0	7	12
1837–1841	Van Buren	0	0	1	1
1841–1841	Harrison	0	0	0	0
1841–1845	Tyler	6	1	4	10
1845–1849	Polk	2	0	1	3
1849–1850	Taylor	0	0	0	0
1850–1853	Fillmore	0	0	0	0
1853–1857	Pierce	9	5	0	9
1857–1861	Buchanan	4	0	3	7
1861–1865	Lincoln	2	0	5	7
1865–1869	A. Johnson	21	15	8	29
1869–1877	Grant	45	4	48	93
1877–1881	Hayes	12	1	1	13
1881–1881	Garfield	0	0	0	0
1881–1885	Arthur	4	1	8	12

Presidents employed the veto power infrequently until the administration of Andrew Johnson, but it has been used with increasing vigor since then (see Table 11-2). The total number of vetoes from George Washington through George Bush was 2,494, with about two-thirds of those vetoes being exercised by Cleveland, Franklin Roosevelt, Truman, and Eisenhower.

A veto is a clear-cut indication of the president's dissatisfaction with congressional legislation. It is a very effective tool as well, because it denies the legislative power of the Congress. Nonetheless, Congress rarely overrides a regular presidential veto. Consider that two-thirds of the members of each house who are present must vote to override the president's veto in a roll-call vote. This means that if only one-third plus one of the members voting in one of the houses of Congress do not agree to override the veto, the veto holds. Table 11-2 tells us that it was not until the administration of John Tyler that Congress overrode a presidential veto. In the first sixty-five years of American federal government his-

TABLE 11-2 (continued)

Years	President	Regular Vetoes	Vetoes Overridden	Pocket Vetoes	Total Vetoes
1885–1889	Cleveland	304	2	110	414
1889–1893	Harrison	19	1	25	44
1893–1897	Cleveland	42	5	128	170
1897–1901	McKinley	6	0	36	42
1901–1909	T. Roosevelt	42	1	40	82
1909–1913	Taft	30	1	9	39
1913–1921	Wilson	33	6	11	44
1921–1923	Harding	5	0	1	6
1923–1929	Coolidge	20	4	30	50
1929–1933	Hoover	21	3	16	37
1933–1945	F. Roosevelt	372	9	263	635
1945–1953	Truman	180	12	70	250
1953–1961	Eisenhower	73	2	108	181
1961–1963	Kennedy	12	0	9	21
1963–1969	L. Johnson	16	0	14	30
1969–1974	Nixon	26[a]	7	17	43
1974–1977	Ford	48	12	18	66
1977–1981	Carter	13	2	18	31
1981–1989	Reagan	39	9	28	67
1989–1992	Bush	31	1	15	46
Total		1,450	104	1044	2,494

[a]Two pocket vetoes, overruled in the courts, are counted here as regular vetoes.

SOURCE: Louis Fisher, *The Politics of Shared Power: Congress and the Executive,* 2d ed. (Washington, D.C.: Congressional Quarterly Press, 1987), p. 30; *Congressional Quarterly Weekly Report,* December 19, 1992, pp. 3925–9326.

tory, out of thirty-three regular vetoes, Congress only overrode one, or less than 3 percent. Overall, only about 4 percent of all vetoes have been overridden.

Other Presidential Powers

The powers of the president discussed in the preceding sections are called **constitutional powers** because their basis lies in the Constitution. In addition, Congress has established by law, or statute, numerous other presidential powers—such as the ability to declare national emergencies. These are called **statutory powers.** Both constitutional and statutory powers have been labeled the **expressed powers** of the president because they are expressly written into the Constitution or into congressional law.

Presidents also have what have come to be known as **inherent powers.** These depend on the loosely worded statement in the Constitution that "the executive power shall be vested in a president" and that the president

CONSTITUTIONAL POWERS
The powers vested in the president by Article II of the Constitution.

STATUTORY POWERS
The powers created for the president through laws established by Congress.

EXPRESSED POWERS
The constitutional and statutory powers of the president, which are expressly written into the Constitution or into congressional law.

INHERENT POWERS
Powers of the president derived from the loosely worded statement in the Constitution that "the executive power shall be vested in a president" and that the president should "take care that the laws be faithfully executed"; defined through practice rather than through constitutional or statutory law.

should "take care that the laws be faithfully executed." The most common example of inherent powers are those emergency powers invoked by the president during wartime. Franklin Roosevelt used his inherent powers to relocate the Japanese living in the United States during World War II.

The President As Party Chief and Super Politician

Presidents are by no means above political partisanship, and one of their many roles is that of chief of party. Although the Constitution says nothing about the function of the president within a political party (the mere concept of political parties was abhorrent to most of the authors of the Constitution), today presidents are the actual leaders of their parties.

As party leader, presidents choose the national committee chairperson and can try to discipline those party members who fail to support presidential policies. One way of exerting political power within the party is by the use of **patronage**—appointing individuals to government or public jobs. This power was more extensive in the past, before the establishment of the civil service in 1882 (see Chapter 12), but the president still retains impressive patronage power. As we noted earlier, the president can appoint several thousand individuals to jobs in the cabinet, the White House, and the federal regulatory agencies.

Presidents have a number of other ways of exerting influence as party chief. They may make it known that they will not appoint a particular congressperson's choice for federal judge unless that member of Congress is more supportive of their legislative program.[10] They may agree to campaign for a particular program or for a particular candidate. The president is often called on to mend party fences—which was the reason for John F. Kennedy's trip to Dallas on November 22, 1963, when he was assassinated.

All politicians worry about their constituencies, and so do presidents. Presidents, however, have numerous constituencies. In principle, they are beholden to the entire electorate—the public of the United States—even to those who did not vote. They are certainly beholden to their party constituency because its members put them in office. The president's constituencies also include members of the opposing party whose cooperation the president needs. Finally, the president has to take into consideration a constituency that has come to be called the **Washington community.** This community consists of individuals who—whether in or out of political office—are intimately familiar with the workings of government, thrive on gossip, and daily measure the political power of the president.

All of these constituencies are impressed by presidents who maintain a high level of public approval, partly because this is very difficult to accomplish. Presidential popularity, as measured by national polls, gives the president an extra political resource to use in persuading legislators or bureaucrats, who realize that in refusing the president, they may be going against public sentiment. President Reagan showed amazing strength in the public opinion polls for a second-term chief executive, as Figure 11-1

PATRONAGE
Rewarding faithful party workers and followers with government employment and contracts.

WASHINGTON COMMUNITY
Individuals regularly involved with the political circles in Washington, D.C.

---

[10]"Senatorial courtesy" (see Chapter 13) often puts the judicial appointment in the hands of the Senate, however.

indicates. A Gallup poll of June 1985 showed that President Reagan was also improving his image in history, with the public ranking him as sixth on the list of the nation's greatest presidents, behind Kennedy, Lincoln, Franklin Roosevelt, Truman, and Washington.[11]

The presidential preoccupation with public opinion has been criticized by at least one scholar as changing the balance of national politics. Samuel Kernell proposed that the style of presidential leadership since World War II has changed, partly owing to the influence of television.[12] Presidents frequently go over the heads of Congress and the political elites, taking their case directly to the people. This strategy, which Kernell dubbed "going public," gives the president additional power through the ability to persuade and manipulate public opinion. By identifying their own positions so clearly, presidents make compromise with the Congress much more difficult and weaken the legislators' positions. Furthermore, Kernell asserts, legislators who follow the president are not rewarded by their constituents, whereas those congresspersons who oppose the president may be punished at the polls. Given the increasing importance of the media as the major source of political information for citizens and elites, presidents will continue to use public opinion as part of their arsenal of weapons to get support from Congress and to achieve their policy goals.

The Special Uses of Presidential Power

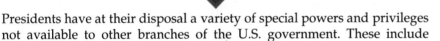

Presidents have at their disposal a variety of special powers and privileges not available to other branches of the U.S. government. These include

[11]*The Gallup Poll*, 1985.
[12]Samuel Kernell, *Going Public: New Strategies of Presidential Leadership*, (Washington, D.C.: Congressional Quarterly Press, 1986).

FIGURE 11-1 ■ Public Popularity of Bush and His Predecessors

SOURCE: *Public Opinion*, February/March 1988, pp. 36–39; Gallup Poll, March 1992.

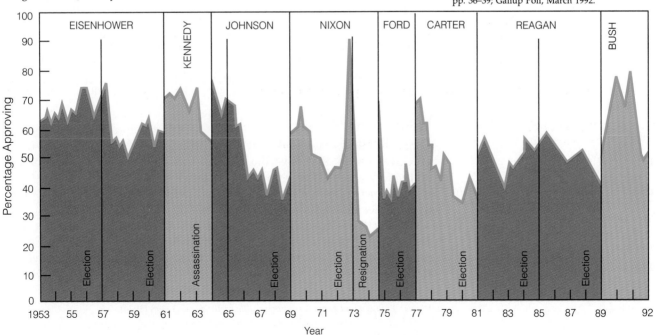

EMERGENCY POWERS
Inherent powers exercised by the president during a period of national crisis, particularly in foreign affairs.

(1) emergency powers, (2) executive orders, (3) executive privilege, and (4) impoundment of funds.

Emergency Powers

If you were to read the Constitution, you would find no mention of the additional powers that the executive office may exercise during national emergencies. Indeed, the Supreme Court has indicated that an "emergency does not create power."[13] But it is clear that presidents have used their inherent powers during times of emergency, particularly in the realm of foreign affairs. The **emergency powers** of the president were first enunciated in the Supreme Court's decision in *United States v. Curtiss-Wright Export Corporation*.[14] In that case, President Franklin Roosevelt, without authorization by Congress, ordered an embargo on the shipment of weapons to two warring South American countries. The Court recognized that the president may exercise inherent powers in foreign affairs and that the national government has primacy in foreign affairs.

Examples of emergency powers are abundant, coinciding with real or contrived crises in domestic and foreign affairs. Abraham Lincoln's suspension of civil liberties at the beginning of the Civil War, his calling of the state militias into national service, and his subsequent governance of conquered areas and even of areas of northern states were justified by claims that such actions were essential to preserve the Union. Franklin Roosevelt declared an "unlimited national emergency" following the fall of France in World War II and mobilized the federal budget and the economy for war.

A more recent example occurred when President Harry S Truman authorized the federal seizure of steel plants and their operation by the national government in 1952 during the Korean war. Truman claimed that he was using his inherent emergency power as chief executive and commander in chief to safeguard the nation's security, as the ongoing steel mill strike threatened the supply of weapons to the armed forces. The Supreme Court did not agree, holding that the president had no authority under the Constitution to seize private property or to legislate such action.[15] According to legal scholars, this was the first time a limit was placed on the exercise of the president's emergency powers.

Executive Orders

Congress allows the president (and administrative agencies) to issue **executive orders** that have the force of law. These executive orders can do the following: (1) give force to legislative statutes, (2) enforce the Constitution or treaties with foreign nations, and (3) establish or modify practices of executive administrative agencies.

An executive order, then, represents the president's legislative power. The only apparent requirement is that under the Administrative Procedure Act of 1946, all executive orders must be published in the *Federal Register.*

EXECUTIVE ORDER
A rule or regulation issued by the president that has the effect of law. Executive orders can implement and give administrative effect to provisions in the Constitution, to treaties, and to statutes.

FEDERAL REGISTER
A publication of the executive branch that prints executive orders, rules, and regulations.

---

[13]*Home Building and Loan Association v. Blaisdell*, 290 U.S. 398 (1934).
[14]229 U.S. 304 (1936).
[15]*Youngstown Sheet and Tube Co. v. Sawyer*, 343 U.S. 579 (1952).

Executive orders have been used to establish some procedures for appointing noncareer administrators, to implement national affirmative-action regulations, to restructure the White House bureaucracy, to ration consumer goods and to administer wage and price controls under emergency conditions, to classify government information as secret, and to regulate exports of restricted items. More than thirteen thousand executive orders have been promulgated in a numbered series officially compiled by the State Department, and many more have never been compiled.

Executive Privilege

Another inherent executive power that has been claimed by presidents concerns the ability of the president and his executive officials to refuse to appear before, or to withhold information from, Congress or the courts. This is called **executive privilege,** and it relies on the constitutional separation of powers for its basis. Critics of executive privilege believe that it can be used to shield from public scrutiny actions of the executive branch that should be open to Congress and to the American public.

Limits to executive privilege went untested until the Watergate affair in the early 1970s. The Supreme Court subpoenaed secret tapes containing Richard Nixon's Oval Office conversations during his tenure at the White House. Nixon refused to turn them over, claiming executive privilege. He argued that "no president could function if the private papers of his office, prepared by his personal staff, were open to public scrutiny." In 1974, in one of the Court's most famous cases, *United States v. Nixon,*[16] the justices unanimously ruled that Nixon had to hand over the tapes to the Court. Executive privilege could not be used to prevent evidence from being heard in criminal proceedings.

Impoundment of Funds

By law, the president proposes a budget, and Congress approves it. But there is no clear-cut constitutional indication that the president, as chief executive, is required by law to *spend* all of the funds appropriated by Congress, and many presidents have not done so. In 1803, Thomas Jefferson deferred a $50,000 appropriation for gunboats. Ulysses Grant returned to the Treasury unspent money for public works. In 1932, Herbert Hoover canceled projects funded by Congress. Franklin Roosevelt deferred spending on a number of appropriations to later fiscal years. Truman did not spend all of the money that Congress had allocated for the military, nor did Johnson the money allocated for highway construction, nor did Kennedy the money for weapons systems.

The question came to a head during the Nixon administration after a number of confrontations over this issue between the president and an antagonistic, Democratic-controlled Congress. When Nixon vetoed appropriations bills, Congress often overrode his veto. In retaliation, Nixon impounded the appropriated funds and refused to spend them, claiming that he wanted to reduce overall federal spending. As part of its Budget and Impoundment Control Act of 1974, Congress required that the president

Did You Know . . . That John Kennedy was the first president to hold a live television news conference, although Dwight Eisenhower had permitted television cameras to film his press conferences?

EXECUTIVE PRIVILEGE
The right of executive officials to refuse to appear before, or to withhold information from, a legislative committee. Executive privilege is enjoyed by the president and by those executive officials accorded that right by the president.

---

[16]318 U.S. 683 (1974).

IMPEACHMENT
As authorized by Article I of the Constitution, impeachment is an action by the House of Representatives and the Senate to remove the president, vice president, or civil officers of the United States from office for crimes of "treason, bribery, or other high crimes and misdemeanors."

Nixon (right) leaving the White House after his resignation. Next to him are his wife, Pat, Betty Ford, and Gerald Ford, the new president.

spend all appropriated funds, although Congress gave the president some leeway. A president who is not going to spend all appropriated funds must tell Congress, and only if Congress agrees within forty-five days can the president withhold spending. If the president simply wishes to delay spending, this must be indicated to Congress. If Congress does not agree, it can pass a resolution requiring immediate spending of the appropriated funds. While Congress was deliberating on the budget bill, cities, states, and certain members of Congress sued President Nixon over the impoundment issue. The Supreme Court in 1975 unanimously ruled that the president had to spend money appropriated by Congress because of his obligation to "take care that the laws be faithfully executed."[17]

Abuses of Executive Power and Impeachment

Presidents normally leave office either because their first term has expired and they do not seek (or win) reelection or because, having served two full terms, they are not allowed to seek reelection (owing to the Twenty-second Amendment, passed in 1951). Eight presidents have died in office. But there is still another way for a president to leave office—by **impeachment.** Article I of the Constitution authorizes the House and Senate to remove the president, the vice president, or other civil officers of the United States for crimes of "treason, bribery, or other high crimes and misdemeanors." No one has really defined "high crimes and misdemeanors," but at least twice Congress and the American public were pretty sure that a president had engaged in them.

The authority to impeach is vested in the House of Representatives, and formal impeachment proceedings are initiated there. The power to try impeachment cases rests with the Senate. In the House, a representative must list the charges against the president, vice president, or other civil officer. The impeachment charges are referred either to the Judiciary Committee or to a special investigating committee. If a majority in the House votes for impeachment, then Articles of Impeachment are drawn up, which set forth the basis for the removal of the executive-branch officer. When the president is on trial, the chief justice of the United States Supreme Court presides over the Senate. A two-thirds vote of the senators present is required for conviction. The only punishment that Congress can mete out is removal from office and disqualification from holding any other federal office. The convicted official, however, is subject to further punishment according to law.

In the history of the United States, no president has ever been impeached and also convicted. The only president who was actually impeached by the House was Andrew Johnson, but he was acquitted by the Senate by the margin of a single vote in 1868. Some argue that Johnson's impeachment was simply a case of partisan politics. Impeachment attempts were made against Tyler, Hoover, and Vice President Schuyler Colfax.

The case of Richard Nixon, however, was more serious and certainly less questionable in terms of its political motivation (see the feature entitled *Politics and the Law* in this chapter). In 1974, the House was ready to

---

[17]*Train v. City of New York*, 420 U.S. 35 (1975).

POLITICS AND THE LAW

Watergate: A Crime of Power?

On June 17, 1972, at 2:30 A.M., five men were arrested in the headquarters of the Democratic National Committee in the Watergate apartment complex in Washington, D.C. It was obvious from the outset that this was no ordinary burglary. The five men, dressed in business suits and wearing surgical gloves, were also found to have in their possession some extraordinary items: two cameras, forty rolls of film, lock picks, pen-sized tear-gas guns, bugging devices, a walkie-talkie, and nearly $2,300 in cash among them. In the following days and months, as investigations of the Watergate break-in continued, a story was pieced together that shocked the nation.

The five men had been searching for documents that would connect Senator George McGovern, the Democratic nominee for president, with Fidel Castro and thereby discredit McGovern in the eyes of the American public. They were also looking for any information the Democratic National Committee might have stumbled on that could prove embarrassing to the Nixon administration.

Six days after the break-in, President Nixon and his White House chief of staff, H. R. (Bob) Halderman, formulated a plan by which the Central Intelligence Agency would impede the investigation of the affair that was being undertaken by the Federal Bureau of Investigation.

By early 1973, however, a select Senate committee was established, under the chairmanship of Senator Sam Ervin of North Carolina, to in-

John Dean testifying at Nixon's impeachment hearing.

vestigate the Watergate affair. During the Senate investigation, information about the White House–sponsored criminal activities and subsequent cover-up began to leak out. John Dean III, President Nixon's legal counsel, eventually told the committee that the president himself was responsible for the cover-up. The committee also learned that the Oval Office conversations had been tape-recorded.

Archibald Cox, the Watergate special prosecutor in charge of legal investigations into the affair, subpoenaed several of the tapes, an action upheld by the federal district and appeals courts. The "Saturday Night Massacre" ensued, in which Nixon fired Cox, and the attorney general and deputy attorney general were both forced to resign because

they refused to obey Nixon's orders to fire Cox. Many of Nixon's closest White House aides were indicted in the scandal, and Nixon himself was named an unindicted co-conspirator by the grand jury. A new special prosecutor and Congress subpoenaed a large number of tapes, which the president refused to make available—except in edited form—to Congress. On July 24, 1974, the U.S. Supreme Court ruled that Nixon had to give up the information requested by the special prosecutor. Three days later, the House Judiciary Committee passed the first of three Articles of Impeachment against President Nixon. On August 9, Nixon resigned, and his vice president, Gerald Ford, became president.

vote on Nixon's impeachment and to send the Articles of Impeachment to the Senate when Nixon resigned.

The Executive Organization

Gone are the days when presidents answered their own mail, as George Washington did. It was not until 1857 that Congress authorized a private secretary for the president, to be paid by the federal government. Woodrow Wilson typed most of his correspondence, even though he did have several secretaries. At the beginning of Franklin Roosevelt's long tenure in the White House, the entire staff consisted of thirty-seven individuals. It was not until the New Deal and World War II that the presidential staff became a sizable organization. Today, the executive organization includes a White House Office staff of about 600, including some workers who are part-time and others who are detailed from their departments to the White House. Not all of these employees have equal access to the president, nor are all of them likely to be equally concerned about the administration's political success. The more than 350 employees who work in the White House Office itself are closest to the president. They often include many individuals who worked in the president's campaign. These assistants are most concerned with preserving the president's reputation. Also included in the president's staff are a number of councils and advisory organizations, such as the National Security Council (NSC). Although the individuals who hold staff positions in these offices are appointed by the president, they are really more concerned with their own area than with the president's overall success. The group of appointees who perhaps are least helpful to the president is the cabinet, whose members are each the principal officer of a government department.

The Cabinet

Although the Constitution does not include the word *cabinet*, it does state that the president "may require the Opinion, in writing, of the principal Officer in each of the executive Departments." Since the time of our first president, there has always been an advisory group, or **cabinet,** to which the president turns for counsel. Originally, the cabinet consisted of only four individuals—the secretaries of state, treasury, and war and the attorney general. Today the cabinet numbers thirteen secretaries and the attorney general. Table 11-3 shows the chronological growth of the president's cabinet.

The cabinet may consist of more than the secretaries of the various departments. The president at his discretion can, for example, ascribe cabinet rank to his National Security Council adviser, to the ambassador to the United Nations, or to others. Because neither the Constitution nor statutory law requires the president to consult with the cabinet, its use is purely discretionary. Some presidents have relied on the counsel of their cabinets more than others. Eisenhower frequently turned to his cabinet for advice on a wide range of governmental policies—perhaps because he was used to the team approach in solving problems. Other presidents solicited the opinions of their cabinets and then did what they wanted to do anyway. Lincoln supposedly said—after a cabinet meeting in which a vote was

---

THE CLINTON CABINET

- **Les Aspin,**
  Secretary of Defense
- **Bruce Babbitt,**
  Secretary of Interior
- **Lloyd M. Bentsen,**
  Secretary of the Treasury
- **Jesse Brown,**
  Secretary of Veterans Affairs
- **Ronald H. Brown,**
  Secretary of Commerce
- **Warren M. Christopher,**
  Secretary of State
- **Henry G. Cisneros,**
  Secretary of Housing and Urban Development
- **Mike Espy,**
  Secretary of Agriculture
- **Hazel R. O'Leary,**
  Secretary of Energy
- **Federico Pena,**
  Secretary of Transportation
- **Robert B. Reich,**
  Secretary of Labor
- **Janet Reno**
  Attorney General
- **Richard W. Riley,**
  Secretary of Education
- **Donna E. Shalala,**
  Secretary of Health and Human Services

CABINET

An advisory group selected by the president to aid him in making decisions. The cabinet presently numbers thirteen department secretaries and the attorney general. Depending on the president, the cabinet may be highly influential or relatively insignificant in its advisory role.

TABLE 11–3 ■ **The Cabinet Departments in Order of Their Creation**

Department	Function
State (1789)	Foreign policy making and treaties
Treasury (1789)	The federal government's banker
War (1789)	Administration of the Army only (this department was merged with the Department of the Navy and, with the addition of the Air Force, was called the National Military Establishment in 1947)
Attorney General (1789)	Government's attorney (became the Justice Department in 1870)
Navy (1798)	Administration of the Navy (became part of the National Military Establishment in 1947)
Interior (1849)	Manager of national natural resources, including public lands
Justice (1870)	Government's attorney with attorney general as head
Post Office (1872)	Operation of the mails (became an independent federal agency in 1970)
Agriculture (1889)	Administration of farm programs and, currently, the food stamp program
Commerce and Labor (1903)	Conducts U.S. Census, aids business and labor organizations (split into two separate departments in 1913)
Commerce (1913)	Formerly part of Commerce and Labor
Labor (1913)	Formerly part of Commerce and Labor
Defense (DOD) (1949)	Combined departments of Army and Navy, with Air Force added
Health, Education and Welfare (HEW) (1953)	Health and welfare programs, Social Security, and education (split in 1980)
Housing and Urban Development (HUD) (1965)	The nation's public housing program
Transportation (DOT) (1966)	Federally funded highway program and mass transportation
Energy (DOE) (1977)	Research, atomic energy, and overall national energy policy
Health and Human Services (HHS) (1980)	From HEW
Education (1980)	From HEW
Veterans Affairs (1989)	Elevation of Veterans Administration

seven nays against his one aye—"Seven nays and one aye, the ayes have it."[18] In general, few presidents have relied heavily on the advice of their cabinet members. Carter thought he could put his cabinet to good use and held regular cabinet meetings for the first two years of his tenure. Then he fired three cabinet members and forced two others to resign, while

---

[18]Quoted in Thomas E. Cronin, *The State of the Presidency*, 2d ed. (Boston: Little, Brown, 1980), p. 11.

reorganizing his "inner government." He rarely met with the members of his cabinet thereafter. In recent years, the growth of other parts of the executive branch has rendered the cabinet relatively insignificant as an advisory board to the president.

Often, a president will use a **kitchen cabinet** to replace the formal cabinet as a major source of advice. The term *kitchen cabinet* originated during the presidency of Andrew Jackson, who relied on the counsel of close friends who often met with him in the kitchen of the White House. A kitchen cabinet is a very informal group of advisers, such as Reagan's trusted California coterie, who may or may not be otherwise connected with the government.

It is not surprising that presidents only reluctantly meet with their cabinet heads. Often the departmental heads are more responsive to the wishes of their own staffs or to their own political ambitions than they are to the president. They may be more concerned with obtaining resources for their departments than with helping presidents achieve their goals. So there is often a strong conflict of interest between presidents and their cabinet members. It is likely that formal cabinet meetings are held more out of respect for the cabinet tradition than for their problem-solving value.

The Executive Office of the President

When President Franklin Roosevelt appointed a special committee on administrative management, he knew that the committee would conclude that the president needed help. Indeed, the committee proposed a major reorganization of the executive branch. Congress did not approve the entire reorganization, but it did create the **Executive Office of the President (EOP)** to provide staff assistance for the chief executive and to help coordinate the executive bureaucracy. Since that time, a number of agencies have been created to supply the president with advice and staff help. These agencies are as follows:

- White House Office (1939).
- Council of Economic Advisers (1946).
- National Security Council (1947).
- Office of the United States Trade Representative (1963).
- Council on Environmental Quality (1969).
- Office of Management and Budget (1970).
- Office of Science and Technology Policy (1976).
- Office of Administration (1977).
- Office of Policy Development (1977).
- National Economic Council (1992).

The White House Office.   One of the most important of the agencies within the EOP is the **White House Office,** which includes most of the key personal and political advisers to the president. Among the jobs held by these aides are those of legal counsel to the president, secretary, press secretary, and appointments secretary. Often, the individuals who hold these positions are recruited from the president's campaign staff, and their duties, mainly protecting the president's political interests, are similar to campaign functions. In some administrations, one member of the White

---

KITCHEN CABINET
The informal advisers to the president.

EXECUTIVE OFFICE OF THE PRESIDENT (EOP)
Established by President Franklin D. Roosevelt by executive order under the Reorganization Act of 1939. It currently consists of nine staff agencies that assist the president in carrying out major duties.

WHITE HOUSE OFFICE
The personal office of the president, which tends to presidential political needs and manages the media.

PROFILE

Janet Reno

"I approved the plan and I'm responsible for it."

More than three weeks after being sworn in as president of the United States, Bill Clinton named Janet Reno, the state attorney of Dade County, Florida, as his nominee for attorney general. After being confirmed by the Senate, Reno, a fifty-four year old woman, became the first female ever to hold the office of attorney general.

Less than a month after entering office, she was faced with deciding how to end the siege of the Branch Davidian compound in Waco, Texas that had lasted fifty-one days. After consulting with the FBI, the Bureau of Alcohol, Tobacco, and Firearms (ATF), and many other experts, Reno approved a plan to break down the walls of the compound and pump tear gas into it with the hope that many of the members of the cult would flee. What followed was confusion, explosions, and fires that swiftly turned the compound into a holocaust. Only nine of the roughly ninety members of David Koresh's group escaped. Reno quickly called a press conference to face the media; she accepted full responsibility for the decision. She offered to resign if the president wished her to do so. Generally, the public supported Reno in her decision and admired her willingness to take the blame. President Bill Clinton, who did not speak publicly about the Waco disaster until almost a day later, was criticized for not backing up his attorney general more quickly.

Janet Reno proved to many that she was the right choice for the job in the Waco situation. The nomination had come to her, however, after the rest of the Clinton cabinet was formed. Clinton's first choice, Zoë Baird, an attorney from Connecticut, withdrew from consideration after it was discovered that she had employed illegal aliens to care for her child and had not paid appropriate taxes on their wages. Clinton's second nominee, New York judge Kimba Wood, was asked by the president to withdraw from consideration when it became known that she had also employed aliens. In Wood's case, however, she had paid the appropriate taxes and had helped her employee to obtain legal residency when the law made it possible. Many feminists used these unsuccessful nominations to demonstrate how difficult it is for women to obtain child care so that they can work outside the home. Janet Reno, a single woman without children, did not present a child care problem for the president.

A native Floridian, Janet Reno was the daughter of two Miami journalists, Henry and Jane Wood Reno. For all of her life, she lived in her parents' rural home on a wild plot of land south of Miami, Florida. After her father's death, she continued to maintain the home, living with her mother and tending to an assortment of pets.

Janet Reno attended Cornell University, earning a degree in chemistry in 1960. She then entered Harvard University Law School, completing her studies in 1963. After practicing law in the Miami area for a dozen years, she was appointed state attorney for Dade County, which includes Miami, in 1978. Since that time she was re-elected five times by very large margins.

During her years as state attorney in Miami, Reno has directed an office of more than 900 employees whose job is to prosecute criminals. Her tenure included the explosion of drug trafficking in Florida, the immigration of thousands of Cubans and Haitians, and conflicts sparked by poor race relations among some Miami communities. Her reputation is that of a tough prosecutor particularly concerned with ending violence in families and developing new programs to rehabilitate offenders. Reno has also worked to end child abuse and neglect in the Miami area. She has never shied away from difficult situations. Obviously, the strength of character that Janet Reno showed in the Waco crisis has been developed in fifteen years as Miami's chief prosecutor.

The president's airplane, the 747 Air Force One, was inaugurated in 1990. It costs $26,000 per hour to operate Air Force One.

CHIEF OF STAFF
Directs the White House Office and advises the president.

COUNCIL OF ECONOMIC ADVISERS (CEA)
A staff agency in the Executive Office that advises the president on measures to maintain stability in the nation's economy. Established in 1946, the council develops economic plans and budget recommendations for maintaining the nation's "employment, production, and purchasing power" and helps the president prepare an annual economic report to Congress.

House Office is named **chief of staff.** This person, who is responsible for coordinating the office, is one of the president's chief advisers. Some chiefs of staff, such as Donald Regan during the Reagan administration, have been criticized for keeping the president too isolated, while others have been praised for facilitating compromise within the administration.

Employees of the White House Office have been both envied and criticized. The White House Office, according to most ex-staffers, grants its employees access and power. They are able to use the resources of the White House to contact virtually anyone in the world by telephone or cable, as well as to use the influence of the White House to persuade legislators and citizens. Because of this influence, staffers are often criticized for overstepping the bounds of the office. It is the appointments secretary who is able to grant or deny access to the president to senators, representatives, and cabinet secretaries. It is the press secretary who grants access to any information about the president to the press and television journalists. White House staff are closest to the president and may have considerable influence over the administration's decisions. Often, when presidents are under fire for their decisions, the staff is accused of keeping the chief executive too isolated from criticism or help. Presidents insist that they will not allow the staff to become too powerful, but, given the difficulty of the office, each president eventually turns to staff members for loyal assistance and protection.

Several other of the nine offices within the EOP are especially important.

The Council of Economic Advisers. The Employment Act of 1946 created a three-member **Council of Economic Advisers (CEA)** to advise the president on economic matters. Their advice serves as the basis for the president's annual economic report to Congress. Each of the three members is appointed by the president and can be removed at will. In principle, the CEA was also created to advise the president on economic policy, but for the most part the function of the CEA has been to prepare the annual report.

Office of Management and Budget. The **Office of Management and Budget (OMB)** was originally the Bureau of the Budget, which was created in 1921 within the Department of the Treasury. Recognizing the importance of this agency, President Franklin Roosevelt moved it into the White House Office in 1939. Nixon reorganized the Bureau of the Budget in 1970 and changed its name to reflect its new managerial function. It is headed by a director who must make up the annual federal budget that the president presents to Congress each January for approval (which is rarely forthcoming without months of haggling over changes). In principle, the director of the OMB has broad fiscal powers in planning and estimating various parts of the federal budget, as all agencies must submit their proposed budget to OMB for approval. In reality, it is not so clear that the OMB truly can affect the greater scope of the federal budget. The OMB may be more important as a clearinghouse for legislative proposals initiated in the executive agencies.

National Security Council. The **National Security Council (NSC)** is a link between the president's key foreign and military advisers and the president. Its members consist of the president, the vice president, and the secretaries of state and defense, plus other informal members. The NSC has the resources of the National Security Agency (NSA) at its disposal in giving counsel to the president. Included in the NSC is the president's special assistant for national security affairs. Nixon had Henry Kissinger in this post; Carter had the equally visible Zbigniew Brzezinksi. In the Reagan years, staff members of the NSC, including Lieutenant Colonel Oliver North and Admiral John Poindexter, became involved in an illegal plan to aid the contras in Nicaragua (see the feature entitled *Politics and Ethics* in this chapter).

OFFICE OF MANAGEMENT AND BUDGET (OMB)
A division of the Executive Office created by executive order in 1970 to replace the Bureau of the Budget. OMB's main functions are to assist the president in preparing the annual budget, to clear and coordinate all departmental agency budgets, to help set fiscal policy, and to supervise the administration of the federal budget.

NATIONAL SECURITY COUNCIL (NSC)
A staff agency in the Executive Office established by the National Security Act of 1947. The NSC advises the president on domestic and foreign matters involving national security.

The Vice Presidency

Vice presidents usually have not been overly ecstatic about their position. Franklin Roosevelt's vice president for his first two terms, John Nance Garner, said that "the vice presidency isn't worth a pitcher of warm spit." Harry Truman, himself Franklin Roosevelt's last vice president, was even more forthright: "[Vice presidents are] about as useful as a cow's fifth tit." Walter Mondale, Carter's hard-working vice president and one of the few who truly took an active role in the executive branch, said, "They know who Amy is, but they don't know me." He was referring to Carter's grammar school–aged daughter.

The Vice President's Job

The Constitution does not give much power to the vice president. The only formal duty is to preside over the Senate—which is rarely necessary. This obligation is fulfilled when the Senate organizes and adopts its rules and when the vice president is needed to decide a tie vote. In all other cases, the president pro tempore manages parliamentary procedures in the Senate. The vice president is expected only to participate informally in senatorial deliberations, if at all.

POLITICS AND ETHICS

The Tower Commission and the Iran–*Contra* Investigations

The risks created by the unchecked presidential advisers were made clear in the Iran–*contra* affair. The Reagan administration was shaken by the revelation that government officials had sold weapons to Iran in return for Iranian promises to help negotiate the release of American and other hostages held by pro-Iranian terrorist groups in the Middle East. Profits from these arms sales had then been used to finance operations of the contras in Nicaragua who were attempting to overthrow the Sandinista government there.

These efforts began to unravel after an American C123K cargo plane carrying guns and other weapons to the contras was shot down over Nicaragua on October 5, 1986. The Justice Department launched a full-scale investigation by the Federal Bureau of Investigation into the Iran weapons shipments. President Reagan announced on the same day the appointment of the President's Special Review Board, chaired by former Republican Texas senator John G. Tower and including former secretary of state and former Democratic Maine senator Edmund S. Muskie, and former national security adviser Brent Scowcroft. This special review board, which became known as the Tower Commission, was charged with studying the role of the National Security Council in the scandal.

In early March 1987, the Tower Commission released its report on what had come to be called variously the Iran–*contra* affair, "Iran-scam," "Iranamok," or "Contragate." The report concluded that

Reagan had let his emotional commitment to obtain release of the hostages overrule better judgment, faulted him for failing to conduct a forceful review of the programs once they were under way, and determined that the president's aides had manipulated him and had made their own private foreign policy through a process of lying, surreptitiously diverting arms-deal profits, and trying to cover up the scandal.

The Tower Commission did not give detailed answers to basic questions, such as exactly who had approved and who had knowledge of the Iran and *contra* dealings, when the relevant decisions had been made, or whether any illegal activities had indeed taken place. The joint congressional hearings on the affair, however, supplied dramatic and contradictory testimony on these and other questions. It became clearer that control over the general policy in this regard and control over operational details had rested with National Security Adviser John Poindexter and with his aide, Marine Lieutenant Colonel Oliver North, rather than with the Central Intelligence Agency. A former Air Force general, Richard Secord, had been instrumental in assisting North's execution of the plan.

Oliver North, who testified under a congressional grant of immunity, argued that Congress did not have a right to oversee the activities in which he was engaged and did not even have the right to know what he was up to.

Testimony from Richard Secord revealed some details behind the shipments of arms to the contras.

North's secretary, Fawn Hall, testified about the shredding of important documents, while former national security adviser John Poindexter argued before the committee that it had been necessary to preserve the secret nature of the operation from a probing Congress.

North, Poindexter, Secord, and an arms dealer were all indicted on charges that included conspiracy to divert government funds to buy arms for the *contras*. North was convicted on three counts but found innocent on five charges by a jury that reportedly felt he was the "fall guy" for those higher up. A federal court overturned one of North's convictions in July, 1990, however, because he had been granted immunity for his congressional testimony. Poindexter was convicted and sentenced to six months in prison, but his conviction was overturned in late 1991 on the same grounds as North's had been.

As virtually his last presidential act, George Bush pardoned two Reagan administration officials—Caspar Weinberger and Duane Clarridge—of any wrongdoing in the case. Four other officials who had been found guilty and sentenced were also pardoned. In Bush's view, "the prosecutions of these men represented not law enforcement but criminalization of policy differences."

What remains unresolved is how to control the activities of presidential aides and how presidents can be held responsible for what their aides do.

Traditionally, vice presidents have been chosen by presidential nominees to balance the ticket or to reward or appease party factions. If a presidential nominee is from the North, it is not a bad idea to have a vice presidential nominee who is from the South or the West. If the presidential nominee is from a rural state, perhaps someone with an urban background would be most suitable as a running mate. Presidential nominees who are strongly conservative or strongly liberal would do well to have vice presidential nominees who are more in the middle of the political road.

In 1992, presidential nominee Bill Clinton broke with tradition by naming Senator Al Gore as his vice presidential nominee. Gore, like Clinton, was a moderate, Southern politician of Clinton's own generation. Rather than a "balanced" ticket, Clinton and Gore offered a "team" approach.

Vice presidents have infrequently become elected presidents in their own right. John Adams and Thomas Jefferson were the first to do so. Then Martin Van Buren was elected president in 1836 after he had served as Jackson's vice president. Nixon became president in 1968, having been Eisenhower's vice president eight years earlier. In 1988, George Bush was elected to the presidency after eight years as Ronald Reagan's vice president.

The job of the vice president is certainly not time consuming, even when the president gives some specific task to the vice president. Typically, vice presidents spend their time supporting the president's activities. All of this changes, of course, if the president becomes disabled or dies in office.

Presidential Succession

Eight vice presidents have become president because of the death of the president. John Tyler, the first, took over William Henry Harrison's po-

Did You Know . . . That every president from William Henry Harrison to John Kennedy who was elected in the first year of a new decade died in office (Harrison was elected in 1840, Lincoln in 1860, Garfield in 1880, McKinley in 1900, Harding in 1920, Roosevelt in 1940, and Kennedy in 1960)?

The attempted assassination of Ronald Reagan on March 31, 1981. In the foreground, press secretary James Brady lies seriously wounded. In the background, two men bend over President Reagan.

Did You Know . . . That David Atchison, president pro tempore of the Senate in 1849, was briefly president of the United States because Zachary Taylor refused to be sworn into office on a Sunday and that Atchison spent most of his term asleep?

TWENTY-FIFTH AMENDMENT
An amendment to the Constitution adopted in 1967 that establishes procedures for filling vacancies in the two top executive offices and that makes provisions for situations involving presidential disability.

sition after only one month. No one knew whether Tyler should simply be a caretaker until a new president could be elected three and a half years later or whether he actually should be president. Tyler assumed that he was supposed to be the chief executive and he acted as such—although he was commonly referred to as "His Accidency." On all occasions since then, vice presidents taking over the position of the presidency because of the incumbent's death have assumed all of the presidential powers.

But what should a vice president do if a president becomes incapable of carrying out necessary duties while in office? When Garfield was shot in 1881, he stayed alive for two and a half months. What was Vice President Chester Arthur's role?

This question was not addressed in the original Constitution. Article II, Section 1, says only that "in the case of the removal of the president from office, or of his death, resignation, or inability to discharge the powers and duties of the said office, the same shall devolve on the vice president." There have been many instances of presidential disability. When Eisenhower became ill a second time in 1958, he entered into a pact with Nixon, which provided that the vice president could determine whether the president was incapable of carrying out his duties if the president could not communicate. Kennedy and Johnson entered into similar agreements with their vice presidents. Finally, the **Twenty-fifth Amendment** was passed in 1967, establishing procedures in case of presidential incapacity.

The Twenty-fifth Amendment

According to the Twenty-fifth Amendment, when the president believes that he is incapable of performing the duties of office, he must inform the Congress in writing. Then the vice president serves as acting president until the president can resume his normal duties. When the president is unable to communicate, a majority of the cabinet, including the vice president, can declare that fact to Congress. Then the vice president serves as acting president until the president resumes his normal duties.

If a dispute arises over the president's ability to discharge his normal functions, a two-thirds vote of Congress is required to decide whether the vice president shall remain acting president or whether the president shall resume his duties.

Although President Reagan did not formally invoke the Twenty-fifth Amendment during his surgery for the removal of a cancerous growth in his colon on July 13, 1985, he followed its provisions in temporarily transferring power to the vice president, George Bush. At 10:32 A.M., before the operation began, Reagan signed letters to the speaker of the House and the president pro tem of the Senate directing that the vice president "shall discharge those powers and duties in my stead commencing with the administration of anesthesia to me." In early evening of that same day, Reagan transmitted another letter to both officials announcing that he was again in charge. During this period, Vice President Bush signed no bills and took no actions as acting president. Although the Reagan administration claimed that the president's action set no precedents, most legal experts saw Reagan's acts as the first official use of the Twenty-fifth Amendment.

When the Vice Presidency Becomes Vacant

The Twenty-fifth Amendment also addresses the issue of how the president should fill a vacant vice presidency. Section 2 of the amendment simply states, "Whenever there is a vacancy in the office of the vice president, the president shall nominate a vice president who shall take office upon confirmation by a majority vote of both houses of Congress." This is exactly what occurred when Nixon's vice president, Spiro Agnew, resigned in 1973 because of his alleged receipt of construction contract kickbacks during his tenure as governor of Maryland. Nixon turned to Gerald R. Ford as his choice for vice president. After extensive hearings, both houses confirmed the appointment. Then, when Nixon resigned on August 9, 1974, Ford automatically became president and nominated as his vice president Nelson Rockefeller. Congress confirmed Ford's choice. For the first time in the history of the country, both the president and the vice president were individuals who were not elected to their positions.

The question of who shall be president if both the president and vice president die is answered by the Succession Act of 1947. If the president and vice president die, resign, or are disabled, the speaker of the House will act as president, after resigning from Congress. Next in line is the president pro tempore of the Senate, followed by the cabinet officers in order of creation of the department (see Table 11-4).

Spiro Agnew, Nixon's vice president from 1969 to 1973.

Conclusion: Is the Power of the Presidency Increasing or Decreasing?

After the Watergate scandal in 1972 and immediately following the end of the Vietnam war, many people feared that the American presidency had become far too powerful. As commander in chief, the president could engage U.S. military forces anywhere in the world. Control over the budget process established authority over Congress and the executive agencies. And the constant expansion of the Executive Office of the President provided better information and assistance than that available to the other branches of government.

Congressional response to this augmented presidential power was quite striking. Among the techniques forged by Congress to maintain a balance of power with the president were the War Powers Act of 1973, which required the president to consult with Congress before committing American troops; the Budget and Impoundment Control Act of 1974, which restrained the president's power to impound funds; and the Case–Zablocki Act of 1972, which required secret executive agreements to be reported to Congress with safeguards for the sake of security. Congress also resorted more frequently to the legislative veto to control presidential policy making.

The ability of President Reagan to get his first tax plan and budget passed in 1981 by a Democratic House suggests that the balance of power has not swung too heavily to Congress. Reagan reaffirmed the power of the president as commander in chief with his use of military forces in Lebanon and Central America and against Libya. He convinced the Con-

TABLE 11-4 ■ Line of Succession to the Presidency of the United States

1. Vice president.
2. Speaker of the House of Representatives.
3. Senate president pro tempore.
4. Secretary of State.
5. Secretary of the Treasury.
6. Secretary of Defense.
7. Attorney General.
8. Secretary of the Interior.
9. Secretary of Agriculture.
10. Secretary of Commerce.
11. Secretary of Labor.
12. Secretary of Health and Human Services.
13. Secretary of Housing and Urban Development.
14. Secretary of Transportation.
15. Secretary of Energy.
16. Secretary of Education.
17. Secretary of Veterans Affairs.

gress to support aid for the contras in Nicaragua and to work for, and complete, serious tax reform.

Similarly, it was not all that clear that Congress had the upper hand in the executive-legislative power struggle during the Bush administration. Although President Bush stated in 1992 that the "gridlock" in Congress had prevented him from implementing some of his key domestic programs, there did not seem to be any significant diminution in presidential power. Bush had no difficulty, for example, in sending troops to Panama and to the Middle East, and he vetoed more than thirty bills without an override. President Bill Clinton, with the support of Democratic majorities in both the House and the Senate, quickly won legislative victories on the family leave plan and his overall budget. His initial proposals for an economic stimulus package were thwarted and reduced in scope, however, owing to filibuster tactics by Senate Republicans. Complicated negotiations with Congress were required before the narrow approval of his initiatives to attempt to balance the federal budget.

GETTING INVOLVED

Influencing the Presidency

On June 14, 1990, James Baker, the secretary of state, rebuked Israel for not responding to the U.S. peace plan to resolve the Israel–Palestinian conflict, saying, "When you're serious about peace, call us. The phone number is 202-456-1414." In the next twenty-four hours, the White House switchboard received about eight thousand calls.

If you wish to contact the president, that switchboard is open twenty-four hours a day. If you ask for the president, you will be directed to the appropriate department or to the comment line. If you call the comment line (202-456-7639), an operator will take down your comment or question and forward it to the president's office.

Expressions of public support or opposition are important either to legitimize the administration's actions or to voice disapproval. Although you will probably not have the opportunity to express your personal opinions directly to the president, your views and those of others who think the same way can be brought to the president's attention. If you strongly agree with, or oppose, certain actions taken by the president, call the White House or write a letter to the president, addressing your letter to:

The President of the United States
The White House
1600 Pennsylvania Ave., N.W.
Washington, DC 20500

The Clinton administration, representing a more technologically literate generation, also welcomed electronic mail (E-mail). On-line computer networks such as Compuserve and Internet can send and receive messages from the White House. The President's staff make speeches, press releases, and photographs electronically transmitable.

CHAPTER SUMMARY

1. The office of the presidency, combining as it does the functions of chief of state and chief executive, is unique. The framers of the Constitution were divided over whether the president should be a weak executive controlled by the legislature or a strong executive.

2. The requirements for the office are outlined in Article II, Section 1, of the Constitution. The president's roles include both formal and informal duties. The president is commander in chief, chief executive, chief of state, chief diplomat, chief legislator, and party chief.

3. As chief of state, the president is ceremonial head of the government. As chief executive, the president is bound to enforce the acts of Congress, the judgments of the federal courts, and treaties. The chief executive has the power of appointment and the power to grant reprieves.

4. As commander in chief, the president is the ultimate decision maker in military matters. As chief diplomat, the president negotiates treaties, signs agreements, recognizes foreign governments, and nominates and receives ambassadors.

5. The role of chief legislator includes recommending legislation to Congress, approving laws, exercising the veto power, and lobbying for the legislation. The president also has statutory powers written into law by Congress.

6. The president is also leader of his political party. Presidents use their power to persuade and their access to the media to fulfill this function.

7. Abuses of executive power are dealt with by Article I of the Constitution, which authorizes the House and Senate to impeach and remove the president, vice president, or other officers of the government for crimes of "treason, bribery or other high crimes and misdemeanors."

8. The president gets assistance from the cabinet, from the Executive Office of the President, and from the White House Office.

9. The vice president is the constitutional officer assigned to preside over the Senate and to assume the presidency in case of the death, resignation, removal, or disability of the president. The Twenty-fifth Amendment, passed in 1967, established procedures to be followed in case of presidential incapacity and when filling a vacant vice presidency.

QUESTIONS FOR REVIEW AND DISCUSSION

1. The roles of the president often require difficult decisions. What should the president do when Congress sends him a law that violates his own party platform? Can you think of other situations in which the political needs of the president may not be consistent with national needs?

2. The president is frequently seen as the chief legislator of the nation. How much power does the president have to get laws passed? What restraints does the Congress have on this role?

3. What is the process for impeaching the president? Can a president be impeached for political reasons—that is, by offending enough members of Congress?

4. Why has the Executive Office of the President grown so dramatically in the last quarter century? Does the existence of so many advisory and staff offices really assist the president in his job?

SELECTED REFERENCES

James D. Barber, *The Presidential Character: Predicting Performance in the White House,* 5th ed. (Englewood Cliffs, N.J.: Prentice Hall, 1991). A major typology of the personal traits of presidents and the consequences of how we are governed.

John P. Burke, *The Institutional Presidency* (Baltimore, Md.: The Johns Hopkins University Press, 1992). A detailed examination of the interplay between the White House staff system and the style and management abilities of particular presidents, from Franklin Roosevelt to George Bush.

John Hart, *The Presidential Branch* (Elmsford, N.Y.: Pergamon Press, 1987). This book traces the history of the Executive Office from 1857 to the mid-1980s, analyzing the role of staff power, accountability, and the importance of the Executive Office in the post-Watergate period.

Barbara Hinkley, *The Symbolic Presidency: How Presidents Portray Themselves* (New York: Routledge, 1990). This excellent book looks at how presidents, in their speeches and other actions, reinforce the symbolism surrounding the presidential office.

Samuel Kernell, *Going Public: New Strategies of Presidential Leadership* (Washington, D.C.: Congressional Quarterly Press, 1986). This fascinating book explores how presidents have increasingly bypassed the traditional process of bargaining with Congress and have "gone public" with presidential priorities in an effort to bring direct public pressure on Congress.

Thomas S. Langston, *Ideologues and Presidents: From the New Deal to the Reagan Revolution* (Baltimore, Md.: The Johns Hopkins University Press, 1992). In this study of the influence of ideologues on the American presidency and presidential administrations, the author concludes that U.S. presidents are increasingly dependent on unelected ideologues ("people of ideas") who are not accountable to the electorate.

Sydney M. Milkis and Michael Nelson, *The American Presidency: Origins and Development, 1776–1990* (Washington, D.C.: Congressional Quarterly Press, 1990). A comprehensive overview of the American presidential office, how it has changed over time, and the factors influencing that change.

Peggy Noonan, *What I Saw at the Revolution* (New York: Random House, 1990). The author of this book, President Reagan's favorite speechwriter who also wrote for George Bush's first campaign (coining such phrases as "a kinder, gentler nation," "a thousand points of light," and "Read my lips: no new taxes"), provides a unique and often very funny perspective on the Reagan presidency and its cast of characters.

Mark Peterson, *Legislating Together: The White House and Capitol Hill from Eisenhower to Reagan* (Cambridge, Mass.: Harvard University Press, 1990). This is one of the most thorough studies ever undertaken of the process by which presidential domestic policy proposals are made and how they become law or fail to be enacted. The author's conclusions are based on his study of over five thousand proposals.

Kenneth W. Thompson, ed., *Papers on Presidential Disability and the Twenty-fifth Amendment by Six Medical, Legal, and Political Authorities.* Vol. 2. (Lanham, Md.: University Press of America, 1991). An in-depth study of presidential disability and the transfer of presidential powers in accordance with the Twenty-fifth Amendment.

CHAPTER 12
The Bureaucracy

CHAPTER CONTENTS

WHAT IF ... ALL INDEPENDENT AGENCIES HAD TO MAKE A PROFIT?

The federal government is big. It employs millions of individuals. It provides millions of services to Americans every day. As you will read in this chapter, the federal bureaucracy consists of the fourteen departments in the executive branch, independent regulatory agencies, government corporations, and independent executive agencies. The last two categories include the National Aeronautics and Space Administration, the Tennessee Valley Authority, the U.S. Postal Service, and AMTRAK—the nation's nationalized passenger railroad system.

Currently, there is no legal requirement that independent agencies and government corporations make a profit. Indeed, one might suspect that the legal requirement is the reverse—that they must lose money—because they almost always do. The U.S. Postal Service, for example, routinely loses billions of dollars a year.

What if independent agencies and government corporations had to make a profit each year? What if a law were passed that required such agencies to charge enough money for their services to cover all of their costs? Now to make this scenario somewhat more realistic, we will assume that each government agency and corporation is given, say, five years until it has to be profitable.

The first thing that would happen is that certain government agencies and corporations would have to start charging user fees for the services they render to the public. Those agencies that are already

charging user fees would have to raise them significantly. For example, the Tennessee Valley Authority—if forced to take account of the true costs of all its operations—would have to raise the price of electricity to its customers. The U.S. Postal Service would have to raise its rates probably more than it already periodically does. The Small Business Administration would have to charge small businesses for any services rendered. The National Mediation Board would have to bill unions and businesses for its mediation services in labor–management disputes.

But what about those agencies that were not put into existence with the idea of charging for their services? They would have to rethink their charter. The National Aeronautics and Space Administration would basically have to become a commercial satellite-launching operation. It might even advertise throughout the world. It would have to refocus its efforts away from big, bold plans, such as a manned space station, to more mundane operations, such as communication satellites.

Something else might have to happen on the cost side with all government independent agencies and corporations. They might actually

have to be run like private businesses. Managers would be required under law to contain costs to enable such agencies to make a profit. The U.S. Postal Service, for example, would be run more like Federal Express. U.S. postal workers, who are now part of a very strong union, would find postal management much less willing to accept union demands for higher wages. After all, the profit requirement means keeping costs down, and labor accounts for 83 percent of the U.S. Postal Service's budget.

Nationwide, the requirement that independent agencies and corporations make a profit would certainly lead to the elimination of a large number of them. Many publicly offered services in the areas of medical care, welfare, the arts, science, and technology would disappear. Other services, now being furnished at bargain rates, would become much more expensive and would reflect more accurately the true cost to the nation of providing those services. Some groups would undoubtedly be hurt. The American taxpayer in general, however, would see smaller federal budget deficits and less federal government spending.

1. *What government agencies and corporations would be good candidates for the requirement that they turn a profit?*
2. *Why should some government agencies never be required to make a profit?*

Every presidential candidate, regardless of party affiliation or political ideology, has attacked the federal bureaucracy for, among other things, its inefficiency and wastefulness. Indeed, candidates find that they can usually get a round of applause when they blast the federal bureaucracy. What is curious is that even sitting presidents, such as Ronald Reagan (1981–1989) and George Bush (1989–1993), could assail the federal bureaucracy and garner votes, even though they presided over that very same bureaucracy.

Presidents have been virtually powerless to affect significantly the structure and operation of the federal bureaucracy. It has been called the "fourth branch of government," even though you will find no reference to the bureaucracy in the original Constitution or in the twenty-seven amendments that have been passed since 1787. But Article II, Section 2, of the Constitution gives the president the power to appoint "all other officers of the United States, whose appointments are not herein otherwise provided for." Article II, Section 3, states that the president "shall take care that the laws be faithfully executed, and shall commission all the officers of the United States." Constitutional scholars believe that the legal basis for the bureaucracy rests on these two sections in Article II.

The Nature of Bureaucracy

▼

A **bureaucracy** is the name given to a large organization that is structured hierarchically to carry out specific functions. Generally, most bureaucracies are characterized first and foremost by an organization chart. According to the German sociologist Max Weber, bureaucracies share certain qualities. Every person who works in the organization has a superior to whom he or she reports. The units of the organization are divided according to the specialization and expertise of the employees. There are elaborate rules that everyone in the organization is expected to accept and follow. Finally, tasks are supposed to be done in a neutral manner—that is, for the sake of the organization rather than for personal gain.[1]

BUREAUCRACY
A large organization that is structured hierarchically to carry out specific functions.

Public and Private Bureaucracies

We should not think of bureaucracy as unique to government. Any large corporation or university can be considered a bureaucratic organization. The fact is that the handling of complex problems requires a division of labor. Individuals must concentrate their skills on specific, well-defined aspects of a problem and depend on others to solve the rest of it.

But public or government bureaucracies differ from private organizations in some important ways. Unlike a private corporation, such as General Motors (GM), public bureaucracies do not have a single set of leaders such as GM's board of directors. Although the president is the chief administrator of the federal system, all bureaucratic agencies are subject to the desires of Congress for their funding, staffing, and, indeed, for their continued existence. Furthermore, public bureaucracies supposedly serve the citizen rather than the stockholder.

---

[1]Max Weber, *Theory of Social and Economic Organization*, ed. Talcott Parsons (New York: Oxford University Press, 1974).

The Department of Agriculture inspects meat-packing facilities throughout the United States, certifying the healthfulness and quality of the meat to be sold.

One other important difference is that government bureaucracies are not organized to make a profit. Rather, they are supposed to perform their functions as efficiently as possible to conserve the taxpayers' dollars. Perhaps it is this aspect of government organization that makes citizens hostile toward government employees when citizens experience inefficiency and red tape.

These characteristics, together with the prevalence and size of the government bureaucracies, make them an important factor in American life.

Theories of Bureaucracy

Several theories have been offered to help us understand better the ways in which bureaucracies function. Each of these theories focuses on specific features of bureaucracies.

The Weberian Model

WEBERIAN MODEL
A model of bureaucracy developed by the German sociologist, Max Weber, who viewed bureaucracies as rational, hierarchical organizations in which power flows from the top downward and decisions are based on logical reasoning and data analysis.

The classic model, or **Weberian model,** of the modern bureaucracy was proposed by Max Weber. He argued that the increasingly complex nature of modern life, coupled with the steadily growing demands placed on governments by their citizens, made the formation of bureaucracies inevitable. According to Weber, most bureaucracies—whether in the public or private sector—are hierarchically organized and governed by formal procedures. The power in a bureaucracy flows from the top downward. Decision-making processes in bureaucracies are shaped by detailed technical rules that promote similar decisions in similar situations. Bureaucrats are specialists who attempt to resolve problems through logical reasoning and data analysis instead of "gut feelings" and guesswork. Individual advancement in bureaucracies is supposed to be based on merit rather than political connections. Indeed, the modern bureaucracy, according to Weber, should be an apolitical organization.

The Acquisitive Model

Other theorists do not view bureaucracies in such benign terms. Some believe that bureaucracies are acquisitive in nature. Proponents of the **acquisitive model** argue that top-level bureaucrats will always try to expand, or at least avoid any reductions in, the size of their budgets. Although government bureaucracies are not-for-profit enterprises, bureaucrats want to maximize the size of their budgets and staffs because these things are the most visible trappings of power in the public sector. These efforts are also prompted by the desire of bureaucrats to "sell" their product—national defense, public housing, agricultural subsidies, and so on—to both Congress and the public.

The Monopolistic Model

Because bureaucracies seldom have competitors, some theorists have suggested that bureaucratic organizations may best be explained by using a **monopolistic model.** The analysis is similar to that used by economists to examine the behavior of monopolistic firms. Monopolistic bureaucracies—like monopolistic firms—are less efficient and more costly to operate because they have no competitors. Because monopolistic bureaucracies are not usually penalized for chronic inefficiency, they have little reason to adopt cost-saving measures or to make more productive uses of their resources. Some economists have argued that such problems can be cured only by privatizing certain bureaucratic functions. This strategy has been most successful on the local level. Municipalities, for example, can form contracts with private companies for such things as trash collection. Such an approach is not a cure-all, however, as there are many functions, particularly on the national level, that cannot be contracted out in any meaningful way. For example, the federal government could not contract out national defense to a private firm.

The Garbage Can Model

The image of a bumbling, rudderless organization is offered by proponents of the **garbage can model** of bureaucracy. This theory presupposes that bureaucracies rarely act in any purposeful or coherent manner but instead bumble along aimlessly in search of solutions to particular problems. This model views bureaucracies as having relatively little formal organization. The solutions to problems are obtained not by the smooth implementation of well-planned policies but instead by trial and error. Choosing the right policy is tricky because it is not usually possible to determine in advance which solution is best. Thus, bureaucrats may have to try one, two, three, or even more policies before they obtain a satisfactory result.

The Size of the Bureaucracy

In 1789, the new government's bureaucracy was miniscule. There were three departments—State (with nine employees), War (with two employees), and Treasury (with thirty-nine employees). This bureaucracy was still

Did You Know . . . That the Internal Revenue Service (IRS), with 125,000 employees, is the largest federal law-enforcement agency?

ACQUISITIVE MODEL
A model of bureaucracy that views top-level bureaucrats as constantly seeking to expand the size of their budgets and staffs of their departments or agencies so as to gain greater power and influence in the public sector.

MONOPOLISTIC MODEL
A model of bureaucracy that compares bureaucracies to monopolistic business firms. Lack of competition within a bureaucracy leads to inefficient and costly operations, just as it does within monopolistic firms. Because bureaucracies are not penalized for inefficiency, there is no incentive to save costs or use resources more productively.

GARBAGE CAN MODEL
A model of bureaucracy that characterizes bureaucracies as rudderless entities with little formal organization in which solutions to problems are based on trial and error rather than rational policy planning.

FIGURE 12-1 ■ **Federal Agencies and Their Respective Numbers of Civilian Employees**

SOURCE: *Statistical Abstract of the United States, 1992.*

EXECUTIVE OFFICE OF THE PRESIDENT 1,767

JUDICIAL BRANCH 24,664

LEGISLATIVE BRANCH 38,387

EXECUTIVE DEPARTMENTS 2,039,059	INDEPENDENT AGENCIES (including postal service) 997,012
• Agriculture 118,403 • Commerce 40,092 • Defense 1,009,371 • Education 4,862 • Energy 18,712 • Health and Human Services 126,768 • Housing and Urban Development 13,745 • Interior 77,808 • Justice 87,265 • Labor 18,123 • State 25,534 • Transportation 68,049 • Treasury 175,150 • Veterans Affairs 255,217	

small in 1798. At that time, the secretary of state had seven clerks and spent a total of $500 (about $5,300 in 1993 dollars) on stationery and printing. In that same year, the Appropriations Act allocated $1.4 million to the War Department (or $14.5 million in 1993 dollars).[2]

Times have changed, as we can see in Figure 12-1, which lists the various federal agencies and the number of employees in each. Excluding the military, approximately 3.1 million government employees constitute the federal bureaucracy. That number has remained relatively stable for the last several decades. It is somewhat deceiving, however, because there are many others working directly or indirectly for the federal government as subcontractors or consultants and in other capacities.

The figures for federal government employment are only part of the story. Figure 12-2 shows the growth in government employment on federal, state, and local levels. Since 1950, this growth has been mainly at the state and local levels, so that if all government employees are counted, 14 percent of the entire civilian population over the age of sixteen works directly for the government.

The costs of the bureaucracy are commensurately high and growing. The share of the gross national product taken up by government spending was only 8.5 percent in 1929, but today it exceeds 40 percent.

FIGURE 12-2 ■ **Growth in Government Employment on Federal, State, and Local Levels**

By the 1980s, there were more local government employees than federal and state employees.

SOURCE: Department of Commerce, 1992; 1993 data are estimates.

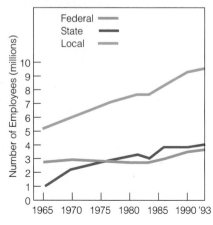

The Organization of the Federal Bureaucracy

Within the federal bureaucracy are a number of different types of government agencies and organizations. Figure 12-3 outlines the several bureaucracies within the executive branch, as well as the separate organizations that provide services to Congress, to the courts, and directly to the pres-

[2]Leonard D. White, *The Federalists: A Study in Administrative History, 1789–1801* (New York: The Free Press, 1948).

ident. In Chapter 11, we discussed those agencies that are considered to be part of the Executive Office of the President.

The executive branch, which employs most of the bureaucrats, has four major types of bureaucratic structures. They are (1) cabinet departments, (2) independent executive agencies, (3) independent regulatory agencies, and (4) government corporations. Each has a distinctive relationship to the president, and some have unusual internal structures, overall goals, and grants of power.

Cabinet Departments

The fourteen **cabinet departments** are the major service organizations of the federal government. They can also be described in management terms as **line organizations.** This means that they are directly accountable to the

CABINET DEPARTMENTS
The fourteen departments of the executive branch (State, Treasury, Defense, Justice, Interior, Agriculture, Commerce, Labor, Health and Human Services, Housing and Urban Development, Education, Energy, Transportation, and Veterans Affairs).

LINE ORGANIZATION
Government or corporate units that provide direct services or products for the public.

FIGURE 12-3 ■ Organization Chart of the Federal Government

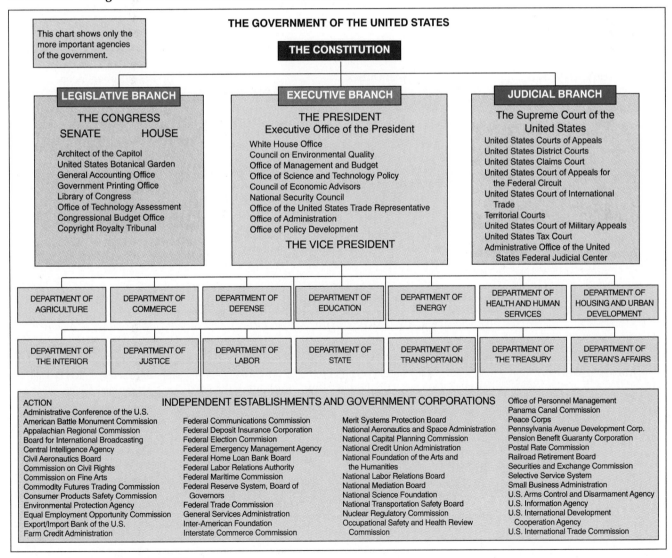

SOURCE: *U.S. Government Manual, 1991–1992.*

president and are responsible for performing government functions, such as printing money or training troops. These departments were created by Congress when the need for each department arose. The first department to be created was State, and the most recent one was Veterans Affairs, established in 1989. A president might ask that a new department be created or an old one abolished, but the president has no power to do so without legislative approval from Congress.

Each department is headed by a secretary (except for the Justice Department, which is headed by the attorney general) and several levels of undersecretaries, assistant secretaries, and so on. Presidents theoretically have considerable control over the cabinet departments because they are able to appoint or fire all of the top officials. As Franklin Roosevelt suggested, however, even cabinet departments do not always respond to the president's wishes. One reason for the frequent unhappiness of presidents with their departments is that the entire bureaucratic structure below the top political levels is staffed by permanent employees, many of whom are

FIGURE 12-4 ■ Executive Departments

Department and Year Established	Principal Duties	Most Important Subagencies
State (1789) (25,534 employees)	Negotiates treaties; develops foreign policy; protects citizens abroad	Passport Agency; Bureau of Diplomatic Security; Foreign Service; Bureau of Human Rights and Humanitarian Affairs; Bureau of Consular Affairs; Bureau of Intelligence and Research
Treasury (1789) (175,150 employees)	Pays all federal bills; borrows money; collects federal taxes; mints coins and prints paper currency; operates the Secret Sevice; supervises national banks.	Internal Revenue Service (IRS); Bureau of Alcohol, Tobacco, and Firearms; United States Secret Service; U.S. Mint; Customs Service
Interior (1849) (77,808 employees)	Supervises federally owned lands and parks; operates federal hydroelectric power facilities; supervises Native-American affairs.	United States Fish and Wildlife Service; National Park Service; Bureau of Indian Affairs; Bureau of Land Management
Justice (1870)[1] (87,265 employees)	Furnishes legal advice to the president; enforces federal criminal laws; supervises the federal corrections system (prisons).	Federal Bureau of Investigation (FBI); Drug Enforcement Administration (DEA); Bureau of Prisons (BOP); United States Marshals Service; Immigration and Naturalization Service (INS)
Agriculture (1889) (118,403 employees)	Provides assistance to farmers and ranchers; conducts research to improve agricultural activity and to prevent plant disease; works to protect forests from fires and disease.	Soil Conservation Service; Agricultural Research Service; Food and Safety Inspection Service; Federal Crop Insurance Corporation; Farmers Home Administration
Commerce (1903) (40,902 employees)	Grants patents and trademarks; conducts a national census; monitors the weather; protects the interest of businesses.	Bureau of the Census; Bureau of Economic Analysis; Minority Business Development Agency; Patent and Trademark Office; National Oceanic and Atmospheric Administration; United States Travel and Tourism Administration
Labor (1913) (18,123 employees)	Administers federal labor laws; promotes the interest of workers.	Occupational Safety and Health Administration (OSHA); Bureau of Labor Statistics; Employment Standards Administration; Office of Labor–Management Standards; Employment and Training Administration

committed to established programs or procedures and who resist change. As we can see from Figure 12-4, each cabinet department employs thousands of individuals, only a handful of whom are under the control of the president. The figure also describes the functions of each of the cabinet departments.

Independent Executive Agencies

Independent executive agencies are bureaucratic organizations that have a single function. They are not located within a department and report directly to the president, who appoints their chief officials. When a new federal agency is created—the Environmental Protection Agency, for example—a decision is made by the president and Congress about where it will be located in the bureaucracy. In this century, presidents have often asked that a new organization be kept separate or independent rather than added to an existing department, particularly if a department may in fact

INDEPENDENT EXECUTIVE AGENCY
A federal agency having a single function that is not part of a cabinet department but reports directly to the president.

FIGURE 12-4 ■ Executive Departments (continued)

Department and Year Established	Principal Duties	Most Important Subagencies
Defense (1947)[2] (1,009,371 employees)	Manages the armed forces (army, navy, air force, and marines); operates military bases; responsible for civil defense.	National Guard; Defense Investigation Service; National Security Agency; Joint Chiefs of Staff; Departments of the Air Force, Navy, Army
Health and Human Services (1979)[3] (126,728 employees)	Administers the Social Security and Medicare programs; promotes public health; enforces pure food and drug laws; is involved in health-related research.	Social Security Administration; Family Support Administration; Office of Human Development Services; Public Health Service
Housing and Urban Development (1965) (13,745 employees)	Concerned with the nation's housing needs; develops and rehabilitates urban communities; promotes improvement in city streets and parks.	Office of Block Grant Assistance; Emergency Shelter Grants Program; Office of Urban Development Action Grants; Assistant Secretary for Fair Housing and Equal Opportunity
Transportation (1967) (68,049 employees)	Finances improvements in mass transit; develops and administers programs for highways, railroads, and aviation; involved with off-shore maritime safety.	Federal Aviation Administration (FAA); Federal Highway Administration; National Highway Traffic Safety Administration; United States Coast Guard; Urban Mass-Transit Administration
Energy (1977) (18,712 employees)	Involved in the conservation of energy and resources; analyzes energy data; conducts research and development.	Energy Information Administration; Economics Regulatory Administration; Bonneville Power Administration; Office of Nuclear Energy; Energy Information Administration; Office of Conservation and Renewable Energy
Education (1979)[4] (4,862 employees)	Coordinates federal programs and policies for education; administers aid to education; promotes educational research.	Office of Special Education and Rehabilitation Services; Office of Elementary and Secondary Education; Office of Postsecondary Education; Office of Vocational and Adult Education
Veterans Affairs (1989) (255,217 employees)	Promotes the welfare of veterans of the U.S. armed forces.	Health Care Service Benefit Programs; Memorial Affairs; Medical Training

[1] Formed from the Office of the Attorney General (created in 1789).
[2] Formed from the Department of War (created in 1789) and the Department of Navy (created in 1798).
[3] Formed from the Department of Health, Education, and Welfare (created in 1953).
[4] Formed from the Department of Health, Education, and Welfare (created in 1953).

be hostile to the agency's creation. Figure 12-5 describes the functions of several selected independent executive agencies.

Independent Regulatory Agencies

The **independent regulatory agencies** are typically responsible for a specific type of public policy. Their function is to make and implement rules and regulations in a particular sector of the economy to protect the public interest. The earliest such agency was the Interstate Commerce Commission (ICC), which was established in 1887 when Americans began to seek some form of government control over the rapidly growing business and industrial sector. This new form of organization, the independent regulatory commission, was supposed to make technical, nonpolitical decisions about rates, profits, and rules that would be for the benefit of all and that did not require congressional legislation. In the years that followed the creation of the ICC, other agencies were formed to regulate aviation (the Civil Aeronautics Board), communication (the Federal Communications Commission), nuclear power (the Nuclear Regulatory Commission), and so on.

The regulatory commissions are administered independently of all three branches of government. They were set up because Congress felt it was unable to handle the complexities and technicalities required to carry out specific laws in the public interest. The regulatory commissions in fact combine some functions of all three branches of government—executive, legislative, and judicial. They are legislative in that they make rules that have the force of law. They are executive in that they provide for the

FIGURE 12-5 ■ Selected Independent Executive Agencies

Name	Date Formed	Principal Duties
Central Intelligence Agency (CIA)	1947	Gathers and analyzes political and military information about foreign countries so that the United States can improve its own political and military status; conducts activities outside the United States, with the goal of countering the work of intelligence services operated by other nations whose political philosophies are inconsistent with our own.
General Services Administration (GSA)	1949	Purchases and manages all property of the federal government; acts as the business arm of the federal government in overseeing federal government spending projects; discovers overcharges in government programs.
National Science Foundation	1950	Promotes scientific research; provides grants to all levels of schools for instructional programs in the sciences.
Small Business Administration (SBA)	1953	Protects the interests of small businesses; provides low-cost loans and management information to small businesses.
Commission on Civil Rights	1957	Evaluates information on discrimination that is based on sex, race, national origin, religion, or handicap.
National Aeronautics and Space Administration (NASA)	1958	Responsible for the U.S. space program, including building, testing, and operating space vehicles.
Federal Election Commission (FEC)	1974	Ensures that candidates and states follow the rules established by the Federal Election Campaign Act.

enforcement of those rules. They are judicial in that they decide disputes involving the rules they have made.

Regulatory commission members are appointed by the president with the consent of the Senate, although they do not report to the president. By law, the members of regulatory commissions cannot all be from the same political party. Presidents can influence regulatory agency behavior by appointing people of their own parties or who share their political views when vacancies occur, in particular when the chair is vacant. Figure 12-6 describes the functions of several selected independent agencies.

Over the last several decades, some observers have concluded that these agencies, although nominally independent of the three branches of the federal government, may in fact not always be so. They contend that many independent regulatory commissions have been **captured** by the very industries and firms that they were supposed to regulate. The results have been less competition rather than more competition, higher prices rather than lower prices, and less choice rather than more choice for consumers.

Not surprisingly, the 1980s have been called the **era of deregulation.** An important part of Reagan's 1980 campaign was his promise to reduce the regulation of American business. But deregulation had already started before Reagan was elected. President Carter pushed for, and obtained, the Motor Carrier Deregulation Act of 1978. He also appointed a chairperson of the Civil Aeronautics Board (CAB) who waged a war against the reg-

CAPTURE
The act of gaining direct or indirect control over agency personnel and decision makers by the industry that is being regulated.

ERA OF DEREGULATION
The early 1980s, characterized by deregulation of several industries, including trucking, air transport, and banking.

FIGURE 12-6 ■ Selected Independent Regulatory Agencies

Name	Date Formed	Principal Duties
Interstate Commerce Commission (ICC)	1887	Regulates interstate surface transportation via trucks, buses, trains, and inland waterways.
Federal Reserve System Board of Governors (Fed)	1913	Determines policy with respect to interest rates, credit availability, and the money supply.
Federal Trade Commission (FTC)	1914	Prevents businesses from engaging in unfair trade practices; stops the formation of monopolies in the business sector; protects consumer rights.
Securities and Exchange Commission (SEC)	1934	Regulates the nation's stock exchanges, in which shares of stocks are bought and sold; requires full disclosure of the financial profiles of companies that wish to sell stocks and bonds to the public.
Federal Communications Commission (FCC)	1934	Regulates all communications by telegraph, cable, telephone, radio, and television.
National Labor Relations Board (NLRB)	1935	Protects employees' rights to join unions and bargain collectively with employers; attempts to prevent unfair labor practices by both employers and unions.
Equal Employment Opportunity Commission (EEOC)	1964	Works to eliminate discrimination based on religion, sex, race, national origin, or age; examines claims of discrimination.
Environmental Protection Agency (EPA)	1970	Undertakes programs aimed at reducing air and water pollution; works with state and local agencies to help fight environmental hazards. (It has been suggested recently that its status be elevated to that of a department.)
Nuclear Regulatory Commission (NRC)	1974	Ensures that electricity-generating nuclear reactors in the United States are built and operated safely; regularly inspects operations of such reactors.

PROFILE

Henry Cisneros

"There are 22 million Hispanics and in the next 15 years we will see the Hispanization of the United States."

Although Henry Cisneros' career track took a few detours in recent years, he reached Washington, D.C., and an opportunity to gain national prominence as the secretary of housing and urban development. Cisneros will be challenged by the massive problems of the big agency, with its dilapidated stock of public housing, its more than 3.4 million tenants, and the continuously increasing problem of homelessness in America.

Henry Cisneros grew up in San Antonio, Texas, in a Mexican-American family. He attended Texas A&M University for his undergraduate work, went to Harvard University to complete a masters degree in public administration, and then received a doctorate in public administration from George Washington University. Quickly identified as a bright and ambitious young man, Cisneros served for a time as a White House Fellow during the Nixon years and as an assistant to secretary of health, education, and welfare Elliott Richardson.

After returning to Texas, he achieved political success almost immediately, becoming the mayor of San Antonio in 1981 at the very young age of thirty-one. Like Bill

Clinton, who gained an East Coast education and returned to the South for the beginning of a career, Cisneros established himself as one of the bright young leaders of the Democratic party. He was an activist mayor, working closely with business to bring economic development to his city. A moderate, pro-growth Democrat, he seemed likely to be the first Hispanic politician to be nominated for vice president or even president.

In 1989, Cisneros' career hit a snag. Although he had built a reputation for being a good family man, Cisneros was faced with allegations that he was having an affair with a

San Antonio woman. He admitted the affair and did not run for mayor again. He founded a private corporation, Cisneros Asset Management, a financial consulting corporation, and worked on his relationships with the Hispanic community. He and his wife reconciled, brought together in part by the heart problems of their young son. In 1991, he gave his support to Bill Clinton and worked on the campaign team, focusing particularly on gaining Hispanic votes for the Clinton/Gore ticket.

With his expertise in city government, his excellent credentials, and his activist style of leadership, Henry Cisneros seemed a natural choice for the Clinton cabinet. Indeed, his predecessor in the secretary's job, Jack Kemp, noted that, "If there is one man who was born to be HUD secretary, it is Henry Cisneros." His experience and enthusiasm will, however, be needed if he is to resolve some portion of the nation's housing problems. Not only must he find a way to improve thousands of housing units that are unsafe and crime ridden, he must do so in an era when the federal budget will be curtailed to reduce the deficit. This situation will challenge Cisneros to find ways to engage both the tenants and private-sector businesses in solving America's housing problems.

ulation of airline tariffs and routes. The result has been the almost complete deregulation of the airline industry. The CAB ceased to exist on January 1, 1985.

Deregulation has not been entirely successful. In perhaps the most conspicuous example, when restrictions were lifted on how savings and loan institutions could invest their depositors' savings, many institutions invested in highly risky business ventures. By the beginning of the 1990s, bad investments, fraud, and insider abuse had resulted in failures of an estimated one thousand savings and loan institutions at a cost to taxpayers of an estimated $500 billion. Calls for reregulation of many businesses mounted, and the Bush administration responded. Legislation and regulations affecting the environment (the Clean Air Act of 1991), employers (Americans with Disabilities Act of 1990 and the Civil Rights Act of 1991), the banking industry, oil spills, and a number of other areas led one national magazine to refer to President Bush as "the regulatory president." In early 1992, however, with an election year before him, President Bush placed a ninety-day moratorium on new federal regulations, which was later further extended, but was dropped by Clinton.

Government Corporations

The newest form of bureaucratic organization to be adopted in the United States is the **government corporation.** Although the concept is borrowed from the world of business, distinct differences exist between the public and private corporations.

A private corporation has shareholders (stockholders) who elect a board of directors, who in turn choose the corporate officers, such as president and vice president. When a private corporation makes a profit, it must pay taxes (unless it avoids them through various legal loopholes), and it either distributes part or all of the after-tax profits to shareholders as dividends or plows the profits back into the corporation to make new investments.

GOVERNMENT CORPORATION
An agency of government that administers a quasi-business enterprise. Used when an activity is primarily commercial, produces revenue for its continued existence, and requires greater flexibility than is permitted for departments.

The Postmaster General unveiled two versions of a stamp commemorating Elvis Presley's life. The public was given the chance to "vote" for the version of the stamp that it preferred. Millions of Americans responded to the opportunity.

A government corporation has a board of directors and managers, but it does not have any stockholders. We cannot buy shares of stock in a government corporation. If the government corporation makes a profit, it does not distribute the profit as dividends. Also, if it makes a profit, it does not have to pay taxes; the profits remain in the corporation. Figure 12-7 describes the functions of selected government corporations.

Staffing the Bureaucracy

There are two categories of bureaucrats: political appointees and civil servants. As noted earlier, the president is able to make political appointments to most of the top jobs in the federal bureaucracy and can appoint ambassadors to the most important foreign posts. All of the jobs that are considered "political plums" and that usually go to the politically well connected are listed in *Policy and Supporting Positions,* published by the Government Printing Office after each presidential election. This has been informally (and correctly) called "The Plum Book." The rest of the individuals who work for the national government belong to the civil service and obtain their jobs through a much more formal process.

Political Appointees

To fill the positions listed in "The Plum Book," the president and the president's advisers solicit suggestions from politicians, businesspersons, and other prominent individuals. Appointments to these positions offer the president a way to pay outstanding political debts. But the president must also take into consideration such things as the candidate's work

FIGURE 12-7 ■ Selected Government Corporations

Name	Date Formed	Principal Duties
Tennessee Valley Authority (TVA)	1933	Operates a Tennessee River control system and generates power for a seven-state region and for the U.S. aeronautics and space programs; promotes the economic development of the Tennessee Valley region; controls floods and promotes the navigability of the Tennessee River.
Federal Deposit Insurance Corporation (FDIC)	1933	Insures individuals' bank deposits up to $100,000; oversees the business activities of banks.
Commodity Credit Corporation (CCC)	1933	Attempts to stabilize farm prices and protect farmers' income by purchasing designated farm products at prices above what they would get in the marketplace.
Export/Import Bank of the United States (Ex/Im Bank)	1933	Promotes American-made goods abroad; grants loans to foreign purchasers of American products.
National Railway Passenger Corporation (AMTRAK)	1970	Provides a balanced national and intercity rail passenger service network; controls 23,000 miles of track with 505 stations.
U.S. Postal Service[1]	1970	Delivers mail throughout the United States and its territories; is the largest government corporation, with almost 800,000 employees.

[1] Formed from the Office of the Postmaster General in the Department of the Treasury (created in 1789).

experience, intelligence, political affiliations, and personal characteristics. Presidents have differed over the importance they attach to appointing women and minorities to plum positions. Presidents often use ambassadorships, however, to reward selected individuals for their campaign contributions.

Political appointees are in some sense the aristocracy of the federal government. But their powers, while appearing formidable on paper, are often exaggerated. Like the president, a political appointee will occupy his or her position for a comparatively brief time. Political appointees often leave office before the president's term actually ends. The average term of service for political appointees is less than two years. As a result, the professional civil servants who serve under the political appointee may not feel compelled to carry out their new boss's directives quickly because they know that he or she will not be around for very long. This inertia is compounded by the fact that it is extremely difficult to discharge civil servants. In recent years, less than one-tenth of 1 percent of federal employees have been fired for incompetence. Because discharged employees may appeal their dismissals, many months or even years may pass before the issue is resolved conclusively. This occupational rigidity helps to ensure that most political appointees, no matter how competent or driven, will not be able to exert much meaningful influence over their subordinates, let alone implement dramatic changes in the bureaucracy itself.

A Short History of the Federal Civil Service

When the federal government was formed in 1789, it had no career public servants but rather consisted of amateurs who were almost all Federalists. When Jefferson took over as president, he found that few in his party were holding federal administrative jobs, so he fired more than one hundred officials and replaced them with members of the so-called **natural aristocracy**—that is, with his own Jeffersonian Republicans. For the next twenty-five years, a growing body of federal administrators gained ex-

Did You Know . . . That the secret U.S. government intelligence fund, which finances the Central Intelligence Agency as well as intelligence activities in other departments, exceeds $35 billion per year?

NATURAL ARISTOCRACY
A small ruling clique of the state's "best" citizens, whose membership is based on birth, wealth, and ability. The Jeffersonian era emphasized government rule by such a group.

United States Post Office employees sort the mail during the night shift at the New York post office.

perience and expertise, becoming in the process professional public servants. These administrators stayed in office regardless of who was elected president. The bureaucracy had become a self-maintaining, long-term element within government.

To the Victor Belongs the Spoils.   When Andrew Jackson took over the White House in 1828, he could not believe how many appointed officials (appointed before him, that is) were overtly hostile toward him and his Democratic party. The bureaucracy—indeed an aristocracy—considered itself the only group fit to rule. But Jackson was a man of the people, and his policies were populist in nature. As the bureaucracy was reluctant to carry out his programs, Jackson did the obvious: He fired federal officials—more than had all his predecessors combined. The **spoils system**—an application of the principle that to the victor belongs the spoils—reigned.

The Civil Service Reform Act of 1883.   Jackson's spoils system survived for a number of years, but it became increasingly corrupt. Also, the size of the bureaucracy increased by 300 percent between 1851 and 1881. Reformers began to examine the professional civil service that was established in several European countries, which operated under a **merit system** in which job appointments were based on competitive examinations. The cry for civil service reform began to be heard more loudly.

The ruling Lincoln–Grant Republican party was divided in its attitude toward reform, the "stalwart" faction opposing reform of any sort. When President James A. Garfield, a moderate reformer, was assassinated in 1881 by a disappointed office seeker, Charles J. Guiteau, the latter was heard to shout "I am a stalwart, and Arthur is president now!" He was correct: Chester A. Arthur, a stalwart vice president, became president. Ironically, it was under the stalwart Arthur that civil service reform actually occurred—partly as a result of public outrage over Garfield's assassination. The movement to replace the spoils system with a permanent career civil service had the cause that would carry it to victory.

SPOILS SYSTEM
The awarding of government jobs to political supporters and friends; generally associated with President Andrew Jackson.

MERIT SYSTEM
The selection, retention, and promotion of government employees on the basis of competitive examinations.

The assassination of President Garfield by a disappointed office seeker. The effect of this event was to replace the spoils system with a permanent career civil service.

In 1883, the **Pendleton Act**—or **Civil Service Reform Act**—was passed, bringing to a close the period of Jacksonian spoils. The act established the principle of employment on the basis of open competitive examinations and created the **Civil Service Commission** to administer the personnel service. Only 10 percent of federal employees were initially covered by the merit system. Later laws, amendments, and executive orders, however, increased the coverage to more than 90 percent of the federal civil service.

The Supreme Court put an even heavier lid on the spoils system in *Elrod v. Burns*[3] in 1976 and *Branti v. Finkel*[4] in 1980. In those two cases, the Court used the First Amendment to forbid government officials from discharging or threatening to discharge public employees solely for not being supporters of the political party in power unless party affiliation is an appropriate requirement for the position. Additional curbs on political patronage were added in *Rutan v. Republican Party of Illinois*[5] in 1990. The Court's ruling effectively prevented the use of partisan political considerations as the basis for hiring, promoting, or transferring most public employees. An exception was permitted, however, for senior policy-making positions, which usually go to officials who will support the programs of the elected leaders.

The Hatch Act of 1939. The growing size of the federal bureaucracy created the potential for political manipulation. In principle, a civil servant is politically neutral. But civil servants certainly know that it is politicians who pay the bills through their appropriations and that it is politicians who decide about the growth of agencies. In 1933, when President Franklin D. Roosevelt set up his New Deal, a virtual army of civil servants was hired to staff the numerous new agencies that were created to cope with the problems of the Great Depression. Because the individuals who worked in these agencies owed their jobs to the Democratic party, it seemed natural for them to campaign for Democratic candidates. The Democrats controlling Congress in the mid-1930s did not object. But in 1938, a coalition of conservative Democrats and Republicans took control of the Congress and forced through the **Hatch Act**—or the **Political Activities Act**—of 1939.

The main provision of this act is that civil service employees cannot take an active part in the political management of campaigns. It also prohibits the use of federal authority to influence nominations and elections and outlaws the use of bureaucratic rank to pressure federal employees to make political contributions.

In 1972, a federal district court declared the Hatch Act prohibition against political activity to be unconstitutional. The U.S. Supreme Court, however, reaffirmed the challenged portion of the act in 1973, stating that the government's interest in preserving a nonpartisan civil service was so great that the prohibitions should remain.[6]

In June 1990, Congress passed legislation that would have significantly changed the Hatch Act by allowing more than three million federal civil service and postal employees to organize voter registration drives, hold

PENDLETON ACT (CIVIL SERVICE REFORM ACT)
This law, as amended over the years, remains the basic statute regulating federal employment personnel policies. It established the principle of employment on the basis of merit and created the Civil Service Commission to administer the personnel service.

CIVIL SERVICE COMMISSION
The central personnel agency of the national government; created in 1883.

HATCH ACT (POLITICAL ACTIVITIES ACT)
This act prohibits the use of federal authority to influence nominations and elections or the use of rank to pressure federal employees to make political contributions. It also prohibits civil service employees from active involvement in political campaigns.

---

[3]427 U.S. 347 (1976).

[4]445 U.S. 507 (1980).

[5]497 U.S. 62 (1990).

[6]*United States Civil Service Commission v. National Association of Letter Carriers*, 413 U.S. 548 (1973).

POLITICS AND PEOPLE

A Guide to Running Government Like a Business

David Osborne

Many people believe that the government is increasingly unable or unwilling to govern the country. Politicians seem to have few ideas as to how to make government institutions more effective. What compounds the problem is that most state governments, as well as the federal government itself, are beset by huge deficits as well as eroding tax bases. The attitude of federal legislators has been to play politics as usual, but an increasing number of state governments are beginning to experiment with a variety of schemes to run their operations more efficiently and capably. These legislators and officials realize that taxpayers are increasingly unwilling to fund what they view as wasteful or excessive government spending and are more willing to take out their anger on incumbent politicians.

One inspiration behind this new willingness to try unorthodox solutions in government is David Osborne, a forty-two-year-old journalist who has become something of a celebrity in government circles. Osborne has worked as a consultant for literally hundreds of state and local governments around the country, urging that they run their operations more like businesses. Osborne's focus is not on making government operations profitable but on maximizing the efficiency and productivity of government workers by providing incentives for improved performance.

Growing Support

Although Osborne has been preaching his message for years, it is only recently that tough economic times have forced many governors, may-

ors, and city administrators to consider ways in which government can be made more entrepreneurial. Some of the more promising measures have included such tactics as permitting agencies that do not spend their entire budget to keep some of the difference and rewarding employees with performance-based bonuses. The difficulty of restructuring government is not lost upon these state and local officials, but they have accepted to varying degrees Osborne's message that centralized governments are increasingly obsolete.

Unchanging Government Structures

Osborne asserts that the nation's diverse economic base cannot be administered competently by traditional bureaucratic organizations. Consequently, government must become more responsive to cope with the increasing number of demands placed on it.

Some unions have attacked Osborne's ideas as little more than thinly veiled efforts to lay off government workers. Indeed, some researchers question whether it is even possible to measure the performance of government employees, given the nature of the tasks they perform and the absence of an objective yardstick, such as the wage rates set by supply and demand signals in the private market.

Osborne's ideas attracted the attention of Bill Clinton when he was the governor of Arkansas. He continued to offer advice to President Clinton after the inauguration of the former governor.

office in political party organizations, and serve as delegates to presidential nominating conventions. The act also would have allowed the solicitation of campaign funds from coworkers on behalf of federal employee union political action committees. Opponents of the legislation argued that it would significantly weaken the Hatch Act, politicize the bureaucracy, and erode public trust in government. President Bush vetoed the legislation, saying that he did not want to change a law that has "successfully insulated the federal service from the undue political influence that would destroy its essential political neutrality." Congress failed to override the veto. Some of Bush's critics argued that his veto was purely political, pointing out that a majority of federal civil servants are Democrats.

Current Attempts at Bureaucratic Reform

As long as federal bureaucracy exists, there will continue to be attempts to make it more open, efficient, and responsive to the needs of American citizens. The most important actual and proposed reforms in the last few years include sunshine and sunset laws, privatization, and more protection for so-called whistle blowers.

Sunshine Laws

In 1976, Congress enacted the **Government in the Sunshine Act.** It required for the first time that all multiheaded federal agencies—about fifty of them—hold their meetings regularly in public session. The bill defined *meetings* as almost any gathering, formal and informal, of agency members, including conference telephone calls. The only exceptions to this rule of openness are discussions of matters such as court proceedings or personnel problems, and these exceptions are specifically listed in the bill.

Sunset Laws

A potential type of control on the size and scope of the federal bureaucracy is **sunset legislation,** which would place government programs on a definite schedule for congressional consideration. Unless Congress specifically reauthorized a particular federally operated program at the end of a designated period, it would automatically be terminated; that is, its sun would set.

The idea of sunset legislation was first suggested by Franklin D. Roosevelt when he created the plethora of New Deal agencies. His assistant, William O. Douglas, recommended that each agency's charter should include a provision allowing for its termination in ten years. Only an act of Congress could revitalize it. Obviously, the proposal was never adopted. It was not until 1976 that a state legislature—Colorado's—adopted sunset legislation for state regulatory commissions, giving them a life of six years before their sun set. Today most states have some type of sunset law.

Privatization

One approach to bureaucratic reform is **privatization,** or **contracting out.** Privatization is replacing government services with services from the pri-

GOVERNMENT IN THE SUNSHINE ACT
Requires that all multiheaded federal agencies conduct their business regularly in public session.

SUNSET LEGISLATION
A law requiring that an existing program be regularly reviewed for its effectiveness and terminated unless specifically extended as a result of this review.

PRIVATIZATION, OR CONTRACTING OUT
The replacement of government-paid-for products and services by private firms.

vate sector. For example, the government might contract with private firms to operate prisons. Supporters of privatization argue that some services could be provided more efficiently by the marketplace. Another privatization scheme is to furnish vouchers to clients in lieu of services. For example, it has been proposed that instead of federally supported housing assistance, the government should offer vouchers that recipients could use to "pay" for housing in privately owned buildings. Privatization also includes selling government assets. The Reagan administration proposed selling the naval petroleum reserve oil fields at Elk Hills, California, and Teapot Dome, Wyoming, to private companies. Another proposal is that AMTRAK passenger rail service be sold to private business or to states or local governments.

Helping Out the Whistle Blowers

WHISTLE BLOWER
Someone who brings to public attention gross governmental inefficiency or an illegal action.

The term **whistle blower** as applied to the federal bureaucracy has a special meaning: It is someone who blows the whistle on a gross governmental inefficiency or illegal action. Whistle blowers may be clerical workers, managers, or even specialists, such as scientists. Dr. Aldric Saucier is an army research scientist who had claimed since 1987 that the Strategic Defense Initiative, known as "Star Wars," was plagued by mismanagement. Saucier asserted that the army tried to dismiss him for reporting his criticisms about the program to his superiors. In particular, Saucier charged that the program had been beset by wasteful and flawed research and that his dismissal was ordered after he submitted detailed reports documenting those criticisms to the military. Representative John Conyers (D., Mich.) intervened on Saucier's behalf and obtained the assistance of the Federal Office of Special Counsel. The office conducted a preliminary examination and concluded in March 1992 that some of Saucier's claims might have merit. Shortly after, the army agreed to suspend Saucier's dismissal until his claims could be fully investigated.

The 1978 Civil Service Reform Act prohibits reprisals against whistle blowers by their superiors, and it set up the Merit Systems Protection Board as part of this protection. There is little evidence, though, that potential whistle blowers truly have received more protection as a result. An attempt by Congress to increase protection for whistle blowers was vetoed by President Reagan in 1988.

Many federal agencies also have toll-free hot lines that employees can use to anonymously report bureaucratic waste and inappropriate behavior. About 35 percent of all calls result in agency action or follow up. Some calls lead to dramatic savings for the government. The General Accounting Office (GAO) hot line was reported to have generated $22 million in savings in 1991 alone. Excluding crank calls, the GAO hot line received more than ten thousand calls during that period, which resulted in the conviction or reprimand of 300 federal employees.

Bureaucrats As Politicians and Policy Makers

Agencies in the federal bureaucracy are created by Congress to implement legislation. Because Congress is unable to oversee the day-to-day administration of its programs, it must delegate certain powers to administrative agencies. In theory, the agencies should put into effect laws passed by Congress. Laws are often drafted in such vague and general terms, however, that they provide little guidance to administrators as to how they should be put into effect. This means that the agencies themselves must decide how best to carry out the wishes of Congress.

The discretion given to administrative agencies is not accidental. Congress has long realized that it lacks the technical expertise and the resources to monitor the implementation of its laws. Hence, the administrative agency is created to fill the gaps. This gap-filling role requires the agency to formulate administrative rules (regulations) to put flesh on the bones of the law. But it also forces the agency itself to assume the role of an unelected policy maker.

The Rule-Making Environment

Rule making does not occur in a vacuum. Suppose that Congress passes a new air pollution law. The Environmental Protection Agency (EPA) might decide to implement the new law by a technical regulation relating to factory emissions. This proposed regulation would be published in the *Federal Register* so that interested parties would have an opportunity to comment on it. Individuals and companies that opposed parts or all of these rules might then try to convince the EPA to revise or redraft it. Some parties might try to persuade the agency to withdraw the proposed regulation altogether. In any event, the EPA would consider these comments in drafting the final version of the regulation following the expiration of the comment period.

Once the final regulation has been published, it might be challenged in court by a party having a direct interest in the rule, such as a company that could expect to incur significant costs in complying with the rule. The company could argue that the rule misinterprets the applicable law or goes beyond the agency's statutory purview. An allegation by the company that the EPA made a mistake in judgment would probably not be

Did You Know . . . That the U.S. Postal Service, with over 811,000 employees, is the largest civilian employer in the United States?

Members of a Federal Aviation Administration investigation team try to find the cause of a crash at the Los Angeles airport. The federal government essentially controls all air traffic in the United States and sets the regulations for commercial and private aircraft.

Did You Know ... That a recent study by the General Accounting Office revealed that, in one month alone, twenty federal programs incorrectly paid more than $4.3 million to dead people?

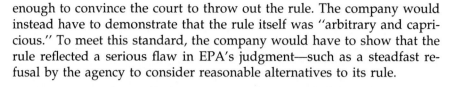

enough to convince the court to throw out the rule. The company would instead have to demonstrate that the rule itself was "arbitrary and capricious." To meet this standard, the company would have to show that the rule reflected a serious flaw in EPA's judgment—such as a steadfast refusal by the agency to consider reasonable alternatives to its rule.

Negotiated Settlements

Since the end of World War II, companies have filed lawsuits regularly to block the implementation of agency regulations. Environmentalists and other special interest groups have also challenged government regulations. In the 1980s and 1990s, however, the sheer wastefulness of attempting to regulate through litigation has become more and more apparent, particularly in an era when the government is beseiged by high deficits. A growing number of federal agencies have begun encouraging businesses and public interest groups to become directly involved in the drafting of regulations. Agencies hope that such participation might help to prevent later courtroom battles over the meaning, applicability, and legal effect of the regulations.

One example of this trend was the EPA's decision to seek an agreement with business interests and environmental groups about implementing certain provisions of the Clean Air Act of 1990. The only condition was that the participants—which included such perennial targets of environmentalists as the National Petroleum Refiners Association (NPRA)—promise not to challenge in court the outcome of any agreement to which they were a party and to support the agreement if one of the other participating companies filed suit to have the agreement overturned. Representatives of the NPRA and other business organizations have hailed this process as being more productive than the past practice of simply challenging agency regulations in court. This new approach has also been supported by environmental groups, such as the Environmental Defense Fund, which view such agreements as a way to conserve their own limited resources and to deal with potential pollution problems before they arise.

Bureaucrats Are Policy Makers

PUBLIC ADMINISTRATION
The science of managing public organizations.

Theories of **public administration** once assumed that bureaucracies do not make policy but only implement the laws and policies promulgated by the president and legislative bodies. A more realistic view of the role of the bureaucracy in policy making, which is now held by most bureaucrats and elected officials, is that the agencies and departments of government play important roles in policy making. As we have seen, many government rules, regulations, and programs are in fact initiated by the bureaucracy, based on its expertise and scientific studies. How a law passed by Congress is eventually translated into concrete action—from the forms to be filled out to decisions about who gets the benefits—is usually determined within each agency or department. Even the evaluation of whether a policy has achieved its purpose is usually based on studies that are commissioned and interpreted by the agency administering the program.

IRON TRIANGLE
The three-way alliance among legislators, bureaucrats, and interest groups to make or preserve policies that benefit their respective interests.

Policy is made by several groups. The bureaucracy's policy-making role can be better understood by examining what has been called the "**iron triangle.**"

The Iron Triangle

Consider the bureaucracy within the Department of Agriculture. It consists of 118,403 individuals working directly for the federal government and thousands of other individuals who, directly or indirectly, work as contractors, subcontractors, or consultants to the department. Now consider that there are various interest, or client, groups that are concerned with what the federal government does for farmers. These include the American Farm Bureau Federation, the National Cattleman's Association, the National Milk Producers Association, the Corn Growers Association, and the Citrus Growers Association. Finally, go directly to Congress and you will see that there are two major congressional committees concerned with agriculture—the House Committee on Agriculture and the Senate Committee on Agriculture, Nutrition, and Forestry—each of which has seven subcommittees.

Figure 12-8 is a schematic view of the iron triangle. This triangle, or subgovernment, is an alliance of mutual benefit among some unit within the bureaucracy, its interest or client group, and committees or subcommittees of Congress and their staff members. The workings of iron triangles are complicated, but they are well established in almost every subgovernment.

Consider again the Department of Agriculture. The secretary of agriculture is nominated by the president (and confirmed by the Senate) and is nominally the head of the Department of Agriculture. But that secretary cannot even buy a desk lamp if Congress does not approve the appropriations for Agriculture's budget. Within Congress, the responsibility for considering the Department of Agriculture's request for funding belongs first to the House and Senate Appropriations committees and to the Agriculture subcommittees under them. The members of those committees, most of whom represent agricultural states, have been around a long time. They have their own ideas about what amount of funds is appropriate for the Agriculture Department's budget. They have their own program concepts. They carefully scrutinize the ideas of the president and the secretary of agriculture.

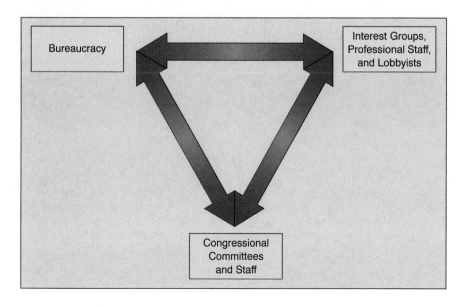

FIGURE 12-8 ■ The Iron Triangle

Did You Know . . . That the federal government owns one-third of the land in the United States (744 million acres), an area the size of all the states east of the Mississippi River plus Texas?

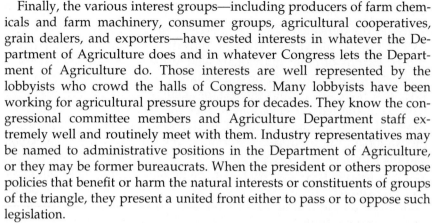

Finally, the various interest groups—including producers of farm chemicals and farm machinery, consumer groups, agricultural cooperatives, grain dealers, and exporters—have vested interests in whatever the Department of Agriculture does and in whatever Congress lets the Department of Agriculture do. Those interests are well represented by the lobbyists who crowd the halls of Congress. Many lobbyists have been working for agricultural pressure groups for decades. They know the congressional committee members and Agriculture Department staff extremely well and routinely meet with them. Industry representatives may be named to administrative positions in the Department of Agriculture, or they may be former bureaucrats. When the president or others propose policies that benefit or harm the natural interests or constituents of groups of the triangle, they present a united front either to pass or to oppose such legislation.

Such iron triangles—of which there are many, not only on Capitol Hill, but also in state capitals—at times have completely thwarted efforts by the president to get the administration's programs enacted.

Congressional Control of the Bureaucracy

Although Congress is the ultimate repository of political power under the Constitution, many political pundits doubt whether it can meaningfully control the burgeoning federal bureaucracy. These commentators forget that Congress has the power of the purse and could, theoretically, refuse to authorize or appropriate money for a particular agency. Whether Congress would actually take such a drastic measure in exercising its responsibility of legislative oversight would depend on the circumstances. It is clear, however, that Congress does have the legal authority to decide whether to fund or not to fund administrative agencies.

Creating Administrative Agencies.   Nearly every administrative agency is created through an act of Congress. The legislation that results in the creation of an agency is usually proposed to address a pressing national problem. The Occupational Safety and Health Act of 1970, for example, was created to redress the problem of workplace hazards. But the act itself would have been rendered nearly useless had it not included provisions for the creation of a regulatory agency, the Occupational Safety and Health Administration (OSHA), to create and enforce safety standards. Although Congress delegated significant powers to OSHA in the enabling legislation, Congress did define the parameters within which the agency could operate.

AUTHORIZATION
A formal declaration by a legislative committee that a certain amount of funding may be available to an agency. Some authorizations terminate in a year; others are automatically renewable without further congressional authorization.

Authorizing Funds.   Once an agency is created, Congress must authorize funds for it. The **authorization** is a formal declaration by the appropriate legislative committee that a certain amount of funding may be available to the agency. The authorization itself may terminate in a year, or it may be renewed automatically without further action by Congress. The National Aeronautics and Space Administration (NASA) is one agency in which authorizations must be periodically renewed; Social Security, in contrast, is funded through a permanent authorization. Periodic authorizations enable Congress to exercise greater control over the spending programs of an agency, while permanent authorizations free Congress from the task of having to review the authorization each year. The drawback of permanent authorizations is that they can become almost impossible to control politically.

Appropriating Funds.   After the funds are authorized, they must be appropriated by Congress. The Appropriations committees of both the House and the Senate forward spending bills to their respective bodies. The **appropriation** of funds occurs when the final bill is passed. Congress is not required to appropriate the entire authorized amount. It may appropriate less if it so chooses. If the appropriated funds are substantially less than the authorized amount, however, it may signal that the agency's agenda soon may be revamped by Congress.

The Legislative Veto.   The appropriations process is not the only way in which Congress may assert control over federal agencies. Congress also may try to limit the power of executive agencies through the use of a **legislative veto,** a procedural device by which Congress requires that executive actions be placed before Congress for a specified period of time before becoming effective. During that time, Congress may disapprove the action by a vote of either the House or the Senate—or both. In general, the legislative veto has been used by Congress as a way to assert greater control over the president's conduct of foreign policy. In 1983, however, the U.S. Supreme Court declared legislative vetoes to be unconstitutional in the case of *Immigration and Naturalization Service v. Chadha.*[7] The Court's decision was apparently not the last word on the subject, however, because Congress has since passed laws that contain provisions for legislative vetoes. How this particular legislative device will fare if it is legally challenged in the future remains to be seen.

Conclusion: The Important Function of the Bureaucracy

The federal bureaucracy is often viewed as a monolithic organization that is beyond the control of either the president or Congress. But is this really the case? Although presidents periodically complain about their inability to rein in the bureaucracy, they are able to nominate political appointees to top positions in most federal agencies. Also, through the annual budget process, Congress retains considerable power over the bureaucracy.

Despite the public's widespread distaste for bureaucracies, most Americans realize that federal agencies perform a variety of important tasks, ranging from the building of public housing to the maintenance of federal parks. Moreover, federal agencies are the primary means by which the laws of Congress are put into practice. This "gap filling" power gives federal agencies significant discretion to make policy. Such policy making—despite the insularity of the bureaucracy itself—is not without its advantages. Bureaucrats are often specialists in their fields and more knowledgeable than congresspersons about specific issues relating to the legislation passed by Congress.

APPROPRIATION
Occurs when Congress passes a spending bill specifying the amount of authorized funds that will actually be allocated for an agency's use.

LEGISLATIVE VETO
A procedural device that allows Congress to veto executive actions before they become effective and thus control, to some extent, the bureaucracy.

[7]462 U.S. 919 (1983).

GETTING INVOLVED

What Does the Government Know about You?

The federal government collects billions of pieces of information on tens of millions of Americans each year. These are stored in files and gigantic computers and often are exchanged between agencies. You probably have at least several federal records (for example, those in the Social Security Administration, the Internal Revenue Service, and, if you are a male, the Selective Service).

The 1966 Freedom of Information Act requires that the federal government release, on your request, any identifiable information it has in the administrative agencies of the executive branch. This information can be about you or about any other subject; however, ten categories of material are exempted (classified material, confidential material dealing with trade secrets, internal personnel rules, personal medical files, and the like). To request material, you must write the Freedom of Information Act officer directly at the agency in question (let's say the Department of Education). You must also have a relatively specific idea about the document or information you wish to obtain.

A second law, the Privacy Act of 1974, gives you access specifically to information the government may have collected about you. This is a very important law because it allows you to review your records on file with federal agencies (for example, with the Federal Bureau of Investigation) and to check those records for possible inaccuracies. Cases do exist in which two people with similar or the same names have had their records confused. In some cases, innocent persons have had the criminal records of another person erroneously inserted in their files.

If you wish to look at any records or find out if an agency has a record on you, write to the Agency Head or Privacy Act Officer, address it to the specific agency, state that "under the provisions of the Privacy Act of 1974, 5 U.S.C. 522a, I hereby request a copy of (or access to) _____ ," and then describe the record that you wish to investigate.

If you have trouble finding out about your records or wish to locate an attorney in Washington, D.C., to help you with this matter, you can contact:

Lawyer Referral Service
Washington Bar Association
1819 H St., N.W., Suite 300
Washington, D.C. 20036
202-223-1484

CHAPTER SUMMARY

1. Bureaucracies are rigid hierarchical organizations in which the tasks and powers of lower-level employees are clearly defined. Job specialties and extensive procedural rules set the standards for behavior. Bureaucracies are the primary form of organization of most major corporations and universities. Presidents have long complained about their inability to control the federal bureaucracy. There is no reference to the bureaucracy itself in the Constitution, but Article II gives the president the power to appoint officials to execute the laws of the United States. Most scholars cite Article II as the constitutional basis for the federal bureaucracy.

2. Several theories have been offered to explain bureaucracies. The Weberian model posits that bureaucracies have developed into centralized hierarchical structures in response to the increasing demands placed on governments by their citizens. The acquisitive model views top-level bureaucrats as pressing for ever greater funding, staffs, and privileges to augment their own sense of power and security. The monopolistic model focuses on the environment in which most gov-

ernment bureaucracies operate, stating that bureaucracies are inefficient and excessively costly to operate because they often have no competitors. Finally, the garbage can model posits that bureaucracies are rudderless organizations that flounder about in search of solutions to problems.

3. Since the founding of the United States, the federal bureaucracy has grown from 50 to approximately 3.1 million employees. Federal, state, and local employees together make up some 14 percent of the nation's labor force. The federal bureaucracy consists of fourteen cabinet departments, as well as numerous independent executive agencies, independent regulatory agencies, and government corporations. These entities enjoy varying degrees of autonomy, visibility, and political support.

4. A self-sustaining federal bureaucracy of career civil servants was formed during Thomas Jefferson's presidency. Andrew Jackson implemented a spoils system through which he appointed his own political supporters. A civil service based on professionalism and merit was the goal of the Civil

Service Reform Act of 1883. Concerns that the civil service be freed from the pressures of politics prompted the passage of the Hatch Act in 1939.

5. Congress delegates much of its authority to federal agencies when it creates new laws. The bureaucrats that run these agencies may become important policy makers because Congress has neither the time nor the technical expertise to oversee the administration of its laws. In the agency rule-making process, a proposed regulation is published, followed by a comment period during which interested parties may offer suggestions for changes. Because companies have challenged many regulations in court, federal agencies are now trying to engage them in the actual drafting of certain regulations.

6. Congress exerts ultimate control over all federal agencies because it controls the federal government's purse strings. It also establishes the general guidelines by which regulatory agencies must abide. The appropriations process may also provide a way to send messages of approval or disapproval to particular agencies.

QUESTIONS FOR REVIEW AND DISCUSSION

1. Why has the federal bureaucracy grown so tremendously in the twentieth century? Why has the growth of the federal bureaucracy remained relatively stable in recent decades, while state and local bureaucracies continue to grow?

2. Although Congress often attacks the bureaucracy as overgrown and inefficient, it has done little to reform it. Why is Congress unlikely to make major reforms in the bureaucracy?

3. Tales of $5,000 screwdrivers being purchased by the army and of other bureaucratic wastefulness abound. Who is responsible for such inefficiencies? What role do private interests play in making the government inefficient?

4. If you were on a government commission to streamline the federal bureaucracy, how would you reorganize the departments, independent agencies, and regulatory commissions? Could some of these organizations be combined so that the president would have more direct control over them? Or would you grant them more independence from the president's authority?

SELECTED REFERENCES

David Burnham, *A Law unto Itself: The IRS and the Abuse of Power* (New York: Random House, 1990). A very critical study of the role of the Internal Revenue Service, the largest, most powerful, and least accountable enforcement agency in the federal government.

Edward Erler and John Marini, *Bureaucracy and the American Constitution* (Bristol, Pa.: Crane Russak, 1992). The authors look at the historical growth of bureaucracy within the American system of government and argue that the separation of powers envisioned by the framers of the Constitution is jeopardized by the institutional size and strength of today's bureaucracy.

Cole Blease Graham, Jr., and Steven W. Hays, *Managing the Public Organization* (Washington, D.C.: Congressional Quarterly Press, 1986). This book distinguishes sharply between private and public sector management and thoroughly explores such practical topics as planning, organization, staffing, coordination, reporting, budgeting, and evaluation.

Naomi B. Lynn and Aaron Wildavsky, *Public Adminstration: The State of the Discipline* (Chatham, N.J.: Chatham House, 1990). This book addresses the lamentable lack of interest in the science of adminstration, the state that public administration is in today, and the benefits that an alliance between the disciplines of administration and political science would produce.

Kenneth J. Meyer, *Politics and the Bureaucracy: Policymaking in the Fourth Branch of Government* (Monterey, Calif.: Brooks/ Cole, 1986). The impact of bureaucracy on policy making (as opposed to simple policy implementation) is explored in this book. Includes suggestions on how to channel, structure, and control bureaucratic policy making.

Bogdan Mieczkowski, *Dysfunctional Bureaucracy* (Lanham, Md.: University Press of America, 1991). A look at the history of bureaucracy through the ages, its present forms both in America and abroad, and the conditions under which a functional bureaucracy becomes dysfunctional.

Dennis D. Riley, *Controlling the Federal Bureaucracy* (Philadelphia: Temple University Press, 1987). An analysis of the power of the bureaucracy and its relationship to other political institutions.

Chester A. Robinson, *The Bureaucracy and the Legislative Process: A Case Study of the Health Care Financing Administration* (Lanham, Md.: University Press of America, 1991). Using the Health Care Administration as a concrete example, Robinson examines the legislative role of the bureaucracy in American politics.

Bernard Rosen, *Holding Government Bureaucracies Accountable* (New York: Praeger, 1984). The principal focus of this book is the question of accountability of the bureaucracy to the executive, legislative, and judicial branches of government and to interest groups and citizens, with suggestions on how such accountability can be strengthened.

CHAPTER 13
The Judiciary

CHAPTER CONTENTS

WHAT IF ... FEDERAL JUDGES WERE ELECTED?

It is commonly argued that the federal judiciary is, and many say ought to be, insulated from the fierce winds of politics. The notion of a Supreme Court justice having to go out to the populace to attempt to save his or her job on the Court every few years would be unseemly to many Americans. While there certainly is a lot to be said for having the federal courts act impartially, it must be kept in mind that judges in most states have long been elected.

Many state judicial officers would not be in power except by the will of the voters. Even appointed judges, such as the justices on the U.S. Supreme Court, are nominated to office through the highly political apparatus of presidential appointment, followed by either the confirmation or rejection of that nomination by the U.S. Senate. Moreover, judges on the federal courts are not necessarily out of tune with changing political attitudes.

There is the general sense among judicial experts, as expressed pointedly by the humorist Finley Peter Dunne, that "'th' Supreme Court follows th' iliction returns." In fact, the surest way to get a federal judiciary that is to your liking politically is to vote for presidents and U.S. senators who have taken campaign positions in support of hiring judges with certain specific views on major issues. The federal courts, in this sense, have always been part of the electoral process.

What might happen if we did elect federal judges, up to and including the Supreme Court justices? One possibility is that the public's wishes, as measured, for example, in public opinion polls or in national referenda on key issues, could be put into effect more rapidly and more certainly. If strong majorities of the public were to favor, say, a federal flag-burning law or an end to legalized abortion, then that is the way that the courts might be expected to rule. The uneven track record of Congress and the presidents of the United States in translating popular will into public policy, however, suggests that success through this process is not at all assured.

Another real possibility is that the federal judiciary would become as thoroughly influenced by special interest groups (such as large corporations, labor unions, or ideologically motivated political action committees) as the Congress and the presidency. That would undoubtedly increase the cost of the electoral process overall, as judicial candidates would be added to those running for legislative and executive office who seek millions of dollars from organized interests. It may even happen that judges would run on "tickets" with candidates for the presidency or for other offices, so that when you voted for a new team in the White House you also would be voting for a set of judges.

Think, too, about what might happen if your judicial candidates lost and you, as, say, a registered Republican, were in court against a Democrat and had to have your case argued before a panel of Democratic judges. The federal judicial system as it is currently constituted is, of course, not always fair or free of bias. Nonetheless, the chances that overt partisanship might enter into the administration of justice may increase the likelihood of decisions that are arbitrary and capricious or vindictive against the losing party. Would the political affiliation of a candidate judge make any difference? After all, judges are supposed to rule on issues of law—not advance their own personal political agendas. But judges are human, and their court rulings are colored to varying degrees by their political and ideological convictions. Many people would not be surprised to find that Republican judges have been more conservative than their Democratic counterparts, particularly on issues relating to the rights of criminal defendants and abortion.

Keep in mind, though, that many of the decisions that are made by judges are about obscure clauses in tax laws, bureaucratic regulations, or other complicated points regarding statutes and rules that even expert lawyers cannot disentangle. Voters would not pay attention to these arcane arguments and would probably vote much as they do for congressional representatives or U.S. senators, with the candidate's party label (if the elections are partisan), personality, and name recognition deciding most elections.

1. *Who might benefit if federal judges were popularly elected?*
2. *Is it possible for any judiciary to be free of political motivation?*

We have just examined a hypothetical federal judiciary in which judges and justices are elected rather than appointed. Of course, the federal judiciary is 100 percent appointed in the United States, but that does not mean the judicial branch of the federal government is apolitical. Indeed, our courts play a larger role in making public policy than in any other country in the world today. This quasi-legislative role was not envisioned by the framers of the Constitution, who were primarily concerned with abuses of power by the national government. Rather, it evolved over time, particularly after Chief Justice John Marshall devised the doctrine of judicial review to resolve the impasse in *Marbury v. Madison*, which is discussed in the *Politics and Political Analysis* feature in this chapter.

As Alexis de Tocqueville, the nineteenth-century French commentator on American society, noted, "Scarcely any political question arises in the United States that is not resolved, sooner or later, into a judicial question."[1] Our judiciary forms part of our political process. The instant judges interpret the law, they become actors in the political arena—policy makers working within a political institution. As such, the most important political force within our judiciary is the United States Supreme Court. Because of its preeminence, we devote the major portion of this chapter to it. The remainder of the chapter deals with the lower federal courts and the state court system.

The Foundation of American Law: The Courts and *Stare Decisis*

Because of its colonial heritage, most of American law is based on the English legal system. In 1066, the Normans conquered England, and William the Conqueror and his successors began the process of unifying the country under their rule. One of the ways they did this was to establish the King's Court, or *Curia Regis.* Before the conquest, disputes had been settled according to local custom. The King's Court sought to establish a common or uniform set of rules for the whole country. As the number of courts and cases increased, the more important decisions of each year were gathered together and recorded in *Year Books.* Judges settling disputes similar to ones that had been decided before used the *Year Books* as the basis for their decisions. If a case was unique, judges had to create new laws, but they based their decisions on the general principles suggested by earlier cases. The body of judge-made law that developed under this system is still used today and is known as the **common law.**

The practice of deciding new cases with reference to former decisions, that is, according to **precedent,** became a cornerstone of the English and American judicial systems and is embodied in the doctrine of *stare decisis* ("to stand on decided cases").

The rule of *stare decisis* performs many useful functions. First, it helps the courts to be more efficient. It would be time consuming if each judge had to establish reasons for deciding what the law should be for each case brought before the court. If other courts have confronted the same

COMMON LAW
Judge-made law that originated in England from decisions shaped according to prevailing custom. Decisions were reapplied to similar situations and gradually became common to the nation. Common law forms the basis of legal procedures in the American states.

PRECEDENT
A court rule bearing on subsequent legal decisions in similar cases. Judges rely on precedents in deciding cases.

STARE DECISIS
"To stand on decided cases." The policy of courts to follow precedents established by the decisions of the past.

---

[1]Alexis de Tocqueville, *Democracy in America* (New York: Harper and Row, 1966), p. 248.

issue and reasoned through the case carefully, their opinions can serve as guides.

Second, *stare decisis* makes for a more uniform system. All courts try to follow precedent, and thus different courts will often use the same rule of law. (Some variations occur, however, because different states and regions follow different precedents.) Also, the rule of precedent tends to neutralize the personal prejudices of individual judges to the degree that they feel obliged to use precedent as the basis for their decision. Finally, the rule makes the law more stable and predictable than it otherwise would be. If the law on a subject is well settled, someone bringing a case to court can usually rely on the court to make a decision based on what the law has been.

More Recent Sources of Law

Today, courts have sources other than precedents to consider when making their decisions. These sources are described below.

Constitutions

The constitutions of the federal government and the states set forth the general organization, powers, and limits of government. The U.S. Constitution is the supreme law of the land. A law in violation of the Constitution, no matter what its source, may be declared unconstitutional and

A jury is being sworn in. Most jury trials have between six and twelve jurors. Some trials are held without juries.

thereafter cannot be enforced. Similarly, the state constitutions are supreme within their respective borders (unless they conflict with the U.S. Constitution or laws and treaties made in accordance with it). The Constitution thus defines the political playing field on which state and federal powers are reconciled. The idea that the Constitution should be supreme in certain matters stemmed from widespread dissatisfaction with the weak federal government that had existed previously under the Articles of Confederation adopted in 1781 (see Chapter 2).

Statutes and Administrative Regulations

Although the English common law provides the basis for both our civil and criminal legal systems, statutes have become increasingly important in defining the rights and obligations of individuals. Federal statutes may relate to any subject that is a concern of the federal government and cover areas ranging from hazardous wastes to federal taxation. State statutes include criminal codes, commercial laws, and laws relating to a variety of other matters. Cities, counties, and other local political bodies also pass statutes, which are called ordinances. These ordinances may deal with such things as zoning schemes and public safety. Rules and regulations issued by **administrative agencies** are another source of law. Today, much of the work of courts consists of interpreting these laws and regulations and applying them to circumstances in cases before the courts.

Judicial Review

The process for deciding whether a law is contrary to the mandates of the Constitution is known as **judicial review.** The power of judicial review is nowhere mentioned in the U.S. Constitution. Those in attendance at the Constitutional Convention probably expected that the courts would have some authority to review the legality of acts by the executive and legislative branches. Otherwise, there would be no one to decide whether Congress or the executive branch was overstepping its bounds. But it fell to the Supreme Court itself and its Chief Justice, John Marshall, to claim this power. The doctrine of judicial review was first established in the famous case of *Marbury v. Madison*, which determined that the Supreme Court had the power to decide that a law passed by Congress violated the Constitution:

> It is emphatically the province and duty of the Judicial Department to say what the law is. Those who apply the rule to a particular case, must of necessity expound and interpret that rule. If two laws conflict with each other, the courts must decide on the operation of each.[2]

The Supreme Court has ruled parts or all of acts of Congress to be unconstitutional only about 150 times in its history. State laws, however, have been declared unconstitutional by the Court much more often—about 1,000 times. Most of these rulings date from the period after the Civil War, before which time only two acts of Congress were declared unconstitutional. There have been two periods of relatively extensive use of the process of judicial negation—from 1921 to 1940, when a conserva-

ADMINISTRATIVE AGENCIES
Agencies that usually form part of the executive branch, plus independent regulatory agencies and independent agencies; for example, the Federal Trade Commission, the Securities and Exchange Commission, and the Federal Communications Commission.

JUDICIAL REVIEW
The power of the courts to declare acts of the executive and legislative branches unconstitutional; first established in *Marbury v. Madison.*

---

[2]1 Cranch 137 (1803).

POLITICS AND POLITICAL ANALYSIS

Judicial Review—*Marbury v. Madison* (1803)

In the edifice of American public law, the *Marbury v. Madison* decision in 1803 can be viewed as the keystone of the constitutional arch. The story is often told, and for a reason—it shows how seemingly insignificant cases can have important and enduring results.

Consider the facts behind *Marbury v. Madison.* John Adams had lost his bid for reelection to Thomas Jefferson in 1800. Adams, a Federalist, thought the Jeffersonian Republicans (Anti-Federalists) would weaken the power of the national government by asserting states' rights. He also feared the Anti-Federalists' antipathy toward business. During the final hours of Adams's presidency, he worked feverishly to "pack" the judiciary with loyal Federalists by giving what came to be called "midnight appointments," just before Jefferson took office.

All of the judicial commissions had to be certified and delivered. The task of delivery fell on Adams's secretary of state, John Marshall. Out of the fifty-nine midnight appointments, Marshall delivered only

John Marshall

James Madison

forty-two. He assumed that the remaining seventeen would be sent out by Jefferson's new secretary of state, James Madison. Of course, the new administration refused to cooperate in packing the judiciary: Jefferson refused to deliver the remaining commissions. William Marbury, along with three other Federalists to whom the commissions had not been delivered, decided to sue. The suit was brought directly to the Supreme Court seeking a **writ of**

mandamus, authorized by the Judiciary Act of 1789.

As fate would have it, the man responsible for the lawsuit, John Marshall, had stepped down as Adams's secretary of state only to become chief justice. He was now in a position to decide the case for which he was responsible.* Marshall was

*Today any justice who has been involved in an issue before the Court would probably disqualify himself or herself because of a conflict of interest.

WRIT OF *MANDAMUS*
An order issued by a court to compel the performance of an act.

tive Court upheld private interests over public statutes, and in the 1960s and 1970s, when more liberal justices upheld individual and group rights to racial and political equality.

A significant modern case of judicial review was the ruling by the Supreme Court in 1983 that outlawed the practice of the *legislative veto,* by which one or both chambers of Congress could overturn decisions made by the president or by executive agencies.[3] This single declaration of unconstitutionality affected several hundred separate statutes and reinforced the Court's position as an enforcer of the separation of powers principle.

[3]*Immigration and Naturalization Service v. Chadha,* 462 U.S. 919 (1983).

POLITICS AND POLITICAL ANALYSIS

faced with a dilemma: If he ordered the commissions delivered, the new secretary of state could simply refuse. The Court had no way to compel action because it has no police force. Also, Congress was controlled by the Jeffersonian Republicans. It might impeach Marshall for such an action.[**] But if Marshall simply allowed Secretary of State Madison to do as he wished, the Court's power would be severely eroded.

Marshall stated for the unanimous Court that Jefferson and Madison had acted incorrectly in refusing to deliver Marbury's commission. Marshall also stated, however, that the highest court did not have the power to act as a court of **original jurisdiction** in this particular case, because the section of the law that gave it original jurisdiction was unconstitutional. The Judiciary Act of 1789 specified that the Supreme Court could issue writs of manda-

[**]In fact, in 1805, Congress did impeach Supreme Court Justice Samuel Chase, a Federalist, though he was not convicted. The charge was abusive behavior under the Sedition Act.

mus as part of its original jurisdiction, but Marshall pointed out that Article III of the Constitution, which spelled out the Supreme Court's original jurisdiction, did not mention writs of mandamus. In other words, Congress did not have the right to expand the Court's jurisdiction, so this section of the Judiciary Act of 1789 was unconstitutional and hence void.

The decision avoided a showdown between the Federalists and the Jeffersonian Republicans. The power of the Supreme Court was enlarged: "A law repugnant to the Constitution is void."

Was the Marshall Court's assumption of judicial review power justified by the Constitution? Whether it was or not, *Marbury v. Madison* confirmed a doctrine that was part of the legal tradition of the time. Indeed, judicial review was a major premise (although not articulated) on which the movement to draft constitutions and bills of rights was ultimately based, as well as being part of the legal theory underlying the Revolution of 1776. During the

decade before the adoption of the federal Constitution, cases in at least eight states involved the power of judicial review. Also, the Supreme Court had considered the constitutionality of an act of Congress in *Hylton v. United States*,[***] in which Congress's power to levy certain taxes was challenged. But because that particular act was ruled constitutional, rather than unconstitutional, this first federal exercise of true judicial review was not clearly recognized as such.

In any event, because Marshall masterfully fashioned a decision that did not require anyone to do anything, there was no practical legal point to challenge. It still stands today as a judicial and political masterpiece.

[***]3 Dallas 171 (1796).

Our Court System Today

The United States has a dual court system. There are state courts and federal courts. Each of the fifty states, as well as the District of Columbia, has its own fully developed, independent system of courts. The federal court system derives its power from the U.S. Constitution, Article III, Section 1. Both the federal and state court systems have several tiers of authority. Figure 13-1 shows the components of the federal judiciary. There are ninety-six federal district courts, which are the basic **trial courts** in the federal system. The majority of cases that are appropriately within the **jurisdiction** of the federal courts start here.[4]

[4]The jurisdiction of the federal courts is limited by Article III, Section 2, of the U.S. Constitution.

ORIGINAL JURISDICTION
The authority of a court to hear a case in the first instance.

TRIAL COURTS
Those courts in which most cases usually begin and in which questions of fact are examined.

JURISDICTION
The authority of a court to decide certain cases. Not all courts have the authority to decide all cases. Where a case arises and what its subject matter is are two jurisdictional factors.

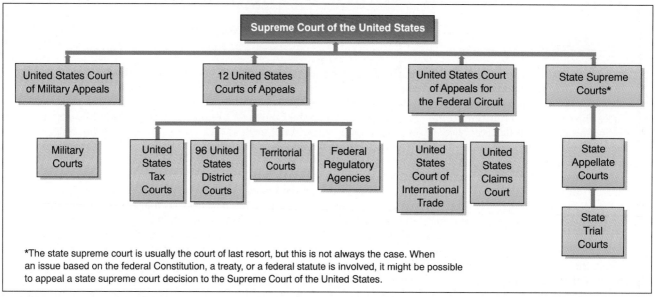

*The state supreme court is usually the court of last resort, but this is not always the case. When an issue based on the federal Constitution, a treaty, or a federal statute is involved, it might be possible to appeal a state supreme court decision to the Supreme Court of the United States.

FIGURE 13-1 ■ **The Federal Court System**

APPELLATE COURTS
Those courts having jurisdiction of appeal and review of cases and issues that were originally tried in lower courts.

GRAND JURY
A jury called to hear evidence and determine whether indictments should be issued against persons suspected of having committed crimes.

PETIT JURY
The ordinary jury for the trial of a civil or criminal case

There are other federal trial courts. These have special, or limited, jurisdiction. They include the tax courts, which decide cases involving taxpayers' challenges to tax assessments, and the bankruptcy courts, which interpret and apply the federal bankruptcy laws. The U.S. Claims Court hears lawsuits against the government based on the Constitution, federal laws, and contracts. The Claims Court also decides cases concerning salaries of public officials, payment of money to persons unjustly imprisoned for federal crimes, and some Native-American claims. The Court of International Trade hears cases involving taxes on imported merchandise.

When cases that have been decided in a federal trial court are appealed, they usually go to one of the judicial circuit courts of appeals (including the District of Columbia and federal circuit courts of appeal), the boundaries of which are outlined in Figure 13-2. Under normal circumstances, the decisions of the courts of appeals are final, but appeal to the United States Supreme Court is possible. At the top of the federal judiciary is the Supreme Court of the United States. According to the language of Article III of the U.S. Constitution, there can only be one Supreme Court, with all other courts in the federal system "inferior" to it.

State court systems are similar to the federal court system, except that only thirty-seven states have intermediate courts of appeals, or **appellate courts,** between the trial courts, in which the majority of cases originate, and the highest reviewing courts of the states. Many cases that appear before trial courts require juries. A **grand jury** consists of at least twelve persons who are called to hear evidence and determine whether indictments should be issued against persons suspected of having committed a crime. Grand juries decide whether there is enough evidence to warrant a formal accusation by the state of wrongdoing; they do not determine guilt. A **petit jury,** in contrast, consists of six or twelve jurors and determines the innocence or guilt of the defendant in criminal and civil trials. The decisions of each state's highest court on questions of state law are final. Only when issues relating to the U.S. Constitution or other federal

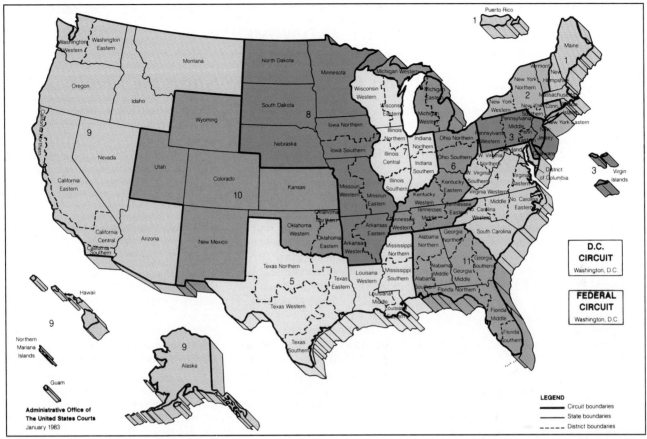

FIGURE 13-2 ■ Geographical Boundaries of Federal Circuit Courts

laws are involved can the Supreme Court of the United States overrule a state court's decision. The United States Supreme Court has no power to hear appeals from a state supreme court concerning issues of purely state law. Recall that the Constitution reserves all powers to the states that are not expressly granted to the federal government. The federal courts, which derive their power from the Constitution, thus have no authority to rule on issues solely relating to state law.

The Early Years of the Supreme Court

Alexander Hamilton, writing in *Federalist Paper* No. 78, believed that the Supreme Court would be the "least dangerous branch" of the federal government because it had no enforcement powers, nor could it raise money. The other two branches had to cooperate with it and the public had to accept its decisions, or the Supreme Court would be superfluous.

In its earliest years, it appeared that Hamilton's prediction would come true. The first Supreme Court chief justice, John Jay, resigned to become governor of New York because he thought the Court would never play an important role in American society. The next chief justice, Oliver Ellsworth, quit to become envoy to France. In 1801, when the federal cap-

POLITICS AND WOMEN

The New Majority on the Minnesota Supreme Court

Women lawyers have always been conscious of their role as a highly visible minority in the still largely male-dominated legal profession. Indeed, women did not begin to enter the legal profession in significant numbers until the 1960s. Today, women make up nearly 40 percent of all law students. Moreover, record numbers of women are winning elections or appointments to judgeships in state and federal trial courts around the country. Despite these advances, however, there are comparatively few women who are state supreme court justices.

State governors are usually charged with the task of appointing new justices to the state supreme court. They are aware of the desirability of having at least one woman justice on the state's highest court. But this concern is apparently not great enough to ensure that more than one woman or, at most, two women sit on the bench of the highest court in any given state. More than half of all state supreme courts can claim to have at least one woman as a member. But women jurists are still not numerous enough to alter the masculine orientation that pervades the rulings issued by most courts.

Given this relative paucity of female state supreme court justices, the recent appointment of a fourth woman justice, Sandra Gardebring, by outgoing Governor Rudy Perpich, to Minnesota's seven-seat supreme court is all the more remarkable. Although Minnesota has long been known for its progressive social policies, the appointment of Gardebring represents a first in the United States—a high court in which the women justices outnumber the men. Whether this new majority will significantly alter the future course of the court is yet to be seen.

Some lawyers have speculated that the Minnesota court will now be more interested in hearing cases involving spousal or child abuse, sexual harassment, and employment discrimination. Others believe that the court will continue to chart a moderate course in reviewing its cases. In spite of the predictions about a new sensitivity on the part of the court toward "women's issues," few feel that the women justices are any more likely to vote as a cohesive bloc than are their male counterparts. After all, the court's four female justices have different political and ideological perspectives that are not likely to be bridged merely because the justices are of the same gender.

Another distinction claimed by the Minnesota Supreme Court is the recent election of a former National Football League star, Alan Page. Page, a member of the Pro Football Hall of Fame, earned a law degree following his sports career, provided commentary on National Public Radio, and in 1992 became the first African-American member of Minnesota's highest court.

ital was moved to Washington, somebody forgot to include the Supreme Court in the plans: It met in the office of the clerk of the Senate until 1935.

Of the total number of cases that are decided each year, those reviewed by the Supreme Court represent less than one-half of 1 percent. Included in these, however, are decisions that profoundly affect our lives—even issues of life and death. In recent years, the U.S. Supreme Court has dealt with capital punishment, affirmative-action programs, abortion, busing, and pornography. Because the Supreme Court exercises a great deal of discretion over the types of cases it hears, it can influence the nation's policies by issuing decisions in some types of cases and refusing to hear appeals in others, thereby allowing lower court decisions to stand.

Which Cases Reach the Supreme Court?

Many people are surprised to learn that in a typical case there is no absolute right of appeal to the United States Supreme Court. The Supreme Court is given original, or trial court, jurisdiction in a small number of situations. Under Article III, Section 2, Paragraph 2, the Supreme Court has original jurisdiction in all cases affecting foreign diplomats and in all cases in which a state is a party. The Eleventh Amendment, passed in 1798, removed from the judicial power of the United States suits commenced by, or prosecuted against, citizens of another state or by citizens or subjects of any foreign state. Therefore, the Supreme Court today rarely acts as a court of original jurisdiction except in cases involving suits by one state against another, such as suits relating to territorial disputes or cross-border pollution. In all other cases, its jurisdiction is appellate "with such Exceptions, and under such Regulations as the Congress shall make." Appellate jurisdiction means the authority of the Court to review decisions of a lower court.

Writ of *Certiorari*

With a **writ of *certiorari*,** the Supreme Court orders a lower court to send it the record of a case for review. A party can petition the Supreme Court to issue a writ of *certiorari*. Typically, however, only petitions that raise the possibility of important constitutional questions or problems of statutory interpretation are granted writs of *certiorari*. Within these limits, the granting of *certiorari* (or "cert," as it is popularly called) is done entirely at the discretion of the Court and seems to depend on such factors as who the petitioners are, the kinds of issues, and the ideologies of the individual justices.

The following situations indicate when the Court will issue a writ, although they are not a limit on the Court's discretion:

1. When a state court has decided a substantial federal question that has not been determined by the Supreme Court before, or the state court has decided it in a way that is probably in disagreement with the trend of the Supreme Court's decisions.
2. When two federal courts of appeals are in disagreement with each other.
3. When a federal court of appeals has decided an important state question in conflict with state law, has decided an important federal question not yet addressed by the Court but which should be decided by the Court, has decided a federal question in conflict with applicable decisions of the Court, or has departed from the accepted and usual course of judicial proceedings.
4. When a federal court of appeals holds a state statute to be invalid because it violates federal law.
5. When the highest state court holds a federal law invalid or upholds a state law that has been challenged as violating a federal law.
6. When a federal court holds an act of Congress unconstitutional and the federal government or one of its employees is a party.

WRIT OF *CERTIORARI*
An order issued by a higher court to a lower court to send up the record of a case for review. It is the principal vehicle for U.S. Supreme Court review.

Most petitions for writs of *certiorari* are denied. A denial is not a decision on the merits of a case, nor does it indicate agreement with the lower court's opinion. (The judgment of the lower court remains in force, however.) Therefore, denial of the writ has no value as a precedent.[5] The Court will not issue a writ unless at least four justices approve of it. This is called the **rule of four.**[6]

Decisions and Opinions

The United States Supreme Court normally does not hear any evidence, as is true with all appeals courts. The Court's decision in a case is based on the abstracts, the record, and the briefs. The attorneys can present **oral arguments,** after which the case is taken under advisement. When the Court has reached a decision, the decision is written. It contains the **opinion** (the Court's reasons for its decision), the rules of law that apply, and the judgment. In general, the Court will not **reverse** findings of fact unless the findings are unsupported or contradicted by the evidence. Rather, it will review the record for errors of law. If the Supreme Court feels that a reversible error was committed during the trial or that the jury was improperly instructed, the judgment will be reversed. Sometimes the case will be **remanded** (sent back to the court that originally heard the case) for a new trial or other proceeding. In many cases, the decision of the lower court is **affirmed,** resulting in enforcement of that court's judgment or decree.

The Court's written opinion is sometimes brief and unsigned; this is called a *per curiam* opinion. Often, it is long and is signed by all those justices who agree with it. Usually, when in the majority, the chief justice will write the opinion or assign it to another justice who agrees with the majority opinion. Whenever the chief justice is in the minority, the senior justice on the majority side decides who writes the opinion.

There are four types of written opinions for any particular case decided by the Supreme Court. When all justices unanimously agree on an opinion, the opinion is written for the entire Court (all the justices) and can be deemed a **unanimous opinion.** When there is not a unanimous opinion, a **majority opinion** is written, outlining the views of the majority of the justices involved in the particular case. Often, one or more justices who feel strongly about making or emphasizing a particular point that is not made or emphasized in the unanimous or majority written opinion will write a **concurring opinion.** That means the justice writing the concurring opinion agrees (concurs) with the conclusion given in the unanimous or majority written opinion but for different reasons. Finally, in other than unanimous opinions, one or more dissenting opinions are usually written by those justices who do not agree with the majority. The **dissenting opinion** is important because it often forms the basis of the arguments used years later that cause the Court to reverse the previous decision and establish a new precedent.

---

[5]*Singleton v. Commissioner of Internal Revenue,* 439 U.S. 940 (1978).
[6]The "rule of four" is modified when seven or fewer justices participate, which occurs from time to time. When that happens, as few as three justices can grant *certiorari* to go to a full-scale appeal.

RULE OF FOUR
A U.S. Supreme Court procedure requiring four affirmative votes to hear the case before the full Court.

ORAL ARGUMENTS
The verbal arguments presented in person by opposing counsel.

OPINION
The statement by a judge or a court of the decision reached in a case tried or argued before them. It expounds the law as applied to the case and details the reasons on which the judgment was based.

REVERSE
To annul or make void a judgment on account of some error or irregularity.

REMAND
To send a case back to the court that originally heard it.

AFFIRM
To declare that a judgment is valid and right and must stand.

UNANIMOUS OPINION
Agreement of all judges on the same opinion or determination.

MAJORITY OPINION
The views of the majority of the judges.

CONCURRING OPINION
A separate opinion, prepared by a judge who supports the decision of the majority of the court but who wants to make or clarify a particular point or to voice disapproval of the grounds on which the decision was made.

DISSENTING OPINION
A separate opinion in which a judge dissents from the conclusion reached by the majority of the court and expounds his or her own views about the case.

Group-Sponsored Litigation and the Supreme Court

In Chapter 7, we discussed the role of interest groups in the United States. Interest groups play an important role in our judicial system, because they **litigate**—bring to trial—most cases of race or sex discrimination and virtually all civil liberties cases, as well as more than one-third of criminal cases and those involving business matters. In 1928, for example, interest groups filed *amicus curiae* **briefs** in fewer than 2 percent of the cases decided by the Supreme Court, but more than 50 percent are accompanied by such briefs today.

Interest groups see litigation as a political strategy complementing other activities, such as helping individuals favorable to the groups' causes to be elected to Congress or to the presidency. There are numerous litigating organizations today, such as the Washington Legal Foundation, the Capital Legal Foundation, and the Pacific Legal Foundation (which normally seek pro-business judicial outcomes), and the Center for the Study of Responsive Law and the Public Interest Research Group (which normally seek pro-consumer and pro-environment judicial outcomes). The interest group (or the litigating organization it supports) will directly challenge a law or administrative ruling and take it to court. Alternatively, such a group may have an individual test a law in court, while the interest group lends financial and legal support to the case.

Sometimes interest groups will start a **class-action suit** in which whatever the court decides will affect all members of a class "similarly situated." Significant recent class-action suits were brought on behalf of individuals suffering injuries associated with use of the Dalkon Shield, individuals suffering from asbestos-related injuries, and individuals claiming injuries associated with automobiles, tampons, and chemicals such as formaldehyde, diethylstilbesterol (DES), and Agent Orange.

Refusing to Hear a Case—Political Questions

The Supreme Court (and other courts, too) will only hear what are called **justiciable disputes,** which are disputes that arise out of actual cases and that can be settled by legal methods. When the Court deems a dispute to be a **political question,** it will refuse to rule under the doctrine of political questions. Basically, any dispute deemed a political question by the Supreme Court is one that it declares should be decided by the executive branch, or the legislative branch, or those two branches together. For many years, for example, the Supreme Court refused to rule on the constitutionality of laws concerning legislative apportionment, even when they resulted in grossly obvious gerrymandering (see Chapter 10). It was not until 1962 in *Baker v. Carr*[7] that the doctrine of political questions was put aside. No political scientist or legal expert has been able to develop a consistent definition of "political questions" that applies to all of the reasoning of the Court.

After a Decision Is Reached

President Andrew Jackson was once supposed to have said, after Chief Justice John Marshall made an unpopular decision, that "John Marshall

LITIGATE
To engage in a legal proceeding.

AMICUS CURIAE **BRIEFS**
Latin for "friend of the court"; refers here to persons or groups who are not parties to a case but who have an interest in its outcome. These briefs are documents filed with the court that contain legal arguments supporting a particular desired outcome in a case.

CLASS-ACTION SUIT
A lawsuit filed by an individual seeking damages for "all persons similarly situated."

JUSTICIABLE DISPUTES
Disputes that raise questions about the law and are appropriate for resolution before a court of law.

POLITICAL QUESTION
An issue that a court believes should be decided by the executive or legislative branches.

---

[7]369 U.S. 186 (1962).

JUDICIAL IMPLEMENTATION
The way in which court decisions are translated into policy.

has made his decision; now let him enforce it."[8] This purported quote goes to the heart of **judicial implementation,** or whether court decisions are actually translated into policy and thereby affect the behavior of individuals, businesspersons, police personnel, and the like. The Court does not have the executive power to implement its decisions, nor does it have control of the budget to pay for such implementation when government funds are required. Other units of government have to carry out the Court's decisions.

That means that the process of judicial implementation may take time or it may never occur at all. Prayers were banned in public schools in 1962, yet it was (and is still) widely known that the ban was ignored in many southern districts. After the Court ordered schools to desegregate "with all deliberate speed" in 1955,[9] the inflammatory rhetoric against desegregation expounded by the governor and state legislators in Little Rock, Arkansas, encouraged citizens to take the law into their own hands. A riot broke out in 1957, and the president finally decided to act. President Eisenhower federalized the state's national guard, which quelled the riot.

Initially, the media reporting on Supreme Court decisions provide the most widespread information about what the Court has decided. Often, though, such paraphrased information may be inaccurate. The consumer population of Supreme Court decisions somehow has to become aware of its new-found rights (or the stripping of existing rights). For example, the Supreme Court in *Miranda v. Arizona*[10] in 1966 set guidelines for police questioning of suspects (see Chapter 4). It has been estimated that it took seventeen months before all of the police departments around the country were aware of the decision, and it certainly took even longer for suspected criminals to be aware that they should be "read their Miranda rights."

The Supreme Court at Work

The Supreme Court, by law, begins its regular annual term on the first Monday in October and usually adjourns in late June or early July of the next year. Special sessions may be held after the regular term is over, but only a few cases are decided in this way. More commonly, cases are carried over until the next regular session.

The Court hears oral arguments on Monday, Tuesday, Wednesday, and sometimes Thursday, usually for seven two-week sessions scattered from the first week in October to the end of April or the first week in May. Recesses are held between periods of oral argument to allow the justices to consider the cases and handle other Court business. Oral arguments run from 10 A.M. to noon and again from 1 to 3 P.M., with thirty minutes for each side unless a special exception is granted. All statements and the justices' questions are tape recorded during these sessions. Unlike in most courts, lawyers addressing the Supreme Court can be questioned by the justices at any time during oral argument.

Deciding a Case: Private Research.   All of the crucial work on accepted cases is done through private research and reflection. Each justice is en-

---

[8]The decision referred to was *Cherokee Nation v. Georgia,* 5 Pet. 1 (1831).
[9]*Brown v. Board of Education,* 349 U.S. 294 (1955), (the second *Brown* decision).
[10]384 U.S. 436 (1966).

titled to four law clerks, recent graduates of law schools, who undertake much of the research and preliminary drafting necessary for the justice to form an opinion. It is sometimes suspected that because of their extensive assistance, the law clerks form a kind of junior court in themselves, deciding the fate of appeals and petitions to the Court. Some disgruntled lawyers have even suggested that the Senate should no longer confirm the appointment of justices but rather the appointment of law clerks. Such criticism is probably too harsh. Clerks do help in screening the large volume of petitions and in the preliminary research work for cases under review, but the justices make the decisions.

Deciding a Case: The Friday Conference. Each Friday during the annual Court term, the justices meet in conference to discuss cases then under consideration and to decide which new appeals and petitions the Court will accept. These conferences take place in the oak-paneled chamber and are strictly private—no stenographers, tape recorders, or video cameras are allowed. There used to be two pages in attendance who waited on the justices while they were in conference, but fear of information leaks caused the Court to stop this practice.[11]

In the justices' conference, certain procedures are traditionally observed. On entering the room, each justice shakes hands with all present. The justices then sit by order of seniority around a large, rectangular table. Each case is discussed by each justice in that order, with the chief justice starting the discussion. The chief justice determines the order in which the cases are called, guides the discussion generally, and, in most cases, sets the tone for the proceedings.

Starting with the Court of John Marshall, after each discussion, a vote was taken in reverse order of seniority. Today, the justices seldom vote formally. Rather, the chief justice gets a sense of what the majority wants by listening to the justices' individual arguments. When each conference is over, the chief justice, if in the majority, will assign the writing of opinions. When the chief justice is not in the majority, the most senior justice in the majority assigns the writing. Since 1965, decisions have been announced on any day that they are ready to be released. They are usually presented orally, in summary form, in open session by the author of the decision. Other views may be stated by members who have written concurring or dissenting opinions. After the necessary editing and the publication of preliminary prints, the official Court decision is placed in the *United States Reports,* the official record of the Court's decisions, which is available in most college libraries.

Cases that are brought on petition or appeal to the Court are scheduled for an oral argument or denied a hearing in a written "orders list" released on Mondays.

The Selection of Federal Judges: Politics Again

All federal judges are appointed. The Constitution, in Article II, Section 2, states that the president appoints the justices of the Supreme Court with

---

[11]Even though it turned out that one supposed information leak came from lawyers making educated guesses.

the advice and consent of the Senate.[12] Congress has provided the same procedure for staffing other federal courts. This means that the Senate and the president jointly decide who shall be a federal judge, no matter what the level.

Nominating Judicial Candidates

Judicial candidates for federal judgeships are suggested to the president by the Department of Justice, senators, other judges, the candidates themselves, and bar associations and other interest groups.

Since the Truman administration, the American Bar Association, through its Committee on the Federal Judiciary, furnishes the president with evaluations of those individuals being considered. No president is required to refer any nominees to the committee, but most presidents have done so.

The nomination process—no matter how the nominees are obtained—always works the same way: The president does the actual nomination, transmitting the name to the Senate. The Senate then either confirms or rejects. To reach a conclusion, the Senate Judiciary Committee (operating through subcommittees) invites testimony, both written and oral, at its various hearings. In the case of federal district court judgeship nominations, a practice used in the Senate, called **senatorial courtesy,** is a constraint on the president's freedom to appoint whomever the administration chooses. Senatorial courtesy allows a senator of the president's political party to veto a judicial appointment in his or her state.

Nominating Candidates for Federal District Courts and Courts of Appeals

There are approximately seven hundred important federal judgeships in the United States. Once appointed to such a judgeship, a person holds that job for life. Judges serve until they resign, retire voluntarily, or die. Federal judges may be removed through impeachment, although such action is extremely rare.

District Court Judgeship Nominations.   Although the president nominates federal judges, the nomination of district court judges typically originates with a senator or senators of the president's party from the state in which there is a vacancy. If the Committee on the Federal Judiciary of the American Bar Association deems the nominee unqualified, as a matter of senatorial courtesy the president will discuss with the senator or senators who originated the nomination whether the nomination should be withdrawn. Also, when a nomination is politically unacceptable to the president, the president will consult with the appropriate senator or senators to indicate that the nomination is unacceptable and to seek an alternative candidate.

Courts of Appeals Appointments.   Although there are many fewer courts of appeals appointments than district court appointments, they are

SENATORIAL COURTESY
In regard to federal district court judgeship nominations, a Senate tradition allowing a senator of the president's political party to veto a judgeship appointment in his or her state simply by indicating that the appointment is personally "obnoxious." At that point, the Senate may reject the nomination or the president may withdraw consideration of the nominee.

[12]The terms *justice* and *judge* are two designations given to judges in various courts. All members of the U.S. Supreme Court are referred to as justices. In most states' highest appellate courts, the formal title given to the judge is justice also, although the converse is true in the state of New York.

more important because federal appellate judges handle more important matters, at least from the point of view of the president, and therefore, presidents take a keener interest in the nomination process for such judgeships. Also, appointments to the United States courts of appeals have become "stepping stones" to the Supreme Court. Typically, the president culls the Circuit Judge Nominating Commission's list of nominees for potential candidates. The president may also use this list to oppose senators' recommendations that may be politically unacceptable to the president.

Supreme Court Appointments and Ideology

The nomination of Supreme Court justices belongs solely to the president. That is not to say the president's nominations are always confirmed, however. In fact, almost 20 percent of presidential nominations for the Supreme Court have been either rejected or not acted on by the Senate. Numerous acrimonious battles over Supreme Court appointments have ensued when the Senate and the president have not seen eye to eye about political matters. The U.S. Senate had a long record of refusing to confirm the president's judicial nominations from the beginning of Jackson's presidency in 1829 to the end of Grant's presidency in 1877. During a fairly long period of relative acquiescence on the part of the Senate to presidential nominations, from 1894 until 1968, only three nominees were not confirmed. From 1968 through 1983, however, there were two rejections of presidential nominees to the highest court. Both were Nixon appointees—G. Harold Carswell and Clement Haynsworth. Both were from the South because Nixon wanted to shore up his southern support. Both were rejected because of questions about their racial attitudes. In addition, one of Lyndon Johnson's nominations was not acted on, and his choice for chief justice in 1968—Abe Fortas, a member of the Court—was withdrawn after a question arose during confirmation hearings involving Fortas's association with an industrialist convicted of securities irregularities. That problem resulted in Fortas's eventual resignation from the Court.

President Reagan found two of his nominees for a Supreme Court vacancy rejected by the Senate. Both were sitting judges on federal courts of appeals. In 1987, he nominated Robert Bork, who faced sometimes caustic grilling by the Senate on his views of the Constitution. His nomination was rejected. Next, Reagan nominated Douglas Ginsburg, who ultimately withdrew his nomination when the press reported information about his alleged social use of marijuana during the 1970s. Finally, the Senate approved Reagan's third choice, Anthony M. Kennedy.

President Bush decided to use a different strategy when Justice Brennan announced his retirement from the bench in 1989. Bush chose David Souter, a recent appointee to the federal court of appeals with extensive experience as a justice on the New Hampshire Supreme Court. Souter was dubbed a "stealth" candidate because he had not written extensively on controversial social issues, such as abortion or racial equality. During the Senate Judiciary Committee hearings, various members attempted to elicit Souter's views on these subjects, but he refused to speculate as to how he would rule in any particular hypothetical case. The same tactic was followed by Bush's second nominee, Clarence Thomas, who underwent an

Demonstrators protest the possible confirmation of Judge Clarence Thomas after Professor Anita Hill charged him with sexually harassing her while she was his employee. After long and difficult hearings on the subject, the Senate voted to confirm Judge Thomas.

extremely volatile confirmation hearing replete with charges of sexual harassment. Were it not for the dramatic and televised allegations by his former aide Anita Hill, Thomas's confirmation hearings might have been more similar in tone to those of Souter. Both men were confirmed, however, although members of the Senate Judiciary Committee complained about the lack of information about the nominees' views.

Ideology plays an important role in the president's choices for the Supreme Court (and the lower federal courts, too), and ideology plays a large role in the Senate's confirmation hearings. There has been an extremely partisan distribution of presidential appointments to the federal judiciary. In the almost two hundred years of the U.S. Supreme Court's history, fewer than 13 percent of the justices nominated by a president have been from an opposing political party. Presidents see their federal judiciary appointments as the one sure way to institutionalize their political views long after they have left office. By 1993, Presidents Reagan and Bush together had appointed nearly three-quarters of all federal court judges.[13] This preponderance of Republican-appointed federal judges will probably further strengthen the legal moorings of the conservative social agenda on a variety of issues, ranging from abortion to civil rights, well into the next century. More generally, this shift in the demographic makeup of the federal judiciary is likely to entrench the doctrine of judicial restraint and render it increasingly unlikely that the Supreme Court will resume a more activist stance in the near future.

Who Becomes a Supreme Court Justice?

The makeup of the federal judiciary is far from typical of the American public. Table 13-1 summarizes the background of all of the 106 Supreme

---

[13]Sheldon Goldman, ''The Bush Imprint on the Judiciary: Carrying on a Tradition,'' *Judicature*, Vol. 74 (1991), p. 306.

TABLE 13-1 ■ Background of Supreme Court Justices to Summer, 1993

	Number of Justices (106 = Total)
Occupational Position before Appointment	
Private legal practice	25
State judgeship	21
Federal judgeship	27
U.S. attorney general	7
Deputy or assistant U.S. attorney general	2
U.S. solicitor general	2
U.S. senator	6
U.S. representative	2
State governor	3
Federal executive posts	9
Other	3
Religious Background	
Protestant	83
Roman Catholic	10
Jewish	5
Unitarian	6
No religious affiliation	1
Age on Appointment	
Under 40	5
41–50	31
51–60	56
61–70	15
Political Party Affiliation	
Federalist (to 1835)	13
Democratic Republican (to 1828)	7
Whig (to 1861)	1
Democrat	43
Republican	42
Independent	1
Educational Background	
College graduate	91
Not a college graduate	16
Sex	
Male	105
Female	2
Race	
Caucasian	105
Other	2

SOURCES: Congressional Quarterly, *Congressional Quarterly's Guide to the U.S. Supreme Court* (Washington, D.C.: Congressional Quarterly Press, 1992).

Court justices to the summer, 1993. In general, the justices' partisan attachments have been mostly the same as those of the president who appointed them. There have been some exceptions, however. Nine nominal Democrats have been appointed by Republican presidents, three Republicans by Democratic presidents, and one Democrat by Whig President John Tyler.[14]

---

[14]Actually, Tyler was a member of the Democratic party who ran with Harrison on the Whig ticket. When Harrison died, much to the surprise of the Whigs, Tyler—a Democrat—became president, although they tried to call him "acting president." Thus, there are historians who quibble over the statement that Tyler was a Whig.

POLITICS AND CULTURAL DIVERSITY

Does Our Legal System Reflect Our Diversity?

Obviously, we are living in a culturally diverse society. Nonwhite minorities account for an increasing percentage of the U.S. population, and the traditional "white" complexion of many of our social institutions is changing to reflect this fact. But one very significant institution—the legal system—would seem to be an exception to this rule.

Consider, for example, the graph below.

As you can see, of the 356 judges who currently sit on the highest

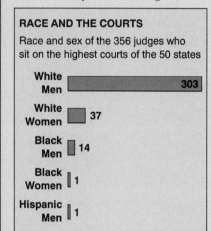

RACE AND THE COURTS

Race and sex of the 356 judges who sit on the highest courts of the 50 states

White Men   303
White Women   37
Black Men   14
Black Women   1
Hispanic Men   1

state courts, only 40 are women, 15 are African American, and only 1 is of Hispanic descent. In other words, women account for 11 percent of the judges, African Americans for 4 percent, and Hispanic Americans for less than 1 percent. The situation is somewhat—but not much—brighter in the federal court system.

What do these statistics mean for women and members of minority groups who enter the nation's courtrooms? Can justice be meted out impartially in a justice system composed largely of white males? Some observers are doubtful. Many African Americans maintain, for example, that even though 44 percent of prison inmates are African Americans, it is not because they are committing such a disproportionate share of crimes relative to the rest of the population. Rather, it is because of the longer sentences that African Americans receive within the predominantly white-operated criminal justice system. A recent report issued by the Federal Judicial Center, which conducts research for the federal courts, gives weight to their

claim: According to the report, for example, African Americans who are indicted for violating federal drug laws receive sentences that are 49 percent longer than sentences received by whites for the same offenses.*

One element in the judicial system, however, increasingly reflects the cultural and racial diversity of America: the jury. In many states, African Americans and Hispanics are now heavily represented in juries. In large part, this more proportionate representation is due to laws passed since the mid-1960s that prohibit courts from keeping African Americans and other minorities off juries through such requirements as property ownership, qualification examinations, and so on. Also, in 1985, the Supreme Court ruled that attorneys could not bar persons from jury participation on the basis of race.

*Ellen Joan Pollock and Stephen J. Adler, "Justice for All? Legal System Struggles to Reflect Diversity, but Progress Is Slow," *Wall Street Journal*, April 17, 1992, p. A1.

As you will note, the most common occupational background of the justices has been private legal practice or state or federal judgeships at the time of their appointment. Those ten justices who were in federal executive posts at the time of their appointment held the high offices of secretary of state, comptroller of the treasury, secretary of the navy, postmaster general, secretary of the interior, chairman of the Securities and Exchange Commission, and secretary of labor. In the "other" category, under "Occupational Position before Appointment" in Table 13-1, are two justices who were professors of law (including Taft, a former president) and one justice who was a North Carolina state employee with responsibility for organizing and revising the state's statutes.

Most justices were in their fifties when they assumed office, although two were as young as thirty-two and one as old as sixty-six. The average age of newly sworn justices is about fifty-three.

Note also that the great majority of justices have had a college education. By and large, those who did not attend college or receive a degree
lived in the late eighteenth and early nineteenth centuries, when a college
education was much less common than it is today. In recent years, degrees
from such schools as Yale, Harvard, Columbia, and other prestigious institutions have been typical. It is interesting that many of the earlier
college-educated justices did not hold their degrees in law. In fact, it was
not until 1957 that all of the members of the Court were graduates of law
schools.

The religious background of Supreme Court justices is strikingly untyp-
ical of that of the American population as a whole, even making allowances for changes over time in the religious composition of the nation.
Catholics (and certain Protestant denominations, notably Baptists and Lutherans) have been underrepresented, whereas Protestants in general
(Episcopalians, Presbyterians, Methodists, and others), as well as Unitar-
ians, have been overrepresented among the justices. Typically, there has
been a ''Catholic seat'' on the Court, with interruptions, and a ''Jewish
seat'' existed without a break from 1916 until 1969, when Fortas resigned.

The Rehnquist Court

William H. Rehnquist (see the *Profile*) became the sixteenth chief justice of
the Supreme Court in 1986 after fifteen years as an associate justice. He
was known as a strong anchor of the Court's conservative wing. With
Rehnquist's appointment as chief justice, it seemed to observers that the
Court would necessarily become more conservative. In the past, Rehnquist
had dissented from numerous majority opinions. His views on individual
liberties seemed to favor a strong state, because the Constitution, according to him, had as its purpose a government that would have direct authority over individuals. Proponents of civil liberties feared that the
Rehnquist Court would eventually erode many of those liberties that the

Did You Know . . . That only
four American presidents,
William Henry Harrison,
Zachary Taylor, Andrew
Johnson, and Jimmy Carter,
appointed no Supreme Court
justices?

The Supreme Court in spring, 1993.

PROFILE

Chief Justice Rehnquist

"It is basically unhealthy to have so much authority concentrated in a small group of lawyers who have been appointed to the Supreme Court and enjoy virtual life tenure."

On Tuesday, June 17, 1986, Warren Burger, chief justice of the Supreme Court, announced that he would retire after seventeen years of service. President Ronald Reagan named Supreme Court Justice William Rehnquist to replace Burger as chief justice. Rehnquist had been on the Supreme Court since 1971, when he was nominated by Richard Nixon. Since that time, he has been viewed as one of the Court's more conservative members. He faced a hard chief justice confirmation fight in the Senate because of his conservative views. The Senate ultimately approved his nomination by the smallest margin in the history of the U.S. Senate.

His background includes a B.A. from Stanford University, a master's degree in political science from Harvard, and a degree from Stanford Law School where he graduated first in his class in 1952. He clerked for Supreme Court Justice Robert Jackson in 1952 and 1953 and then practiced law in Arizona, where in 1964 he worked on conservative

Barry Goldwater's presidential campaign. Under the Nixon administration in 1969, he became a deputy attorney general and later head of the Department of Justice, Office of Legal Counsel, from which he successfully defended the government's program of secret surveillance of anti-Vietnam war groups in the United States.

On many issues, Rehnquist is an almost doctrinaire conservative. For example, he has been the leader in the Court conservatives' efforts to narrow the interpretation of defendants' rights in criminal cases. In recent decisions, he has dissented forcefully when the Court reaffirmed women's rights to abortion and wrote a strong decision uphold-

ing Missouri's restrictions on abortion rights.

Personal acquaintances say that Rehnquist is affable and friendly, with great skills in interpersonal relations. One University of Virginia law professor has indicated that he is one of the brightest justices ever to sit on the bench because he writes with style, force, and assurance, as no one else has in recent times. "It is hard to match his agility in shaping a record and marshalling arguments to reach a conclusion."*

Despite the concerns voiced by prominent civil libertarians, Rehnquist's tenure as chief justice has not seen dramatic erosions in the liberal precedents bequeathed by the Warrent Court and, to a lesser extent, the Burger Court. Instead, the increasingly conservative Court has gradually chipped away at some of the more expansive Court decisions in areas ranging from racial discrimination to freedom of speech. Whether such hallmarks of past eras such as *Roe v. Wade,*** the 1973 decision legalizing abortion, will continue to pass the scrutiny of a Court that no longer can claim to have a "liberal" voting bloc is uncertain.

*Professor of Law A. E. Dick Howard, University of Virginia, quoted in *U.S. News & World Report*, June 30, 1986, p. 18.
**410 U.S. 113 (1973).

previous Courts under Earl Warren (1953–1969) and Warren Burger (1969–1986) had established or maintained.

In the late 1980s, the Rehnquist Court ruled on several extremely important matters that raised the question of the direction in which the Court was moving ideologically. It also caused renewed speculation about the impact on the court if one or more of the aging "liberal" justices should die or resign and be replaced with Bush appointees. That is precisely what did happen following the resignations of William Brennan and Thurgood Marshall in 1990 and 1991, respectively, and the subsequent appointments by President Bush of conservative justices David Souter and Clarence Thomas.

The perception that the Rehnquist court accelerated the rightward shift of the Court in the late 1980s and early 1990s appears to be borne out by its conservative rulings in cases involving criminal confessions, racial disparities in death-penalty sentencing, the burden of proof placed on litigants in civil rights cases, and the availability of abortion. Indeed, a primary impetus behind Congress's passage of the 1991 Civil Rights Act was its desire to overrule a group of four 1989 Supreme Court cases that had greatly restricted the ease with which discrimination suits could be brought by increasing the burden of proof on plaintiffs. The conservative shift of the Rehnquist court also forced many special interest groups, including the American Civil Liberties Union and the National Association for the Advancement of Colored People, to view the Court as a brake on, rather than an accelerator of, the engine of social progress. Consequently, these groups began petitioning Congress to enact laws to overturn Court rulings they considered to be undesirable such as the Civil Rights Act of 1990 (discussed in Chapter 10).

Soon after the inauguration of President Bill Clinton, Justice Byron White announced that he would retire at the end of the spring term. His retirement opens the door for Clinton to be the first Democratic president to nominate a Supreme Court justice in twenty-six years. In June 1993, Clinton announced the selection of Ruth Bader Ginsburg, who had amassed a generally liberal judicial record on abortion and other issues.

Justice Ruth Bader Ginsburg

Judicial Activism and Judicial Restraint

Judicial scholars like to characterize different Supreme Courts and different Supreme Court justices as being either activist or restraintist. Those advocating the doctrine of **judicial activism,** such as former justices William Brennan and Thurgood Marshall, believe that the Court should use its power to alter the direction of the activities of Congress, state legislatures, and administrative agencies to expand individual freedoms. Those advocating the doctrine of **judicial restraint**, such as Chief Justice William Rehnquist and Justice Antonin Scalia, believe that the Court should use its powers of judicial review only rarely. In other words, whatever popularly elected legislatures decide should not be thwarted by the Supreme Court so long as such decisions are not unconstitutional.

Despite the common use of the terms *judicial restraint* and *judicial activism*, the basic concern is about the way in which the justice believes that the Constitution should be interpreted. Should the Court confine itself to interpreting the law, or should it create new laws by issuing specific mandates? In general, most justices who consider themselves to be conservatives would argue that the Constitution should be interpreted based on the intention of the framers who drafted it. According to Robert Bork, this approach does not require the Court to delve into the subjective intentions of the framers, but instead to interpret the law based on the ordinary meaning given to the words being examined.[15] Liberal jurists, such as

JUDICIAL ACTIVISM
A doctrine advocating an active role for the Supreme Court in enforcing the Constitution and in using judicial review. An activist Court takes a broad view of the Constitution and involves itself in legislative and executive matters by altering the direction of activities of Congress, state legislatures, and administrative agencies.

JUDICIAL RESTRAINT
A doctrine holding that the Court should rarely use its power of judicial review or otherwise intervene in the political process.

---

[15]See Robert H. Bork, *The Tempting of America* (New York: Free Press, 1990), pp. 143–146.

LEGISLATIVE HISTORY
The background and events leading up to the enactment of a law. This may include legislative committee reports, hearings, and floor debates.

former Justice William Brennan, have argued that any attempts to divine the original meanings of the Constitution from its text are inappropriate because the social mores and values of society have changed considerably in the past two centuries. Brennan believes that any interpretation given to the Constitution itself must take into account current ideas regarding such concepts as "due process" and "equal protection." Even though all courts will consider what the authors of a particular law meant by examining its **legislative history** (such as statements by the bill's sponsors) prior to enactment, Brennan and other legal experts seem to have decided that such analyses are not appropriate when the Constitution itself is involved.

During the early years of the nation, the Supreme Court certainly was in no position to exercise judicial activism. The Supreme Court during its first decade handled few matters and decided only one important case. Alexis de Tocqueville, an astute French observer of American institutions in the early nineteenth century, appreciated the position of the Court in the American constitutional system, however. He stated that "the supreme court is placed higher than any known tribunal. . . . The peace, the prosperity, and the very existence of the Union are vested in the hands of the seven [now nine] Federal judges."

The difference between activist judges and those who exercise restraint is not the same as the difference between political liberals and conservatives. In the early 1930s, for example, the Supreme Court was activist and conservative, ruling that much regulation of business was unconstitutional. In the later 1930s, however, the Court became restrained and liberal, ruling that similar business regulation was constitutional.

In the 1950s and 1960s, the Court was activist and liberal. Many of the Court's critics believed it should have exercised more restraint. They criticize the first *Brown* decision in 1954, which prohibited racial segregation in public schools, on the grounds that the highest court settled a problem that should have been resolved by Congress or have been left to the states. Critics of the current courts call them "mini-legislatures." They argue, for example, that in *Baker v. Carr*[16] the federal courts wrongly exercised jurisdiction over the issue of state legislative districting plans and that the U.S. Supreme Court had no right to intervene in such a state matter.

Another activist decision in the 1970s was *Roe v. Wade*,[17] in which the Supreme Court gave women the right to an abortion during the first and second trimesters of pregnancy, thereby striking down state statutes permitting abortions only in special cases. Recent Supreme Court decisions have indicated an unmistakable change in the Court's attitude toward civil rights. Some critics fear that the current Court, with its conservative majority, will become increasingly activist in this and other areas in the 1990s.

The fact that all presidents attempt to strengthen their legacy through the appointment of federal judges with similar political and ideological philosophies has already been noted. But the fact that a president appoints a justice who has supported his policies in the past is no guarantee that the newly appointed justice will continue to do so in the future. President

---

[16]369 U.S. 186 (1962).
[17]410 U.S. 113, rehearing denied 410 U.S. 959 (1973).

Eisenhower, a conservative Republican, appointed Earl Warren, the former governor of California, to be Chief Justice of the Supreme Court in 1953. Warren's past moderate-to-conservative policies gave no indication that he would lead the Court in an unprecedented revision of the nation's existing laws, greatly expanding the protections afforded to minorities and criminal defendants. Indeed, Eisenhower later characterized his appointment of Warren as the biggest single mistake of his presidency.

Similarly, Richard Nixon appointed Warren Burger as chief justice in 1969 to replace Warren. Nixon believed that Burger's conservative views would ensure that the court would minimize its involvement in controversial issues such as school desegregation. But within two years, Burger authored the opinion of the Court in *Swann v. Charlotte-Mecklenburg Board of Education*,[18] in which school authorities were directed to desegregate dual school systems. Perhaps the ultimate irony of Nixon's appointment was that Burger wrote the Court's opinion in *United States v. Nixon*,[19] in which the Court unanimously rejected the president's claims of executive privilege.

The question of judicial activism is closely linked to the actual constraints on our judicial system. We examine these next.

What Checks Our Courts?

Our judicial system is probably the most independent in the world. But the courts do not have absolute independence, for they are part of the political process. Political checks limit the extent to which courts can exercise judicial review and engage in an activist policy. These checks are exercised by the legislature, the executive, other courts, and the public.

Legislative Checks

Courts may make rulings, but often the legislatures at local, state, and federal levels are required to appropriate funds to carry out the court's rulings. When such funds are not appropriated, the court, in effect, has been checked. A court, for example, may decide that prison conditions must be improved. Then a legislature has to find the funds to carry out such a ruling.

Courts' rulings can be overturned by constitutional amendments at both the federal and state levels. Many of the amendments to the U.S. Constitution (such as the Eleventh, Fourteenth, Sixteenth, and Twenty-sixth amendments) check the state courts' ability to allow discrimination, for example. Recently, though, proposed constitutional amendments that were created by a desire to reverse courts' decisions on school prayer and abortion have failed.

Finally, legislatures can pass new laws to overturn courts' rulings. This may happen particularly when a court interprets a statute in a way that Congress had not intended or when a court finds no relevant statute to apply in certain cases. The legislature can then pass a new statute to negate the court's ruling, as was the case in 1991.

Did You Know . . . That among the 106 persons who have served on the Supreme Court from 1789 to mid–1993, only two, Thurgood Marshall and Clarence Thomas, have been African American and only one, Sandra Day O'Connor, has been a woman?

---

[18]402 U.S. 1 (1971).
[19]418 U.S. 683 (1974).

Executive Checks

Presidents have the power to change the direction of the Supreme Court and the federal judiciary, for the president can appoint new judges who, in principle, have philosophies more in line with that of the administration. Also, a president, governor, or mayor can refuse to enforce courts' rulings. The possibility that a president might refuse to enforce an order is not merely theoretical. Several presidents, including Abraham Lincoln and Andrew Jackson, have refused to obey orders issued by the Supreme Court.[20] Such conduct does not appear to constitute an explicit violation of the Constitution because there is no language in that document expressly authorizing the federal courts to review the actions of the executive and legislative branches.

Despite its lack of tangible enforcement mechanisms, the Court is widely perceived by the general public to be the final arbiter of national laws. Moreover, its decisions are regarded as the least partisan of all of the three branches of government. Had Richard Nixon refused to hand over the materials for which he claimed executive privilege after the Court's unanimous ruling in *United States v. Nixon*, for example, the Nixon presidency would have seen what little public support it still had further eroded and the chances of a conviction from an impeachment trial increased to a near certainty. In the absence of any threat of impeachment by Congress, however, the main weapon at the Court's disposal would appear to be public pressure. Whether a politician would be able to withstand the public firestorm that would likely result from a deliberate refusal to obey an order from the Supreme Court would depend, in large part, on the factual circumstances of the case and whether the Court's order otherwise appeared to be legally justified.

The Rest of the Judiciary

Higher courts can reverse the decisions of lower courts. Lower courts can put a check on higher courts, too. The Supreme Court of the United States, for example, cannot possibly hear all the cases that go through the lower courts. Lower courts can ignore and have ignored, directly or indirectly, Supreme Court decisions by deciding in the other direction in particular cases. Only if a case goes to the Supreme Court can the Court correct the situation.

The Public Has a Say

History has shown members of the Supreme Court that if its decisions are noticeably at odds with a national consensus, it will lose its support and some of its power. Perhaps the best example was the *Dred Scott* decision of 1857,[21] in which the Supreme Court held that slaves were not citizens of the United States and were not entitled to the rights and privileges of citizenship. The Court ruled, in addition, that the Missouri Compromise

---

[20]Lincoln refused to obey a direct order by the Court in *Ex parte Merryman*, 17 F.Cas. 144 (C.C.D.Md. 1861), whereas Jackson challenged the Court to enforce its order in *Cherokee Nation v. Georgia*, 5 Pet. 1 (1831).

[21]*Dred Scott v. Sanford*, 19 Howard 393 (1857).

banning slavery in the lands of the Louisiana Territory north of latitude 36°30′N, except for Missouri, was unconstitutional. Most observers contend that the *Dred Scott* ruling contributed to making the Civil War inevitable.

Observers of the court system believe that because of the judges' sense of self-preservation, they do act with restraint. Some argue that this self-restraint is the most important of all.

Conclusion: The Conservative Ascendancy in the Federal Judiciary

The federal courts are perhaps the least democratic and representative of our political institutions, consisting overwhelmingly of white, male Protestants. This demographic makeup is slowly changing, however, as increasing numbers of women and minorities enter the legal profession and obtain judicial appointments. Federal judges receive lifetime appointments so that their decisions will not be overly influenced by the vagaries of public passions. But despite their demographic and political insularity, the courts do tend to reflect public opinion over time. Indeed, the issue of school prayer is perhaps the only major constitutional issue that has continued to divide the courts and public opinion for decades.

Most scholars acknowledge that the decisions of the U.S. Supreme Court may encompass legislative as well as judicial functions. Advocates of judicial restraint have criticized many controversial court decisions, such as *Roe v. Wade* and *Brown v. Board of Education of Topeka*, as amounting to legislative decrees. These critics take some comfort in the conservative shift that characterized many Court decisions in the late 1980s and early 1990s.

The virtual demise of the liberal bloc on the Court following the retirements of Justices Brennan and Marshall in 1990 and 1991, respectively, has not led to a full frontal assault on the legacy of the Warren Court and, to a lesser extent, the Burger Court. But the fact that in 1993, before the nomination of Ruth Bader Ginsburg by President Clinton, there was only one remaining justice on the Court who had been appointed by a Democratic president illustrates the ascendancy of conservatives in the federal judiciary. Moreover, nearly three-fourths of all federal judges have been appointed by Presidents Reagan and Bush. This startling reversal from a generation ago has given liberals notice that the federal courts will not be overly sympathetic to many items on their agendas in the short term. Whether President Clinton will have enough judicial appointments to change the ideological balance remains to be seen.

GETTING INVOLVED

Changing the Legal System

Although impressed by the power of judges in American government, Alexis de Tocqueville stated:

> The power is enormous, but it is clothed in the authority of public opinion. They are the all-powerful guardians of a people which respects law; but they would be impotent against public neglect or popular contempt.*

The court system may seem all-powerful and too complex to be influenced by one individual, but its power nonetheless depends on our support. A hostile public has many ways of resisting, modifying, or overturning rulings of the court. Sooner or later a determined majority will prevail. Even a determined minority can make a difference. As Hamilton suggested in *Federalist Paper* No. 1, the people will always hold the scales of justice in their hands, and ultimately all constitutional government depends on their firmness and wisdom.

One example of the kind of pressure that can be exerted on the court system began with a tragedy. On a spring afternoon in 1980, thirteen-year-old Cari Lightner was hit from behind and killed by a drunk driver while walking in a bicycle lane. The driver turned out to be a forty-seven-year-old man with two prior drunk-driving convictions. He was at that time out on bail for a third arrest. Cari's mother, Candy, quit her job as a real estate agent to form MADD (Mothers Against Drunk Driving) and launched a personal campaign to stiffen penalties for drunk-driving convictions.

The organization grew to 20,000 members with 91 regional offices and a staff of 160. Outraged by the estimated 26,000 lives lost every year because of drunk driving, the group not only seeks stiff penalties against drunk drivers but also urges police, prosecutors, and judges to crack down on such violators. MADD, by becoming involved, has gotten results. Owing to its efforts and the efforts of other citizen-activist groups, many states have responded

with stronger penalties and deterrents. If you feel strongly about this issue and want to get involved, contact the following:

MADD
5330 Primrose, Suite 146
Fair Oaks, CA 95628
916-966-6233

Several other organizations have been formed by people who want to change or influence the judicial system. A few of them are as follows:

Legal Defense Research Institute
733 N. Van Buren
Milwaukee, WI 53202
414-272-5995

HALT—An Organization of Americans for Legal Reform
201 Massachusetts Ave., N.E.
Suite 319
Washington, DC 20002
205-546-4258

National Legal Center for the Public Interest
1101 17th St., N.W.
Washington, DC 20036
202-296-1683

If you want information about the Supreme Court, contact the following by telephone or letter:

Clerk of the Court
The Supreme Court of the United States
1 First St., N.E.
Washington, DC
202-393-1640

Democracy in America, Vol. 1 (New York: Schocken Books, 1961), p. 166.

CHAPTER SUMMARY

1. Courts often look to the precedents provided by earlier court decisions in deciding how to resolve a dispute. Although courts take into consideration the merits of past holdings, they will not hesitate to break with earlier cases when justice or changing attitudes in society so require. Courts must weigh any applicable state or federal statutes in deciding cases. As one of the three coequal branches of the gov-

ernment, the courts may pass on the constitutionality of actions taken by either the legislative or executive branches. This power of judicial review permits the courts to act as a check on the actions of the other two branches of government. **2.** The federal court system and most state court systems have a three-tiered structure. All trials are conducted in the trial, or district, courts. The outcome of a trial may then be appealed to an intermediate court, or court of appeals. Whether a litigant can further appeal a claim to the state or federal supreme court will depend on the nature of the claim and the access afforded to litigants by the particular court. The U.S. Supreme Court, for example, exercises almost total discretion over the types of cases it chooses to hear.

3. The U.S. Supreme Court will issue a writ of *certiorari* to a lower court when it wishes to review the record of a particular case. In general, the issue must include a federal question or a conflict between a state law and a federal law before the Court will issue the writ. Some cases may involve political questions, such as those cases relating to the policy decisions of the executive or legislative branches. Courts will generally refrain from hearing cases concerning political questions, believing that such issues should be decided by the other branches of government.

4. Because of the influence wielded by the U.S. Supreme Court and the members of the federal judiciary, the confirmation process for federal judges, particularly those who will sit on the Supreme Court, is often extremely politicized. Democrats and Republicans alike realize that most justices will occupy a seat on the Court for decades and naturally want to have persons appointed who share their basic views. Nearly one-fifth of all U.S. Supreme Court appointments have been rejected by the Senate—often for ideological reasons.

The overwhelming majority of persons appointed to the U.S. Supreme Court have been white, male Protestants. Of the 106 persons who have sat on the Court so far, only two have been African American, and only one has been a woman. The Court is perhaps the least representative government institution in the United States.

5. The Rehnquist Court has become a bastion of conservatism, so much so that liberals now look to Congress to overturn Court decisions that they dislike. With the retirement of Justices Brennan and Marshall, there is no longer a liberal voting bloc to prevent more conservative rulings in areas ranging from civil rights to abortion.

6. Conservatives often argue that judges should exercise judicial restraint and confine themselves to interpreting the law instead of making new laws by issuing decisions having extensive social and political ramifications. Liberals are likely to believe that judges should fashion remedies that reflect today's social, political, and cultural values and needs and not concern themselves with attempts at divining the original meaning of the Constitution.

7. Presidents may influence the federal courts through the use of their appointment power. Congress can limit the jurisdiction of the courts and thereby restrict the types of cases that may be heard.

QUESTIONS FOR REVIEW AND DISCUSSION

1. Define "judicial review." Does the Supreme Court "legislate" using this power? In what areas has the Court made major policy decisions by judicial review?

2. An old political saying declares that "the Supreme Court follows the election returns." What factors in the nomination process, the decision process, and the power of the Court make this true?

3. What are the benefits of being a member of the federal judiciary? Why is this such a sought-after position? How would you go about planning a career in the judicial branch?

4. Why is it possible for the law to change radically within a few decades? For example, after World War II, the Communist party was illegal, women were barred from many activities in our society, and the races were legally segregated in many parts of the country. All of those conditions are now legally reversed, mostly due to Court decisions. How does the Court shape our ideas of what is right or what is fair?

SELECTED REFERENCES

Henry J. Abraham, *The Judiciary: The Supreme Court and the Governmental Process,* 7th ed. (Needham Heights, Mass.: Allyn & Bacon, 1987). A classic textbook that treats in much more detail virtually every aspect in the chapter you have just read.

Henry J. Abraham, *Justices and Presidents: A Political History of Appointments to the Supreme Court* (New York: Oxford University Press, 1992). This classic history of judicial appointments to the Supreme Court since 1789 provides a readable and engaging account of the nomination and selection of each justice who has sat on the Supreme Court, the presidential expectations attending each nomination, and the extent to which each justice's actual conduct on the Court fulfilled, or failed to fulfill, those expectations.

Alan Barth, *Prophets with Honor: Great Dissents and Great Dissenters in the Supreme Court* (New York: Alfred A. Knopf, 1974). Six cases in which dissenting justices had their views vindicated years later when the Court reversed itself.

Sheldon Goldman and Thomas P. Jahnige, *The Federal Courts as a Political System,* 3d ed. (New York: Harper and Row, 1985). Using the systems analysis approach, this book examines inputs, conversions, outputs, feedback, and other processes in a dynamic investigation of the complicated interrelationships of the federal courts' ''political system.''

Joseph Goldstein, *The Intelligible Constitution: The Supreme Court's Obligation to Maintain the Constitution as Something We the People Can Understand* (New York: Oxford University Press, 1992). Goldstein criticizes the Supreme Court for its failure to present its opinions concerning constitutional matters in a clear and comprehensible manner. The author argues that the Supreme Court has an obligation not only to decide cases but also to explicate, with candor and integrity, the principles embedded in the Constitution and to make the Constitution understandable for today's citizens.

William Lasser, *The Limits of Judicial Power: The Supreme Court and American Politics* (Chapel Hill, N.C.: University of North Carolina Press, 1989). The author examines the role of the Supreme Court in shaping American politics, especially the question of judicial activism and what limits are placed on it.

James P. Levine, *Juries and Politics* (Pacific Grove, Calif.: Brooks/Cole 1992). In light of the 1992 California Rodney King trial, involving the issue of police brutality, and the subsequent rebellion in Los Angeles, this engaging book on the role of jury verdicts in shaping American justice is extremely timely and important.

Leonard W. Levy, *Original Intent and the Framers' Constitution* (New York: Macmillan, 1988). The author examines the strict constructionist versus the loose constructionist points of view with respect to what the Supreme Court should do.

Patrick B. McGuigan and Dawn M. Weyrich, *Ninth Justice: The Fight for Bork* (Lanham, Md.: University Press of America, 1990). Through a detailed description of what the parties involved in the Bork nomination did and did not do, the authors give their recommendations and advice on what the conservatives should have done to win the nomination.

David Neubauer, *America's Courts and the Criminal Justice System,* 3d ed. (Pacific Grove, Calif.: Brooks/Cole, 1988). This book thoroughly covers the major issues facing the criminal courts today, including the death penalty, victims' rights, the insanity defense, and the exclusionary rule.

David O'Brien, *Storm Center: The Supreme Court and American Politics,* 2d ed. (New York: W. W. Norton, 1990). This book treats the controversy surrounding the role of the federal judiciary within the U.S. political system.

Sylvia Snowiss, *Judicial Review and the Law of the Constitution* (New Haven, Conn.: Yale University Press, 1990). Using both the opinions of the framers of the Constitution and modern court cases, Snowiss examines the origin and development of judicial review.

Lawrence Tribe, *God Save this Honorable Court* (New York: Random House, 1985). A critical review of the Supreme Court written by an outspoken liberal legal scholar.

Bob Woodward and Scott Armstrong, *The Brethren: Inside the Supreme Court* (New York: Simon and Schuster, 1979). A detailed, behind-the-scenes account of Supreme Court decision making on cases dealing with abortion, busing, the Nixon tapes, and obscenity.

PART FIVE

PUBLIC POLICY

CHAPTER 14
The Politics of Economic and Domestic Policy Making

CHAPTER CONTENTS
▼

451

WHAT IF ... AMERICA HAD A FLAT TAX?

During the 1992 presidential campaign, Democratic primary candidate Jerry Brown proposed a flat tax. In essence, he wanted to get rid of the current federal income tax system and replace it with one that is much simpler. Instead of taxing different brackets of income at higher and higher rates (a so-called progressive tax system), Brown argued for a flat tax: one rate for all—rich or poor. His idea was not new. In the early 1980s, numerous economists argued essentially the same thing. The result was the 1986 Tax Reform Act, which was pushed through by President Ronald Reagan. Rather than a flat tax, the 1986 act gave us a two-tiered federal tax system; 1990 legislation made it officially a three-tiered system. Proposed 1992 legislation would have made it a four- or five-tiered system, but even that would still be a far cry from the fourteen separate tax rates that existed before 1986.

Let's assume that Congress has passed legislation calling for a flat tax. Let's say that the first $10,000 of income has no federal tax applied to it, but everything thereafter is taxed at 15 percent. And there would be no deductions from taxable income for anything. (Today there are deductions for home-mortgage interest payments, charitable contributions, and the like.) How would the flat tax affect each individual and the U.S. economy as a whole?

In the first place, lawyers and accountants specializing in helping individuals and businesses "do their taxes" each year would find themselves without much work. It is esti-

mated that Americans currently pay up to $60 billion each year to have their tax forms filled out. That includes the value of the time they spend themselves and how much they pay accountants and other professionals to help them. Tax accountants and lawyers would have less work for two reasons. First, under this new system, individuals would not be able to deduct anything from their taxable income. Therefore, accountants and lawyers would not be spending time helping individuals and businesses try to find more deductions. Second, individuals would have fewer incentives to pay accountants and lawyers to reduce their taxable income. After all, under current tax laws, high-income-earning individuals save $3,100 for every $10,000 reduction in taxable income because they do not have to pay 31 percent of the $10,000 in taxes. Under the simplified system, they would only save $1,500—or 15 percent of the $10,000. Their incentive to seek out ways to reduce taxable income would therefore also be reduced.

Few individuals would weep for reduced work for highly paid tax accountants and lawyers. But two major political issues would remain. First, would the federal government end up collecting adequate tax revenues with this flat tax rate? Some believe that a lower tax rate would encourage more work, more investment, and more saving and thereby

cause income to grow so rapidly that the government would collect as much as it did before. These proponents of a reduced federal income tax rate also argue that individuals and businesses would not spend as many resources trying to avoid—legally or illegally—paying taxes. Not everybody agrees. Opponents of the flat tax believe that the federal government deficit—the difference between total spending and total revenues—would grow even greater.

Second, would the disparity between the poor and the rich become even greater if we had a flat tax rate? Perhaps not. Many studies have shown that in spite of the progressive nature of federal income taxes, actual taxes paid are roughly proportional to income earned, just as they would be under a flat tax. The reason that progressive income taxes do not work the way they are supposed to—with higher-earning individuals paying a greater proportion of their income in taxes than lower-earning ones—is that those who are in the higher tax brackets devote so many resources to finding ways to avoid those high tax rates. Consequently, proponents of a flat tax believe that, if enacted, such a federal tax system would not worsen the current disparity between the rich and the poor.

1. *Who would benefit most from a shift to a flat tax? Why?*
2. *Would members of Congress be better or worse off with a flat tax system? Why?*

At this point in our text we begin to analyze public policy, or the substance of what government does. In particular, we examine national economic and domestic programs (Chapter 14), and foreign policies (Chapter 15). But before we start, we must look at how national policies are made.

The Policy-Making Process

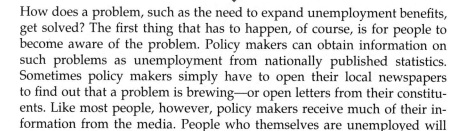

How does a problem, such as the need to expand unemployment benefits, get solved? The first thing that has to happen, of course, is for people to become aware of the problem. Policy makers can obtain information on such problems as unemployment from nationally published statistics. Sometimes policy makers simply have to open their local newspapers to find out that a problem is brewing—or open letters from their constituents. Like most people, however, policy makers receive much of their information from the media. People who themselves are unemployed will certainly be concerned about their plight and about the availability of unemployment benefits. Others who are working will be made aware of the problem by newspapers and television reports or by the plight of their unemployed neighbors.

The Debate over Unemployment Benefits

Unemployment was not a serious problem in 1990. The average unemployment rate was only 5.4 percent, marginally above the decade low of 5.2 percent in the previous year. And 5.4 percent was extremely low relative to other years of the preceding decade. By 1991, however, the unemployment rate was more than 25 percent higher than it had been two years earlier. There was no doubt that millions more Americans were going to be "hitting the financial wall" if their unemployment benefits ran out too soon.

This was the situation when policy makers began searching for ways in which to ease the financial burdens on the millions of persons who had lost their jobs during the recession that had hobbled the American economy since early 1990.

The debate over whether unemployment benefits should be extended was not as clear-cut as one might think. Certainly, the politically popular decision would be to increase benefit payments to the unemployed. But the 1980s had seen the national debt balloon to over $3 trillion following three years of successive tax cuts coupled with huge increases in defense outlays. The federal budget deficit, which had averaged $50 billion per year in the late 1970s, had exploded to more than $300 billion per year by 1991. Lawmakers themselves seemed to lack the political will to deal with the deficit because much of the increase was caused by the growth in politically popular, but untouchable, entitlement programs, such as Social Security. As a result, lawmakers in the early 1990s found themselves increasingly hard pressed to do something about the deficit. It was not necessarily politically advantageous for a member of Congress to push for a multibillion dollar unemployment benefits bill, especially if it would increase the federal budget deficit.

Demonstrators connect the poor economy with Bush's reelection chances as they wait for the president to appear for a speech in Philadelphia in 1992. Political history indicates that a poor economy is one of the strongest factors working against the reelection of an incumbent president.

The issue was further muddied by partisan politics. With the presidential election one year away, the Democratic leadership was trying to paint President Bush as more concerned with foreign affairs—specifically, with the nations of Eastern Europe and the former Soviet Union—than with domestic politics, especially the economy and the problems of unemployed Americans. President Bush, in contrast, was acutely aware of the yawning federal budget deficit and did not want to see it expand further. Bush was concerned that any extension in unemployment benefits would simply be a budget buster that might ultimately prove to be unnecessary if the economy was recovering, as he believed it was.

Although the battle lines were clearly drawn, the parties ultimately resolved their differences and enacted a bill extending unemployment benefits to long-term jobless persons. Although passage of the bill did relieve the immediate financial concerns of many chronically unemployed persons, neither Congress nor the Bush administration viewed the new law as anything more than a stopgap measure. Indeed, legislators in both parties spoke of the need to come up with a more lasting solution before the new benefits were exhausted.

Steps in the Policy-Making Process

The problem, the reaction to the problem, and the solution all form part of public policy making in the United States. No matter how simple or how complex the problem, those who make policy follow a number of steps. Based on observation, we can divide the process of policy making into at least five steps:

1. Agenda building: *The issue must get on the agenda.* This occurs through crises, technological change, or mass media campaigns, as well as through the efforts of strong political personalities. In the case of the extension of jobless benefits, members of Congress with large numbers of constituents who had been laid off or fired from their jobs urged congressional action. Congresspersons who received numerous letters and phone calls from constituents who had lost their jobs or feared losing their jobs also urged action.

2. Agenda formulation: *The proposals are discussed among government officials and the public.* Such discussions may appear in the press, on television, in the halls of Congress, and in scholarly journals. Congress holds hearings, the president voices the administration's views, and the topic may become a campaign issue.

3. Agenda adoption: *A specific strategy is chosen from among the proposals discussed.* That is, Congress must enact legislation, executive departments must write new regulations, or courts must interpret past policies differently. Much of the 1990–1991 congressional year, for example, was taken up by work on the unemployment benefits legislation. After much debate, a bill was passed, and the president signed it.

4. Agenda implementation: *Government action must be implemented by bureaucrats, the courts, police, and individual citizens.* The increased benefits would be paid to the jobless by the same federal and state organizations that had coordinated previous unemployment payment programs.

5. Agenda evaluation: *Increasingly after a policy is implemented, groups undertake policy evaluation.* Groups both inside and outside government perform studies to show what actually happens after a policy has been instituted. Such policy evaluations do not always lead anywhere, though, because proponents of the program tend to exaggerate the positive benefits, whereas critics tend to exaggerate the lack of benefits or any negative side effects. Nonetheless, the test of any program is, more and more, its outcome rather than its content. Presidential commissions are often appointed after an obvious failure or crisis in a program, such as the NASA *Challenger* explosion on January 28, 1986.

It is worth noting that, although the flow of the policy process is well understood, there are competing models of how and for whose benefit that process works. Table 14-1 lists a number of competing models of the policy-making process and gives a brief summary of each.

Did You Know ... That the federal government borrows about $700,000 a minute?

Economic Policy Making

Nowhere are the principles of public policy making clearer than in the area of economic decisions undertaken by our federal government. The president and Congress (and to a growing extent the judiciary) are constantly faced with economic choices. Consider some of them:

1. Should more federal funds be spent on helping the homeless?
2. Should Congress pass laws restricting foreigners' ability to buy U.S. companies and real estate?
3. Should more be spent on health care and, consequently, less on other programs?

TABLE 14-1 ■ Selected Models of the Policy-making Process

1. *The Bureaucratic Politics Model:* In the bureaucratic politics model, the relative power of the large bureaucracies in Washington determines which policy becomes part of the national agenda and which is implemented. This theory of American politics is based on the struggle among competing interest groups.

2. *The Power Elite, or Elitism, Model:* Powerful economic interests determine the outcome of policy struggles, according to the power elite, or elitism, model. The rich and those who know the rich determine what gets done. More important, the power elite decides what items do *not* get on the public agenda and which items get removed if they are already on it.

3. *The Marxist Model:* Closely aligned with the power elite model is the Marxist model of public policy making, in which the ruling class institutes public policy, often at the expense of the working class.

4. *The Incrementalist Model:* Public policy evolves through small changes or adjustments, according to this model. Consequently, policy makers examine only a few alternatives in trying to solve national problems. A good public policy decision is made when there is agreement among contesting interests, and agreement is obtained most easily when changes are minimal.

5. *The Rationalist Model:* This model, sometimes thought of as a pure textbook abstraction, hypothesizes a rational policy maker who sets out to maximize his or her own self-interest, rather than determining what the public, or collective, interest might be. Rational policy makers will rank goals and objectives according to their benefit to the policy maker. Such a model is often viewed as an alternative to the incrementalist model. This model is sometimes known as the theory of public choice.

6. *The Systems Model:* The most general, and perhaps the most ambitious, approach to modeling public policy making is a systems approach, in which policy is a product of the relationships between the institutions of government and the socioeconomic-political environment. Such a model has (a) inputs from public opinion and crises; (b) a political process including legislative hearings, debates, court deliberations, party conventions, and so on; (c) a set of policy outputs consisting of legislation, appropriations, and regulations; and (d) policy outcomes, which may provide, for example, more job security, less unemployment, more research on AIDS, and so on.

4. Should the federal government require welfare recipients to seek work or engage in additional training?

In each of these cases, policy makers cannot have clear-cut answers to their public policy questions. Each policy action carries with it a cost and a benefit known to analysts as a **policy trade-off.** The costs are typically borne by one group and the benefits enjoyed by another group.

Evaluating the Jobless Benefits Bill

The recession that plagued the American economy in the early 1990s had a particularly severe impact on white-collar workers. Hundreds of thousands of these persons, who were on average more educated and more highly skilled than the blue-collar workers who had borne the brunt of the previous recession in 1981–1982, suddenly found themselves without jobs and without immediate prospects for jobs. Many had no choice but to file for unemployment benefits. But by July 1991, nearly 350,000 people had used up their twenty-six weeks of state unemployment benefits.

Although workers are supposed to be eligible for an extra thirteen weeks of benefits in states suffering from extremely high levels of unemployment, very few states actually pay such benefits. In response, the House passed a $6.3 billion unemployment bill on September 17, 1991, that would have provided up to twenty extra weeks of unemployment compensation to workers and thus permanently expanded the unemployment benefits program. In the Senate, Finance Committee Chairman Lloyd Bentsen offered a $5.8 billion bill that would offer temporary benefits to those persons harmed by the recession. Both the House and Senate bills required the federal government to pay the costs of the benefits, but neither abided by the pay-as-you-go requirement that had been a fundamen-

POLICY TRADE-OFFS
The cost to the nation of undertaking any one policy in terms of all of the other policies that could have been taken; for example, an increase in the expenditures on one federal program means a reduction in expenditures on another program or an increase in federal taxes (or the deficit).

With a jobless rate of more than 7% across the country, hundreds of applicants queue up for employment interviews at a federal government facility. More than 2000 unemployed persons waited to apply for 250 jobs at a new hotel in the winter of 1991.

tal part of the previous year's budget agreement between the president and Congress. Each bill also provided that workers could qualify for additional weeks of unemployment benefits if jobless rates in their respective states reached certain specified levels. Under the House bill, for example, a worker living in a state with an unemployment rate of 8 percent would qualify for twenty additional weeks of benefits. Unemployed workers in states having jobless rates below the trigger rates specified in the bills would be eligible to receive four to five weeks of additional benefits.

Bush Vetoes the Bill. On October 16, 1991, President Bush vetoed the House version of the bill, and Congress was unable to override his veto. Stating that the bill would merely add to the government deficit, Bush insisted that any new spending proposals offered by Congress had to be paid for by shifting revenues from existing programs or by raising taxes. Although the 1990 budget agreement allowed the president and Congress to declare an emergency and thereby avoid these constraints, Bush refused to do so, arguing that signs of economic recovery made such an action unnecessary. Bentsen and House Ways and Means Chairman Dan Rostenkowski tried to address the objections of the White House by including pay-as-you-go rules in revised proposals. Democrats also found themselves increasingly pressured by organizations, such as the AFL–CIO, that were concerned because many of their members would see their benefits expire before any effective legislation was passed.

A Political Breakthrough. The breakthrough may have occurred on October 26, 1991, when President Bush asked House Minority Leader Bob Michel to make a deal with Rostenkowski. Bush may have also been motivated by growing signs that the economy was slipping back into a recession and that the tough times had ravaged the managerial ranks of corporate America—a traditional source of Republican voters. Some Democrats, such as Senate Majority Leader George Mitchell, seemed to be in no hurry to stop using the president's opposition to a budget-busting bill for partisan purposes. Others, such as Congressman Thomas Downey, a leading proponent of extended jobs benefits, argued that little additional political capital could be realized by further delays in passage of the bill.

Following extensive posturings by both parties, Congress succeeded in passing a $5.3 billion bill that would extend unemployment benefits to nearly three million workers. President Bush signed the bill on November 20, 1991, but prominent members of both parties voiced their dissatisfaction with the current funding system.

Because the $5.3 billion bill was merely a temporary measure, however, both Congress and the president tentatively agreed on the need to pass a second bill that would add an additional thirteen weeks of unemployment benefits on top of the thirteen to twenty weeks of extended benefits contained in the first bill. Unlike the first bill, this second extension was accompanied by little of the bitterness and rancor that had divided Democrats and Republicans before. Both the House and Senate committees approved identical thirteen-week extensions on January 27, 1992. Another battle over financing the extended benefits was avoided, owing to unexpectedly high estimated tax receipts from corporations, as well as the Bush administration's desire to deal with the issue once and for all. President Bush signed the second extension on February 7, 1992, just three days after Congress passed the bill.

Interest-Group Legislation: The Distribution of Costs and Benefits. The actual costs of the unemployment benefits extensions may exceed $8 billion. This cost will ultimately be paid by the American taxpayer. The beneficiaries will be the recipients of the extended benefits—the newly unemployed as well as the chronically unemployed. But the benefits will not be distributed evenly across the country because the extent of coverage is not dependent on the total number of unemployed workers in each state. As a result, states having similar unemployment levels may receive widely varying amounts of money.

As far as political benefits were concerned, the bill clearly profited the Democrats. They had been able to cite President Bush's opposition to the bill for nearly a year by painting him as a better friend of foreigners than of unemployed Americans. But the gains from continuing to bash Bush for his alleged anti-worker bias had probably been realized by the time Bush signed the first extension into law in late 1991. Interest groups such as the AFL–CIO and other labor organizations—whose members would receive jobless benefits—stood to benefit from the new legislation.

Was the American public concerned with the cost of the two bills? Perhaps, but it was not sufficiently motivated to devote much time, effort, or money to stopping the legislation. But those who would clearly benefit from the legislation would and did donate time and money to make sure it passed. It is always easier for interest groups (such as the AFL–CIO) that are specifically affected by legislation to raise money for candidates and incumbents who will continue to promote and vote for that legislation. The more widespread the costs and the more narrowly focused the benefits of government economic policy making, the more of such policy making we shall see. Indeed, that has been the history of much of our economic legislation at the federal, state, and local levels.

More Lessons in Politics: Taxes and Subsidies

▼

SUBSIDIES
Negative taxes; usually payments to producers given on a per-unit basis according to the amount of production of a particular commodity.

ACTION–REACTION SYNDROME
For every action on the part of government, there is a reaction on the part of the affected public. Then the government attempts to counter the reaction with another action, which starts the cycle all over again.

We can extend our political analysis of government economic activities by examining the areas of taxes and **subsidies** (negative taxes). Let's begin with the premise that in the world of taxes and subsidies, *for every action on the part of the government, there will be a reaction on the part of the public.* Eventually, the government will react with another action, followed by the public's further reaction. The **action–reaction syndrome** is a reality that has plagued government policy makers since before the beginning of the republic.

The Tax Code, Tax Rates, and Tax Loopholes

An examination of the Internal Revenue Code, encompassing thousands of pages, thousands of sections, and thousands of subsections, gives some indication that our tax system is not very simple. The 1986 Tax Reform Act was supposed to simplify it somewhat, but once you understand the action–reaction principle of taxation, you can predict that whatever simplification occurred in 1986 will be undone over time.

PROFILE

Dan Rostenkowski

"When you get a growing resentment about paying taxes, you get a problem with compliance."

Mention tax reform or deficit reduction, and the name Dan Rostenkowski will come up. The Democratic chairman of the powerful House Ways and Means Committee is best known for his work on tax reform in the 1990s. Although a Democrat, "Rosty" worked closely with the Bush and Reagan administrations on domestic tax issues.

An alumnus of the late Chicago Mayor Richard Daley's political machine, Rostenkowski has been a member of Congress for more than thirty years. He has never forgotten his Chicago roots and has received much publicity for his charitable donations to local Illinois organizations, such as the Polish Museum of America. (Its holdings, incidentally, include a bust of Rostenkowski.)

Before his election to the House of Representatives, Rostenkowski served as a member of the Illinois General Assembly. He was originally elected to Congress with the help of Mayor Daley, whose support he won by convincing Daley that younger men were needed to build seniority and break the southern Democrats' hold on committee chairmanships.

Rostenkowski is probably best known to the general public for his stand on tax reform during the Reagan administration. At one point, during a televised rebuttal of a Reagan speech, Rostenkowski asked everyone to write R-O-S-T-Y, Washington, D.C., to express their views on tax reform. He felt that "any reform is better than the current law." In an interview with *U.S. News & World Report*, Rostenkowski complained that it was unfair that his kids paid about a third of their income in taxes, while at the same time some very wealthy people "aren't paying a dime and are living very comfortably."

One recent temporary failure was his fight against the Bush-supported capital gains tax rollback. When President Bush proposed the roll

back, Rostenkowski responded, "I'm not about to tell the wage earners in Chicago that they should pay a higher rate than the stockbrokers."

Rostenkowski's surprise for the 1990s was a deficit reduction proposal that advocated both stiff taxes on gasoline and other special items and sharp cuts in spending for domestic social programs. His motives, however, have come under heavy scrutiny. Some observers see Rostenkowski as a fiscal moderate who has always supported the need for budget reform. Other observers, more cynical in outlook, hypothesize that he wants to regain some power after the capital gains struggle and retire in a few years.

In 1992, it became known that Rostenkowski was under investigation for the illegal purchase of stamps to gain cash from the House Post Office. The Clinton Administration faced a dilemma: Should a rigorous investigation of Rosty be pursued or should Rosty be "saved" so he could lead the fight for new taxes and health insurance reform?

Whatever the outcome, no one can doubt that Dan Rostenkowski is one of the top persuaders in Congress. Although not known as a great orator, he persuades his colleagues by bargaining, by trading favors, and by asking "If I do this, will you do that?" It is an old, familiar style—and it works.

People are not assessed a lump-sum tax each year; each family does not just pay $1,000 or $10,000 or $20,000. Rather, individuals and businesses pay taxes based on tax rates. (In 1992 there were only three federal tax rates applied to income. Before the 1986 Tax Reform Act, individuals had a total of fifteen separate possible tax rates on taxable income.) The higher the tax rate—the action on the part of government—the greater the public's reaction to that tax rate. Again, it is all a matter of costs and benefits. If the tax rate on all the income you make is 15 percent, that means that any method you can use to reduce your taxable income by one dollar saves you fifteen cents in tax liabilities that you owe the federal govern-

LOOPHOLES
Legal methods by which individuals and businesses are allowed to reduce the tax liabilities owed to the government.

ment. Therefore, those individuals paying a 15 percent rate have a relatively small incentive to avoid paying taxes. But consider individuals who were faced with a tax rate of 91 percent in the early 1960s. They had a tremendous incentive to find legal ways to reduce their taxable incomes. For every dollar of income that was somehow deemed nontaxable, the taxpayer would reduce tax liabilities by ninety-one cents.

So, individuals and corporations facing high tax rates will always react by making concerted attempts to get Congress to add **loopholes** in the tax law that allow them to reduce their taxable incomes. Loopholes are defined as legal methods of avoiding taxes. When the Internal Revenue Code imposed very high tax rates on high incomes, it also provided for more loopholes. There were special provisions that enabled investors in oil and gas wells to reduce their taxable income. There were loopholes that allowed people to shift income from one year to the next. There were loopholes that allowed individuals to form corporations outside the United States in order to avoid some taxes completely. The same principles apply to other interest groups. As long as one group of taxpayers sees a specific benefit from getting the law changed and that benefit means a lot of money per individual, the interest group will aggressively support lobbying activities and the election and reelection of members of Congress who will push for special loopholes. In other words, if there is enough of a benefit to be derived from influencing tax legislation, such influence will be exerted by the affected parties.

And Now the Question of Subsidies

Subsidies are just negative taxes. Instead of paying taxes to the governments, you receive money. Subsidies to farmers are often based on amount of output. Dairy producers, beekeepers, peanut farmers, corn farmers, and others have received direct subsidies from the federal government. As a form of negative taxes, the politics of subsidies follows the action–reaction syndrome. If a subsidy is provided to farmers, they will farm more land, buy more fertilizer, and increase output. If a subsidy is given to oil producers by offering tax breaks to investors in oil production, more resources will flow into oil production. If a subsidy is offered to new industry in the form of reduced taxes by a particular state, other things remaining the same, more industry will move into that state than would otherwise.

The main point to remember about subsidies is that they take away government dollars that could be spent elsewhere and induce the private sector to funnel more resources into the subsidized activity. When there were numerous tax benefits to investing in oil exploration, for example, more resources in the United States flowed to oil exploration than would have otherwise been the case. Today, the same is true for the number of resources that flow to subsidized agricultural pursuits, subsidized manufacturing activities, and the like.

The Politics of Monetary and Fiscal Policy

FISCAL POLICY
Changes in government spending or taxes to alter national economic variables, such as the rate of unemployment.

Changes in the tax code sometimes form part of an overall fiscal policy change. **Fiscal policy** is defined as the use of changes in government expenditures and taxes to alter national economic variables, such as the rate of inflation, the rate of unemployment, the level of interest rates, and the rate of economic growth. The federal government also has under its control **monetary policy,** defined as changes in the amount of money in circulation so as to affect interest rates, credit markets, the rate of inflation, and employment. Fiscal policy is the domain of Congress and the president. Monetary policy, as we shall see, is much less under the control of Congress and the president because the monetary authority, the Federal Reserve System—the Fed—is an independent agency not directly controlled by either Congress or the president.

Fiscal Policy: Theory and Reality

The theory behind fiscal policy changes is relatively straightforward: When the economy is going into a recession—a period of rising unemployment—the federal government should stimulate economic activity by increasing government expenditures or by decreasing taxes (or both). When the economy is becoming overheated with rapid increases in employment and rising prices—a condition of inflation—fiscal policy should become contractionary, reducing government expenditures and increasing taxes. That particular view of fiscal policy was first implemented in the 1930s and again became popular during the 1960s. It was an outgrowth of the economic theories of the English economist John Maynard Keynes. Keynes's ideas, published during the Great Depression of the 1930s (see the *Politics and Economics* feature in this chapter), influenced the economic policy makers guiding President Franklin D. Roosevelt's New Deal. **Keynesian economics** has not turned out to be as simple as expected, though. Starting in 1969, the U.S. economy entered a period of simultaneously rising prices and rising unemployment. In such a situation, applying a fiscal policy stimulus is not so obviously appropriate.

Lags in Policy.   Another problem with fiscal policy is that even under the best of circumstances, from the time the economy needs fiscal stimulus—say, at the start of a recession—to the time that any fiscal stimulus is forthcoming, there might be a lag of several years. First, there is a lag between the time a recession starts and when policy makers know that it has started. Next, there is a lag between that time and when policy makers actually decide that fiscal policy should be expansionary. Finally, there is another lag between the time fiscal policy is put into action and when it has its desired effects.

The Reality of the Federal Budgeting Process.   Even if we knew when recessions were beginning the instant they started, the federal budgeting process precludes quick reactions. We examined in Chapter 10 the complexity of the federal budgeting process in which no single agency is responsible for the amorphous concept called fiscal policy. The budget authority is divided between the president and Congress. Moreover, budget policy serves many other goals besides low inflation, low unemployment, and higher economic growth. Indeed, the so-called national goals of full employment, price stability, and economic growth, as outlined, for example, in the Full Employment Act of 1946, often carry little weight in the real budgetary process within Congress. Taxing and spending decisions are made in dozens of subcommittees dominated by interest-group and client politics.

MONETARY POLICY
Changes in the amount of money in circulation to alter credit markets, employment, and the rate of inflation.

KEYNESIAN ECONOMICS
An economic theory, named after English economist John Maynard Keynes, that gained prominence during the Great Depression of the 1930s. Typically associated with the use of fiscal policy to alter national economic variables—for example, increased government spending during times of economic downturns.

POLITICS AND ECONOMICS

The Great Depression, 1929–1941

On October 24, 1929, commonly called "Black Thursday," the New York Stock Exchange suffered through the first of a series of steep declines that made the nation and much of the world aware that a major economic catastrophe was in progress. From 1929 to 1933, the nation's unemployment rate shot up from 3.2 percent to an astronomical 25.2 percent, and income per person (in then current dollars) fell from $846 to $442. Public and private construction fell by nearly 75 percent, the business failure rate increased by 50 percent, and thousands of banks and hundreds of thousands of business firms had closed their doors by the time the Depression hit bottom in 1933.

In this climate of nearly total economic collapse, Republican President Herbert Hoover was voted out of office and replaced by the "New Deal" Democratic administration of Franklin Roosevelt. Roosevelt promised aid to farmers, public development of electric power, a balanced federal budget, and government regulation of private economic power, which many people blamed for causing the depression. He temporarily closed the nation's banks to thwart depositors' panicky withdrawal of funds and implemented measures to economize on government spending. Under his prodding, Congress enacted a bold series of relief measures.

Congress passed legislation in 1933 to create the Federal Emergency Relief Administration, which gave money to state relief agencies; the Civilian Conservation Corps, which employed as many as 500,000 young men at a time in flood con-

Wall Street during the stock market crash.

trol and reforestation work; the Agricultural Adjustment Administration, which aimed to raise farm prices and farmers' incomes through farm commodity subsidies; the Public Works Administration to encourage building and construction; the National Recovery Administration to regulate labor and fair trade practices; the Tennessee Valley Authority to provide flood control, energy, and regional planning for a large segment of lower-income Americans living in Appalachia; and the Securities and Exchange Commission to regulate stock market practices. Other legislation established maximum hours of work, minimum wages, guarantees of labor–management collective bargaining, and abolition of child labor in interstate commerce.

In 1935, the Social Security Act was passed, and the Works Progress Administration (WPA) was created. The WPA employed more than two million workers.

Subsequent opposition from the Supreme Court and from conservative Republicans and many southern Democrats in Congress limited the effectiveness of these and other programs of Roosevelt's New Deal. The Great Depression and its direct economic and political consequences effectively ended by 1941 as the United States rebuilt its industrial base for a wartime economy. Clearly, however, many of the political and economic institutions of today, as well as the debate over their usefulness, can be traced to these events of the Great Depression and the political responses to that crisis.

Monetary Policy: Politics and Reality

The theory behind monetary policy is also relatively straightforward. In periods of recession and high unemployment, we should stimulate the economy by expanding the rate of growth of the money supply (defined loosely as currency plus checking account balances, plus other types of account balances that generally serve as money). An easy-money policy is supposed to lower interest rates and induce consumers to spend more and producers to invest more. With rising inflation, do the reverse: Reduce the rate of growth of the amount of money in circulation. Interest rates should rise, choking off some consumer spending and some business investment. But the world is never so simple as the theory we use to explain it. If the nation experiences stagflation—rising inflation *and* rising unemployment—expansionary monetary policy will lead to even more inflation. Ultimately, the more money there is in circulation, the higher prices will be.

The Monetary Authority—the Federal Reserve System.   Congress established our modern central bank, the Federal Reserve, in 1913. It is governed by a Board of Governors consisting of seven individuals, including the very powerful chair. All of the governors, including the chair, are nominated by the president and approved by the Senate. Their appointments are for fourteen years. Through the Federal Reserve System, or Fed, and its **Federal Open Market Committee (FOMC),** decisions about monetary policy are made eight times a year. The Board of Governors of the Federal Reserve System is independent. The president can "jawbone" the board, and Congress can threaten to merge the Fed with the Treasury, but as long as the Fed retains its independence, its chairperson and governors can do what they please. Hence, talking about "the president's monetary policy" or "Congress's monetary policy" is inaccurate. To be sure, the Fed has, on occasion, yielded to presidential pressure, and for a while the Fed's chairperson felt constrained to follow a congressional resolution requiring

Did You Know . . . That by April 15, 1992, it was estimated that Americans had paid $545 billion in 1991 individual income taxes?

FEDERAL OPEN MARKET COMMITTEE (FOMC)
The most important body within the Federal Reserve System, the FOMC decides how monetary policy should be carried out by the Federal Reserve.

A meeting of the Board of Governors of the Federal Reserve.

Did You Know . . . That the federal budget contains about 190,000 separate accounts and that at the rate of one minute per account, eight hours per day, it would take over a year to think about all of the accounts?

U.S. TREASURY BONDS
Evidences of debt issued by the federal government. Similar to corporate bonds but issued by the U.S. Treasury.

PUBLIC, OR NATIONAL, DEBT
The total amount of debt carried by the federal government.

CONSTANT DOLLARS
Dollars corrected for inflation; dollars expressed in terms of purchasing power for a given year.

TABLE 14-2 ■ Net Public Debt of the Federal Government

Year	Total (billions of current dollars)
1940	$ 42.7
1945	235.2
1950	219.0
1960	237.2
1970	284.9
1980	709.3
1985	1,499.5
1990	2,410.1
1991	2,687.2
1992	3,011.6
1993	3,355.3*

*Estimate

SOURCE: U.S. Office of Management and Budget.

him to report monetary targets over each six-month period. But now, more than ever before, the Fed remains one of the truly independent sources of economic power in the government.

Monetary Policy and Lags. Monetary policy does not suffer from the same lengthy time lags as fiscal policy because the Fed can, within a very short period, put its policy into effect. Nonetheless, researchers have estimated that it takes almost fourteen months for a monetary policy change to become effective, measured from the time the economy either slows down or speeds up too much to the time the economy feels the policy change.[1] This means that by the time monetary policy goes into effect, a different policy might be appropriate.

Reflections on the Public Debt and Big Deficits

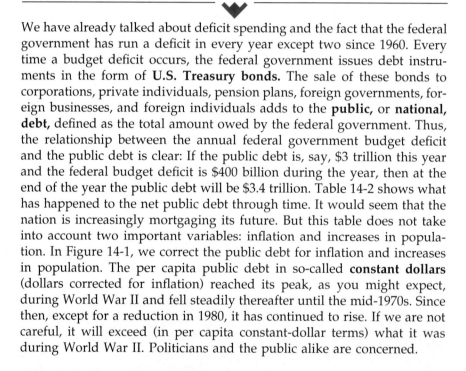

We have already talked about deficit spending and the fact that the federal government has run a deficit in every year except two since 1960. Every time a budget deficit occurs, the federal government issues debt instruments in the form of **U.S. Treasury bonds.** The sale of these bonds to corporations, private individuals, pension plans, foreign governments, foreign businesses, and foreign individuals adds to the **public,** or **national, debt,** defined as the total amount owed by the federal government. Thus, the relationship between the annual federal government budget deficit and the public debt is clear: If the public debt is, say, $3 trillion this year and the federal budget deficit is $400 billion during the year, then at the end of the year the public debt will be $3.4 trillion. Table 14-2 shows what has happened to the net public debt through time. It would seem that the nation is increasingly mortgaging its future. But this table does not take into account two important variables: inflation and increases in population. In Figure 14-1, we correct the public debt for inflation and increases in population. The per capita public debt in so-called **constant dollars** (dollars corrected for inflation) reached its peak, as you might expect, during World War II and fell steadily thereafter until the mid-1970s. Since then, except for a reduction in 1980, it has continued to rise. If we are not careful, it will exceed (in per capita constant-dollar terms) what it was during World War II. Politicians and the public alike are concerned.

Is the Public Debt a Burden?

We often hear about the burden of the public debt. Some argue that the government is eventually going to go bankrupt, but that, of course, cannot happen. As long as the government has the ability to pay for interest payments on the public debt through taxation, it will never go bankrupt. What happens is that when Treasury bonds come due, they are simply "rolled over." That is, if a $1 million Treasury bond comes due today, the U.S. Treasury pays it off and sells another $1 million bond.

What about the interest payments? Interest payments are paid by taxes, so what we are really talking about is taxing some people to pay interest

[1]Robert Gordon, *Macroeconomics*, 6th ed. (New York: HarperCollins, 1993), p. 431.

to others who loaned money to the government. This cannot really be called a burden to all of society. There is one hitch, however. Not all of the interest payments are paid to Americans. A significant amount is paid to foreigners because foreigners own almost 15 percent of the public debt, raising the fear of too much foreign control of U.S. assets. So, it is no longer the case that we "owe it all to ourselves."

Another factor is also important. Even though we are paying interest to ourselves for the most part, the more the federal government borrows, the greater the percentage of the federal budget that is committed to interest payments. The ever-increasing portion of the budget committed to interest payments reduces the federal government's ability to purchase public goods, such as more national parks, in the future. In 1976, interest costs to the government were less than 9 percent of total federal outlays. The estimate for 1993 is about 15 percent. Indeed, if you wish to do a simple projection of current trends, some time in the next century the federal government will be spending almost 100 percent of its budget on interest payments! This, of course, will not occur, but it highlights the problem of running larger and larger deficits and borrowing more and more money to cover them.

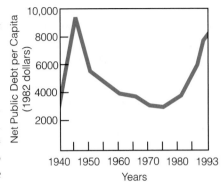

FIGURE 14-1 ■ Per Capita Public Debt of the United States in Constant 1982 Dollars

If we correct the public debt for intergovernmental borrowing, the growth in the population, and changes in the price level (inflation), we obtain a graph that shows the per capita net public debt in the United States expressed in constant 1982 dollars. The public debt reached its peak during World War II and then dropped consistently until about 1975. In the last fifteen years, however, it has risen steadily and is starting to approach World War II levels.

Balancing the Budget: A Constitutional Amendment or Gramm–Rudman?

▼

Some argue that the way not to have deficits is to have a constitutional convention to draft a balanced-budget amendment to the U.S. Constitution. Two-thirds of the state legislatures need to petition the Congress for a convention to be called. To date, the required number of legislative petitions has not been filed. Congress also has the option of passing a constitutional amendment, which it could then submit to the states for ratification.

Perhaps as an alternative to a constitutional amendment for balancing the budget, Congress passed the Gramm–Rudman–Hollings Act, also known as the Balanced Budget and Emergency Deficit Control Act, in December 1985. Its goal was to reach a balanced budget by fiscal year 1991. The act mandated progressive annual cuts in the deficit. At a minimum, the Gramm–Rudman–Hollings Act increased the visibility of deficits as a political issue. Nonetheless, deficits persist, indicating that Congress is not making the necessary painful choices.

After the passage of Gramm–Rudman, the federal government failed for two years to comply with its target deficit reductions. Congress then passed a revised act requiring that the 1988 deficit be no higher than $144 billion and that it drop to zero by 1993. Congress failed to meet the required deficit reductions for the first four years of the revised act. In 1990, a second revision of the Gramm–Rudman set of targets allowed for a deficit of over $200 billion in 1991 (*excluding* the cost of the savings and loan bailout).

The 1990 law presents an overall set of federal deficit reduction targets, but the president has the flexibility to adjust them. Bush has already done so. The estimated $350 billion federal budget deficit for 1993 certainly was not within the limits set by the 1990 law. Moreover, even the most optimistic planners at the General Accounting Office predict that the annual federal budget deficit will remain in the $400 billion range through the year 2000.

Domestic Policy Making

The "big" economic questions of monetary versus fiscal policy and the size of the federal deficit represent only one dimension of domestic public policy. Domestic policy comprises all of the laws, government planning, and government actions that affect each individual's life in the United States. The span of such policies is enormous. Policies range from relatively simple laws, such as those establishing speed limits on interstate highways, to the complex issues involved in protecting our environment. The federal government formulates and implements some of our domestic policies, such as Social Security. Many other policies reflect the combined efforts of state, federal, and local governments. Policies with respect to health issues, poverty, the environment, and public safety normally require multilevel government coordination.

The United States is not a planned society. No national planning commission systematically targets the issues for debate and policy making. Rather, policies are created by governments in response to public concerns as problems arise and as the public demands government action. Sometimes, such public demands originate with interest groups. In other instances—when dealing with the AIDS epidemic or acid rain, for example—the problems force themselves onto the public agenda by the scope of their effects on society.

In this chapter, we focus on four major policy problems currently facing the United States. These four policy domains—health care, poverty and homelessness, the environment, and public safety—furnish examples of how the policy-making process works.

America's Health-Care Crisis

Currently, spending for health care in this country is rapidly approaching three-quarters of a trillion dollars. Expressed as a percentage of the total income generated by our economy during one year, health-care expenditures are estimated to be 14 percent in 1993. Look at Figure 14-2. You can see that in 1965 about 6 percent of annual income was spent on health care, but that percentage has been growing steadily. U.S. spending per person on health care is greater than anywhere else in the world today. Figure 14-3 shows the percentage by which the U.S. spending per capita for health care exceeds that of other countries. Estimated per capita health-care spending in the United States for 1993 is around $2,500. According to Figure 14-3, this means that the United Kingdom spends even less.

Why Have Health-Care Costs Risen So Much?

There are numerous explanations for the steep rise in health-care costs. Among the more important factors are the changing demographics of our population: the U.S. population is getting older; the cost of new tech-

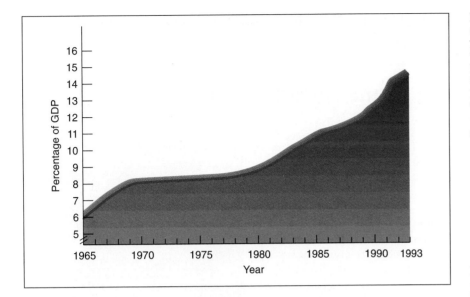

FIGURE 14-2 ■ Growth in Health-Care Expenditures

Health-care expenditures expressed as a percentage of annual national income (gross domestic product, or GDP). In 1965, they were about 6 percent of GDP. The estimate for 1993 is about 14 percent.

SOURCE: Health Care Financing Administration.

nologies; and the effect of third-party financing on the demand for health care.

The Age/Health-Care Expenditure Equation. The top 5 percent of health-care users incur over 50 percent of all health expenditures. The bottom 70 percent of health-care users account for only 10 percent of health-care costs. Not surprisingly, most of the top users of health-care services are elderly persons. Hospital and nursing-home expenditures are now predominantly made by people older than seventy, and elderly persons consume over four times as much health-care service per person as the rest of the population.

Whatever the demand for health-care services is today, it is likely to be considerably higher in the future because the U.S. population is steadily aging. More than 12 percent of the 254 million Americans counted in the 1990 census are over the age of 65. By the year 2030, senior citizens will make up over 21 percent of our population. As the number of elderly persons in our society increases, so will the demand for health care.

New Technologies. Another reason health-care costs have risen so dramatically is the medical profession's increased reliance on high-tech medical equipment. A CT (computerized tomography) scanner costs around a million dollars. An MRI (magnetic resonance imaging) scanner can cost over $2 million. A PET (positron emission tomography) scanner costs around $4 million. All of these machines became available in the 1980s and are in high demand throughout the country. Typical fees for procedures using them run from $300 to $500 for a CT scan to as high as $2,000 for a PET scan. There is no end in sight to the development of new technologies that help physicians and hospitals prolong human life.

Third-Party Financing. Currently, over 40 percent of health-care services are paid for by the government (28 percent by the federal government and 12 percent by the states). Private insurance accounts for a little over

FIGURE 14-3 ■ Per Capita Health-Care Spending

The percentage by which U.S. health-care spending per person ($2,500) exceeds that in other countries. Note that the United States spends nearly twice as much as Luxembourg on per capita health-care spending and about two and a half times as much as Italy.

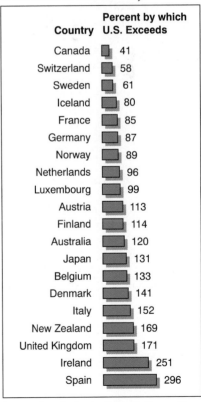

Country	Percent by which U.S. Exceeds
Canada	41
Switzerland	58
Sweden	61
Iceland	80
France	85
Germany	87
Norway	89
Netherlands	96
Luxembourg	99
Austria	113
Finland	114
Australia	120
Japan	131
Belgium	133
Denmark	141
Italy	152
New Zealand	169
United Kingdom	171
Ireland	251
Spain	296

SOURCE: Organization for Economic Cooperation and Development.

POLITICS AND HEALTH-CARE SERVICES

Spending on the AIDS Epidemic

When Los Angeles Lakers' star basketball player Magic Johnson announced to the world in 1992 that he had contracted the virus that causes AIDS, he heightened the nation's awareness about this disease. At least a million Americans have been infected with the HIV virus. Worldwide, the number is much greater. By the year 2000, six million individuals in the world will have been stricken with AIDS, and thirty million more will be infected with the virus. More than three thousand cases of AIDS are reported every month in the United States. The cost of health care in the United States will increasingly reflect the additional expenses incurred in the treatment of AIDS patients.

The initial response of the medical community and the government to the problem of AIDS was not only slow but also political. Gay men and Haitians are the two high-risk groups that were first affected by the virus. These are not people who generate rapid and favorable government response in the form of re-

search and funds for research. Because a primary route of transmission of the AIDS virus is through sexual activity, some conservatives and traditional religious groups even asserted that the disease was a punishment by God for immoral behavior.

Outraged at the slowness and apparent hostility of government, the gay and lesbian communities began to mobilize politically. Rallies, news conferences, and a strategy for inducing wider societal concern about their condition, as well as support for programs to find a cure, were launched. By the mid-1980s, a concerted effort was made to demonstrate that AIDS was a threat to all Americans, not just to high-risk groups. This became dramatically clear when AIDS-contaminated blood was identified as the source of infection of persons falling outside the high-risk groups.

By the late 1980s, AIDS had been taken up as a cause by celebrities, such as Elizabeth Taylor and others. A huge quilt embroidered with the

Magic Johnson announcing to the world that he is HIV positive.

names of AIDS victims was assembled and displayed in many cities throughout the country. Massive demonstrations were organized in Washington, D.C., and elsewhere. The media lent their support to the pressure for more AIDS research

30 percent of health-care payments. The remainder, about 25 percent, is paid directly by individuals. Medicare is the main provider of hospital and other medical benefits to thirty-two million Americans, most of whom are over the age of sixty-five. Medicaid, the joint state–federal program, provides long-term health care, particularly for poor persons living in nursing homes. Medicare, Medicaid, and private insurance companies are considered *third parties* to the medical-care equation. That is, the doctor–hospital is one party, the patient is the second party, and Medicare, Medicaid, and private insurance companies are the third parties. When third parties pay for anything, including medical care, the demand for those services increases. For example, when Medicare and Medicaid went into

POLITICS AND HEALTH-CARE SERVICES

and treatment, while public-service television ads depicted white, middle-class, heterosexual men and women (the lowest-risk group) afflicted with AIDS. After much prodding, Congress began to fund AIDS research, treatment, and education programs. The surgeon general prepared and mailed to every U.S. household a booklet with information on AIDS and its prevention and advocated sex education and the use of condoms.

Current total federal spending on AIDS research and care of AIDS patients exceeds $3 billion a year. Some public health-care experts claim that the money spent for AIDS treatment and prevention is disproportionately large. They point out, for example, that the number of deaths due to breast cancer is ten times that caused by AIDS. Yet the funding for breast-cancer research is only 20 percent of that devoted to AIDS research. The accompanying table shows federal research and development (R&D) funding for various diseases and the number of deaths caused by each disease. As the table indicates, R&D funding in

the AIDS area exceeds that for breast cancer, heart disease, and Alzheimer's disease, even though the number of deaths caused by the latter three diseases is much higher.

AIDS activists dispute these numbers, claiming that most of what the federal government spends is not on research but simply on Medicare and Medicaid payments to AIDS victims. They have pressed for continued increases in research funding. Radical AIDS advocacy groups, such as ACT UP, have done more than dispute numbers. ACT UP disrupted

the 1990 International AIDS conference in San Francisco and completely drowned out the speech by Dr. Louis Sullivan, secretary of the Health and Human Services Department. Other groups have bypassed the extremely slow U.S. Food and Drug Administration (FDA) procedures for the testing and licensing of new drugs. These groups are conducting their own tests on new drugs and medications that may help to reduce AIDS symptoms or prolong the lives of AIDS sufferers. Pressure from AIDS activists on the FDA has produced some changes in the procedures for allowing the experimental use of promising drugs before licensing.

	R&D Funding ($ millions)	U.S. Deaths in 1992
Cancer	$1,984	522,450
HIV/AIDS	**1,164**	**51,000**
Heart disease	729	712,254
Alzheimer's disease	282	100,000
Diabetes	279	50,468
Injuries	162	95,085
Stroke	94	142,524

SOURCES: Public Health Service, Centers for Disease Control, and Alzheimer's Association.

effect in the 1960s, the volume of medical payments reimbursed by third parties increased 75 percent.[2]

The availability of third-party payments for costly medical care has generated large increases in the availability of hospital beds. From 1974 to 1993, the number of hospital beds increased by 50 percent. Present occupancy rates are only around 65 percent.

Physicians Call the Shots, and Hospitals Provide the Services

Third-party payments have allowed physicians to dominate the health-care decision-making process for several decades. Expenditures on phy-

---

[2]Herbert Klarman, "The Difference the Third Party Makes," *Journal of Risk and Insurance*, Vol. 36, No. 5 (December 1969).

sician services rose more rapidly than any other health-care expenditure category in the last decade. Physicians are typically reimbursed on the basis of the medical procedures they undertake. Most physicians have no financial stake in trying to keep hospital costs down. Indeed, many have an incentive to raise costs. They want to protect themselves against malpractice lawsuits. But they also are often paid more by insurance companies if they prescribe more medical procedures per patient.

We see such actions most often with terminally ill patients. A physician may order CT scans or other costly procedures for a terminally ill patient. The physician knows that Medicare or some other type of insurance will pay for the procedure. Then the physician can bill Medicare or the private insurance company for analyzing the CT scan. It is not surprising that 30 percent of Medicare expenditures are for Americans who die within less than a year.

The Clinton Health Care Plan

President Bill Clinton campaigned on the promise that his administration would reform the health care system and make a minimum level of health insurance available to all Americans. In a surprise move, the President appointed his wife, Hillary Rodham Clinton, as the leader of a task force to create a plan for health care reform. Although criticized for operating without public scrutiny and for excluding representatives of the health care industry, the task force proceeded to draft a plan for the Clinton administration. In late spring 1993, it became clear that the new health plan would be costly and controversial. The Clinton administration decided to put its effort into a deficit reduction plan in 1993 and postpone introduction of the health-care plan until after the deficit/economic stimulus package passed the Congress.

Hillary Rodham Clinton presiding over the health care reform task force.

Environmental Policy

In 1989, the supertanker *Exxon Valdez* caused the worst oil spill in North American history in the pristine waters of Prince William Sound in Alaska. A quarter of a million barrels of crude oil—more than ten million gallons—leaked out of the ship's broken hull. Within a month, the slick had spread over 1,600 square miles of ocean waters. A little less than two years later, during the Gulf war between Iraq and the coalition forces led by the United States, a calculated decision was made by Iraq's president, Saddam Hussein, to engage in **eco-destruction.** And so the world's largest oil spill, this time not accidental, ensued. Original estimates of more than 400 million gallons of spilled oil have been reduced. It is now believed that anywhere between 40 and 120 million gallons leaked out of pipelines deliberately opened by Iraqi forces. (At least part of the oil spill may have been caused by the anti-Iraq coalition's aerial bombing campaign.)

ECO-DESTRUCTION
The willful destruction of some part of the ecology as part of an act of war or aggression.

Oil spill disasters in the United States and elsewhere are constant reminders that human actions may create unwanted side effects—often the destruction of the environment and the ecology (the total pattern of environmental relationships). Every day, humans, through their actions, emit pollutants into the air and the water. Each year, the world atmosphere receives twenty million metric tons of sulfur dioxide, eighteen million metric tons of ozone pollutants, and sixty million metric tons of carbon monoxide.

The Government's Response to Pollution Problems

Government has been responding to pollution problems since before the American Revolution, when the Massachusetts Bay Colony issued regulations to try to stop the pollution of Boston Harbor. In the nineteenth century, states passed laws controlling water pollution after scientists and medical researchers convinced most policy makers that dumping sewage into drinking and bathing water caused disease. At the national level, the Water Pollution Control Act of 1948 provided research and assistance to the states for pollution control efforts, but little was done. In 1952, the first state air pollution law was passed in Oregon. The federal Air Pollution Control Act of 1955 gave some assistance to states and cities.

The National Environmental Policy Act.   The year 1969 marked the start of the most concerted national government involvement in pollution problems. In that year, the conflict between oil exploration interests and environmental interests literally erupted when a Union Oil Company's oil well six miles off the coast of Santa Barbara, California, exploded, releasing 235,000 gallons of crude oil. The result was an oil slick, covering an area of 800 square miles, that washed up on the city's beaches and killed plant life, birds, and fish. Hearings in Congress revealed that the Interior Department did not know which way to go in the energy–environment trade-off. Congress did know, however, and passed the National Environmental Policy Act in 1969. This landmark legislation established, among other things, the Council for Environmental Quality. Also, it mandated

Oil wells burned out of control in Kuwait after Iraqi forces retreated from that country in 1991. The cost pollution caused by the oil fires and damage to the coast and ocean from the oil spills reached billions of dollars. The oil fires were controlled, however, in a shorter time period than originally estimated.

Did You Know . . . That the Department of Energy paid a fine of almost $500 million to the Environmental Protection Agency for its improper operation of a uranium foundry twenty miles northwest of Cincinnati?

ENVIRONMENTAL IMPACT STATEMENT (EIS)
As a requirement mandated by NEPA, EISs must show the costs and benefits of major federal actions that could significantly affect the quality of the environment.

ACID RAIN
Rain that has picked up pollutants, usually sulfur dioxides, from industrial areas of the earth that are often hundreds of miles distant from where the rain falls.

that an **environmental impact statement (EIS)** be prepared for every recommendation or report on legislation or major federal action that significantly affected the quality of the environment. The act gave citizens and public interest groups concerned with the environment a weapon against the unnecessary and inappropriate use of natural resources by government.

The Clean Air Act of 1990. The most comprehensive government attempt at cleaning up our environment occurred in 1990. After years of lobbying by environmentalists and counterlobbying by industry, the Clean Air Act of 1990 was passed. This act amended the 1970 Clean Air Act, which, among other things, had required a reduction of 90 percent of the amount of carbon monoxide and other pollutants emitted by automobiles. In spite of the fact that an automobile purchased today emits only 4 percent of the pollutants that a 1970 model did, there is more overall air pollution. This is because so many more automobiles are being driven today. Currently, the urban ground-level ozone is as great as it was before any clean air legislation. The 1990 Clean Air Act requires automobile manufacturers to cut new automobiles' exhaust emissions of nitrogen oxide by 60 percent and the emission of other pollutants by 35 percent. These requirements must be met by 1998.

Stationary sources of air pollution are also subject to more regulation. To reduce **acid rain,** 110 of the oldest coal-burning power plants in the United States must cut their emissions by 40 percent by the year 2001. Controls on other factories and businesses are intended to reduce ground-level ozone pollution in ninety-six cities to healthful levels by 2005 (except in Los Angeles, which has until 2010 to meet the standards). The act also requires that the production of chlorofluorocarbons (CFCs) be stopped completely by the year 2002. CFCs are thought to deplete the ozone layer and increase global warming. CFCs are used in air conditioning and other refrigeration units.

Clean Air Is Not Free. Before the mid-1980s, environmental politics seemed to be couched in terms of "them against us." "Them" was everyone involved in businesses that cut down rain forests, poisoned rivers, and created oil spills. The "us" was the government, and it was the government's job to stop "them." Today, particularly in the United States, more people are aware that the battle lines are blurred. According to the Environmental Protection Agency (EPA), we are already spending well over $100 billion annually to comply with federal environmental rules. When the 1990 Clean Air Act is fully implemented, that amount may be as much as 50 percent higher. So the government, particularly in Washington, D.C., has become interested in how to solve the nation's environmental problems at the lowest cost. Moreover, America's corporations are becoming increasingly engaged in producing recyclable and biodegradable products, as well as pitching in to solve some environmental problems.

Cost concerns were clearly in the minds of the drafters of the Clean Air Act of 1990 when they tackled the problem of sulfur emissions from electric power plants. Rather than tightening these standards, the new law simply limits total sulfur emissions. Companies have a choice of either rebuilding old plants or buying the right to pollute. The result is that polluters have an incentive to not even attempt to deal with exceptionally dirty plants. When closing down such plants, they can sell their pollution rights to those who value them more. The law is straightforward: An electric utility power plant is allowed to emit up to one ton of sulfur dioxide into the air in a given year. If the plant emits one ton of sulfur dioxide, the allowance disappears. If a plant switches to a low-sulfur-dioxide fuel, for example, or installs scrubbing equipment that reduces sulfur dioxide, it may end up emitting less than one ton. In this case, it can sell or otherwise trade its unused pollution allowance, or it can bank it for later use.

These rights to pollution allowances have already started to trade in the marketplace. Indeed, by the time you read this book, there may be a well-established market in "smog futures" offered on the Chicago Board of Trade and the New York Mercantile Exchange.

Global Warming

One of the most pressing environmental concerns is the threat of global warming. Not too many years ago, most commentators and scientists were worried about a new ice age. By 1990, however, scientists had decided that the earth was warming. According to the National Academy of Sciences, "global environmental change [global warming] may well be the most pressing international issue of the next century" and "the future welfare of human society is ... at risk."

Some observers believe there is a silver lining in the cloud of global warming. James R. Udall, a frequent contributor to *Audubon, National Wildlife,* and *Sierra* magazines, wrote:

> A century from now historians may conclude that the threat of global warming was the best thing that ever happened to the environment. Humanity has an enormous investment in a stable climate, and global warming gives us a compelling, selfish, economic incentive to change patterns of energy use that have proved so harmful to the environment.[3]

The Greenhouse Effect and Global Warming

The **greenhouse effect** is the trapping of heat inside the earth's atmosphere as a result of pollution caused largely by the burning of fossil fuels and the emission of carbon dioxide (CO_2). The process is accelerated by deforestation and the burning of trees in places such as the Amazon rain forest. Some of the most reliable computer models of the world's climate, such as one at the National Center for Atmospheric Research, suggest that if the current rate of the greenhouse effect continues, by the year 2050 the earth's temperature will rise by three to nine degrees Fahrenheit. The change in temperature would precipitate ecological changes that in turn would result in dramatic social, economic, and political upheavals. The ice caps would melt, coastal water levels would rise and flood many cities, forests would die, some geographic areas would become deserts, and, in others, farmland and crops would be severely stressed.

The rise in sea levels by the year 2100 would put most of The Netherlands, Bangladesh, and Egypt under water. New Orleans, New York, Ven-

Did You Know ... That Greenpeace USA sends out thirty-five million pieces of mail a year and that the National Wildlife Federation annually mails sixty million pieces?

GREENHOUSE EFFECT
The trapping of heat within the earth's atmosphere as a result of pollution caused largely by the burning of fossil fuels and emissions of carbon dioxide.

---

[3]"Global Warming: Diplomacy's Next Great Challenge," *Phi Kappa Phi Journal,* Winter 1990, p. 36.

Did You Know . . . That less than 5 percent of the 1,200 toxic waste dumps on the EPA's Superfund priority list (Superfund was established by federal legislation in 1980 to fund initially the clean-up of toxic waste dumps) have been cleaned up completely and that about 90 percent of the money used to settle a Superfund environmental claim goes to legal fees and related costs rather than to the clean-up itself?

ice, Bangkok, and other cities would be devastated. Southern Florida, including Miami and Key West, would disappear under the Atlantic Ocean.

Most experts now agree that the greenhouse effect may well pose one of the most serious challenges to U.S. and world leaders in the coming three decades and that the problem must be addressed on a global scale. The revelation of terrible environmental devastation in Eastern Europe and China's and India's continued reliance on coal as a major energy source indicate the urgency of the issue as well as some of the difficulties in reaching solutions. The United States, with 5 percent of the world's population, produces 23 percent of the world's CO_2. The responsibility of American leadership seems clear to many.

Perhaps the most daunting fact is that only drastic reductions in the use of fossil fuels and the use of alternate energy will slow down, stop, and perhaps reverse the damage already done. Those alternative energy sources are not currently cost-effective and safe (nuclear energy, for example), and new, clean energy sources and technologies have yet to be devised, much less put into use.

The Government's Response to Global Environmental Threats

The federal government has responded to the threat of global warming. For example, the Environmental Protection Agency is still requiring ever-improved gas mileage ratings and pollution controls for newly produced automobiles sold in the United States. The purpose is to reduce the amount of carbon dioxide spewed into the air.

Steps also have been taken to halt the destruction of the ozone layer. In 1987, the United States, along with fifty-five other nations, signed a treaty in Montreal, Canada, obligating these nations to reduce the use of chlorofluorocarbons (CFCs) by 50 percent by the year 2000. Federal law in this country now requires special disposal and handling of equipment containing ozone-reducing chemicals that might leak into the atmosphere. In addition, federal law requires the reduction of CFC in widely used consumer products, such as aerosol sprays.

The World's Response to Global Warming and Other Environmental Problems—Rio, 1992

In June 1992, the United Nations (U.N.) held a Conference on Environment and Development in Rio de Janeiro, Brazil. Earlier, 121 governments sent over 22,000 pages to U.N. officials in Geneva, Switzerland, so that the agenda for the conference could be prepared. The impetus behind the Rio conference, commonly called Earth Summit, was statistics like those in Figure 14-4, which shows worldwide CFC consumption as well as carbon dioxide emissions.

From the beginning of the planning stages for the 1992 conference, a disparity of interests and points of view among the various countries was apparent. The developing nations attributed the planet's environmental problems to the "unsustainable production standards" of industrialized nations, such as the United States. Less-developed countries argued that the United States, as well as other developed countries, should cut back

FIGURE 14-4 ■ Some Causes of Global Warming

The United States is responsible for 29 percent of chlorofluorocarbons (CFCs) generated worldwide, even though the United States has less than 5 percent of the world's population. The United States generates less carbon dioxide than Eastern Europe, however.

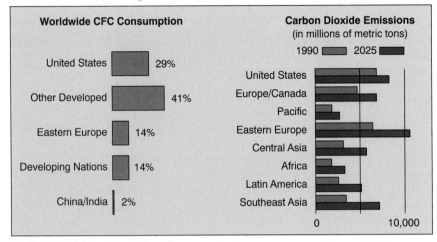

SOURCE: Overseas Development Council.

on everything from energy consumption to water use and help them financially to create sustainable and nonpolluting sources of energy. Nonetheless, despite heavy pressure from environmental groups, President Bush refused to even attend the conference until the rules had been written to his satisfaction.

During the conference, which was attended by virtually all of the 178 U.N. member nations, President Bush made it clear that the United States would not forfeit its control over national environmental policies to the combined world powers. "I'm president of the U.S., not president of the world," he told a news reporter at the conclusion of the conference. Although Bush joined the heads of 152 other nations in signing a global warming treaty—a legally binding agreement to curb emissions of carbon dioxide, methane, and other greenhouse gases that scientists feel are responsible for trapping the sun's heat close to the earth—he did so only after the conference agreed not to set specific targets for reducing carbon-dioxide emissions. The other conference treaty, the Biodiversity Convention, requires that various measures be taken by the signatory countries to protect endangered species. It also includes a provision requiring any country that uses the genetic resources of another nation to share research, profits, and technology with that nation. Although 153 nations signed the Biodiversity Convention, President Bush publicly refused to join them, claiming that the convention did not adequately protect the patents held by U.S. biotechnology firms.

Soon after he took office, President Bill Clinton announced that he *would* sign the Convention. Clinton, along with Vice President Al Gore, took a number of other steps to move the federal government toward a proactive environmental stance.

Public Safety and Crime in America

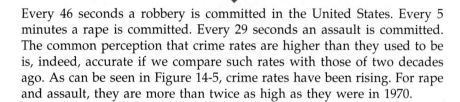

Every 46 seconds a robbery is committed in the United States. Every 5 minutes a rape is committed. Every 29 seconds an assault is committed. The common perception that crime rates are higher than they used to be is, indeed, accurate if we compare such rates with those of two decades ago. As can be seen in Figure 14-5, crime rates have been rising. For rape and assault, they are more than twice as high as they were in 1970.

Crime in American History

In every period in the history of this nation, people have voiced their apprehension about crime. Some criminologists argue that crime was probably as frequent around the time of the American Revolution as it is currently. During the Civil War, mob violence and riots erupted in numerous cities. After the Civil War, people in San Francisco were told that "no decent man is in safety to walk the streets after dark; while at all hours, both night and day, his property is jeopardized by incendiarism and burglary."[4] In 1910, one author stated that "crime, especially in its more violent forms and among the young, is increasing steadily and is threatening to bankrupt the Nation."[5]

From 1900 to the 1930s, social violence and crime increased dramatically. Labor union battles and racial violence were common. Only during the three-decade period from the mid-1930s to the early 1960s did the United States experience, for the first time in its history, stable or slightly declining crime rates.

---

[4]President's Commission on Law Enforcement and Administration of Justice, *Challenge of Crime in a Free Society* (Washington, D.C., 1967), p. 19.
[5]*Ibid.*

FIGURE 14-5 ■ Changes in Violent Crime Rates from 1970 to 1992

Violent crime in the United States rose from 1970 to the beginning of the 1980s. Then crime rates dropped relatively dramatically until about 1986, when they again started to climb. Currently, rape and assault rates are at their highest recorded levels.
SOURCE: U.S. Department of Justice.

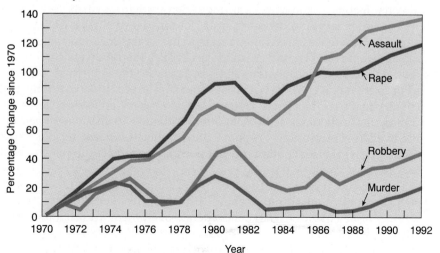

What most Americans are worried about is violent crime. Its rate has been rising relentlessly. Violent crime increased by 5 percent from 1990 to 1991 (after an 11 percent rise in the previous year) and by an estimated 6 percent from 1991 to 1992. The problem may be even worse. Some crime-victim groups estimate that the actual rape totals exceed the Federal Bureau of Investigation's count by over seven times.

Crime Spreads into Mid-Size Cities

Violent crime has started to peak in the major cities of New York and Los Angeles. But violent crimes have had their most significant increase in cities with populations between 100,000 and 500,000. While violent crimes in the 1991 reporting period edged up 2 to 4 percent in the larger cities, they increased by over 8 percent in mid-sized cities. Figure 14-6 shows nine cities in which homicides rose by 50 percent or more in 1991; most are mid-sized cities.

Criminologists argue that the 1990–1992 recession sent young, unemployed males—the group most likely to commit crimes—out from the larger cities to other areas of the country. In addition, gang-related problems seem to have spread from the major cities to the less-populated ones.

The Prison Population Bomb

In 1989, officials in northern California opened a 1,000-bed maximum-security prison at Pelican Bay. A 1,200-bed wing was added soon after, bringing the capacity of the nation's largest state prison system to almost 50,000 inmates. There was one slight problem: By the end of 1989, the California state prison system already had 87,000 people in custody, and 250 were being added every week. The California prison system now routinely operates at almost 200 percent of capacity, with two prisoners packed into one-person cells and prison gyms and dayrooms being used to house inmates for whom there is no cell space. By 1993, an estimated 111,000 criminals were behind bars in the state of California.

The California story is not an anomaly; it is being repeated across the country. The federal prison system was designed to hold 29,000 inmates, but at last count, there were almost 60,000 prisoners crammed into federal jails. The total of state prison populations exceeds 700,000 inmates, up over 100 percent since 1980, and more than 250,000 above the capacity of prisons to hold them. Eighty percent of the states have prison populations at historic highs. Within a few years, *all* states will likely have record numbers of inmates filling their prison systems. At the county and city levels across the country, there are estimated to be 300,000 inmates, far more than those facilities were designed to hold. Overall, there were more than one million Americans in jail at the beginning of the 1990s.

As the number of arrests and incarcerations in the United States increases, so does the cost of building and operating prisons. An additional 1,700 new prison beds are needed each week. The average cost of construction per prison bed ranges from $50,000 at a minimum-security site to $100,000 or more in a maximum-security facility. When operational costs are included and construction costs are amortized over the life of a

A narcotics officer arrests a cocaine dealer in New York. The war against drugs seemed to make little headway during the 1980s and 1990s, although government expenditures on the effort continued to rise.

FIGURE 14-6 ■ Increase in Murders During 1991

In the nine cities listed below, the number of homicides increased by 50 percent or more during 1991. Most of these cities are mid-sized.

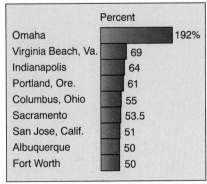

	Percent
Omaha	192%
Virginia Beach, Va.	69
Indianapolis	64
Portland, Ore.	61
Columbus, Ohio	55
Sacramento	53.5
San Jose, Calif.	51
Albuquerque	50
Fort Worth	50

SOURCE: The FBI Uniform Crime Report, 1992.

To help ease overcrowding, inmates at the New York State Prison at Watertown are incarcerated in barrack-style prison blocks.

facility, the cost of sentencing one person to one year in jail averages between $25,000 and $40,000. Thus, the annual nationwide cost of building, maintaining, and operating prisons is about $35 billion today.

The Political Drive for More Punishment

Politically, no man or woman in politics is likely to suffer if he or she argues in favor of stiffer sentences and keeping more criminals behind bars. The Bush administration had a "summit" on punishment policy in May 1992. Attorney General William Barr stated at that meeting, "The choice is clear: More prison space or more crime."

There seems to be no doubt among criminologists that large-scale imprisonment works at a certain level. When it keeps truly violent felons behind bars longer, it prevents them from committing more crimes. The average predatory street criminal commits fifteen or more crimes each year when not behind bars. But most prisoners are in for a relatively short period of time and released on parole early, often because of prison overcrowding. Many find themselves back in prison because they have violated parole, typically by using illicit drugs.

Prisons and Drug Offenders

A major reason why prisons are bursting is the increased enforcement of state and federal drug laws. Between 1984 and 1992, drug arrests increased nearly 75 percent. The number of drug arrests each year totals over one million. Approximately 80 percent of all arrests are for the alleged consumption of illegal drugs. Until about 1988, the majority of arrests were for the possession of marijuana. Cocaine is now more available and cheaper. Consequently, a rising percentage of drug arrests is for the possession of cocaine.

Riots, Public Safety, and Race Relations

In the 1960s, major public-safety problems arose in Detroit, Los Angeles, and other cities. The widespread destruction of the Watts riot in Los Angeles in 1965 stunned the nation. But the summer of 1967—the "long, hot summer"—saw many more riots in the black inner cities of Detroit and elsewhere. According to the federal government's Kerner Commission Report, the root cause of the problem was the existence of two separate and unequal countries in America, one white and one black.

A quarter of a century later, much of the analysis of what caused the riots of the 1960s seemed equally valid in analyzing the causes of Los Angeles's worst riot ever in April 1992. The scene of Los Angeles police beating an African-American motorist, Rodney King, had been videotaped a year earlier by a bystander. A criminal trial ensued. Four police officers were acquitted—by an all-white jury in a courtroom in a predominantly all-white section of Southern California. Within hours of the acquittal, the city's central area erupted into flames. During the course of the riots, more than 50 people died, and 2,116 were injured. A total of 5,273 buildings was damaged by fire and looting. The total damages were in excess of $550 million. Less extensive riots also broke out in Atlanta, Seattle, San Francisco, and Las Vegas.

After the Los Angeles riots, civil rights leaders made race relations a part of the campaign agenda for the 1992 presidential race. African-American Sharon Pratt Kelly, mayor of Washington, D.C., declared publicly that the riots were a result of the Reagan and Bush administrations' failure to face the unmet needs of the African-American community, particularly the needs of African Americans who live in the inner cities. Presidential candidate Bill Clinton said essentially the same thing in numerous speeches. The Bush administration responded initially by claiming that the riots were the result of liberal social programs of the 1960s and 1970s. By May 1992, however, President Bush essentially reversed the administration's earlier claim when he said that this is "no time for name-calling." Bush promised $19 million in federal aid in the form of an anti-crime, anti-poverty grant. Later, he took measures to release current budget restrictions and pledged $300 to $500 million in Small Business Administration loans. He also instituted measures to help low-income persons buy homes and to provide tax breaks for businesses.

Not all African Americans agreed with the prescriptions for government action. Some, including economists Tom Sowell of the Hoover Institution and Walter Williams of George Mason University, believe that the problems of the inner city will not be solved by more government, but rather by less. They argue in favor of changing the incentives facing all of those who live in poverty, not just African Americans. One way is through educational choice. A system of government vouchers would allow all families to send their children to whatever public school they want, public or private. Also, Sowell and Williams point out that the welfare system, as currently constructed, creates a negative incentive for poor people to go to work. One study in California showed, for example, that a person on welfare who decides to go to work and who makes $4,000 ends up no better off. That person loses welfare and other benefits and must also pay Social Security and income taxes.

Conclusion: A Difficult Task

As the four issues discussed in this chapter illustrate, making public policy today is a difficult and exasperating task. Managing the economy is the most important and, possibly, most complex task the government faces. In the case of the environment, the policy problem is not confined to American society, much less to one state or locality. Only through the cooperative efforts of many nations and the development of new technologies can these problems be addressed adequately. The United States spends an increasing amount of money and governmental effort on reducing crime in America, yet the crime rate continues to rise. We also saw that the United States spends more per person on medical care than any other country in the world, yet it has a health-care crisis, with over thirty million Americans lacking any medical insurance at all.

As with most public policy issues, these issues require political decisions that must balance the interests of those affected, deal with the moral choices of human beings, and respect the processes outlined in the Constitution.

GETTING INVOLVED

Working for a Clean Environment

Energy undoubtedly will be among the more important domestic issues in the coming decades. Ultimately, every energy policy involves environmental questions. Not only is this issue central to our everyday lives, but also, it is argued, the fate of the planet may hang in the balance of today's decisions made about energy production and environmental protection. To make things more complicated, these parallel struggles of coping with energy problems and preserving our environment tend to work at cross-purposes. In the pursuit of secure and abundant energy, the interests of clean air, water, and land—as well as people—are sometimes sacrificed.

Over all decisions about nuclear energy hang memories of Three Mile Island, Chernobyl, continuous low-level radiation, the hazards of radioactive waste, and the threat of worldwide proliferation of nuclear weapons. Reliance on oil raises the problem of continuing pollution and of committing the economic well-being of the nation to decisions of other nations. Increasing reliance on coal means encouraging an industry that is hazardous to its workers, as well as increasing the possibility of severe environmental damage through acid rain and global warming.

When objectives clash, difficult political trade-offs must be made. To a large group of environmentalists in this country, the choice is clear. Through citizen action groups, environmentalists have challenged the government on these and other issues. They argue that if we want to improve or even preserve our quality of life, we must stop environmental degradation.

Although these diverse groups work on a host of issues from solar power to mass transit and from wildlife preservation to population control, they are bound by certain commonly held beliefs. Brock Evans describes the traditional goals of the environmental movement:

> We have always sought the highest quality management of public lands for the full spectrum of multiple uses, so that the lands will not be abused but will be passed on to the future intact and not ravaged by short-term exploitation.
> We have always sought special reservations of our finest scenic vistas, our superlative natural and historic wonders, the remnants of once-vast wilderness . . . because they are part of our culture, history, and traditions, too.
> We have always sought the highest degree of protection for our native wildlife in parks, refuges, and wilderness areas, . . . so that future generations as well as our own can enjoy this abundance.[*]

If you feel strongly about these issues and want to get involved, contact the following groups:

Environmental Defense Fund
1616 P St., N.W.
Washington, DC 20036

Environmental Policy Institute
218 D St., S.E.
Washington, DC 20003

Friends of the Earth
537 Seventh St., N.E.
Washington, DC 20003

Greenpeace USA
1611 Connecticut Ave., N.W.
Washington, DC 20009

Izaak Walton League of America
1701 N. Fort Meyer Dr.
Arlington, VA 22209

League of Conservation Voters
320 Fourth St., N.E.
Washington, DC 20002

National Audubon Society
1130 Fifth Ave.
New York, NY 10038

National Parks Conservation Association
1701 Eighteenth St., N.W.
Washington, DC 20009

National Wildlife Federation
1325 Massachusetts Ave., N.W.
Washington, DC 20036

Natural Resources Defense Fund
11350 New York Ave., N.W.
Washington, DC 20005

Sierra Club
730 Polk St.
San Francisco, CA 94109

Wilderness Society
1400 I Street, N.W.
Washington, DC 20005

[*]Brock Evans, "The Environmental Community: Response to the Reagan Administration Program," delivered to the National Symposium on Public Lands and the Reagan Administration, Denver, Colorado, November 19, 1981, and published in *Vital Speeches*, February 1, 1982, p. 231.

CHAPTER SUMMARY

1. The policy-making process is initiated when policy makers become aware—through the media or from their constituents—of a problem that needs to be addressed by the legislature and the president. The process of policy making includes five steps: agenda building, agenda formulation, agenda adoption, agenda implementation, and agenda evaluation. All policy actions necessarily result in both costs and benefits for society. Typically, costs are borne by one group, while benefits are enjoyed by another group.

2. The recent jobless benefits legislation is an example of economic policy making at the national level. The solution to the problem of increased unemployment was not clear-cut. Although increasing unemployment benefits would have been a politically popular decision, the consequent increase in the federal deficit would not have been politically desirable. Partisan politics also made decision making difficult, but the jobless benefits bill was finally signed into law on November 20, 1991. The cost of the legislation, which may exceed $8 billion, will be paid by the American taxpayer. The beneficiaries of the legislation were those without jobs and without immediate prospects for jobs.

3. In the area of taxes and subsidies (negative taxes), policy makers have long had to contend with what is known as the action–reaction syndrome. For every action on the part of the government, there will be a reaction on the part of the public, to which the government will react with another action, to which the public will again react, and so on. In regard to taxes, as a general rule, individuals and corporations that pay the highest tax rates will react to those rates by pressuring Congress into creating exceptions and tax loopholes (loopholes allow high-income earners to reduce their taxable incomes). This action on the part of Congress results in a reaction from another interest group—consisting of those who want the rich to pay more taxes.

4. Fiscal policy is the use of changes in government expenditures and taxes to alter national economic variables, such as the rate of inflation or unemployment. Monetary policy is defined as changes in the amount of money in circulation so as to affect interest rates, credit markets, the rate of inflation, and employment. The problem with fiscal policy and monetary policy is the lag between the time a problem occurs in the economy and when policy changes are actually felt in the economy.

5. Whenever the federal government spends more than it receives, it runs a deficit. The deficit is met by United States Treasury borrowing. This adds to the public debt of the federal government. Although the public debt has grown dramatically, when corrected for increases in population and inflation, it fell from the end of World War II to the middle of the 1970s. Since then, it has increased almost to its previous level at the height of World War II.

6. One congressional option for balancing the federal budget is passing a constitutional amendment. Such an amendment would require that whenever the federal government runs a deficit, Congress and the president would have to eliminate it by either lowering spending or raising taxes. Perhaps as an alternative to a constitutional amendment, Congress passed the Gramm–Rudman–Hollings Act in 1985. Its goal was to force the federal government to balance its budget by fiscal year 1991. A revised plan called for a balanced budget by 1993. Yet a second revision in 1990 placed spending limits in specifically targeted areas but gave the president flexibility to adjust these limits.

7. Those who oppose large increases in government spending argue that one effect of the federal deficit is the crowding out of private investment. The more government spending crowds out private investment, they argue, the poorer our children and grandchildren will be because we will have invested less today in the equipment and research and development necessary to a thriving economy in the future.

8. Health-care spending per person in the United States, which is 14 percent of the total annual income generated by our economy, has risen dramatically in recent years and is higher than in any other country. One of the reasons for the rising cost of medical services is that the U.S. population is aging, and elderly persons are the top users of health-care services. Increased reliance on the use of costly, high-tech medical equipment has also contributed significantly to rising health-care costs. Third-party financing, which acts as a disincentive for both patients and health-care providers to minimize costs, is regarded by many as a leading cause of skyrocketing health-care costs in this country.

9. Pollution problems continue to plague the United States and the world. Since the nineteenth century, at least fifteen significant federal acts have been passed. The National Environmental Policy Act of 1969 established the Council for Environmental Quality. That act also mandated that environmental impact statements be prepared for all legislation or major federal actions that significantly affect the quality of the environment.

10. The Clean Air Act of 1990 requires automobile manufacturers to cut new automobiles' exhaust emissions of nitrogen oxide by 60 percent and the emission of other pollutants by 35 percent by 1998. Controls on factories and other stationary sources of air pollution are intended to reduce ground-level ozone pollution in ninety-six cities to healthful levels by the year 2005 (2010 for Los Angeles). The act also requires that the production of chlorofluorocarbons (CFCs) be stopped completely by the year 2002. The act sets limits on the amount of sulfur dioxide that can be emitted by a company each year. A company that emits less than the allowed amount can sell or trade the unused portion of the allowance.

11. Although in the 1970s the threat of a new ice age seemed to be most in the news, by the 1990s the threat of global warming had taken over. The U.S. government's response has been to participate in several international conferences and to

agree to limit the use of CFCs in widely used products, such as aerosol sprays and refrigeration units, and to require special disposal and handling of equipment containing ozone-reducing chemicals that might leak into the atmosphere.

12. A major step toward international collaboration on environmental issues affecting the planet was a United Nations Conference on Environment and Development held in June 1992 in Rio de Janeiro, Brazil. By the conclusion of the conference, the majority of the member nations had formed two legally binding treaties and had reached a consensus on three statements of principles on environmental protection and economic development. One of the treaties (the Biodiversity Convention) requires that specific measures be taken to preserve endangered species; the other (the Global Warming Convention) recommends reductions in the emissions of carbon dioxide, methane, and other "greenhouse" gases that scientists feel are responsible for trapping the sun's heat close to the earth.

13. American citizens are becoming increasingly alarmed over the rise in violent crime in the United States. Rape and assault rates are now at their highest recorded levels, and mid-sized cities are increasingly witnessing gang-related problems and high crime rates. Drug dealing and drug abusers have contributed significantly, not only to escalating crime rates, but also to overcrowded prisons. The prison "population bomb" presents a major challenge to today's policy makers. The riots in Detroit, Los Angeles, and other cities in the 1960s and, more recently, the Los Angeles rebellion of April 1992 have indicated that there are two countries in America, one for whites and one for blacks. While these riots have caused policy makers to place race relations on the political agenda, some observers believe that the problems of the inner city will not be solved by more government but rather by less. According to these observers, the problem is not so much race relations as it is poverty and the lack of equal opportunities generally.

QUESTIONS FOR REVIEW AND DISCUSSION

▼

1. Does the manner in which the federal government obtains its spending power from the private sector to finance its activities matter to you? That is, do you as an individual care whether the federal government taxes you for the full amount of its expenditures every year or runs a deficit?

2. How can Congress pass a law requiring it to balance the federal budget and not comply with its own legislation?

3. What do you think should be done to solve the health-care crisis in this country?

4. In this chapter, you learned that more federal funds are devoted to research on AIDS than to breast cancer or heart disease, both of which are associated with significantly higher death rates. Nonetheless, many groups still maintain that the federal government is doing too little, too late in regard to AIDS research. What are the arguments in support of this view? What are the arguments against it?

5. How would you argue on behalf of global regulation of environmental policy? How would you argue against global regulation?

SELECTED REFERENCES

▼

Robert L. Bartley, *The Seven Fat Years and How to Do It Again* (New York: The Free Press, 1992). The author, the editor of the *Wall Street Journal*, tells how he and the band of "supply-side" economics advocates helped shape the Reagan economic agenda, which, Bartley argues, was successful in bringing about growth, low interest rates, and low inflation.

Daniel K. Benjamin and Roger LeRoy Miller, *Undoing Drugs: Beyond Legalization* (New York: Basic Books, Inc., 1991). A complete analysis of America's past and present drug policies; plus a new solution—the "constitutional alternative"—to the drug problem.

Robert H. Blank and Andrea L. Bonnicksen, eds., *Emerging Issues in Biomedical Policy*, Vol. 1: *Setting Allocation Priorities: Genetic and Reproductive Technologies* (Irvington, N.Y.: Columbia University Press, 1992). This collection of essays, which focuses on the social implications of recent techno-

logical developments in medicine, touches on a number of policy issues relating to health care.

Forest Chisman and Alan Pifer, *Government for the People— The Federal Social Role* (New York: W. W. Norton, 1988). This book analyzes what the appropriate role of the federal government is in providing social welfare in America.

Robert Crandal et al., eds., *Regulating the Automobile* (Washington, D.C.: Brookings Institution, 1986). The automobile is a source of both pleasure and pollution. The authors of the various papers in this volume examine the facts and fictions relating to the air pollution caused by automobiles.

Matthew A. Crenson, *The Un-Politics of Air Pollution* (Baltimore, Md.: Johns Hopkins University Press, 1971). This twenty-two-year-old treatise on air pollution still presents some insights into the problem and the politics surrounding it.

Benjamin Friedman, *Day of Reckoning: The Consequences of*

American Economic Policy (New York: Random House, 1990). An interesting analysis of the impact of Reaganomics on the American economy and suggestions for new economic policies in the post-Reagan era that will repair the damage the author feels was done during that period.

Milton Friedman and Walter Heller, *Monetary versus Fiscal Policy* (New York: Norton, 1969). A classic presentation of the pros and cons of monetary and fiscal policy given by a noninterventionist (Friedman) and an advocate of federal government intervention in the economy (Heller).

William Greider, *Secrets of the Temple: How the Federal Reserve Runs the Country* (New York: Simon & Schuster, 1987). An insider's view of how our nation's monetary authority, the Fed, actually conducts its policy-making business. Readable and fascinating.

Donald L. Guertin et al., eds., *U.S. Energy Imperatives for the 1990s: Leadership, Efficiency, Environmental Responsibility, and Sustained Economic Growth* (Lanham, Md.: University Press of America, 1992). This book, which contains policy recommendations by some fifty experts on the need for an effective and responsible energy policy, also emphasizes the crucial leadership role that must be played by the United States in working toward environmentally sound economic development.

Andrew Hurrell and Benedict Kingsbury, eds., *The International Politics of the Environment: Actors, Interests, and Institutions* (New York: Oxford University Press, 1992). The contributors to this collection of essays discuss the most pressing environmental issues—including air and water pollution, ozone depletion and global warming, and deforestation—and explore the prospects for global environmental management through international political cooperation.

Robert A. Leone, *Who Profits: Winners, Losers, and Government Regulation* (New York: Basic Books, 1986). The author analyzes the question of who obtains the benefits and who pays the costs of different types of government regulation, including environmental regulation.

Denise E. Markovich and Ronald E. Pynn, *American Political Economy: Using Economics with Politics* (New York: Brooks/Cole, 1988). An integrated overview of how political decision making affects economics and how economic conditions help shape politics.

Roger LeRoy Miller and Daniel K. Benjamin, *The Economics of Macro Issues*, 7th ed. (St. Paul, Minn.: West Publishing Co., 1992). This short paperback consists of twenty-nine topical chapters examining the major issues facing economic policy makers today. Lively, up to date, and easily understood.

Kevin Phillips, *The Politics of Rich and Poor: Wealth and the American Electorate* (New York: Random House, 1990). The author, a well-known student of election politics, analyzes the changing distribution of income and wealth in the United States, primarily as a result of Reagan administration policies that favored the rich. Phillips predicts that populist, liberal policies favoring the middle- and lower-income groups will become a major political force in the 1990s.

The President's Council of Economic Advisers, *Economic Report of the President* (Washington, D.C.: Government Printing Office, published annually). This volume contains a wealth of details concerning current monetary and fiscal policy and what is happening to the economy.

Robert B. Reich, *The Work of Nations: Preparing Ourselves for 21st Century Capitalism* (New York: Random House, 1992). This much-talked-about book offers an analysis of the trends leading to greater globalization, a reduced significance of the nation–state, advances and prosperity for the well prepared and well trained, and alienation and poverty for Americans who fall behind.

Alice Rivlin, *Reviving the American Dream* (Washington, D.C.: The Brookings Institution, 1992). The author, a former director of the Congressional Budget Office and a noted theorist and practitioner of public policy analysis, suggests that undoing the New Deal and returning most domestic government functions to the states would reduce the federal deficit and stimulate private investment in the economy. A crucial aspect of the plan involves the allocation of "common shared taxes" among the states on the basis of population.

Isaac Turiel, *Indoor Air Quality and Human Health* (Stanford, Calif.: Stanford University Press, 1985). Most analysis of air pollution focuses on air outside of the home. This author looks at air inside the home.

CHAPTER 15
Foreign and Defense Policy

CHAPTER CONTENTS

WHAT IF . . . THE UNITED NATIONS ENFORCED HUMAN RIGHTS THROUGHOUT THE WORLD?

The goal of the United Nations (U.N.) is to engage the cooperative efforts of many nations to make the world a better place by reducing the threat of war, improving human conditions, and encouraging multilateral efforts to solve problems. Until recently, the effectiveness of the United Nations at maintaining world peace was limited by the conflict between the two superpowers, the United States and the Soviet Union. Thus, the United States and the Soviet Union carried on the Cold War, engaged each other through surrogates in Vietnam, Central America, and the Middle East, and continued the nuclear arms race. Such actions produced a stalemate in the United Nations. With the end of the Cold War and the breakup of the Soviet Union, however, cooperation under U.N. auspices has achieved conflict resolution in several parts of the world.

Early in the history of the United Nations, the General Assembly passed the Universal Declaration of Human Rights, outlining the fundamental rights of all people on earth. Not all nations, including the United States, have signed the declaration, but it remains a U.N. goal. What if, in this new world of cooperation among former Cold War enemies, the United Nations turned its attention from peacekeeping to enforcing human rights throughout the world?

First, some agency or commission of the United Nations would have to be empowered either to survey the worldwide situation or, more likely, to receive complaints from aggrieved individuals or groups. Once the investigating body was set up and processes agreed to, the United

Nations would be in the human rights business.

Next, priorities would have to be established. The Universal Declaration of Human Rights begins with the basic rights of survival—the need for food, shelter, and safety from violence. Would these basic rights be the first priority for the United Nations? If so, then the starvation of millions in various countries around the world would be the first problem to be confronted. But starvation problems are not always simply problems of scarcity. Sometimes, they are essentially political in nature. Groups in control may try to starve out rebel or opposing groups and resist U.N. intervention. Although the United Nations did intervene in Somalia in 1992, such interventions are attended by political risks. Because of these risks, it may not be possible to obtain widespread support for intervention to assist the starving victims of political struggles in other nations in the future.

Another set of widely agreed-on rights includes freedom of speech, political freedoms (including the right to vote), and freedom of assembly. Would the United Nations be willing, for example, to use force or severe economic sanctions to motivate South Africa to give a greater degree of political freedom to its black citizens? This would be internal intervention, of course, but wouldn't it be justified? Would the United Nations attempt to restore Haiti's democratically elected leader to power? Would the United Nations take on the destiny of the Kurds in Iraq? The gypsies in Eastern Europe? The Palestinians in Israel? The Native Americans in the United States?

Each of these situations involves not only the basic human rights of groups but also internal political problems. Although the United Nations advocates democracy and individual freedom, it has rarely been willing to engage in what might be defined as domestic political issues. Indeed, a nation's internal politics has traditionally been off-limits to direct intervention.

Finally, who would organize and pay for investigations concerning human rights? Which nations would be willing to send investigators or some type of armed police or even military forces to enforce human rights? To date, assembling and paying for peace-keeping operations has been difficult. In 1991 alone, almost $500 million was required for peacekeeping actions in ten regions. It is estimated that peacekeeping operations in Cambodia will cost almost $2 billion in 1992–1993. Not only is money being spent, but also many nations are contributing troops to support these efforts. How many nations would be willing to send troops into military conflicts to preserve human rights in a far-away land? It seems more likely that U.N. authority on these issues will remain mainly moral.

---

1. *Would Americans be willing to send troops to enforce human rights in another country?*
2. *Why would some nations be unwilling to consider human rights violations in other countries?*
3. *Should certain human rights take priority over political considerations?*

If Americans did not have so much faith in what they see on television, they might have thought that the world had turned upside-down in the early 1990s. The Berlin Wall had fallen, and the two Germanies were reunited. The Eastern European countries ousted their communist governments, wrote new constitutions, and held free elections. Lithuania, Latvia, and Estonia declared their independence from the Soviet Union. And, perhaps most astonishing, the Soviet Union ceased to exist, with most of the former Soviet republics becoming either independent states or joining a new Commonwealth of Independent States. As the world watched by satellite-transmitted video, a group opposed to the rapid economic and political disintegration of the Soviet Union attempted to stop these developments, and Boris Yeltsin, the Russian president, defied them. The plotters were arrested, and Yeltsin replaced Gorbachev as the leading Russian statesman. In 1993, Yeltsin forced the Russian parliament to allow a referendum on his reforms. He won a majority vote.

During the same period, Nelson Mandela was freed and began negotiating with the South African government for rights for black South Africans. Sandinistas and *contras* agreed to free elections in Nicaragua, and a woman, Violetta Chamorro, was elected to the presidency in that country. Iraq invaded Kuwait and threatened Saudi Arabia. The United States formed a coalition military force with the Saudis and many European and Arab states and, after a military buildup of more than a half million troops, drove Iraqi forces out of Kuwait in a six-week war.

Five years ago, such events were not even imaginable. No wonder that the United States did not have a plan for the breakup of the Soviet Union. No other nation had considered it either. The United States played multiple roles as these surprising events unfolded. In the Persian Gulf, the United States insisted on military action to curb the Iraqi dictator, Saddam Hussein. In Somalia, the United States mounted a military humanitarian effort. With regard to the Soviet Union and the former satellite states, the United States has watched events unfold, attempting to support anti-communist movements but without official intervention. The United States has worked with the former Soviet republics to continue arms-control negotiations and has been building a coalition to give economic assistance to Russia.

Changes have swept the world. Many of these changes have serious consequences for the United States in terms of its national security and its economic strength. Whatever the future brings, foreign and national security policy will continue to be a priority for the nation and its leaders.

What Is Foreign Policy?

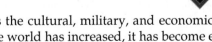

As the cultural, military, and economic interdependence of the nations of the world has increased, it has become even more important for the United States to establish and carry out foreign policies to deal with external situations and to carry out its own national goals. By **foreign policy,** we mean both the goals the government wants to achieve in the world and the techniques and strategies to achieve them. For example, if one national goal is to achieve stability in Eastern Europe and to encourage the formation of pro-American governments there, U.S. foreign policy in that area may be carried out with the techniques of **diplomacy, economic aid,**

FOREIGN POLICY
A nation's external goals and the techniques and strategies used to achieve them.

DIPLOMACY
The total process by which states carry on political relations with each other; settling conflicts among nations by peaceful means.

ECONOMIC AID
Assistance to other nations in the form of grants, loans, or credits to buy American products.

TECHNICAL ASSISTANCE
Sending experts with technical skills in agriculture, engineering, or business to aid other nations.

FOREIGN POLICY PROCESS
The steps by which external goals are decided and acted on.

NATIONAL SECURITY POLICY
Foreign and domestic policy designed to protect the independence and political and economic integrity of the United States; policy that is concerned with the safety and defense of the nation.

NATIONAL SECURITY COUNCIL (NSC)
A board created by the 1947 National Security Act to advise the president on matters of national security.

technical assistance, or military intervention. Sometimes foreign policies are restricted to statements of goals or ideas, such as helping to end world poverty, whereas at other times foreign policies are comprehensive efforts to achieve particular objectives.

United States foreign policy is established through the **foreign policy process,** which usually originates with the president and those agencies that provide advice on foreign policy matters. Foreign policy formulation is often affected by congressional action and national public debate.

National Security Policy

As one aspect of overall foreign policy, **national security policy** is designed primarily to protect the independence and the political integrity of the United States. It concerns itself with the defense of the United States against actual or potential (real or imagined) enemies, domestic or foreign.

U.S. national security policy is based on determinations made by the Department of Defense, the Department of State, and a number of other federal agencies, including the **National Security Council (NSC).** The NSC acts as an advisory body to the president, but it has increasingly become a rival to the State Department in influencing the foreign policy process. This was particularly evident when it was revealed, in November 1986, that the Reagan administration had largely by-passed the Department of State (and Congress) in using the NSC to direct sales of U.S. military equipment to Iran.

Diplomacy

Diplomacy is another aspect of foreign policy but is not coterminous with it. Diplomacy includes all of a nation's external relationships, from routine diplomatic communications to summit meetings among heads of state. More specifically, diplomacy refers to the settling of disputes and conflicts among nations by peaceful methods. Diplomacy is the set of negotiating techniques by which a nation attempts to carry out its foreign policy.

Diplomacy may or may not be successful, depending on the willingness of the parties to negotiate. After years of fruitless disarmament talks, the United States and the Soviet Union moved swiftly to agreement on the Intermediate Range Nuclear Force (INF) Treaty to limit and destroy certain weapons. In contrast, efforts to negotiate a solution to the Palestinian–Israeli conflict have proved so far to be unsuccessful.

Morality versus Reality in Foreign Policy

From the earliest years of the republic, Americans have felt that their nation had a special destiny. The American experiment in democratic government and capitalism, it was thought, would provide the best possible life for men and women and be a model for other nations. As the United States assumed greater status as a power in world politics, Americans came to believe that the nation's actions on the world stage should be guided by American political and moral principles. As Harry Truman stated the premise, "The United States should take the lead in running the world in the way that it ought to be run."

This view of America's mission has led to the adoption of many foreign policy initiatives that are rooted in **moral idealism,** a philosophy that sees the world as fundamentally benign and other nations as willing to cooperate for the good of all.[1] In this perspective, nations should come together and agree to keep the peace, as President Woodrow Wilson proposed for the League of Nations. Nations should see the wrong in violating the human rights of ethnic or religious minorities and should work to end such injustice. Many of the foreign policy initiatives taken by the United States have been based on this idealistic view of the world, but few of these actions have been very successful. The Peace Corps, however, which was created by John Kennedy in 1961, is one example of an effort to spread American goodwill and technology that has achieved some of its goals. In contrast, efforts to influence events in Vietnam, Nicaragua, and El Salvador have been less successful. President Jimmy Carter tried to make human rights the most important priority in his foreign policy, but he failed. Foreign policy based on moral imperatives is often unsuccessful because it assumes that other nations agree with American views of morality and politics.

In opposition to the moral perspective is what we might call **political realism.** Realists see the world as a dangerous place in which each nation strives for its own survival and interests. Foreign policy decisions must be based on a cold calculation of what is best for the United States without regard for morality. Realists believe that the United States must be prepared militarily to defend itself because all other nations are, by definition, out to improve their own situation. A strong defense will show the world that the United States is willing to protect its interests. The practice of political realism in foreign policy allows the United States to sell weapons to military dictators who will support its policies, to support American

MORAL IDEALISM
A philosophy that sees all nations as willing to cooperate and agree on moral standards for conduct.

POLITICAL REALISM
A philosophy that sees each nation acting principally in its own interest.

---

[1]Charles W. Kegley, Jr., and Eugene Wittkopf, *American Foreign Policy, Pattern and Process,* 3d ed. (New York: St. Martin's Press, 1987), p. 73.

The Peace Corps, a program born from moral idealism, has achieved some of its goals for spreading American goodwill. Here a Peace Corps volunteer helps with an irrigation system in Ecuador.

Did You Know . . . That American troops occupied Haiti from 1915 to 1934?

business around the globe, and to repel terrorism through the use of force. Political realism, for example, leads to a policy of never negotiating with terrorists who take hostages, because such negotiations simply will lead to the taking of more hostages.

It is important to note that the United States has never been guided by only one of these principles. Instead, both moral idealism and political realism undergird foreign policy decisions. President George Bush faced this tension when the Soviet republic of Lithuania declared its independence in 1990. Although the United States supported Lithuania's claim on moral grounds, carefully stating that the United States had never recognized the Soviet annexation of Lithuania in 1940, realism demanded that Bush not intervene overtly in the affairs of the Soviet Union.

Who Makes Foreign Policy?

Is foreign policy made by the president, by the Congress, or by joint executive and congressional action? There is no easy answer to this question because, as constitutional authority Edwin S. Corwin once observed, the Constitution created an "invitation to struggle" between the president and Congress for control over the foreign policy process. Let us look first at powers given to the president by the Constitution.

Constitutional Powers of the President

President Franklin D. Roosevelt signs the declaration of war against Japan on December 8, 1941.

The Constitution confers on the president broad powers that are either explicit or implied in key constitutional provisions. Article II vests the executive power of the government in the president. The presidential oath of office given in Article II, Section 1, requires that the president must "solemnly swear" to "preserve, protect and defend the Constitution of the United States."

In addition, and perhaps more important, Article II, Section 2, designates the president as "Commander in Chief of the Army and Navy of the United States." Starting with Abraham Lincoln, all presidents have interpreted this authority dynamically and broadly. Indeed, since the Washington administration, the United States has been involved in at least 125 undeclared wars that were conducted under presidential authority. In 1846, President Polk provoked Mexico into a war. Theodore Roosevelt sent the navy on a cruise around the world (presumably to impress Japan with the nation's naval power). Before entering World War II, Franklin Roosevelt ordered the navy to "shoot on sight" German submarines that appeared in the Western Hemisphere security zone. Harry Truman personally made the decision to drop atomic bombs on Japan. It was also Truman who ordered American armed forces in the Pacific to enter into North Korea's conflict with South Korea. Eisenhower threatened China and North Korea with nuclear weapons if the Korean peace talks were not successfully concluded. From Eisenhower through Nixon, chief executives increasingly involved the United States in a war in Vietnam.

Article II, Section 2, of the Constitution also gives the president the power to make treaties, provided that two-thirds of the senators present concur. Presidents usually have been successful in getting treaties through the Senate. In addition to these formal treaty-making powers, the president makes use of **executive agreements** (discussed in Chapter 11). Since the Second World War, executive agreements have accounted for almost 95 percent of the understandings reached between the United States and other nations.

Executive agreements have a long and significant history. Franklin Roosevelt made his destroyer-base deal with Great Britain in 1940 by executive agreement. More significant in their long-term effects were the several agreements he reached with the U.S.S.R. and other countries, especially at Yalta and Potsdam, during the Second World War. The government of South Vietnam and the government of the United States, particularly under Eisenhower, Kennedy, and Johnson, made a series of executive agreements in which the United States promised support. All in all, between 1946 and 1993, over eight thousand executive agreements with foreign countries were made. There is no way to get an accurate count because perhaps several hundred of these agreements have been secret.

An additional power conferred on the president in Article II, Section 2, is the right to appoint ambassadors, other public ministers, and consuls. In Section 3 of that article, the president is given the power to recognize foreign governments through receiving their ambassadors.

EXECUTIVE AGREEMENT
A binding international obligation made between chiefs of state without legislative sanction.

Informal Techniques of Presidential Leadership

Other broad sources of presidential power in the American foreign policy process are tradition, precedent, and the president's personality. The president can employ a host of informal techniques that give the White House overwhelming superiority within the government in foreign policy leadership.

First, the president has access to information. More information is available to the president from the Central Intelligence Agency (CIA), the State Department, and the Defense Department than to any other governmental authority. This information carries with it the ability to make quick decisions—and that ability is used often.

Second, the president is a legislative leader who can influence the amount of funds that are allocated for different programs. For example, presidents can try, as both Carter and Reagan did, to increase defense spending and decrease nondefense spending.

Third, the president can influence public opinion. President Theodore Roosevelt once made the following statement:

> People used to say to me that I was an astonishingly good politician and divined what the people are going to think. . . . I did not "divine" how the people were going to think; I simply made up my mind what they ought to think and then did my best to get them to think it.[2]

Presidents are without equal in this regard, partly because of their ability to command the media. Depending on their skill in appealing to patriotic sentiment (and sometimes fear), they can make people think that their course in foreign affairs is right and necessary. Public opinion often seems

---

[2]Sidney Warren, *The President as World Leader* (New York: McGraw-Hill, 1964), p. 23.

Did You Know ... That including the Civil War, more than one million American soldiers have been killed in the nation's wars?

to be impressed by the president's decision to make a national commitment abroad. Presidents normally, although certainly not always, receive the immediate support of the American people when reacting to (or creating) a foreign policy crisis.

George Bush used his leadership resources on foreign policy issues to (temporarily) bolster his own popularity. By explaining the December 20, 1989, invasion of Panama as an effort to capture the leader of Panama and alleged drug dealer, Manuel Noriega, he garnered wide approval. Little more than a year later, Bush's approval ratings soared during and immediately after the Persian Gulf war (see Chapter 6).

Finally, the president can commit the nation morally to a course of action in foreign affairs. Because the president is the head of state and the leader of one of the most powerful nations on earth, once the president has made a commitment for the United States, it is difficult for Congress or anyone else to back down on that commitment.

Sources of Foreign Policy Making within the Executive Branch

There are at least four foreign policy making sources within the executive branch, in addition to the president. These are (1) the Department of State, (2) the National Security Council, (3) the intelligence community and informational programs, and (4) the Department of Defense.

The Department of State.   In principle, the State Department is the executive agency that is most directly concerned with foreign affairs. It supervises U.S. relations with the nearly two hundred independent nations around the world and with the United Nations and other multinational groups, such as the Organization of American States. It staffs embassies and consulates throughout the world. It has about 25,000 employees. This may sound impressive, but it is small compared with, say, the Department of Health and Human Services with its more than 126,000 employees. Also, the State Department had an annual operating budget of only $4.5 billion in fiscal year 1992—the smallest budget of the cabinet-level departments.

Newly elected presidents usually tell the American public that the new secretary of state is the nation's chief foreign policy adviser. Nonetheless, the State Department's preeminence in foreign policy has declined rather dramatically since World War II. The State Department's image within the White House Executive Office and Congress (and even other governments) is quite poor—a slow, plodding, bureaucratic maze of inefficient, indecisive individuals. In any event, since the days of Franklin Roosevelt, the State Department has been bypassed and often ignored when crucial decisions are made.

It is not surprising that the State Department has been overshadowed in foreign policy. It has no natural domestic constituency as does, for example, the Department of Defense, which can call on defense contractors for support. Instead, the State Department has what might be called **negative constituents**—U.S. citizens who openly oppose American foreign policy. Also, within Congress, the State Department is often looked on as an advocate of unpopular, costly foreign involvement. It is often called "the Department of Bad News."

NEGATIVE CONSTITUENTS
U.S. citizens who openly oppose government foreign policies.

The National Security Council. The job of the National Security Council (NSC), created by the National Security Act of 1947, is to advise the president on the integration of "domestic, foreign, and military policies relating to the national security." Its larger purpose is to provide policy continuity from one administration to the next. As it has turned out, the NSC—consisting of the president, the vice president, the secretaries of state and defense, the director of emergency planning, and often the chairperson of the joint chiefs of staff and the director of the CIA—is used in just about any way the president wants to use it. Eisenhower made frequent use of the NSC. Kennedy convened it infrequently and on an informal basis. During the Reagan administration, the NSC played a central role in funneling private aid to the *contra* forces in Central America and in arranging the arms deal with Iran, although the agency is not supposed to play an operational role in foreign policy.

The role of national security adviser to the president seems to fit the wearer. Some advisers have come into conflict with heads of the State Department. Henry A. Kissinger, Nixon's flamboyant and aggressive national security adviser, rapidly gained ascendancy over William Rogers, the secretary of state, in foreign policy. When Carter became president, he appointed as national security adviser Zbigniew Brzezinski, who openly competed with Secretary of State Cyrus Vance (who apparently had little power). In contrast, Bush's close friendship with James Baker, his first secretary of state, appeared to put the cabinet officer clearly in charge of foreign policy. President Bill Clinton placed his confidence in his Secretary of State, Warren Christopher.

The Intelligence Community. No discussion of foreign policy would be complete without some mention of what is generally known as the **intelligence community.** This consists of the forty or more government agencies or bureaus that are involved in intelligence activities, informational and otherwise. On January 24, 1978, President Carter issued Executive Order 12036 in which he formally defined the official major members of the intelligence community. They are as follows:

1. Central Intelligence Agency (CIA).
2. National Security Agency (NSA).
3. Defense Intelligence Agency (DIA).
4. Offices within the Department of Defense.
5. Bureau of Intelligence and Research in the Department of State.
6. Federal Bureau of Investigation (FBI).
7. Army intelligence.
8. Air Force intelligence.
9. Department of the Treasury.
10. Drug Enforcement Administration (DEA).
11. Department of Energy.

The CIA was created as part of the National Security Act of 1947. The National Security Agency and the Defense Intelligence Agency were created by executive order. Until recently, Congress voted billions of dollars for intelligence activities with little knowledge of how the funds were being used. On some occasions, the intelligence activities of the CIA have attracted public attention. In 1960, an American U-2 spy plane was shot

INTELLIGENCE COMMUNITY
The government agencies involved in gathering information about the capabilities and intentions of foreign governments and that engages in covert activities to further American foreign policy aims.

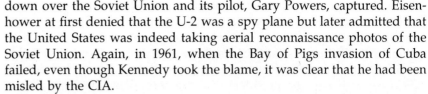

down over the Soviet Union and its pilot, Gary Powers, captured. Eisenhower at first denied that the U-2 was a spy plane but later admitted that the United States was indeed taking aerial reconnaissance photos of the Soviet Union. Again, in 1961, when the Bay of Pigs invasion of Cuba failed, even though Kennedy took the blame, it was clear that he had been misled by the CIA.

Intelligence activities consist mostly of overt information gathering, but covert actions are also undertaken. Covert actions, as the name implies, are done secretly, and rarely does the American public find out about them. In the late 1940s and early 1950s, the CIA covertly subsidized anticommunist labor unions in Western Europe. The CIA covertly aided in the overthrow of the Mossadegh regime in Iran, which allowed the restoration of the shah in 1953. The CIA helped to overthrow the Arbenz government of Guatemala in 1954 and was instrumental in destabilizing the Allende government in Chile from 1970 to 1973.

During the mid-1970s, the "dark side" of the CIA was at least partly uncovered when the Senate undertook an investigation of its activities. One of the major findings of the Senate Select Committee on Intelligence was that the CIA had routinely spied on American citizens domestically— a strictly prohibited activity. Consequently, the CIA came under the scrutiny of six, and later eight, oversight committees within Congress, which restricted the scope of its activity. By 1980, however, the CIA had regained much of its lost power to engage in covert activities. In the early 1990s, as the relationship with the Soviet Union eased, the attention of the CIA and other agencies began to turn from military to economic intelligence. The disintegration of the Soviet Union in 1991 led the director of the CIA, Robert Gates, to seek a new direction for the agency.

In addition to intelligence activities, U.S. foreign policy also makes use of propaganda and information programs. The United States Information Agency (which for a while was called the United States International Communication Agency) is part of an attempt to spread information and propaganda throughout the world on behalf of the American government. One of its major efforts is the Voice of America, a worldwide radio network that broadcasts news and information from an American point of view. Under the Reagan administration, this activity was expanded. In 1983, Congress passed a bill authorizing Radio Marti to transmit specifically to Cuba. A television version (TV Marti) was approved later.

The Department of Defense.   The Department of Defense (DOD) was created in 1947 to bring all of the various activities of the American military establishment under the jurisdiction of a single department headed by a civilian secretary of defense. At the same time, the joint chiefs of staff, consisting of the commanders of each of the military branches and a chairman, was created to formulate a unified military strategy. The DOD is huge. It has more than one million civilian employees and more than two million military personnel. It has an annual budget that in fiscal year 1992 was over $311 billion. Because much of this budget is spent on contracts with civilian firms, it is not surprising that a somewhat symbiotic relationship has developed between civilian defense contractors and the DOD.

Because the Pentagon is unlikely to want to see its power diminished, the Department of Defense responds to the president's foreign policy in-

The Pentagon—a five-story, five-sided building—has become the symbol of the Department of Defense. It has six million square feet of floor space, and over seventeen miles of corridors.

itiatives and world events in light of its own goals. As the Cold War faded from public attention, the Pentagon proposed a decade-long series of military budget cuts. Congress often does not agree with the Pentagon's plans, however, particularly if the plans call for closing a military base in a powerful legislator's state or district. Also, the branches of the military often differ in their points of view, thus weakening the department's political influence.

Limiting the President's Power

One of the major outcomes of the Vietnam war was a new interest in the balance of power between Congress and the president on foreign policy questions. Sensitive to public frustration over the long and costly war and angry at Richard Nixon for some of his other actions as president, Congress attempted to establish some limits on the power of the president in setting foreign and defense policy. In 1973, Congress passed the War Powers Act over President Nixon's veto. The act limited the president's use of troops in military action without congressional approval (see Chapter 11). Most presidents, however, have not interpreted the "consultation" provisions of the act as meaning that Congress should be consulted before military action is taken. Instead, Ford, Carter, Reagan, and Bush ordered troop movements and then informed congressional leaders. Critics note that it is quite possible for a president to commit troops to a situation from which the nation could not withdraw without incurring heavy losses, whether or not Congress is consulted.

In recent years, Congress has also exerted its authority to limit or deny the president's requests for military assistance to Angolan rebels and to the government of El Salvador; for new weapons, such as the B-1 bomber; and for weapons sales through a legislative veto over sales greater than $50 million (although recent court decisions have left the veto technique in doubt). In general, Congress has been far more cautious in supporting the president in situations where military involvement of American troops is possible.

At times, Congress can take the initiative in foreign policy. In 1986, Congress initiated and passed a bill instituting economic sanctions against South Africa to pressure that nation into ending apartheid. President Reagan vetoed the bill, but the veto was overridden by large majorities in both the House and the Senate.

Domestic Sources of Foreign Policy

The making of foreign policy is often viewed as a presidential prerogative because of the president's constitutional power in that area and the resources of the executive branch that the president controls. Foreign policy making is also influenced by a number of other sources, however, including elite and mass opinion, the military–industrial complex, and U.S. multinational business enterprises.

Elite and Mass Opinion

Public opinion influences the making of U.S. foreign policy through a number of channels. Elites in American business, education, communication, labor, and religion try to influence presidential decision making through several strategies. Some individuals, such as former secretary of state Henry Kissinger and former president Richard Nixon, have a longstanding interest in foreign policy and have been active in government service. They may be asked to advise the president privately. Several elite organizations, such as the Council on Foreign Relations and the Trilateral Commission, work to increase international cooperation and to influence foreign policy through conferences, publications, and research.

The members of the American elite establishment also exert influence on foreign policy through the general public by encouraging debate over foreign policy positions, by publicizing the issues, and by use of the media. Generally, the efforts of the president and the elites are most successful with that segment of the population called the **attentive public.** This sector of the mass public, which probably constitutes 10 to 20 percent of all citizens, is more interested in foreign affairs than most Americans. These Americans are also likely to transmit their opinions to the less-interested members of the public through conversation and local leadership.

ATTENTIVE PUBLIC
That proportion of the general public that pays attention to foreign policy issues.

The Military–Industrial Complex

MILITARY–INDUSTRIAL COMPLEX
The mutually beneficial relationship between the armed forces and defense contractors.

Civilian fear of "the generals" and the relationship between the defense establishment and arms manufacturers date back many years. In the 1930s, Franklin Roosevelt raised the specter of mammoth improper military influence in the domestic economy. On the eve of a Senate investigation of the munitions industry, he said that the arms race was a "grave menace ... due in no small measure to the uncontrolled activities of the manufacturers and the merchants of the engines of destruction and it must be met by the concerted actions of the people of all nations."

Eisenhower's Warning.   During his eight years in office, the former five-star general of the army experienced firsthand the kind of pressure that could be brought against him and other policy makers by arms manufacturers. Eisenhower decided to give the country a solemn and, as he saw it, necessary warning of the consequences of this influence. On January 17, 1961, in his last official speech, he said,

> In the councils of government, we must guard against the acquisition of unwarranted influence, whether sought or unsought, by the military-industrial complex. The potential for the disastrous rise of misplaced power exists and will persist. . . . Only an alert and knowledgeable citizenry can compel the proper meshing of the huge industrial and military machinery of defense with our peaceful methods and goals, so that security and liberty may prosper together.[3]

A Symbiotic Relationship. The Pentagon has supported a large sector of our economy through defense contracts, in addition to supplying retired army officers as key executives to large defense-contracting firms.

The military establishment also has a powerful political arm. The Department of Defense is assisted by almost 350 lobbyists on Capitol Hill; it maintains some 2,850 public relations representatives in the United States and in foreign countries. As Russia and the United States worked to conclude treaties reducing their armaments, the Pentagon and defense contractors began to reassess their roles and look for new directions and programs to avoid huge cutbacks in military spending.

The Major Foreign Policy Themes

Although some observers might suggest that United States foreign policy is inconsistent and changes with the current occupant of the White House, the long view of American diplomatic ventures reveals several major themes underlying that policy. In the early years of the nation, presidents and the people generally agreed that the United States should avoid foreign entanglements and concentrate instead on its own development. From the beginning of the twentieth century until today, the theme has been increasing global involvement, with the United States taking an active role in assisting the development of other nations, dominating the world economy, and in some cases acting as a peacemaker. The other major theme of the post–World War II years was the containment of communism. In the following brief review of American diplomatic history, these three themes predominate.

The Formative Years: Avoiding Entanglements

U.S. foreign policy dates back to the colonial uprising against the British Crown. The Declaration of Independence formalized the colonists' desired break from Britain. Then, on September 3, 1783, the signing of the Treaty of Paris not only ended the eight-year War of Independence but also recognized the United States as an independent nation. In addition, the Treaty of Paris probably helped to reshape the world, for the American colonies were the first to secure independence against a "superpower."

Did You Know . . . That U.S. diplomats, troops, and other federal employees in Lebanon, Somalia, Afghanistan, Colombia, Peru, and the Philippines are given "hazardous duty" pay, which adds 15 percent to their normal salary?

---

[3]Congressional Quarterly, *Almanac* (Washington, D.C.: Congressional Quarterly Press, 1961), pp. 938–939.

Did You Know ... That the United States invaded and occupied part of Russia in 1919?

MONROE DOCTRINE
The policy statement included in President Monroe's 1823 annual message to Congress, which set out three principles: (1) European nations should not establish new colonies in the Western Hemisphere; (2) European nations should not intervene in the affairs of independent nations of the Western Hemisphere; and (3) the United States would not interfere in the affairs of European nations.

PERIOD OF ISOLATIONISM
A period of abstaining from an active role in international affairs or alliances, which characterized U.S. foreign policy during most of the nineteenth century.

A 1912 painting shows President James Monroe explaining the Monroe Doctrine to a group of government officials. Essentially, he made the Western Hemisphere the concern of the United States.

Foreign policy was largely negative during the formative years. Remember that the new nation was operating under the Articles of Confederation. The national government had no right to levy and collect taxes, no control over commerce, no right to make commercial treaties, and no power to raise an army (the army was disbanded in 1783). Its lack of international power was clear when the United States was unable to recover American hostages who had been seized in the Mediterranean by Barbary pirates but ignominiously had to purchase the hostages in a treaty with Morocco.

The founders of this nation had a basic mistrust of corrupt European governments. George Washington said it was the U.S. policy "to steer clear of permanent alliances," and Thomas Jefferson echoed this sentiment when he said America wanted peace with all nations but "entangling alliances with none." This was also a logical position at a time when the United States was so weak militarily that it could not directly influence European development. U.S. policy makers chose instead to believe that the United States would set a moral standard that Europe could follow. Moreover, being protected by oceans that took weeks to traverse certainly allowed the nation to avoid entangling alliances. During the 1700s and 1800s, the United States generally stayed out of European conflicts and politics.

Nineteenth-Century Isolationism

The role of the United States as a world power began in the early 1800s. President James Monroe, in his message to Congress on December 2, 1823, stated that this country would not accept foreign intervention in the Western Hemisphere. In return, the United States would not meddle in European internal affairs. The **Monroe Doctrine** was the underpinning of the United States's isolationist foreign policy throughout the nineteenth century, which became known as the **period of isolationism.** More recently, however, the Monroe Doctrine, among other things, was used to justify the invasion of Grenada in the Caribbean in October 1983.

The Beginning of Interventionism and World War I

Although the nineteenth century was not completely devoid of American **interventionism** in the rest of the world, there was relatively little foreign engagement. In 1812, the United States went to war with Great Britain over the ostensible issue of the British navy preying on American commerce. In 1846, President James K. Polk provoked Mexico into a war with the United States when he ordered the army to occupy disputed territory along the Rio Grande River. As a result of the Mexican War, the United States acquired New Mexico, Arizona, California, and other western lands.

But the real end of isolationism started with the Spanish-American War in 1898. Winning that war gave the United States possession of Guam, Puerto Rico, and the Philippines (which gained independence in 1946). Although the United States returned to a policy of isolationism following the Spanish-American War, it lasted only for a brief time—until World War I (1914–1918). Still, reluctant to entangle this country with European internal politics, the United States did not enter the war until late. In his reelection campaign of 1916, President Woodrow Wilson ran on the slogan, "He kept us out of war." Nonetheless, on April 6, 1917, the United States declared war on Germany. It was evident to Wilson that without help, the Allies would be defeated and that American property and lives, already under attack, would be increasingly endangered. Wilson also sought to promote American democratic ideals in Europe and to end international aggression by having the United States enter into the war.

In the 1920s, the United States did indeed go "back to normalcy," as President Warren G. Harding urged it to do. U.S. military forces were largely disbanded, defense spending dropped to about 1 percent of total national income, and the nation once more retreated into isolationism. International power politics ceased to be an issue in U.S. foreign policy—if, in fact, the country can be said to have had a foreign policy.

The Era of Internationalism

Isolationism was permanently shattered and relegated to its place in history by the bombing of the U.S. naval base at Pearl Harbor, Hawaii, on December 7, 1941. The surprise attack by the Japanese resulted in the deaths of 2,403 American servicemen and the wounding of 1,143 others. Eighteen warships were sunk or seriously damaged, and 188 planes were destroyed at the airfields. Tales of the horrors experienced by the wounded survivors quickly reached American shores. The American public was outraged. President Roosevelt asked Congress to declare war on Japan immediately, and the United States entered World War II.

This unequivocal response was certainly due to the nature of the provocation. American soil had not been attacked by a foreign power since the burning of Washington, D.C., by the British in 1814. World War II marked a lasting change in American foreign policy. It also produced a permanent change in the size of the American government. Except for brief periods during the Civil War and World War I, defense spending had been a fairly trivial part of total national income. By the end of World War II in 1945, however, defense spending had increased to almost 40 percent of total national income. The number of U.S. military bases overseas increased from 3 at the beginning of 1940 to almost 450 by the end of World War

INTERVENTIONISM
Involvement in foreign affairs; actions directed at changing or preserving the internal political arrangements of other nations.

The atomic bomb explodes over Nagasaki on August 9, 1945.

Did You Know ... That only 34 percent of Americans say that trade with Japan is good for the U.S. economy?

II. National security had become a priority item on the federal government's agenda.

The United States was the only country to emerge from World War II with its economy intact and even strengthened. The Soviet Union, Japan, Italy, France, Germany, Britain, and a number of minor participants in the war were all economically devastated. The United States was also the only country to have control over operational nuclear weapons. President Harry S Truman had personally made the decision to use two atomic bombs, on August 6 and August 9, 1945, to end the war with Japan. (Historians still dispute the necessity of this action, which ultimately killed more than 100,000 Japanese civilians and left an equal number permanently injured.) The United States had truly become the world's superpower.

The Cold War

SOVIET BLOC
The Eastern European countries that installed communist regimes after World War II.

COLD WAR
The ideological, political, and economic impasse that existed between the United States and the Soviet Union following World War II.

The United States had become an uncomfortable ally of the Soviet Union after it had been invaded by Hitler. Soon after the war ended, relations between the Soviets and the West deteriorated. The Soviets wanted a weakened Germany, and to achieve this they insisted that the country be divided in two, with East Germany becoming a buffer. Little by little, the Soviets helped to install communist governments in Eastern European countries, which collectively became known as the **Soviet bloc.** In response, the United States encouraged the rearming of Western Europe. The "**Cold War**" had begun.[4]

[4]See John Lewis Gaddis, *The United Nations and the Origins of the Cold War* (New York: Columbia University Press, 1972).

Stalin, Roosevelt, and Churchill at Yalta, February 4–11, 1945.

In Fulton, Missouri, on March 5, 1946, Winston Churchill, in a striking metaphor, declared that from the Baltic to the Adriatic seas "an iron curtain has descended across the [European] continent." The term **iron curtain** became even more appropriate when the Soviets built a wall separating East Berlin from West Berlin on August 17–18, 1961.

Containment: A New Foreign Policy

In 1947, a remarkable article was published in *Foreign Affairs.* The article was signed by "X." The actual author was George F. Kennan, chief of the policy-planning staff for the Department of State. The doctrine of **containment** set forth in the article became—according to many—the Bible of Western foreign policy. "X" argued that whenever and wherever the Soviets could successfully challenge Western institutions, they would do so. He recommended that our policy toward the Soviets be "firm and vigilant containment of Russian expansive tendencies."[5]

The containment theory was enunciated quite clearly in the **Truman Doctrine,** which was contained in President Harry S Truman's historic address to Congress on March 12, 1947. In that address, he announced that the United States must help countries in which a communist takeover seemed likely, and he proposed the Greek–Turkish aid program specifically to counter Soviet influence in the eastern Mediterranean. He put the choice squarely before Congress—it either must support those measures required to preserve peace and security abroad or risk widespread global instability and perhaps World War III.[6]

During the cold war, there was never any direct military confrontation between the United States and the Soviet Union. Rather, confrontations among "client" nations were used to carry out the policies of the superpowers. Only on occasion did the United States directly enter into a conflict in a significant way. Two such occasions were in Korea and Vietnam.

In 1950, North Korean troops were embroiled in a war with South Korea. President Truman asked for and received a Security Council order from the United Nations for the North Koreans to withdraw. The Soviet Union was absent from the council on that day and did not participate in the discussion. Truman then authorized the use of American forces in support of the South Koreans. For the next three years, American troops were engaged in a land war in Asia, a war that became a stalemate and a political liability to President Truman. One of Dwight Eisenhower's major 1952 campaign promises was to end the Korean war—which he did. An armistice was signed on July 27, 1953. (American troops have been stationed in South Korea ever since, however.)

U.S. involvement in Vietnam began shortly after the end of the Korean conflict. When the French army in Indochina was defeated by the communist forces of Ho Chi Minh and the two Vietnams were created in 1954, the Americans assumed the role of supporting the South Vietnamese government against the communist North. John Kennedy sent 16,000 "advisers" to help South Vietnam, and after Kennedy's death, Lyndon

IRON CURTAIN
The term used to describe the division of Europe between the Soviet Union and the West. Popularized by Winston Churchill in a speech portraying Europe as being divided by an iron curtain, with the nations of Eastern Europe behind the curtain and increasingly under Soviet control.

CONTAINMENT
A U.S. diplomatic policy adopted by the Truman administration to "build situations of strength" around the globe to contain communist power within its existing boundaries.

TRUMAN DOCTRINE
The policy adopted by President Harry Truman in 1947 to halt communist expansion in southeastern Europe.

---

[5]Mr. X., "The Sources of Soviet Conduct," *Foreign Affairs,* July 1947, p. 575.
[6]*Public Papers of the Presidents of the United States: Harry S Truman, 1947* (Washington, D.C.: Government Printing Office, 1963), pp. 176–180.

Did You Know ... That since 1963, the United States has conducted underground tests of more than four hundred nuclear weapons, whereas the former U.S.S.R. conducted more than three hundred such tests?

DÉTENTE
A French word meaning the relaxation of tension. The term characterizes U.S.–Soviet policy as it developed under President Nixon and Henry Kissinger. Détente stresses direct cooperative dealings with Cold War rivals but avoids ideological accommodation.

MUTUAL ASSURED DESTRUCTION (MAD)
A theory that if the United States and the Soviet Union had extremely large and invulnerable nuclear forces that were somewhat equal, then neither would chance a war with the other.

ANTIBALLISTIC MISSILES (ABMs)
A defense system designed to protect targets by destroying the attacking airplanes or missiles before they reach their destination.

MULTIPLE, INDEPENDENTLY TARGETABLE, WARHEADS (MIRVs)
Multiple warheads carried by a single missile but directed to different targets.

FIRST-STRIKE CAPABILITIES
The launching of an initial strategic nuclear attack before the opponent has used any strategic weapons.

Johnson greatly increased the scope of that support. American forces in Vietnam at the height of the U.S. involvement totaled more than 500,000 troops. More than 56,000 Americans were killed and 300,000 wounded in the conflict. The debate over U.S. involvement in Vietnam divided the American electorate and spurred congressional efforts to limit the ability of the president to commit forces to armed combat. After a peace treaty was signed in 1973 and the prisoners of war were returned, the United States seemed unclear about its national security goals and its commitment to the old containment view of dealing with communism.

Confrontation in a Nuclear World

Nuclear power spread throughout the world. The two superpowers had enough nuclear bombs to destroy everyone at least twice and maybe three times. Obviously, confrontation between the United States and the Soviet Union could have taken on world-destroying proportions. Perhaps the closest we came to such a confrontation was the Cuban missile crisis in 1962. For thirteen days, the United States and the Soviets were close to nuclear war. The Soviets had decided to place offensive missiles ninety miles off the American coast in Cuba. On October 14, 1962, an American U-2 spy plane photographed the missile site being built. President Kennedy and his advisers rejected the possibility of armed intervention, setting up a naval blockade around the island instead. When Soviet vessels, apparently carrying nuclear warheads, appeared near Cuban waters, the tension reached its height. After intense negotiations between Washington and Moscow, the Soviet ships turned around on October 25, and on October 28 the Soviet Union announced the withdrawal of its missile operations from Cuba. In exchange, the United States agreed not to invade Cuba and to remove some of its own missiles that were located near the Soviet border.

A Period of Détente

The French word **détente** means a relaxation of tensions between nations. By the end of the 1960s, it was clear that some efforts had to be made to reduce the threat of nuclear war between the United States and the Soviet Union. The Soviet Union had gradually begun to catch up in the building of strategic nuclear delivery vehicles in the form of bombers and missiles, thus balancing the nuclear scales. In the parlance of nuclear strategy, both nations had acquired **mutual assured-destruction (MAD)** capabilities. Theoretically, this meant that if the forces of both nations were approximately equal, neither would chance a war with each other.

The development of **antiballistic missiles (ABMs)** made the balance unstable. With ABMs, each side could shoot down the other's intercontinental nuclear warhead missiles. The United States also began to put **multiple, independently targetable warheads (MIRVs)** on a single missile, making it impossible for any ABM defensive system to eliminate completely the possibility of nuclear attack. This policy expanded nuclear **first-strike capabilities** without requiring the production of new missiles. These developments in weapons technology made arms control negotiations to reduce the possibility of war imperative.

PROFILE

Colin Powell

"If we listened to some military men, there would never be a step toward peace."

Colin Powell wears more brass on his shoulders than anyone else in the U.S. Army. As chairman of the joint chiefs of staff, Powell is the nation's highest military commander. In exercising full authority over all the branches of the armed forces, Powell answers to no one, with the exception of the president.

A true American success story, Powell grew up in Harlem, New York's African-American ghetto. His parents were poor Jamaican immigrants who had a dream of success for their son. That success was achieved by way of the army, which Powell joined through the Reserve Officers' Training Corps (ROTC) while attending the City College of New York. Commissioned as a second lieutenant in 1958, Powell served as a field officer in Vietnam, where he was seriously wounded. On his return to the states, Powell attended the army's Command and General Staff College and graduated second in his class. Returning to combat duty in Vietnam, Powell ob-

tained a series of promotions and decorations for bravery.

Powell entered the governmental loop in 1972 as a White House fellow, one of a select group of military officers assigned to duties in civilian government. He worked with Caspar Weinberger in the Office of Management and Budget. When Weinberger became secretary of defense under President Reagan, Powell became the secretary's military adviser.

In 1987, the scandal over the sale of missiles to Iran decimated the intelligence community. The top personnel of the National Security Council (NSC) resigned. President Reagan asked Powell to be the new chairman of the NSC, and he served in that capacity until the end of the president's term, in 1989.

The election of 1988 that brought George Bush to power also brought a new head of the NSC—Air Force General Brent Scowcroft. Powell was asked to stay on with the new administration as chairman of the joint chiefs of staff. The fourth general's star on Powell's shoulder that came with the job is another honor among many for a man who has achieved success in life through service.

Powell's image became a familiar one during the U.S. military buildup and Operation Desert Storm in the Persian Gulf in 1990. Although reports suggested that he was less enthusiastic about launching the attack than some other officials, once the war began, he gave every support to the troops in the field. Powell's popularity led many to suggest that he consider a career in national politics in years to come.

As the result of protracted negotiations, in May 1972, the United States and the Soviet Union signed the **Strategic Arms Limitation Treaty (SALT I)**. That treaty "permanently" limited the development and deployment of ABMs, and it limited for five years the number of offensive missiles each country could deploy. To further reduce tensions, under the Kissinger–Nixon policy, new scientific and cultural exchanges were arranged with the Soviets, as well as new opportunities for Jewish emigration out of the Soviet Union.

The policy of détente was not limited to relationships with the Soviet Union. Seeing an opportunity to capitalize on increasing friction between the Soviet Union and the People's Republic of China, Kissinger secretly began negotiations to establish a new relationship with that nation. After some minor cultural exchanges, President Nixon eventually visited the

STRATEGIC ARMS LIMITATION TREATY (SALT I)
A treaty between the United States and the Soviet Union to stabilize the nuclear arms competition between the two countries. SALT I talks began in 1969, and agreements were signed on May 26, 1972.

President Nixon signs the SALT I Treaty, a Cold War agreement with the Soviets, in 1972.

People's Republic of China and set the stage for the formal diplomatic recognition of that country during the Carter administration. Again, new cultural, economic, and scientific exchanges with the Chinese were established to help normalize relations between the two countries.

Historians will certainly mark the late 1970s as threatening détente. Communist military activities increased. The Soviets intervened in Afghanistan on December 27, 1979. The Carter administration, unilaterally and without consulting Congress, retaliated by restricting grain sales to the Soviet Union and by prohibiting Americans from participating in the Olympic Games that were to be held in Moscow in 1980. Beginning in December 1981, the Polish communist regime, backed by the Soviets, crushed the growing Solidarity labor union movement—which had demanded extensive economic, social, and political freedoms—and established martial law.

President Reagan, coming into office in 1981, at first took a hard line against the Soviets, proposing the strategic defense initiative (SDI), or Star Wars, in 1983. Reagan and others in his administration argued that the program would deter nuclear war by shifting the emphasis of defense strategy from offensive to defensive weapons systems. Critics of the program, however, believed it would make the arms race more intense, would be very expensive, and probably would not be technically feasible.

In November 1985, President Reagan and Mikhail Gorbachev, the Soviet leader, held summit talks in Geneva. The two men agreed to reestablish cultural and scientific exchanges and to continue the arms control negotiations. Progress towards an agreement was slow, however. Although the United States, the other member nations of the North Atlantic Treaty Organization, and the Soviet Union agreed to new measures to reduce the possibility of accidental hostilities in 1986, no new nuclear arms treaty was signed.

In 1987, representatives of the United States and the Soviet Union continued work on an arms reduction agreement. Although there were setbacks throughout the year, the negotiations resulted in an historic agreement signed by Reagan and Gorbachev in Washington, D.C., on December 8, 1987. The terms of the Intermediate-Range Nuclear Force (INF) Treaty required the superpowers to dismantle a total of four thousand intermediate-range missiles within the first three years of the agreement. The verification procedures allowed each nation to keep a team of inspectors on the other nation's soil and to conduct up to twenty short-notice inspections of the disassembly sites each year. The Senate ratified the treaty in a vote of ninety-three to five on May 27, 1988, and the agreement was formally signed by Mr. Reagan and Mr. Gorbachev.

George Bush negotiated with the Soviets after he became president, meeting with Gorbachev first in Malta and then in the United States. The goal of both nations was to reduce the number of nuclear weapons and the number of armed troops in Europe. The developments in Eastern Europe, the drive by the Baltic republics for independence, the unification of Germany, and the dissolution of the Soviet Union made the process much more complex, however. American strategists worried as much about who now controlled the Soviet nuclear arsenal as about completing the treaty process. In 1992, the United States signed the Strategic Arms Reduction Treaty (START) with four former Soviet republics—Russia, the Ukraine, Belarus, and Kazakhstan—to reduce the number of long-range nuclear weapons. President Clinton continued the summitry, meeting with President Yeltsin in Vancouver, Canada, early in his administration.

Challenges in World Politics

The end of the cold war, the dissolution of the Soviet Union, the economic unification of Europe, and the political changes in Eastern Europe have challenged U.S. foreign policy in ways that were unimaginable a few years ago. Not only did the United States have no contingency plans for these events, but predicting the consequences of any of these changes for world politics is all but impossible. Furthermore, such sweeping changes mean that not only must the United States adjust its foreign policy to deal with new realities, but it must also consider adjustments in the American military and intelligence establishments.

The Dissolution of the Soviet Union

After the fall of the Berlin Wall in 1989, it was clear that the Soviet Union had relinquished much of its political and military control over the states of Eastern Europe that had formerly been part of the Soviet bloc. Sweeping changes within the Soviet Union had been proposed by Gorbachev, and

Did You Know . . . That poison gases, such as nerve and blood gas, and chemical weapons that use bacteria, viruses, and toxins, including bubonic plague and anthrax agents, are likely to replace nuclear weapons as the greatest threat to world peace?

Russian President Boris Yeltsin celebrating the failure of the August 1991 coup attempt by waving the Russian flag. By 1993, Yeltsin was under severe criticism by the Russian Congress because of the failure of his economic reforms.

talks to reduce nuclear armaments were proceeding, but no one expected the Soviet Union to dissolve into separate states as quickly as it did. While Gorbachev tried to adjust the Soviet constitution and political system to allow greater autonomy for the republics within the union, demands for political, ethnic, and religious autonomy grew. In August 1991, Soviet radio announced that Gorbachev was ill and would be taking a leave of absence from his office. It soon became clear that Gorbachev had been arrested and that military officers were attempting to take control through a coup.

When Soviet troops tried to surround the popular Russian president, Boris Yeltsin, and the Russian government in its offices, the mass public rallied to their support in Moscow and other cities. Some units of the military refused to follow the coup leaders' orders. Yeltsin kept in contact with the media and the West, demanding to see and talk with Gorbachev. In three days, the coup leaders were under arrest, Gorbachev returned to Moscow, and Yeltsin was acclaimed as the new leader. Following the aborted coup, momentum for the states within the Soviet Union to pursue independent status grew rapidly, with most refusing to sign the new Soviet constitution. As state after state declared independence, American military and intelligence officials grew increasingly concerned about the placement and control of the Soviet Union's nuclear weapons arsenal. Diplomats from Europe, the United States, and the new states met to discuss the future of the former superpower. Within a period of months, a new Commonwealth of Independent States was created, with Russia as its pre-

After the dissolution of the Soviet Union, each republic moved to capitalism in its own way. In Moscow, the value of the ruble fell while the rate of pay remained stable. Russians set up private markets to sell whatever goods they could to raise money for survival against rampant inflation and the threat of mass unemployment.

eminent member. Some states, namely Georgia and the Baltic republics, declined to join.

The new commonwealth faced immense problems—an economy that was in shambles, an immediate currency crisis, long-suppressed ethnic conflicts, and the need to create a defense capability. The United States joined with European powers to develop a program for administering technical and financial aid to their former adversary and the newly independent states that had once been part of the Soviet Union.

Regional Conflicts

One of the regions that has traditionally been of great interest to the United States is Central America. In 1823, President Monroe declared a special U.S. interest in the region and, in the twentieth century, the Caribbean was known as an "American lake." The nations of Central America have suffered poverty and turmoil for most of their existence, with the exception of Costa Rica. In an attempt to restore order and to protect American property and lives, the United States has intervened militarily in Central America on many occasions. This interventionist policy did not generate much affection for the United States among Central American nations. In the 1980s, the United States began a serious involvement in at least three Central American states: in El Salvador, where the right-wing government was under attack from leftist terrorist groups; in Nicaragua, where the United States backed the *contras* in their attempt to overthrow the pro-Soviet Sandinista government; and in Panama, where the military leader, General Manuel Noriega, an indicted drug trafficker, refused to leave office.

The Bush administration faced a rapidly changing situation in Central America. In 1989, when Noriega refused to resign from the presidency under pressure of economic sanctions on Panama, Bush ordered military forces into that nation to capture and arrest Noriega for drug dealing.

POLITICS AND ETHICS

Is It Okay to Endanger the Life of a Foreign Head of State?

It took a U.S. invasion to remove General Manuel Noriega from power in Panama in December 1989. General Noriega was seized by U.S. forces and brought to the United States to stand trial in an American court on drug and money-laundering charges. He was subsequently convicted and sentenced to a lengthy prison term. After the invasion, the United States installed the civilian winners of the May 1989 election that had been annulled by Noriega. The Noriega affair exemplifies the complexities of foreign and national security policy.

The Central Intelligence Agency recruited Noriega when he was a young Panamanian officer in the 1950s and put him on its payroll. From then until the early 1980s, Noriega served as an intelligence source for the CIA. Noriega passed on information about Cuba's Fidel Castro, with whom he had extensive dealings, about radicals in various Latin American armed forces, about the Colombian drug cartel, and, af-

ter the 1979 revolution, about the Sandinistas in Nicaragua. But Noriega was a double-dealer, not only helping the United States in its war against the Nicaraguan Marxists during the 1980s by training and arming the U.S.-backed *contra* rebels, but also supplying arms and information to the Marxist Nicaraguan government. He turned in some minor Colombian drug dealers but was implicated in alleged drug activities himself and is assumed to have protected and even given safe haven to some of Colombia's Medellin cocaine cartel bosses. He also allegedly passed on *to* Castro as much information as he got *from* Castro to give to the United States.

By 1989, the United States wanted Noriega out. But because of a presidential executive order issued by Gerald Ford (and reissued by all subsequent presidents), the United States could not support any action that might lead to the death of a foreign head of state. In 1989, Panamanian military officers tried to

overthrow Noriega. Their aborted effort and Noriega's brutal reprisals led Congress and the president to reach an understanding that liberalized the interpretation of the executive order. Until it is changed or reinterpreted again, the U.S. president is presumably empowered to act in the interest of the United States *even when this may lead to the death of a foreign head of state*. This represents a major revision of U.S. foreign policy principles.

Although Noriega surrendered and was returned to the United States for trial, the invasion killed a large number of Panamanian civilians and leveled many blocks of the capital, Panama City. Most Panamanians were glad to be rid of Noriega, but the invasion worsened the country's economic problems.

The situation in El Salvador went from bad to worse. Five Jesuit faculty members at a leading Salvadoran university and their housekeeper were massacred, possibly by a squad detailed by the rightist military in 1989. The United States continued to support the regime, although the administration expressed outrage at the murders and demanded, to no avail, that the perpetrators be found and brought to trial. Nicaragua has been more successful in ending its civil war. Elections were held, monitored by U.S. observers, and the Marxist president, Daniel Ortega, lost to Violetta

Chamorro, a well-known opponent of Ortega and the Sandanistas. Chamorro assumed office, and most of the *contras* surrendered their arms, at least temporarily.

The United States has also played a role in the Middle East. As a long-time supporter of Israel, the United States has undertaken to persuade the Israelis to agree to some kind of negotiations with the Palestinians who live as refugees within the occupied territories of the state of Israel. The conflict, which has been ongoing since 1948, is extremely hard to resolve because it requires the Arab states of the region to recognize Israel's right to exist and requires Israel to make some settlement with the Palestine Liberation Organization (PLO), which has launched attacks on Israel from within and outside its borders and which Israel regards as a terrorist organization. In December 1988, the U.S. began talking directly to the PLO and in 1991, under great pressure from the United States, the Israelis opened talks with representatives of the Palestinians and other Arab states. Further east, in the Persian Gulf, the Iran–Iraq war lasted ten years before the combatants agreed to a cease-fire and the conflict, which had destabilized the region, ended. Most analysts attributed the cease-fire to the high cost of the war for Iran.

U.S. Response to Iraq's Invasion of Kuwait

On August 2, 1990, the Middle East became the setting for a major challenge to the authority of the United States and its ability to buy oil from its allies there. President Saddam Hussein of Iraq initially sent more than 100,000 troops into the neighboring oil sheikdom of Kuwait, occupying the entire nation. The government of Kuwait fled the country. In addition, Iraqi troops took up positions on the Kuwaiti–Saudi Arabian border, close to the oil fields that are the key to the Saudis' wealth.

Within less than two days, President George Bush took the position that the annexation of Kuwait must not be tolerated by the Western World

Did You Know . . . That the largest trading partner of the United States is Canada?

American tanks on maneuvers in Saudi Arabia.

Did You Know ... That 40 percent of Eastern Europeans surveyed in a regional poll in 1991 said they disliked the major minority ethnic group within their own nations?

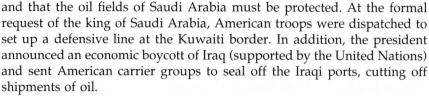

and that the oil fields of Saudi Arabia must be protected. At the formal request of the king of Saudi Arabia, American troops were dispatched to set up a defensive line at the Kuwaiti border. In addition, the president announced an economic boycott of Iraq (supported by the United Nations) and sent American carrier groups to seal off the Iraqi ports, cutting off shipments of oil.

Although the NATO alliance did not respond as an institution to this threat to the oil supply, individual nations—including England, France, and Canada—sent ships to assist. Following a vote at an Arab summit meeting, Egypt and Morocco sent troops to join the U.S. and Saudi forces in the desert. The Security Council of the United Nations voted to impose economic sanctions against Iraq, and the Soviet Union stopped its arms shipments to Saddam Hussein.

Bush continued to send troops—including reserve units called up from the United States—to Saudi Arabia. By the end of 1990, more than a half-million troops were in place. After the United Nations approved a resolution authorizing the use of force if Saddam Hussein did not respond to sanctions, the U.S. Congress reluctantly also approved such an authorization. On January 17, 1991, two days after the deadline for Saddam to withdraw, the coalition forces launched a massive air attack on Iraq. After several weeks of almost unopposed aerial bombardment, the ground offensive began. Iraqi troops retreated from Kuwait a few days later, and the war ended within another week. One hundred forty-three Americans were killed in action, and many others died in war-related accidents.

After the end of the armed conflict, many Americans criticized the Bush administration for not sending troops to Baghdad, where they might have deposed Saddam Hussein. Others faulted the effort for raising the expectations of the Kurdish people that the United States would eliminate Saddam if they revolted. When no one helped their uprising, the entire community risked retaliation by the Iraqi dictator. Belatedly, American troops were sent to preserve peace. The Persian Gulf war also created an enormous environmental disaster owing to the destruction of the oil fields by the Iraqis when they retreated from Kuwait. Not only were millions of barrels of oil burned, but also the coastline of the Gulf and many miles of land were damaged by the pollution and fires. Finally, many Americans were surprised by Saddam Hussein's ability to survive the devastating attack on his country. He has remained in power and continues to resist terms of the truce as well as to foster hatred toward the West.

In the early months of Clinton's presidency, it was learned that an attempt would be made on the life of George Bush while he visited Kuwait. On June 26, President Clinton ordered a cruise missile attack on the Iraqi intelligence headquarters to punish Hussein for the assassination attempt. Hussein threatened retaliation.

Eastern Europe

Eastern Europe, a region that had been extremely stable while under Soviet domination, suddenly became an unknown quantity in U.S. policy. With the decision of the Soviet Union to allow free elections and non-Marxist governments in Eastern Europe, these nations began separate paths to anticommunist states with mixed or market-oriented economies.

Bosnian and Croatian prisoners taken by the Serbian forces in the civil war that has shattered the former nation of Yugoslavia since 1991. Although European nations tried to provide humanitarian aid to the civilians involved, many of the bitter combatants resisted any outside interference.

Some nations moved immediately to hold new elections; some struggled first to repair damaged economies, and others attempted to deal with ethnic tensions within their populations.

It is difficult to overestimate the potential for civil disorder in these nations, particularly with regard to ethnic differences. The world watched in 1991 as Yugoslavia split into a number of independent states. As the former provinces of Yugoslavia—Slovenia, Croatia, and Bosnia-Herzegovina—tried to declare independence, Serbian military and government leaders launched attacks on their neighbors. The fighting was caused by historic conflicts and by strong ethnic and religious differences. Neither European nor U.N. efforts, which fell short of intervention, seemed able to stop the bloodshed in the Balkan region. As the fighting intensified and the world became aware that Bosnian women were being raped as a technique of war, public demands for stopping the conflict escalated. The Clinton administration faced hard choices as to how the United States could intervene to stop the bloodshed.

During his presidential election campaign against George Bush, Bill Clinton had called for tougher action against the likelihood of a Serb (and Croat) military success in predominantly Muslim Bosnia. The United States and the European countries came under heavy criticism from Islamic governments and proIslamic movements around the world for being unprepared to take military action in Yugoslavia. In mid-1993, Clinton dispatched American military units to the former Yugoslavian republic of Macedonia in an attempt to prevent the war from spreading beyond Bosnia.

The Global Economy

Although the United States derives only about 10 percent of its total national income from world trade, it is deeply dependent on the world economy. The stock market crash of 1987 showed how closely other markets watch the economic situation of the United States and, conversely, how

POLITICS AND ECONOMICS

Exporting Arms to the Third World

Although the United States has been unable to eliminate its overall trade deficit, it has been a net exporter to a number of developing countries. A part of that export trade has been arms sales. With the dissolution of the Soviet Union, the United States has taken the lead among nations in the world in selling arms to the Third World. As indicated in the figure, American arms sales to Third-World nations rose by more than $7.8 billion in 1990. Much of the increase was accounted for by armament contracts with Saudi Arabia. These contracts had been concluded before the Iraqi invasion of Kuwait and the Persian Gulf conflict.

SOURCE: *New York Times*, August 11, 1991.

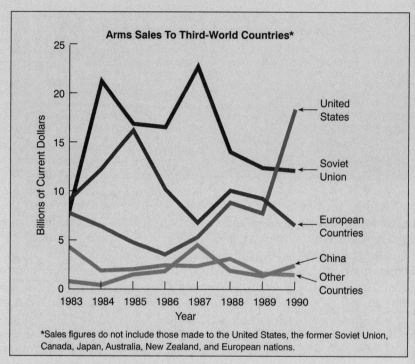

Arms Sales To Third-World Countries*

*Sales figures do not include those made to the United States, the former Soviet Union, Canada, Japan, Australia, New Zealand, and European nations.

SOURCES: Congressional Research Service and *New York Times*, August 11, 1991.

U.S. markets follow those of London and Japan. Furthermore, since the 1980s the United States has become a debtor nation, meaning that we owe more to foreigners than foreigners owe to us. The reason for this is a huge trade deficit and the willingness of foreign individuals and nations to finance part of the national debt by purchasing U.S. government securities.

Because the United States imports more goods and services than it exports, it has a net trade deficit. These imports include BMWs, Sonys, Toshibas, and Guccis, as well as cheaper products such as shoes manufactured in Brazil and clothes from Taiwan. As Figure 15-1 shows, the biggest trade deficit is with Japan.

No one can predict how "Europe 1992" will affect world trade. With the European Community having supposedly become one true economic

FIGURE 18-1 ■ U.S. Exports and Imports, 1992

SOURCE: U.S. Department of Commerce.

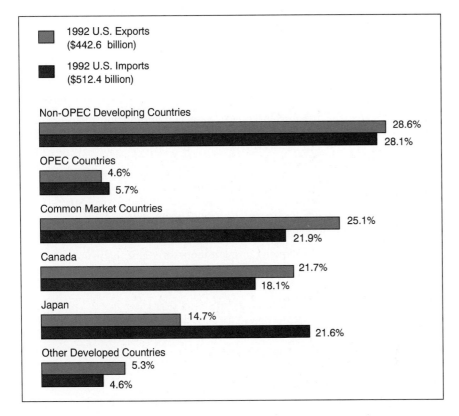

■ 1992 U.S. Exports
($442.6 billion)

■ 1992 U.S. Imports
($512.4 billion)

Non-OPEC Developing Countries
28.6%
28.1%

OPEC Countries
4.6%
5.7%

Common Market Countries
25.1%
21.9%

Canada
21.7%
18.1%

Japan
14.7%
21.6%

Other Developed Countries
5.3%
4.6%

"nation" on December 31, 1992, some expect Europe to close some markets to outside powers. Others see united Europe as a market opportunity for American and multinational corporations.

Conclusion: Facing an Uncertain World

In one sense, the United States is well positioned to plan and implement foreign policy in a world that is changing at a rate faster than at any other time since the conclusion of World War II. The United States is economically relatively strong, militarily powerful, and politically stable. In fact, the United States finds itself in the curious position of needing to assist the former republics of the Soviet Union in their quest for economic and political reform. The world, however, is filled with "hot spots" that may become threats to peace. Only the United States seems to be able to take action in troubled areas, such as Somalia in 1992.

It remains to be seen whether the American people and their leaders have the patience and motivation to pursue a foreign policy of restrained leadership and economic competitiveness. The future shape of world politics will require these characteristics to deal with the period of extreme change that lies ahead.

As part of the military effort to safeguard the delivery of food to Somalia, U.S. Marines patrol a street in the Somali capital, Mogadishu.

GETTING INVOLVED

Working for Human Rights

In many countries throughout the world, human rights are not protected to the extent that they are in the United States. In some nations, people are imprisoned, tortured, or killed because they oppose the current regime. In other nations, certain ethnic or racial groups are oppressed by the majority population. In nations such as Somalia, in which civil war has caused starvation among millions of people, international efforts to send food relief to the refugee camps has been hampered by the fighting among rival factions that rages within that country.

What can you do to work for the improvement of human rights in other nations? One way is to join one of the many national and international organizations listed here that attempt to keep watch over human rights violations. By publicizing human rights violations, these organizations try to pressure nations into changing their tactics. Sometimes, such organizations are able to apply enough pressure and cause so much embarrassment that selected individuals may be freed from prison or allowed to emigrate.

Another way to work for human rights is to keep informed about the state of affairs in other nations and to write personally to those governments or to their embassies asking them to cease these violations. Again, most of the organizations listed here have newsletters or other publications to keep you aware of developments in other nations.

If you want to receive general information about the position of the United States on human rights violations, you could begin by writing to the State Department at the following address:

U.S. Department of State
Bureau of Human Rights and Humanitarian Affairs
U.S. Department of State, Room 7802
Washington, DC 20520

The following organizations are best known for their watch-dog efforts in countries that violate human rights for political reasons. These include both leftist and rightist regimes.

Amnesty International U.S.A.
304 W. 58th St.
New York, NY 10017

American Friends Service Committee
1501 Cherry St.
Philadelphia, PA 19102

Clergy and Laity Concerned
198 Broadway
New York, NY 10038

CHAPTER SUMMARY

1. Foreign policy includes national goals and the techniques used to achieve them. National security policy, which is one aspect of foreign policy, is designed to protect the independence and the political and economic integrity of the United States. Diplomacy involves the nation's external relationships and is an attempt to resolve conflict without resort to arms. Sometimes U.S. foreign policy is based on moral idealism, the belief that the world can be improved and that it is the duty of the United States to lead in this effort. At other times, U.S. policies stem from political realism, the belief that the world is a dangerous place and that every nation must do what it can to survive.

2. The formal power of the president to make foreign policy derives from the Constitution, which makes the president responsible for the preservation of national security and designates the president as commander in chief of the army and navy. Presidents have interpreted this authority broadly.

They also have the power to make treaties and executive agreements. In principle, the State Department is the executive agency most directly involved with foreign affairs. In the last several administrations, it has often been bypassed, however. The National Security Council (NSC) advises the president on the integration of "domestic, foreign, and military policies relating to national security." Presidents' use of the NSC has varied. The intelligence community consists of forty or more government agencies engaged in intelligence activities varying from information gathering to covert actions. In response to presidential actions in the Vietnam war, Congress attempted to establish some limits on the power of the president in foreign policy by passing the War Powers Act in 1973.

3. Three major themes have guided U.S. foreign policy. In the early years of the nation, isolationism was the primary focus. With the start of the twentieth century, this view gave way to global involvement. From World War II until the end of the 1980s, the major goal was to contain communism and the influence of the Soviet Union.

4. During the 1700s and 1800s, the United States had little international power and generally stayed out of European conflicts and politics. The nineteenth century has been called the period of isolationism. The Monroe Doctrine of 1823 stated that the United States would not accept foreign intervention in the Western Hemisphere and would not meddle in European affairs. The end of the period of isolationism started with the Spanish-American War of 1898. The first major entanglement in European politics began when the United States entered World War I on April 6, 1917. Following the signing of the Treaty of Versailles in 1919, the United States once more retreated into isolationism, rejecting membership in the League of Nations and largely disbanding its military forces. World War II marked a lasting change in American foreign policy. The United States was the only country to emerge from the war with its economy intact and the only country with operating nuclear weapons.

5. Soon after the war ended, the uncomfortable alliance between the United States and the Soviet Union ended and the Cold War began. A policy of containment, which assumed an expansionist Soviet Union, was enunciated in the Truman Doctrine. Following the frustrations of the Vietnam war and the apparent arms equality of the United States and the Soviet Union, the United States was ready for détente. As the arms race escalated, arms control became a major foreign policy issue. Although President Reagan established a tough stance toward the Soviet Union in the first term of his administration, the second term saw serious negotiations toward arms reduction, culminating with the signing of the Intermediate-Range Nuclear Forces Treaty at the Moscow summit in 1988. Negotiations toward further arms reduction continued in the Bush administration. The Strategic Arms Reduction Treaty, which limited long-range nuclear missiles, was signed in 1992 with Russia and several other states of the former Soviet Union.

6. One very serious threat to world stability is the persistence of regional conflicts in such areas as Central America and the Middle East. Other threats include the ethnic rivalries in Eastern Europe and the rapid changes taking place in the former Soviet Union.

7. The United States is deeply dependent on the world economy, as shown by the vulnerability of its stock market to world forces, its status as a debtor nation, and its huge trade deficit.

QUESTIONS FOR REVIEW AND DISCUSSION

1. Some critics have argued that the United States alternates between internationalism and isolationism, never quite able to decide whether to take a leadership role. What historical experiences might account for this indecisiveness? What would be the consequences for American citizens and for the world community if the United States did withdraw from world affairs?

2. Which branches and agencies of the national government are influential in making foreign policy? Think of at least one issue or foreign policy question on which the Departments of State and Defense would be likely to hold different views. What are the sources of power in foreign policy decision making that would determine which department might be more influential?

3. Foreign economic policy is increasingly important not only for the United States but also for its allies and for the less-developed nations. Should economic policy be used as a tool to serve other foreign policy goals, as in the earlier grain embargo against the Soviet Union, or should economic policy only serve the cause of American prosperity?

4. While the breakup of the Soviet Union has lessened the chance of nuclear war, nuclear weapons remain a serious concern. How can the United States prevent the spread of these weapons to other states, such as Iraq or Libya?

SELECTED REFERENCES

Graham Allison and Gregory F. Treverton, eds., *Rethinking America's Security: Beyond the Cold War to New World Order* (New York: W. W. Norton, 1992). This book, which was sponsored by the American Assembly and the Council on Foreign Relations, brings together the insights of leading experts on foreign policy and provides an in-depth scrutiny of national security in the post–Cold War period.

Jean-Claude Derian, *America's Struggle for Leadership in Technology* (Cambridge, Mass.: MIT Press, 1990). This interesting and important book analyzes the role government has played and can play in stimulating successful technological innovation and business practices among corporations. It compares Japan, the United States, and Europe and discusses the role of U.S. defense spending.

Murray Feshbach and Alfred Friendly, Jr., *Ecocide in the USSR: Health and Nature under Seige* (New York: Basic Books, 1992). The authors chronicle the ecological problems caused by the former Soviet model of industrialization. They conclude that a major refocus of economic priorities in the post–Soviet era is essential to improve this situation and that the problems confronting the successor states of the U.S.S.R. serve as a warning to other countries of the dangers of ecological mismanagement.

Graham E. Fuller, *The Democracy Trap: The Perils of the Post–Cold War World* (New York: Dutton, 1992). The author, a former Foreign Service official and currently a senior political analyst at the RAND Corporation, argues that Americans may be unable to cope with the problems confronting the world following the end of the Cold War because they are trapped in the democratic politics of immediate gratification, interest-group parochialism, positive-news propaganda, and the dominance of individualism over communal effort.

Harry Harding, *A Fragile Relationship: The United States and China since 1972* (Washington, D.C.: Brookings Institution, 1992). This book reviews and analyzes U.S.–China relations since President Nixon's visit to Beijing. The author envisions more tenuous relationships in the future based on mutual economic interests, replacing the previous tacit strategic alliance against the former Soviet Union.

Shintaro Ishihara, *The Japan That Can Say No* (New York: Simon & Schuster, 1990). The author, a Japanese legislator and former member of the government, argues, in one of the most controversial books on Japan and the United States to be published so far, that Japan has a technological advantage over the United States, is a rising power while the United States is in decline, and should no longer defer to the United States.

Saul Landau, *The Dangerous Doctrine: National Security and U.S. Foreign Policy* (Boulder, Colo.: Westview Press, 1988). This book traces and sharply critiques the history of "national security" as a justification for U.S. policy overseas from Truman through the Reagan administration, using excellent case studies to illustrate the issue.

John Mueller, *Retreat from Doomsday: The Obsolescence of Major War* (New York: Basic Books, 1990). The author argues that the likelihood of nuclear war has declined, not just because of the fear of nuclear annihilation but also because people have changed, learned from past mistakes, and become more civilized.

Paul A. Volcker and Toyoo Gyohten, *Changing Fortunes: The World's Money and the Threat to American Leadership* (New York: Times Books/Random House, 1992). This book emphasizes the decline of American economic supremacy in international finance and focuses on the incompatibility of the governments' desires for stable foreign exchange rates, highly mobile private capital, and autonomous national economic policy.

APPENDIX A

The Declaration of Independence

In Congress, July 4, 1776

A Declaration by the Representatives of the United States of America, in General Congress assembled. When in the Course of human Events, it becomes necessary for one People to dissolve the Political Bands which have connected them with another, and to assume among the Powers of the Earth, the separate and equal Station to which the Laws of Nature and of Nature's God entitle them, a decent Respect to the Opinions of Mankind requires that they should declare the causes which impel them to the Separation.

We hold these Truths to be self-evident, that all Men are created equal, that they are endowed by their Creator with certain unalienable Rights, that among these are Life, Liberty, and the Pursuit of Happiness—That to secure these Rights, Governments are instituted among Men, deriving their just Powers from the Consent of the Governed, that whenever any Form of Government becomes destructive of these Ends, it is the Right of the People to alter or to abolish it, and to institute new Government, laying its Foundation on such Principles, and organizing its Powers in such Forms, as to them shall seem most likely to effect their Safety and Happiness. Prudence, indeed, will dictate that Governments long established should not be changed for light and transient Causes; and accordingly all Experience hath shewn, that Mankind are more disposed to suffer, while Evils are sufferable, than to right themselves by abolishing the Forms to which they are accustomed. But when a long Train of Abuses and Usurpations, pursuing invariably the same Object, evinces a Design to reduce them under absolute Despotism, it is their Right, it is their Duty, to throw off such Government, and to provide new Guards for their future Security. Such has been the patient Sufferance of these Colonies; and such is now the Necessity which constrains them to alter their former Systems of Government. The History of the present King of Great-Britain is a History of repeated Injuries and Usurpations, all having in direct Object the Establishment of an absolute Tyranny over these States. To prove this, let Facts be submitted to a candid World.

He has refused his Assent to Laws, the most wholesome and necessary for the public Good.

He has forbidden his Governors to pass Laws of immediate and pressing Importance, unless suspended in their Operation till his Assent should be obtained; and when so suspended, he has utterly neglected to attend to them.

He has refused to pass other Laws for the Accommodation of large Districts of People, unless those People would relinquish the Right of Representation in the Legislature, a Right inestimable to them, and formidable to Tyrants only.

He has called together Legislative Bodies at Places unusual, uncomfortable, and distant from the Depository of their Public Records, for the sole Purpose of fatiguing them into Compliance with his Measures.

He has dissolved Representative Houses repeatedly, for opposing with manly Firmness his Invasions on the Rights of the People.

He has refused for a long Time, after such Dissolutions, to cause others to be elected; whereby the Legislative Powers, incapable of Annihilation, have returned to the People at large for their exercise; the State remaining in the mean time exposed to all the Dangers of Invasion from without, and Convulsions within.

He has endeavoured to prevent the Population of these States; for that Purpose obstructing the Laws for Naturalization of Foreigners; refusing to pass others to encourage their Migrations hither, and raising the Conditions of new Appropriations of Lands.

He has obstructed the Administration of Justice, by refusing his Assent to Laws for establishing Judiciary Powers.

He has made Judges dependent on his Will alone, for the Tenure of their offices, and the Amount and payment of their Salaries.

He has erected a Multitude of new Offices, and sent hither Swarms of Officers to harrass our People, and eat out their Substance.

He has kept among us, in Times of Peace, Standing Armies, without the consent of our Legislatures.

He has affected to render the Military independent of, and superior to the Civil Power.

He has combined with others to subject us to a Jurisdiction foreign to our Constitution, and unacknowledged by our

Laws; giving his Assent to their Acts of pretended Legislation:

For quartering large Bodies of Armed Troops among us:

For protecting them, by a mock Trial, from Punishment for any Murders which they should commit on the Inhabitants of these States:

For cutting off our Trade with all Parts of the World:

For imposing Taxes on us without our Consent:

For depriving us, in many cases, of the Benefits of Trial by Jury:

For transporting us beyond Seas to be tried for pretended Offences:

For abolishing the free System of English Laws in a neighbouring Province, establishing therein an arbitrary Government, and enlarging its Boundaries, so as to render it at once an Example and fit Instrument for introducing the same absolute Rule into these Colonies:

For taking away our Charters, abolishing our most valuable Laws, and altering fundamentally the Forms of our Governments:

For suspending our own Legislatures, and declaring themselves invested with Power to legislate for us in all Cases whatsoever.

He has abdicated Government here, by declaring us out of his Protection and waging War against us.

He has plundered our Seas, ravaged our Coasts, burnt our towns, and destroyed the Lives of our People.

He is, at this Time, transporting large Armies of foreign Mercenaries to compleat the works of Death, Desolation, and Tyranny, already begun with circumstances of Cruelty and Perfidy, scarcely parelleled in the most barbarous Ages, and totally unworthy the Head of a civilized Nation.

He has constrained our fellow Citizens taken Captive on the high Seas to bear Arms against their Country, to become the Executioners of their Friends and Brethren, or to fall themselves by their Hands.

He has excited domestic Insurrections amongst us, and has endeavoured to bring on the Inhabitants of our Frontiers, the merciless Indian Savages, whose known Rule of Warfare, is an undistinguished Destruction, of all Ages, Sexes and Conditions.

In every state of these Oppressions we have Petitioned for Redress in the most humble Terms: Our repeated Petitions have been answered only by repeated Injury. A Prince, whose Character is thus marked by every act which may define a Tyrant, is unfit to be the Ruler of a free People.

Nor have we been wanting in Attentions to our British Brethren. We have warned them from Time to Time of Attempts by their Legislature to extend an unwarrantable Jurisdiction over us. We have reminded them of the Circumstances of our Emigration and Settlement here. We have appealed to their native Justice and Magnanimity, and we have conjured them by the Ties of our common Kindred to disavow these Usurpations, which, would inevitably interrupt our Connections and Correspondence. They too have been deaf to the Voice of Justice and of Consanguinity. We must, therefore, acquiesce in the Necessity, which denounces our Separation, and hold them, as we hold the rest of Mankind, Enemies in War, in Peace, Friends.

We, therefore, the Representatives of the UNITED STATES OF AMERICA, in General Congress Assembled, appealing to the Supreme Judge of the World for the Rectitude of our Intentions, do, in the Name, and by the Authority of the good People of these Colonies, solemnly Publish and Declare, That these United Colonies are, and of Right ought to be, Free and Independent States; that they are absolved from all Allegiance to the British Crown, and that all political Connection between them and the State of Great-Britain, is and ought to be totally dissolved; and that as Free and Independent States, they have full Power to levy War, conclude Peace, contract Alliances, establish Commerce, and to do all other Acts and Things which Independent States may of right do. And for the support of this declaration, with a firm Reliance on the Protection of divine Providence, we mutually pledge to each other our lives, our Fortunes, and our sacred Honor.

The Constitution of the United States of America*

The Preamble

We the People of the United States, in Order to form a more perfect Union, establish Justice, insure domestic Tranquility, provide for the common defence, promote the general Welfare, and secure the Blessings of Liberty to ourselves and our Posterity, do ordain and establish this Constitution for the United States of America.

The Preamble declares that "We the People" are the authority for the Constitution (unlike the Articles of Confederation, which derived their authority from the states). The Preamble also sets out the purposes of the Constitution.

Article I. (Legislative Branch)

The first part of the Constitution is called Article 1; it deals with the organization and powers of the lawmaking branch of the national government, the Congress.

Section 1. Legislative Powers

All legislative Powers herein granted shall be vested in a Congress of the United States, which shall consist of a Senate and House of Representatives.

Section 2. House of Representatives

Clause 1: Composition and Election of Members. The House of Representatives shall be composed of Members chosen every second Year by the People of the several States, and the Electors in each State shall have the Qualifications requisite for Electors of the most numerous Branch of the State Legislature.

Each state has the power to decide who may vote for members of Congress. Within each state, those who may vote for state legislators may also vote for members of the House of Representatives (and, under the Seventeenth Amendment, for U.S. senators). When the Constitution was written, nearly all states limited voting rights to white male property owners or taxpayers at least twenty-one years old. Subsequent amendments granted voting power to African-American men, all women, and eighteen-year-olds.

Clause 2: Qualifications. No Person shall be a Representative who shall not have attained to the Age of twenty five Years, and been seven Years a Citizen of the United States, and who shall not, when elected, be an Inhabitant of that State in which he shall be chosen.

Each member of the House must (1) be at least twenty-five years old, (2) have been a U.S. citizen for at least seven years, and (3) be a resident of the state in which she or he is elected.

Clause 3: Apportionment of Representatives and Direct Taxes. Representatives [and direct Taxes][1] shall be apportioned among the several States which may be included within this Union, according to their respective Numbers [which shall be determined by adding to the whole Number of free Persons, including those bound to Service for a Term of Years, and excluding Indians not taxed, three fifths of all other Persons].[2] The actual Enumeration shall be made within three Years after the first Meeting of the Congress of the United States, and within every subsequent Term of ten Years, in such Manner as they shall by Law direct. The Number of Representatives shall not exceed one for every thirty Thousand, but each State shall have at Least one Representative; and until such enumeration shall be made, the State of New Hampshire shall be entitled to chuse three, Massachusetts eight, Rhode Island and Providence Plantations one, Connecticut five, New York six, New Jersey four, Pennsylvania eight, Delaware one, Maryland six, Virginia ten, North Carolina five, South Carolina five, and Georgia three.

A state's representation in the House is based on the size of its population. Population is counted in each decade's census, after which Congress reapportions House seats. Since early in this century, the number of seats has been limited to 435.

---

*The spelling, capitalization, and punctuation of the original have been retained here. Brackets indicate passages that have been altered by amendments to the Constitution.
[1]Modified by the Sixteenth Amendment.
[2]Modified by the Fourteenth Amendment.

Clause 4: Vacancies.   When vacancies happen in the Representation from any State, the Executive Authority thereof shall issue Writs of Election to fill such Vacancies.

The "Executive Authority" is the state's governor. When a vacancy occurs in the House, the governor calls a special election to fill it.

Clause 5: Officers and Impeachment.   The House of Representatives shall chuse their Speaker and other Officers; and shall have the sole Power of Impeachment.

The power to impeach is the power to accuse. In this case, it is the power to accuse members of the executive or judicial branch of wrongdoing or abuse of power. Once a bill of impeachment is issued, the Senate holds the trial.

Section 3. The Senate
Clause 1: Term and Number of Members.   The Senate of the United States shall be composed of two Senators from each State [chosen by the Legislature thereof],[3] for six Years; and each Senator shall have one Vote.

Every state has two senators, each of whom serves for six years and has one vote in the upper chamber. Since the Seventeenth Amendment in 1913, all senators are elected directly by voters of the state during the regular election.

Clause 2: Classification of Senators.   Immediately after they shall be assembled in Consequence of the first Election, they shall be divided as equally as may be into three Classes. The Seats of the Senators of the first Class shall be vacated at the Expiration of the second Year, of the second Class at the Expiration of the fourth Year, and of the third Class at the Expiration of the sixth Year, so that one third may be chosen every second Year; [and if Vacancies happen by Resignation, or otherwise, during the Recess of the Legislature of any State, the Executive thereof may make temporary Appointments until the next Meeting of the Legislature, which shall then fill such Vacancies].[4]

One-third of the Senate's seats are open to election every two years (unlike the House, all of whose members are elected simultaneously).

Clause 3: Qualifications.   No Person shall be a Senator who shall not have attained to the Age of thirty Years, and been nine Years a Citizen of the United States, and who shall not, when elected, be an Inhabitant of that State for which he shall be chosen.

Every senator must be at least thirty years old, a citizen of the United States for a minimum of nine years, and a resident of the state in which he or she is elected.

Clause 4: The Role of the Vice President.   The Vice President of the United States shall be President of the Senate, but shall have no Vote, unless they be equally divided.

The vice-president presides over meetings of the Senate but cannot vote unless there is a tie. The Constitution gives no other official duties to the vice-president.

Clause 5: Other Officers.   The Senate shall chuse their other Officers, and also a President pro tempore, in the Absence of the Vice President, or when he shall exercise the Office of President of the United States.

The Senate votes for one of its members to preside when the vice-president is absent. This person is usually called the president pro tempore because of the temporary situation of the position.

Clause 6: Impeachment Trials.   The Senate shall have the sole Power to try all Impeachments. When sitting for that Purpose, they shall be on Oath or Affirmation. When the President of the United States is tried, the Chief Justice shall preside: And no Person shall be convicted without the Concurrence of two thirds of the Members present.

The Senate conducts trials of officials that the House impeaches. The Senate sits as a jury, with the vice-president presiding if the president is not on trial.

Clause 7: Penalties for Conviction.   Judgment in Cases of Impeachment shall not extend further than to removal from Office, and disqualification to hold and enjoy any Office of honor, Trust, or Profit under the United States: but the Party convicted shall nevertheless be liable and subject to Indictment, Trial, Judgment, and Punishment, according to Law.

On conviction on impeachment charges, the Senate can only force an official to leave office and prevent him or her from holding another office in the federal government. The individual, however, can still be tried in a regular court.

Section 4. Congressional Elections: Times, Manner, and Places
Clause 1: Elections.   The Times, Places and Manner of holding Elections for Senators and Representatives, shall be prescribed in each State by the Legislature thereof; but the Congress may at any time by Law make or alter such Regulations, except as to the Places of chusing Senators.

Congress set the Tuesday after the first Monday in November in even-numbered years as the date for congressional elections. In states with more than one seat in the House, Congress requires that representatives be elected from districts within each state. Under the Seventeenth Amendment, senators are elected at the same places as other officials.

Clause 2: Sessions of Congress.   [The Congress shall assemble at least once in every Year, and such Meeting shall be on

---

[3]Repealed by the Seventeenth Amendment.
[4]Modified by the Seventeenth Amendment.

the first Monday in December, unless they shall by Law appoint a different Day.][5]

Congress has to meet every year at least once. The regular session now begins at noon on January 3 of each year, subsequent to the Twentieth Amendment, unless Congress passes a law to fix a different date. Congress stays in session until its members vote to adjourn. Additionally, the president may call a special session.

Section 5. Powers and Duties of the Houses
Clause 1: Admitting Members and Quorum. Each House shall be the Judge of the Elections, Returns, and Qualifications of its own Members, and a Majority of each shall constitute a Quorum to do Business; but a smaller Number may adjourn from day to day, and may be authorized to compel the Attendance of absent Members, in such Manner, and under such Penalties as each House may provide.

Each chamber may exclude or refuse to seat a member-elect.
  The quorum rule requires that 218 members of the House and 51 members of the Senate be present in order to conduct business. This rule is normally not enforced in the handling of routine matters.

Clause 2: Rules and Discipline of Members. Each House may determine the Rules of its Proceedings, punish its Members for disorderly Behaviour, and, with the Concurrence of two thirds, expel a Member.

The House and the Senate may adopt their own rules to guide their proceedings. Each may also discipline its members for conduct that is deemed unacceptable. No member may be expelled without a two-thirds majority.

Clause 3: Keeping a Record. Each House shall keep a Journal of its Proceedings, and from time to time publish the same, excepting such Parts as may in their Judgment require Secrecy; and the Yeas and Nays of the Members of either House on any question shall, at the Desire of one fifth of those Present, be entered on the Journal.

The journals of the two houses are published at the end of each session of Congress.

Clause 4: Adjournment. Neither House, during the Session of Congress, shall, without the Consent of the other, adjourn for more than three days, nor to any other Place than that in which the two Houses shall be sitting.

Congress has the power to determine when and where to meet, provided, however, that both houses meet in the same city. Neither house may recess in excess of three days without the consent of the other.

Section 6. Rights of Members
Clause 1: Compensation and Privileges. The Senators and Representatives shall receive a Compensation for their services, to be ascertained by Law, and paid out of the Treasury of the United States. They shall in all Cases, except Treason, Felony and Breach of the Peace, be privileged from Arrest during their Attendance at the Session of their respective Houses, and in going to and returning from the same; and for any Speech or Debate in either House, they shall not be questioned in any other Place.

Congressional salaries are to be paid by the U.S. Treasury rather than by the members' respective states. The original salaries were $6 per day; in 1857 they were $3,000 per year. Both representatives and senators currently are paid $129,500 each year.

Members cannot be arrested for things they say during speeches and debates in Congress. This immunity applies to the Capitol Building itself and not to their private lives.
  Treason is defined in Article III, Section 3. A felony is any serious crime. A breach of the peace is any indictable offense less than treason or a felony. Members cannot be arrested for anything they say in speeches or debates in Congress.

Clause 2: Restrictions. No Senator or Representative shall, during the Time for which he was elected, be appointed to any civil Office under the Authority of the United States, which shall have been created, or the Emoluments whereof shall have been encreased during such time; and no Person holding any Office under the United States, shall be a Member of either House during his Continuance in Office.

During the term for which a member was elected, he or she cannot concurrently accept another federal government position.

Section 7. Legislative Powers: Bills and Resolutions
Clause 1: Revenue Bills. All Bills for raising Revenue shall originate in the House of Representatives; but the Senate may propose or concur with Amendments as on other Bills.

All tax and appropriation bills for raising money have to originate in the House of Representatives. The Senate, though, often amends such bills and may even substitute an entirely different bill.

Clause 2: The Presidential Veto. Every Bill which shall have passed the House of Representatives and the Senate, shall, before it becomes a Law, be presented to the President of the United States; If he approve he shall sign it, but if not he shall return it, with his Objections to the House in which it shall have originated, who shall enter the Objections at large on their Journal, and proceed to reconsider it. If after such Reconsideration two thirds of that House shall agree to pass the Bill, it shall be sent together with the Objections, to the other House, by which it shall likewise be reconsidered, and if approved by two thirds of that House, it shall become a Law. But in all such Cases the Votes of both Houses shall be de-

---

[5]Changed by the Twentieth Amendment.

termined by Yeas and Nays, and the Names of the Persons voting for and against the Bill shall be entered on the Journal of each House respectively. If any Bill shall not be returned by the President within ten Days (Sundays excepted) after it shall have been presented to him, the Same shall be a Law, in like Manner as if he had signed it, unless the Congress by their Adjournment prevent its Return in which Case it shall not be a Law.

When Congress sends the president a bill, he or she can sign it (in which case it becomes law) or send it back to the house in which it originated. If it is sent back, a two-thirds majority of each house must pass it again for it to become law. If the president neither signs it nor sends it back within ten days, it becomes law anyway, unless Congress adjourns in the meantime.

Clause 3: Actions on Other Matters.
Every Order, Resolution, or Vote to which the Concurrence of the Senate and House of Representatives may be necessary (except on a question of Adjournment) shall be presented to the President of the United States; and before the Same shall take Effect, shall be approved by him, or being disapproved by him, shall be repassed by two thirds of the Senate and House of Representatives, according to the Rules and Limitations prescribed in the Case of a Bill.

The president must either sign or veto everything that Congress passes, except votes to adjourn and resolutions not having the force of law.

Section 8. The Powers of Congress

Clause 1: Taxing.
The Congress shall have Power To lay and collect Taxes, Duties, Imposts and Excises, to pay the Debts and provide for the common Defence and general Welfare of the United States; but all Duties, Imposts and Excises shall be uniform throughout the United States;

Duties are taxes on imports and exports. Impost is a generic term for tax. Excises are taxes on the manufacture, sale, or use of goods.

Clause 2: Borrowing.
To borrow Money on the credit of the United States;

Congress has the power to borrow money, which is normally carried out through the sale of U.S. treasury bonds on which interest is paid. Note that the Constitution places no limit on the amount of government borrowing.

Clause 3: Regulation of Commerce.
To regulate Commerce with foreign Nations, and among the several States, and with the Indian Tribes;

This is the Commerce Clause, which gives to the Congress the power to regulate interstate and foreign trade. Much of the activity of Congress is based on this clause.

Clause 4: Naturalization and Bankruptcy.
To establish a uniform Rule of Naturalization, and uniform Laws on the subject of Bankruptcies throughout the United States;

Only Congress may determine how aliens can become citizens of the United States. Congress may make laws with respect to bankruptcy.

Clause 5: Money and Standards.
To coin Money, regulate the Value thereof, and of foreign Coin, and fix the Standard of Weights and Measures;

Congress mints coins and prints and circulates paper money. Congress can establish uniform measures of time, distance, weight, etc. In 1838 Congress adopted the English system of weights and measurements as our national standard.

Clause 6: Punishing Counterfeiters.
To provide for the Punishment of counterfeiting the Securities and current Coin of the United States;

Congress has the power to punish those who copy American money and pass it off as real. Currently, the fine is up to $5,000 and/or imprisonment for up to fifteen years.

Clause 7: Roads and Post Offices.
To establish Post Offices and post Roads;

Post roads include all routes over which mail is carried—highways, railways, waterways, and airways.

Clause 8: Patents and Copyrights.
To promote the Progress of Science and useful Arts, by securing for limited Times to Authors and Inventors the exclusive Right to their respective Writings and Discoveries;

Authors' and composers' works are protected by copyrights established by copyright law, which currently is the 1978 Copyright Act. Copyrights are valid for the life of the author or composer plus fifty years. Inventors' works are protected by patents, which vary in length of protection from three and a half to seventeen years. A patent gives a person the exclusive right to control the manufacture or sale of her or his invention.

Clause 9: Lower Courts.
To constitute Tribunals inferior to the supreme Court;

Congress has the authority to set up all federal courts, except the Supreme Court, and to decide what cases those courts will hear.

Clause 10: Punishment for Piracy.
To define and punish Piracies and Felonies committed on the high Seas, and Offences against the Law of Nations;

Congress has the authority to prohibit the commission of certain acts outside U.S. territory and to punish certain violations of international law.

Clause 11: *Declaration of War.* To declare War, grant Letters of Marque and Reprisal, and make Rules concerning Captures on Land and Water;

Only Congress can declare war, although the president, as commander in chief, can make war without Congress's formal declaration. Letters of marque and reprisal authorized private parties to capture and destroy enemy ships in wartime. Since the mid-nineteenth century, international law has prohibited letters of marque and reprisal, and the United States has honored the ban.

Clause 12: *The Army.* To raise and support Armies, but no Appropriation of Money to that Use shall be for a longer Term than two Years;

Congress has the power to create an army; the money used to pay for it must be appropriated for no more than two-year intervals. This latter restriction gives ultimate control of the army to civilians.

Clause 13: *Creation of a Navy.* To provide and maintain a Navy;

This clause allows for the maintenance of a navy. In 1947 Congress created the air force.

Clause 14: *Regulation of the Armed Forces.* To make Rules for the Government and Regulation of the land and naval Forces;

Congress sets the rules for the military mainly by way of the Uniform Code of Military Justice, which was enacted in 1950 by Congress.

Clause 15: *The Militia.* To provide for calling forth the Militia to execute the Laws of the Union, suppress Insurrections and repel Invasions;

The militia is known today as the National Guard. Both Congress and the president have the authority to call the National Guard into federal service.

Clause 16: *How the Militia is Organized.* To provide for organizing, arming, and disciplining the Militia, and for governing such Part of them as may be employed in the Service of the United States, reserving to the States respectively, the Appointment of the Officers, and the Authority of training the Militia according to the discipline prescribed by Congress;

This clause gives Congress the power to "federalize" state militia (National Guard). When called into such service, the National Guard is subject to the same rules that Congress has set forth for the regular armed services.

Clause 17: *Creation of the District of Columbia.* To exercise exclusive Legislation in all Cases whatsoever, over such District (not exceeding ten Miles square) as may, by Cession of particular States, and the Acceptance of Congress, become the Seat of the Government of the United States, and to exercise like Authority over all Places purchased by the Consent of the Legislature of the State in which the Same shall be, for the Erection of Forts, Magazines, Arsenals, dock-Yards, and other needful Buildings;—And

Congress established the District of Columbia as the national capital in 1791. Virginia and Maryland had granted land for the District, but Virginia's grant was returned because it was believed it would not be needed. Today, the District is sixty-nine miles square.

Clause 18: *The Elastic Clause.* To make all Laws which shall be necessary and proper for carrying into Execution the foregoing Powers, and all other Powers vested by this Constitution in the Government of the United States, or in any Department or Officer thereof.

This clause—the Necessary and Proper Clause, or the Elastic Clause—grants no specific powers, and thus it can be stretched to fit different circumstances. It has allowed Congress to adapt the government to changing needs and times.

Section 9. The Powers Denied to Congress

Clause 1: *Question of Slavery.* The Migration or Importation of such Persons as any of the States now existing shall think proper to admit, shall not be prohibited by the Congress prior to the Year one thousand eight hundred and eight, but a Tax or duty may be imposed on such Importation, not exceeding ten dollars for each Person.

"Persons" referred to slaves. Congress outlawed the slave trade in 1808.

Clause 2: *Habeas Corpus.* The privilege of the Writ of Habeas Corpus shall not be suspended, unless when in Cases of Rebellion or Invasion the public Safety may require it.

A writ of habeas corpus is a court order directing a sheriff or other public officer who is detaining another person to "produce the body" of the detainee so the court can assess the legality of the detention.

Clause 3: *Special Bills.* No Bill of Attainder or ex post facto Law shall be passed.

A bill of attainder is a law that inflicts punishment without a trial. An ex post facto law is a law that inflicts punishment for an act that was not illegal when it was committed.

Clause 4: *Direct Taxes.* [No Capitation, or other direct, Tax shall be laid, unless in Proportion to the Census or Enumeration herein before directed to be taken.][6]

---

[6]Modified by the Sixteenth Amendment.

A capitation is a tax on a person. A direct tax is a tax paid directly to the government, such as a property tax. This clause was intended to prevent Congress from levying a tax on slaves per person and thereby taxing slavery out of existence.

Clause 5: Export Taxes.   No Tax or Duty shall be laid on Articles exported from any State.

Congress may not tax any goods sold from one state to another or from one state to a foreign country. (Congress does have the power to tax goods that are bought from other countries, however.)

Clause 6: Interstate Commerce.   No Preference shall be given by any Regulation of Commerce or Revenue to the Ports of one State over those of another: nor shall Vessels bound to, or from, one State, be obliged to enter, clear, or pay Duties in another.

Congress may not treat different ports within the United States differently in terms of taxing and commerce powers. Congress may not tax goods sent from one state to another. Finally, Congress may not give one state's port a legal advantage over those of another state.

Clause 7: Treasury Withdrawals. No Money shall be drawn from the Treasury, but in Consequence of Appropriations made by Law; and a regular Statement and Account of the Receipts and Expenditures of all public Money shall be published from time to time.

Federal funds can be spent only as Congress authorizes. This is a significant check on the president's power.

Clause 8: Titles of Nobility.   No Title of Nobility shall be granted by the United States: And no Person holding any Office of Profit or Trust under them, shall, without the Consent of the Congress, accept of any present, Emolument, Office, or Title, of any kind whatever, from any King, Prince, or foreign State.

No person in the United States may be bestowed a title of nobility such as a duke or duchess. This clause also discourages bribery of American officials by foreign governments.

Section 10. Those Powers Denied to the States
Clause 1: Treaties and Coinage.   No State shall enter into any Treaty, Alliance, or Confederation; grant Letters of Marque and Reprisal; coin Money; emit Bills of Credit; make any Thing but gold and silver Coin a Tender in Payment of Debts; pass any Bill of Attainder, ex post facto Law, or Law impairing the Obligation of Contracts, or grant any Title of Nobility.

Prohibiting state laws "impairing the Obligation of Contracts" was intended to protect creditors. (Shays's Rebellion—an attempt to pre-vent courts from giving effect to creditors' legal actions against debtors—occurred only one year before the Constitution was written.)

Clause 2: Duties and Imposts.   No State shall, without the Consent of the Congress, lay any Imports or Duties on Imports or Exports, except what may be absolutely necessary for executing its inspection Laws; and the net Produce of all Duties and Imposts, laid by any State on Imports or Exports, shall be for the Use of the Treasury of the United States; and all such Laws shall be subject to the Revision and Controul of the Congress.

Only Congress can tax imports. Further, the states cannot tax exports.

Clause 3: War.   No State shall, without the Consent of Congress, lay any Duty of Tonnage, keep Troops, or Ships of War in time of Peace, enter into any Agreement or Compact with another State, or with a foreign Power or engage in War, unless actually invaded, or in such imminent Danger as will not admit of delay.

A duty of tonnage is a tax on ships according to their cargo capacity. No states may effectively tax ships according to their cargo unless Congress agrees. Additionally, this clause forbids any state to keep troops or warships during peacetime or to make a compact with another state or foreign nation unless Congress so agrees. States can, in contrast, maintain a militia, but its use has to be limited to internal disorders that occur within a state—unless, of course, the militia is called into federal service.

Article II. (Executive Branch)

Section 1. The Nature and Scope of Presidential Power
Clause 1: Four-Year Term.   The executive Power shall be vested in a President of the United States of America. He shall hold his Office during the Term of four Years, and, together with the Vice President, chosen for the same Term, be elected, as follows.

The president has the power to carry out laws made by Congress, called the executive power. He or she serves in office for a four-year term after election. The Twenty-second Amendment limits the number of times a person may be elected president.

Clause 2: Choosing Electors From Each State.   Each State shall appoint, in such Manner as the Legislature thereof may direct, a Number of Electors, equal to the whole Number of Senators and Representatives to which the State may be entitled in the Congress; but no Senator or Representative, or Person holding an Office of Trust or Profit under the United States, shall be appointed an Elector.

The "Electors" are more commonly known as the "electoral college." The president is elected by electors—that is, representatives chosen by the people—rather than by the people directly.

Clause 3: The Former System of Elections. [The Electors shall meet in their respective States, and vote by Ballot for two Persons, of whom one at least shall not be an Inhabitant of the same State with themselves. And they shall make a List of all the Persons voted for, and of the Number of Votes for each; which List they shall sign and certify, and transmit sealed to the Seat of the Government of the United States, directed to the President of the Senate. The President of the Senate shall, in the Presence of the Senate and House of Representatives, open all the Certificates, and the Votes shall then be counted. The Person having the greatest Number of Votes shall be the President, if such Number be a Majority of the whole Number of Electors appointed; and if there be more than one who have such Majority, and have an equal Number of Votes, then the House of Representatives shall immediately chuse by Ballot one of them for President; and if no Person have a Majority, then from the five highest on the List the said House shall in like Manner chuse the President. But in chusing the President, the Votes shall be taken by States, the Representation from each State having one Vote; A quorum for this Purpose shall consist of a Member or Members from two thirds of the States, and a Majority of all the States shall be necessary to a Choice. In every Case, after the Choice of the President, the Person having the greater Number of Votes of the Electors shall be the Vice President. But if there should remain two or more who have equal Votes, the Senate shall chuse from them by Ballot the Vice President.][7]

The original method of selecting the president and vice-president was replaced by the Twelfth Amendment. Apparently, the framers did not anticipate the rise of political parties and the development of primaries and conventions.

Clause 4: The Time of Elections. The Congress may determine the Time of chusing the Electors, and the Day on which they shall give their Votes; which Day shall be the same throughout the United States.

Congress set the Tuesday after the first Monday in November every fourth year as the date for choosing electors. The electors cast their votes on the Monday after the second Wednesday in December of that year.

Clause 5: Qualifications for President. No person except a natural born Citizen, or a Citizen of the United States, at the time of the Adoption of this Constitution, shall be eligible to the Office of President; neither shall any Person be eligible to that Office who shall not have attained to the Age of thirty five Years, and been fourteen Years a Resident within the United States.

The president must be a natural-born citizen, be at least thirty-five years of age when taking office, and have been a resident within the United States for at least fourteen years.

Clause 6: Succession of the Vice President. [In Case of the Removal of the President from Office, or of his Death, Resignation or Inability to discharge the Powers and Duties of the said Office, the same shall devolve on the Vice President, and the Congress may by Law provide for the Case of Removal, Death, Resignation or Inability, both of the President and Vice President, declaring what Officer shall then act as President, and such Officer shall act accordingly, until the Disability be removed, or a President shall be elected.][8]

This former section provided for the method by which the vice-president was to succeed to the presidency, but its wording is ambiguous. It was replaced by the Twenty-fifth Amendment.

Clause 7: The President's Salary. The President shall, at stated Times, receive for his Services, a Compensation, which shall neither be encreased nor diminished during the Period for which he shall have been elected, and he shall not receive within that Period any other Emolument from the United States, or any of them.

The president maintains the same salary during each four-year term. Moreover, she or he may not receive additional cash payments from the government. Originally set at $25,000 per year, it is currently $200,000 a year plus a $50,000 taxable expense account.

Clause 8: The Oath of Office. Before he enter on the Execution of his Office, he shall take the following Oath or Affirmation: "I do solemnly swear (or affirm) that I will faithfully execute the Office of President of the United States, and will to the best of my Ability, preserve, protect and defend the Constitution of the United States."

The president is "sworn in" prior to beginning the duties of the office. Currently, the taking of the oath of office occurs on January 20, following the November election. The ceremony is called the inauguration. The oath of office is administered by the chief justice of the United States Supreme Court.

Section 2. Powers of the President

Clause 1: Commander in Chief. The President shall be Commander in Chief of the Army and Navy of the United States, and of the Militia of the several States, when called into the actual Service of the United States; he may require the Opinion, in writing, of the principal Officer in each of the executive Departments, upon any Subject relating to the Duties of their respective Offices, and he shall have Power to grant Reprieves and Pardons for Offences against the United States, except in Cases of Impeachment.

---

[7]Changed by the Twelfth Amendment.

[8]Modified by the Twenty-fifth Amendment.

The armed forces are placed under civilian control because the president is a civilian, but still commander in chief of the military. The president may ask for the help of the heads of each of the executive departments (thereby creating the Cabinet). The Cabinet members are chosen by the president with the consent of the Senate, but they can be removed without Senate approval.

The president's clemency powers extend only to federal cases. In those cases, he or she may grant a full or conditional pardon, or reduce a prison term or fine.

Clause 2: *Treaties and Appointment.*   He shall have Power, by and with the Advice and Consent of the Senate, to make Treaties, provided two thirds of the Senators present concur; and he shall nominate, and by and with the Advice and Consent of the Senate, shall appoint Ambassadors, other public Ministers and Consuls, Judges of the supreme Court, and all other Officers of the United States, whose Appointments are not herein otherwise provided for, and which shall be established by Law; but the Congress may by Law vest the Appointment of such inferior Officers, as they think proper, in the President alone, in the Courts of Law, or in the Heads of Departments.

Many of the major powers of the president are identified in this clause, including the power to make treaties with foreign governments (with the approval of the Senate by a two-thirds vote) and the power to appoint ambassadors, Supreme Court justices, and other government officials. Most such appointments require Senate approval.

Clause 3: *Vacancies.*   The President shall have Power to fill up all Vacancies that may happen during the Recess of the Senate, by granting Commissions which shall expire at the end of their next Session.

The president has the power to appoint temporary officials to fill vacant federal offices without Senate approval if the Congress is not in session. Such appointments expire automatically at the end of Congress's next term.

Section 3. Duties of the President
He shall from time to time give to the Congress Information of the State of the Union, and recommend to their Consideration such Measures as he shall judge necessary and expedient; he may, on extraordinary Occasions, convene both Houses, or either of them, and in Case of Disagreement between them, with Respect to the Time of Adjournment, he may adjourn them to such Time as he shall think proper; he shall receive Ambassadors and other public Ministers; he shall take Care that the Laws be faithfully executed, and shall Commission all the Officers of the United States.

Annually, the president reports on the state of the union to Congress, recommends legislative measures, and proposes a federal budget. The State of the Union speech is a statement not only to

Congress but also to the American people. After it is given, the president proposes a federal budget and presents an economic report. At any time he or she so chooses, the president may send special messages to Congress while it is in session. The president has the power to call special sessions, to adjourn Congress when its two houses do not agree for that purpose, to receive diplomatic representatives of other governments, and to ensure the proper execution of all federal laws. The president further has the ability to empower federal officers to hold their positions and to perform their duties.

Section 4. Impeachment
The President, Vice President and all civil Officers of the United States, shall be removed from Office on Impeachment for, and Conviction of, Treason, Bribery, or other high Crimes and Misdemeanors.

Treason denotes giving aid to the nation's enemies. The definition of high crimes and misdemeanors is usually given as serious abuses of political power. In either case, the president or vice-president may be accused by the House (called an impeachment) and then removed from office if convicted by the Senate. (Note that impeachment does not mean removal, but rather the state of being accused of treason or high crimes and misdemeanors.)

Article III. (Judicial Branch)

Section 1. Judicial Powers, Courts, and Judges
The judicial Power of the United States, shall be vested in one supreme Court, and in such inferior Courts as the Congress may from time to time ordain and establish. The Judges, both of the supreme and inferior Courts, shall hold their Offices during good Behaviour, and shall, at stated Times, receive for their Services a Compensation, which shall not be diminished during their Continuance in Office.

The Supreme Court is vested with judicial power, as are the lower federal courts that Congress creates. Federal judges serve in their offices for life unless they are impeached and convicted by Congress. The payment of federal judges may not be reduced during their time in office.

Section 2. Jurisdiction
Clause 1: *Cases Under Federal Jurisdiction.*   The judicial Power shall extend to all Cases, in Law and Equity, arising under this Constitution, the Laws of the United States, and Treaties made, or which shall be made, under their Authority;—to all Cases affecting Ambassadors, other public Ministers and Consuls;—to all Cases of admiralty and maritime Jurisdiction;—to Controversies to which the United States shall be a Party;—to Controversies between two or more States; [—between a State and Citizens of another State;—][9]

---

[9]Modified by the Eleventh Amendment.

between Citizens of different States;—between Citizens of the same State claiming Lands under Grants of different States, [and between a State, or the Citizens thereof, and foreign States, Citizens or Subjects.][10]

The federal courts take on cases that concern the meaning of the U.S. Constitution, all federal laws, and treaties. They also can take on cases involving citizens of different states and citizens of foreign nations.

Clause 2: Cases for the Supreme Court.   In all Cases affecting Ambassadors, other public Ministers and Consuls, and those in which a State shall be a Party, the supreme Court shall have original Jurisdiction. In all the other Cases before mentioned, the supreme Court shall have appellate Jurisdiction, both as to Law and Fact, with such Exceptions, and under such Regulations as the Congress shall make.

In a limited number of situations, the Supreme Court acts as a trial court and has original jurisdiction. These cases involve a representative from another country or involve a state. In all other situations, the cases must first be tried in the lower courts and then can be appealed to the Supreme Court. Congress may, however, make exceptions. Today the Supreme Court acts as a trial court of first instance on rare occasions.

Clause 3: The Conduct of Trials.   The Trial of all Crimes, except in Cases of Impeachment, shall be by Jury; and such Trial shall be held in the State where the said Crimes shall have been committed; but when not committed within any State, the Trial shall be at such Place or Places as the Congress may by Law have directed.

Any person accused of a federal crime is granted the right to a trial by jury in a federal court in that state in which the crime was committed. Trials of impeachment are an exception.

Section 3. Treason
Clause 1: The Definition of Treason.   Treason against the United States, shall consist only in levying War against them, or, in adhering to their Enemies, giving them Aid and Comfort. No Person shall be convicted of Treason unless on the Testimony of two Witnesses to the same overt Act, or on Confession in open Court.

Treason is the making of war against the United States or giving aid to its enemies.

Clause 2: Punishment.   The Congress shall have Power to declare the Punishment of Treason, but no Attainder of Treason shall work Corruption of Blood, or Forfeiture except during the Life of the Person attainted.

Congress has provided that the punishment for treason range from a minimum of five years in prison and/or a $10,000 fine to a maximum of death. "No Attainder of Treason shall work Corruption of Blood" prohibits punishment of the traitor's heirs.

Article IV. (Relations Among the States)

Section 1. Full Faith and Credit
Full Faith and Credit shall be given in each State to the public Acts, Records, and judicial Proceedings of every other State. And the Congress may by general Laws prescribe the Manner in which such Acts, Records and Proceedings shall be proved, and the Effect thereof.

All states are required to respect one another's laws, records, and lawful decisions. There are exceptions, however. A state does not have to enforce another state's criminal code. Nor does it have to recognize another state's grant of a divorce if the person obtaining the divorce did not establish legal residence in the state in which it was given.

Section 2. Treatment of Citizens
Clause 1: Privileges and Immunities.   The Citizens of each State shall be entitled to all Privileges and Immunities of Citizens in the several States.

A citizen of a state has the same rights and privileges as the citizens of another state in which he or she happens to be.

Clause 2: Extradition.   A Person charged in any State with Treason, Felony, or other Crime, who shall flee from Justice, and be found in another State, shall on Demand of the executive Authority of the State from which he fled, be delivered up, to be removed to the State having Jurisdiction of the Crime.

Any person accused of a crime who flees to another state must be returned to the state in which the crime occurred.

Clause 3: Fugitive Slaves.   [No Person held to Service or Labour in one State, under the Laws thereof, escaping into another, shall, in Consequence of any Law or Regulation therein, be discharged from such Service or Labour, but shall be delivered up on Claim of the Party to whom such Service or Labour may be due.][11]

This clause was struck down by the Thirteenth Amendment, which abolished slavery in 1865.

Section 3. Admission of States
Clause 1: The Process.   New States may be admitted by the Congress into this Union; but no new State shall be formed

---

[10]Modified by the Eleventh Amendment.

[11]Repealed by the Thirteenth Amendment.

or erected within the Jurisdiction of any other State; nor any State be formed by the Junction of two or more States, or Parts of States, without the Consent of the Legislatures of the States concerned as well as of the Congress.

Only Congress has the power to admit new states to the union. No state may be created by taking territory from an existing state unless the state's legislature so consents.

Clause 2: Public Land.   The Congress shall have Power to dispose of and make all needful Rules and Regulations respecting the Territory or other Property belonging to the United States; and nothing in this Constitution shall be so construed as to Prejudice any Claims of the United States, or of any particular State.

The federal government has the exclusive right to administer federal government public lands.

Section 4. Republican Form of Government
The United States shall guarantee to every State in this Union a Republican Form of Government, and shall protect each of them against Invasion; and on Application of the Legislature, or of the Executive (when the Legislature cannot be convened) against domestic Violence.

Each state is promised a form of government in which the people elect their representatives, called a republican form. The federal government is bound to protect states against any attack by foreigners or during times of trouble within a state.

Article V. (Methods of Amendment)
The Congress, whenever two thirds of both Houses shall deem it necessary, shall propose Amendments to this Constitution, or on the Application of the Legislatures of two thirds of the several States, shall call a Convention for proposing Amendments, which, in either Case, shall be valid to all Intents and Purposes, as Part of this Constitution, when ratified by the Legislatures of three fourths of the several States, or by Conventions in three fourths thereof, as the one or the other Mode of Ratification may be proposed by the Congress; Provided that no Amendment which may be made prior to the Year One thousand eight hundred and eight shall in any Manner affect the first and fourth Clauses in the Ninth Section of the First Article; and that no State, without its Consent, shall be deprived of its equal Suffrage in the Senate.

Articles may be proposed in either of two ways: a two-thirds vote of each house (Congress) or at the request of two-thirds of the states. Ratification of amendments may be carried out in two ways: by the legislatures of three-fourths of the states or by the voters in three-fourths of the states. No state may be denied equal representation in the Senate.

Article VI. (National Supremacy)
Clause 1: Existing Obligations.   All Debts contracted and Engagements entered into, before the Adoption of this Constitution shall be as valid against the United States under this Constitution, as under the Confederation.

During the Revolutionary War and the years of the Confederation, Congress borrowed large sums. This clause pledged that the new federal government would assume those financial obligations.

Clause 2: Supreme Law of the Land.   This Constitution, and the Laws of the United States which shall be made in Pursuance thereof; and all Treaties made, or which shall be made, under the Authority of the United States, shall be the supreme Law of the Land; and the Judges in every State shall be bound thereby, any Thing in the Constitution or Laws of any State to the Contrary notwithstanding.

This is typically called the Supremacy Clause; it declares that federal law takes precedence over all forms of state law. No government, at the local or state level, may make or enforce any law that conflicts with any provision of the Constitution, acts of Congress, treaties, or other rules and regulations issued by the president and his or her subordinates in the executive branch of the federal government.

Clause 3: Oath of Office.   The Senators and Representatives before mentioned, and the Members of the several State Legislatures, and all executive and judicial Officers, both of the United States and of the several States, shall be bound by Oath or Affirmation, to support this Constitution; but no religious Test shall ever be required as a Qualification to any Office or public Trust under the United States.

Every federal and state official must take an oath of office promising to support the U.S. Constitution. Religion may not be used as a qualification to serve in any federal office.

Article VII. (Ratification)
The Ratification of the Conventions of nine States shall, be sufficient for the Establishment of this Constitution between the States so ratifying the Same.

Nine states were required to ratify the Constitution. Delaware was the first and New Hampshire the ninth.

Done in Convention by the Unanimous Consent of the States present the Seventeenth Day of September in the Year of our Lord one thousand seven hundred and Eighty seven and of the Independence of the United States of America the Twelfth. In witness whereof we have hereunto subscribed our Names,

                              Go. WASHINGTON
Attest   Presid't. and deputy from Virginia
WILLIAM JACKSON
Secretary

DELAWARE
Geo. Read
Gunning Bedfordjun
John Dickinson
Richard Basset
Jaco. Broom

MASSACHUSETTS
Nathaniel Gorham
Rufus King

CONNECTICUT
Wm. Saml. Johnson
Roger Sherman

NEW YORK
Alexander Hamilton

NEW JERSEY
Wh. Livingston
David Brearley.
Wm. Paterson.
Jona. Dayton

PENNSYLVANIA
B. Franklin
Thomas Mifflin
Robt. Morris
Geo. Clymer
Thos. FitzSimons
Jared Ingersoll
James Wilson.
Gouv. Morris

NEW HAMPSHIRE
John Langdon
Nicholas Gilman

MARYLAND
James McHenry
Dan of St. Thos. Jenifer
Danl. Carroll.

VIRGINIA
John Blair
James Madison Jr.

NORTH CAROLINA
Wm. Blount
Richd. Dobbs Spaight.
Hu. Williamson

SOUTH CAROLINA
J. Rutledge
Charles Cotesworth
   Pinckney
Charles Pinckney
Pierce Butler.

GEORGIA
William Few
Abr. Baldwin

Articles in addition to, and amendment of the Constitution of the United States of America, proposed by Congress and ratified by the Legislatures of the several states, pursuant to the Fifth Article of the original Constitution.

Amendments to the Constitution of the United States

The Bill of Rights[12]

Amendment I.
Religion, Speech, Assembly, and Politics
Congress shall make no law respecting an establishment of religion, or prohibiting the free exercise thereof; or abridging the freedom of speech, or of the press; or the right of the people peaceably to assembly, and to petition the Government for a redress of grievances.

[12]On September 25, 1789, Congress transmitted to the state legislatures twelve proposed amendments, two of which, having to do with Congressional representation and Congressional pay, were not adopted. The remaining ten amendments became the Bill of Rights.

Congress may not create an official church or enact laws limiting the freedom of religion, speech, the press, assembly, and petition. These guarantees, like the others in the Bill of Rights (the first ten amendments), are not absolute—each may be exercised only with regard to the rights of other persons.

Amendment II.
Militia and the Right to Bear Arms
A well regulated Militia, being necessary to the security of a free State, the right of the people to keep and bear Arms, shall not be infringed.

To protect itself, each state has the right to maintain a volunteer armed force. States and the federal government regulate the possession and use of firearms by individuals.

Amendment III.
The Quartering of Soldiers
No Soldier shall, in time of peace be quartered in any house, without the consent of the Owner, nor in time of war, but in a manner to be prescribed by law.

Before the Revolutionary War, it had been common British practice to quarter soldiers in colonists' homes. Military troops do not have the power to take over private houses during peacetime.

Amendment IV.
Searches and Seizures
The right of the people to be secure in their persons, houses, papers, and effects, against unreasonable searches and seizures, shall not be violated, and no Warrants shall issue, but upon probable cause, supported by Oath or affirmation, and particularly describing the place to be searched, and the persons or things to be seized.

Here the word warrant *means "justification" and refers to a document issued by a magistrate or judge indicating the name, address, and possible offense committed. Anyone asking for the warrant, such as a police officer, must be able to convince the magistrate or judge that an offense probably has been committed.*

Amendment V.
Grand Juries, Self-incrimination, Double Jeopardy, Due Process, and Eminent Domain
No person shall be held to answer for a capital, or otherwise infamous crime, unless on a presentment or indictment of a Grand Jury, except in cases arising in the land or naval forces, or in the Militia, when in actual service in time of War or public danger; nor shall any person be subject for the same offence to be twice put in jeopardy of life or limb; nor shall be compelled in any criminal case to be a witness against himself, nor be deprived of life, liberty, or property, without

due process of law; nor shall private property be taken for public use, without just compensation.

There are two types of juries. A grand jury considers physical evidence and the testimony of witnesses, and decides whether there is sufficient reason to bring a case to trial. A petit jury hears the case at trial and decides it. "For the same offence to be twice put in jeopardy of life or limb" means to be tried twice for the same crime. A person may not be tried for the same crime twice or forced to give evidence against herself or himself. No person's right to life, liberty, or property may be taken away except by lawful means, called the due process of law. Private property taken for use in public purposes must be paid for by the government.

Amendment VI.
Criminal Court Procedures

In all criminal prosecutions, the accused shall enjoy the right to a speedy and public trial, by an impartial jury of the State and district wherein the crime shall have been committed, which district shall have been previously ascertained by law, and to be informed of the nature and cause of the accusation; to be confronted with the witnesses against him; to have compulsory process for obtaining witnesses in his favor, and to have the assistance of counsel for his defence.

Any person accused of a crime has the right to a fair and public trial by a jury in the state in which the crime took place. The charges against that person must be so indicated. Any accused person has the right to a lawyer to defend him or her and to question those who testify against him or her, as well as the right to call people to speak in his or her favor at trial.

Amendment VII.
Trial by Jury in Civil Cases

In Suits at common law, where the value in controversy shall exceed twenty dollars, the right of trial by jury shall be preserved, and no fact tried by jury, shall be otherwise reexamined in any Court of the United States, than according to the rules of the common law.

A jury trial may be requested by either party in a dispute in any case involving more than $20. If both parties agree to a trial by a judge without a jury, the right to a jury trial may be put aside.

Amendment VIII.
Bail, Cruel and Unusual Punishment

Excessive bail shall not be required, nor excessive fines imposed, nor cruel and unusual punishments inflicted.

Bail is that amount of money that a person accused of a crime may be required to deposit with the court as a guarantee that she or he will appear in court when requested. The amount of bail required or the fine imposed as punishment for a crime must be reasonable

compared with the seriousness of the crime involved. Any punishment judged to be too harsh or too severe for a crime shall be prohibited.

Amendment IX.
The Rights Retained by the People

The enumeration in the Constitution, of certain rights, shall not be construed to deny or disparage others retained by the people.

Many civil rights that are not explicitly enumerated in the Constitution are still hailed by the people.

Amendment X.
Reserved Powers of the States

The powers not delegated to the United States by the Constitution, nor prohibited by it to the States, are reserved to the States respectively, or to the people.

Those powers not delegated by the Constitution to the federal government or expressly denied to the states belong to the states and to the people. This clause in essence allows the states to pass laws under its "police powers."

Amendment XI
(Ratified on February 7, 1795).
Suits Against States

The Judicial power of the United States shall not be construed to extend to any suit in law or equity, commenced or prosecuted against one of the United States by Citizens of another State, or by Citizens or Subjects of any Foreign State.

This amendment has been interpreted to mean that a state cannot be sued in federal court by one of its citizens, by a citizen of another state, or by a foreign country.

Amendment XII
(Ratified on June 15, 1804).
Election of the President

The Electors shall meet in their respective states, and vote by ballot for President and Vice-President, one of whom, at least, shall not be an inhabitant of the same State with themselves; they shall name in their ballots the person voted for as President, and in distinct ballots the person voted for as Vice-President, and they shall make distinct lists of all persons voted for as President, and of all persons voted for as Vice-President, and of the number of votes for each, which lists they shall sign and certify, and transmit sealed to the seat of the government of the United States, directed to the President of the Senate;—The President of the Senate shall, in the presence of the Senate and House of Representatives, open all the certificates and the votes shall then be counted;—The person having the greatest number of votes for President, shall be the President, if such number be a majority of the whole number of Electors appointed; and if no person have such majority, then from the persons having the highest numbers not exceeding three on the list of those voted for as President, the House of Representatives shall choose immediately, by ballot, the President. But in choosing the President, the votes shall be taken by States, the representation from each State having one vote; a quorum for this purpose shall consist of a member or members from two-thirds of the States, and a majority of all States shall be necessary to a choice. [And if the House of Representatives shall not choose a President whenever the right of choice shall devolve upon them, before the fourth day of March next following, then the Vice-President shall act as President, as in the case of the death or other constitutional disability of the President.][13]—The person having the greatest number of votes as Vice-President, shall be the Vice-President, if such number be a majority of the whole number of Electors appointed, and if no person have a majority, then from the two highest numbers on the list, the Senate shall choose the Vice President; a quorum for the purpose shall consist of two-thirds of the whole number of Senators, and a majority of the whole number shall be necessary to a choice. But no person constitutionally ineligible to the office of President shall be eligible to that of Vice-President of the United States.

The original procedure set out for the election of president and vice-president in Article II, Section 1, resulted in a tie in 1800 between Thomas Jefferson and Aaron Burr. It was not until the next year that the House of Representatives chose Jefferson to be president. This amendment changed the procedure by providing for separate ballots for president and vice-president.

Amendment XIII
(Ratified on December 6, 1865).
Prohibition of Slavery

Section 1.
Neither slavery nor involuntary servitude, except as a punishment for crime whereof the party shall have been duly convicted, shall exist within the United States, or any place subject to their jurisdiction.

Some slaves had been freed during the Civil War. This amendment freed the others and abolished slavery.

Section 2.
Congress shall have power to enforce this article by appropriate legislation.

Amendment XIV
(Ratified on July 9, 1868).
Citizenship, Due Process, and Equal Protection of the Laws

Section 1.
All persons born or naturalized in the United States, and subject to the jurisdiction thereof, are citizens of the United States and of the State wherein they reside. No State shall make or enforce any law which shall abridge the privileges or immunities of citizens of the United States; nor shall any State deprive any person of life, liberty, or property, without due process of law; nor deny to any person within its jurisdiction the equal protection of the laws.

Under this provision, states cannot make or enforce laws that take away rights given to all citizens by the federal government. States cannot act unfairly or arbitrarily toward, or discriminate against, any person.

Section 2.
Representatives shall be apportioned among the several States according to their respective numbers, counting the whole number of persons in each State, excluding Indians not taxed. But when the right to vote at any election for the choice of electors for President and Vice President of the United States, Representatives in Congress, the Executive and Judicial officers of a State, or the members of the Legislature thereof, is denied to any of the male inhabitants of such State, being [twenty-one][14] years of age, and citizens of the United States, or in any way abridged, except for participation in rebellion, or other crime, the basis of representation therein shall be reduced in the proportion which the number of such male citizens shall bear to the whole number of male citizens twenty-one years of age in such State.

Section 3.
No person shall be a Senator or Representative in Congress, or elector of President and Vice President, or hold any office, civil or military, under the United States, or under any State, who having previously taken an oath, as a member of Congress, or as an officer of the United States, or as a member of any State legislature, or as an executive or judicial officer of any State, to support the Constitution of the United States, shall have engaged in insurrection or rebellion against the same, or given aid or comfort to the enemies thereof. But Congress may by a vote of two-thirds of each House, remove such disability.

This provision forbade former state or federal government officials who had acted in support of the Confederacy during the Civil War to hold office again. It limited the president's power to pardon those persons. Congress removed this "disability" in 1898.

---

[13]Changed by the Twentieth Amendment.

[14]Changed by the Twenty-sixth Amendment.

Section 4.
The validity of the public debt of the United States, authorized by law, including debts incurred for payment of pensions and bounties for services in suppressing insurrection or rebellion, shall not be questioned. But neither the United States nor any State shall assume or pay any debt or obligation incurred in aid of insurrection or rebellion against the United States, or any claim for the loss or emancipation of any slave, but all such debts, obligations and claims shall be held illegal and void.

Section 5.
The Congress shall have power to enforce, by appropriate legislation, the provisions of this article.

Amendment XV
(Ratified on February 3, 1870).
The Right to Vote

Section 1.
The right of citizens of the United States to vote shall not be denied or abridged by the United States or by any State on account of race, color, or previous condition of servitude.

No citizen can be refused the right to vote simply because of race or color or because that person was once a slave.

Section 2.
The Congress shall have power to enforce this article by appropriate legislation. *

Amendment XVI
(Ratified on February 3, 1913).
Income Taxes

The Congress shall have power to lay and collect taxes on incomes, from whatever source derived, without apportionment among the several States, and without regard to any census or enumeration.

This amendment allows Congress to tax income without sharing the revenue so obtained with the states according to their population.

Amendment XVII
(Ratified on April 8, 1913).
The Popular Election of Senators

The Senate of the United States shall be composed of two Senators from each State, elected by the people thereof, for six years; and each Senator shall have one vote. The electors in each State shall have the qualifications requisite for electors of the most numerous branch of the State legislatures.

When vacancies happen in the representation of any State in the Senate, the executive authority of such State shall issue writs of election to fill such vacancies: *Provided,* That the legislature of any State may empower the executive thereof to make temporary appointments until the people fill the vacancies by election as the legislature may direct.

This amendment shall not be so construed as to affect the election or term of any Senator chosen before it becomes valid as part of the Constitution.

This amendment modified portions of Article I, Section 3, that related to election of senators. Senators are now elected by the voters in each state directly. When a vacancy occurs, either the state may fill the vacancy by a special election, or the governor of the state involved may appoint someone to fill the seat until the next election.

Amendment XVIII
(Ratified on January 16, 1919).
Prohibition.

Section 1.
After one year from the ratification of this article the manufacture, sale, or transportation of intoxicating liquors within, the importation thereof into, or the exportation thereof from the United States and all territory subject to the jurisdiction thereof for beverage purposes is hereby prohibited.

Section 2.
The Congress and the several States shall have concurrent power to enforce this article by appropriate legislation.

Section 3.
This article shall be inoperative unless it shall have been ratified as an amendment to the Constitution by the legislatures of the several States, as provided in the Constitution, within seven years from the date of the submission hereof to the States by the Congress.[15]

This amendment made it illegal to manufacture, sell, and transport alcoholic beverages in the United States. It was ended by the Twenty-first Amendment.

Amendment XIX
(Ratified on August 18, 1920).
Women's Right to Vote.

The right of citizens of the United States to vote shall not be denied or abridged by the United States or by any State on account of sex.

---

[15]The Eighteenth Amendment was repealed by the Twenty-first Amendment.

Congress shall have power to enforce this article by appropriate legislation.

Women were given the right to vote by this amendment, and Congress was given the power to enforce this right.

Amendment XX
(Ratified on January 23, 1933).
The Lame Duck Amendment

Section 1.
The terms of the President and Vice President shall end at noon on the 20th day of January, and the terms of Senators and Representatives at noon on the 3d day of January, of the years in which such terms would have ended if this article had not been ratified; and the terms of their successors shall then begin.

This amendment modified Article I, Section 4, Clause 2, and other provisions relating to the president in the Twelfth Amendment. The taking of the Oath of Office was moved from March 4 to January 20.

Section 2.
The Congress shall assemble at least once in every year, and such meeting shall begin at noon on the 3d day of January, unless they shall by law appoint a different day.

Congress changed the beginning of its term to January 3. The reason the Twentieth Amendment is called the Lame Duck Amendment is because it shortens the time between when a member of Congress is defeated for reelection and when he or she leaves office.

Section 3.
If, at the time fixed for the beginning of the term of the President, the President elect shall have died, the Vice President elect shall become President. If a President shall not have been chosen before the time fixed for the beginning of his term, or if the President elect shall have failed to qualify, then the Vice President elect shall act as President until a President shall have qualified; and the Congress may by law provide for the case wherein neither a President elect nor a Vice President elect shall have qualified, declaring who shall then act as President, or the manner in which one who is to act shall be selected, and such person shall act accordingly until a President or Vice President shall have qualified.

This part of the amendment deals with problem areas left ambiguous by Article II and the Twelfth Amendment. If the president dies before January 20 or fails to qualify for office, the presidency is to be filled in the order given in this section.

Section 4.
The Congress may by law provide for the case of the death of any of the persons from whom the House of Representatives may choose a President whenever the rights of choice shall have devolved upon them, and for the case of the death of any of the persons from whom the Senate may choose a Vice President whenever the right of choice shall have devolved upon them.

Congress has never created legislation subsequent to this section.

Section 5.
Sections 1 and 2 shall take effect on the 15th day of October following the ratification of this article.

Section 6.
This article shall be inoperative unless it shall have been ratified as an amendment to the Constitution by the legislatures of three-fourths of the several States within seven years from the date of its submission.

Amendment XXI
(Ratified on December 5, 1933).
The Repeal of Prohibition.

Section 1.
The eighteenth article of amendment to the Constitution of the United States is hereby repealed.

Section 2.
The transportation or importation into any State, Territory, or possession of the United States for delivery or use therein of intoxicating liquors, in violation of the laws thereof, is hereby prohibited.

Section 3.
This article shall be inoperative unless it shall have been ratified as an amendment to the Constitution by conventions in the several States, as provided in the Constitution, within seven years from the date of the submission hereof to the States by the Congress.

The amendment repealed the Eighteenth Amendment but did not make alcoholic beverages legal everywhere. Rather, they remained illegal in any state that so designated them. Many such "dry" states existed for a number of years after 1933. Today, there are still "dry" counties within the United States, in which alcoholic beverages are illegal.

Amendment XXII
(Ratified on February 27, 1951).
Limitation of Presidential Terms.

Section 1.
No person shall be elected to the office of the President more than twice, and no person who has held the office of Presi-

dent, or acted as President, for more than two years of a term to which some other person was elected President shall be elected to the office of President more than once. But this Article shall not apply to any person holding the office of President when this Article was proposed by the Congress, and shall not prevent any person who may be holding the office of President, or acting as President, during the term within which this Article becomes operative from holding the office of President or acting as President during the remainder of such term.

Section 2.

This article shall be inoperative unless it shall have been ratified as an amendment to the Constitution by the legislatures of three-fourths of the several States within seven years from the date of its submission to the States by the Congress.

No president may serve more than two elected terms. If, however, a president has succeeded to the office after the halfway point of a term in which another president was originally elected, then that president may serve for more than eight years, but not to exceed ten years.

Amendment XXIII
(Ratified on March 29, 1961).
Presidential Electors for
the District of Columbia.

Section 1.

The District constituting the seat of Government of the United States shall appoint in such manner as the Congress may direct:

A number of electors of President and Vice President equal to the whole number of Senators and Representatives in Congress to which the District would be entitled if it were a State, but in no event more than the least populous State; they shall be in addition to those appointed by the States, but they shall be considered, for the purposes of the election of President and Vice President, to be electors appointed by a State; and they shall meet in the District and perform such duties as provided by the twelfth article of amendment.

Section 2.

The Congress shall have power to enforce this article by appropriate legislation.

Citizens living in the District of Columbia have the right to vote in elections for president and vice-president. The District of Columbia has three presidential electors, whereas before this amendment it had none.

Amendment XXIV
(Ratified on January 23, 1964).
The Anti-Poll Tax Amendment.

Section 1.

The right of citizens of the United States to vote in any primary or other election for President or Vice President, for electors for President or Vice President, or for Senator or Representative in Congress, shall not be denied or abridged by the United States, or any State by reason of failure to pay any poll tax or other tax.

Section 2.

The Congress shall have power to enforce this article by appropriate legislation.

No government shall require a person to pay a poll tax in order to vote in any federal election.

Amendment XXV
(Ratified on February 10, 1967).
Presidential Disability and Vice
Presidential Vacancies.

Section 1.

In case of the removal of the President from office or of his death or resignation, the Vice President shall become President.

Whenever a president dies or resigns from office, the vice-president becomes president.

Section 2.

Whenever there is a vacancy in the office of the Vice President, the President shall nominate a Vice President who shall take office upon confirmation by a majority vote of both Houses of Congress.

Whenever the office of the vice-presidency becomes vacant, the president may appoint someone to fill this office, provided Congress consents.

Section 3.

Whenever the President transmits to the President pro tempore of the Senate and the Speaker of the House of Representatives his written declaration that he is unable to discharge the powers and duties of his office, and until he transmits to them a written declaration to the contrary, such powers and duties shall be discharged by the Vice President as Acting President.

Whenever the president believes she or he is unable to carry out the duties of the office, she or he shall so indicate to Congress in writing. The vice-president then acts as president until the president declares that she or he is again able to properly carry out the duties of the office.

Section 4.

Whenever the Vice President and a majority of either the principal officers of the executive departments or of such other body as Congress may by law provide, transmit to the President pro tempore of the Senate and the Speaker of the

House of Representatives their written declaration that the President is unable to discharge the powers and duties of his office, the Vice President shall immediately assume the powers and duties of the office as Acting President.

Thereafter, when the President transmits to the President pro tempore of the Senate and the Speaker of the House of Representatives his written declaration that no inability exists, he shall resume the powers and duties of his office unless the Vice President and a majority of either the principal officers of the executive department or of such other body as Congress may by law provide, transmit within four days to the President pro tempore of the Senate and the Speaker of the House of Representatives their written declaration that the President is unable to discharge the powers and duties of his office. Thereupon Congress shall decide the issue, assembling within forty-eight hours for that purpose if not in session. If the Congress, within twenty-one days after receipt of the latter written declaration, or, if Congress is not in session, within twenty-one days after Congress is required to assemble, determines by two-thirds vote of both Houses that the President is unable to discharge the powers and duties of his office, the Vice President shall continue to discharge the same as Acting President; otherwise, the President shall resume the powers and duties of his office.

Whenever the vice-president and a majority of the members of the Cabinet believe that the president cannot carry out his or her duties, they shall so indicate in writing to Congress. The vice-president shall then act as president. When the president believes that she or he is able to carry out her or his duties again, she or he shall so indicate to the Congress. If, though, the vice-president and a majority of the Cabinet do not agree, Congress must decide by a two-thirds vote within three weeks who shall act as president.

Amendment XXVI
(Ratified on July 1, 1971).
The Eighteen-Year-Old Vote.

Section 1.

The right of citizens of the United States, who are eighteen years of age or older, to vote shall not be denied or abridged by the United States or by any State on account of age.

No one over eighteen years of age can be denied the right to vote in federal or state elections by virtue of age.

Section 2.

The Congress shall have power to enforce this article by appropriate legislation.

Amendment XXVII
(Ratified on May 7, 1992).
Congressional Pay.

No law varying the compensation for the services of the Senators and Representatives shall take effect, until an election of representatives shall have intervened.

APPENDIX C

The Presidents of the United States

	Term of Service	Age at Inauguration	Political Party	College or University	Occupation or Profession
1. George Washington	1789–1797	57	None		Planter
2. John Adams	1797–1801	61	Federalist	Harvard	Lawyer
3. Thomas Jefferson	1801–1809	57	Democratic-Republican	William and Mary	Planter, Lawyer
4. James Madison	1809–1817	57	Democratic-Republican	Princeton	Lawyer
5. James Monroe	1817–1825	58	Democratic-Republican	William and Mary	Lawyer
6. John Quincy Adams	1825–1829	57	Democratic-Republican	Harvard	Lawyer
7. Andrew Jackson	1829–1837	61	Democrat		Lawyer
8. Martin Van Buren	1837–1841	54	Democrat		Lawyer
9. William H. Harrison	1841	68	Whig	Hampden-Sydney	Soldier
10. John Tyler	1841–1845	51	Whig	William and Mary	Lawyer
11. James K. Polk	1845–1849	49	Democrat	U. of N. Carolina	Lawyer
12. Zachary Taylor	1849–1850	64	Whig		Soldier
13. Millard Fillmore	1850–1853	50	Whig		Lawyer
14. Franklin Pierce	1853–1857	48	Democrat	Bowdoin	Lawyer
15. James Buchanan	1857–1861	65	Democrat	Dickinson	Lawyer
16. Abraham Lincoln	1861–1865	52	Republican		Lawyer
17. Andrew Johnson	1865–1869	56	Nat/l. Union†		Tailor
18. Ulysses S. Grant	1869–1877	46	Republican	U.S. Mil. Academy	Soldier
19. Rutherford B. Hayes	1877–1881	54	Republican	Kenyon	Lawyer
20. James A. Garfield	1881	49	Republican	Williams	Lawyer
21. Chester A. Arthur	1881–1885	51	Republican	Union	Lawyer
22. Grover Cleveland	1885–1889	47	Democrat		Lawyer
23. Benjamin Harrison	1889–1893	55	Republican	Miami	Lawyer
24. Grover Cleveland	1893–1897	55	Democrat		Lawyer
25. William McKinley	1897–1901	54	Republican	Allegheny College	Lawyer
26. Theodore Roosevelt	1901–1909	42	Republican	Harvard	Author
27. William H. Taft	1909–1913	51	Republican	Yale	Lawyer
28. Woodrow Wilson	1913–1921	56	Democrat	Princeton	Educator
29. Warren G. Harding	1921–1923	55	Republican		Editor
30. Calvin Coolidge	1923–1929	51	Republican	Amherst	Lawyer
31. Herbert C. Hoover	1929–1933	54	Republican	Stanford	Engineer
32. Franklin D. Roosevelt	1933–1945	51	Democrat	Harvard	Lawyer
33. Harry S Truman	1945–1953	60	Democrat		Businessman
34. Dwight D. Eisenhower	1953–1961	62	Republican	U.S. Mil. Academy	Soldier
35. John F. Kennedy	1961–1963	43	Democrat	Harvard	Author
36. Lyndon B. Johnson	1963–1969	55	Democrat	Southwest Texas State	Teacher
37. Richard M. Nixon	1969–1974	56	Republican	Whittier	Lawyer
38. Gerald R. Ford‡	1974–1977	61	Republican	Michigan	Lawyer
39. James E. Carter, Jr.	1977–1981	52	Democrat	U.S. Naval Academy	Businessman
40. Ronald W. Reagan	1981–1989	69	Republican	Eureka College	Actor
41. George H. W. Bush	1989–1993	64	Republican	Yale	Businessman
42. Bill Clinton	1993–	43	Democrat	Georgetown	Lawyer

*Church preference; never joined any church.
†The National Union Party consisted of Republicans and War Democrats. Johnson was a Democrat.
**Inaugurated Dec. 6, 1973, to replace Agnew, who resigned Oct. 10, 1973.
‡Inaugurated Aug. 9, 1974, to replace Nixon, who resigned that same day.
§Inaugurated Dec. 19, 1974, to replace Ford, who became President Aug. 9, 1974.

Religion	Born	Died	Age at Death	Vice President	
1. Episcopalian	Feb. 22, 1732	Dec. 14, 1799	67	John Adams	(1789–1797)
2. Unitarian	Oct. 30, 1735	July 4, 1826	90	Thomas Jefferson	(1797–1801)
3. Unitarian*	Apr. 13, 1743	July 4, 1826	83	Aaron Burr	(1801–1805)
				George Clinton	(1805–1809)
4. Episcopalian	Mar. 16, 1751	June 28, 1836	85	George Clinton	(1809–1812)
				Elbridge Gerry	(1813–1814)
5. Episcopalian	Apr. 28, 1758	July 4, 1831	73	Daniel D. Tompkins	(1817–1825)
6. Unitarian	July 11, 1767	Feb. 23, 1848	80	John C. Calhoun	(1825–1829)
7. Presbyterian	Mar. 15, 1767	June 8, 1845	78	John C. Calhoun	(1829–1832)
				Martin Van Buren	(1833–1837)
8. Dutch Reformed	Dec. 5, 1782	July 24, 1862	79	Richard M. Johnson	(1837–1841)
9. Episcopalian	Feb. 9, 1773	Apr. 4, 1841	68	John Tyler	(1841)
10. Episcopalian	Mar. 29, 1790	Jan. 18, 1862	71		
11. Methodist	Nov. 2, 1795	June 15, 1849	53	George M. Dallas	(1845–1849)
12. Episcopalian	Nov. 24, 1784	July 9, 1850	65	Millard Fillmore	(1849–1850)
13. Unitarian	Jan. 7, 1800	Mar. 8, 1874	74		
14. Episcopalian	Nov. 23, 1804	Oct. 8, 1869	64	William R. King	(1853)
15. Presbyterian	Apr. 23, 1791	June 1, 1868	77	John C. Breckinridge	(1857–1861)
16. Presbyterian*	Feb. 12, 1809	Apr. 15, 1865	56	Hannibal Hamlin	(1861–1865)
				Andrew Johnson	(1865)
17. Methodist*	Dec. 29, 1808	July 31, 1875	66		
18. Methodist	Apr. 27, 1822	July 23, 1885	63	Schuyler Colfax	(1869–1873)
				Henry Wilson	(1873–1875)
19. Methodist*	Oct. 4, 1822	Jan. 17, 1893	70	William A. Wheeler	(1877–1881)
20. Disciples of Christ	Nov. 19, 1831	Sept. 19, 1881	49	Chester A. Arthur	(1881)
21. Episcopalian	Oct. 5, 1829	Nov. 18, 1886	57		
22. Presbyterian	Mar. 18, 1837	June 24, 1908	71	Thomas A. Hendricks	(1885)
23. Presbyterian	Aug. 20, 1833	Mar. 13, 1901	67	Levi P. Morton	(1889–1893)
24. Presbyterian	Mar. 18, 1837	June 24, 1908	71	Adlai E. Stevenson	(1893–1897)
25. Methodist	Jan. 29, 1843	Sept. 14, 1901	58	Garret A. Hobart	(1897–1899)
				Theodore Roosevelt	(1901)
26. Dutch Reformed	Oct. 27, 1858	Jan. 6, 1919	60	Charles W. Fairbanks	(1905–1909)
27. Unitarian	Sept. 15, 1857	Mar. 8, 1930	72	James S. Sherman	(1909–1912)
28. Presbyterian	Dec. 29, 1856	Feb. 3, 1924	67	Thomas R. Marshall	(1913–1921)
29. Baptist	Nov. 2, 1865	Aug. 2, 1923	57	Calvin Coolidge	(1921–1923)
30. Congregationalist	July 4, 1872	Jan. 5, 1933	60	Charles G. Dawes	(1925–1929)
31. Friend (Quaker)	Aug. 10, 1874	Oct. 20, 1964	90	Charles Curtis	(1929–1933)
32. Episcopalian	Jan. 30, 1882	Apr. 12, 1945	63	John N. Garner	(1933–1941)
				Henry A. Wallace	(1941–1945)
				Harry S Truman	(1945)
33. Baptist	May 8, 1884	Dec. 26, 1972	88	Alben W. Barkley	(1949–1953)
34. Presbyterian	Oct. 14, 1890	Mar. 28, 1969	78	Richard M. Nixon	(1953–1961)
35. Roman Catholic	May 29, 1917	Nov. 22, 1963	46	Lyndon B. Johnson	(1961–1963)
36. Disciples of Christ	Aug. 27, 1908	Jan. 22, 1973	64	Hubert H. Humphrey	(1965–1969)
37. Friend (Quaker)	Jan. 9, 1913			Spiro T. Agnew	(1969–1973)
				Gerald R. Ford**	(1973–1974)
38. Episcopalian	July 14, 1913			Nelson A. Rockefeller§	(1974–1977)
39. Baptist	Oct. 1, 1924			Walter F. Mondale	(1977–1981)
40. Disciples of Christ	Feb. 6, 1911			George H. W. Bush	(1981–1989)
41. Episcopalian	June 12, 1924			J. Danforth Quayle	(1989–1993)
42. Baptist	Aug. 19, 1946			Al Gore	(1993–)

APPENDIX D

⌄

Federalist Papers #10 and #51

#10

Among the numerous advantages promised by a well-constructed Union, none deserves to be more accurately developed than its tendency to break and control the violence of faction. The friend of popular governments never finds himself so much alarmed for their character and fate as when he contemplates their propensity to this dangerous vice. He will not fail, therefore, to set a due value on any plan which, without violating the principles to which he is attached, provides a proper cure for it. The instability, injustice, and confusion introduced into the public councils have, in truth, been the mortal diseases under which popular governments have everywhere perished, as they continue to be the favorite and fruitful topics from which the adversaries to liberty derive their most specious declamations. The valuable improvements made by the American constitutions on the popular models, both ancient and modern, cannot certainly be too much admired; but it would be an unwarrantable partiality to contend that they have as effectually obviated the danger on this side, as was wished and expected. Complaints are everywhere heard from our most considerate and virtuous citizens, equally the friends of public and private faith and of public and personal liberty, that our governments are too unstable, that the public good is disregarded in the conflicts of rival parties, and that measures are too often decided, not according to the rules of justice and the rights of the minor party, but by the superior force of an interested and overbearing majority. However anxiously we may wish that these complaints had no foundation, the evidence of known facts will not permit us to deny that they are in some degree true. It will be found, indeed, on a candid review of our situation, that some of the distresses under which we labor have been erroneously charged on the operation of our governments; but it will be found, at the same time, that other causes will not alone account for many of our heaviest misfortunes; and, particularly, for that prevailing and increasing distrust of public engagements and alarm for private rights which are echoed from one end of the continent to the other. These must be chiefly, if not wholly, effects of the unsteadiness and injustice with which a factious spirit has tainted our public administration.

By a faction I understand a number of citizens, whether amounting to a majority or minority of the whole, who are united and actuated by some common impulse of passion, or of interest, adverse to the rights of other citizens, or the permanent and aggregate interests of the community.

There are two methods of curing the mischiefs of faction: the one, by removing its causes; the other, by controlling its effects.

There are again two methods of removing the causes of faction: the one, by destroying the liberty which is essential to its existence; the other, by giving to every citizen the same opinions, the same passions, and the same interests.

It could never be more truly said than of the first remedy that it was worse than the disease. Liberty is to faction what air is to fire, an aliment without which it instantly expires. But it could not be a less folly to abolish liberty, which is essential to political life, because it nourishes faction than it would be to wish the annihilation of air, which is essential to animal life, because it imparts to fire its destructive agency.

The second expedient is as impracticable as the first would be unwise. As long as the reason of man continues fallible, and his is at liberty to exercise it, different opinions will be formed. As long as the connection subsists between his reason and his self-love, his opinions and his passions will have a reciprocal influence on each other; and the former will be objects to which the latter will attach themselves. The diversity in the faculties of men, from which the rights of property originate, is not less an insuperable obstacle to a uniformity of interests. The protection of these faculties is the first object of government. From the protection of different and unequal faculties of acquiring property, the possession of different degrees and kinds of property immediately results; and from the influence of these on the sentiments and views of the respective proprietors ensues a division of the society into different interests and parties.

The latent causes of faction are thus sown in the nature of man; and we see them everywhere brought into different degrees of activity, according to the different circumstances of civil society. A zeal for different opinions concerning religion, concerning government, and many other points, as well of speculation as of practice; an attachment to different leaders ambitiously contending for pre-eminence and power; or to persons of other descriptions whose fortunes have been interesting to the human passions, have, in turn, divided mankind into parties, inflamed them with mutual animosity, and rendered them much more disposed to vex and oppress each other than to co-operate for their common good. So strong is this propensity of mankind to fall into mutual animosities that where no substantial occasion presents itself the most frivolous and fanciful distinctions have been sufficient to kindle their unfriendly passions and excite their most violent conflicts. But the most common and durable source of factions has been the various and unequal distribution of property. Those who hold and those who are without property have ever formed distinct interests in society. Those who are creditors, and those who are debtors, fall under a like discrimination. A landed interest, a manufacturing interest, a mercantile interest, a moneyed interest, with many lesser interests, grow up of necessity in civilized nations, and divide them into different classes, actuated by different sentiments and views. The regulation of these various and interfering interests forms the principal task of modern legislation and involves the spirit of party and faction in the necessary and ordinary operations of government.

No man is allowed to be a judge in his own cause, because his interest would certainly bias his judgment, and, not improbably, corrupt his integrity. With equal, nay with greater reason, a body of men are unfit to be both judges and parties at the same time; yet what are many of the most important acts of legislation but so many judicial determinations, not indeed concerning the rights of single persons, but concerning the rights of large bodies of citizens? And what are the different classes of legislators but advocates and parties to the causes which they determine? Is a law proposed concerning private debts? It is a question to which the creditors are parties on one side and the debtors on the other. Justice ought to hold the balance between them. Yet the parties are, and must be, themselves the judges; and the most numerous party, or in other words, the most powerful faction must be expected to prevail. Shall domestic manufacturers be encouraged, and in what degree, by restrictions on foreign manufacturers? are questions which would be differently decided by the landed and the manufacturing classes, and probably by neither with a sole regard to justice and the public good. The apportionment of taxes on the various descriptions of property is an act which seems to require the most exact impartiality; yet there is, perhaps, no legislative act in which greater opportunity and temptation are given to a predominant party to trample on the rules of justice. Every shilling with which they overburden the inferior number is a shilling saved to their own pockets.

It is in vain to say that enlightened statesmen will be able to adjust these clashing interests and render them all subservient to the public good. Enlightened statesmen will not always be at the helm. Nor, in many cases, can such an adjustment be made at all without taking into view indirect and remote considerations, which will rarely prevail over the immediate interest which one party may find in disregarding the rights of another or the good of the whole.

The inference to which we are brought is that the *causes* of faction cannot be removed and that relief is only to be sought in the means of controlling its *effects*.

If a faction consists of less than a majority, relief is supplied by the republican principle, which enables the majority to defeat its sinister views by regular vote. It may clog the administration, it may convulse the society; but it will be unable to execute and mask its violence under the forms of the Constitution. When a majority is included in a faction, the form of popular government, on the other hand, enables it to sacrifice to its ruling passion or interest both the public good and the rights of other citizens. To secure the public good and private rights against the danger of such a faction, and at the same time to preserve the spirit and the form of popular government, is then the great object to which our inquiries are directed. Let me add that it is the great desideratum by which alone this form of government can be rescued from the opprobrium under which it has so long labored and be recommended to the esteem and adoption of mankind.

By what means is this object attainable? Evidently by one of two only. Either the existence of the same passion or interest in a majority at the same time must be prevented, or the majority, having such coexistent passion or interest, must be rendered, by their number and local situation, unable to concert and carry into effect schemes of oppression. If the impulse and the opportunity be suffered to coincide, we well know that neither moral nor religious motives can be relied on as an adequate control. They are not found to be such on the injustice and violence of individuals, and lose their efficacy in proportion to the number combined together, that is, in proportion as their efficacy becomes needful.

From this view of the subject it may be concluded that a pure democracy, by which I mean a society consisting of a small number of citizens, who assemble and administer the government in person, can admit of no cure for the mischiefs of faction. A common passion or interest will, in almost every case, be felt by a majority of the whole; a communication and concert results from the form of government itself; and there is nothing to check the inducements to sacrifice the weaker party or an obnoxious individual. Hence it is that such democracies have ever been spectacles of turbulence and contention; have ever been found incompatible with personal security or the rights of property; and have in general been as short in their lives as they have been violent in their deaths. Theoretic politicians, who have patronized this species of government, have erroneously supposed that by reducing mankind to a perfect equality in their political rights, they would at the same time be perfectly equalized and assimilated in their possessions, their opinions, and their passions.

A republic, by which I mean a government in which the scheme of representation takes place, opens a different prospect and promises the cure for which we are seeking. Let us examine the points in which it varies from pure democracy, and we shall comprehend both the nature of the cure and the efficacy which it must derive from the Union.

The two great points of difference between a democracy and a republic are: first, the delegation of the government, in the latter, to a small number of citizens elected by the rest; secondly, the greater number of citizens and greater sphere of country over which the latter may be extended.

The effect of the first difference is, on the one hand, to refine and enlarge the public views by passing them through the medium of a chosen body of citizens, whose wisdom may best discern the true interest of their country and whose patriotism and love of justice will be least likely to sacrifice it to temporary or partial considerations. Under such a regulation it may well happen that the public voice, pronounced by the representatives of the people, will be more consonant to the public good than if pronounced by the people themselves, convened for the purpose. On the other hand, the effect may be inverted. Men of factious tempers, of local prejudices, or of sinister designs, may, by intrigue, by corruption, or by other means, first obtain the suffrages, and then betray the interests of the people. The question resulting is, whether small or extensive republics are most favorable to the election of proper guardians of the public weal; and it is clearly decided in favor of the latter by two obvious considerations.

In the first place it is to be remarked that however small the republic may be the representatives must be raised to a certain number in order to guard against the cabals of a few; and that however large it may be they must be limited to a certain number in order to guard against the confusion of a multitude. Hence, the number of representatives in the two cases not being in proportion to that of the constituents, and being proportionally greatest in the small republic, it follows that if the proportion of fit characters be not less in the large than in the small republic, the former will present a greater option, and consequently a greater probability of a fit choice.

In the next place, as each representative will be chosen by a greater number of citizens in the large than in the small republic, it will be more difficult for unworthy candidates to practise with success the vicious arts by which elections are too often carried; and the suffrages of the people being more free, will be more likely to center on men who possess the most attractive merit and the most diffusive and established characters.

It must be confessed that in this, as in most other cases, there is a mean, on both sides of which inconveniencies will be found to lie. By enlarging too much the number of electors, you render the representative too little acquainted with all their local circumstances and lesser interests; as by reducing it too much, you render him unduly attached to these, and too little fit to comprehend and pursue great and national objects. The federal Constitution forms a happy combination in this respect; the great and aggregate interests being referred to the national, the local and particular to the State legislatures.

The other point of difference is the greater number of citizens and extent of territory which may be brought within the compass of republican than of democratic government; and it is this circumstance principally which renders factious combinations less to be dreaded in the former than in the latter. The smaller the society, the fewer probably will be the distinct parties and interests composing it; the fewer the distinct parties and interests, the more frequently will a majority be found of the same party; and the smaller the number of individuals composing a majority, and the smaller the compass within which they are placed, the more easily will they concert and execute their plans of oppression. Extend the sphere and you take in a greater variety of parties and interests; you make it less probable that a majority of the whole will have a common motive to invade the rights of other citizens; or if such a common motive exists, it will be more difficult for all who feel it to discover their own strength and to act in unison with each other. Besides other impediments, it may be remarked that, where there is a consciousness of unjust or dishonorable purposes, communication is always checked by distrust in proportion to the number whose concurrence is necessary.

Hence, it clearly appears that the same advantage which a republic has over a democracy in controlling the effects of faction is enjoyed by a large over a small republic—is enjoyed by the Union over the States composing it. Does this advantage consist in the substitution of representatives whose enlightened views and virtuous sentiments render them superior to local prejudices and to schemes of injustice? It will not be denied that the representation of the Union will be most likely to possess these requisite endowments. Does it consist in the greater security afforded by a greater variety of parties, against the event of any one party being able to outnumber and oppress the rest? In an equal degree does the increased variety of parties comprised within the Union increase this security. Does it, in fine, consist in the greater obstacles opposed to the concert and accomplishment of the secret wishes of an unjust and interested majority? Here again the extent of the Union gives it the most palpable advantage.

The influence of factious leaders may kindle a flame within their particular States but will be unable to spread a general conflagration through the other States. A religious sect may degenerate into a political faction in a part of the Confederacy; but the variety of sects dispersed over the entire face of it must secure the national councils against any danger from that source. A rage for paper money, for an abolition of debts, for an equal division of property, or for any other improper or wicked project, will be less apt to pervade the whole body of the Union than a particular member of it, in the same proportion as such a malady is more likely to taint a particular county or district than an entire State.

In the extent and proper structure of the Union, therefore, we behold a republican remedy for the diseases most incident to republican government. And according to the degree of pleasure and pride we feel in being republicans ought to be our zeal in cherishing the spirit and supporting the character of federalists.

#51

To what expedient, then, shall we finally resort, for maintaining in practice the necessary partition of power among the several departments as laid down in the Constitution? The only answer that can be given is that as all these exterior provisions are found to be inadequate the defect must be supplied, by so contriving the interior structure of the government as that its several constituent parts may, by their mutual relations, be the means of keeping each other in their proper places. Without presuming to undertake a full development of this important idea I will hazard a few general observations which may perhaps place it in a clearer light, and enable us to form a more correct judgment of the principles and structure of the government planned by the convention.

In order to lay a due foundation for that separate and distinct exercise of the different powers of government, which to a certain extent is admitted on all hands to be essential to the preservation of liberty, it is evident that each department should have a will of its own; and consequently should be so constituted that the members of each should have as little agency as possible in the appointment of the members of the others. Were this principle rigorously adhered to, it would require that all the appointments for the supreme executive, legislative, and judiciary magistracies should be drawn from the same fountain of authority, the people, through channels having no communication whatever with one another. Perhaps such a plan of constructing the several departments would be less difficult in practice than it may in contemplation appear. Some difficulties, however, and some additional expense would attend the execution of it. Some deviations, therefore, from the principle must be admitted. In the constitution of the judiciary department in particular, it might be inexpedient to insist rigorously on the principle: first, because peculiar qualifications being essential in the members, the primary consideration ought to be to select that mode of choice which best secures these qualifications; second, because the permanent tenure by which the appointments are held in that department must soon destroy all sense of dependence on the authority conferring them.

It is equally evident that the members of each department should be as little dependent as possible on those of the others for the emoluments annexed to their offices. Were the executive magistrate, or the judges, not independent of the legislature in this particular, their independence in every other would be merely nominal.

But the great security against a gradual concentration of the several powers in the same department consists in giving to those who administer each department the necessary constitutional means and personal motives to resist encroachments of the others. The provision for defense must in this, as in all other cases, be made commensurate to the danger of attack. Ambition must be made to counteract ambition. The interest of the man must be connected with the constitutional rights of the place. It may be a reflection on human nature that such devices should be necessary to control the abuses of government. But what is government itself but the greatest of all reflections on human nature? If men were angels, no government would be necessary. If angels were to govern men, neither external nor internal controls on government would be necessary. In framing a government which is to be administered by men over men, the great difficulty lies in this: you must first enable the government to control the governed; and in the next place oblige it to control itself. A dependence on the people is, no doubt, the primary control on the government; but experience has taught mankind the necessity of auxiliary precautions.

This policy of supplying, by opposite and rival interests, the defect of better motives, might be traced through the whole system of human affairs, private as well as public. We see it particularly displayed in all the subordinate distributions of power, where the constant aim is to divide and arrange the several offices in such a manner as that each may be a check on the other—that the private interest of every individual may be a sentinel over the public rights. These inventions of prudence cannot be less requisite in the distribution of the supreme powers of the State.

But it is not possible to give to each department an equal power of self-defense. In republican government, the legislative authority necessarily predominates. The remedy for this inconveniency is to divide the legislature into different branches; and to render them, by different modes of election and different principles of action, as little connected with each other as the nature of their common functions and their common dependence on the society will admit. It may even be necessary to guard against dangerous encroachments by still further precautions. As the weight of the legislative authority requires that it should be thus divided, the weakness of the executive may require, on the other hand, that it should be fortified. An absolute negative on the legislature appears, at first view, to be the natural defense with which the executive magistrate should be armed. But perhaps it would be neither altogether safe nor alone sufficient. On ordinary occasions it might not be exerted with the requisite firmness, and on extraordinary occasions it might be perfidiously abused. May not this defect of an absolute negative be supplied by some qualified connection between this weaker department and the weaker branch of the stronger department, by which the latter may be led to support the constitutional rights of the former, without being too much detached from the rights of its own department?

If the principles on which these observations are founded be just, as I persuade myself they are, and they be applied as a criterion to the several State constitutions, and to the federal Constitution, it will be found that if the latter does not perfectly correspond with them, the former are infinitely less able to bear such a test.

There are, moreover, two considerations particularly applicable to the federal system of America, which place that system in a very interesting point of view.

First. In a single republic, all the power surrendered by the people is submitted to the administration of a single government; and the usurpations are guarded against by a division of the government into distinct and separate departments. In the compound republic of America, the power surrendered by the people is first divided between two distinct governments, and then the portion allotted to each subdivided among distinct and separate departments. Hence a double security arises to the rights of the people. The different governments will control each other, at the same time that each will be controlled by itself.

Second. It is of great importance in a republic not only to guard the society against the oppression of its rulers, but to guard one part of the society against the injustice of the other part. Different interests necessarily exist in different classes of citizens. If a majority be united by a common interest, the rights of the minority will be insecure. There are but two methods of providing against this evil: the one by creating a will in the community independent of the majority—that is, of the society itself; the other, by comprehending in the society so many separate descriptions of citizens as will render an unjust combination of a majority of the whole very improbable, if not impracticable. The first method prevails in all governments possessing an hereditary or self-appointed authority. This, at best, is but a precarious security; because a power independent of the society may as well espouse the unjust views of the major as the rightful interests of the minor party, and may possibly be turned against both parties. The second method will be exemplified in the federal republic of the United States. Whilst all authority in it will be derived from and dependent on the society, the society itself will be broken into so many parts, interests and classes of citizens, that the rights of individuals, or of the minority, will be in little danger from interested combinations of the majority. In a free government the security for civil rights must be the same as that for religious rights. It consists in the one case in the multiplicity of interests, and in the other in the multiplicity of sects. The degree of security in both cases will depend on the number of interests and sects; and this may be presumed to depend on the extent of country and number of people comprehended under the same government. This view of the subject must particularly recommend a proper federal system to all the sincere and considerate friends of republican government, since it shows that in exact proportion as the territory of the Union may be formed into more circumscribed Confederacies, or States, oppressive combinations of a majority will be facilitated; the best security, under the republican forms, for the rights of every class of citizen, will be diminished; and consequently the stability and independence of some member of the government, the only other security, must be proportionally increased. Justice is the end of government. It is the end of civil society. It ever has been and ever will be pursued until it be obtained, or until liberty be lost in the pursuit. In a society under the forms of which the stronger faction can readily unite and oppress the weaker, anarchy may as truly be said to reign as in a state of nature, where the weaker individual is not secured against the violence of the stronger; and as, in the latter state, even the stronger individuals are prompted, by the uncertainty of their condition, to submit to a government which may protect the weak as well as themselves; so, in the former state, will the more powerful factions or parties be gradually induced, by a like motive, to wish for a government which will protect all parties, the weaker as well as the more powerful. It can be little doubted that if the State of Rhode Island was separated from the Confederacy and left to itself, the insecurity of rights under the popular form of government within such narrow limits would be displayed by such reiterated oppressions of factious majorities that some power altogether independent of the people would soon be called for by the voice of the very factions whose misrule had proved the necessity of it. In the extended republic of the United States, and among the great variety of interests, parties, and sects which it embraces, a coalition of a majority of the whole society could seldom take place on any other principles than those of justice and the general good; whilst there being thus less danger to a minor from the will of a major party, there must be less pretext, also, to provide for the security of the former, by introducing into the government a will not dependent on the latter, or, in other words, a will independent of the society itself. It is no less certain than it is important, notwithstanding the contrary opinions which have been entertained, that the larger the society, provided it lie within a practicable sphere, the more duly capable it will be of self-government. And happily for the *republican cause*, the practicable sphere may be carried to a very great extent by a judicious modification and mixture of the *federal principle*.

Publius
(James Madison)

How to Do Research
in Political Science

You are expected to complete a political science research project for your class and present the results in a paper. Research, you have learned, is a tool of science. At first you may ask, what is there about politics that is "scientific"? You can't study people the way you do rats in a maze, nor can you conduct experiments in the same manner as in the biology lab. Yet much of what we know today about how political processes work, and especially about how people act in political situations, is the result of scientific research. For the modern political scientist, the acts of voters, the decisions of presidents and Supreme Court justices, and the policy decisions of state and municipal governments are data to be analyzed according to the methods of science.

I. The Scientific Approach to Politics

When you conduct a research project, it is essential to adhere to certain rules of *epistemology*. Epistemology has to do with *how* we know what we think is true, and the answer to this question lies in whether our work is valid and reliable. A research result is *valid* if it tells you something that actually is true, and it is *reliable* if you or other researchers could reproduce the same results (or at least get approximately the same findings). Validity and reliability are the two hallmarks of the scientific method, which is applied to political science research as much as it is to other scientific research.

How do you know when your results are valid and reliable? The validity of your findings is difficult to establish, but your results are more likely to be valid if you follow these steps in the research process:

1. Formulate a fairly narrow problem to research in such a way that you can make a conclusion based on empirical evidence, that is, evidence based on observation or experience.
2. Set up one or more concrete research hypotheses, which are statements about what you expect to find from your observations.
3. Put together a research design, or a strategy for getting your observations (which might involve doing a sample survey, observing a city council meeting, or gathering information from an almanac or a computer file.
4. Find an appropriate way to measure the key pieces of information, or data, that you need in order to determine whether your research hypotheses are supported by the factual evidence of your observations.
5. Go out and collect the data.
6. Conduct a careful analysis of the data that you have gathered (usually with appropriate statistical procedures).
7. Make some general conclusions about whether the data tend to support your research hypotheses.

This list of procedures makes empirical research in political science look very mechanical. In part, it is. However it takes intuition and clear thinking to decide how to study political phenomena. There are certain pitfalls to be avoided in analyzing data.

Pitfalls to Avoid. For one thing, you must show that there is some meaningful relationship, or covariation, between or among the variables on which you have collected information. For example, before you claim that Republicans tend to be in higher-income brackets, you must be able to show that the percentage of people who are Republicans is greater among those who have incomes over, say, $50,000 a year than the percentage of Republicans you find among those with incomes under $50,000 a year. The simple fact that you find this pattern of covariation, by itself, though, doesn't necessarily mean that income is what really causes people to choose political sides. It turns out that people's income level is closely related to how much education they have, what kind of job they hold (medical doctors make more money than secretaries), and even how old they are and whether they are married. In other words, you must attempt to eliminate possibly spurious relationships, that is, explanations that don't take into account the complex relationships among variables.

Sometimes empirical covariation can be completely misleading. You probably remember the old story about how storks bring babies. Well, it really is true that birthrates in Europe are higher when storks are busy with their own nesting activities. This empirical fact, however, doesn't mean that the storks bring human babies with them; it just means that there is a similar pattern of human and stork behavior. As another example, you can easily find that the more fire trucks that go to fight a fire, the greater is the amount of damage from the fire. Does sending more fire trucks actually cause the fire to be worse? Of course not. Rather, the correct conclusion would be that a bigger fire requires that more trucks be called in to help fight it, and the bigger fire also produces more property damage. The covariation between the number of fire trucks and the amount of damage is spurious, because both of those variables are affected by the severity of the fire.

The fire truck example also brings us to another point of caution—deciding what "causes" what. You might be led astray in your conclusions if you aren't careful about the order of causal patterns. The fact that you took an examination in your American government course before you went to the polls and voted a straight Democratic ticket doesn't mean that your course (or the exam) caused you to vote that way. Such an incorrect conclusion would be an example of the *post hoc ergo propter hoc* (after, and therefore because of) fallacy. As another example, consider the relationship between your decision to protest ROTC on your campus and your parents' views on whether it is legitimate for people to engage in protest behavior. What "causes" what here? Assume your parents in general support public protests. Does your parents' general approval of protesting tend to determine whether you participate in the protest, or does your protesting gradually intensify your parents' view? Or could your behavior and their attitudes be mutually "casual"? Probably, the fact that you grew up under your parents' influence (not that you listened to or did everything they said) meant that you absorbed their tolerance for protest behavior. They had a much better chance to influence your behavior than you had a chance to influence their attitudes. In other words, it is important to take into consideration the *time ordering* of the variables that you might measure. In general, a later event logically is not able to "cause" an earlier event. Still, there likely is some tendency for parents to modify their previous views if they can be persuaded that your way of doing things politically is legitimate.

How to Increase Reliability. For your results to be valid, they must first be reliable. Whether your conclusions are reliable depends on how carefully you designed the study to take into account random variation from what otherwise might be observed. There are four different ways to test for reliability in your work.

1. Measure everything a second time. This is called the **test–retest method.**
2. Measure the same phenomenon in more than one way. This is the **parallel forms method** for assessing reliability.
3. Split your sample of observations into two groups and see if the results correspond closely. This is the **split-half method.**
4. Conduct an **item analysis,** which entails looking at the degree to which any one item that you have measured relates to the entire set of results. Any variable that doesn't fit closely with the overall pattern may need to be thrown out, or at least be remeasured. (Incidentally, this is precisely what many university instructors do when they prepare computer analyses for the results of a multiple-answer examination).

II. Choosing a Topic

Choosing a topic is the most important decision you'll make. Avoid being too broad ("Civil Rights in the U.S."). Avoid being too current (you will find almost nothing published and little analysis on the subject). Your freedom to choose will depend on the instructions you have received. In any case, make sure the topic fits the course. Be specific and focused. Consider the data or variables you will need to complete your project, keeping in mind the need to present valid and reliable facts. Also pick a subject that interests and even excites you. Your research will be more fun and your written report more lively if your heart is really in the project.

III. Writing the paper

After you have read the pamphlet that accompanies your text entitled, *Handbook on Critical Thinking and Writing in American Politics,* you are ready to start.

Begin with an outline. It is your road map, so, for most research papers, make sure you cover at least the following:

Title page (title, your name, class, date.)

1. Introduction (what you plan to do).
2. Problem statement or thesis (what you plan to prove; why this is an important topic).
3. Body of project (logically arranged discussion of facts; interpretation/analysis of the information).
4. Conclusion (what generalizations or overall insights you have gained from the study. Make sure these relate back to 2).
5. Endnotes or footnotes.
6. Appendix (put tables, charts, and other material here that are important to the paper but are not directly relevant in the body of the study).
7. Sources (bibliography).

Other Tips: Take notes on index cards or a yellow pad. Write down the complete citation, including page numbers of material. You may think it will be easy to do that later but it won't! The book or magazine may be gone, checked out, or missing. You may forget where it was. Label cards or pages so you can sort and organize them to fit the structure of your project.

Try to Be Objective. Let the facts lead you to conclusions. DON'T start with a conclusion (or bias) and then look for facts to prove you are right!

Type Your Paper. Make sure you number all pages. Cite sources, especially quotations or close paraphrasing. DON'T PLAGIARIZE (in other words, don't use ideas, analysis, or conclusions from other sources and pretend they are your own).

IV. Where to Find Information

Knowing where to find information quickly and efficiently is every researcher's goal. The following are excellent places to start:

We assume that you are familiar with the card catalog in your library and know how to search for books and other items indexed there. However, you will want to go beyond books (perhaps the subject is too recent for books or no one has quite focused on the subject the way you plan to approach it). You should also be familiar with the *Reader's Guide to Periodical Literature*, which cites material in popular periodicals such as *Time* and *People* magazines.

The Public Affairs Information Service (PAIS) publishes the *PAIS Bulletin*, which is an index (cumulated each year) with diverse citations on public affairs including books, journals, government documents, periodicals, fliers, and pamphlets.

Facts on File may be helpful in pinpointing and succinctly informing you about an event or person in the news. Its index is very complete and cross referenced. The *New York Times Index* is an annotated reference to the articles and stories that have appeared in the nation's complete newspaper, the *New York Times*.

The periodicals section of your library should have what we call *scholarly journals*. These are research-oriented publications in which political scientists report the results of their studies. Look for articles on your topic in *ABC POL SCI A Bibliography of Contents; Political Science and Government, Santa Barbara, CA: American Bibliographical Center, Clio Press*. This index is published five times a year and leads you to nearly 300 periodicals.

Familiarize yourself with some of the following scholarly journals: *The American Political Science Review, The Journal of Politics, Comparative Politics, Political Science Quarterly, The Western Political Quarterly, The American Journal of Political Science, Polity, Foreign Affairs, Presidential Studies Quarterly, Public Administration Review*.

For public opinion one of the most widely used sources is the *Gallup Opinion Index*.

The *Congressional Quarterly Weekly Report (CQWR)* is absolutely essential for every researcher. It comes to your library every week, is indexed, and is bound by volume every year. This source contains useful information on members of Congress, issues, scandals, political action committees, legislation, international affairs, and other material related to Congress. Tables and charts are excellent sources of information.

The *National Journal* covers material similar to the *CQWR*.

The *Supreme Court Reporter* (West Publishing) is one of the best-annotated sources of Supreme Court cases. It provides detailed information about the case and background as well as reference to other relevant cases.

The *Book of the States* is the authoritative source on the structure of state government, statistics, finances, and other information about the fifty states. This is published every two years.

The *Encyclopedia of Associations* is a multivolume source of information on organizations. You will be amazed at the number and diversity of organized groups, associations, and other organizations that exist. The *Encyclopedia* tells you the objectives, organizations, budget, membership, names of officers, address, and telephone numbers.

V. Using Government Publications

One of the best sources of information for research is the U.S. government, the largest publisher in the world. There are federal government publications for virtually every research topic. Because of the sheer volume, only specially designated *depository libraries* receive most of these publications. As your librarian where the nearest one is located. Remember that you can obtain this material through interlibrary loan.

Federal publications include statistics; congressional material including hearings, pamphlets, and bulletins; technical reports; presidential statements and documents; court rulings; and agency-specific publications. To find this material, you may want to use the following:

The *CIS* (Congressional Information Service) *Index*. This is published monthly and bound into a volume each year. It covers congressional hearings, reports, and special publications. Each item listed includes an abstract.

The *Congressional Monitor* is the best source of information on congressional hearings, which are listed by subject area for each House and Senate committee.

The *American Statistics Index* covers over five hundred federal government sources of information including numerical data.

The *Guide to U.S. Government Publications*, by John L. Andriot, is an annual guide to the reports and regular publications (magazines, for example) that are produced by more than 2,000 government agencies.

The following are selected United States government publications by topic:

Foreign Policy: *United States Foreign Policy: A Report of the Secretary of State*. This annual report reviews U.S. foreign policy, military and technical assistance, and other international activities country by country.

Federalism: *Catalog of Federal Domestic Assistance*. This publication is compiled by the Office of Management and Budget and lists virtually all federal grant programs to state and local governments. *Intergovernmental Perspective* is published by the Advisory Commission on Intergovernmental Relations four times a year and contains statistical information, analysis, and listings on all aspects of intergovernmental relations.

Voting/Elections: The *Journal of Election Administration* is published by the Federal Election Commission (FEC), which also publishes an array of statistical information on campaigns, voting, and related matters (call toll free, 800-424-9530).

Congress: The *Congressional Record* is published every day Congress is in session and contains the proceedings as well as supplemental documents inserted by members of Congress.

Presidency: The *Weekly Compilation of Presidential Documents* is issued every week and compiled annually as *Public Powers of the President of the United States*. It contains the speeches, messages, statements, and press conferences of the president.

The Supreme Court: The *United States Reports,* published since 1790, is the official publication of Supreme Court decisions. Citation of a case is usually to the *Reports*. For example Miranda v. Arizona, 348 U.S. 436 (1966) means volume 348 of the U.S. Reports, page 436 in the year 1966.

Domestic Policy: One of the best sources of information is the *Budget of the United States* and its appendices or the *United States Budget in Brief,* which contain the specific spending plans and revenue sources of the federal government.

Public Welfare Policy: The book *Characteristics of General Assistance in the United States* provides state-by-state data on federal and state assistance programs for the needy.

Education: data are found in the *Digest of Educational Statistics* published by the Department of Education each year.

The Economy and the Society: Statistics on general aspects of the society and the economy can be found in *Social Indicators: Selected Statistics on Social Conditions and Trends in the U.S.,* published by the Office of Management and Budget.

The U.S. Federal Government: The *United States Government Manual,* describes the agencies of the executive branch, their activities and the names and addresses of key officials. This book can be considered the "official" directory of U.S. government agencies. Government publication can also be obtained from your representative and senators. Find their nearest office in the government section of your local phone book. Ask for the publication by title, date, publication number, and issuing agency. (Have as much of this information as possible.) You can also write or call their office and tell them what general topic you are researching; they will send you material. However, be aware that this will be a random selection from publications they have in their office. You will still need to do further research to make certain you've covered the subject fully.

VI. Computerized Research Sources

Computerized searching capabilities are rather recent. The following are useful for students doing research in American government:

The *Social Science Index* is available on CD-ROM floppy disks and also on-line through various library services.

DIALOG Information Service Inc. contains over 350 databases with more than 200 million individual records (units of information generally citations to sources). A typical ten-minute search costs from $5 to $15. It is available twenty-four-hours a day except from 3 A.M. to 1 P.M. EST on Sundays.

One of the most useful files is *U.S. Political Science Documents #93*. This contains 48,970 records starting in 1975 and consisting of detailed abstracts and indexes from roughly 150 of the major American scholarly journals in political science.

Social Science #7 contains over 2.5 million records indexed from the 1,500 most important social science journals throughout the world. It covers every area of the social and behavioral sciences.

PAIS International #49 has 338,817 records with bibliographic information on the public policy literature in a range of disciplines.

Another separate computerized source is the *Monthly Catalog of Government Publications,* which is available on CD-ROM disks under the name MARCIVE, GPO CAT/PAC.

The research librarian at your library is an excellent source for other and computerized sources of information for research projects and papers.

VII. More on Research

For a more detailed discussion of how to do research in political science, the following are excellent: Carl Kalvelage, Albert P. Melone, and Morley Segal, *Bridges to Knowledge in Political Science: A Handbook for Research,* (Pacific Palisades, CA: Palisades Publishers, 1984), or Robert Weissberg, *Politics: A Handbook for Students* (New York: Harcourt Brace Jovanovich, Publishers, 1985).

Jay M. Shafritz, *The Dorsey Dictionary of American Government and Politics* (Chicago: The Dorsey Press, 1988) is a 661-page treasure of detailed information and reference that you should consider owning. It is richly illustrated and very easy to use.

GLOSSARY

ACID RAIN   Rain that has picked up pollutants, usually sulfur dioxides, from industrial areas of the earth that are often hundreds of miles distant from where the rain falls.

ACQUISITIVE MODEL   A model of bureaucracy that views top-level bureaucrats as constantly seeking to expand the size of their budgets and staffs of their departments or agencies so as to gain greater power and influence in the public sector.

ACTIONABLE   Furnishing grounds for a lawsuit.

ACTION–REACTION SYNDROME   For every action on the part of government, there is a reaction on the part of the affected public. Then the government attempts to counter the reaction with another action, which starts the cycle all over again.

ACTUAL MALICE   Actual desire and intent to see another suffer by one's actions.

ADMINISTRATIVE AGENCIES   Agencies that usually form part of the executive branch, plus independent regulatory agencies and independent agencies; for example, the Federal Trade Commission, the Securities and Exchange Commission, and the Federal Communications Commission.

ADVICE AND CONSENT   The power vested in the U.S. Senate by the Constitution (Article II, Section 2) to give its advice and consent to the president concerning treaties and presidential appointments.

AFFIRM   To declare that a judgment is valid and right and must stand.

AFFIRMATIVE ACTION   Policies issued in job hiring that give special consideration or compensatory treatment to traditionally disadvantaged groups in an effort to overcome present effects of past discrimination.

AGENDA SETTING   The power to determine which public policy questions will be debated or considered by Congress.

AID TO FAMILIES WITH DEPENDENT CHILDREN (AFDC)   A state-administered program that furnishes assistance for families in which dependent children do not have the financial support of the father, owing to the father's desertion, disability, or death. The program is partially financed by federal grants.

AMICUS CURIAE **BRIEFS**   Latin for "friend of the court"; refers here to persons or groups who are not parties to a case but who have an interest in its outcome. These briefs are documents filed with the court that contain legal arguments supporting a particular desired outcome in a case.

ANARCHY   The state of having no government and no laws. Each member of the society governs himself or herself.

ANTIBALLISTIC MISSILES (ABMs)   A defense system designed to protect targets by destroying the attacking airplanes or missiles before they reach their destination.

ANTI-FEDERALISTS   The Anti-Federalists opposed the adoption of the Constitution because of its centralist tendencies and attacked the failure of the Constitution's framers to include a bill of rights.

APPELLATE COURTS   Those courts having jurisdiction of appeal and review of cases and issues that were originally tried in lower courts.

APPOINTMENT POWER   The authority vested in the president to fill a government office or position. Positions filled by presidential appointment include those in the executive branch, the federal judiciary, commissioned officers in the armed forces, and members of the independent regulatory commissions.

APPROPRIATION   Occurs when Congress passes a spending bill specifying the amount of authorized funds that will actually be allocated for an agency's use.

ATTENTIVE PUBLIC   That proportion of the general public that pays attention to foreign policy issues.

AUSTRALIAN BALLOT   A secret ballot prepared, distributed, and tabulated by government officials at public expense. Since 1888, all states have used the secret Australian ballot rather than an open, public ballot.

AUTHORITY   The features of a leader or an institution that compel obedience, usually because of ascribed legitimacy. For most societies, government is the ultimate authority in the allocation of values.

AUTHORIZATION   A formal declaration by a legislative committee that a certain amount of funding may be available to an agency. Some authorizations terminate in a year; others are automatically renewable without further congressional authorization.

BAD-TENDENCY RULE   Speech or other First Amendment freedoms may permissibly be curtailed if there is a possibility that such expression might lead to some "evil."

BEAUTY CONTEST A presidential primary in which contending candidates compete for popular votes but the results have little or no impact on the selection of delegates to the national convention, which is made by the party elite.

BICAMERALISM The division of a legislature into two separate assemblies.

BICAMERAL LEGISLATURE A legislature made up of two chambers, or parts. The United States Congress, composed of the House of Representatives and the Senate, is a bicameral legislature.

BILL OF RIGHTS The first ten amendments to the United States Constitution. They contain a listing of the rights a person enjoys and which cannot be infringed upon by the government, such as the freedoms of speech, press, and religion.

BLANKET PRIMARY A primary in which all candidates' names are printed on the same ballot, regardless of party affiliation. The voter may vote for candidates of more than one party.

BLOCK GRANTS Federal programs that provide funding to the state and local governments for general functional areas, such as criminal justice or mental health programs.

BUREAUCRACY A large organization that is structured hierarchically to carry out specific functions.

BUSING The transportation of public school students from areas where they live to schools in other areas to eliminate school segregation based on residential patterns.

CABINET An advisory group selected by the president to aid him in making decisions. The cabinet presently numbers thirteen department secretaries and the attorney general. Depending on the president, the cabinet may be highly influential or relatively insignificant in its advisory role.

CABINET DEPARTMENTS The fourteen departments of the executive branch (State, Treasury, Defense, Justice, Interior, Agriculture, Commerce, Labor, Health and Human Services, Housing and Urban Development, Education, Energy, Transportation, and Veterans Affairs).

CADRE The nucleus of political party activists carrying out the major functions of American political parties.

CANVASSING BOARD An official group on a county, city, or state level that receives vote counts from every precinct in the area, tabulates the figures, and sends them to the state canvassing authority, which certifies the winners.

CAPTURE The act of gaining direct or indirect control over agency personnel and decision makers by the industry that is being regulated.

CASEWORK Personal work for constituents by members of Congress.

CATEGORICAL GRANTS-IN-AID Federal grants-in-aid to states or local governments that are for very specific programs or projects.

CAUCUS A closed meeting of party leaders to select party candidates or to decide on policy. Also, a meeting of party members designed to select candidates and propose policies.

CHALLENGE An allegation by a poll watcher that a potential voter is unqualified to vote or that a vote is invalid; designed to prevent fraud in elections.

CHECKS AND BALANCES A major principle of the American governmental system whereby each branch of the government exercises a check on the actions of the others. Separation of powers, divided power, and checks and balances limit government's power by pitting power against power. For example, the president checks Congress by holding veto power, Congress has the purse strings, and the Senate approves presidential appointments.

CHIEF DIPLOMAT The role of the president in recognizing foreign governments, making treaties, and making executive agreements.

CHIEF EXECUTIVE The role of the president as head of the executive branch of the government.

CHIEF LEGISLATOR The role of the president in influencing the making of laws.

CHIEF OF STAFF Directs the White House Office and advises the president.

CHIEF OF STATE The role of the president as ceremonial head of the government.

CIVIL LAW The law regulating conduct between private persons over noncriminal matters. Under civil law, the government provides the forum for the settlement of disputes between private parties in such matters as contracts, domestic relations, and business relations.

CIVIL SERVICE A collective term for the body of employees working for the government. Generally, civil service is understood to apply to all those who gain government employment through a merit system.

CIVIL SERVICE COMMISSION The central personnel agency of the national government; created in 1883.

CLASS-ACTION SUIT A lawsuit filed by an individual seeking damages for "all persons similarly situated."

CLASS POLITICS Political preferences based on income level and/or social status.

CLEAR AND PRESENT DANGER TEST The test proposed by Justice Holmes for determining when government may restrict free speech. Restrictions are permissible, he argued, only when speech provokes a "clear and present danger" to the public order.

CLIMATE CONTROL The use of public relations techniques to create favorable public opinion toward an interest group, industry, or corporation.

CLOSED PRIMARY The most widely used primary, in which voters may participate only in the primary of the party with which they are registered.

CLOTURE A method invoked to close off debate and to bring the matter under consideration to a vote in the Senate.

COATTAIL EFFECT The influence of a popular or unpopular candidate on the electoral success or failure of other candidates on the same party ticket. The effect is increased by the party-column ballot, which encourages straight-ticket voting.

COLD WAR The ideological, political, and economic impasse that existed between the United States and the Soviet Union following World War II.

COMMANDER IN CHIEF The role of the president as supreme commander of the military forces of the United States and of the state national guard units when they are called into federal service.

COMMERCE CLAUSE The section of the Constitution in which Congress is given the power to regulate trade among the states and with foreign countries.

COMMERCIAL SPEECH Advertising statements that have increasingly been given First Amendment protection.

COMMON LAW Judge-made law that originated in England from decisions shaped according to prevailing custom. Decisions were reapplied to similar situations and gradually became common to the nation. Common law forms the basis of legal procedures in the American states.

COMMON SENSE Thomas Paine's best-selling pamphlet that argued for a new government in the colonies.

COMPARABLE WORTH The idea that compensation should be based on the worth of the job to an employer and that factors unrelated to the worth of a job, such as the sex of the employee, should not affect compensation. Supporters of the comparable-worth doctrine argue that women should be entitled to comparable wages for doing work that is different from, but of comparable worth and value to, work done by higher-paid men.

COMPLIANCE Accepting and carrying out authoritative decisions.

CONCURRENT MAJORITY A principle advanced by John C. Calhoun whereby democratic decisions could be made only with the concurrence of all segments of society affected by the decision. Without their concurrence, a decision should not be binding on those whose interests it violates.

CONCURRING OPINION A separate opinion, prepared by a judge who supports the decision of the majority of the court but who wants to make or clarify a particular point or to voice disapproval of the grounds on which the decision was made.

CONFEDERAL SYSTEM A system of government consisting of a league of independent states, each having essentially sovereign powers. The central government created by such a league has only limited powers over the states.

CONFEDERATION A political system in which states or regional governments retain ultimate authority except for those powers they expressly delegate to a central government. A voluntary association of independent states, in which the member states agree to limited restraints on their freedom of action.

CONFERENCE COMMITTEES Special joint committees appointed to reconcile differences when bills pass the two houses of Congress in different forms.

CONSENSUS General agreement among the citizenry on an issue.

CONSENT OF THE PEOPLE The idea that governments and laws derive their legitimacy from the consent of the governed.

CONSERVATISM A set of beliefs that includes a limited role for the national government in helping individuals, support for traditional values and life-styles, and a preference for the status quo.

CONSERVATIVE COALITION An alliance of Republicans and southern Democrats that can form in the House or the Senate to oppose liberal legislation and support conservative legislation.

CONSOLIDATION The union of two or more governmental units to form a single unit.

CONSTANT DOLLARS Dollars corrected for inflation; dollars expressed in terms of purchasing power for a given year.

CONSTITUTIONAL INITIATIVE An electoral device whereby citizens can propose a constitutional amendment through petitions signed by the required number of registered voters.

CONSTITUTIONAL POWERS The powers vested in the president by Article II of the Constitution.

CONTAINMENT A U.S. diplomatic policy adopted by the Truman administration to "build situations of strength" around the globe to contain communist power within its existing boundaries.

CONTINUING RESOLUTIONS Temporary laws that Congress passes when various appropriations bills have not been decided by the beginning of the new fiscal year on October 1.

COOLEY'S RULE The view that cities should be able to govern themselves, presented in an 1871 decision by Michigan Judge Thomas Cooley.

COOPERATIVE FEDERALISM The theory that the states and the national government should cooperate in solving problems.

CORRUPT PRACTICES ACTS A series of acts passed by Congress in an attempt to limit and regulate the size and sources of contributions and expenditures in political campaigns.

COUNCIL OF ECONOMIC ADVISERS (CEA) A staff agency in the Executive Office that advises the president on measures to maintain stability in the nation's economy. Established in 1946, the council develops economic plans and budget recommendations for maintaining the nation's "employment, production, and purchasing power" and helps the president prepare an annual economic report to Congress.

COUNCILS OF GOVERNMENTS (COGs) Voluntary organizations of counties and municipalities concerned with area-wide problems.

COUNTY The chief government unit set up by the state to administer state law and business at the local level. Counties are drawn up by area, rather than by rural or urban criteria.

CREDENTIALS COMMITTEE A committee used by political parties at their national convention to determine which delegates may participate. The committee inspects the claim of each prospective delegate to be seated as a legitimate representative of his or her state.

CRIMINAL LAW The law that defines crimes and provides punishment for violations. In criminal cases, the government is the prosecutor because crimes are against the public order.

DE FACTO SEGREGATION Racial segregation that occurs not as a result of deliberate intentions but because of past social and economic conditions and residential patterns.

DE JURE SEGREGATION Racial segregation that occurs because of laws or administrative decisions by public agencies.

DEFAMATION OF CHARACTER Wrongfully hurting a person's good reputation. The law has imposed a general duty on all persons to refrain from making false, defamatory statements about others.

DEMOCRACY A system of government in which ultimate political authority is vested in the people. Derived from the Greek words *demos* ("the people") and *kratos* ("authority").

DEMOCRATS One of the two major American political parties evolving out of the Democratic Republican (Jeffersonian) group supporting Thomas Jefferson.

DÉTENTE A French word meaning the relaxation of tension. The term characterizes U.S.–Soviet policy as it developed under President Nixon and Henry Kissinger. Détente stresses direct cooperative dealings with cold war rivals but avoids ideological accommodation.

DILLON'S RULE The narrowest possible interpretation of the legal status of local governments, outlined by Judge John F. Dillon, who in 1811 stated that a municipal corporation can exercise only those powers expressly granted by state law.

DIPLOMACY The total process by which states carry on political relations with each other; settling conflicts among nations by peaceful means.

DIRECT DEMOCRACY A system of government in which political decisions are made by the people directly, rather than by their elected representatives; probably possible only in small political communities.

DIRECT PRIMARIES An intraparty election in which the voters select the candidates who will run on a party's ticket in the subsequent general election.

DIRECT TECHNIQUES Interest group activities that involve interaction with government officials to further the group's goals.

DISCHARGE PETITION A procedure by which a bill in the House of Representatives may be forced out of a committee (discharged) that has refused to report it for consideration by the House. The discharge motion must be signed by an absolute majority (218) of representatives and is used only on rare occasions.

DISSENTING OPINION A separate opinion in which a judge dissents from the conclusion reached by the majority of the court and expounds his or her own views about the case.

DIVISIVE OPINION Public opinion that is polarized between two quite different positions.

DUAL CITIZENSHIP The condition of being a citizen of two sovereign political units; being a citizen of both a state and the nation.

DUAL FEDERALISM A system of government in which the states and the national government each remain supreme within their own spheres. The doctrine looks on nation and state as coequal sovereign powers. It holds that acts of states within their reserved powers could be legitimate limitations on the powers of the national government.

ECO-DESTRUCTION The willful destruction of some part of the ecology as part of an act of war or aggression.

ECONOMIC AID Assistance to other nations in the form of grants, loans, or credits to buy American products.

ECONOMIC REGULATION The regulation of business practices by government agencies.

ELASTIC CLAUSE, OR NECESSARY AND PROPER CLAUSE The clause in Article I, Section 8, that grants Congress the power to do whatever is necessary to execute its specifically delegated powers.

ELECTOR The partisan slate of electors is selected early in the presidential election year by state laws and applicable political party apparatus, and the electors cast ballots for president and vice president. The number of electors in each state is equal to that state's number of representatives in both houses of Congress.

ELECTORAL COLLEGE A group of persons called electors who are selected by the voters in each state; this group officially elects the president and the vice president of the United States. The number of electors in each state is equal to the number of each state's representatives in both houses of Congress.

ELECTRONIC MEDIA Broadcasting media (radio and television). The term derives from their method of transmission, in contrast to printed media.

ELITE THEORY A perspective holding that society is ruled by a small number of people who exercise power in their self-interest.

ELITES The upper socioeconomic classes that control political and economic affairs.

EMERGENCY POWERS Inherent powers exercised by the president during a period of national crisis, particularly in foreign affairs.

ENUMERATED POWERS The powers specifically granted to the national government by the Constitution. The first seventeen clauses of Article I, Section 8, specify most of the enumerated powers of Congress.

ENVIRONMENTAL IMPACT STATEMENT (EIS) As a requirement mandated by NEPA, EISs must show the costs and benefits of major federal actions that could significantly affect the quality of the environment.

EQUAL EMPLOYMENT OPPORTUNITY COMMISSION (EEOC) A commission established by the 1964 Civil Rights Act to (1) end discrimination based on race, color, religion, gender, or national origin in conditions of employment and (2) promote voluntary action programs by employers, unions, and community organizations to foster equal job opportunities.

EQUALITY A concept that all people are of equal worth.

EQUALIZATION A method for adjusting the amount of money that a state must put up to receive federal funds that takes into account the wealth of the state or its ability to tax its citizens.

ERA OF DEREGULATION The early 1980s, characterized by deregulation of several industries, including trucking, air transport, and banking.

ERA OF GOOD FEELING The years from 1817 to 1825 when James Monroe was president and there was, in effect, no political opposition.

ERA OF PERSONAL POLITICS An era when attention centers on the character of individual candidates rather than on party identification.

ESTABLISHMENT CLAUSE The part of the First Amendment prohibiting the establishment of a church officially supported by the national government. It is applied to questions of state and local government aid to religious organizations and schools, of the legality of allowing or requiring school prayers, and of the teaching of evolution versus fundamentalist theories of creation.

EUTHANASIA Killing incurably ill people for reasons of mercy.

EXCISE TAXES A tax on certain commodities, such as liquor and tobacco, levied on their manufacture or sale within a country.

EXCLUSIONARY RULE A policy forbidding the admission at trial of illegally seized evidence.

EXECUTIVE AGREEMENT A binding international obligation made between chiefs of state without legislative sanction.

EXECUTIVE BUDGET The budget prepared and submitted by the president to Congress.

EXECUTIVE OFFICE OF THE PRESIDENT (EOP) Established by President Franklin D. Roosevelt by executive order under the Reorganization Act of 1939. It currently consists of nine staff agencies that assist the president in carrying out major duties.

EXECUTIVE ORDER A rule or regulation issued by the president that has the effect of law. Executive orders can implement and give administrative effect to provisions in the Constitution, to treaties, and to statutes.

EXECUTIVE PRIVILEGE The right of executive officials to refuse to appear before, or to withhold information from, a legislative committee. Executive privilege is enjoyed by the president and by those executive officials accorded that right by the president.

EXPRESSED POWERS The constitutional and statutory powers of the president, which are expressly written into the Constitution or into congressional law.

EXTRADITE To surrender an accused or convicted criminal to the authorities of the state from which he or she has fled; to return a fugitive criminal to the jurisdiction of the accusing state.

EXTRAORDINARY MAJORITY A majority that is greater than 50 percent plus one. For example, ratification of amendments to the U.S. Constitution requires the approval of two-thirds of the House and the Senate and three-fourths of the states.

FACTION A group or bloc in a legislature or political party acting together in pursuit of some special interest or position.

FAIRNESS DOCTRINE An FCC regulation affecting broadcasting media, which required that fair or equal opportunity be given to legitimate opposing political groups or individuals to broadcast their views.

"FAITHLESS" ELECTORS Electors voting for candidates other than those within their parties. They are pledged, but not required by law, to vote for the candidate who has a plurality in the state.

FALL REVIEW Every year, after receiving formal federal agency requests for funding for the next fiscal year, the Office of Management and Budget reviews the requests, makes changes, and submits its recommendations to the president.

FEDERAL ELECTION COMMISSION Created by the 1974 Federal Election Campaign Act to enforce compliance with the requirements of the act; the commission consists of six nonpartisan administrators.

FEDERAL MANDATES Requirements in federal legislation that force states and municipalities to comply with certain rules.

FEDERAL OPEN MARKET COMMITTEE (FOMC) The most important body within the Federal Reserve System, the FOMC decides how monetary policy should be carried out by the Federal Reserve.

FEDERAL REGISTER A publication of the executive branch that prints executive orders, rules, and regulations.

FEDERAL SYSTEM A system of government in which power is divided by a written constitution between a central government and regional, or subdivisional, governments. Each level must have some domain in which its policies are dominant and some genuine political or constitutional guarantee of its authority.

FEDERAL SYSTEM A system of government in which power is divided by a written constitution between a central government and regional, or subdivisional, governments. Each level must have some domain in which its policies are dominant and some genuine political or constitutional guarantee of its authority.

FEDERALISTS The name given to those who were in favor of the adoption of the U.S. Constitution and the creation of a federal union. They favored a strong central government.

FIGHTING WORDS Words that when uttered by a public speaker are so inflammatory that they could provoke the average listener to violence; the words are usually of a racial, religious, or ethnic type.

FILIBUSTER In the Senate, unlimited debate to halt action on a particular bill.

FIRESIDE CHATS Warm, informal talks by Franklin D. Roosevelt to a few million of his intimate friends—via the radio. Roosevelt's fireside chats were so effective that succeeding presidents have been urged by their advisers to emulate him by giving more radio and television reports to the nation.

FIRST BUDGET RESOLUTION A resolution passed by Congress in May that sets overall revenue and spending goals and hence, by definition, the size of the deficit for the following fiscal year.

FIRST CONTINENTAL CONGRESS   The first gathering of delegates from the thirteen colonies, held in 1774.

FIRST-STRIKE CAPABILITIES   The launching of an initial strategic nuclear attack before the opponent has used any strategic weapons.

FISCAL POLICY   Changes in government spending or taxes to alter national economic variables, such as the rate of unemployment.

FISCAL YEAR   The twelve-month period that is used for bookkeeping, or accounting, purposes. Usually, the fiscal year does not coincide with the calendar year. For example, the federal government's fiscal year runs from October 1 through September 30.

FLUIDITY   The extent to which public opinion changes over time.

FOOD STAMPS   Coupons issued by the federal government to low-income individuals to be used for the purchase of food.

FOREIGN POLICY   A nation's external goals and the techniques and strategies used to achieve them.

FOREIGN POLICY PROCESS   The steps by which external goals are decided and acted on.

FRANCHISE   The legal right to vote, extended to African Americans by the Fifteenth Amendment, to women by the Nineteenth Amendment, and to all citizens age eighteen and over by the Twenty-sixth Amendment.

FRANKING   A policy that enables members of Congress to send material through the mail by substituting their facsimile signature (frank) for postage.

FRATERNITY   From the Latin *fraternus* ("brother"), the term *fraternity* came to mean, in the political philosophy of the eighteenth century, the condition in which each individual considers the needs of all others; a brotherhood. In the French Revolution of 1789, the popular cry was "liberty, equality, and fraternity."

FREE EXERCISE CLAUSE   The provision of the First Amendment guaranteeing the free exercise of religion.

FULL FAITH AND CREDIT CLAUSE   A section of the Constitution that requires states to recognize one another's laws and court decisions. It ensures that rights established under deeds, wills, contracts, and other civil matters in one state will be honored by other states.

FUNCTIONAL CONSOLIDATION   The cooperation of two or more units of local government in providing services to their inhabitants.

"GAG ORDERS"   Orders issued by judges restricting publication of news about a trial in progress or a pretrial hearing in order to protect the accused's right to a fair trial.

GARBAGE CAN MODEL   A model of bureaucracy that characterizes bureaucracies as rudderless entities with little formal organization in which solutions to problems are based on trial and error rather than rational policy planning.

GENDER GAP   Most often used to describe the difference between the percentage of votes a candidate receives from women voters and the percentage the candidate receives from men. The term was widely used after the 1980 presidential election.

GENERAL LAW CITY   A city operating under general state laws that apply to all local government units of a similar type.

GENERAL SALES TAX   A tax levied as a proportion of the retail price of a commodity at the point of sale.

GENERATIONAL EFFECTS   The long-lasting effects of events of a particular time period on the political opinions or preferences of those who came of political age at that time.

GERRYMANDERING   The drawing of legislative district boundary lines for the purpose of obtaining partisan or fractional advantage. A district is said to be gerrymandered when its shape is manipulated by the dominant party in the state legislature to maximize electoral strength at the expense of the minority party.

GOVERNMENT   A permanent structure (institution) composed of decision makers who make society's rules about conflict resolution and the allocation of resources and who possess the power to enforce them.

GOVERNMENT CORPORATION   An agency of government that administers a quasi-business enterprise. Used when an activity is primarily commercial, produces revenue for its continued existence, and requires greater flexibility than is permitted for departments.

GOVERNMENT IN THE SUNSHINE ACT   Requires that all multiheaded federal agencies conduct their business regularly in public session.

GRAND JURY   A jury called to hear evidence and determine whether indictments should be used against persons suspected of having committed crimes.

GRANDFATHER CLAUSE   A device used by southern states to exempt whites from state taxes and literacy laws originally intended to disenfranchise African-American voters. It restricted the voting franchise to those who could prove that their grandfathers had voted before 1867.

GREAT COMPROMISE   The compromise between the New Jersey and the Virginia plans that created one chamber of the Congress based on population and one chamber that represented each state equally. Also called the Connecticut Compromise.

GREENHOUSE EFFECT   The trapping of heat within the earth's atmosphere as a result of pollution caused largely by the burning of fossil fuels and emissions of carbon dioxide.

HATCH ACT (POLITICAL ACTIVITIES ACT)   This act prohibits the use of federal authority to influence nominations and elections or the use of rank to pressure federal employees to make political contributions. It also prohibits civil service employees from active involvement in political campaigns.

HECKLERS' VETO   Boisterous and generally disruptive behavior by listeners of public speakers that, in effect, vetoes the public speakers' right to speak.

HOME RULE CITY   A city with a charter allowing local voters to frame, adopt, and amend their own charter.

HORIZONTAL FEDERALISM   Activities, problems, and policies that require state governments to interact with one another.

HOUSE MINORITY LEADER   The party leader elected by the minority party in the House.

HYPERPLURALISM   An extreme form of pluralism in which government is so decentralized and authority so fragmented that it does not get much accomplished.

IDEOLOGUE   A term applied to an individual whose political opinions are carefully thought out and relatively consistent with one another. Ideologues are often described as having a comprehensive world view.

IDEOLOGY   A comprehensive and logically ordered set of beliefs about the nature of people and the institutions of government.

IMAGE BUILDING   Using public and private opinion polls, the candidate's image is molded to meet the particular needs of the campaign. Image building is done primarily through the media.

IMPEACHMENT   As authorized by Article I of the Constitution, impeachment is an action by the House of Representatives and the Senate to remove the president, vice president, or civil officers of the United States from office for crimes of "treason, bribery, or other high crimes and misdemeanors."

INALIENABLE RIGHTS   Rights held to be inherent in natural law and not dependent on government; as asserted in the Declaration of Independence, the rights to "life, liberty, and the pursuit of happiness."

INCOME TRANSFER   A transfer of income from some individuals in the economy to other individuals. This is generally done by way of the government. It is a transfer in the sense that no current services are rendered by the recipients.

INCORPORATION THEORY   The view that most of the protections of the Bill of Rights are incorporated into the Fourteenth Amendment's protection against state governments.

INDEPENDENT CANDIDATE   A political candidate who is not affiliated with a political party.

INDEPENDENT EXECUTIVE AGENCY   A federal agency having a single function that is not part of a cabinet department but reports directly to the president.

INDEPENDENT REGULATORY AGENCY   An agency outside the major executive departments charged with making and implementing rules and regulations to protect the public interest.

INDEPENDENT VOTERS   Voters who disavow any party affiliation and cast their ballots based on their views of who is the best candidate.

INDIRECT TECHNIQUES   Strategies employed by interest groups that use third parties to influence government officials.

INDUSTRIAL POLICY   Any systematic attempt by a government to direct the way in which resources are used in a capitalist economy such as that of the United States.

INHERENT POWERS   Powers of the president derived from the loosely worded statement in the Constitution that "the executive power shall be vested in a president" and that the president should "take care that the laws be faithfully executed"; defined through practice rather than through constitutional or statutory law.

INITIATIVE   A procedure by which voters can propose a change in state and local laws by gathering signatures on a petition and submitting it to the legislature for approval.

INJUNCTION   An order issued by a court to compel or restrain the performance of an act by an individual or government official.

IN-KIND SUBSIDIES   Goods and services—such as food stamps, housing, or medical care—provided by the government to lower-income groups.

INSTITUTIONS   Long-standing, identifiable structures or associations that perform functions for society.

INSTRUCTED DELEGATES   The concept that legislators are agents of the voters who elected them and that they should vote according to the views of their constituents regardless of their own personal assessments.

INTELLIGENCE COMMUNITY   The government agencies involved in gathering information about the capabilities and intentions of foreign governments and that engages in covert activities to further American foreign policy aims.

INTENSITY   The strength of a pro or con position concerning public policy or an issue. Intensity is often critical in generating public action; an intense minority can often win on an issue of public policy over a less intense majority.

INTEREST GROUP   An organized group of individuals sharing common objectives who actively attempt to influence government policy makers through direct and indirect methods, including the marshalling of public opinion, lobbying, and electioneering.

INTERPOSITION   The act in which a state places itself between its citizens and the national government as a protector, shielding its citizens from any national legislation that may be harmful to them. The doctrine of interposition has been rejected by the federal courts as contrary to the national supremacy clause of Article VI in the Constitution.

INTERSTATE COMPACT   An agreement between two or more states to cooperate on a policy or problem, such as sharing water resources. It must first be approved by Congress.

INTERVENTIONISM   Involvement in foreign affairs; actions directed at changing or preserving the internal political arrangements of other nations.

IRON CURTAIN   The term used to describe the division of Europe between the Soviet Union and the West. Popularized by Winston Churchill in a speech portraying Europe as being divided by an iron curtain, with the nations of Eastern Europe behind the curtain and increasingly under Soviet control.

IRON TRIANGLE   The three-way alliance among legislators, bureaucrats, and interest groups to make or preserve policies that benefit their respective interests.

ISSUE VOTING   Voting for a candidate based on how he or she stands on a particular issue.

ITEM VETO   The power exercised by the governors of most states to veto particular sections or items of an appropriations bill, while signing the remainder of the bill into law.

JOINT COMMITTEE   A legislative committee composed of members from both houses of Congress.

JUDICIABLE DISPUTES   Disputes that raise questions about the law and are appropriate for resolution before a court of law.

JUDICIAL ACTIVISM   A doctrine advocating an active role for the Supreme Court in enforcing the Constitution and in using judicial review. An activist Court takes a broad view of the Constitution and involves itself in legislative and executive matters by altering the direction of activities of Congress, state legislatures, and administrative agencies.

JUDICIAL IMPLEMENTATION   The way in which court decisions are translated into policy.

JUDICIAL RESTRAINT   A doctrine holding that the Court should rarely use its power of judicial review or otherwise intervene in the political process.

JUDICIAL REVIEW   The power of the courts to declare acts of the executive and legislative branches unconstitutional; first established in *Marbury v. Madison.*

JURISDICTION   The authority of a court to decide certain cases. Not all courts have the authority to decide all cases. Where a case arises and what its subject matter is are two jurisdictional factors.

JUSTICIABLE QUESTION   A question that may be raised and reviewed in court.

KANGAROO COURT   A mock hearing in which norms of justice and judicial procedure are ignored.

KEYNESIAN ECONOMICS   An economic theory, named after English economist John Maynard Keynes, that gained prominence during the Great Depression of the 1930s. Typically associated with the use of fiscal policy to alter national economic variables—for example, increased government spending during times of economic downturns.

KITCHEN CABINET   The informal advisers to the president.

LABOR MOVEMENT   In general, the term refers to the full range of economic and political expression of working-class interests; politically, it describes the organization or working-class interests.

LATENT INTERESTS   Interests that are dormant or unexpressed. The group that holds these interests has never organized or articulated them.

LATENT PUBLIC OPINION   Unexpressed political opinions that have the potential to become manifest attitudes or beliefs.

LAWMAKING   The process of deciding the legal rules that govern our society. Such laws may regulate minor affairs or establish broad national policies.

LEGISLATIVE HISTORY   The background and events leading up to the enactment of a law. This may include legislative committee reports, hearings, and floor debates.

LEGISLATIVE VETO   A provision in a bill reserving to Congress or to a congressional committee the power to reject an act or regulation of a national agency by majority vote; declared unconstitutional by the Supreme Court in 1983.

LEGISLATURE   A government body primarily responsible for the making of laws.

LEGITIMACY   A status conferred by the people on the government's officials, acts, and institutions through their belief that the government's actions are an appropriate use of power by a legally constituted governmental authority following correct decision-making policies. These actions are regarded as rightful and entitled to compliance and obedience on the part of citizens.

LIBEL   Defamation of character in writing.

LIBERALISM   A set of beliefs that includes the advocacy of positive government action to improve the welfare of individuals, support for civil rights, and a tolerance for political and social change.

LIBERTY   The greatest freedom of individuals that is consistent with the freedom of other individuals in the society.

LIMITED GOVERNMENT   A form of government based on the principle that the powers of government should be clearly limited either through a written document or through wide public understanding; characterized by institutional checks to ensure that government serves the public rather than private interests.

LINE ORGANIZATION   Government or corporate units that provide direct services or products for the public.

LITIGATE   To engage in a legal proceeding.

LOBBYING   The attempt by organizations or by individuals to influence the passage, defeat, or contents of legislation and the administrative decisions of government. The derivation of the term may be traced back to over a century ago, when certain private citizens regularly congregated in the lobby outside the legislative chambers before a session to petition legislators.

LOGROLLING   An arrangement by which two or more members of Congress agree in advance to support each other's bills.

LOOPHOLES   Legal methods by which individuals and businesses are allowed to reduce the tax liabilities owed to the government.

MADISONIAN MODEL   The model of government devised by James Madison in which the powers of the government are separated into three branches: executive, legislative, and judicial.

MAJORITY   Full age; the age at which a person is entitled by law to the management of his or her own affairs and to the full enjoyment of civil rights; more than 50 percent.

MAJORITY FLOOR LEADER   The chief spokesperson of the major party in the Senate who directs the legislative program and party strategy.

MAJORITY LEADER OF THE HOUSE A legislative position held by an important party member in the House of Representatives. The majority leader is selected by the majority party in caucus or conference to foster cohesion among party members and to act as spokesperson for the majority party in the House.

MAJORITY OPINION The views of the majority of the judges.

MAJORITY RULE A basic principle of democracy asserting that the greatest number of citizens in any political unit should select officials and determine policies.

MANAGED NEWS Information generated and distributed by the government in such a way as to give governmental interests priority over candor.

MANDATORY RETIREMENT Forced retirement when a person reaches a certain age.

MATCHING FUNDS For many categorical grant programs, the state must "match" the federal funds. Some programs only require the state to raise 10 percent of the funds, whereas others approach an even share.

MATERIAL INCENTIVES Reasons or motives having to do with economic benefits or opportunities.

MEDIA The technical means of communication with mass audiences. The media have become extremely important in American political life as a means of informing and influencing millions of citizens.

MEDIA ACCESS The public's right of access to the media. The Federal Communications Commission and the courts have gradually taken the stance that citizens do have a right to media access.

MERIT SYSTEM The selection, retention, and promotion of government employees on the basis of competitive examinations.

MILITARY–INDUSTRIAL COMPLEX The mutually beneficial relationship between the armed forces and defense contractors.

MINORITY FLOOR LEADER The party officer in the Senate who commands the minority party's opposition to the policies of the majority party and directs the legislative program and strategy of his or her party.

MONETARY POLICY Changes in the amount of money in circulation to alter credit markets, employment, and the rate of inflation.

MONOPOLISTIC MODEL A model of bureaucracy that compares bureaucracies to monopolistic business firms. Lack of competition within a bureaucracy leads to inefficient and costly operations, just as it does within monopolistic firms. Because bureaucracies are not penalized for inefficiency, there is no incentive to save costs or use resources more productively.

MONROE DOCTRINE The policy statement included in President Monroe's 1823 annual message to Congress, which set out three principles: (1) European nations should not establish new colonies in the Western Hemisphere; (2) European nations should not intervene in the affairs of independent nations of the Western Hemisphere; and (3) the United States would not interfere in the affairs of European nations.

MORAL IDEALISM A philosophy that sees all nations as willing to cooperate and agree on moral standards for conduct.

MULTIPLE, INDEPENDENTLY TARGETABLE, WARHEADS (MIRVs) Multiple warheads carried by a single missile but directed to different targets.

MUNICIPAL HOME RULE The power vested in a local unit of government to draft or change its own charter and to manage its own affairs.

MUTUAL ASSURED DESTRUCTION (MAD) A theory that if the United States and the Soviet Union had extremely large and invulnerable nuclear forces that were somewhat equal, then neither would chance a war with the other.

NARROW CASTING Broadcasting that is targeted to one small sector of the population.

NATIONAL COMMITTEE A standing committee of a national political party established to direct and coordinate party activities during the four-year period between national party conventions.

NATIONAL CONVENTION The meeting held every four years by each major party to select presidential and vice presidential candidates, to write a platform, to choose a national committee, and to conduct party business. In theory, the national convention is at the top of a hierarchy of party conventions (the local and state conventions are below it) that considers candidates and issues.

NATIONAL POLITICS The pursuit of interests that are of concern to the nation as a whole.

NATIONAL SECURITY COUNCIL (NSC) A staff agency in the Executive Office established by the National Security Act of 1947. The NSC advises the president on domestic and foreign matters involving national security.

NATIONAL SECURITY POLICY Foreign and domestic policy designed to protect the independence and political and economic integrity of the United States; policy that is concerned with the safety and defense of the nation.

NATURAL ARISTOCRACY A small ruling clique of the state's "best" citizens, whose membership is based on birth, wealth, and ability. The Jeffersonian era emphasized government rule by such a group.

NATURAL RIGHTS Rights held to be inherent in natural law, not dependent on governments. John Locke stated that natural law, being superior to human law, specifies certain rights of "life, liberty, and property." These rights, slightly altered to become "life, liberty, and the pursuit of happiness," are asserted in the Declaration of Independence.

NECESSARIES In contract law, necessaries include whatever is reasonably necessary for suitable subsistence as measured by age, state, condition in life, and so on.

NEGATIVE CONSTITUENTS U.S. citizens who openly oppose government foreign policies.

NEW ENGLAND TOWN Combines the roles of city and county

into one governmental unit in the New England states.

NEW FEDERALISM A plan to limit the national government's power to regulate and to restore power to state governments. Essentially, the new federalism was designed to give the states greater ability to decide for themselves how government revenues should be spent.

NULLIFICATION The act of nullifying, or rendering void. John C. Calhoun asserted that a state had the right to declare a national law to be null and void and therefore not binding on its citizens, on the assumption that ultimate sovereign authority rested with the several states.

OFFICE-BLOCK, OR MASSACHUSETTS, BALLOT A form of general election ballot in which candidates for elective office are grouped together under the title of each office. It emphasizes voting for the office and the individual rather than for the party.

OFFICE OF MANAGEMENT AND BUDGET (OMB) A division of the Executive Office created by executive order in 1970 to replace the Bureau of the Budget. OMB's main functions are to assist the president in preparing the annual budget, to clear and coordinate all departmental agency budgets, to help set fiscal policy, and to supervise the administration of the federal budget.

OMBUDSMAN An individual in the role of hearing and investigating complaints by private individuals against public officials or agencies.

OPEN PRIMARY A direct primary in which voters may cast ballots in the primary of either party without having to declare their party registration. Once voters choose which party primary they will vote in, they must select among only the candidates of that party.

OPINION The statement by a judge or a court of the decision reached in a case tried or argued before them. It expounds the law as applied to the case and details the reasons on which the judgment was based.

OPINION LEADERS Those who are able to influence the opinions of others because of position, expertise, or personality. Such leaders help to shape public opinion either formally or informally.

OPINION POLL A method of systematically questioning a small, selected sample of respondents who are deemed representative of the total population. Widely used by government, business, university scholars, political candidates, and voluntary groups to provide reasonably accurate data on public attitudes, beliefs, expectations, and behavior.

ORAL ARGUMENTS The verbal arguments presented in person by opposing counsel.

ORIGINAL JURISDICTION The authority of a court to hear a case in the first instance.

OVERSIGHT The responsibility Congress has for following up on laws it has enacted to ensure that they are being enforced and administered in the way in which they were intended.

PAID-FOR POLITICAL ANNOUNCEMENT A message about a political candidate conveyed through the media and designed to elicit positive public opinion.

PARDON The granting of a release from the punishment or legal consequences of a crime; a pardon can be granted by the president before or after a conviction.

PARTY-COLUMN, OR INDIANA, BALLOT A form of general election ballot in which candidates for elective office are arranged in one column under their respective party labels and symbols. It emphasizes voting for the party rather than for the office or individual.

PARTY IDENTIFICATION Linking oneself to a particular political party.

PARTY IDENTIFIERS Those who identify themselves with a political party.

PARTY-IN-ELECTORATE Those members of the general public who identify with a political party or who express a preference for one party over the other.

PARTY-IN-GOVERNMENT All of the elected and appointed officials who identify with a political party.

PARTY ORGANIZATION The formal structure and leadership of a political party, including elective committees, local, state, and national executives, and paid professional staff.

PARTY PLATFORM A document drawn up by the platform committee at each national convention, outlining the policies, positions, and principles of the party; it is then submitted to the entire convention for approval.

PATRONAGE Rewarding faithful party workers and followers with government employment and contracts.

PEER GROUPS Groups consisting of members sharing common relevant social characteristics. They play an important part in the socialization process, helping to shape attitudes and beliefs.

PENDLETON ACT (CIVIL SERVICE REFORM ACT) This law, as amended over the years, remains the basic statute regulating federal employment personnel policies. It established the principle of employment on the basis of merit and created the Civil Service Commission to administer the personnel service.

PERIOD OF ISOLATIONISM A period of abstaining from an active role in international affairs or alliances, which characterized U.S. foreign policy during most of the nineteenth century.

PERSONAL ATTACK RULE The rule promulgated by the Federal Communications Commission that allows individuals or groups air time to replay to attacks that have previously been aired.

PETIT JURY The ordinary jury for the trial of a civil or criminal case.

PLURALISM A political doctrine in which autonomous groups in society actively compete in the decision-making process for resources and services.

PLURALITY The winning of an election by a candidate who

receives more votes than any other candidate but not necessarily a majority. Most national, state, and local electoral laws provide for winning elections by a plurality vote.

POCKET VETO A special veto power exercised by the chief executive after a legislative body has adjourned. Bills not signed by the chief executive die after a specified period of time. If Congress wishes to reconsider such a bill, it must be reintroduced in the following session of Congress.

POLICE POWERS The authority to legislate for the protection of the health, morals, safety, and welfare of the people. In the United States, most police power is a reserved power of the states. The federal government is able to legislate for the welfare of its citizens through specific congressional powers, such as its power to regulate interstate commerce.

POLICY TRADE-OFFS The cost to the nation of undertaking any one policy in terms of all of the other policies that could have been taken; for example, an increase in the expenditures on one federal program means a reduction in expenditures on another program or an increase in federal taxes (or the deficit).

POLITICAL ACTION COMMITTEES (PACs) Committees set up by and representing corporations, labor unions, or special interest groups; PACs raise and give campaign donations on behalf of the organizations or groups they represent.

POLITICAL CONSULTANT A paid professional hired to devise a campaign strategy and manage a campaign. Image building is the crucial task of the political consultant.

POLITICAL CULTURE That set of beliefs and values regarding the political system that are widely shared by the citizens of a nation.

POLITICAL PARTY A group of political activists who organize to win elections, to operate the government, and to determine public policy.

POLITICAL QUESTION An issue that a court believes should be decided by the executive or legislative branches.

POLITICAL REALISM A philosophy that sees each nation acting principally in its own interest.

POLITICAL SOCIALIZATION The process through which individuals learn a set of political attitudes and form opinions about social issues. The family and the educational system are two of the most important forces in the political socialization process.

POLITICAL TOLERANCE The degree to which individuals are willing to grant civil liberties to groups that have opinions differing strongly from their own.

POLITICAL TRUST The degree to which individuals express trust in the government and political institutions. This concept is usually measured through a specific series of survey questions.

POLITICO The legislative role that combines the delegate and trustee concepts. The legislator varies the role according to the issue under consideration.

POLITICS According to David Easton, the "authoritative allocation of values" for a society; according to Harold Lass-well, "who gets what, when, and how" in a society.

POLL TAX A special tax that must be paid as a qualification for voting. The Twenty-fourth Amendment to the Constitution outlawed the poll tax in national elections, and in 1966 the Supreme Court declared it unconstitutional in all elections.

POLL WATCHER An individual appointed by a political party to scrutinize the voting process on election day. Usually, there are two poll watchers at every voting place, representing the Democratic and the Republican parties, both attempting to ensure the honesty of the election.

POPULAR SOVEREIGNTY The concept that ultimate political authority rests with the people.

POSITIVE LAW Laws made in and by legislatures to fit a particular circumstance.

POWER The ability to cause others to modify their behavior and to conform to what the power holder wants.

PRECEDENT A court rule bearing on subsequent legal decisions in similar cases. Judges rely on precedents in deciding cases.

PREFERRED-POSITION TEST A court test used in determining the limits of free expression guaranteed by the First Amendment, requiring that limitations only be applied on speech to avoid imminent, serious, and important evils.

PRESIDENTIAL PRIMARY A statewide primary election of delegates to a political party's national convention to help a party determine its presidential nominee. Such delegates are either pledged to a particular candidate or unpledged.

PRESIDENT PRO TEMPORE The temporary presiding officer of the Senate in the absence of the vice president.

PRESS SECRETARY The individual responsible for representing the White House before the media. The press secretary writes news releases, provides background information, sets up press conferences, and so on.

PRIOR RESTRAINT Restraining an action before the activity has actually occurred. It involves censorship as opposed to subsequent punishment.

PRIVATIZATION, OR CONTRACTING OUT The replacement of government-paid-for products and services by private firms.

PRIVILEGES AND IMMUNITIES Special rights and exceptions provided by law. Article IV, Section 2, of the Constitution requires states not to discriminate against one another's citizens. A resident of one state cannot be treated as an alien when in another state; he or she may not be denied such privileges and immunities as legal protection, access to courts, travel rights, or property rights.

PROJECT GRANT An assistance grant that can be applied for directly by state and local agencies; established under a national program grant. Project grants allow Congress (and the administration) to bypass state governments and thereby to place the money directly where it is supposedly the most needed.

PROPERTY As conceived by the political philosopher John

Locke, a natural right superior to human law (laws made by government).

PROPERTY TAX A tax on the value of real estate; limited to state and local governments and a particularly important source of revenue for local governments.

PUBLIC ADMINISTRATION The science of managing public organizations.

PUBLIC AGENDA Issues that are commonly perceived by members of the political community as meriting public attention and governmental action. The media play an important role in setting the public agenda by focusing attention on certain topics.

PUBLIC DEBT FINANCING Government spending more than it receives in taxes and paying for the difference by issuing U.S. Treasury bonds, thereby adding to the public debt.

PUBLIC INTEREST The best interests of the collective, overall community; the national good, rather than the narrow interests of a self-serving group.

PUBLIC OPINION The aggregate of individual attitudes or beliefs shared by some portion of adults. There is no one public opinion because there are many different "publics."

PUBLIC POLICIES What the government decides to do or not to do.

PUBLIC, OR NATIONAL, DEBT The total amount of debt carried by the federal government.

PURPOSIVE INCENTIVES Reasons or motives having to do with ethical beliefs or ideological principles.

RATIFICATION Formal approval.

RATIONAL IGNORANCE EFFECT When people purposely and rationally decide not to become informed on an issue because they believe that their vote on the issue is not likely to be a deciding one; a lack of incentive to seek the necessary information to cast an intelligent vote.

REAPPORTIONMENT The redrawing of legislative district lines to accord with the existing population distribution.

RECALL A procedure allowing the people to vote to dismiss an elected official from state office before his or her term has expired.

RECOGNITION POWER The president's power, as chief diplomat, to extend diplomatic recognition to foreign governments.

REDISTRICTING The redrawing of district lines within the states.

REFERENDUM An act of referring legislative (statutory) or constitutional measures to the voters for approval or disapproval.

REGISTRATION The entry of a person's name onto the list of eligible voters for elections. Registration requires meeting certain legal requirements, such as age, citizenship, and residency.

RELEVANCE The extent to which an issue is of concern at a particular time. Issues become relevant when the public views them as pressing or of direct concern to them.

REMAND To send a case back to the court that originally heard it.

REPRESENTATION The function of Congress as elected officials to represent the views of their constituents.

REPRESENTATIVE ASSEMBLY A legislature composed of individuals who represent the population.

REPRESENTATIVE DEMOCRACY A form of government in which representatives elected by the people make and enforce laws and policies.

REPRESENTATIVE DEMOCRATIC GOVERNMENT A democracy in which representatives are empowered by the people to act on behalf of those represented.

REPRIEVE The president has the power to grant a reprieve to postpone the execution of a sentence imposed by a court of law; usually done for humanitarian reasons or to await new evidence.

REPUBLICAN FORM OF GOVERNMENT A system of government in which the supreme power rests with the voters, who elect representatives to operate the government for them.

REPUBLICAN PARTY One of the two major American political parties, which emerged in the 1850s as an antislavery party. It was created to fill the vacuum caused by the disintegration of the Whig party. The Republican party traces its name—but not its ideology—to Jefferson's Democratic Republican party.

REVERSE To annul or make void a judgment on account of some error or irregularity.

REVERSE DISCRIMINATION The charge that affirmative action programs requiring preferential treatment or quotas discriminate against those who do not have minority status.

RULES COMMITTEE A standing committee of the House of Representatives that provides special rules under which specific bills can be debated, amended, and considered by the House.

RULE OF FOUR A U.S. Supreme Court procedure requiring four affirmative votes to hear the case before the full Court.

RUN-OFF PRIMARY An election that is held to nominate candidates within the party if no candidate receives a majority of the votes in the first primary election.

SAFE SEAT A district that returns the legislator with 55 percent of the vote or more.

SECESSION The act of formally withdrawing from membership in an alliance; the withdrawal of a state from the federal union.

SECOND BUDGET RESOLUTION A resolution passed by Congress in September that sets "binding" limits on taxes and spending for the next fiscal year beginning October 1.

SECOND CONTINENTAL CONGRESS The 1775 Congress of the colonies that established the Continental Army.

SECTIONAL POLITICS The pursuit of interests that are of special concern to a region or section of the country.

SELECTPERSONS The governing group of a town.

SELECT COMMITTEE A temporary legislative committee established for a limited time period for a special purpose.

SENATORIAL COURTESY In regard to federal district court judgeship nominations, a Senate tradition allowing a senator of the president's political party to veto a judgeship appointment in his or her state simply by indicating that the appointment is personally "obnoxious." At that point, the Senate may reject the nomination or the president may withdraw consideration of the nominee.

SENIORITY SYSTEM A custom followed in both houses of Congress specifying that members with longer terms of continuous service will be given preference when committee chairpersons and holders of other significant posts are selected.

SEPARATE-BUT-EQUAL DOCTRINE The doctrine holding that segregation in schools and public accommodations does not imply the superiority of one race over another; rather, it implies that each race is entitled to separate but equal facilities.

SEPARATION OF POWERS The principle of dividing governmental powers among the executive, the legislative, and the judicial branches of government.

SERVICE SECTOR The sector of the economy that provides services—such as food services, insurance, and education—in contrast to the sector of the economy that produces goods.

SEX DISCRIMINATION Overt behavior in which people are given differential or unfavorable treatment on the basis of sex. Any practice, policy, or procedure that denies equality of treatment to an individual or to a group because of gender.

SEXUAL HARASSMENT Harassment on the basis of sex, in violation of Title VII. This includes unwanted physical or verbal conduct or abuse of a sexual nature that interferes with a recipient's job performance or carries with it an implicit or explicit threat of adverse employment consequences.

SLANDER The public uttering of a statement that holds a person up for contempt, ridicule, or hatred. This means the defamatory statement is made to, or within the hearing of, persons other than the defamed party.

SLIDING-SCALE TEST The courts must carefully examine the facts of each individual case before restricting expression.

SOCIAL CONFLICT Disagreements arising in society because of differing beliefs, values, and attitudes; conflicts over society's priorities and competition for scarce resources.

SOCIAL CONTRACT An agreement among individuals to establish a government and to abide by its rules.

SOCIAL MOVEMENT A movement that represents the demands of a large segment of the public for political, economic, or social change.

SOCIAL SECURITY A federal program that provides monthly payments to millions of people who are retired or unable to work.

SOCIOECONOMIC STATUS A category of people within a society who have similar levels of income and similar types of occupations.

SOLIDARY INCENTIVES Reasons or motives having to do with the desire to associate with others and to share with others a particular interest or hobby.

SOLID SOUTH A term describing the disposition of the post-Civil War southern states to vote for the Democratic party. (Voting patterns in the South have changed.)

SOUND BITE A brief, memorable comment that can easily be fit into news broadcasts.

SOVIET BLOC The Eastern European countries that installed communist regimes after World War II.

SPEAKER OF THE HOUSE The presiding officer in the House of Representatives. The speaker is always a member of the majority party and is the most powerful and influential member of the House.

SPIN An interpretation of campaign events or election results that is most favorable to the candidate's campaign strategy.

SPIN DOCTORS Political campaign advisers who try to convince journalists of the truth of a particular interpretation of events.

SPIN-OFF PARTY A new party formed by a dissident faction within a major political party. Usually, spin-off parties have emerged when a particular personality was at odds with the major party.

SPOILS SYSTEM The awarding of government jobs to political supporters and friends; generally associated with President Andrew Jackson.

SPRING REVIEW Every year, the Office of Management and Budget requires federal agencies to review their programs, activities, and goals and submit their requests for funding for the next year.

STABILITY The extent to which public opinion remains constant over a period of time.

STANDING COMMITTEE A permanent committee within the House or Senate that considers bills within a certain subject area.

STARE DECISIS "To stand on decided cases." The policy of courts to follow precedents established by the decisions of the past.

STATE A group of people occupying a specific area and organized under one government; may be either a nation or a subunit of a nation.

STATE CENTRAL COMMITTEE The principal organized structure of each political party within each state. Responsible for carrying out policy decisions of the party's state convention.

STATE OF THE UNION MESSAGE An annual message to Congress in which the president proposes a legislative program. The message is addressed not only to Congress but also to the American people and to the world. It offers the opportunity to dramatize policies and objectives and to gain public support.

STATUTORY POWERS The powers created for the president through laws established by Congress.

STRATEGIC ARMS LIMITATION TREATY (SALT I) A treaty between the United States and the Soviet Union to stabilize the nuclear arms competition between the two countries. SALT I talks began in 1969, and agreements were signed on May 26, 1972.

SUBPOENA A legal writ requiring a person's appearance in court to give testimony.

SUBSIDIES Negative taxes; usually payments to producers given on a per-unit basis according to the amount of production of a particular commodity.

SUFFRAGE The right to vote; the franchise.

SUNSET LEGISLATION A law requiring that an existing program be regularly reviewed for its effectiveness and terminated unless specifically extended as a result of this review.

SUPPLEMENTAL SECURITY INCOME (SSI) A federal program established to provide assistance to the aged, the blind, and the disabled.

SUPREMACY CLAUSE The constitutional provision that makes the Constitution and federal laws superior to all state and local legislation.

SUPREMACY DOCTRINE A doctrine that asserts the superiority of national law over state or regional laws. This principle is rooted in Article VI of the Constitution, which provides that the Constitution, the laws passed by the national government under its constitutional powers, and all treaties constitute the supreme law of the land.

SYMBOLIC SPEECH Nonverbal expression of beliefs, which is given substantial protection by the courts.

TAX PREFERENCES Another name for loopholes, or reduced taxes, legally mandated by Congress for particular activities, individuals, or businesses.

TECHNICAL ASSISTANCE Sending experts with technical skills in agriculture, engineering, or business to aid other nations.

THIRD PARTY A political party other than the two major political parties (Republican and Democratic). Usually, third parties are composed of dissatisfied groups that have split from the major parties. They act as indicators of political trends and as safety valves for dissident groups.

THIRD-PARTY CANDIDATE A political candidate running under the banner of a party other than the two major political parties.

TICKET SPLITTING Voting for candidates of two or more parties for different offices. For example, a voter splits her ticket if she votes for a Republican presidential candidate and for a Democratic congressional candidate.

TOTALITARIAN REGIME A form of government that controls all aspects of the political and social life of a nation. All power resides with the government. The citizens have no power to choose the leadership or policies of the country.

TOWN MANAGER SYSTEM Form of city government in which voters elect three selectpersons who then appoint a professional town manager, who in turn appoints other officials.

TOWN MEETING The governing authority of a New England town. Qualified voters may participate in the election of officers and in the passage of legislation.

TOWNSHIP Rural units of government based on federal land

surveys of the American frontier in the 1780s. They have declined significantly in importance.

TRACKING POLLS Polls taken for the candidate on a nearly daily basis as election day approaches.

TRIAL COURTS Those courts in which most cases usually begin and in which questions of fact are examined.

TRUMAN DOCTRINE The policy adopted by President Harry Truman in 1947 to halt communist expansion in southeastern Europe.

TRUSTEES The idea that a legislator should act according to his or her conscience and the broad interests of the entire society, often associated with the British statesman Edmund Burke.

TWELFTH AMENDMENT An amendment to the Constitution, adopted in 1804, that specifies the separate election of the president and vice president by the electoral college.

TWENTY-FIFTH AMENDMENT An amendment to the Constitution adopted in 1967 that establishes procedures for filling vacancies in the two top executive offices and that makes provisions for situations involving presidential disability.

TWO-PARTY COMPETITION Two strong and solidly established political parties in competition for political control; both parties have a strong chance of winning an election.

TWO-PARTY SYSTEM A political system in which only two parties have a reasonable chance of winning.

UNANIMOUS OPINION Agreement of all judges on the same opinion or determination.

UNICAMERAL LEGISLATURES Legislatures with only one legislative body, as compared with bicameral (two-house) legislatures, such as the United States Congress. Nebraska is the only state in the Union with a unicameral legislature.

UNINCORPORATED AREAS Areas not located within the boundaries of municipalities.

UNITARY SYSTEM A centralized governmental system in which local or subdivisional governments exercise only those powers given to them by the central government.

UNIT RULE All of a state's electoral votes are cast for the presidential candidate receiving a plurality of the popular vote.

UNIVERSAL SUFFRAGE The right of all adults to vote for their representatives.

U.S. TREASURY BONDS Evidences of debt issued by the federal government. Similar to corporate bonds but issued by the U.S. Treasury.

VETO MESSAGE The president's formal explanation of a veto when legislation is returned to the Congress.

VOTER TURNOUT The percentage of citizens taking part in the election process; the number of eligible voters that actually "turn out" on election day to cast their ballots.

WAR POWERS ACT A law passed in 1973 spelling out the conditions under which the president can commit troops without congressional approval.

WASHINGTON COMMUNITY Individuals regularly involved with the political circles in Washington, D.C.

WATERGATE BREAK-IN The 1972 illegal entry into the Democratic campaign offices engineered by participants in Nixon's reelection campaign.

WEBERIAN MODEL A model of bureaucracy developed by the German sociologist, Max Weber, who viewed bureaucracies as rational, hierarchical organizations in which power flows from the top downward and decisions are based on logical reasoning and data analysis.

WHIGS One of the foremost political organizations in the United States during the first half of the nineteenth century, formally established in 1836. The Whig party was dominated by the same anti-Jackson elements that organized the National Republican faction within the Jeffersonian Republicans and represented a variety of regional interests. It fell apart as a national party in the early 1850s.

WHIPS Assistant floor leaders who aid the majority and minority floor leaders.

WHISTLE BLOWER Someone who brings to public attention gross governmental inefficiency or an illegal action.

WHITE HOUSE OFFICE The personal office of the president, which tends to presidential political needs and manages the media.

WHITE HOUSE PRESS CORPS A group of reporters assigned full time to cover the presidency.

WHITE PRIMARY A state primary election that restricts voting only to whites; outlawed by the Supreme Court in 1944.

WRIT OF CERTIORARI An order issued by a higher court to a lower court to send up the record of a case for review. It is the principal vehicle for U.S. Supreme Court review.

WRIT OF HABEAS CORPUS Literally, "you should have the body." An order that requires jailers to bring a party before a court or judge and explain why the party is being held in prison.

WRIT OF MANDAMUS An order issued by a court to compel the performance of an act.

YELLOW JOURNALISM A term for sensationalistic, irresponsible journalism. Reputedly, the term is short for "Yellow Kid Journalism," an allusion to the cartoon "The Yellow Kid" in the old *New York World*, a paper especially noted for its sensationalism.

INDEX

Photo Credits

1 © Dennis Brack, Black Star; 3 © Peter Miller, Photo Researchers, Inc.; 5 © Gyorgy Sugar, Gamma Liaison; 6 Barry Thumma, AP/Wide World; 9 © Rick Friedman, Black Star; 11 © Bettmann; 12 © Lisa Quinones, Black Star; 14 © Arnaldo Magnani, Gamma Liaison; 16 © Brooks Kraft, Sygma; 18 © Andrew Holbrooke, Black Star; 19 © Ira Wyman, Sygma; 21 Marinovich, AP/Wide World; 25 © Michael Evans, Sygma; 27 © The Granger Collection; 28 © The Granger Collection; 30 From the Studio of A. Ramsay, © 1767, Courtesy of the National Portrait Gallery, London; 32 © Photo Researchers; 35 © The Granger Collection; 37 © The Granger Collection; 38 The Library of Congress; 41 © Bettmann; 57 © Brooks Kraft, Sygma; 62 © Bettmann; 66 © J. Berry, Gamma Liaison; 68 © Eunice Harris, Photo Researchers; 72 The Library of Congress; 74 The Library of Congress; 76 The Library of Congress; 77 © Ellis Herwig, Stock, Boston; 79 © Dirck Halstead, Gamma Liaison; 87 © Bob Adelman, Magnum; 89 © Joyce R. Wilson, Photo Researchers; 94 © Bob Nelson, Picture Group; 95 © Bruce Flynn, Picture Group; 100 © UPI/Bettmann; 102 © Andrew Holbroke, Black Star; 103 © Scott Nelson, Sygma; 104 John Duricka, Wide World Photos; 108 © Paul Miller, Black Star; 111 (left) © Dennis Brack, Black Star; 111 (right) © Rick Friedman, Black Star; 113 © KTLA, Sygma; 115 © Flip Schulke, Black Star; 117 © Phil Huber, Black Star; 123 © Spenser Grant, Stock, Boston; 125 © Missouri Historical Society; 126 © The Granger Collection; 128 From the Dorthy Sterling Collection at the Amistad Research Center; 130 © Ellis Herwig, Stock, Boston; 132 © Edwin H. Remsberg, Gamma Liaison; 134 UPI/Bettmann; 135 © Flip Schulke, Black Star; 141 © Ira Wyman, Sygma; 143 © Donald Dietz, Stock, Boston; 147 © J. P. Laffont, Sygma; 150 © Bettmann; 151 © Bettmann; 153 © Sygma; 154 © Rob Crandall, Picture Group; 155 © Donna Ferrato, Black Star; 158 © Paul Fusco, Magnum; 162 © Mark Lenihan, Associated Press Photo; 164 © Burt Bartholomew, Black Star; 166 © R. Maiman, Sygma; 173 © Jeff Jacobson, Archive; 175 © Billy Barnes, Uniphoto; 179 © Arthur Grace, Stock, Boston; 184 UPI/Bettmann; 185 © Andy Levin, Photo Researchers; 188 G. Widman, Wide World Photos; 189 © Todd Buchanan, Black Star; 199 (top) © Rob Crandall, Picture Group; 199 (bottom) © Allan Tannenbaum; 205 © Paul Conklin, PhotoEdit; 207 © The Bettmann Archive; 212 © Renee Lynn, Photo Researchers; 213 © David Sutton, Picture Group; 216 © Mark D. Phillips, Photo Researchers; 217 © Brad Markel, Gamma Liaison; 218 © A. Berliner, Gamma Liaison; 219 © Dennis Brack, Black Star; 224 © Lisa Quinones, Black Star; 227 © Michael Evans, Sygma; 228 UPI/Bettmann; 231 © R. Maiman, Sygma; 233 © Lisa Quinones, Black Star; 236 Library of Congress; 237 © Bettmann; 238 (top) The Granger Collection; 238 (bottom) The Smithsonian; 241 © R. F. Owen, Black Star; 242 © Lisa Quinones, Black Star; 243 © R. Maiman, Sygma; 246 © Steven Leonard, Black Star; 249 © Roger Sandler, Picture Group; 252 © Lisa Quinones, Black Star; 254 © Bettmann; 256 National Archives; 261 © Dennis Brack, Black Star; 267 © John Ficara, Woodfin Camp; 270 © Mark McKenna; 271 © Wide World Photos; 272 © Mike Fletcher, Gamma Liaison; 274 © Paul Conklin, Monkmeyer; 277 © Dennis Brack, Black Star; 278 © Ira Wyman, Sygma; 283 © R. Maiman, Sygma; 287 © Brad Markel, Gamma Liaison; 288 © Mark Phillips, Photo Researchers; 292 © Roger Sandler, Picture Group; 296 © Dennis Brack, Black Star; 299 With the permission of Doyle Dane Bernbach, Inc.; 301 Library of Congress; 302 © Dirck Halstead, Gamma Liaison; 304 Photo Researchers; 307 © Baker, Picture Group; 313 © Ellis Herwig, Stock, Boston; 315 © J. L. Atlan, Sygma; 317 © Sygma; 325 UPI/Bettmann; 327 UPI/Bettmann; 330 (from left to right) Kevork Djansezian, © Wide World Photos; John Duricka, Wide World Photos; Wide World Photos; John Duricka, Wide World Photos; 331 © Karl Gehring, Gamma Liaison; 336 © Dennis Brack, Black Star; 338 © R. Cheny, Gamma Liaison; 340 © Dennis Brack, Black Star; 341 © Shepard Sherbell, Picture Group; 342 © Dennis Brack, Black Star; 346 Charles TasnadiAP/Wide World; 347 © Pam Price, Picture Group; 357 © J. L. Atlan, Sygma; 359 © Ellis Herwig, Stock, Boston; 360 The Black Star Pool; 361 © Bettmann; 365 © Sygma; 366 © 1993 Matthew McVay; 368 © Sygma; 376 © Don Carl Steffan, Photo Researchers; 377 © Fred Ward, Black Star; 381 © Dennis Brack, Black Star; 382 © Sygma; 385 © Sebastio Salgado, Jr., Magnum; 387 UPI/Bettmann Newsphotos; 391 © Lawrence Migdale, Photo Researchers; 394 © David Frazier, Photo Researchers; 402 © David Sams, Stock, Boston; 403 © Christopher Farina, Sygma; 405 © J. P. Laffont, Sygma; 406 © Bettmann; 408 © Steven Liss, Gamma Liaison; 411 © David Butow, Black Star; 419 © Oliver Martel, Black Star; 422 © Stacy Pick, Stock, Boston; 424 Library of Congress; 424 Library of Congress; 436 © Lee Corkran, Sygma; 439 © Sygma; 440 © Shepard Sherbell, Picture Group; 441 © Pam Price, Picture Group; 449 © Sean Haffey, Sygma; 451 © Terry Ashe, Gamma Liaison; 454 © Brad Bower, Picture Group; 456 © Dennis Brack, Black Star; 459 © Gamma Liaison; 462 UPI/Bettmann; 463 © Markel, Gamma Liaison; 468 © Bill Nation, Sygma; 470 © Ira Wyman, Sygma; 471 © S.